saudi arabia | A **MEED** PRACTICAL GUIDE
SECOND EDITION

King Fahd of Saudi Arabia

saudi arabia
A **MEED** PRACTICAL GUIDE
SECOND EDITION

Compiled and edited by
TREVOR MOSTYN

Middle East Economic Digest

21 John Street, London WC1N 2BP
Telephone: 01-404 5513
Telex: London 27165 MEEDAR
Cables: MEEDARR London WC1

Published by
Middle East Economic Digest Ltd
21 John Street,
London WC1N 2BP

All rights reserved © 1983
Middle East Economic Digest

Designed and typeset
by MEED Studios

ISBN 0 946510 00 8

Printed by Eyre & Spottiswoode Ltd
Northarbour Road, Cosham, Portsmouth

Distributed by
Croom Helm Ltd
Provident House
Burrell Row
Beckenham
Kent BR3 1AT
England
Tel: 01-658 7813

Colour plates: MEPhA/individual photographers as listed.

Full-page plates: city park, Jeddah/Peter Ryan; modern farming in Wadi Birk/MB; visitors palace, Riyadh/M Sparrow; villages and terraced fields north of Abha/Peter Ryan.

¼ page plates: Saudi children/David Shirreff; coffee — the heart of hospitality/R Webster; pivot irrigation, Wadi Birk/MB; stud farm near Riyadh/Alistair Duncan; office in old Jeddah/Peter Ryan; spring floods near Raudhat al-Khuraim/Roger Webster; Shammar bedu/Roger Webster; Jeddah museum/Peter Ryan; Yemeni stonemason, Abha/Peter Ryan; eating a kabsa in Yanbu/Peter Ryan; village south of Abha/Peter Ryan; terraced fields in the Asir/MB; television tower, Riyadh/M Sparrow; National Guard in Riyadh/MB; schoolchildren in Jeddah/A Duncan; cement works, Jeddah/A Duncan; operating rock drill, quarry north of Najran/Peter Ryan; Airport road roundabout, Jeddah/MB; Madain Salih/Peter Ryan; Jeddah Islamic port — ro-ro terminal/MB; Riyadh — looking southeast/MB; vegetable market; Riyadh/Roger Webster; primary school, Jeddah/Alistair Duncan; luxury homes, Jeddah/B Morris; visitors' palace, Riyadh/M Sparrow; Jeddah Islamic port/MB; rockcutting equipment, Najran/Peter Ryan; Jeddah fountain by night/MB; Saudi Mercedes factory/D Shirreff; Saptco double-deck bus, Jeddah/MB; Jubail-Yanbu pipeline/Peter Ryan; Jaramax 17 dropping anchors/R Newman.

Black and white photographs MEPhA pages 23, 27, 40, 61, 67, 86, 89, 102, 108, 113, 115, 120, 131, 133, 151, 171, 172, 178, 180, 226, 229, 240, 245, 250, 251, 263, 269, 298, 323, 332; P Ryan/MEPhA pages 24, 33, 36, 39, 43, 44, 68, 82, 97, 101, 116, 118, 121, 139, 153, 196, 197, 199, 216, 238, 283, 305, 318, 320, 321, 331; David Shirreff/MEPhA pages 21, 25, 42, 47, 99, 247, 255, 319; Alistair Duncan/MEPhA pages 6, 12, 45, 136, 138, 146; J Caldow/MEPhA pages 68, 274, 284, 204; Christine Osborne/MEPhA pages 20, 210, 228; M Petrie-Ritchie/MEPhA pages 55, 56, 130; Trevor Mostyn pages 74, 164, 170; Herbie Knott/Camera Press pages 3, 4; Central Press Photos pages 105, 213, MB/MEPhA pages 152, 232; J Wallace/MEPhA pages 232, 242; Ministry/MEPhA pages 256, 299; Camera Press pages 3, 19, 99; Rachad el-Koussy/Camera Press page 4; Royal Geographic Society/Captain Shakespear pages 9, 11; Jill Brown/MEPhA page ii; Royal Geographic Society page 5; Popperfoto page 14; Jean Claude Sauer/Camera Press page 15; Kuwait Ministry/Camera Press page 15; Kuwait Ministry/MEPhA page 30; Kenneth W Fink/MEPhA page 31; Michael Rice & Co/MEPhA page 34; Ted Rosen/MEPhA page 49; A Hutt/MEPhA page 77; Tom Hanley/Camera Press page 80; Construction News/MEPhA page 91; Financial Times page 95; Eddie O'Sullivan/MEPhA page 124; Inter-Continental Hotels page 140; M Sparrow/MEPhA page 208; R Simonds/Albert Abela/MEPhA page 306; A Stagg page 324; Werkfoto page 330.

PREFACE

This book is a completely updated, revised and expanded edition of MEED's first guide to Saudi Arabia, published in 1981 as the first in the Practical Guide series. The first edition was warmly reviewed as the first comprehensive guide to treat the kingdom of Saudi Arabia with the seriousness it deserves. It was short-listed for the 1981 Thomas Cook Guide Book of the year award, as was the UAE guide the following year. In 1982 a guide to Oman was published, and in 1983 guides to Jordan, Bahrain and Qatar.

The MEED Practical Guides aim to serve as comprehensive, practical, learned and highly readable guides for business people, tourists, resident expatriates and even academics. To achieve both the broadest and most accurate viewpoint of life in Saudi Arabia today, experts in every field have contributed on subjects ranging from history and bedouin life to expatriate schooling and leisure. The detailed travel sections are the most comprehensive ever to be published on Saudi Arabia. Thanks for these must go to the Saudi Arabian Natural History Society for much of the Jeddah region travel section, to Peter Shurville, on whose Day Trips from Riyadh the Riyadh travel section is based, and to Rosalind Ingrams, who wrote on the Riyadh-Najran road south and on Buraydah and Anayzah. For these and other contributors see Notes on Contributors.

MEED itself was first published in 1957 in the aftermath of the Suez conflict. The magazine — the first business weekly on the Middle East — was founded by Elizabeth Collard. She was farsighted enough to see then that Arab countries would play a prominent role in international affairs. Today her ideals are perpetuated by Jonathan Wallace, MEED's publisher and chief executive, Peter Kilner, MEED's chairman, and by MEED's dedicated team of journalists.

My special thanks go to Kathy Turton, who made a major contribution to both the first edition and this edition of the guide. She compiled and cross-checked much of the practical and domestic detail, and her support has been essential to the success of the project.

Within MEED House my thanks go to Mary-Rose Wakefield who was a reliable and friendly assistant throughout; to Jane Collin, who meticulously sub-edited the book; to Clare Whelan, who made the index, and to Roger Emmerson and his staff who designed and typeset the book. His staff, who worked long hours, are Jacqui Apthorpe, Paul Bell, Judith Charlton, Diana Dryden, Joanne Gardiner, Karen Henderson, Pat Hill, Margaret Joseph, Veloria Mullings, John Walker and Paul Webster.

I would also like to thank Jane Greening, who researched the photographs, and the MEED Library, which researched the Bibliography.

I believe this guide to be the most wide-ranging of any published so far and hope it will be of invaluable help to visitors and residents alike.

Trevor Mostyn
Editor
April 1983

The Editor

The editor and part writer of this guide, Trevor Mostyn, has travelled throughout the Middle East for the past 19 years since making an overland trip to India and Nepal in 1964. He took an MA degree in Arabic and Persian at Edinburgh University, also studying at the Middle East Centre for Arabic Studies at Shemlan in Lebanon and than at the American University in Cairo. After a period teaching English literature at Algiers University, he spent a year travelling in Saudi Arabia and Iran as a consultant, followed by three years visiting the Arab World and Iran as Macmillan Publishers' Middle East manager. He has written regularly on the Middle East for The Times' special reports, The New Statesman, The Scotsman and in MEED, and has broadcast on Arab affairs on the BBC World Service. He is managing editor of MEED Books.

Notes on contributors

Part One — The Background

Trevor Mostyn, the editor, wrote, among other sections, on History and on Islam

William Facey, a museum planner, is on the staff of Michael Rice & Company. He has worked for several years for the Department of Antiquities & Museums in Saudi Arabia

George Popov is principal scientific officer at the Centre for Overseas Pest Research, London

John and Patricia Gasperetti live in Jeddah, where he is an eminent zoologist

Peter Ryan is a science writer and photographer who has worked in Saudi Arabia

Ashkhain Skipwith, who lives in Jeddah, is author of Ashkhain's Desert Cookery, and wrote on Saudi Cuisine

Part Two — Practical Guide

Thanks for much of the information in this section must go to the **Riyadh Group of British Businessmen** (see Riyadh). The Desert Driving survival checklist is based on advice given by **Avis'** Abu Dhabi office. The information on Freight Forwarding comes from **Don Clarke** of Schenkers International Freight Forwarders. Useful Arabic words and phrases are based on a simplified version of a text by **Leslie McLoughlin,** director, Arabic Services UK

Part Three — The Expatriate Experience

Laron L Jensen was for several years Saudi Arabia specialist, Commerce Action Group for the Near East (CAGNE), US Department of Commerce

Dr Anthony Turner is honorary associate physician at the Hospital for Tropical Diseases, London

Vernon Cassin Jr is attorney-at-law with Hussein M El-Sayed in Riyadh

Part Four — The Economy

Edmund O'Sullivan is MEED's specialist on Saudi Arabia and MEED's news editor

William Lee is MEED's Washington correspondent

David Shirreff is assistant editor at Euromoney, and was for several years MEED's Saudi Arabia specialist

Jonathan Fenby is MEED's former Paris correspondent

Part Five — Doing Business

Chris Syer is chairman of the Riyadh Group of British Businessmen (see Riyadh)

Part Six — The Regions

Jeddah

The major contribution to this section came from **Primrose and Christopher Arnander,** who live in Jeddah. Additional advice and help was given by **Philip Dew,** who also lives in the city

Justin Harris wrote on antique souqs

James Syrett, who wrote on sea sports, has been a diver since 1971

Trips to make in the Jeddah region are based on journeys made by the Saudi Arabian Natural History Society (see Jeddah)

Yanbu

Information on Yanbu is supplied by Saudi Arabian Parsons and by the Royal Commission for Jubail & Yanbu

Makkah

Haroon Sugich is a businessman, freelance writer and journalist working for the Information Ministry. A US citizen, he lives with his Saudi wife and three children in Makkah

Riyadh

Most of this section was revised by **Pam Coleridge,** who also wrote for the first edition. She and her husband lived in Riyadh for several years before returning to the UK in early 1983

Trips to make in the Najd Region are based on Day Drives Around Riyadh by **Peter Shurville**

The section on Qassim Province and the Riyadh-Najran trip are by **Rosalind Ingrams,** who has lived for several years in Riyadh

Eastern Province

Robert and **Jean Fraga** who wrote this section live in the Province

Arthur Stagg, who lives in Khamis Mushait, revised some of the Khamis Mushait section and contributed to the section on places of interest in the Asir

CONTENTS

Part 1 The Background
Introduction	1
Government and monarchy	2
Historical background	5
Islam	18
The geography of Saudi Arabia	24
Vegetation	26
Arabian fauna	29
Mineral resources	35
Antiquities and museums	39
Manners and customs	41
The Muslim woman in Saudi Arabia	43
Saudi cuisine	46
Map of Saudi Arabia	48

Part 2 Practical guide
Basic information	49
Entering the kingdom: visas; identity cards; when to visit; health regulations	52
Getting about: driving, air travel; bus system; road distances in kilometres	55
Communications: telephone, telex and postal services	58
Islamic calendar	62
Useful Arabic words and phrases	63
Desert driving survival checklist	65

Part 3 The Expatriate Experience
Advice for expatriates	69
Health	73
Housing	77
Saudi criminal law	78

Part 4 The Economy
Introduction to the economy	83
Oil and gas	86
Construction	90
Manufacturing	94
Banking	98
Telecommunications	102
Trade with the UK	103
US-Saudi relations	106
US government agencies	110
USACE	110
Trade with France	112
Agriculture	115
Education	117

Part 5 Doing Business
The Business setting	119
Courier services	126
Exporter's checklist	126
Doing business	127
Incentives for industrial investment	129
Chambers of commerce and industry	130
Freight forwarding	131
Business events 1983-84	132
Budget allocations	134

Part 6 The Regions
The Hejaz (the western region)
Makkah al-Mukarama	135
Air communications	139
Hotels	139
Courier service	142
Banks	142
Eating out	142
Shopping	142
Other shopping areas	144
Hospitals	145
Entertainment	145
Places of interest	145
Al-Madinah	148
Hotels	148
Air communications	149
Local transport	149
Chamber of commerce	149
Medical	149
Jeddah	150
Ministries	154
Embassies	154
Map	156
Getting around	159
Car hire	162
Hotels	164
Communications	168
Courier services	168
Travel agents	169
Eating out	169
Shopping	171
Medical	179
Estate agent	182
Jeddah for the expatriate	182
Education	183
Housing	185
Sport	186
Recreation	188
Banking	188
Lawyers	190
Places to visit around Jeddah	191
Taif	198
Hotels	199
Communications	200
Courier service	200
Travel agents	200
Restaurants	200
Shops	200
Medical	200
Yanbu	201
Government department	202
Getting around	202
Car hire	202
Hotels	202
Communications	203
Restaurants	203

Shopping	203
Education	204
Libraries	204
Housing	204
Medical	204
Other facilities	205
Recreation	205
The media	206
Places to visit	206
The Najd (the central region)	
Riyadh	207
Ministries	211
Diplomatic services	212
Getting around	213
Map	214
Car hire	216
Hotels	217
Communications	220
Courier services	221
Travel agents	221
Eating out	221
Shopping	223
Medical	227
King Saud University	232
Libraries and museums	233
Riyadh international book fair	233
Education	233
Housing	235
Recreation	239
Sport	241
Banking	244
Lawyers	244
Doing business	245
Trips in the Najd region	246
Qassim Province	253
Buraydah	254
Aneyzah	256
The Rabadi'yah oasis	258
Hail	259
Tabuk	261
The road south	262
Hasa (Eastern province)	
Living in Eastern province	273
Diplomatic services	276
Getting around	279
Map of Al-Khobar	280
Map of Dammam	281
Car hire	282
Hotels	283
Al-Khobar	283
Dammam	284
Dhahran	286
Communications	286
Courier services	287
Travel agents	287
Eating out	289
Shopping	292
Services	296
Housing	297
Medical	298
Education	299
Recreation	301
Sports	303
Media	305
Lawyers	305
Aramco	306
Communications	306
Getting around	306
Eating out	306
Shopping	307
Banking	307
Medical	307
Recreation	307
Housing	308
Media	308
Trips to make	309
Jubail	312
Hotels	313
Communications	313
Courier services	313
Car hire	313
Travel agencies	313
Shopping	314
Banks	314
Eating out	314
Medical	315
Education	315
Media	315
Recreation	315
Sports	316
The South	
Abha	317
Baha	317
The Asir	317
Places to visit	321
Khamis Mushait	325
Hotels	325
Communications	326
Courier service	326
Restaurants	327
Shopping	327
Banks	328
Useful telephone numbers	328
Medical	329
Housing	329
Education	329
Recreation	330
Jizan	330
Part 7 Appendices	
Statistics	333
Bibliography	338
Index	345

PART 1 THE BACKGROUND

Introduction

Saudi Arabia's economic development is, today, virtually overshadowed by the kingdom's pivotal diplomatic role. The kingdom's position as the richest country in the Middle East is only one factor behind the political and moral influence it exerts. It is by far the largest country in the Arab world — and the twelfth largest globally — and possesses the two holiest cities in Islam, Makkah and Al-Madinah. Perhaps most important, the very existence of Saudi Arabia, formally created in 1932, is concomitant with one of the most important reformations in the history of Islam — the puritan reformation of 1744 which sought a return to the purity of early Islam based on the Quran and the Hadith (sayings) of the Prophet Muhammed (see History and Islam).

Fahd succeeded as king on the death of Khaled on 3 June 1982. His international experience, authority and confidence to act decisively are important factors in the role that he and the kingdom are playing today. Saudi Arabia is making a crucial effort in seeking a comprehensive Middle East settlement. It was prominent in moves to ensure the safety of the Palestinian resistance in summer 1982, while Fahd was the author of the eight-point plan drawn up in 1981 which entailed the Israeli withdrawal from Jerusalem and the creation of a Palestinian state. Israel's terrible onslaught on Lebanon in mid-1982 led to the Arab summit in Fes in September, in which peace plans were drawn up on the basis of the Fahd plan.

Saudi Arabia has also played a key role in forging closer links with other Gulf states, with the founding in 1981 of the Gulf Co-operation Council (GCC). Other members are Bahrain, Kuwait, Oman, the United Arab Emirates (UAE) and Qatar. The GCC's aims include reducing trade and investment barriers among its members, and waiving the need for visas. Every member airport now has a GCC passport control point. The council's formation was quickly followed by bilateral security agreements between Saudi Arabia and four of its GCC colleagues.

At the start of 1983, world economic developments did not seem to favour the kingdom. Saudi Arabia has the world's largest oil reserves: proven reserves at the end of 1981 were officially reported at 116,700 million barrels, with probable reserves up to 70 per cent higher (see Oil & Gas). Demand for OPEC oil collapsed in the spring and summer of 1982, following a decline since 1979. At the time of writing an agreement was concluded by OPEC whereby the price of Saudi marker crude — the base for fixing other oil prices — was cut by $5 to $29, and total OPEC production was fixed at 17.5 million barrels a day (b/d). In autumn 1982 Saudi Arabia had cut its own output to about 5.5 million b/d, from 8.5 million b/d at the start of the year.

The next year is expected to see major developments in the new industrial cities of Jubail and Yanbu, with the first two petrochemicals plants in the downstream programme due to start operating. Start-up at the Jubail Fertiliser Company and the Saudi Methanol Company, both Jubail-based, will coincide with the opening of the Saudi Iron & Steel Company, also based in Jubail. The other six heavy industrial plants are due to start operating in 1985.

Saudis are today being trained to fill key jobs in every sector, particularly in the oil industry, where Aramco is training nationals to top executive positions. This is one of the main features of the present development plan and almost certainly the key to the kingdom's influence and security in the coming decade. Saudi Arabia's aim is not only to use its wealth to create a self-supporting infrastructure for the future, but also to act as a guide for the whole Muslim world, a role made more crucial by Iran's diminished authority since its 1979 revolution.

Government of Saudi Arabia

as at 1 July 1983

Head of state
King Fahd Ibn-Abdel-Aziz
—also prime minister

First Deputy Premier
Crown Prince Abdullah Ibn-Abdel-Aziz
Second Deputy Premier, Defence & Aviation
Prince Sultan Ibn-Abdel-Aziz
Interior
Prince Nayef Ibn-Abdel-Aziz
Foreign Affairs
Prince Saud al-Faisal
Agriculture & Water
Abdel-Rahman Ibn-Abdel-Aziz Ibn-Hasan al-Shaikh
Commerce
Sulaiman Abdel-Aziz al-Solaim
Communications
Hussain Ibrahim al-Mansouri
Education
Abdel-Aziz al-Abdullah al-Khuwaiter
Finance & National Economy
Mohammad Ali Abalkhail
Health (acting)
Ghazi Abdel-Rahman al-Gosaibi
Higher Education
Hasan Ibn-Abdullah al-Shaikh
Industry & Electricity
Ghazi Abdel-Rahman al-Gosaibi
Information
Ali Hasan al-Shaer
Justice
Ibrahim Ibn-Mohammad Ibn-Ibrahim al-Shaikh
Labour & Social Affairs
Mohammad Ali al-Fayez
Municipal & Rural Affairs
Ibrahim Ibn Abdullah al-Angari
Petroleum & Minerals
Ahmad Zaki Yamani
Pilgrimage Affairs & Awqaf (Religious Endowments)
Abdel-Wahhab Ahmad Abdel-Wasi
Planning
Hisham Nazer
Posts, Telegraphs & Telecommunications
Alawi Darwish Kayyal
Public Works & Housing
Prince Moutib Ibn-Abdel-Aziz
Transport
Hussain Mansouri
Governor of Makkah
Prince Majid Ibn-Abdel-Aziz

Ministers of State
Mohammad Ibrahim Masoud, Mohammad Abdel-Latif al-Milhim, Abdullah Mohammad al-Omran, Omar Abdel-Qader Faqih

Deputy Interior Minister
Prince Ahmad Ibn-Abdel Aziz
Adviser to Defence & Aviation Minister
General Othman al-Humaid
President of Youth Welfare
Prince Faisal Ibn-Fahd

Ministers without portfolio
Fayez Badr, Abdel-Hadi Taher

Supreme Petroleum Council
King Fahd
Petroleum & Minerals Minister Ahmad Zaki Yamani
Foreign Affairs Minister Prince Saud al-Faisal
Industry & Electricity Minister Ghazi Abdel-Rahman al-Gosaibi
Planning Minister Hisham Nazer

The Monarchy

King Fahd

King Fahd was born in 1923 and has spent half his life in very senior government posts. In 1953, at the age of 30, he joined the kingdom's first council of ministers as education minister. He became interior minister in 1963, and was appointed second deputy premier four years later.

He became king on the death of his half brother, Khaled, on 3 June 1982.

As effective chief executive since the death of his older half-brother, king Faisal, in 1975 Fahd had played a key part in many aspects of the modernisation programme. Posts he still holds include chairmanship of the key Supreme Petroleum Council and the recently created Military Service Organisation.

The eleventh son of king Abdel-Aziz, King Fahd is a staunch supporter of modernisation and industrialisation, and is one of the most important motivating forces behind the creation of a national consultative council (Majlis al-Shoura). He had some formal education in Riyadh and Makkah, and sent his children to study in the West.

Fahd is the eldest of the seven children of king Abdel-Aziz's favourite wife, Hassa Bint-Ahmad al-Sudairi. His full brothers include Second Deputy Premier and Defence & Aviation Minister Prince Sultan, Riyadh governor Prince Salman and Deputy Interior Minister Prince Ahmad.

Crown Prince Abdullah

First Deputy Premier Crown Prince Abdullah represents the traditional side of the Saudi regime. Born in Riyadh in 1924 he has headed the 40,000-strong National Guard, which draws its recruits exclusively from leading Saudi tribes, since 1963. There is no evidence that Abdullah had a formal education; he is said to have been trained by "noted scholars and intellectuals." Most of his early years were spent in the desert.

Abdullah was appointed second deputy premier in 1975 following king Faisal's assassination. He is the thirteenth son of king Abdel-Aziz; his mother was Princess Hassa Bint-Asi al-Shuraim of the Shammar tribal confederation. He is King Fahd's half-brother.

Abdullah's strengths include excellent relations with tribal leaders and a substantial knowledge of Levantine politics.

Prince Sultan

Prince Sultan was appointed second deputy premier one day after the death of his elder brother and the confirmation of Crown Prince Fahd as king and his half-brother, Prince Abdullah, as heir to the throne. Sultan, sixteenth son of king Abdel-Aziz, was born in Riyadh in 1928.

minister and, seven years later, took the defence and aviation portfolio, a post he still holds.

Prince Turki al-Faisal

Born in 1946, Prince Turki is head of the intelligence services and the youngest of king Faisal's sons. After graduating from the University of California, Prince Turki continued his studies in Islamic law at London university. He played a courageous role in the recapture of the Great Mosque in Makkah in 1979.

Prince Sultan was appointed governor of Riyadh at the age of 18 and helped draft the kingdom's administrative system. He joined the cabinet in 1953 as agriculture minister and worked on early plans to encourage the bedu to settle on modern farms. In 1955, Prince Sultan was apppointed communications

Prince Saud al-Faisal

Born in 1943, Prince Saud has been minister of foreign affairs since 1975. He is the eldest of the five sons of king Faisal by his last and favourite wife, Iffat. The five brothers tend to support a policy of modernisation and economic liberalisation. Educated at Princeton university in the US, Prince Saud has been particularly effective in dealing with western public opinion. ▼

Historical background

"The Arab is a democrat and the greatest and most powerful Arab ruler of the present day is proof of it. Ibn Saud is no more than primus inter pares; his strength lies in the fact that he has for twenty years accurately interpreted the aspirations and will of his people."

St John, later Abdullah, Philby

With the massive figure — in terms both of charisma and height — of Abdel-Aziz Bin Abdel-Rahman al-Saud (commonly known as Ibn Saud) the history of modern Saudi Arabia begins. It was his concept of governance, based on a literal interpretation of the Quran and on the consultative traditions of the bedu, which forms the bedrock of the relationship between monarchy and people today. Indeed, in contrast with the government of the Shah's Iran, which enjoyed little contact with the Iranian people, the House of Saud is connected at every level and in every region, thanks to Ibn Saud's many dynastic marriages. According to David Holden (The House of Saud: see Bibliography): "With about 500 princes descending from Abdel-Aziz, together with wives, daughters and collateral branches of the family, the House of Saud today cannot number less than 20,000 people."

When Ibn Saud conquered Makkah, Islam's holiest city, in 1924 its people, frightened of his over-zealous Ikhwan (brethren — bedu turned missionary warriors) were reassured by his pragmatically generous treatment. "We have a proverb familiar to everyone," he told them. "The people of Makkah know best their valley. . . . I do not see what is more desirable for you than that responsibility for affairs should be placed on your shoulders and I want you to appoint a time for a select group of ulema (religious scholars), dignitaries and merchants to meet together in order for each group to choose a specified number (of its members). . . . to look into its general interest and to investigate its affairs." Ibn Saud became king in 1926. In 1932 the Arabian peninsula, with the exception of the Arabian Gulf states, trucially allied with Britain and the two Yemens (North Yemen, now the Yemen Arab Republic, and South Yemen, now the People's Democratic Republic of Yemen) officially became the kingdom of Saudi Arabia.

The foundations

The history of the religious alliance of temporal ruler and religious reformer which was to become the cornerstone both of Saudi rule and the kingdom's religious fundamentalism began in 1744 with an oath between two men, Muhammad Ibn Abdel-Wahhab and Muhammad Ibn Saud, the ancestor of the present rulers. Muhammad Ibn Abdel-Wahhab gave his name to Wahhabism — an anglicism, as the correct term for the followers of the religious reformer is Muwahhidun (literally, unitarians). Ibn Abdel-Wahhab came from a long line of

Riyadh at the turn of the century

theologians. After preliminary teaching by his father and in Makkah, he studied first in Al-Madinah, Islam's second holiest city, and then in Basra, in modern Iraq. On his return his obsession was to root out the decadence of popular Islam in Arabia and initiate an era of moral reform. After early abortive attempts, he met the ruler of the small desert town of Dir'iya, a few kilometres from Riyadh (see Dir'iya).

The Al al-Shaikh

From the moment the two men made their oath of unity of purpose, based on a common religious ideology, the hegemony of the House of Saud began. Ibn Abdel-Wahhab became known as the shaikh (an honorific literally meaning old man) and Muhammad Ibn Saud as Imam, or guide. The family of the reformer, now known as the Al al-Shaikh (of the family of the Shaikh), today remains one of the four families with whom the Al-Saud intermarry and is pre-eminent within the ulema and the Council of Ministers. At the time of writing the ministers of higher education, justice and agriculture are all members of the Al al-Shaikh.

According to a contemporary Arab chronicler Ibn Bishr, "no camels were mounted and no opinions were voiced by Muhammad Ibn Saud or his son Abdel-Aziz without his (the shaikh's) approval." The eighteenth century traveller Garston Niebuhr wrote of Muhammad Ibn Abdel-Wahhab: "He takes zakat (tax destined for the poor and obligatory in the Quran from every Muslim — see Islam) from all his subjects. . . in order to provide for the poor and to maintain his religion against those he calls unbelievers."

Ibn Abdel-Wahhab was calling for the recognition of the absolute unity of God encompassed in the key words of Islam: "There is no God but God; Muhammad is the Prophet of God (La illah illa Allah; Muhammad Rasoul Allah)." These words are inscribed on the green flag of the kingdom of Saudi

The Al-Fatiha Sura in a Quran in Jeddah

Arabia and are the second of the twice-repeated phrases of the muezzin (Mu'addin, announcer of the hour of prayer) when, five times a day, he calls believers to prayer from the minaret attached to a mosque.

Wahhabism follows the Hanbalite doctrine in its attack on the cult of saints and its insistence on a return to the purity of Islam as it existed at the time of the Prophet Muhammad and the four Caliphs (Khalifa; plural Khulafa) who followed him: Abu Bakr, Omar, Uthman and Ali.

Expansion and defeat

Muhammad Ibn Saud was succeeded as Imam by his son, Abdel-Aziz, who took Riyadh soon after his accession in 1765. Converts flocked to the Saudi banner, drawn by its spiritual ideology. By 1787 most of the Najd, the kingdom's central region, had been absorbed. In 1792 Muhammad Ibn Abdel-Wahhab died. In 1803 Abdel-

Aziz's son, Saud — heir apparent and his father's leading general — marched on the Hejaz in response to an attack by the army of the Sharif of Makkah. Saud took the Holy City and performed the Hajj in company with his warriors (see Islam). By this time Saudi rule extended west to the Hasa and south towards Najran.

However, Saudi hegemony was short-lived. Alarmed by the military and political power of the reforming dynasty, the Ottoman Sultan Mahmoud II commissioned his recalcitrant viceroy in Egypt, Muhammad Ali, to reconquer the Hejaz. Saud died at the moment when, having taken the Hejaz, Ali's army — led by his son Ibrahim — prepared to march on Najd. Saud's son, Abdallah, failed to halt the invaders' advance and Dir'iya was taken and laid waste — as visitors today can see. Abdallah was sent to Istanbul where he was executed.

After the Ottoman forces' withdrawal, Abdallah's son Turki resurrected the family fortunes and retook Riyadh. Although Turki was assassinated in 1834 by a relative, the latter was himself defeated by Turki's eldest son, Faisal, who became Imam. However, Muhammad Ali's forces returned to Najd in 1838, defeated the Imam and sent him captive to Cairo. Five years later he escaped and began a second, 20-year reign. These were years of development. By the end of his reign he had reconquered most of Najd and Hasa. After his death Saudi fortunes again waned, with internal squabbles and the rise of the Rashid family based in Hail. By 1884 Muhammad Ibn Rashid was ruler of Riyadh and within five years most of the Saudi clan had fled into exile in Kuwait.

Traditions of the bedu

Ibn Saud's reconquest of the kingdom of his ancestors must be seen in the context of the bedouin environment from which the Saudis — like all other tribes, clans and families — emerged.

At the turn of the century the Hejaz was ruled by the Sharif of Makkah. With Makkah the focus of the Hajj since the time of the Prophet Muhammad and Jeddah a cosmopolitan seaport, the Hejaz had for long had cosmopolitan populations absorbing eclectic cultural and social influences. But the region had lapsed into a state of decadence which shocked both the pilgrims (Hajjis) and the fundamentalist followers of Ibn Saud.

Apart from the eastern seaboard — centred today on the neighbouring towns of Al-Khobar, Dammam and Dhahran, and the new industrial city of Jubail - most of desert Arabia was the preserve of bedouin tribes who moved from pasture to pasture according to the season and sought to increase their marginal wealth by raiding camel caravans. Such raids were usually nonviolent. The weaker side would normally flee from the stronger and seize back its plundered camels on a more propitious day. Sir John Bagot Glubb (Glubb Pasha), who lived long among the bedu when the ghazzu, or raid, was still a way of life described them as "a cross between Arthurian chivalry and county cricket." There were rules: "You raided to take camels, not merchandise, land or life, and the protocol was precise: no raiding between midnight and dawn, no stealing of sheep and goats — and no molesting of women. . . . To touch or harm (women) would be haram, a shameful thing, and, should you destroy other tents, you should always leave at least one for the women, with provisions, cooking things and coffee pots: for though you might be the visitor today, tomorrow it might be your own mother or sisters at the mercy of someone else's ghazzu" (Lacey: The Kingdom — see Bibliography). Speaking of the early battles between Ibn Saud and the Al-Rashid, Al-Mana (Arabia Unified — see Bibliography) writes: "The unique kind of warfare that resulted was a cat-and-mouse affair, made up of a great deal of marching and counter-marching coupled with frequent small raids and skirmishes; it only rarely culminated in full-scale battle."

Conventions among the bedu were simple, but always pragmatic and usually honourable. The best of them have survived to the present day. Hospitality to a guest was an absolute duty. A man had only to take water or tea with a tribe or merely kiss the tribe's tent to secure protection without question for "three days and one third," at the end of which the tribe had the right to ask him who he was. Even if he turned out to be a deadly foe the tribe would let him go in peace. The nineteenth century British traveller Charles Doughty often invoked this tradition, reminding potentially unfriendly tribes that he had shared "bread and salt" with them. The Austrian convert to Islam, Muhammad Asad (The Road to Makkah — see Bibliography) remarked: "To be the guest of an Arab means to enter for a few hours into the lives of people who want to be your brothers and your sisters."

In bedouin tradition the tribal shaikh is first among equals, selected for his wisdom to arbitrate rather than rule. This tradition of consensus survives today in Saudi Arabia. Even the poorest man will call the king brother when he makes his petition at the weekly majlis (meeting). Foreign businessmen are often astonished to see princes and ministers arguing with servants and teaboys as equals.

The extraordinary taking of Riyadh

In 1902 the 21-year-old Ibn Saud, filled with dreams nurtured in Kuwaiti exile of re-asserting the dynasty of his family and the religious ideology of the shaikh, carried out one of the most bizarre, and certainly one of the most significant, raids in modern history. Under cover of night and accompanied by about nine men he scaled a crumbling part of Riyadh's adobe walls and crept through the sleeping streets to the Musmak Palace where the governor, Ibn Ajlan, was asleep.

The group came to a cowherd's house owned by a family retainer of the House of Saud. Pretending they had come to buy cows they gained access and waited for the governor. The governor arrived at dawn and was killed in a hand-to-hand scuffle. Within 20 minutes the fort, and with it the city, had submitted and the Sauds were again supreme.

Expansion of the House of Saud

The next few years saw almost constant fighting. The Rashid hankered after vengeance. The Hejaz had become soft and corrupt under the rule of the Sharif. In 1904 Ibn Saud took Anayzah in a gruesome battle. "And we broke them and slaughtered of them three hundred and seventy men," he wrote to Shaikh Mubarak, the ruler of Kuwait and the Sauds' host during the years of exile. Throughout this period the Saud's main adversary was Ibn Rashid, whose capital was Hail in the Jebel Shammar region of northern Najd. Ibn Rashid was supported by the Ottoman Turks who still held nominal sway over most of Arabia and effective dominion over Hasa and the Hejaz. Ibn Saud was to capture Hasa in 1913 when the Turkish troops were allowed to depart in peace. As one observer had noted, the Turks had only brought Arabia "discipline, artillery and cholera."

A model society

Ibn Saud aimed to break the freebooting anarchy of the tribes and replace it with a disciplined society in which government was centralised, and law and the constitution based on the Quran. At first he had to depend on the unreliable bedu for his armies. They tended to disperse if they became bored, or if the duration of campaigns interfered with their grazing movements or if victory offered booty which they could carry away.

Ibn Saud's armies on the march

Mercy in victory

In 1906, at a battle near Buraydah, Ibn Rashid was killed. The city, however, was treated kindly. Indeed, Ibn Saud usually embodied the bedouin tradition of mercy in victory, rarely executing his enemies. He even spared the Ikhwan warrior Faisal ad-Dawish, who twice rebelled against Ibn Saud, the second time at the latter's decisive victory over the Ikhwan at the battle of Sibilla in 1929. According to Holden it was said of Faisal ad-Dawish that he could execute a man without consulting the elders; "with Abdel-Aziz (Ibn Saud) it was never true." Ibn Saud's usual policy was to reinstate his opponents with the proviso that ultimate authority was his, and by 1911 he had worn down the peoples of central Arabia into a state of baffled peace.

The Ikhwan

Although Ibn Saud did not found the Ikhwan, religious diehards who established their first commune at Artawiya, east of Riyadh, he quickly realised their value, both militarily and ideologically, in spearheading the parallel conquest and reformation that lay at the roots of the first Saudi dynasty. The Ikhwan of Saudi Arabia are quite distinct from the Ikhwan, or Muslim Brethren, founded in Egypt in the 1930s.

Lacey calls them "God's soldiers, heedless of death and thirsty for glory." Had they been present at the battle of Jarrab, where the young English officer Captain Shakespear died standing in full uniform alongside the Saudi forces, the battle would probably not have been lost (Captain Shakespear: see Bibliography). "In their twenty-year history," writes Lacey, "the Ikhwan never wavered in battle as the Ajman (tribe) had done at Jarrab." According to Lawrence Gouldrup, one of Ibn Saud's main objects in developing the Ikhwan colonies, absorbing the anarchic bedu into disciplined and ideologically motivated communes, was "to reduce divisive tribal feuds in the interest of improving the striking power of the community." (see Bibliography: Arabia Studies VI). After the establishment of the Artawiya settlement, more than 125 others were formed. Ibn Saud soon depended heavily on the Ikhwan, who were both to play a major role in the reconquest of the peninsula and to become a threat when they tried to carry their fanaticism beyond practical bounds.

British friendship

Britain's political agent in Kuwait in 1910 was Captain Shakespear, the successor to Percy Cox. Shakespear quickly built up a friendship with Ibn Saud based on integrity and courage; this mutual empathy may have done much to create a wider empathy between Ibn Saud and the British, and may well have influenced Ibn Saud in overriding the pleas of some of his advisers to support the axis powers during the second world war. Unlike his predecessors, Shakespear made no hypocritical attempts to disguise himself as a Muslim. He remained sternly British and continued to wear his uniform until he died with reckless heroism, alongside Ibn Saud's troops, at the hands of the Rashid in 1914. Ibn Saud wrote to Sir Percy Cox: "We pressed him to leave us, but he refused ...." According to Lacey, when asked to name the most remarkable non-Muslim he knew, Ibn Saud replied without hesitation: "Shakespear." Glubb, who had asked the question, initially took this to mean Ibn Saud had a greater command of English literature than in fact was the case then. It says much for Ibn Saud that he retained his affection for Britain despite the latter's support of his enemy, the Sharif of Makkah, and its equivocal position regarding Palestine, in whose freedom from Zionist domination Ibn Saud passionately believed. The Balfour Declaration of 2 November 1917 had pledged British support for a "national" home for the Jews in Palestine — a promise which totally contradicted the British promises which lay behind the Arab Revolt led by Sharif's son, Faisal, and T E Lawrence (Lawrence of Arabia).

The story of the revolt is well-known in the West (see Bibliography: The Seven Pillars of Wisdom). The Sharif proclaimed the Arab Revolt against the Turks in the Hejaz in June 1916 with full British backing. To inspire Arab disaffection from the Turks during the first world war, the British high commissioner in Egypt, Sir Henry McMahon, had promised the Sharif "independence of Arabia and its inhabitants" in exchange. But these promises were made against promises to the Jews which made any Arab independence in Palestine a non-starter. Lawrence's campaign with Faisal, the attack on Aqaba in which the Turkish guns were pointing the wrong way, the glorious march on Damascus and the final defeat of the Turks are well covered elsewhere.

In 1924 Sharif Hussain infuriated the Islamic world by declaring himself Caliph when the new republican regime in Istanbul abolished the Ottoman Caliphate under Kemal Ataturk.

Describing the Hejaz during the Sharif's rule, one British Arabist remarked: "The population has exchanged the virtues of the bedouin for the worst corruption of eastern town life without casting off the ferocity of the desert. The unspeakable vices of Makkah are a scandal to all Islam and a constant wonder to the Makkans." The Sharif — obstinate and temperamental — was a strong contrast to Ibn Saud, whose religious discipline and courage were balanced by broad-mindedness and humour. Shakespear described him as "straightforward and frank." When the English traveller Gertrude Bell met him in Basra in 1925, she said: "He combines with his qualities as a soldier that grasp of statecraft which is yet more highly prized by the tribesmen." The Dutch consul in Jeddah said of him: "His smile

Ibn Saud as a young man

made his face radiate kindness. In repose his face was grim and forbidding but when he smiled it was completely transformed. . . ." The explorer Philby, who as convert to Islam became Abdullah Philby, immediately fell under Ibn Saud's spell.

Philby — Westminster School, Trinity College, Cambridge, and the father of the British double-agent, Kim — met Ibn Saud in 1917 and built up a long friendship, which on his side took the form of dedication but which left Ibn Saud perpetually puzzled. In 1925 Philby resigned from the British Indian Civil Service and settled as a businessman in Jeddah, and in 1930 he became a Muslim.

The liberation of Makkah

Ibn Saud's peaceful conquest of Makkah followed a tragic event in Taif when his Ikhwan soldiers were said to have run amok. According to Al-Mana: "The account of the loss of Taif given by the Sharifan government to the outside world included allegations that the Ikhwan had behaved with the utmost barbarity and had brutally murdered women and children. Foreigners writing on the subject have repeated these allegations as if they were undisputed fact. For my part I believe them to be entirely false."

When Ibn Saud entered Makkah, it was in peace. He even called an international conference to seek guidance about the type of government the city should enjoy. As he approached the Haram, the shrine that encloses the Ka'aba (see Islam) he sent forward four of his men, unarmed and dressed as pilgrims. Makkah was silent, its beautiful wooden lattice buildings bolted. The four men, riding to the four main points of the city, called out to the Makkans, telling them they were safe for they enjoyed the protection of God and Ibn Saud.

On the following day, the Saudi army, dressed as pilgrims and unarmed, entered the city and set about destroying the ornaments and decorations which were abhorrent to their puritan creed. But they did not harm the people. "Now that the rule of injustice and tyranny is over," Ibn Saud told the people, "our most cherished desire is that the land of Islam be open to all Muslims and that the ordinances of the sacred places be decided by all Muslims."

As Ibn Saud entered the Haram the warrior became the pilgrim. He laid down his sword and took off his headdress (gutra) and gown (thobe). Taking the two simple pieces of cloth which pilgrims wear, he wrapped one piece around his loin and one piece around his shoulder. Bareheaded and wearing sandals, he rode unarmed, as he rode constantly repeating the talbiyah prayer:

"Here I am, Oh God, at thy command. Thou are One and Alone. Here am I."

Jeddah was to take a year to fall to Ibn Saud's son, Faisal. Ibn Saud simply waited for it to do so.

The absorption of the Hejaz jolted the Saudis into a cosmopolitan world and exacerbated the social tensions between the Hejazis and the diehard Ikhwan of the Najd. It has been the ability of Saudi rulers from Ibn Saud onwards to unite these contrasting cultures that has led to the unity of the kingdom today, when people in the most senior positions have names that reflect races from central Asia to Egypt.

However, a conflict of identity did ensue between Ibn Saud — who sought to absorb the best of the modern world — and the Ikhwan extremists, who opposed innovations such as cars, telephones and radio. This conflict reached its nadir in the rebellion of three Ikhwan leaders — Dhaidan Ibn Hithlain, Faisal ad-Dawish and Sultan Ibn Humaid — whose soldiers had been flinging themselves against the British Iraqi armoured cars of Glubb Pasha's Arab Legion. After repeated rebellion against Ibn Saud's centralised state he defeated them at the crucial battle of Sibilla in 1929. As the battle ended Faisal ad-Dawish's women sought shelter in the Saudi camp, a traditional bedouin gesture of submission.

In 1926 Ibn Saud became king of Najd, and the Hejaz, and on 18 September 1932 he proclaimed the unity of the Najd and the Hejaz by announcing the creation of the kingdom of Saudi Arabia. Yet even after his absorption of the Hejaz, which had enjoyed marginal wealth

The Ka'aba at Makkah

from pilgrims' dues, the kingdom remained poor. The world depression of the 1930s affected Saudi Arabia like everywhere else. Later, when oil wealth was bringing in about $2 million a week, the king would recall the days when he would joke with friends such as Philby about storing the kingdom's entire wealth in his saddlebags.

In 1932, Standard Oil Company of California (Socal), to which the king had awarded a concession for Hasa province, struck oil in Bahrain. In 1937 the firm, renamed the Arabian American Oil Company (Aramco), discovered the vital Bahrain cap at the Ayn Hit waterhole near Riyadh (see Ayn Hit). It was then confirmed that immense oil reserves lay beneath the eastern deserts (see The Economy). Ibn Saud made the journey to Dhahran for the ceremonial start-up of production in May 1939. In the 1940s Aramco began work on the trans-Arabian pipeline (Tapline), 1,710 kilometres from the Gulf to the Lebanese port of Sidon. Between 1946 and 1949, Saudi oil production leapt from 164,000 barrels a day (b/d) to 476,000 b/d (see page 333).

On 9 November 1953 Ibn Saud died in Taif. He was buried, as is the Wahhabi custom, in an unmarked grave — an anonymous grave offers no incentive to potential worshippers, such veneration being anathema to Wahhabis. Ibn Saud was succeeded by his son, Crown Prince Saud. In 1958 Saud gave his far-sighted and pious brother, Faisal, full authority for foreign, economic and internal affairs. In 1960, however, Faisal resigned and the king resumed full powers.

In 1964 Saud relinquished all real power to Faisal, who had acted as prime minister since the previous year. His decision to step down in 1964 was supported by the ulema "in the light of developments, the king's condition of health, and his inability to attend to state affairs." In November Saud was formally deposed, Faisal became king and his brother Khaled crown prince.

King Faisal

Faisal was as charismatic as his father. Although an austere and deeply pious Muslim who treasured his role of Islamic preacher as well as politician, Faisal was also a pragmatist. He recognised that the kingdom must absorb the best from western technology without compromising its spiritual culture. "Like it or not," he was quoted as saying, "we must join the modern world and find an honourable place in it."

His foreign policy was characterised by his hatred of communism, whose atheism was anathema to his Wahhabi creed, and by an unbending hostility to Zionism. The latter represented the displacement of his brother Palestinians and, after the 1967 war with Israel, the usurpation of Jerusalem, Islam's holiest city after Makkah and Al-Madinah. When asked by a correspondent about his attitude to socialism, the king said: "We have the Holy Quran and the Sharia law. Why do we need socialism, capitalism, communism or any other ideology?"

Faisal inherited the kingdom when its finances were in chaos, but also when it was on the point of an economic take-off unparalleled in world history. With the world's largest oil reserves (about a quarter of total global resources) Saudi Arabia was producing 33.5 per cent of the total output of Middle East countries when Faisal died in 1975. Aware of the impact such wealth would have on the country, Faisal laid down the goals of the first and second development plans (1970-75 and 1975-80). The plans were designed "to maintain the religious and moral values of Islam, to assure the defence and internal security of the kingdom, to maintain a high rate of economic growth by developing economic resources, to maximise earnings from oil over the long- term and conserve depletable resources, to reduce economic dependence on the export of crude oil, to develop human resources by education, training and raising standards of health, to increase the well-being of all groups within the society and foster social stability under circumstances of rapid social change, and to develop the physical infrastructure to support the achievement of such goals."

The key to the first plan was the decision to process resources into marketable commodities by tapping world demand, particularly in Africa and Asia. To achieve this, the kingdom had to acquire western technology and to diversify from a purely oil-based economy. This implied the ability to maintain such an economy. Faisal was quoted as saying: "In my opinion, it is far better to equip ourselves with the ability to do things on our own without relying on foreigners or on anyone else."

King Faisal's background

Faisal was as well-suited to consolidating Saudi Arabia's position in the world as Ibn Saud was to forging disparate parts into unity. In 1919, aged 14, he had been sent to England to represent his father at a series of meetings designed to show British gratitude for Saudi loyalty to the Allies during the war. Although the trip was ill-prepared on the British side, the young prince made quite an impression on his hosts. Faisal was taken to Greenwich, the Houses of Parliament and Cambridge. There he visited the college of his guide and interpreter, St John Philby. In his biography of Faisal (see Bibliography), Gerald de Gaury says: "(Faisal) exhibited the always splendid manners and equanimity of his race, adapting himself with perfect ease to western life."

Although Faisal had had no more formal education, apart from the vital Quranic studies, than his brothers, the combination of foreign travel and innate intelligence was later to make him the epitome of a visionary ruler. After Ibn Saud's conquest of the Hejaz, Faisal was made its viceroy. It was a wise choice. The wordly Hejazis were at first suspicious of the simple but idealistic peoples of central Arabia who had conquered them. The miracle today is that the contrast between two regional cultures is not more distinct. Faisal had besieged Jeddah, but the province was treated with pragmatic moderation and respect when it finally fell. Harsh treatment was meted out for murder and theft, and the bedouin lawlessness which had made the Hajj a nightmare was stamped out. Faisal identified himself with the Hejazis, an attitude which helped the reabsorption of this important province.

King Faisal's regional role

Faisal played a vital role in the 1950s, when pan-Arabism was emergent and Nasserism — reaching its peak with Nasser's nationalisation of the Suez Canal in 1956 — was the dominant force in Arab countries. In 1957, Egypt and Syria joined to form the United Arab Republic. Soon after, Lebanon was engulfed in a civil war between the proponents and opponents of the union, with the ideological rivalry that this implied. To protect himself, Yemen's Imam Ahmad joined the union; in 1958 a group of army officers slaughtered the Iraqi royal family and established a republic. Against the atheist ideologies which were now in fashion, Faisal countered with Islam, which can today be seen to have far stronger roots than new ideologies.

When Imam Ahmad died in 1962

King Faisal and Queen Elizabeth II during the king's state visit to the UK in May 1967

King Faisal respected the traditions of his people and was accessible to all

and was succeeded by his son, a group of Yemeni army officers, led by Colonel Abdullah al-Sallal, seized control and proclaimed a pro-Nasser republic. From 1962 until soon after the 1967 Arab-Israeli war there was civil war in Yemen. Egypt backed the republicans and Saudi Arabia the royalists. Faisal called for pan-Islamic solidarity.

The defeat of the Arabs by the Israelis in 1967 left Egypt militarily weak. With the withdrawal of aid to both sides by Egypt and Saudi Arabia the Yemeni civil war came to an end. After Nasser's death in 1970 King Faisal attracted the mantle of authority in the Arab world. Two years later, President Sadat dismissed Egypt's Soviet advisers. Faisal's goal of harnessing Saudi money to Egyptian manpower to implement the kingdom's development plans became a reality.

Although the 1973 war with Israel failed to restore Jerusalem, the West Bank and the Gaza Strip, it demonstrated a strong Arab morale and constituted a near-victory for the Arab states. Despite its friendship with the US, Saudi Arabia felt obliged to put pressure on the Americans to influence Israel to withdraw from Jerusalem and the occupied territories by cutting oil production. Saudi Arabia used the oil weapon for ideological rather than economic purposes. The establishment of the state of Israel in 1948 and the resulting flight of most Palestinians from their natural home has always represented a deep-rooted agony to Arabs of all persuasions. The Israeli occupation of Jerusalem in 1967 shocked all Muslims, particularly the Saudis. Saudi Arabia sees itself as an Islamic state par excellence and is protector of the holy cities of Makkah and Al-Madinah.

The war and oil

On 17 October 1973 the members of the Organisation of Arab Petroleum Exporting Countries (OAPEC) met in Kuwait. They agreed to cut back oil production and exports by 5 per cent from the September 1973 levels. The cutback was to be increased by an additional 5 per cent each month until all Israeli forces were withdrawn from occupied Arab lands. The following month, OAPEC's members decided to increase the production cutback by 25 per cent. When the US announced its intention of granting $2,200 million in military aid to Israel, the Arab states decided to embargo all exports to the US. In the same month, the Arab oil producers decided to raise the price of a barrel of oil from $1.77 to $3.05, and then to $7. By January 1974, oil prices had increased fourfold. The embargo was lifted two months later.

Death of King Faisal

On 25 March 1975, seated at a majlis to greet well-wishers at his Riyadh palace, King Faisal was shot dead by his nephew, Prince Faisal Ibn Musaid. The king was buried in an unmarked grave, according to Wahhabi custom. Although the king had been murdered for no apparent political motive, it was a relief when the succession passed without fuss to Faisal's brother, Prince Khaled. His other brother, Prince Fahd, was declared crown prince and first deputy prime minister, and Prince Abdullah, commander-in-chief of the National Guard, as second deputy prime minister.

The reign of King Khaled

No major policy change was effected by the succession. King Khaled confirmed that he would follow Faisal's campaign for Arab solidarity and the strengthening of Arab unity. He also pledged to continue his main political objectives: the recovery of occupied Arab territories seized by Israel and the "liberation of the City of Jerusalem from the claws of Zionism."

The following year, Saudi Arabia established diplomatic relations with the People's Democratic Republic of Yemen (South Yemen).

In November 1979 the Great Mosque at Makkah was occupied by about 250 followers of Juhaiman Bin Saif al-Otaibi, a Muslim fanatic who aimed to proclaim the Mahdi (the Chosen One) within the mosque that day, the first day of the Islamic year 1400. Two weeks of bloody fighting ensued before the siege ended, by which time 102 rebels and 27 Saudi soldiers had died. On 9 January 1980, 63 of the rebels were led out to the squares of various towns to which they had been taken and publicly beheaded.

Following this unhappy episode the subject of the Majlis al-Shora (consultative assembly), first suggested by Ibn Saud on his entry into Makkah in 1924, was raised again by Crown Prince Fahd. "New government concepts are needed," he said, setting up a committee under his brother Naif. A year later Naif proposed a new consultative council — "men of wisdom, knowledge and high morals to advise the government in policy making." He also suggested a heavy decentralisation plan. Meanwhile, the regional situation became more tense. South Yemen was clearly in the Soviet camp while North Yemen concluded a weapons deal with the Soviet Union in November 1979. The following month the Soviet Union threatened the entire Islamic world by invading Afghanistan. In September 1980 war broke out between Iraq and Iran, and Saudi Arabia felt bound to support an Arab ally. The kingdom was meanwhile building up its military defence systems by buying F-15 fighter aircraft from the US. In March 1981 the US, despite much local opposition, agreed to sell Saudi Arabia five airborne warning and control systems (AWACS) aircraft in addition to the four sold soon after the outbreak of the Iran/Iraq war. In May 1981 Saudi Arabia joined five other states in establishing the Gulf Co-operation Council, set up

> **Gulf Co-operation Council charter**
>
> In recognition of the special ties which bind each of the UAE, Bahrain, Saudi Arabia, Oman, Qatar and Kuwait to one another, arising from their common ideology and heritage, and the similarity between their social, political and demographic structures, and out of a desire to promote their peoples' prosperity, growth and stability through closer co-operation, the foreign ministers of these states met in Riyadh, Saudi Arabia, on 4 February, 1981, corresponding to 29 Rabi al-Awwal, 1401 AH.
>
> The talks at this meeting were aimed at drawing up a practical framework for the consolidation and development of co-operation between the states concerned. As a result it was decided to establish a co-operation council between these Arab Gulf states, which would have a general secretariat and hold regular meetings, both on summit and foreign minister level, in order to achieve the goals of the states and their peoples in all fields.
>
> *Issued 4 February 1981 in Riyadh*

both as an economic alliance and as a military security pact (see above).

Palestine

Saudi diplomacy has become increasingly involved in seeking a solution to the Arab-Israeli conflict, particularly since the Israelis' tragic invasion of Lebanon in June 1982. The basis of Saudi policy regarding Palestine is contained in King Fahd's eight-point plan — the Fahd plan — published in August 1981.

Review of King Khaled's reign

Khaled's role during his reign was far more assertive than had been expected in view of his recurring ill-health. One of his first acts on becoming king on 25 March 1975 was to declare an amnesty for political prisoners. On 13 October he formed a new government in which 15 of the 25 portfolios were held by commoners. His mediation during the Riyadh summit of October 1976 between Egypt's President Sadat and Syria's President Assad was a key factor in ending the Lebanese civil war. In December that year Khaled opposed the hawks in OPEC by pushing for a 5, rather than a 10, per cent increase in oil prices. On 17-19 February 1979 he received the UK's Queen Elizabeth on her state visit to the kingdom, a visit reciprocated in June 1981. In January of that year he had chaired the crucial Makkah/Taif Islamic summit.

Prone, however, to ill health — he had a serious heart attack in February 1980 — King Khaled died of a heart attack on 14 June 1982, aged 69.

King Fahd

Prince Fahd, the fifth surviving son of Ibn Saud and a member of the Sudairi Seven (see Bibliographies of Princes), was the obvious choice of successor because of his intelligence, understanding of world affairs and interest in development. Fahd is expected to rely heavily on the support of his full brothers such as Prince Salman, the governor of Riyadh (see Riyadh). Continuity should be assured by the fact that Fahd has, for the past eight years, been the chief formulator of Saudi policy.

In March 1982 the then Crown Prince Fahd pledged that the consultative council and the basic statutes of government would soon be promulgated. In early 1983, several new cabinet ministers were appointed; since 1975 there had only been one change in the council of ministers. One of King Fahd's main achievements has been his contribution to the creation of the GCC. However, his task is likely to be made more difficult by the US' ambivalence towards the Israeli invasion of Lebanon and the consequent crushing of Palestinian resistance, of which Fahd is an ardent and sincere supporter.

Trevor Mostyn

Islam

As the historic heartland of Islam, Saudi Arabia plays a pre-eminent role within the Islamic world, a world that extends from Morocco in the west to Indonesia in the east. Both Islam's holiest cities, Makkah and Al-Madinah, lie on the kingdom's western seaboard and its history, culture and society are rooted in the puritan Islamic ideology of the eighteenth-century reformer, Muhammad ibn Abdel-Wahhab (see History).

As dawn breaks behind the palms, the mountains, the lovely coastlines and the modern buildings of Saudi Arabia, the muezzin climbs the minaret beside the mosque and calls the faithful to prayer with these simple words, the Muslim Shahada:

> "God is most great.
> I testify that
> There is no god but God
> and that Mohammad
> Is the Prophet of God.
> Come to the prayer!
> Come to the salvation!
> Prayer is better than sleep,
> God is most great,
> There is no god but God."

The call to prayer is made five times a day — only the dawn prayer includes the phrase "Prayer is better than sleep" — with each phrase twice repeated. Unlike the bells of Christianity or the horns of the Jews, the first Muslims chose the simplest instrument of all, the human voice. For anyone who has visited a Muslim country the two opening phrases "Allahu Akbar" and "Ash-hadu an la illah illa Allah; Mohammad Rasoul Allah" will linger in the mind.

Islam is an Arabic word meaning submission, implying man's duty to submit himself to worship and obey the One True God of Abraham. Islam was not founded. It existed before all time.

When, in the early seventh century AD, the Prophet Mohammad called upon the people of Makkah to turn away from the pagan goddesses they worshipped and submit to the one true God of Abraham, he was speaking of the same one God of Judaism and Christianity. He maintained, however, that the Jews and the Christians had adulterated their holy books and that the Quran was the true and unadulterated word of God.

Muslims, therefore, do not regard God as separate from the God in the Torah or the New Testament. Their principal disagreement with Christianity is in their rejection of Jesus' divinity. The Quran says: "He (God) was neither born, nor gave birth (to anyone)."

Although Islam has become better known in the West, it is still misunderstood by many westerners. Misunderstanding, and even antipathy, has been fuelled by historical conflicts such as the struggles between Christian and Moor in Spain; attempts by the mercenary Crusaders to take the Holy Land by force, and since the second world war, Israeli propaganda attempting to justify the Zionist occupation of Palestine.

How many westerners realise that Muslims revere Jesus as a prophet second only to Mohammad, and Mary as the mother of Jesus, or that one of the Quran's most lovely surahs (chapters) is called Miriam (Mary) and is a mirror-image of the New Testament story? How many realise that Islam and Christianity share the principles of compassion, honesty, justice and love (words on the lips of every Muslim as he prays)?

Of Mary, God tells Mohammad to recite in the Quran: "And she who guarded her chastity, we breathed of our spirit into her and made both her and her son as a sign for (everyone in) the universe."

The Quran is God's word spoken to Mohammad in Al-Madinah and Makkah in the seventh century AD. Muslims consider it the uncreated word of

God and the greatest of God's miracles. In Islam, the spiritual and temporal worlds are not separated. Rules for man's spiritual and temporal behaviour are clearly laid down in the Quran and in the Hadith (Sayings of the Prophet).

Islamic law (Sharia) is based on the Quran and the Hadith. Muslims believe that everything in a man's life — even in the modern, technological world — can be guided by Islam.

The Prophet Mohammad was an orphan member of the merchant Quraysh clan in Makkah, born in the early seventh century AD. As he grew up, he abhorred the corruption he saw gripping the city. Pagan worship of three goddesses was widespread — baby girls were buried alive, because girls were considered an economic curse — and women's status was inferior.

At this time, God spoke to Mohammad, calling on his people to repent and return to the one God of Abraham. The voice told him to take down the words, saying "read" (iqra) — the verbal noun Quran is derived from the word iqra.

When Mohammad recited the words to the pagan Makkans, they threatened him and his followers. So they decided to migrate (Hijra) to Al-Madinah, where Mohammad had been invited to arbitrate in a dispute. The Hijra marked the starting point of the Islamic calendar — AH 1.

The Madinans submitted immediately to Islam — many of the longer Quranic surahs are Madinan. There followed a series of battles with the Quraysh, who eventually submitted to the Islamic ideal. As a prelude to his final return to the holy city of Makkah, Mohammad and his followers made the pilgrimage, or Hajj, to Makkah during the holy month.

From the moment the Prophet returned to Makkah, the expansion of Islam throughout most of Arabia began. On Mohammad's death, temporal authority was inherited by an elected successor or Khalifah (Caliph). During

A hajji places his head inside the protective silver sheath to kiss the Black Stone in the Ka'aba at Makkah

this period of the Rashidun (or rightly-guided) caliphs — Abu Bakr (632-634), Umar (634-644), Uthman (644-656) and Ali (656-661) — Islam conquered Syria, Iraq, Persia and Egypt. Most of the Middle East and North Africa was firmly Muslim by the time of the battle of Siffin, which was to lead to the end of the khalifate of the Rashidun and the emergence of the Umayyad empire, based in Damascus.

The five pillars of Islam

The religious duties of a Muslim centre on the five pillars (arkan) of Islam. The first is the Shahada or Profession of Faith; the second is prayer (salah). A Muslim must turn towards Makkah and recite the prescribed prayer five times a day: at dawn, midday, midafternoon, sunset and nightfall.

King Khaled's bodyguards pray at Riyadh airport

In all Islamic countries, whether in the mosque, on a carpet in front of a grocer's shop, beside a convoy of lorries in the desert, or merely at home, the believing Muslim will stop work, check his bearing on Makkah, line up with his companions, and perform the prayer.

It is a moving sight in Saudi Arabia to see men of all classes and races praying together, wherever they may be, with the same bodily postures and genuflections, facing Makkah. The most important prayer, the Friday prayer, includes a sermon (khutbah) delivered by the prayer-leader (imam) from the pulpit (minbar) of the mosque.

The third pillar is almsgiving (Zakat). The zakat has developed from a voluntary act of love and charity towards the poor, to an obligatory property tax destined for the needy. In the surah Everyman, God tells Mohammad to recite: "They offer food to the needy, the orphan and the captive out of love for Him. 'We are only feeding you for God's sake. We want no reward from you, nor thanks'."

Ramadan

The fourth pillar is fasting (Sawm). Every Muslim must fast from dawn to dusk during the holy month of Ramadan. Ramadan commemorates the month during which the Quran was first revealed and in which Mohammad's followers were victorious over the Makkans at the battle of Badr. Ramadan varies according to the cycle of the moon. In 1982 it lasted from mid-June to mid-July (see Practical Guide).

The breaking of the fast

The joyous Eid al-Fitr marks the end of Ramadan with an explosion of feasting and entertainment. Throughout Saudi Arabia and the Gulf, you will hear the familiar greeting: "Eidkum mbarek" (May your Eid be blessed.) Another Arabic greeting used at the Eid as well as at the New Year and birthdays is "Kul am winta bkhair" (May you be happy every year).

Eid al-Fitr, like the start of Ramadan itself, is heralded by cannon shots, usually before 2300 on the eve of the feast. Children shout with joy in the streets when they hear the first shot, knowing that the following day will be a holiday and bring presents.

The men and boys must get up at

Pilgrims arriving at Jeddah airport en route for Makkah

dawn on the morning of the feast to pray in the mosque, after the family exchanges greetings. Depending on the family's standing, the head of the household will often hold a majlis for neighbours and friends. The visitors then return to their neighbourhood to distribute cash and food to their poorer neighbours. Meanwhile, the women spend much of the first morning and the previous night cooking immense feasts. Hotels throughout Saudi Arabia arrange special Eid feasts which are widely advertised in the press.

The Hajj

The fifth, and last, pillar is the pilgrimage to Makkah (the Hajj). Every Muslim who can afford it, and who is fit enough, should make the journey at least once in his lifetime.

At the time of the pilgrimage, the pilgrim (hajji) enters the holy precincts of Makkah, wearing a white, seamless garment (ihram). He walks seven times round the Kaabah, the black stone in the centre of the holy mosque, and performs the sevenfold course between the little hills of Safa and Marwah near Makkah. Muslims perform this in memory of Haggar, of the Old Testament, who ran seven times between Safa and Marwah seeking a spring for her thirsty son.

The Hajj begins with the march to Arafat. This lasts from the seventh to the eighth of the Islamic month of Dhu-l-Hijjah. The pilgrims' halts (wuquf) take place at the sanctuaries of Arafat, Al-Muzdalifah and Mina. The stone-throwing ceremony is at Jamrat al-Aqabah, on the way to the valley of Mina. The pilgrimage formally ends with the Eid al-Adha (festival of sacrifice), in which a camel, sheep or horned domestic animal is sacrificed at Mina on the tenth of Dhu-l-Hijjah. After the shaving of the head, the ihram is discarded and secular dress (ihlal) is resumed. As long as the hajji is muhrim (in a sanctified place) he must refrain from sexual intercourse, shedding blood, hunting and uprooting plants (for fuller details, see Makkah under Regions).

The Islamic way of life

Muslims see their religion as an integral part of daily life. By contrast, to many Muslims, Christianity seems otherworldly and without practical application to life. When Mohammad began preaching to the Makkans, corruption was rife, polytheism was the order of the day, women had no financial security. Mohammad brought to Arabia an ordered society, in which man's social, spiritual, political and economic status was clearly defined.

For example, the Quran lays down clear economic guidelines: "Oh you who believe, do not forbid yourself the good things which God made lawful to you and do not exceed the limits." According to one Hadith, the Prophet said: "Your faith is incomplete unless you desire for your fellow brother what you desire for yourself." The Quran condemns all unearned income — usury, gambling, monopolistic trade and the meddling of middlemen: "God has permitted trading and forbidden taking interest" (The Cow 2:275).

Islam calls for the fulfilment of life and condemns the inordinate. "Eat and drink, and do not be extravagant; He does not love the extravagant" (The Heights 7:31). Some western critics have long recognised the intrinsic justice of Islam; H G Wells commented: "Islam has created a society more free from widespread cruelty and social oppression than any society has ever been in the world before."

Islam sees itself as a religion of mercy and love. Indeed, the opening phrase of the Quran — and one of the most commonplace expressions used by Muslims is "B'ism Illahi ar-Rahman ar-Rahim" (in the name of God, the Merciful, the Compassionate). Some of the loveliest lines in the Quran concern love and kindness. Mohammad is told to recite: "Did he not find thee an orphan and give thee shelter; did he not find thee erring and guide thee?" and later in the same surah: "As for the orphan, do not avoid him; as for the man who has lost his way, do not reject him." In Small Kindness (surah 107:1-3) the Prophet is told to recite: "Have you seen someone who rejects religion? That is the person who pushes the orphan aside and does not encourage feeding the needy." As in Christianity, the only unforgivable crime in Islam is apostasy — abandonment of faith.

Women — an Islamic view

In the West, many people believe that Islam treats women as inferior. Muslims believe the opposite. Although the Prophet encouraged monogamy, polygamy was allowed. This was because the death of Muslim warriors in battle led to widowhood and, at that time, widowhood could mean starvation. However, the Quranic line in which a man is permitted to take up to four wives is followed immediately by one which reads: "If you cannot deal equitably and justly with all, you shall marry only one." The meaning of equity (adl) is equity both in social treatment and in love.

The demand that women should dress and behave modestly is seen by Muslims as a symbol of the importance of women as mothers and guardians of the family. In the Quran, women are told to remain chaste: "Tell believing women to avert their glances and guard their private parts, and not to display their charms. . . They should fold their shawls over their bosoms..." (The Light 24:30-31). (see Background: The Muslim woman in Saudi Arabia.)

Islamic law — Sharia

Sharia law derives from four sources — the Quran, the Sunnah, Ijma and Qiyas. The Quran is the primary and most important source. When a judge (qadi) needs further guidance to make his decision he may draw on the Sunnah. The Sunnah consists of those of the Prophet's deeds and utterances (Hadith) which have been passed down the generations and backed up by a chain of authority accepted by the Islamic umma (nation). Ijma and Qiyas are of less importance than either the Quran or the Sunnah; Ijma is the consensus of ulema (religious scholars) on problems whose solutions are not directly found in the Quran or the Sunnah. The final source, Qiyas, means "reasoning by analogy" with regard to the first three sources, where a clear decision cannot be made on the basis of those three.

As in most western systems, a man is deemed innocent in Sharia law until proved guilty. Likewise, the burden of proof falls not on the accused but on the accuser. Again, as in the West, a system of appeals exists. In Sharia law all men are equal before the court — the plaintiff and the defendant sit side by side while the case is being heard.

The qadi's role is an active one. He will question all sides at will, there being neither jury nor (usually) lawyers between himself and the parties at dispute. Sometimes the qadi will conclude a case by "sulh" or reconciliation, when he will usually recommend which party is in the right.

To prove his case, the plaintiff must produce two or, in certain cases, four eye-witnesses. If he cannot produce such witnesses he may, instead, demand an oath from the defendant. The latter will automatically be judged guilty if he refuses to take it. Christians and Jews — to Muslims the protected "People of the Book" — take a separate oath. The Christian oath is "In the name of God, who gave Jesus, son of Mary, the Holy Bible and made him cure the sick, the leper, and the deaf, I swear."

Muslims maintain that few men would dare risk the fires of hell by making a false oath.

Sunnis and Shia

The great majority of Saudis are Sunnis (from Sunnah, the "path" of the Prophet, i e orthodox). The Sunnis differ from the Shia (from "sect" of Ali) in that they support the traditional method of election to the caliphate and accept the caliphs of the Ummayads (the dynasty which followed the period of the Rashidun). The Shias' main disagreement with the Sunnis is in their support for the claims of Ali, the Prophet Mohammad's son-in-law, to the caliphate. The Saudi Shia are almost entirely restricted to the Eastern province.

Modern mosque in Dhahran

The geography of Saudi Arabia

As those who have driven out of the sands of the Rub' al-Khali (Empty Quarter) desert of Saudi Arabia into the green palm oasis of Najran will know, the term desert is usually meaningless. Even true desert can be deceptive, as travellers learn to their astonishment, passing through a sea of sand one day only to return through a carpet of flowers where light rainfall has suddenly activated patient seeds.

As a geographical unit, Arabia stretches from central Syria in the north to the Indian Ocean in the south and from the Red Sea in the west to the Arabian Gulf in the east. The Arabian platform is a huge, detached piece of ancient rock between the even larger platform of Africa and the fold systems of Turkey and Iran. It experiences extremes of heat, dryness and humidity. Rainfall exceeds 250 millimetres a year only in the extreme southwest.

The Hejaz

The coastal territory between the Gulf of Aqaba in Jordan and Al-Madinah, Islam's holiest city after Makkah, is known as the Hejaz (barrier). The mountains in southern Hejaz reach heights of up to 3,000 metres, with a northern plateau of 1,000-1,500 metres. In the west they fall steeply to a narrow coastal plain. Rainfall is rare but torrents lasting several days sweep down the mountainsides every few years cutting both deep and shallow valleys.

The eastern side of the Hejaz mountains is less precipitous and — despite the scarcity of water — better suited to agriculture. The valleys are wider and shallower so water can be stored more easily. The area, ideal for oasis settlements, became the obvious route for the caravans that have passed from north to south for millenia. The oases have also encouraged the garden cultivation of cereals, vegetables and fruit that has supported towns such as Tabuk and Al-Ula.

On the seaward side of the Hejaz mountains the run-off water is swift. The coastal plain, particularly in the north, offers little scope for cultivation. Narrow inlets (shurum) penetrate from the sea at intervals but extensive coral reefs make much of the coastline difficult of access for shipping. Some shurum are clear of reefs but Jeddah, despite its immense artificial ports, is not favoured in this way. The Red Sea coastal plain, known as the Tihama, varies in width from 15-50 kilometres and extends into the Asir region below and beyond into North Yemen.

Asir

Most of the Asir region, which starts where the Tihama narrows south of latitude 20 degrees north, stands above 1,500 metres, although some peaks reach as high as 3,000 metres. Asir enjoys rainfall of 150-300 millimetres

Luxuriant crops near Najran

City park, Jeddah

Office in old Jeddah

Spring floods near Raudhat al-Khuraim

Shammar bedu

Jeddah museum

a year and is for part of the year under the influence of the Indian Ocean monsoons. Fast streams pour down the mountains for some months but these rarely reach the sea. On the higher slopes forests of palms, thorns and evergreen bushes proliferate and millet, wheat and dates are grown. The government recognises the region's agricultural potential and has undertaken irrigation schemes in the Wadi Jizan and Abha areas (see Regions — The South).

The Najd

The topography of the Najd, the heartland of Arabia around Riyadh, with its diversity of regions, differs from the great desert — the Nafud — in the north and the Rub al-Khali (Empty Quarter) in the southeast. The Najd varies between areas of uplands and escarpments, small plateaux, scarps, broad valleys and dry rivers.

In some regions the mountains reach heights of more than 500 metres above the plateau level. The region is characterised by sedimentary series of mainly Jurassic and later rocks. The most prominent of these is the Jabal Tuwaiq escarpment which rises 300 metres above the plateau. Rainfall is slight on the plains but heavier in the highlands and hollows, such as the Ayn Hit waterhole.

One of the main features of Najd is oasis agriculture, the largest oases being Riyadh, Buraydah, Hail, Jabrin and Anayzah. Nomadism has been a traditional feature of the region, although with the advent of oil wealth the bedu have been drawn increasingly to the cities. Staple crops in the oases are dates and fruits ranging from figs to oranges.

The Rub al-Khali (The Empty Quarter)

The Empty Quarter, one of the biggest sand deserts in the world, covers an area of more than 500,000 square kilometres and measures 1,200 by 500 kilometres. It has been made famous by its crossing by three British

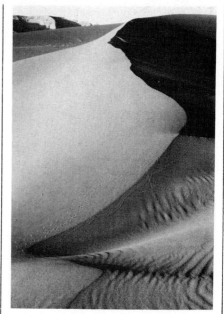

Treacherous, beautiful dunes in the Empty Quarter

travellers. Bertram Thomas first crossed it in 1930 and described it in his Arabia Felix. St John Philby crossed it in 1932 describing it in his Rub al-Khali. In the 1940s Wilfred Thesiger crossed it and described it memorably in Arabian Sands. Thomas crossed by a well-watered route across the central sands by Dakaka to the Qatar peninsula, a route used by the bedu. Philby crossed further to the west, reaching the Wadi Dawasir. Thesiger made two crossings, one in 1946-47 and the other in 1947-48.

Thesiger's first crossing took him from Salala in Oman through the Ramlat al-Ghafa and the 'Uruq al-Shaiba in the unexplored eastern section up into the Liwa oasis, which is in the present-day United Arab Emirates (UAE). His second crossing took him from the Hadramaut, now in South Yemen, through the territory of the Saar tribe across the southern portion to the Wadi Dawasir and up along the Tuwaiq escarpment through Sullaiyil and Layla (see Layla).

The Eastern Region (Hasa)

The eastern coastal region between the Musandam peninsula of Oman and the Shatt al-Arab, the bight which links Iran with Iraq and Kuwait, is never higher than 200 metres. It consists mainly of an undulating plain with occasional low hills. Much of the surface is covered with sand and gravel. Dunes are formed by winds blowing soft sand from the interior towards the coast. Other areas are characterised by gravel plains with dry river beds (wadis). The coastline is mostly shallow with coral reefs. From the air formations of dunes and of coral beneath the blue waters can easily be seen. Another prominent feature of the landward regions is sabkhat (salt marshes) fed either by the sea or by evaporated underground waters. The Hasa region lies between Qatar and Kuwait within Saudi Arabia. Huge water tables lie beneath the Hasa, coming from upland regions of the Tuwaiq escarpment and even the Hejaz mountains. The water sometimes rises as natural springs.

The Nafud

The Nafud desert in the north is one of the driest in Saudi Arabia although some light rainfall in parts leads to the bizarre appearance of annual spring grasses. Between the sandstone escarpments of the Nafud, dunes of loose sand can reach heights of 100 metres. Daytime summer temperatures can reach 49°C while in winter frost is common. Sandstorms, caused by temperamental and violent winds, are frequent. These winds create crescent-shaped dunes. Water lies beneath the surface in the lowland depressions where oasis agriculture produces fruit, barley, dates and vegetables. The western oases obtain water from artesian wells fed by rainwater from the Hejaz mountains. The well at Tayma, for example (see Tayma), is 20 metres deep and 37 metres in diameter. □

Vegetation

It is natural to think of Arabia as a great desert. Early travellers such as Burton, Doughty, Bertram Thomas, Philby and, more recently, Wilfred Thesiger — the last of the great explorers of the old school — all pitted their wits and stamina against cruel waterless wastes and, in great peril and hardship, crossed them to get from A to B, or simply because they were there.

The impression that the desert is there is strengthened by the glimpse from the aircraft window crossing Arabia when, dust haze permitting, you see from some 10,000 metres bleak barren mountains, or a limitless tawny plain, where nothing apparently grows.

It is all a matter of rain and water — the acute shortage of it. The Arabian peninsula is part of the great Sindo-Saharan desert, which lies between two weather systems — the Mediterranean to the north, and the tropical to the south. The first gets most of its rain from the eastward-travelling depressions which form over the eastern Atlantic and the Mediterranean, principally in winter and spring, and the second, from the tropical monsoon in summer. The desert in between may get a splash from both, either, or neither.

Most of the Arabian peninsula gets less than 100 millimetres a year. But even the notorious Rub al-Khali (Empty Quarter) has rain sometimes, although rarely twice in the same place in the same year. The desert plants have to be able to survive several successive years with scarcely any rain. Several species of plants have adapted so that few parts of the desert are devoid of all vegetation permanently, although it is often sparse, localised, or absent during the rainless periods.

Plants adapt to the desert in two main ways: the first is opportunism, and applies to a group of predominantly annual or ephemeral plants; the second

Harvesting the wheat fields of Al-Ghat

is resistance to drought and ability to extract and store whatever moisture there is, with minimal loss.

The opportunist, ephemeral plants, sprout quickly after rain, flower and produce seed within a few weeks — seeds which then remain dormant in the ground, perhaps for several years, until the next fall of rain. Even a moderate fall of rain brings a transformation that is nothing short of miraculous; for a while the desert blooms where there was virtually nothing before.

To the Arab pastoralists — the bedu — this annual desert vegetation (the ushb) is more than a thing of beauty — it is their livelihood. They must be quick to spot these annual pastures to bring out and fatten their flocks of camels, goats and sheep before it disappears once again. So the scouts are constantly looking for areas of more recent rain and new pastures. A nomadic life is thus a matter of necessity rather than choice. It is a precarious existence and it is not surprising that with the discovery of oil and the modernisation of Arabia the bedu have left the desert to seek jobs and an easier life in towns, or with oil companies.

But some bedu remain and to these, modern transport and technology have brought improvements, albeit at some cost to the values of their traditional way of life. Scouting is now done by fast cars; sheep and goats are often transported by truck from pasture to pasture, and water is brought by tanker. Fodder crops and hay are produced where possible for the drought periods.

The way plants survive the desert through resistance cum adaptation takes ingenious, sometimes bizarre forms. There is the extensive root system, both just below the surface and in depth, which seeks out moisture wherever it might be; leaves may be greatly reduced in size to cut water loss through evaporation, as in acacias, or change their shape, or be lost altogether as in tamarix, or the desert shrubs, calligonum and haloxylon. Conversely, the leaves may be fleshy to store water, as in the many salt bushes, or moisture may be stored in stems and trunks as in the cactiform euphorbias, or adenium arabicum with its grotesquely swollen trunk.

Drainage is all-important. The amount of water accumulating in even a shallow depression can be several times that of direct rainfall, thanks to the run-off from the surrounding higher ground, and will thus support a much better plant growth.

Fertile regions

A bigger catchment area will collect proportionately more rain water. Wadis (seasonal streams and rivers) support dense groves of tamarix and acacias and a variety of salt bushes and tussock grasses, even in desert areas. Larger wadis may flow for several months after rain and when the flow stops, the water table will remain high for some time after. Here traditional agriculture of the oasis type can be developed. The main crop is the date palm — a plant which, as the Arabs say, likes to have "its feet in water and its head in fire." Here it finds optimal conditions for growth because it must not rain while the dates are ripening. In small irrigated plots — partly protected by palms — fruit trees such as pomegranate, peach, apricot, lime and quince grow. This is as well as grapes, vegetables, melons, water melons, fodder crops, a little wheat, barley and even rice. In recent years, artesian water and the generally fertile desert soils have been exploited and oasis agriculture has been expanded and modernised, especially in the Hasa, Al-Kharj and Qassim provinces.

But by no means all of Arabia is desert. Enough rain falls in the highlands of the southern Hejaz and particularly of Asir for dry farming of wheat and barley — perhaps as much as 800 millimetres a year in the wetter parts. Rainfall here is spread through the year and, with occasional mists, provides good conditions for both wild and cultivated plants. The celebrated Mocha coffee is grown on terraced mountain slopes not only in Yemen, but also in Asir province of Saudi Arabia. Cereal crops — barley and wheat from winter to spring and sorghum millet, in summer — are grown extensively, as well as fruit and some vegetables.

Inevitably the demands of agriculture and other forms of land use by a large human population have exerted a considerable pressure on the natural vegetation, probably from early Himyaritic times. Although little original forest or woodland remains in Yemen, some still survives in Asir and the southern Hejaz. Here on the highest peaks — rising to some 3,000 metres at Suda, above the town of Abha — and on the somewhat lower ones at Bilahmar, Bilasmar and Bilad Zahran, patches of juniper (Juniperus procera), woodland and groves of wild olive (Olea chrysophylla) are found, especially around Bilad Zahran.

Elsewhere in the highlands are thorn trees (Acacia spp), wild figs (Ficus spp) and a variety of smaller trees, shrubs and bushes. Some of the latter, especially the wild lavenders and other labiates and composites, are very aromatic, while species of aloe, caralluma, kalanchoe and cactiform euphorbias form rock communities. The scenery throughout the highlands is enchanting and reminiscent of parts of Lebanon. Now a highway has been built linking Taif and Abha with Najran, access to the highlands is easy.

Scrubby vegetation growing on the lower mountain slopes and the intervening valleys at best may develop into a xerophilous woodland with many species of plants, but dominated by acacia. The larger wadis are usually lined with trees.

Arabian fauna

A wide variety of fauna have their habitat in the Arabian peninsula, despite the often harsh physical conditions. Zoologically, the most interesting region is the high rim of the escarpment running from Taif southward to North Yemen where the climate is conducive to a more extensive range of flora and fauna. Here there are many relict species — those which came from further north during quaternary glaciations and in the late pluvial periods — and remnants of the recent geological past when Africa and Arabia were joined.

Birds

There are about 500 recorded and recognised species of the animal class AVES, more than 10 of which are considered endemic.

The Arabian ostrich, Struthio camelus syriacus, was once native to the vast desert steppes and sands. Its eggs and young were eagerly sought for food and the adult bird was the hunter's greatest prize. Eventually, this human assault restricted the ostrich to the waterless sand wastes. The advent of guns, and cars fitted with sand tyres, sealed its fate. The last ostrich may have been shot and killed as early as 1939; it is almost certainly extinct.

Many birds are passing migrants — moving south in autumn to escape inclement northern climates, they return with spring — including small flocks of geese and ducks, rollers, bee-eaters, kingfishers, wheatears, warblers, swallows, swifts, martins, wagtails and pipits, many shore birds, doves, quail and the houbara.

There is a winter influx of birds of prey, including vultures. Of these, the falcons — particularly the saker, Falco cherrug — are particularly valued. They are caught uninjured, in an ingenious trap baited with pigeons. Within 10 days to two weeks the falcon is trained to catch and kill hares and houbara. Several more falcon species are found, as well as harriers, buzzards and several species of eagle.

The vultures include several noteworthy species. Winter visitors include the black vulture, Aegypius monachus, the lappet-faced vulture, Torgos tracheliotus — which can be seen in the northwest — and Ruppell's vulture, Gyps Ruppelli, in central and western areas. The Egyptian vulture, Neophron percnopterus, and the huge griffon vulture, Gyps fulvus, as well as the lammergeyer or bearded vulture, Gypaetus barbatus, are to be seen all year round, as they nest in the higher, remote mountain areas.

The owls are a mysterious group. Some are doubtless migrant, while others are probably resident breeders. The latter group includes the rare Hume's tawny owl, Strix butleri; the large eagle owl, Bubo bubo; the much smaller Scops owl, Otus scops; the barn owl, Tyto alba; the little owl Athene noctua — measuring only about 20cm — and the long-eared and short-eared owls, Asio otus and Asio flammeus.

Improved water supplies and food sources have allowed some birds to propagate and increase their range dramatically. These include the sparrows, Passer; the rose-ringed parakeet, Psittacula Krameri; the house (or carrion) crow, Corvus corone spp, and the black kite, Milvus migrans.

The hoopoe, Upupa epops, is widespread during the cooler months; in the summer it lives in the higher mountain areas. Mentioned in the Quran as a special messenger of King Solomon, the hoopoe has — more than any other bird — achieved fame in story and legend. Parts of its body were important in ancient medicine.

Larks are the main residents of the desert steppes and sand wastes. The most widespread is the hoopoe lark Alaemon alaudipes. A true desert bird, it is seen on the hottest days, far from water. Also widespread in the deserts is the nocturnal stone curlew, Burhinus oedicnemus.

On the Gulf coast, the endemic Socotra cormorant, Phalacrocorax nigrogularis, is common with nesting colonies on many of the islands. On the Red Sea coast are the white-eyed gull, Larus leucophthalmus, and Hemprich's Sooty gull, Larus hemprichii. There are resident colonies of the greater flamingo, Phoenicopterus ruber. The western reef heron, Egretta gularis, is common to all the Arabian coasts. Pelicans are seen occasionally — the pink-backed Pelecanus rufescens is believed to be a resident breeding bird on rocky crags near the sea in the southwest. In the southern coastal areas, the red-billed tropicbird, Phaethon aethereus, may be sighted.

The southwest has the most remarkable bird population. Near Abha is a relict population of the black-billed magpie, Pica pica asirensis, which occupies a restricted distribution area. Other relicts — all considered endemic — are the Yemen linnet, Carduelis yemenensis; the Arabian woodpecker, Dendrocopos dorae; the blackstart, Cercomela melanura; the Yemen thrush, Turdus menachensis; the yellow-rumped serin, Serinus atrogularis; and more widespread in the extreme north to the Dead Sea, Tristram's Grackle, Onychognathus Tristramii; the golden-winged grosbeak, Rhynchostruthus socotramus, and two species of partridge; the Arabian red-legged partridge, Alectoris melanocephala, and Philby's chukar, Alectoris Phylbyi.

Here also is the remarkable and majestic Arabian bustard, Ardeotis arabs. However, the bustard's status is precarious, with nest robbing and pot hunting taking a heavy toll. The Arabian guinea fowl, Numida meleagris, is similarly threatened.

Occasionally seen overhead are the stately lammergeyer and the striking bateleur eagle, Teratropius ecaudatus. Both inhabit the cliff faces of the steep escarpment. The bateleur is one

The hawk is the traditional hunting bird of the Arabian desert

of the world's most colourful eagles; it has a red beak and talons, a reddish back, white breast, black and white under-wings and purplish-black wing coverts and head.

The chanting goshawk, Melierax metabates, is common in the southwest during the winter. The scarce waldrapp or bald-headed ibis, Geronticus eremita, has been reported on the Red Sea coast — the present world population (Morocco and Turkey) is believed to be 275 pairs in southwest Arabia.

Mammals

Arabia has an interesting cross-section of the class MAMMALIA. There are almost 70 species of 24 families in 10 orders.

In the mountains and foothills from Taif to the southwest corner of the peninsula lives the baboon, Papio hamadryas, of the family CERCOPITHECIDAE of the order of PRIMATES — also found in Somalia, eastern Ethiopia and eastern Sudan. It has long been extinct in Egypt, where it was considered sacred.

Baboons are large and powerfully built with elongated dog-like muzzles, small ears and rather sunken eyes. The male has a long, shaggy, grey mane covering the back of the head, neck and shoulders. In both sexes the genitals are prominent. These omnivorous animals live in bands of 12-20, foraging in the wadis and hills for berries, grasses and roots. Several bands may congregate in troops at water-holes, as water availability controls their movements. More recently, huge troops have been seen searching for food on city rubbish dumps.

The baboons' greatest natural enemy, once thought to be the leopard, may be schistosomiasis (bilharzia). This is a liver fluke, incubated in a snail and transmitted on contact in streams, ponds and water holes.

Baboons can still be seen near Taif

Jackals, foxes and wolves of the family CANIDAE are common. The wolf, Canis lupus, is the age-old enemy of the nomads. Except on the desert steppes and in the sands where cars can travel, it is still fairly common. Canis lupus is large — a measured specimen was 114cm total length — and closely resembles the German shepherd, Alsatian, or police dog.

Similar, but smaller than the wolf is the jackal, Canis aureus, found in the oasis area of the east only.

The common fox, Vulpes vulpes, is found all over the peninsula, as is Ruppell's fox, Vulpes Ruppelli, a rare endemic species.

The fennec, Fennecus zerda, is a wary denizen of the huge waterless sand wastes. A small, pale buff-coloured animal with very large ears, it is known from only one specimen from Kuwait.

All these relatives of the domestic dog will survive, adapting to the times and resisting all intentional or incidental threats.

The family MUSTELIDAE is represented by the stone marten, Martes foina, and the ratel, or honey badger, Mellivora capensis. The stone marten is a secretive, nocturnal animal. Slender and graceful, it is about 60cm long, with a bushy tail and fine, brownish fur. The ratel, once common throughout the peninsula, is now extremely rare. A sturdily built creature, about 80cm long, its coarse hair is black, apart from a white stripe extending from the forehead to about half way along the tail. An excellent digger, it obtains its prey by excavating burrows of rodents, lizards or snakes. It too is nocturnal and seldom seen.

The family VIVERRIDAE — genets and mongooses — is represented by the common genet, Genetta genetta, and two mongooses: the Indian grey mongoose, Herpestes Edwardsi, and the white-tailed mongoose, Ichneumia albicauda. The genet is a beautiful animal, slender and cat-like with a rather pointed muzzle and a long tail. Found in the southwest, it is a nocturnal predator and seldom seen, so the full extent of its distribution is not clear.

The Indian grey mongoose is common in the eastern oasis areas. The white-tailed mongoose, previously known from Africa and Oman, has recently been recorded in the southwest.

The striped hyena, Hyaena hyaena, is still extant. Once common even on the desert steppes and sand areas, it is now restricted to the lava flows, steep escarpments and rugged jebel areas where cars find difficulty in running it to death. The hyena's forelegs are more developed and larger than those in the rear, with the front shoulders taller than the hindquarters. This tall frontal appearance is accentuated by a greyish mane. Powerful jaws and a comically vicious appearance belie a docile nature — the hyena needs the help of man, its only real enemy, to survive today.

The cat family, FELIDAE, is well-represented. The Arabian leopard, Panthera pardus nimr, is endemic in subspecific form, and still found in remoter parts of the western and southern mountains and highlands. The cheetah, Acinonyx jubatus, although never common, was once widespread on the desert steppes and in the sand areas. It is now believed to be extinct in the peninsula, although some may survive either on the lava flows or, perhaps, in the remotest sand deserts.

The caracal, Caracal caracal, is widespread, but rare. It is a uniform reddish sand colour and distinguished by ear tufts up to 4cm long.

Felis margarita, the small "sand cat," is more widespread than scientific records indicate. About 70cm long, it is a pale sandy drab colour, with the forelegs marked with contrasting black bars.

The ancestor of all domestic cats, Felis silvestris, is probably widespread, except in the deserts. Resembling a large domestic cat, it is pale ashy grey, with fine speckling. The tail has four or five black rings and a black tip.

All wild cats are wary and seldom seen. However, they are particularly vulnerable to traps and baits and their numbers are drastically decreasing.

The rock hyrax, family PROVAVIIDAE order HYRACOIDEA, is the "coney" referred to in the Bible (Proverbs 30:26). Procavia capensis syriacus is found in the north, northwest and north central mountain areas; Procavia capensis jayakari is found in the southwest and southern mountains.

The gazelles, antelope, sheep and goats of the family BOVIDAE, order ARTIODACTYLA, were once plentiful. But sport and hunters have nearly wiped them out.

The Arabian tahr, Hemitragus jayakari, is a small, wild goat endemic to the mountains of Oman. Once widespread, the ibex, Capra ibex, still exists in the high mountains and lava flows of the northwest and, perhaps, the south. Capra aegagrus, the wild goat, is larger than the ibex. Its status in Arabia is unknown, as is that of the wild sheep, Ovis ammon.

Large numbers of the Arabian oryx, Oryx leucoryx, once roamed from the deserts of Syria and Iraq to the southern end of the peninsula. But man encroached until, by the turn of the century, the oryx was restricted to the great Nefud desert in the north and the Rub al-Khali (Empty Quarter) in the south. Even in these remote wastes it could not withstand the wantonness of men in vehicles armed with breech-loading shotguns.

Preserving the oryx

Just as the oryx was disappearing, however, the Fauna Preservation Society organised an expedition to southern Arabia, where several animals were captured for preservation in American zoos. The society's efforts may not alone have saved enough oryx to ensure the continuation of the species, but the action created enthusiasm, resulting in gifts of animals from then unknown captive herds. This small number was nurtured and carefully bred. Although the oryx became extinct in its wild state in 1962, it was saved from total extinction. It is now estimated that there may be more than 300 in the world and they have started to be reintroduced to the wild in Jordan and Oman.

The oryx has almost straight horns 48-71cm long. Standing up to 100cm at the shoulders, it weighs about 60 kilos. Total length is up to 180cm, with the tail 30cm long ending in a bushy tuft. The body colour is white, with dark chocolate markings on the head, neck, legs and tip of the tail.

Oryx have been saved from extinction — just

Gazelle were once abundant in three species: the idhmi, Gazella gazella arabica; the afri, Gazella dorcas saudiya, and the rheem, Gazella subgutturosa. Their numbers have been sadly reduced by huntsmen, but some are believed to survive in remoter areas.

In the seas surrounding the peninsula are mammals of the order CETACEA, the dolphins and whales. Three species of whale and six species of dolphin have been recorded from the Arabian Gulf. Records from the Red Sea include Bryde's whale, Balaenoptera Brydei, and the Red Sea bottle-nosed dolphin, Tursiops aduncus.

Of much greater interest is another order of mammals found in the Red Sea: the SIRENIA family DUGONGIDAE, represented by an extremely endangered species — the Red sea dugong, Dugong dugong, actually thought to be a subspecies, Dugong dugong tabernaculi. Sadly, it may be extinct except in Australia, where it has been protected, and on the Arabian Red Sea coast, where it has not been historically exploited for its much sought-after flesh and skin — except perhaps in the northern areas. A huge animal, considered to be completely stupid, its flesh is said to taste like beef. Its leather, made into sandals, will never wear out.

The dugong has a fish-like shape up to 300cm long, and weighs nearly 200 kilos. The males have two large incisors, or tusks, in the upper jaw. The tail is slightly forked and broadened horizontally. The skin is wrinkled, and bluish-grey above, paler beneath. The sexual organs are very prominent.

Skeletal finds indicate the presence of a colony of dugongs between Bahrain and Uqair.

In the past, when caught in fishermen's nets, the dugong broke loose. Modern nylon nets will contain it, however, and it is usually hauled ashore as a curiosity and allowed to die from heat and exposure — it sorely needs intervention by the proper authorities to preserve it for posterity.

Amphibians and Reptiles

With at least 10 species of AMPHIBIA, 100 species of lizards and 53 species of snakes (10 of which are sea snakes), this group is well-represented.

Seven species of toad, the genus Bufo, are found wherever there is water. A small green tree frog — genus Hyla — inhabits higher altitudes from Taif to the southwest. Two frogs of the genus Rana are to be noted. Rana ridibunda is found in the eastern oases and Rana cyanophlyctis is found in the southwest.

Two freshwater turtles — the Caspian pond turtle, Mauremyscaspica, and a side-necked turtle, Pelomedusa subrufa — are extant and five species of sea turtle have been reported. They are the green sea turtle, the hawksbill turtle, the Olive Ridley turtle, and, less frequently, the loggerhead turtle and the largest living turtle, the leatherback. The first three have important breeding grounds on some of the remote islands of the Arabian Gulf and the Red Sea and off the southern coasts.

Of the lizards, the family GEKKONIDAE comprises 38 species in nine genera. These small lizards are mainly nocturnal, and can be seen on walls, fences and in dwellings at night, near the lights, where they await their insect prey.

A desert lizard

Seven families of snakes are represented and those of the TYPHLOPIDAE and LEPTOTYPHLOPIDAE families are widely distributed. Fossorial and wholly nocturnal, they are seldom seen. The family BOIDAE, the family of the huge boa constrictors and pythons, is represented in Arabia by three species of the genus Eryx, small sand burrowers.

The family COLUBRIDAE is represented by 27 species in 16 genera. The genus Coluber has some seven species, mostly small snakes. One of the most beautiful colubers is C. elegantissimus, found in the northwest. It is a small snake, 60-70cm total length. Across the back are 29-39 black bands over a ground colour of greyish-white. In about half the specimens there is a broad reddish-orange vertebral stripe from between the eyes to the tip of the tail. The underparts are irridescent pearly grey.

Of the genus Dasypeltis, the egg-eating snake, Dasypeltis scabra, is found in the southwest, although it is more common in Africa. It is small — up to 100cm — and said to eat only eggs: it has a special apparatus in the gullet to break the egg, swallow the contents and disgorge the shell. The genus Lytorhynchus has an enlarged rostral shield (leaf-nose) for burrowing into the sand. These, like the snakes noted above, are aglyphous snakes, having teeth, no fangs and no venom glands.

Two species of the cobra family ELAPIDAE are known. The cobras are proteroglyphous — having fangs fixed in the front of the mouth, just anterior to the position of the eyes.

Naja haje arabica, an endemic subspecies, is common in the mountainous areas of the southwest. When alarmed, it raises the front third of its body vertically and its neck forms a hood. From this position it strikes downward at its adversary. It attains a relatively large size, probably well over 200cm. The colour is usually blackish, brown, copper, yellow or yellowish green but the head and the tip of the tail are always black with dark irregular splotches on the ventral parts.

Walterinesia aegyptia, the black desert cobra, does not have a "hood." It is an extremely aggressive animal, although seldom seen as it is fossorial. Black, with bluish-black ventral parts, it attains a total length of 128cm.

Sea snakes occur in the Arabian Gulf and the Gulf of Oman. There are none in the Red Sea. They have fixed front fangs like the cobra's and most specimens measure about 90-100cm. Sea-snakes are the most poisonous of snakes. Dr H Alistair Reid, a world authority on venomous snakes, says: "15 drops of viper venom could be fatal to an adult man, three drops of cobra venom could be lethal. One such drop of sea-snake venom could kill five men." These animals are wholly aquatic, feeding on fish and eels. As they are extremely numerous in the Arabian Gulf, it can only be concluded that sea-snakes seldom bite people.

The horned viper (or sand viper), Cerastes cerastes gasperettii, is the most widely distributed poisonous snake. It is found everywhere apart from the higher areas and the extreme deserts. It is sand coloured, with dark stripes through the eyes and dark irregular transverse markings. Curiously, some of these snakes have horns 5 or 6mm in length, while some have only scaly protrusions over the eyes. They are "sidewinders," moving in a fashion which almost defies description. The sidewinder throws a loop of the front end of its body forward and places its neck on the ground. The rest of the body then leaves the ground and is twisted forward. The tracks show the full length of the body lying diagonal to the direction of progress.

The genus Echis has two species, both of which are found in Arabia. Medically, these are the most important snakes. Their venom is highly toxic, and they are aggressive and numerous in their area of distribution.

Echis coloratus is found throughout western Arabia. Up to 70cm long, it has a great colour variation — from bluish-grey to silver-grey to dark grey, with ligher spots edged with a darker shade. The underparts are speckled.

Echis carinatus is also widely distributed. Again, quoting Reid: "Echis are the snakes most dangerous to man." Known as the "carpet viper," this snake is usually reddish in colour, with a blackish trident mark on the head, whitish transverse bars on the back and a dark serrated pattern edged in white on the flanks.

John and Patricia Gasperetti

Mineral resources

Saudi Arabia's wealth is derived from the export of oil from the inland and offshore fields of Eastern province. As well as its huge reserves of oil, the kingdom has much smaller but still economically significant reserves of other minerals, ranging from precious metal ores to building stone. The former are found mainly in the western part of the country where some of the rocks are geologically similar to those of mineral-rich regions in other parts of the world such as Australia and Canada. Another novel and potentially important source of metals is the mineral-rich mud found at the bottom of Red Sea trenches

The exploitation of mineral reserves other than oil is the responsibility of the Deputy Ministry for Mineral Resources, an offshoot of the Petroleum & Minerals Ministry. The deputy ministry's own staff of geologists is supplemented by specialists in earth sciences and mineral exploration from resident missions of the US Geological Survey (USGS), the French Bureau de Recherches Geologiques & Minieres (BRGM), and Riofinex, a subsidiary of the UK's Rio-Tinto Zinc.

The deputy ministry also uses specialist commercial enterprises to carry out surveys and exploratory drilling, and retains the services of consultants for advice and research. Satellite imagery at various scales and in various formats is also being used in the search for minerals.

Precious metal ores were mined in ancient times. Well preserved by the dry climate, prehistoric trenches and tips can be seen today at many sites in western Saudi Arabia. Exploration around and beneath these sites has revealed new reserves. At the start of the third five-year plan, the deputy ministry had an inventory of more than 2,000 mineral occurrences in computerised storage.

Gold

Saudi Arabia's best known gold prospect is at Mahd adh Dhahab, about 275 kilometres northeast of Jeddah along an ancient caravan route between present-day Yemen and Jordan.

In Arabic the place name means "cradle of gold." Some people think Mahd adh Dhahab may have been one of the legendary mines of Ophir, the long lost source of a biblical king's 1,086 talents (34 tonnes) of gold. The evidence is a series of deep trenches, cut into the eastern flank of Jabal Mahd more than 2,900 years ago. From these a parallel series of gold-bearing veins of quartz were extracted.

Records show that the site was mined for gold during the Abbasid Caliphate, between about 625 and 950 AD.

From 1939-54 the Saudi Arabian Mining Syndicate extracted 23 tonnes of gold from Mahd adh Dhahab. Much of this was recovered from the waste dumps left behind by the miners of ancient times.

Until the early 1970s it looked as if the syndicate had exhausted the area but then, with the price of gold beginning to rise, USGS geologists found another ore body, 700 metres south of the old workings.

In 1976, the UK's Consolidated Gold Fields was awarded an exploration licence. In 1978, following promising results from drilling, a joint-venture enterprise — Gold Fields Mahd adh Dhahab — was formed to exploit the deposit. The partners were Consolidated Gold Fields and the state-owned Petromin.

Within a year a tunnel — decline, in mining technology — had been driven more than a kilometre into the southern flank of Jabal Mahd. By the end of 1980 15 kilometres of core samples had been extracted by underground drilling. Sample analysis showed that there is still enough gold at Mahd adh Dhahab for a mine to be developed.

By mutual agreement, Petromin in January 1982 became the sole owner of the rights to the Mahd adh Dhahab deposit, and awarded a preliminary contract for developing and operating the mine to Gold Fields Mahd adh Dhahab.

The new Mahd adh Dahab mine will cost around $100 million to develop. The feasibility study recommends an

Employees at Mahd adh-Dhahab

ore processing rate of 400 tonnes a day for 10 years. This should yield an average 2.9 tonnes of gold a year, as well as some useful quantities of silver, copper and zinc (see below).

With a profitable mine, the Mahd adh Dhahab region will benefit as today's collection of hamlets expands into a small town, with power and water, social services, and paved roads to Al-Madinah in the north and Makkah in the south.

Several other ore bodies containing gold are being evaluated. At Al-Masane, 145 kilometres east of Abha, several million tonnes of ore reserves contain useful traces of gold. The deposit is being investigated with the aid of an interest-free government loan by a joint venture. The partners are the Saudi/US firm Arabian Shield Development Company and the Saudi-owned National Mining Company.

Not far away, the same partnership has investigated gold-bearing quartz veins in Jabal Guyan and its surroundings in which flecks of the metal are visible to the naked eye.

Northeast of Al-Madinah, it has been exploring the area around the ancient gold mines of Jabal al-Safra and Nuqrah where Petromin, in partnership with a Swedish company, Granges International, has proved two small workable deposits.

Economically significant levels of gold are present in ore deposits at Jabal Said, near Mahd adh Dhahab, and at Al-Masane. Gold is also found in the mineral-rich muds of the Red Sea Atlantis II Deep (see below).

Silver

Gold-bearing rock often contains useful amounts of ores of other metals, including silver. At Mahd adh Dhahab, mining between 1939-54 yielded 31 tonnes of silver along with the gold. Provided the 400-tonne-a-day ore processing rate is attained, annual output of nine tonnes of silver is now expected.

Gold-bearing ore bodies in the Al-Masane and Nuqrah regions also contain silver in economically significant concentrations. The mineral-rich muds of the Red Sea Atlantis II Deep may contain as much as 9,000 tonnes of silver.

Copper

The projected mine at Mahd adh Dhahab is expected to yield around one tonne of copper for every 180 tonnes of ore treated. The Jabal Said copper deposit was discovered in 1968. Awarded an exploration licence in 1974, US Steel and a French company, Sorem, began a programme of surface mapping and drilling to further define this deposit, which contains useful quantities of gold, silver and zinc as well as copper.

In 1980 the two companies, in partnership with Petromin, contracted a Saudi company, Red Sea Mining, to dig a two-kilometre decline into the ore bodies at Jabal Said. This is being done, in a subcontract, by Sweden's Boliden. The decline, with about six kilometres of core sampling, is due to be completed by 1984.

Copper is also found in ore deposits at Nuqrah and Al-Masane, while the muds of the Atlantis II Deep are estimated to contain around 600,000 tonnes of the metal.

Zinc

There are economically significant quantities of zinc in the ore deposits of Mahd adh Dhahab, Jabal Said, Knaiguiyah, Nuqrah and Al-Masane. At Al-Masane a small mine is being considered, following the discovery of an ore body rich in gold, silver, copper and zinc.

The expected yield at Madh adh Dhahab is 2.5 tonnes of zinc for every 120 tonnes of ore treated. The deposits at Knaiguiyah contain as much as 5.3 per cent zinc. Estimated reserves in the Atlantis II Deep are 2.5 million tonnes of the metal.

Lead

Lead is found in significant amounts in the Nuqrah ore deposits; it would be a useful by-product of precious metal mining at this site.

Iron

About 450 kilometres north of Al-Madinah lies the potential source of raw material for Jubail's planned steelmaking industry: the huge Wadi Sawawin iron ore deposit. In a contract with Petromin, British Steel has been carrying out a major feasibility study to determine how this 300 million tonne ore deposit might be successfully exploited.

The ore contains 42 per cent iron and is rich in silica. Jubail's steelmaking process requires that it be converted into pellets containing around 65 per cent iron with a low silica content. Although the conversion process will be costly, home-produced pellets are likely to be economically competitive in the 1990s.

Magnesite

Potentially useful as the raw material for the manufacture of refractory surfaces needed in steel-making processes, magnesite is found in a deposit at Zarghat, 250 kilometres northeast of Al-Madinah.

Bauxite

Bauxite, the ore from which aluminium is extracted, is converted into the metal by a process involving the use of large amounts of electricity. For an energy-rich nation such as Saudi Arabia, a bauxite deposit is an attractive proposition. Such a deposit was found in 1980 at Al-Zabirah, 490 kilometres northwest of Riyadh. It is estimated the deposit contains about 90 million tonnes of bauxite.

Fertiliser minerals

In the north of the country, Riofinex has been exploring phosphate-bearing strata which extend across the Jordanian border into about 46,000 square kilometres of the Sirham-Turaif basin.

Oil exploration boreholes have revealed potash in association with deeply buried salt beds along the margins of the Red Sea.

Atlantis II Deep

As its shape suggests, the Red Sea fills a geologically recent rift between what is termed the Arabian Shield and its counterpart, the Nubian Shield. Mineral-rich muds, 2,000 metres down, lie in the deeps forming the middle of the rift. These muds are being evaluated by the Saudi-Sudanese Commission for the Development of Red Sea Resources.

Atlantis II – one of 18 such deeps midway between Saudi Arabia and Sudan – has muds containing 17 metallic elements including zinc, copper, silver and gold in economically significant amounts.

Led by West Germany's Preussag, several specialists in offshore mining technology have been demonstrating the feasibility of bringing this novel resource to the surface.

Mining on a pilot scale, and processing mud concentrate at a rate of 10 tonnes a day at a Yanbu plant, was due to begin in 1983-84.

Construction materials

Other sought-after minerals are those used for making various grades of cement and plaster. Granite, sandstone, coral stone and marble are being exploited for use by the building industry.

The future

On and offshore the search continues for useful raw materials and revenue-producing minerals. Although the generous Saudi mining code attracts foreign mining companies, most of the impetus and finance comes from the government, which believes that exploitation of its own resources should be an integral part of the kingdom's industrial future.

Peter Ryan

Antiquities and museums

The economic strength of the Arabian peninsula is widely assumed to be without precedent in the experience of its peoples. Arabia of antiquity — as in more recent times — was protected by its inhospitable climate and arid terrain, and would-be invaders generally had second thoughts.

Yet ancient Arabia also boasted societies which became legendary for their wealth. "Arabia Felix" was how Romans referred to the Yemens, grown rich on the centuries-old trade in aromatics. If oil is the currency of prosperity today, aromatics were its equivalent in the ancient world, and important cities sprang up on the overland trade routes across what is now Saudi Arabia.

Again — and more significantly — it was from here that exploded the far-reaching religious, political and social movement of Islam in the seventh century AD, which changed the cultural face of much of the known world (see History).

Such observations help to suggest the potential richness of Saudi Arabia's archaeological resources. The heritage has, until recently, gone largely uninvestigated — in sharp contrast to Egypt, the Levant, Iraq and Iran, where excavators have been hard at it for over a century.

But this has advantages. The Directorate-General of Antiquities & Museums (DGAM) has been able to start from scratch, unencumbered by the randomly accumulated habits and institutions of a haphazard past.

Between 1976-80 a comprehensive survey of archaeological resources was carried out by survey teams of Saudis, Americans, Britons and French. Their results, as well as comparative studies of their finds, are published in Atlal, the annual journal of Saudi Arabian antiquities.

The first modern museum, the Museum of Archaeology & Ethnography in Riyadh, was completed in 1976. It presents, in archaeological terms, the most complete conspectus anywhere of Saudi Arabia's past, from the Early Old Stone Age until the Islamic period.

The museum is intended to be temporary — a prelude to the much more ambitious project to establish a national museum in Riyadh, the scope of which will extend beyond archaeology, history and ethnography.

Local museums are being set up at Hofuf, Jawf, Taima, Al-Ula, Najran, on the coastal Tihama near Jizan, in the Wadi Dawasir and in Qassim. These museums, near sites of outstanding archaeological importance, are part of an integrated museum network which will include regional and Islamic museums. They are intended to be site protection agencies and bases for

Madain Salih

research teams, as well as conventional museums, with exhibition and educational centres.

Much has emerged during these recent years. The Stone Age has already demonstrated its richness in surface finds. Sophisticated third and second millennium BC urban societies in the eastern region had strong maritime contacts with the Indus valley and the cities of Sumer in southern Iraq. A flourishing Midianite culture in the northwest between 1200-600 BC has been established, and more is now known about their successors, the Nabataeans, who built Petra in Jordan and Madain Salih in Saudi Arabia.

Perhaps most important, the network of ancient overland trade routes, whose development was stimulated by the domestication of the camel in Arabia at some time before 1000 BC, is becoming clearer. Most of Saudi Arabia's most spectacular archaeological remains — such as at Najran, Al-Ula, Madain Salih, Taima and Jawf — can be appreciated properly only in the context of these overland routes, which formed the commercial link between the Indian Ocean and Mediterranean worlds between 1000 BC-600 AD.

Finally a note of caution. The DGAM is not yet encouraging tourists to visit sites until those sites are adequately protected. But, as partial compensation, it has published a series of films and books on the antiquities. So, always, if possible, request permission to visit a site from the directorate-general in Riyadh. When you are in the area where you wish to visit sites, first go to the amir's office to pay your respects and obtain permission from the local Department of Education. This is customary courtesy rather than formal regulation but, if neglected, your activities will be regarded with suspicion.

William Facey

The Directorate-General of Antiquities & Museums, PO Box 3734, Riyadh, tel: Riyadh 4355821.

The Museum of Archaeology & Ethnography is in the same building as the directorate-general, in Imam Saud Ibn Abdul-Aziz Ibn Muhammad street (known generally as Al-Asarat street), Riyadh. The museum is open to the public at the following times:

Saturday-Thursday 0800-1400; 1700-2000; women only on Monday 1700-2000 and Thursday 0800-1400.

For details of museum see Riyadh. For details of archaeological sites see individual regions.

Museum of Archaeology & Ethnography in Riyadh

OUR SPECIAL WAY TO THE FAR EAST AND USA

You can fly with us any Thursday or Sunday evening from Dhahran to Singapore, arriving there early next morning. Just in time for our same-day connecting flights to 12 key cities in the Far East and to Honolulu, San Francisco and Los Angeles. Or, if you like, enjoy a relaxing break in our garden city. For only US$19 for one night and up to US$106 for four nights,* our Singapore Stopover Holiday gives you first class hotel accommodation, daily breakfast, transfers and a sightseeing tour. And of course, when you fly with us, you'll enjoy all the comforts of the world's most modern fleet plus inflight service even other airlines talk about. **SINGAPORE AIRLINES**

*Call your Travel Agent or SIA Reservations:
Al Khobar Tel. 8646025/8645545/8640515. Jeddah Tel. 6674345/
6671813/6671690. Dhahran Tel. 8951515/8951564/8954636.
Prices valid till 31 March 1983.

10R82 A

RIYADH

Hyatt Regency brings special elegance to Saudi Arabia's capital. Enjoy modern luxury. Dine elegantly. Refresh in the outdoor pool. Shop. Business center and 6 meeting rooms.

JEDDAH

Luxury Hyatt Regency hotel only minutes from Commercial Center. Enjoy European cuisine, modern athletic facilities in the heart of the commercial area. Indoor pool. Fascinating tea lounge.

YANBU

Hyatt welcomes you to the shores of the Red Sea. Luxuriate in handsomely decorated guestrooms. Continental cuisine. Swim in the outdoor pool. Join friends in the elegant lobby lounge.

GIZAN

Discover the splendour of a new Hyatt on this Red Sea harbour. Just 3.5 km. from the airport. Revive in the swimming pool or at nearby beach. Enjoy continental or Middle East dishes.

PEOPLE ON THE SPOT KNOW BETTER

**b international arab inter
urance services insurance
nal arab international ara
ces insurance services ins
ernational arab internati
ce services insurance serv**

WHO ARE WE?
Small enough to listen, big enough to help . . . AIIS are best suited to meet your insurance needs with a wide experience of the local market and the support of a first class international insurance group.

WHAT DO WE DO?
We offer all classes of corporate insurance:
- C.A.R. E.A.R. 10 Year Liability,
- Fire, Machinery Breakdown, Loss of Profit,
- Marine,
- Staff Insurance Packages (local staff and expatriates)

General Agents for:

assurances
GROUPE VICTOIRE

A.I.I.S.
RIYADH OFFICE:

P.O. BOX 2322, 11451 RIYADH. TEL 4780282 4773603, TLX 202463 AIIS SJ

Manners and customs

From the moment a man is offered food or drink by the Arabian bedu (singular: bedawi), he becomes their guest. As a guest his life is inviolable and must be protected by them to the death. In the history of Arabia there are numerous instances of the stranger running to kiss the hem of a tribe's tent to claim the status of guest even if the tribe is otherwise antagonistic. In Travels in Arabia Deserta Charles Doughty passionately reminded unfriendly tribes that he had shared their "salt and bread." Another bedu tradition is protecting the traveller through regions of foreign tribes. In Arabian Sands Wilfred Thesiger, who explored the Duru country of Oman, had to take a guide (rabia) belonging to the Duru. The guide would take an oath: "You are my companions and your safety, both of your blood and of your possessions, is in my face."

Tradition

The bedu are no longer representative of the Arabian peninsula but their traditions of honour and hospitality are still at the root of Arabian culture even in the Western region where many Saudis do not claim Arabian stock. In modern Saudi Arabia the duty of the host to his guest is a crucial ethic. Linked with this ethic is that of covenant. Negotiations for a contract can be extremely protracted and success, apparently assured, may be snatched away. But it is very rare for a Saudi to go back on his word once he has positively made it. Breaking a troth is considered a severe dishonour.

When a man visits a traditional Saudi house with his wife she will normally be invited to spend the evening separately with the women of the household in the Women's (or Hareem) Quarters. Traditionally, men and women do not mix in public in Saudi Arabia, although in modern circles they may be invited to dine together.

The Majlis

Traditional Saudis often have an open office akin to the ruler's majlis (meeting place). Here people can come and go without an appointment, although it would be discourteous for a foreigner to turn up without one. The host will talk to several people at the same time, even answering the the telephone. The skill with which he will hold several simultaneous conversations without getting impatient and without forgetting a word of any one can be impressive. The visitor should never show impatience and should arrange his itinerary to allow for long waits and longer meetings than he had envisaged.

Various social customs are well known. One must always eat with the right hand. The left hand is considered unclean. It is impolite to point the sole of the foot at the man you are speaking to. Major deals have been lost in this way. It is discourteous to ask after a man's wife or daughters. You should ask after "his family and sons." When tea and coffee are brought it is polite to take at least one cup. The coffee cup should be held, not put down. When you have finished drinking, oscillate the cup to show you have had enough, otherwise the server will pour more.

Doing business

When you meet your client or host, do not start talking business immediately. A time, sometimes considerable, should first be spent exchanging courtesies. Because familiarity is an important concept among Arabians, it may be necessary to make frequent visits to win a contract. Trust and understanding are important. The man who flies home on the scheduled day, although his host has asked for further meetings, will usually fail in his enterprise.

It should be added that today

Tea is drunk throughout the day in town and desert

some Saudis have to a certain extent adopted western norms in business matters. The pleasantly human preamble to a business discussion will, in these cases, be done away with and be replaced by the immediate, hard negotiating familiar in the West. The visitor must judge for himself what behaviour to adopt according to his host's attitude.

The Muslim woman in Saudi Arabia

Many westerners who have never been exposed to the Islamic way of life believe that its treatment of women, especially, is harsh and puritanical. Yet Saudi women do not see their role as that of shackled victims longing to move to a more public world. From time to time a western writer, reporter or broadcaster has the notion that Muslim women are intended to remain simply virtuous mothers and wives, with nothing else to aspire to — conditions externally imposed from which women are trying to escape. Yet many Muslim women themselves see their role as that of wife and mother, and many repudiate the new freedoms they may have adopted in the West, either when studying or living abroad. It is the women from the rich and middle classes who tend to speak out on the question of women, and while they cannot yet influence common practice, there is an intelligentsia which operates quietly and conscientiously.

The choice between marriage and career which faces many western women is not yet a problem in Saudi Arabia. Those women working in schools, colleges, hospitals, social welfare institutions, banks, private shops, airlines and radio and television have managed to combine marriage and career either because they have help at home or live in an extended family where there is usually someone to look after the children.

Nearly 70 per cent of working women live in nuclear families which maintain close ties with relations. Saudi husbands have become more supportive of wives who want to work, and often encourage them to continue studying after marriage. The enormous work potential of women in the kingdom is undeniable but, rather than join the feminists of the West, women seek a role derived more directly from the Quran and early Islamic tradition. This leaning towards greater understanding of Islam is considered fanaticism by many westerners, who naively see it as a rebellion against imported western ways. Thus the use of the veil is widespread; it affords women a certain anonymity not available in the West, where the intention of dress is to reveal the figure.

The family is the hub of Saudi society. Women are the custodians of morality within the family and responsible for the children's upbringing. There is an Arabic saying: "The mother is a school." The law is perhaps harder on women because the consequences of their misbehaviour are more devastating, threatening the very fabric of the family. Religious practices are observed at home and, according to the Quran, women should impart moral and religious teaching to their offspring. A westerner who comes into contact with Saudi families

Woman and child of the Asir

cannot fail to be struck by the love and respect afforded parents and old people — a direct consequence of the principles of Islam which are taught children from a very early age.

Women in Europe seem to have social freedom but are still campaigning for total legal freedom. In contrast, Saudi women possess legal freedoms as stipulated in the Quran, but very often lack "social freedom." A woman may own her own property, run her own business, inherit in her own right, with her husband having no right to any property she may bring with her after marriage. She is accorded full spiritual and intellectual equality with men — each of the five pillars of Islam is as important for women as for men, with the rewards to be gained the same.

The definition of the relationship between man and wife is that of interdependence. The Quran says, "He created you as helpmates for yourselves that you might find rest in them, and he ordained between you love and mercy." Such a description involves mutual care, consideration, respect and affection. There is no servility on the part of the wife, only a recognition of her duties towards her husband and her rights as a wife. The behaviour due to her from men is certainly not emphasised enough and local paternalistic interpretation of the Quran has often affected women negatively, detracting from their privileged Quranic position.

No one would deny the tremendous advances made in the kingdom with regard to the position of women in the past decade. The government recognises the need for women's labour and at the same time is committed to preserving the mother's nurturing role in the Saudi family.

There is a women's section on all public buses in order not to offend traditional sensibilities. Many enterprises which employ women have altered their work schedules to conform to the staff's childcare and home responsibilities. Women's banks and a clothes factory allow their employees a long lunch break — customary in hot countries — which allows women some time to go home to be with their families. An office has been opened in Jeddah municipality, run by women, to deal specifically with women's complaints. A group of 45 women from the Women's Awareness Society in Riyadh recently visited King Khaled hospital to discover what is happening in the kingdom's health programme.

Three social welfare institutions in Riyadh, Jeddah and Dammam care for children whose mothers have either died or are too ill to care for them. There are also 12 social education institutes countrywide looking after more than 1,000 children who have either been orphaned or become the

Schoolgirls in old Jeddah

victims of divorce. Saudi Arabia has only four institutions for juvenile delinquents — perhaps a sign that delinquency is not so great in the kingdom as it is in other societies. There are also 70 private philanthropic societies with revenues exceeding SR 150 million. The two largest women's welfare societies in Jeddah did a wonderful job in collecting clothes, blankets and gifts for the refugees in Lebanon and for the earthquake victims in North Yemen.

Saudi Arabia's first girls' school was set up in 1956 while secondary education for girls began in 1963. It is worth keeping these dates in mind when talking about women's progress in the kingdom. While education for them is a relatively recent phenomenon, it has already spread within reach of most of the population. Most of the teachers were initially foreign, simply because there were no women's training colleges. However, school curricula have now expanded to include sciences and languages, as well as Islamic studies. Girls now have the chance to go on to university, where they can watch lectures by male professors on closed-circuit television, while generous scholarships are given to those who would like to do post-graduate study abroad.

The government recently declared a day dedicated to the eradication of illiteracy — still a major problem, especially among older women. Nearly 100 schools have been built nationwide to combat this problem, from the village level up.

The prophet Muhammad is reported to have said: "To seek knowledge is obligatory on every Muslim, male and female." As more women begin to participate in the life of the country, the more likely it becomes that they will soon play a greater role in industry and government, thus replacing the large number of foreign workers. As more women receive higher education and gain professional qualifications, the government will have to find new

Saudi women enjoy limitless opportunities to study

ways of incorporating them into the workforce.

As the cultural, social and even religious awareness of these women increases, the more likely they are to exercise their right according to Islam and have a greater say in their choice of husband, choosing men with whom they have more in common. This does not mean that women will marry someone against their parents' wishes because, no matter how "emancipated" they become, they are unlikely to shed their traditional feeling towards the family.

There is still much that could be said about women in Saudi Arabia — their aspirations, their problems, their hopes for their country. Their position is growing stronger daily and their confidence increasing. In this they can remember the words of Muhammad and take heart — there could be no better platform on which to stand. "The rights of women are sacred. See that women are maintained in the rights assigned to them."

by a Muslim woman living in Saudi Arabia

Saudi cuisine

Pure Saudi cuisine is hard to find. As a result of the influence of immigrants from neighbouring Arab countries, dishes have become more varied. In cities such as Jeddah and Riyadh it is more common to be offered tabbulah and sambousik than it is to be served traditional mutton and rice. In the towns, such as Tabuk, Taif, or Najran, chicken and rice compete with shawarma, falafel and liver sandwiches — all common, popular, and increasingly part of the Saudi cuisine. In the heart of the desert the small tin-shack groceries are stacked with canned foul mudammas — very Egyptian — and hummus, and rarely, if ever, sell camel or sheep-milk biscuits.

Traditional cuisine has, however, survived and comes to the fore at the innumerable feasts given for weddings, births, visits by relatives — indeed any excuse. Here, meat and rice or chicken and rice is the main and most prominent dish. The meat — mutton, goat, or camel — is cooked either unadorned or stuffed with rice, nuts and herbs in special ovens, and placed on a bed of rice. The guests then reach in and pluck the food with their fingers. The main dish can be accompanied by soups and salads in which chives, coriander and dill are widely used. This cuisine can be rather bland — little seasoning is used and it is never hot and spicy. The ceremony of preparing, serving and eating it in the festive atmosphere is what makes it such a special dish.

In the coastal areas there is, of course, fish, in an amazing variety of colours and shapes. Traditional cuisine includes 10 or 20 fish recipes, such as samkah harrah (fish in tahini) and maglubat samak (fish cooked with rice, nuts and spices). Here again, however, custom is strong, and the most common dish is fried fish accompanied by rice, salad and bread.

Saudis eat bread — shami and samuli — with every meal and in great quantities. The flat bread, more common in the south, is when hot and fresh out of the traditional conical ovens still found in small village bakeries, the most delicious in the world.

Vegetables are part of the new cuisine, and intensive cultivation programmes are under way in various parts of the kingdom. Locally grown vegetables are, however, more expensive and you usually find imported vegetables in cities and towns. Most vegetables are cooked with meat or chicken in a tomato-based sauce and eaten as a stew, accompanied — of course — by rice and bread. One of the most delicious dishes is a mixture of four or six vegetables prepared with pieces of lamb and tomato sauce, and baked.

Dates used to be one of the staple diets of the desert, but modernisation, industrialisation and inflation have taken their toll and many palm groves are dying of neglect.

The date is a versatile fruit. It can be eaten fresh when it is bright red or yellow, and hard, juicy and sweet — an acquired taste because it puckers the lips. When the red dates turn black and the yellow ones brown — the stage called rutab — the fruit is at its most delicious. It has to be skinned as eaten, and is served as a dessert. The final, and most common, way of eating them is when they are dried and pressed. The quality of dried dates varies, depending on where they were grown and the method of preparing them. One of the better versions, found in supermarkets, is the Al-Madinah date, served when drinking Arabic coffee or as a dessert.

In the modern Saudi cuisine, the date has been replaced as a dessert by other sweets — and they are sweet. Muhallabiyah, a milky pudding, is at the less sweet end of the scale. Then there are the sticky, syrupy, Middle Eastern sweets such as kneifah, baklawa, and nammurah, filled with honey and nuts. The sweetest of them all is

Cheap meals can be had in the kingdom's many small restaurants

katayef, a Ramadan speciality, which used to be found only at the month of fasting.

No gathering or meal is considered truly complete, however, without Arabic coffee. It is prepared by boiling ground coffee and cardamom, placing it in pots and then pouring it into small coffee cups and serving it direct to guests.

Ashkhain Skipwith

Mashwi

The recipe here is one of the more traditional ways of preparing a sheep or goat. It is time-consuming and involves slaughtering the animal — something which is best to have done by someone else.

Ingredients
1 sheep or goat (alive)
Salt and black pepper
Rice
Pine nuts
Raisins
Saffron

Utensils
Shovel
Strong wire (two two-metre lengths)
1 large barrel (open at both ends)
1 metal lid to cover the barrel
Charcoal
4 pegs (tent pegs will do)
Large platter for serving
3-4 sacks

Method:
Slaughter the animal on the spot — not in advance — and skin
Remove the innards, and put the edible parts to one side
Wash, drain and cut up the animal into four or six hunks. Also wash and drain the edible innards to be used
Season the hunks well with salt and pepper, string them on the lengths of wire and let stand
Prepare the fire by:
    digging a hole in the ground, deep enough and wide enough to contain the barrel;
    placing the barrel upright in the hole, so its top stands a few inches above ground;
    filling the bottom of the barrel with charcoal about 12 inches deep, and lighting the fire.
When the flames have died down and the embers are red-hot your oven is ready
Knock the pegs into the ground on either side of the barrel, and hang the meat over the embers in the barrel by tying the ends of the wire to the pegs — the meat is now suspended
Cover the barrel with the metal lid. Then cover the lid and some of the ground around it with the sacks so they overlap
Shovel sand over the sacks to form a mound about 50 centimetres high, and leave the meat to cook for at least one hour
About half an hour before the meat is ready, wash and cook the rice in a large pan of boiling water containing the edible innards of the animal and saffron
When the rice is cooked, drain it and mix in raisins and pine nuts, then cover and leave to stand until the meat is ready
After the meat has cooked for about one hour, gently clear the sand covering the "oven," remove the sacks, flip away the lid, and withdraw the hunks

To serve
Place the cooked rice on a large platter and place the hunks of cooked meat on top. Serve as a single dish, on the floor, with spring onions and yogurt as side dishes. The meat should traditionally be eaten by hand from the communal dish, but as this is an art it is best to provide spoons.

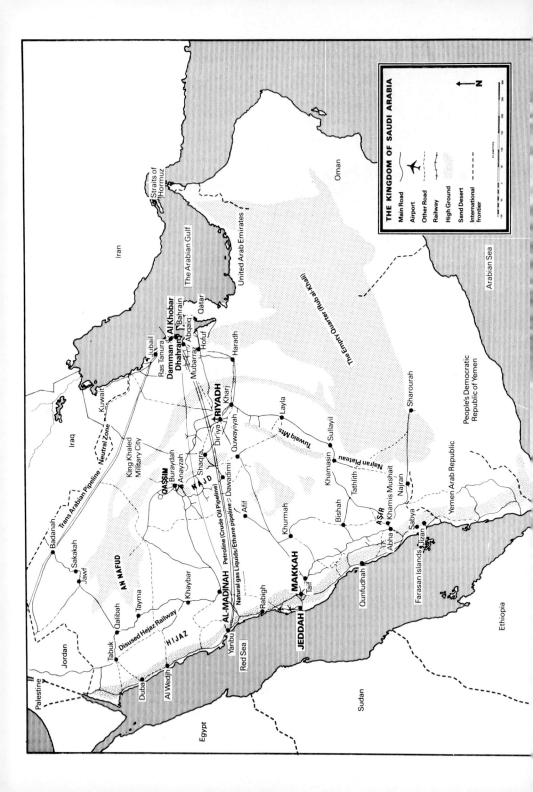

PART 2 PRACTICAL GUIDE FOR THE VISITOR

Basic information

Official name
Kingdom of Saudi Arabia — Al-Mamlaka al-Arabiyya al-Saudiyyah.

Government
Monarchy. The king and council of ministers form the executive and legislative branches of government.

Religion
Islam. No other religious practices are allowed.

Legal system
Islamic law (Sharia), based on the Quran.

National flag and symbol
Sword and inscription in white on green. The inscription is the Muslim profession of faith, the shahada: "There is no God but God; Muhammad is the messenger of God." The symbol is a date palm and crossed swords. The palm symbolises life and growth, and the crossed swords justice and strength rooted in faith.

Area
About 1.6 million square kilometres (1 million square miles).

Elevation
Altitude of 1,000-1,500 metres in northern plateau rising to 2,000-3,000 metres in the Madian mountains in the south. East of the mountains a plateau gradually extends east sloping down to the coast.

Geographic location
Saudi Arabia is bounded to the north by Jordan, to the west by the Red Sea, to the northeast by Iraq, the Neutral Zone and Kuwait, to the east by the Gulf, Bahrain, Qatar, the UAE and Oman, and to the south by North and South Yemen. The border with Iraq was originally established with a 7,044-square-kilometre neutral zone between them, allowing nomads to pass unhindered. In 1975 the zone was divided equally between the two countries. The border with Kuwait was also established with a neutral zone of 5,770 kilometres. Since 1966 the zone has been divided between the two with revenue from the oil found there shared equally.

Climate
Rainfall rarely exceeds 250 millimetres, except in the extreme southwest. Maximum temperatures are 100°F/38°C in summer, and the winter minimum 56°F/13°C. The summers are generally hot and dry, with humidity in some areas reaching 90 per cent, and the winters cold. In Riyadh, and elsewhere inland, it is less humid and temperatures are more extreme, with occasional rain in winter. Coastal towns tend to be hot and

humid all year. In Jeddah, humidity is greater and temperature variations slight; Eastern province's climate is similar, although temperatures are harsher. Sand and dust storms — shamals — occur in late spring and early summer.

Capital
Riyadh. Although embassies are still in Jeddah, they are due to move to a new diplomatic quarter in Riyadh (see Riyadh).

Population
The first full census, in 1974, put the population at just over 7 million. Government officials believe this is an overestimate, and recent reports by the Saudi Arabian Monetary Agency (SAMA — central bank authority) are based on an estimate of 6.9 million in fiscal 1974/75, rising annually by 2.9-3 per cent to 7.95 million in 1979/80. UN figures for 1974 are 7,012,642 — including 73,000 Saudis living abroad — in accordance with the census.

Subsequent estimates were: 1977 — 7,918,000; 1978 — 8,259,000; 1979 — 8,606,000; 1980 — 8,960,000.

A breakdown of nationals and expatriates is not given, although the ratio is believed to be 3:1.

Currency
The monetary unit is the riyal, which is divided into 100 halalahs. Notes are in 1, 5, 10, 50 and 100 riyal denominations, and coins in 5, 10, 25 and 50 halalah denominations. The riyal is quoted in dollars but based on the IMF's special drawing right (SDR). As the SDR/dollar rate varies, so the official riyal/dollar rate is revalued at intervals to keep within a narrow band around SDR 1 = SR 4.28.

In May 1983 the exchange rate was $1 = SR 3.4505; £1 = SR 5.4052; DM 1 = SR 1.4191; SF 1 = SR 1.6981; FF 1 = SR 0.4689; 1 yen = 0.014970.

Currency regulations
There are no restrictions on currency taken in or out of the country.

Credit cards
The main credit cards used in hotels are American Express, Diners Club and Visa, although Masterchage, Access, Eurocard and Carte Blanche are also accepted. Many shops and restaurants also accept American Express and Diners Club.

Tipping
In hotels and restaurants a service charge is usually included, so tips are optional. Hairdressers usually get SR 5 and porters expect SR 5 a suitcase. Taxi drivers are not normally tipped.

Customs regulations
Alcohol, drugs, pork produce and pornographic material are strictly illegal. However, tobacco can be imported in unlimited quantities, and articles for personal use are not restricted. Mechanical and electronic equipment such as cameras and typewriters may be subject to some levies. These will be returned if the goods are re-exported within three months.

Weights and measures
The metric system is used.

Electricity
Homes are usually supplied with alternative voltages which allow for using 220 V for heavier duty appliances and 110 V for most ordinary appliances. Homes in Riyadh, Jeddah and Dhahran all operate on 220/110 V and a frequency of 60 cycles. More outlying areas operate on 380/220 V and 50 cycles. As voltages vary, you can't rely on using electrical appliances in strange areas.

Light bulbs are bayonet or screw-type. Plugs are round two-pin continental plugs or American flat two-pin.

A proposal has been made to unify

all electrical supplies at 220/380V and 50 cycles — however, nothing has yet been done.

Public holidays
There are no official public holidays. However, business usually stops for two days during Eid al-Fitr, "the breaking of the fast" at the end of Ramadan. This feast lasts about a week from the end of the month of Ramadan to the beginning of the month of Shawwal. The second important feast day is the Id al-Adha, on the tenth of Dhu-I-Hijjah (see Islamic calendar).

Friday is the official Islamic weekly holiday. Most businesses and offices close then, although a few food shops may remain open. Government offices, banks and schools also close on Thursday, although most businesses are open for half a day.

Business hours
Government departments: Saturday-Wednesday 0730-1430; Ramadan 0930-1430.

Banks: Saturday-Wednesday 0830-1200, 1700-1900; Thursday 0830-1130; Ramadan 1000-1330.

Shops: opening hours vary slightly, but in general are Saturday-Thursday 0900-1200, 1600-2100; during Ramadan they are closed until sunset but then open until 0200.

Businesses: Saturday-Thursday 0800-1300, 1700-2000.

Prayer times
Every Muslim must pray five times a day. All offices and shops are obliged to close for each prayer for up to half an hour. Exact prayer times are published daily in the Arab News and Saudi Gazette.

The five daily prayers are: Fajr — dawn, Dhuhr — mid-day; Asr — mid-afternoon, Maghreb — early evening (usually 1800-1900); Asha — late evening (usually 1900-2000).

Administrative divisions
There are 14 administrative divisions, each with its own capital. From north to south these are Qurayyat (capital An-Nabk); Jawf (cap Sakakah); Northern Frontier (cap Arar); Tabuk (cap Tabuk); Hail (cap Hail); Al-Madinah (cap Al-Madinah); Qassim (cap Buraydah); Makkah (cap Makkah); Riyadh (cap Riyadh), Baha (cap Baha); Asir (cap Abha), Jizan (cap Jizan), and Najran (cap Najran). Eastern (formerly Hasa) province absorbs the entire eastern segment from the Iraqi and Kuwaiti borders in the north to the South Yemen border in the south, and the seaboard on the east from Kuwait to the UAE bar the Qatari peninsula. It also contains the Rub al-Khali (Empty Quarter), one of the biggest and most arid deserts in the world.

Provincial governors

Riyadh Prince Salman Ibn Abdul-Aziz
Makkah Prince Majid Ibn Abdul-Aziz
Al-Madinah Prince Abdul-Muson Ibn Abdul-Aziz
Asir Prince Khalid Ibn Faisal Ibn Abdul-Aziz
Qassim Prince Abdulillah Ibn Abdul-Aziz
Tabuk Prince Abdul-Mujid Ibn Abdel-Aziz
Hail Prince Mugrin Ibn Abdul-Aziz
Eastern province Prince Abdel-Muhsin Ibn Jiluwi
Northern borders Prince Abdullah Ibn Abdul-Aziz Ibn Musaid Ibn Jiluwi
Hofuf Prince Muhammad Ibn Fahd Ibn Jiluwi
Al-Jawf Amir Abdul-Rahman Ibn Ahmad Ibn Muhammad al-Sudairi
Najran Amir Fahd Ibn Khalid al-Sudairi
Qurayyat Amir Sultan Ibn Abdul-Aziz al-Sudairi
Al-Baha Shaikh Ibrahim Ibn Abdul-Aziz al-Ibrahim
Khamis Mushait Abdul-Aziz Ibn Said Ibn Mushait

Entering the kingdom

(see RGBB page vi)

Before visiting and working in the kingdom, you will need a visa stamped in your passport. You will be unable to obtain this if you have an Israeli visa stamped in your passport or any indication of a visit to Israel. Passports are required by all visitors except Muslim pilgrims who hold pilgrim passes, tickets and other documents for their onward or return journey, and who are entering the kingdom via Jeddah or Dhahran. No visa is required by nationals of Saudi Arabia, Bahrain, Kuwait, Oman, Qatar or the UAE. Passengers proceeding to a third country do not need a transit visa, but they must have a confirmed onward ticket and are forbidden to leave the airport.

Business visit visa

This is obtained through the local Saudi consulate on production of a letter from the Saudi sponsor stating that the visitor is required to enter. It is valid from two weeks to three months, although the period can be extended for two weeks by applying to the passport office in Saudi Arabia.

Work visa

This is required by all foreigners working in Saudi Arabia. It is obtained by the sponsor or employer, who applies to the relevant department at the Interior Ministry, submitting the employee's name, nationality and job. The application is usually dealt with in one month, when the Interior Ministry confirms its approval to the Foreign Affairs Ministry, which then contacts the relevant Saudi consulate abroad. Employees can then obtain their work visa, valid for three months, from their local consulates. Within three days of an employee's arrival, the employer should apply for a residence permit on the employee's behalf.

Sponsorship

Anybody working in Saudi Arabia must have a sponsor. Imprisonment is now the penalty for employing a non-sponsored worker — one week to one month plus a fine of SR 2,000-10,000.

Block visas

When a company needs several staff, it is usual to apply to the Interior Ministry for a block visa, which states the number and categories of employees permitted to be issued with work visas. Once the Interior Ministry has approved the block visa, it will notify the Foreign Affairs Ministry, which advises the local consulate through which the visas are to be issued. If all the work visas allocated are not used over the valid period of the block visa, this has to be renewed. At the time of writing, block visas were valid for six months. Before renewals can be applied for, the local consulate has to issue a certificate stating the number of visas issued during the valid period of the block visa.

Residence permit/Iqama *(white card with employee's photograph)*

All foreigners working in the kingdom need a residence permit, which can be obtained on submission of work visa and application form to the passport office. A residence permit is available for one or two years, and is renewable. Employees usually surrender their passport to their employer in exchange for the Iqama, which must be carried at all times as evidence of the residence permit's issue.

Family visa

Having obtained a residence permit, employees can ask their sponsor or employer to apply to the Interior Ministry on their behalf for a family visa for wives and children under 18. The visa, which allows the family to take up residence, will only be issued to certain categories of employee —

usually of professional status and earning a minimum SR 5,000 a month. Approval will be passed from the Interior Ministry to the Foreign Affairs Ministry, which will notify the local consulate.

On arrival, details of dependants are entered on the Iqama, while their residence status is written into their passports (which they are allowed to keep). It is sensible if dependants always carry photocopies of their Iqama or passport.

Work permit *(blue card)*
This is obtained by applying to the local labour office at any time during the term of employment and is usually essential for the renewal of residence permits.

Family visit visa
This is needed by wives and children under 18 visiting a resident in the kingdom. Only certain categories of resident — including doctors, engineers, lawyers, teachers, and senior and general managers — are allowed to obtain them.

Exit and re-entry visa
This is needed by all those on work visas — including dependants — wanting to leave the kingdom for not more than six months. It is usually available within one or two months of application and, if not used, must be cancelled. Where wives have children entered on their passports, it is worth checking that the visa allows all family members to travel — don't wait until you're at the airport to do this. Similarly, check the return date, as this sometimes varies. In some cases, it may be better to get individual passports for all family members, as this will avoid possible problems or confusion. Children must be cancelled from the parent's passport before a residence visa is granted.

Exit-only visa
This is obtained on final departure from the kingdom at the end of a contract and automatically terminates the residence permit. To prove final departure, a departure certificate can be obtained from the airport authorities. This is important if a company intends to replace an employee, as it may have to prove the number of workers brought into the country under a particular contract before new work visas will be issued.

How to obtain visas and permits
It is possible for employees to obtain some visas and permits themselves, although it is more usual for the company to deal with them. No visas can be obtained without the company's written consent.

Submitting the application
The family visa
1) Collect the forms from the importation of foreign labour office (IFLO) in the Interior Ministry.
2) Complete them in Arabic.
3) Return the application to the IFLO in person, accompanied by a Saudi national to answer any questions. The application should be accompanied by originals and photocopies of the following documents:

☐ husband or father's academic or professional qualifications. These should be authenticated by the Department of Education & Science, the Foreign & Commonwealth Office, the London Chamber of Commerce & Industry and the Saudi consulate in London. It is preferable for the husband to do this before he leaves the UK;

☐ a copy of the company's commercial registration certificate — where applicable — or other authorisation for the company to operate in the kingdom;

☐ social insurance documents proving — where applicable — the firm has more than 20 employees;

☐ marriage certificate of wife and birth certificate of children, to be translated and attested by the Foreign Affairs Ministry;

☐ passport with husband's valid residence visa;
☐ letter from the husband to the IFLO manager asking permission to bring the dependant or relative into the kingdom;
☐ letter from the company supporting the application and quoting the employee's conditions of service — salary, accommodation, and so on, and
☐ declaration from the General Organisation of Social Insurance confirming that the husband's salary has been paid.

4) The copies will be compared with the originals and the originals returned immediately. Be careful to get your passport back.

5) The Saudi interpreter may be called back to answer queries as the documents are processed. This can be lengthy as queries are dealt with individually and not together, so be prepared for some delay.

6) When the application is approved, the Interior Ministry will pass the visa's reference number to the Foreign Affairs Ministry and authorise it to send the number to the Saudi embassy in London. This may take two or three weeks.

7) Report to the Foreign Affairs Ministry once you are informed that the application has been approved. Get the visa's reference number and present it to the Saudi embassy in London, which will issue the visa. This may also take two or three weeks.

The visit visa

Application for a family visit visa is made in Arabic to the Foreign Affairs Ministry on completion of the appropriate form, with a copy of the resident's passport, marriage certificate and resident permit. A certificate from the resident's sponsor is also needed, accepting responsibility for the members of the family arriving in the kingdom. Details of the resident's salary and accommodation must be included in this certificate, which usually has to be endorsed by the Riyadh Chamber of Commerce.

The extension of visit visa

There is no way of predicting how long a visit visa may last — it might be for as little as two weeks or for as long as three months. Before December 1980 it was possible to overstay a short while on a visit visa and, on payment of a small fine, to obtain an exit visa. Since then, however, penalties for overstaying have been severe, consisting of a large fine and possible prison sentence for both the sponsor and the visitor.

Conversion of a visit visa

It is not generally possible to convert a visit visa into a residence visa without leaving the kingdom.

It is wise to keep photocopies of passports, visas and permits in case of loss. Except for the Iqama and driving licence — where originals are necessary — photocopies are enough to carry round. It is essential to have the Arabic details on all permits checked by a translator to ensure that details such as dates of expiry and validity are understood. It is also vital to remember that if an emergency in the UK requires employees to leave the kingdom in a hurry, **written** evidence (copy of a telex) must be produced to obtain prompt attention from the immigration authorities.

Identity cards

All non-Saudis employed in the kingdom must always carry identity cards, residence permits or passports. The police may stop you at any time and request identification — people not carrying such documents are liable to serious penalties. Companies should supply full information about non-Saudi employees to the passport authorities so identity cards can be issued.

When to visit

When planning a short business trip, Islamic holidays should be borne in mind. During the month of Dhu-l-Hijjah and the feast of Eid al-Adha, which vary from year to year, business meetings are difficult to arrange and flights are heavily booked. In Jeddah, because of its proximity to Makkah, hotels tend to be fully booked.

Ramadan is another time to avoid if you can, as business tends to be restricted. Businessmen are available briefly around noon and after sunset. Most offices close two days before Eid al-Fitr at the end of Ramadan.

You should also be wary of going in summer, both because of climate and because businessmen are often abroad.

Health regulations
These should be checked at the Saudi embassy before departure as requirements may vary. However, in general, those arriving from the West do not need inoculations, except during the Hajj period (see Islamic Calendar), when a certificate of inoculation against cholera may be requested. Anyone arriving from cholera-infected areas will be expected to show proof of inoculation — an international vaccination certificate, proof of having left the area five days previously and a certificate showing two doses of tetracycline tablets have been taken on two consecutive days, either while still in the area or in the ensuing five days in the cholera-free zone.

Anyone intending to visit areas outside the main cities should take preventive medicine against malaria, particularly if going to the south. For smallpox and yellow fever, valid certificates of vaccination are also required if you are coming from an infected area.

For further information contact the Ministry of Foreign Affairs, tel Jeddah 6421322, telex 40104 kharjia. There are also chambers of commerce in Riyadh, Jeddah, Al-Madinah, Dammam, Taif and Buraydah.

In the US contact: US-Arab Chamber of Commerce, tel 212 4320655, One World Trade Center, Suite 4657, New York, NY 10048.

In the UK contact: Arab-British Chamber of Commerce, tel London 6291249, PO Box 4BL, 42 Berkeley Square, London W1X 5DB.

Getting about

Driving
Driving is on the right. Women may not drive under any circumstances. Valid licences from most countries will be accepted for up to 45 days and a temporary licence can be issued quickly from the town traffic department after completion of the necessary forms. A five-year licence will be issued against most clean foreign licences and can be obtained within three days.

To get a licence it is best to go accompanied by an Arabic speaker. Take a valid driving licence, passport, iqama (residence permit), three passport-size photos and a blood group certificate. Applicants are sometimes required to give half a litre of blood and to take an eye test. Those who do not give blood are occasionally given only a one-year licence.

Most car hire firms stipulate a minimum age of 21 and will not accept a driving licence of less than one year's standing. Visitors are only allowed to drive private vehicles — only Saudi nationals can drive taxis.

Driving is a challenge but petrol is cheap

Driving conditions can be rough and every precaution should be taken (see Advice to Expatriates). At junctions, the car on the right has priority — but even then take great care.

Although car insurance is not

This government warning speaks for itself

compulsory, visitors are advised to carry maximum third party risk for their own protection. If an accident does occur and someone is killed, the family may demand compensation. If you are uninsured, there is a risk of long-term imprisonment. Drivers must always carry vehicle and private documentation, and it is wise to keep duplicates of these elsewhere. The police carry out regular checks of such documents and the penalties for being without them can be up to SR 300 and/or one month's jail. If a licence is confiscated a receipt should be issued. If not, the police car number or officer number should be noted and it is probably wise not to make too many objections.

Air travel
There are three main airports: Riyadh international, about seven kilometres from the city centre, Dhahran international, 10 kilometres from Al-Khobar and 15 kilometres from Dhahran, and King Abdul-Aziz international, 20 kilometres from Jeddah city centre.

All domestic services are operated by the national airline Saudia. International lines can only operate in and out of Jeddah and Dhahran; they cannot fly between the two.

If you have a contract with the Saudi government it usually contains a clause stating that employees must travel with Saudia. Tickets for Saudia flights are only available direct from the airline or its approved agents. Tickets for other airlines can be bought from general service agents. As there are no regulations covering agents it is best to deal only with those which are IATA-approved.

The usual check-in times are one hour before departure on internal flights; two hours for international flights from Riyadh, and 90 minutes for international flights from Jeddah and Dhahran.

If you intend to go to Riyadh it is best to avoid entering the kingdom via Jeddah or Dhahran, as problems may arise.

The bus system
The bus services of the Saudi Arabian Public Transport Company (Saptco) started in Riyadh in July 1979 and now run in Riyadh, Jeddah, Eastern province, Makkah, Taif and Al-Madinah. Internal city buses charge SR 1 for any journey while Dhahran airport to Dammam and Al-Khobar costs SR 5. Inter-city routes connect towns throughout Saudi Arabia (Jeddah, Makkah, Taif, Al-Madinah, Riyadh, Buraydah, Al-Kharj, Dammam and Jubail). Single inter-city fares vary: Jeddah-Makkah SR 15, Jeddah-Al-Madinah SR 50, Jeddah-Dammam Express (luxury) SR 190 one way.

The city buses have a back section reserved for women, with a separate entrance. Passengers are expected to have a SR 1 coin ready as change is not given; this is put in the box by the driver at the men's end and by the entrance to the women's section.

Saptco's city buses are fast and comfortable with stops every 200 metres recognisable by the motif of a cubist man leaping on to a bus. Routes are published in the Saudi Gazette and the Arab News and complete route networks and information are available from Saptco — Riyadh Tel: 4545000, Jeddah Tel: 6474900/6672828, Taif Tel: 7384648, Al-Madinah Tel: 8236107, Dammam Tel: 8266833, Qassim Tel: 3334618.

Modern farming in Wadi Birk

Saudi children

Coffee – the heart of hospitality

Pivot irrigation, Wadi Birk

Stud farm near Riyadh

Road distances in kilometres

	Buraydah	Dhahran	Dammam	Hofuf	Jeddah	Makkah	Al-Madinah	Riyadh	Taif
Abha	1,355	1,485	1,499	1,346	678	606	1,053	1,018	528
Abqaiq	876	71	85	83	1,443	1,371	1,387	376	1,277
Al-Kharj	550	527	541	408	1,141	1,069	1,091	80	981
Al-Khobar	927	10	18	164	1,528	1,452	1,468	457	1,358
Al-Madinah	541	1,458	1,472	1,339	424	447	0	1,011	535
Al-Mudawwarah	1,326	2,245	2,257	2,126	1,214	1,286	785	1,798	1,374
Al-Zarqani	1,295	378	371	532	1,892	1,820	1,836	835	1,727
Aneyzah	30	887	901	768	945	968	521	440	1,056
Badanah	1,959	1,042	1,035	1,196	2,556	2,484	2,931	1,489	2,396
Buraydah	0	917	931	798	965	915	541	470	827
Dammam	931	14	0	168	1,528	1,456	1,472	461	1,362
Dhahran	917	0	14	154	1,514	1,442	1,458	447	1,348
Doha	1,048	376	390	250	1,639	1,567	1,589	578	1,479
Hail	284	1,201	1,215	1,073	822	894	398	745	982
Hofuf	798	154	168	0	1,389	1,317	1,337	328	1,229
Jeddah	965	1,514	1,528	1,389	0	72	424	1,061	160
Kuwait	1,354	437	423	591	1,951	1,879	1,895	884	1,785
Makkah	988	1,442	1,456	1,317	72	0	447	989	88
Najran	1,736	1,713	1,727	1,594	970	898	1,345	1,266	810
Qaisumah	1,379	462	455	616	1,976	1,904	1,920	909	1,810
Qatif	947	30	18	184	1,544	1,472	1,488	477	1,378
Rafha	1,675	758	750	912	2,272	2,200	2,216	1,205	2,106
Ras Tanura	986	69	63	223	1,583	1,511	1,527	516	1,417
Riyadh	470	447	461	328	1,061	989	1,011	0	901
Salwa	948	301	315	150	1,545	1,473	1,476	484	1,385
Taif	1,076	1,348	1,362	1,229	160	88	535	901	0
Tabuk	1,227	2,144	2,158	2,025	1,110	1,133	686	1,697	1,221
Turaif	2,197	1,280	1,272	1,425	2,794	2,722	2,725	1,733	2,634

Communications

Telephones

The telephone system is administered for the Posts, Telegraphs & Telecommunications Ministry by Saudi Telephone.

If renting a home or office it is best to take one with a telephone already installed, as it can be difficult to get one put in. Telephone lines can only be transferred to different premises if requested by the registered subscriber, who may be an absentee landlord.

Bills are quarterly and should be paid in at a Saudi Telephone office promptly, to avoid disconnection. Bills are either sent to a PO box or can be collected from a Saudi Telephone office. Local calls are free from private telephones; trunk and international calls are charged on a time basis. A one minute call to the UK costs SR 15. There are no off-peak reductions.

The kind of telephone equipment you have is your own affair — many companies offer exchange and internal extension systems of varying prices and complexity.

Dialling from abroad

From abroad dial international code 010 + country code 966 + area code (Jeddah 2; Makkah 2; Riyadh 1; Dammam, Al-Khobar and Dhahran 3) + number required. Calls to other areas must be booked through the operator.

International subscriber dialling (ISD)

Dial 00 + country code + city code + numbers
Where no city code is shown, number should be dialled after country code

Country	Code	Charge per minute (SR)
Algeria*	213	8.40
Andorra	33 (+078 all points)	14.00
Argentina	54 (+1 Buenos Aires)	17.00
Australia	61 (+2 Sydney)	17.00
Austria	43 (+222 Vienna)	13.00
Bahrain*	973	Rate varies
Belgium	32 (+2 Brussels)	14.00
Brazil	55 (+21 Rio de Janeiro)	17.00
Cameroon	237	22.00
Canada	1 (+613 Ottawa)	15.00
Caribbean	1+809	Rate varies
Cyprus	357 (+21 Nicosia)	22.00
Denmark	45 (+1 Copenhagen)	14.00
Egypt	20 (+2 Cairo)	7.00
Finland	358 (+0 Helsinki)	13.00
France	33 (+1 Paris)	14.00
Germany (West)	49 (+2221 Bonn)	13.00
Greece	30 (+1 Athens)	13.00

Country	Code	Charge per minute (SR)
Hongkong	852 (+5 Capital)	13.00
India	91 (+11 Delhi)	12.00
Indonesia	62 (+21 Jakarta)	17.00
Iran	98 (+21 Tehran)	7.00
Iraq	964 (+1 Baghdad)	5.60
Ireland	353 (+1 Dublin)	14.00
Italy	39 (+6 Rome)	14.00
Ivory Coast	225 (+2 all points)	17.00
Japan	81 (+3 Tokyo)	17.00
Kenya	254 (+2 Nairobi)	16.00
Korea (South)	82 (+2 Seoul)	13.00
Kuwait*	965	5.60
Lebanon*	961	8.40
Libya	218 (+21 Tripoli)	8.40
Liechtenstein	41 (+75 all points)	8.40
Luxembourg*	352	14.00
Malaysia	60 (+3 Kuala Lumpur)	17.00
Malta*	356	14.00
Mexico	52 (+5 Mexico City)	17.00
Monaco	33 (+93 all points)	14.00
Morocco	212 (+5 Rabat)	8.40
Netherlands	31 (+20 Amsterdam)	13.00
New Zealand	64 (+0 Auckland)	22.00
Nigeria	234 (+33 Lagos)	16.00
Norway	47 (+2 Oslo)	13.00
Oman*	968	Rate varies
Pakistan	92 (+21 Karachi)	8.40
Peru	51 (+14 Lima)	22.00
Philippines	63 (+2 Manila)	18.00
Portugal	351 (+19 Lisbon)	13.00
Qatar*	974	Rate varies
San Marino	39 (+541 all points)	14.00
Senegal*	221	22.00
Seychelles*	248	17.00
Singapore*	65	13.00
South Africa	27 (+11 Johannesburg) (+21 Cape Town)	13.00

		Charge per minute (SR)
Spain	34 (+1 Madrid)	13.00
Sri Lanka	94 (+1 Colombo)	14.00
Sweden	46 (+8 Stockholm)	13.00
Switzerland	41 (+1 Zurich) (+22 Geneva)	13.00
Taiwan	886 (+6 all points)	16.00
Thailand	66 (+2 Bangkok)	22.00
Tunisia	216 (+1 Tunis)	8.40
Turkey	90 (+41 Ankara)	14.00
United Arab Emirates	971 (+2 Abu Dhabi) (+4 Dubai)	Rate varies
UK	44 (+1 London)	15.00
US	1 (+212 New York) (+202 Washington)	9.00
Upper Volta*	226	22.00
Venezuela	58 (+2 Caracas)	17.00
Yemen (North)*	967	8.40

At the time of writing some rates were being reduced considerably. Calls to Italy, for example, have been reduced from SR 14 to SR 9 a minute

* Area code not required

Local zone codes

07	Abha	02	Al-Hada	04	Al-Madinah	01	Sajir
03	Abqaiq	06	Hail	02	Makkah	04	Sakakah
01	Afif	02	Hawiyah	06	Midnab	03	Seihat
06	Aneyzah	03	Hofuf	03	Mobarraz	01	Shaqra
04	Arar	04	Al-Jawf	01	Murat	07	Sharora
06	Badayah	02	Jeddah	07	Najran	04	Tabuk
07	Baha	07	Jizan	03	Qatif	02	Taif
07	Bisha	03	Jubail	01	Al-Qawiyah	03	Tarut
06	Bukairiyah	06	Khabra	04	Qurayyat	04	Turaif
06	Buraydah	03	Al-Khafji	02	Rabigh	02	Obhor
03	Dammam	07	Khamis Mushait	03	Ras Tanura	04	Umm Lajj
01	Dawadmi	01	Al-Kharj	06	Ar-Rass	04	Al-Wedjh
03	Dhahran	04	Khaybar	01	Rimah	04	Yanbu
01	Dir'iya	03	Al-Khobar	01	Riyadh	06	Az-Zilfi
01	Durma	01	Leyla	06	Riyadh al-Khabra		
07	Faisalia	06	Majmaah	03	Safwa		
06	Al-Ghat	01	Mazahimiyah				

Emergency and information

Long distance operator	900
Accident reporting	993
Ambulance	997
Fire service	998
Emergency and police patrol	999
Telephone repairs	904
Information	905
Time (Arabic)	961
Time (English)	962
Cable location bureau	906

* For directory enquiries, dial zone code for the number required followed by 905

Telex
Telex facilities are available on application to the Posts, Telegraphs & Telecommunications Ministry. As telex machines use existing telephone lines, an extra line is essential.

Telexing from abroad
From abroad dial 007 for the exchange. When your own answerback appears type 495 then the number. All Saudi numbers have six digits.

Facsimile (fax) machines
Details of facsimile machines and systems can be obtained from local equipment agents such as Binladin Telecommunications.

Post
Post is delivered only to boxes at post offices. These can be obtained, by individuals or companies, by applying to the head postmaster and paying a rental of SR 300 for two years.

Until a company obtains its own box it should arrange to use a box belonging to a sponsor or client.

Registered mail can be collected from the post office only by personnel authorised by the employer. A note is placed in boxes when mail awaits collection.

Postal codes
A five-digit postal code is being introduced, while a new system of numbering and naming houses and streets began in major cities in mid-1982.

Philips mobile telephones represent the kingdom's high-tech approach

Time differentials*

Local Saudi time is GMT + 3 hours. Times shown are plus or minus local time

Algeria	−1
Andorra	−2
Australia	+5/+7
Bahrain	same
Bangladesh	+3
Belgium	−2
Bermuda	−7
Canada	−6/−11
Cyprus	−1
Denmark	−2
Egypt	−1
France	−2
Greece	−1
Hongkong	+5
India	+2
Iran	+ 30 mins
Iraq	same
Italy	−2
Japan	+6
Jordan	−1
Kuwait	same
Luxembourg	−2
Morocco	−3
Netherlands	−2
New Zealand	+9
Norway	−2
Oman	+1
Qatar	same
Singapore	+4½
Spain	−2
Sri Lanka	+2
Sweden	−2
Switzerland	−2
UAE	+1
UK	−3
US	−8/−12
Vatican City	−2
West Germany	−2

*Differentials may alter by one hour if summer time is observed

General information

Islamic Calendar

Gregorian year AD	Hijra year AH (after Hijra)	First day of new year	Ramadan begins	Eid al-Fitr	Eid al-Adha	Dhu-l-Hijjah begins
1980	1400/1	9 Nov	14 Nov	12 Aug	19 Oct	10 Oct
1981	1401/2	29 Oct	3 July	1 Aug	8 Oct	29 Sept
1982	1402/3	18 Oct	22 June	21 July	27 Sept	18 Sept
1983	1403/4	7 Oct	11 June	10 July	16 Sept	7 Sept
1984	1404/5	26 Sept	31 May	29 June	5 Sept	27 Aug
1985	1405/6	15 Sept	20 May	18 June	25 Aug	16 Aug

The Islamic calendar starts from the year 622 AD, the year of the Prophet Muhammad's Migration (Hijra) from Makkah to Al-Madinah. There are 12 Hijri months (see calendar conversion) making 354 or 355 days. The Hijri year is thus 11 days shorter than the Gregorian year. The calendar depends on the sighting of the moon. Therefore, like everything else in a lunar calendar, the year and events, such as the fast of Ramadan, move back against the Gregorian calendar by 10-12 days annually. The Hijri months are Muharram, Safar, Rabi' I, Rabi' II, Jumada I, Jumada II, Rajab, Sha'aban, Ramadan, Shawwal, Dhu-l-Qa'dah, Dhu-l-Hijjah. Ramadan corresponds to the month of fasting (see Introduction to Islam). Dhu-l-Hijjah corresponds with the month of the Pilgrimage to Makkah.

Population of main towns at 1974 census

Riyadh	666,840
	(1980 1 million)
Jeddah	561,104
	(1980 1.35 million)
Makkah	366,801
Taif	204,857
Al-Madinah	198,186
Dammam	127,844
Hofuf	101,271
Tabuk	74,825
Buraydah	69,940
Mobarraz	54,325
Khamis Mushait	49,581
Al-Khobar	48,817
Najran	47,501
Hail	40,502

Education

Education is free to all Saudis. Although it is not compulsory, more than 90 per cent of all children attend school.

There are 16 university and college campuses countrywide. The major universities are: King Faisal university, Eastern province; University of Petroleum & Minerals, Dhahran; King Saud and Imam Muhammad Ibn Saud Islamic universities, Riyadh; King Abdul-Aziz university, Makkah and Jeddah, and the Islamic university, Al-Madinah. In 1981 the number of people studying at school or university totalled 1.5 million, 100,000 more than the previous year. The state's allocation for education amounted to SR 21,200 million — about SR 14,000 a student, official statistics show.

In 1980 about 10,000 Saudis were studying abroad, 6,896 of them in the US.

Male students outnumber females by 10 to 1. Engineering is studied by about one in four students; other popular subjects are social sciences and medicine (see page 117).

Language

Arabic is the official language and all official documents are published initially in Arabic. However, many government officials have been educated partly in the West and in these and business circles English is spoken almost universally. A knowledge of Arabic is not essential for visiting businessmen but a little Arabic will naturally please the Saudis with whom they come in contact.

All Arabs take immense pride in the Arabic language which, as the language of the Quran, is held in a peculiar esteem. Iconography is condemned by Islam and the condemnation is particularly severe among the Wahhabis. The Arabs' main graphic art-form, therefore, is calligraphy. Pictures of ships or animals, for example, are sometimes drawn in calligraphic suras from the Quran. The Arabic language, therefore, is far more than a mere vehicle for communication.

Westerners are sometimes surprised by the florid nature of Arabic conversations. They should remember that language among the Arabs is not merely used to express ideas but also to create mood. In medieval times a bedouin army would sometimes flee as a result of the vituperous language of the poet of the opposing forces, even if they were weaker in physical terms.

Commercial interpreter and translation services are available but are usually unnecessary, as most companies have at least one English speaker.

Useful words and phrases

Saudi dialects vary a good deal as is only natural in a country almost 10 times as big as West Germany. However, the foreign student of Arabic need not be too discouraged — there are many more features which unite the dialects than divide them. The main unifying factor — and indeed that which prevents Arabic dialects in general from becoming too disparate — is the Holy Quran. The following selection of words and phrases is intended to illustrate genuine Saudi usage without being confined to one particular area of the Hejaz or Najd or the Eastern province. Since Makkah is the birthplace of the Prophet Muhammad, it is natural to head the list with religious phrases

Religion

There is no God but God, Muhammad is the Messenger of God	Laa illaah illa Allaah Muhammad rasool Allaah.
The Quran	Al-Quraan
The Quran's opening verses (recited on all great occasions, solemn or joyful)	Al-faatiha
Times of prayer	
Dawn	Al-fajr
Noon	Adh-dhuhr
Afternoon	Al-'asr
Sunset	Al-maghrib
Evening	Al-'ashaa

(Saudis use these as indications of time, eg, for appointments.)

The Pillars of Islam

Testifying to God's oneness	Ash-shahaada
Prayer	As-salaat
Fasting	As-sawm
Pilgrimage	Al-hajj
Almsgiving	Az-zakaat

The Islamic Months — universally used; the Christian calendar is secondary:

The twelve months in the Hijri calendar (dating from Mohammad's "hijra" from Makkah to Al-Madinah) do not coincide with the Gregorian months since the Islamic calendar is lunar. Months have alternately, 29 and 30 days, 354 days a year. Hence the AH year recedes by approximately 11 days a year against the AD calendar.	Muharram Safar Rabi' al-awwal Rabi' ath-thaani Jumaada-l-oolaa Jumaada-l-ukhraa Rajab Sha'abaan Ramadhaan Shawwaal Dhu-l-qa'da Dhu-l-hijja

Feast Days — strictly speaking two only

End of Ramadan ('Feast of the breaking' of the fast)	Eed al-fitr
Pilgrimage Feast	Eed al-adha

Money

A great deal of money	Fuloos katheer
I owe you 20 riyals	Alayi lak 'ashreen riyal
The car cost me 20,000 riyals	As-sayaara kalafatnee 'ashreen alf riyaal
The price is fixed	As-si'r mahdood
Where is the money-changer?	Wayn maktab as-sarraaf?
How many riyals to the dollar today?	Ad-doolaar bi-kam al-yawm?
How much is this?	Haadha bi-kam?
Do you take travellers' cheques?	Btakhudh sheekaat siyaaha?

Travel

I want to book to London (first/economy)	Abghee ahjiz illaa Landan (daraja oolaa/siyaaheeya)
What time is take-off?	At-tayaara btitla' as-saa'a kam?
Is there any delay?	Fee taakheer?
What is arrival time?	At-tayaara bitawassul as-saa'a kam?
What is the taxi fare to the airport?	Ujrat it-taksee kam illa-l-mataar?
Take my luggage, please	Khudh al-'afsh, min fadlak.

Courtesies

Welcome!	Ahlan wa sahlan!
Welcome! Hullo!	Yaa halaa
Good morning	Sabaah al-khayr!
(Reply)	Sabaah an-noor
Good evening	Masaa al-khayr
(Reply)	Masaa an-noor
Goodbye (or leaving — lit: "with your permission")	'An idhnak (fem: 'an idhnik)
Goodbye (to someone leaving)	Ma'a as-salaama
(Reply — lit: "God bless you!")	Allaah yisalmak! (fem: Allaah yisalmik)
Goodbye (to someone leaving — lit: "In the safekeeping of God!")	Fee amaan Illah!
(Reply)	Fee amaan il-Kareem!
Please!	Min fadlak! (fem: min fadlik)
Thank you!	Shukran!
(Reply — lit: "I beg pardon of God")	'Afwan

On being introduced (lit: "We are honoured") — Natasharraf
(Reply — lit: "May God increase your honour!") — Allaah yazeedak sharaf! (fem' Allah yazeedik sharaf)

Won't you come this way? — Tfaddal (fem: tfaddali)

Titles

Your highness	Yaa saahib as-sumoo
Your majesty	Yaa saahib al-jalaala
You (respectfully — lit: "May your life be long!")	Taal 'amrak (fem: taal 'amrik)

"Father of X" — either literally, or as a term of respect.
Traditionally some names are "converted" eg,
Hassan — Aboo 'alaa
Ibrahim — Aboo khaleel
Mohammad — Aboo-l-qaasim

Directions

Right	Yameen
Left	Shimaal/Yisaar
North	Shimaal
South	Janoob
East	Sharq
West	Gharb
Straight on!	'Alaa tool!
Stop!	Waqqif!
Slowly!	'Alaa mahlak!
Go on, further	Imshee kemaan shway
In front of	Amaama
Behind	Waraa
Turn right	Khush yameen
Turn left	Khush yisaar
Take me to...	Wadeenee illaa
Drop me here	Nazalnee hawn
Upstairs	Fawq
Downstairs	Taht
Bring me...	Haat...
Take this away	Sheel haadha

Go!	Rooh!
Come!	Ta'aal!
Go away!	Imshee
Wait for me here	Istanaanee hawn!

Language Problems

Do you speak English?	Tatakallam inkleezee? (fem: tatakallami inkleezee?)
Please speak slowly!	Takallim shway shway min fadlak! (fem: takallimi shway shway min fadlik)
Is there anyone here who speaks English?	Fee had hawn bya'rif inkleezee?
I can't read/write/speak English & Arabic	Maa ba'rif iqraa/uktub/atakallam inkleezee/'arabee.

Miscellaneous Expressions

The Eastern Province	Al-mantiqa ash-sharqiya
The Najd	Najd
The Hejaz	Al-Hejaaz
The Wahhabis literally "the unitarians" (the term is never used by Saudis) ie those who testify that "There is but one God"	Al-muwahhidoon
Quickly	Bi-sur'a
Be patient	Tawwil baalak (fem: tawwili baalik)
Not yet	Lissa
Like this/in this way	Kadhaa
He hasn't come yet	Maa jaa ba'ad
It's impossible	Mish mumkin
The same thing	Nafs ish-shee
I am busy	Ana mashghool (fem: ana mashghoola)
I'm sorry	Muta'assif (fem: muta'assifa)

He contacted us	Zahama 'alayna
A long time ago	Min zamaan
Two weeks ago	Qabla usboo'ayn
Is there a good Arabic restaurant here?	Fee mat'am 'arabee kwayyis hawn?
And finally, since all depends on God's will,	
If God wills	In shaa' Allaah

Numbers

One wahid; *two* ithnain; *three* thalatha; *four* arba'a *five* khamsa; *six* sitta; *seven* sab'a; *eight* thamaniya; *nine* tis'a; *ten* 'ashara; *eleven* ihda 'ashar; *twelve* ithna 'ashar; *twenty* 'ashreen; *hundred* mi'a; *thousand* alf

Days of the week

Sunday Yom al-ahad;
Monday Yom al-ithnain;
Tuesday Yom al-thalatha;
Wednesday Yom al-arba'a;
Thursday Yom al-khamees;
Friday Yom al-jum'a;
Saturday Yom as-sabt

Simplified from a text compiled by Leslie McLoughlin, director of UKAS, London, UK

Desert driving survival checklist

The deserts are among the most inhospitable and potentially dangerous areas for the unsuspecting and unwary traveller — to underestimate the dangers and to ignore expert advice is to court disaster. Remember: your vehicle and its contents will be your sole means of survival. Four-wheel-drive is usually essential off the road.

The following is based on advice given by Avis' Abu Dhabi office to all users of its cars.

Documents and legal requirements

You must always carry identification. A check list for a desert trip: passport, iqama (residence permit), driving licence, car registration, warning triangle, fire extinguisher, insurance, letter of permission from a sponsor, preferably stamped by a chamber of commerce, which must be valid for a fixed period of time.

Before starting your journey

Carry out these checks yourself — don't rely on somebody else.

☐ Check fuel tank is full — don't rely on fuel gauge, it may be faulty. Check radiator water level.

☐ Check tyres for condition and pressure (including spare).

☐ Check tool kit — take one jack, one wheel spanner, one block of wood on which to place the jack, one foot pump.

☐ Take a survival pack.

☐ Allow 10 litres of drinking water a head — excluding any soft drinks. Carry a food supply although this is not as important.

☐ Identify destination and route. Take a compass.

Before you leave

Make sure someone knows the following:

☐ Name and number of passengers.

☐ Your route

☐ Type and colour of vehicle

☐ Departure time

☐ Estimated time of return/arrival and arrival point.

In the desert

Whatever happens:
- ☐ Never leave your vehicle
- ☐ Try to travel with at least two vehicles.
- ☐ Avoid travelling across the sand at midday in summer (May-October). The higher the sun, the hotter the ground and the softer the sand — also lack of shadows make it harder to see bumps and holes.
- ☐ Unless essential, never travel at night.
- ☐ Follow existing well-used tracks, wherever possible. If anything happens there is a chance that someone else will come along and be able to help. When travelling after rain keep to the tracks — in low-lying areas the sand can become waterlogged quickly and you will get stuck.
- ☐ If you should get stuck, or find someone else stuck, the vehicle able to move should never drive up to the vehicle in difficulties. Stop on firm ground and then go to help. If travelling in convoy, don't follow too close — the vehicle in front may stick and so might you.
- ☐ Try to find a way around a steep sand dune or hill. It is easy to roll a vehicle, especially driving down it. If you have to drive down, do so slowly in first or second gear in low four-wheel drive. Try not to brake: the vehicle may swing round. The low gear will give you enough engine braking on its own.
- ☐ On sand, avoid hard braking and sudden acceleration — either may cause the tyres to "dig in."
- ☐ If you do get lost or stuck — don't panic. You will do something stupid and your body will use up its reserves of energy and fluid at double the normal rate. Remember — 95 per cent of deaths of desert travellers are caused by stupidity and/or panic. Sit down; calm down; have a cigarette; look at the situation — don't panic.

If you get stuck

Get out of the vehicle and look for the nearest firm ground. Note the slope of the land; it may be better to travel down a slope over a longer stretch of soft sand than to try to reverse up a slope over a shorter stretch of soft sand.

The following procedures should be followed, according to the circumstances:

- ☐ Straighten the front wheels — never try to drive out of soft sand in anything but a straight line, until you are clear and travelling at some speed.
- ☐ If the tyres are not deep in the sand, try digging the sand away in front of all the tyres to provide a gradual ramp up which you should try to drive.
- ☐ If deeply bogged down, and if you have enough people, try to lift the vehicle corner by corner with one person pushing the sand back under the wheel being raised, until the vehicle is on level ground again. Or use the jack to achieve the same result. Put something solid under the jack to prevent it sinking into the sand.
- ☐ When ready to drive select low ratio four-wheel drive. Release the clutch slowly and try to drive away as slowly as possible. Do not over-rev the engine and spin the tyres as you will only dig yourself in again.

If all the above fails, follow the same procedure to free the wheels, but this time let down the tyres to about half the normal pressure. Lighten the load in the vehicle, then try again — slowly. **Remember** if you have deflated the tyres, **it is dangerous to drive at more than about 40 kilometres an hour on hard tracks or tarmac roads.**

- ☐ Provide a better grip for the tyres — collect scrub, grass and branches, anything to cover the sand.
- ☐ If you are stuck in a "bowl" — a natural hollow or depression — don't give up. There are two ways of getting out.

1) Run or "rock" the vehicle backwards and forwards across the floor of the bowl, aiming at what you think is the firmest slope — don't forget, the gentlest or easiest slope will probably be the slope with the softest sand — and then drive out over the rim.

2) Drive in a circle around the bowl, gradually spiralling upwards until you reach the top.

If you still cannot get out, stay with your vehicle.

Waiting for rescue

If you are on a track, someone may come along. Even if you are away from the track you still have an excellent chance of being rescued, provided you follow these rules:

- ☐ Stay with your vehicle.
- ☐ Keep out of direct sun. Use the vehicle — covering the windows — to provide as much shade for yourself and passengers as possible. Re-position the car if possible to allow whatever wind is available to pass through. Or take advantage of whatever is around you to give you shade.

☐ Check how much water you have and store it in the coolest place: In the shade, you can each make do on 2¼ litres a day. Try to drink in early morning and evening. Drinking during the middle of the day can lead to excessive perspiration and loss of body salts.

☐ If you are short of water, remember condensation or dew will often form at night. Gather it on metallic objects, glass and non-absorbent sheets such as plastic or tin foil. With plastic or foil, dig a hole in the sand and line it with the sheet. Put smooth objects on the sheet in the hole to attract the moisture, which will collect in the bottom.

☐ The car's window washer may have a small supply of water. The vehicle's radiator also contains water, but be careful. Check to see if it is coloured — if it is don't drink it because it may contain a poisonous corrosion inhibitor.

☐ It may be advisable to take salt tablets to replace salt lost through perspiration and to prevent heat exhaustion. Salt loss makes itself felt by giddiness and stiffness of the joints. If your own perspiration does not taste of salt, you definitely need to take salt tablets.

☐ Check food supplies, but food is considerably less important than water. A person can survive for more than 28 days without food. If you have food, but little water, don't eat, as the digestion of food will take water from your body.

Attracting help

Use your survival pack — smoke flares, flares and mirror.

☐ Additional smoke can be made by burning the tyres of the vehicle. Remove the wheel, deflate and ignite with petrol — from a distance.

☐ Remove the driving and/or wing mirrors. Flash the mirror at searching aircraft or land vehicles.

☐ The lights of the vehicle can be used at night, but only if you can see or hear someone.

☐ Make a fire from local vegetation. Smoke in the daytime, if available grass is not too dry, or flames at night.

☐ Collect any available material lying around and lay it out on the ground, together with Dayglo strips forming the shape of a large cross, with the vehicle at the centre. This will make it more easily visible from the air.

Desert survival pack

The following are advised: water, plastic cups, salt tablets, first-aid kit, matches, toilet roll, tinned food, smoke flares, flares, Dayglo strips, two sheets — one plastic, one bright red canvas — string mirror and a compass.

Caution is the rule — this kind of driving is only for the absolute expert

Expatriates at a riding club in Jeddah

Expatriates from East Asia

PART 3 THE EXPATRIATE EXPERIENCE

Advice for Expatriates

In one phrase: "Be sensitive and careful." Saudi Arabia is a strictly Islamic kingdom, some of whose laws and customs differ from those practised in western countries. Foreign visitors to the kingdom frequently become embroiled in serious problems with the authorities because of the foreigners' ignorance of Saudi regulations and social customs, or in the mistaken belief that foreigners are either above the law or treated magnanimously when they break it.

There is little that governments or their embassies in Saudi Arabia can do to save their nationals from the consequences of their own actions. Many foreigners who have not travelled abroad before find it hard to understand that their government cannot (a) spring them from jail, (b) immunise them from police raids, (c) prevent them from being fired by local employers or deported from the kingdom against their will. Foreigners are often dismayed when they learn, too late, that assistance from their embassy generally is limited to ensuring that their treatment during imprisonment is fair according to local law.

Areas which cause the most concern and problems to western expatriates visiting or living in the kingdom include the sponsorship process, traffic accidents, alcohol, drugs, visas, photography or death (accidental and natural). These and other issues are explored below and in Saudi criminal law.

Items from an expatriate notebook:

— A Saudi customer complains about items missing from a shipment. The foreign supplier travels to Jeddah to look into the problem personally. Both parties agree that certain items are indeed missing from several previous shipments. The foreigner is told that until the missing parts are delivered he will be prevented from leaving the kingdom. The foreign businessman eventually puts up as personal security a bank bond equivalent to the value of the missing goods and is allowed to leave.

— A foreigner travels to the kingdom for the first time, using a third-party consultant to arrange visas and appointments. After discussing several business deals with contacts arranged by the consultant, the foreigner is introduced to the sponsor of his visa. The sponsor demands that all business done by the foreigner be done through him. The foreigner refuses and shortly thereafter is denied permission to leave by airport police. The foreigner is allowed to leave the kingdom only after signing a business agreement satisfactory to the sponsor.

Sponsorship

As used in Saudi Arabia, sponsorship refers either to sponsoring a visa for a foreign visitor or prospective resident, or a business relationship. This section deals with the former use of the term — the impact of sponsorship on people.

By his sponsorship of a foreign business visitor or prospective resident, a Saudi incurs legal obligations to answer for his client's conduct and to pay his debts or claims made upon him during his stay in the kingdom or even after his departure. For these reasons, sponsorship is not treated frivolously by Saudis, nor do they readily agree to sponsor a stranger at a moment's notice.

In the case of foreigners going to live and work in Saudi Arabia, there is a direct and generally well-understood link between them and their Saudi sponsor, who is most commonly their employer or their firm's local partner. This link between sponsor and sponsored party is equally true, but less understood, in the case of people who visit the kingdom on short-term business. The sponsor, in the latter case, carries the same implicit obligations towards the party as is true for expatriates taking up residence. In most cases, sponsors of business visitors do not oblige the visitor to strike up a permanent relationship unless there is common interest in doing so. In such cases, the sponsorship arrangement amounts only to a short-term marriage of convenience permitting the foreigner access for business exploration purposes.

However, despite the normally innocuous nature of sponsorship for short-term business visitors, problems may be encountered. The sponsor, for example, can block the sponsored party's departure by swearing out a complaint against him. Until investigation of the case is completed, the foreigner will be prevented from leaving and may even be incarcerated. In rare cases, a sponsor may demand compensation or a percentage if the sponsored party has undertaken business deals with third parties during his stay in the kingdom.

Dependants' visas
In most cases, only "professionals" with university or technical degrees can enjoy family status and bring dependant wives and children to Saudi Arabia. Only individuals with valid work permits are allowed to work in the kingdom. Dependants are generally granted residence visas, which means that they cannot legally work. If such individuals are discovered working, the employer may be fined, the firm's personnel manager jailed, and the individual and her spouse deported. Dependants who come to the kingdom on a short-duration family visit visa generally cannot change their visa into a resident visa to remain. Dependant children over the age of 17 are not readily given family visit visas (see Entering the kingdom).

Photography
There are obvious sensitivities when cameras are trained at donkey carts or a traditional souq, rather than at a modern school or high-rise office building. Anti-Arab propagandists have made some Saudis wary by photographing certain scenes to make it appear that the kingdom's oil wealth is not reaching the people. It is culturally taboo to take pictures of women and illegal to photograph certain military or government installations, such as airports or palace gates.

Use of Arabic
Saudi government regulations require that all signs, place names, posters, printed matter and public notices issued, erected or posted by companies working in the kingdom be in Arabic, as well as other languages (eg English) as desired, with the Arabic above or to the right of the foreign language. These regulations apply to signs or notices posted on buildings, at work places, by access roads or at entrances to work camps or office sites. Vehicles which carry a company name or other information must carry the information in Arabic, in a position as prominent as the foreign language if one is used. Foreign firms resident in the kingdom must correspond with the government in Arabic.

Local customs
Certain things illegal elsewhere are

similarly illegal or strictly controlled in Saudi Arabia: drugs, weapons, etc. Pornography is banned. The definition of pornography can extend to the pictures displayed in womens' and mens' magazines which may not be considered pornographic in western societies. Alcohol and pork products, including pigskin, are banned according to the Quran's precepts.

Dress

If you intend wearing a suit, make sure it is made of lightweight material. Although a tie for men is de rigueur for business, a jacket is not. Shirts should be long-sleeved for business or formal occasions. Even on informal occasions long trousers and shirts which do not open below the collar bone are advised because of traditional Saudi puritanism. Cotton is preferable to man-made fibres for shirts and underclothes. For winters in Riyadh, Eastern province in particular, some warm clothes are needed for the evenings. It is amazing how cold Riyadh can become in winter if the heating system breaks down.

Although it is not necessary for women to wear ankle-length skirts, they should come well below the knee. Sleeves should be at least elbow length and necklines modest. In general, women's clothing should be loose fitting and concealing; trousers and trouser suits are not recommended. In late 1982 many western, non-Muslim women believed that an order had gone out to non-Muslims as well as Muslim women which obliged them to wear the abaya (see Manners and Customs). This was a misunderstanding — indeed, western embassies actually discourage western women from wearing the abaya.

In dress, women should veer towards the conservative. Tiny swim-suits on the beach, for example, should be avoided.

Hints to motorists

Great care needs to be taken when driving in the kingdom. Advice given by the Riyadh Group of British Businessmen is: be patient; be extra cautious; make sure your papers and those of the car are in order; always be courteous and — expect the unexpected (see Driving).

As well as licence and vehicle documents, you must also remember to carry a fire extinguisher, reflective triangle and first-aid kit at all times.

Women must not sit next to the driver unless the driver is their husband.

Insurance

Whether you own the car or not, make sure you have third-party insurance. In all offences, the principle applied by the courts is that the offender must make full restitution to the injured party, or to his family in the case of death. This is the "private right." Only then will the question of punishment — "the public right" — for the offence be considered. A driver who may not be to blame for the death or injury of another driver or pedestrian in a traffic accident will nonetheless have to pay compensation (see below). If you are not insured you risk imprisonment.

Accidents

As in all countries, it is possible for the parties involved in an accident to settle the matter amicably without recourse to higher authority. It is therefore as well to keep SR 300 or 500 on you specifically for such an event.

Generally, however, a police report will have to be made. In such a case, phone the police and an ambulance, if it is needed — but *don't* attempt to move injured people yourself or you will be held responsible for any further injuries.

Don't move your car until the police have arrived and made their inspection. Anyone moving a vehicle before inspection will usually be considered completely at fault. Once the police have determined fault, repair estimates can be obtained and the cost apportioned among the parties in relation to their fault. You *must* get an official accident report from the traffic police. Without this damages will not be covered by the insurance company and garages will not carry out repairs.

If someone has been seriously injured, those at fault will often be jailed or kept in hospital until the full extent of injuries is determined. Compensation will normally be demanded from the culpable party or parties, and criminal penalties may also be levied if traffic regulations have been violated.

If someone is killed in an accident, "blood money" will have to be paid to the relatives by those deemed at fault. The blood price depends on religion and sex — for adult male Muslims it is SR 100,000, and for Muslim women and non-Muslim men SR 50,000. Culpable parties will usually be jailed until the amount due is determined and paid.

Burglary

If you return home and find you have been burgled, don't touch or disturb anything. Call the police, who will usually come and inspect the premises and take fingerprints.

Draw up a written report in Arabic for the local police station and your insurance company. You will also have to make a statement for the police on a standard printed form.

If you follow these procedures promptly, you may get your property back.

Accident or natural death*

If the death occurs in hospital, you will need to get a medical report from the hospital for registration of the death at the Central Hospital in Jeddah.

Any death which occurs outside hospital must be investigated by the police, who should be called immediately. Whether or not death is apparently from natural causes, they will wish to be satisfied that neither the body nor anything near it has been touched, disturbed or even covered. The police will make a report, which will be needed for registration of the death at the Central Hospital. They will also, on request, give a certificate stating they have no objection to the body being handed over for burial outside the kingdom.

You should also contact the British embassy, giving as many of the following particulars as possible:

☐ full name of the deceased;
☐ place and date of birth;
☐ passport number, date and place of issue, and
☐ name of next-of-kin, address and telephone number.

The embassy will enter the death in the consular register once it has a completed application form, Saudi death certificate, British passport and consular fee (SR 32 for registration and SR 14 for certified copy).

When the death has been entered in the consular register, death certificates are immediately available from the embassy, and early the following year from the General Register Office in London.

The Central Hospital is in Bab Sharif, tel Jeddah 6314857. As well as registering the death and issuing the death certificate, its functions include making a medical report on a death occurring elsewhere than at another hospital; mortuary services; embalming; providing and sealing an airtight coffin suitable for carrying overseas; issuing embalming certificate, which usually also confirms that the body is free of contagious and epidemic diseases, and issuing a burial permit.

The emirate (governorate) should also be asked for a certificate confirming it has no objection to the body being taken outside Saudi Arabia. The application should state the relationship to the deceased of the person wishing the body to be repatriated. On approving the application, the

---

* *These details, provided by the British embassy in Jeddah, relate to the death of a UK national.*

emirate will issue a "no objection letter" addressed to Jeddah police headquarters, airport customs, the airport passport office and the health affairs department.

The airline will need copies of the police certificate, the embalming certificate and the emirate certificate. British Airways' requirements are four photocopies of these documents at least 24 hours in advance of the flight. Further information from British Airways Customer Service, tel 6853261, 6853027.

Health

As soon as you know you are going to Saudi Arabia it is sensible to arrange to have all your inoculations carried out. These are of two kinds: those internationally or legally required, and those medically recommended. The only one at present legally required for Saudi Arabia is the yellow fever inoculation, which should be taken by anyone arriving in the country within six days of leaving a yellow fever area — west, central and east Africa, and parts of central and South America. Those medically recommended are, first, typhoid, tetanus and poliomyelitis. Typhoid and tetanus vaccinations both involve three injections, with four to six weeks between first and second, and six to 12 months between second and third — the combined vaccine is no longer available in the UK. For typhoid a booster should be given every three years and for tetanus every five years. However, if you wound yourself you should be given a tetanus booster if it is more than one year since the last injection.

Poliomyelitis vaccination, with a booster every five years, is essential for overseas travellers. Prophylactic rabies is not recommended, other than for vets and those working with vets, but anyone bitten by a stray dog must seek medical advice immediately.

Immune gamma globulin injections are given to prevent infective hepatitis, fairly common throughout the Middle East. Protection is fairly brief:smaller doses give protection for about two months and larger doses for four to six months.

Heat
It is very important to know how to keep cool, especially in the summer. The body's natural response to heat is to perspire more freely. Provided you are sensible, reasonably young and fit,

and not too overweight, acclimatisation will take about two weeks. In addition, excess fatigue should be avoided. Three things will help you acclimatise:

Maintaining fluids In every 24 hours you should drink one pint of fluid for every 10 degrees of Fahrenheit temperature — at 80ºF drink eight pints of fluid between 0800 one morning and 0800 the next — or two litres in 24 hours plus one litre for every 10ºC — four litres at 20ºC, five litres at 30ºC, and so on. Make sure your urine remains nearly colourless — once it becomes a definite yellow it is concentrating and you are beginning to dehydrate.

Maintaining salt This is important, as you lose salt when you sweat. You should aim to take in 15-25 grams in each 24 hours, depending on the heat and the amount of physical work. The best method of taking extra salt is to add it to your food and drink. Salt tablets and pills are not always absorbed, especially if you have an attack of diarrhoea, when it is even more important to take in extra. Once you have acclimatised fully — about six weeks — the need for extra fluid and salt decreases slightly.

Clothing Cotton is by far the best material because it absorbs half its weight in water and is therefore a great help when you sweat. Most man-made fibres have very poor absorptive factors — from zero to 12 per cent — hence their "drip-dry properties." If your clothes do not absorb sweat your skin remains bathed in moisture and you develop prickly heat, a trying skin problem. Loose-fitting clothes allow a layer of air between the clothes and the skin which encourages evaporation, while wearing an aertex or string vest also encourages evaporation.

In dry heat when humidity is low sweat evaporates quickly and you may not think you are sweating as much. This is not so — keep up fluid and salt intake.

Hats should be worn when there is a clear sky. When it is humid and overcast it is probably best not to;

Health care for the expatriate is excellent today

one-quarter of perspiration comes from the head so if you wear a hat unnecessarily it may impede sweating.

Sun

Most heat disorders result from failure to maintain the necessary intake of fluids. Good sunglasses are better for avoiding glare than a hat. Plastic lenses are lighter than glass but they scratch more easily, and sunburn lotions and creams, insect repellents and some cosmetic creams can make the lenses opaque.

Be very careful sunbathing whether intentionally or while sailing, swimming or walking — as the sun can be very hot, especially when the sky is clear. Use good quality lotions or creams, not oils. Most high quality preparations have a factor number and the higher the number the greater the screening. For the mildly sun-sensitive a factor number of at least 6 should be used, but for the more sensitive numbers 10 to 15 — the maximum — are better. Painful burning can be avoided by taking Sylvasun, a vitamin A/calcium carbonate pill. Take two a day for the first two weeks. However, as Sylvasun is a South African preparation it is not available in many countries. The best substitute is Ro-A-Vit vitamin A capsules — take one a day, also for two weeks.

What is most important, though, is to be very careful about the length of time you spend in the sun. Fifteen minutes is plenty on the first day; 30 minutes on the second, an hour on the third, and then an hour more each day.

Stomach upsets

Many people have diarrhoea attacks lasting two or three days during their first two or three weeks abroad. While not serious, they can be incapacitating and a real problem to a businessman on a short trip. More serious forms of diarrhoea result from dysenteries, typhoid and cholera. All, including travellers' diarrhoea, are caused by infections spread by poor food hygiene or poor sanitation. You can guard against these by observing simple food hygiene rules:

Unless you are absolutely certain that tap water is safe — it often isn't — you should boil it before drinking or treat it with proprietary sterilising tablets such as Halozone or Steritabs. In the US you can also buy Potable Aqua iodine-based tablets. If you don't use tablets you can add four drops of tincture of iodine to one litre of water and leave it to stand for half an hour. However, neither chlorine nor iodine is effective if the water is cloudy; it must be filtered first. Similarly, all milk should be boiled unless you know it has been satisfactorily pasteurised.

Malaria prevention

Malaria is a serious and very unpleasant disease which, if inadequately treated, can recur. Visiting Europeans or Americans with no acquired immunity are far more likely to be very ill than locals who have been infected throughout their lives and have acquired immunity. The disease is spread by the anopheline mosquito which bites humans from dusk to dawn.

Diethyl Toluamide is the most effective repellent and is contained in Skeet-o-Stik, Sect-O-Stik and Flypel. Repellent usually lasts up to three or four hours, but less when you are sweating — and remember to avoid eyes, lips, spectacles and rayon clothing. Use an insecticidal aerosol spray in the bedroom. If the room is not satisfactorily airconditioned with tight fitting fixtures, attach a mosquito net to the window frame or over the bed.

Take an anti-malaria tablet regularly while in a malarial area, and for at least 28 days after you have left. Although the malaria parasite has become resistant to certain anti-malaria drugs in the Far East and South America, resistance has not developed in Saudi Arabia. The best anti-malaria tablets are either Proguanil or Paludrine. Take one a day when in the area and for 28 days after leaving the area. It is better to take a daily tablet than a weekly one, and easier to remember important, as it is essential to take the tablet regularly.

Bilharzia
Bilharzia (schistosomiasis), a parasitic infection which has two hosts, occurs in the kingdom. The primary hosts are humans and the intermediate host a freshwater snail. Larvae develop in the snail and are then discharged into fresh water where the snail lives. If you bathe or even paddle in this water the larvae will penetrate your skin, and if you drink the water they will penetrate the mucous membrane in your mouth. The infection takes two forms — one type infects the lower bowel and causes blood-stained diarrhoea and the other the bladder causing blood stained urine. Bilharzia can be avoided completely by not bathing in water unless you have been told by the local health authority that the water is free from infection. It is another good reason for ensuring drinking water is always boiled.

Snakes and scorpions
Snakes are not very common in Saudi Arabia. Although only about one in four people bitten by a snake develops general poisoning, you must, if bitten, seek medical advice and treatment immediately. First-aid treatment must be simple. The first thing is reassurance. Wipe the site of the bite with a clean cloth and don't incise, as has been done in the past. If the bite is on the arm, leg, hand or foot apply a tourniquet just above the bite. Don't apply this too tightly — the idea is to prevent the poison spreading, not to cut off the blood supply to the limb. Then get the victim to hospital. Aspirin can be given for the pain.

Scorpions again are not common. Like a beetle and about five centimetres long with a slightly longer tail, they are nocturnal creatures, spending their day hiding under stones. They often hide in shoes, so it is a good idea to shake a shoe upside down before wearing it. The sting, from the tail, is similar to a severe bee or wasp sting. There may be associated muscular cramps, sweating, fever and vomiting, but usually only in children. Pain is often relieved by a local anaesthetic so it is worth visiting a doctor or hospital.

Danger from the sea
Stone fish are found on the shore. Resembling a stone, they inject poison into the feet of unwary bathers who tread on them. There is usually severe and immediate pain, often accompanied by severe shock. You should bathe the foot in water — as hot as is bearable — or in a solution of Epsom salts, but the sting can be fatal unless anti-stonefish serum is administered quickly. This should be available at local hospitals although it cannot be guaranteed.

Jelly fish poisoning is also very unpleasant. A sting from the Portuguese man-of-war is probably one of the worst, extremely painful, causing acute shock and even collapse. Morphine may be necessary, and calamine lotion should be applied locally and antihistamines taken orally.

Sea snakes are also found in the Arabian Gulf. They are recognised by their flat rudder-like tail, unlike that of the harmless water snake which is rounded. Sea snakes are very poisonous but they do not inhabit shallow water and their victims are usually local fishermen.

Insurance
If you are not covered by a company sickness scheme take out sickness insurance for at least $50,000, and preferably $100,000. If you fall ill within a few weeks of your return tell your doctor where you have been.

Housing

According to Royal Decree M/22, foreigners are not — except in very rare cases — allowed to own land. Short-term leases are, however, tacitly permitted. Foreign companies licensed to operate in the kingdom may obtain permission to own land but, again, this is the exception.

Lease agreements do not need to be certified or registered — or even translated — to be binding. However, in the event of court proceedings, a certified translation of the lease will be needed. It is therefore wise to sign any lease in English and Arabic to avoid doubt, although the Arabic will take precedence.

Rents are controlled by royal decree during the period of the lease and thereafter according to a formula based on the original date of the lease.

Estate agents

Estate agents act purely as middlemen in transactions, having few — if any — responsibilities to either the owner of the property or the tenant. Many agents have standard lease agreements on pre-printed forms — as most are in Arabic, obtain a translation before signing.

Agents' fees range from 2½-5 per cent for the duration of the initial lease. Extensions can be negotiated between landlord and tenant, and no further commission should be payable. It is important to establish who is to pay commission.

In general, it is no longer necessary to pay two or more years' rent in advance. Most landlords now accept a minimum two-year lease, with rent payable yearly in advance.

Before signing a lease or paying rent, find out:

Has the property been completed and is it ready for possession? If not, will it be ready for possession on the

One of Jeddah's new housing estates

agreed date, which should be written into the lease?

Are all mains services available? In some areas, the answer to this will be "not yet." In the long term it may prove financially advantageous to pay less rent for a property without mains water, and live with the inconvenience of bringing water by road for the first three or four months.

Do all the plumbing and lighting fixtures work? If not, insist they are replaced before paying.

Is there a swimming pool? If not, and you intend to install one, you may be able to negotiate a reduction in rent in return for increasing the property's value. This will probably be stipulated in the agreement.

Is the water table high in the area of the property? If it is, sewage disposal could be a nuisance, as well as costly. The landlord should contribute to the cost of emptying the septic tank, although try to avoid on-going dues from landlords, as the latter can often prove difficult to contact.

Once you are satisfied with the property and ready to sign a lease, remember the following:

It is not usual to leave expensive fixtures, such as airconditioners, carpets and curtains, in the property on expiry of the lease. As landlords often try to obtain this, make sure there is no such clause in the agreement.

Although structural faults and defective workmanship are the landlord's sole responsibility, repairing accidental damage is not. In the event of fire, it is the tenant's responsibility to restore the property to its original condition. Consult your insurance adviser.

Saudi criminal law

Saudi law, which derives from religious tradition, governs both legal relationships and everyday social behaviour. Because of the wide range of activities covered and the severe consequences which can result from failing to obey the law, every expatriate — whether resident or merely visiting — should have at least a passing acquaintance with the law and the way it is enforced. It is not uncommon for foreigners to be prosecuted and imprisoned in Saudi Arabia for activities legal in their own country, nor is it uncommon for them to be held for days or weeks during investigations of what they would consider a minor administrative violation or a commercial dispute.

The law
Saudi law is Islamic law — Sharia — and is derived from the Quran, which, by tradition, was handed down by God to Muhammad in the seventh century AD. The Quran deals with many aspects of social life and sets out specific rules for certain types of commercial and serious criminal behaviour. It also sets out general rules for civil liability between individuals and for less serious criminal violations. Civil authorities are allowed to issue and enforce administrative regulations, provided these do not contravene the Quran. Islamic law also provides for certain "private rights" which enable individuals to bring actions to recover damages for wrongs done them by others.

Islamic law in Saudi Arabia governs the activities of anyone in the kingdom, whether Muslim or non-Muslim, Saudi or non-Saudi.

Customs offences
Among the legal problems most often encountered by expatriates are customs offences. Certain items, such

as alcohol, drugs, pornographic material and firearms, are strictly forbidden. Customs searches are usually very thorough, sometimes including body searches, and are carried out by officials trained to detect prohibited items. Unsuccessful attempts, even by visitors, to smuggle alcohol can result in imprisonment for up to six months, and attempts to smuggle drugs are usually treated more harshly. Anyone carrying prescribed drugs should also carry a prescription describing the substance, as customs may detain the individual for several days while the drug is analysed. Age is not a mitigating factor, and foreigners who would have been treated as juveniles in their own countries have received long prison sentences in Saudi Arabia. The Saudi definition of pornography includes magazines showing whole or partial nudity as well as films or video cassettes which contain partial nudity or semi-explicit sexual encounters. Customs officials regularly leaf through magazines and examine video cassettes on a screen during entry searches. The penalty for illegally importing pornography is usually a fine and confiscation of the offending material, although in at least one recent case an offender was fined SR 1,000 and imprisoned for two months. Saudi definitions of pornography are very broad, and fashion or other magazines not usually considered pornographic in the West will often be seized.

As well as these items, other items such as pork products, certain shortwave and FM radios, certain foods, and books about Saudi Arabia or the Arab world are often confiscated.

Alcohol

The import, possession, use, manufacture and sale of alcohol are strictly forbidden. Detection of alcohol on an individual's breath may result in up to two months' imprisonment and a lashing. Possession of alcohol or driving while under the influence of alcohol may result in six months' imprisonment, a fine and lashes. Making alcohol and serving or selling it to others may result in sentences of one or more years, as well as a fine and lashes. In one recent case an expatriate was given an 18-month prison sentence and 150 lashes, and deported — after serving the sentence — when he admitted making wine and serving it to western friends. This was despite the fact that there was no suggestion that any sale had taken place.

Although the authorities do not generally concern themselves with what goes on in an individual's home, they will enter houses to search for alcohol if its presence is brought to their attention, whether by a disgruntled servant, a minor traffic accident or some other event.

Drugs

Automatic jail terms are: for possession two years, for distribution (giving or selling any amount to a third party) five years, for smuggling 15 years.

More serious crimes

Expatriates generally manage to avoid involvement in the more serious crimes. Of these, four carry the death penalty: murder, rape, adultery — for a married person — and renouncing the Islamic faith. The death penalty is usually carried out in public after the main Friday prayers, and is usually by decapitation for murder and rape, and stoning for adultery. Theft — including embezzlement — may be punished by imprisonment and a fine or, in cases of serious or repeated theft, by amputation of the right hand. Application of the penalty for repeated theft need not require repeated convictions. Confession of repeated theft at the first arrest may be sufficient.

Bribery

Offering or accepting a bribe is illegal. Penalties may be severe, as shown by

Palace of Justice of the Amir of Riyadh on Deera Square. Tribal leaders are seen leaving soon after the king's weekly public majlis

a recent case which resulted in a three-year jail term and a SR 50,000 fine for the person offering the bribe.

Blasphemy
Blasphemy, or insulting Islam, is also a crime. It occasionally occurs when an expatriate loses his temper with another driver or fellow worker, and is usually punished by detention and a fine.

Traffic offences
Given the number of traffic accidents in the kingdom, the average expatriate's most likely encounter with the law is on the road (see Hints to Motorists).

Jails
Jails are intentionally unpleasant. A typical cell is a medium-size room with a bare floor, little or no ventilation and a hole in the ground for a lavatory. Up to 60 people may be kept there. There are no mattresses so prisoners sleep on the floor and pay for their food, which they may order through a jail official. Once convicted, conditions tend to be worse — up to 200 prisoners can share a single room. Basic food is provided, usually eaten by hand from the floor, although prisoners' families often supplement the prisoners' diet.

Unpleasant as they are, Saudi prisons are not dangerous, and little violence occurs.

Procedure
When a crime has been committed or is suspected, the individual thought to be responsible will usually be jailed during the investigation, which may take from a few days to several months. The suspect has to make a statement — without a lawyer or consular official present — and answer questions concerning the case. Questions are asked and recorded in Arabic. If the suspect does not speak Arabic, a translator will be provided. After the interrogation is concluded, the suspect will be asked to sign his statement as recorded in Arabic.

In view of the difficulty of explaining away a bad translation later in court, most lawyers and consular officials advise non-Arabic reading suspects to have an embassy official or company translator examine the translation before signing the statement. However, in practice, this can be difficult. During the investigation, the suspect should also be aware that police and investigating officials may, without authority, offer promises of leniency in exchange for a confession. Courts are not bound to keep such promises.

When the investigation is complete, the case officer writes a report including his recommendation for the disposition of the case and submits it to the governor of the province for the actual disposition. Until the report and recommendation leave the case officer's desk, charges may very occasionally be dropped in less serious cases on intervention by the suspect's sponsor or government. After the recommendation reaches the governor's desk, the case is virtually certain to proceed if the case officer has so recommended.

Criminal cases are referred to the Sharia courts where the case is tried in Arabic — again with a translator provided. Depending on the city in which the trial is held, consular officials may be allowed to attend trials involving their nationals, although as observers only. Cases are usually dealt with without delay by the Sharia courts with a decision given as little as three or four weeks after the case has been referred to the courts. Procedures are usually very informal and may be conducted across a simple table. The judge is granted wide discretion to inquire into the case and to determine an appropriate punishment. Cases involving commercial disputes are usually decided by the Committee for the Settlement of Commercial Disputes, part of the Commerce Ministry. These cases may take more than a year to decide.

Evidence rules in Islamic law are very strict and virtually all convictions result from the testimony of witnesses or confession by the criminal. As a result, appeals, while in theory possible, are most unlikely to result in the overturning of a conviction.

When a prison sentence is handed down, it is calculated from the time of initial incarceration. While there are no provisions for parole, most prisoners are released for good behaviour after serving three-quarters of their sentence.

Vernon Cassin, Jr

Santa Fe oil rig — representing the kingdom's tremendous economic and industrial energy

PART 4 THE ECONOMY

Introduction to the Economy

Increasing world recession will provide the greatest test of the achievements of Saudi Arabia's golden era of economic expansion. With western demand for Saudi crude forecast to stagnate in the next few years, the non-oil sector will be expected to make its biggest contribution to national income since before the 1973/74 price rises. Can the economy rise to the challenge? The past decade's experience provides mixed evidence, but suggests planners can face the future with confidence.

Growth statistics since 1973 are only a partial guide to the economy's performance. Gross domestic product (GDP) in this period has risen in real terms at a rate almost unmatched elsewhere. With the exception of 1975, growth in constant prices has never been less than 8 per cent, and has often been in double figures.

However, closer examination reveals considerably less buoyancy. The state has accounted for most of the spending increases in the Saudi economy itself. Although real total per capita consumption by both the government and private sector rose by up to 39 per cent between 1973-79, private consumption generally increased by less than 10 per cent.

The slow rise in personal living standards can be attributed to the fact that the state was pre-empting private spending. However, other factors played their part.

Inflation — which topped 30 per cent in 1974 and 1975 — rapidly eroded increases in nominal income. A second factor was the unequal distribution of the oil boom's benefits. These went mainly to the urban population, while the living standards of those in rural areas — the majority of Saudi nationals — improved much more slowly.

Defenders of the kingdom's economic performance point to the mass of non-monetary benefits passed on to the people — improved services and infrastructure, education and social welfare. Food subsidies have helped push down the cost of living, while low-cost government loans have been made available to home builders and agriculturalists. It can be argued that slower than expected increases in consumption have helped conserve resources for future investment in the industries and services that will provide the kingdom with new sources of income.

The figures seem to confirm this view. Gross capital formation — an approximate measure of investment — has been growing at a remarkable rate. It rose by an average of nearly 40 per cent a year between 1970-78. The government is the biggest investor in the kingdom's future, mainly in infrastructure, but increasingly in productive sectors such as industry and agriculture.

Expanding in other areas

However, eye-catching GDP growth figures are deceptive in other respects. They camouflage less exciting expansion in sectors which will be important to Saudi Arabia long after the oil fields are exhausted. The government has worked hard to stimulate the non-oil economy, and can claim a substantial degree of success. Growth in the non-oil sector — which now represents slightly more than half GDP — in the second five-year plan (1975-80) averaged 12 per cent a year in real terms.

But the expansion is largely the result of state spending on infrastructure. Construction accounted for more than 10 per cent of GDP in the 1970s, making it the second largest component after oil. The value of spending on construction per head of the population is more than 10 times that in developed countries. Other sectors of GDP which have recorded similar growth — electricity, gas and water — also depend heavily on state spending.

In contrast, the kingdom's oldest-established activity has not only declined dramatically as a proportion of GDP in the past decade, but has also fallen in absolute terms. Agriculture's share of GDP fell from 8.3 per cent in real terms in 1965 to 3.7 per cent in 1975 and 3.3 per cent in 1980, a reflection of the massive urban shift in the population.

Manufacturing, in which considerable progress has been made, is the new hope of Saudi planners. Nevertheless, its contribution to GDP remains relatively minor: 1 per cent in real terms in 1975, rising to 3 per cent in 1980.

Heavy oil dependence

But even these signs of diversification away from oil may be illusory. Both industry and agriculture are richly financed by the state and it is uncertain what proportion of both could survive without its support. The conclusion drawn by some analysts is that the Saudi economy is now more dependent on income from the oil industry than at any previous stage.

However, there are many positive achievements. The first oil-financed economic boom started immediately after the oil price rises lifted the financial constraints on the kingdom's development strategy. But the burst of project spending, principally in the main cities, was more than the ports and roads could take. Within months, the significant delays which built up in the ports had reached critical levels. This in turn sparked off competitive bidding for the goods available in the kingdom, including labour services. The horrifying inflationary spiral which ensued at times approached 50 per cent a year and threatened the entire development programme.

Six years after the crisis, Saudi Arabia's ports are among the most valued elements of an increasingly comprehensive domestic transport and distribution system. Exporters can now expect their goods to reach destinations almost anywhere in the kingdom without significant delay.

Mini-recession

The inflation was eventually cured by a short, sharp dose of deflation. This threw the Saudi economy into a mini-recession, but laid the basis for a fresh burst of expansion in 1979. By then, a new round of oil price rises had replenished Saudi Arabia's treasury and provided the government with the resources to make a new dash for development. Public spending in fiscal 1979/80 rose to SR 188,400 million ($ 54,601 million), 27 per cent up on 1978/79's figure. Allocations in 1980/81 and 1981/82 were up by 25 and 22 per cent respectively. In real terms, the 1980/81 budget was more than 60 per cent greater than spending in fiscal 1974/75.

These figures indicate how much the economy's absorptive capacity has grown in less than a decade. And, despite the flood of public spending, inflation has been kept under control. Measured by the cost-of-living index, it totalled only 3.6 per cent in fiscal 1980/81, and by the GDP deflator — a wider index of inflation — 7.8 per cent.

New fiscal restraint

With the slump in oil prices, Saudi Arabia has embarked on a new era of fiscal restraint after three years of dramatically expanded government spending. The 1982/83 budget calls for spending of SR 313,400 million ($ 90,827 million), equivalent to a rise of just 8.8 per cent on the 1981/82 budget. The Finance Ministry is uncertain about the trend in government revenues in the year, and has forecast a balanced budget after three years of massive surpluses. Even if oil prices and output match the most optimistic estimates, no-one expects a repetition of 1980/81's SR 111,530 million ($ 32,323 million) budget surplus, which helped to push the kingdom's reserves to about $ 150,000 million at the beginning of 1982.

With the monetary problems of massive spending on state projects under control, Saudi Arabia can look forward confidently to 1985, the start of the fourth development plan. Provided oil revenues do not fall below levels needed to finance projects the kingdom should achieve most of the targets in its present plan.

Although completion of outstanding infrastructure projects — including the new international airports at Jeddah and Riyadh — is one of the present plan's targets, the underlying emphasis is on shifting the economy towards activities involving production of goods and services. The biggest obstacle in the way is the shortage of nationals willing and able to work productively.

Manpower challenge

The kingdom's manpower challenge is formidable. The present population can only be guessed. The government estimate, implicit in the economic reports of its own departments, is about 8.4 million. However, this probably overestimates the number of nationals, often put at 7 million or less.

Problems arising from the shortage are compounded by the lack of skills possessed by most adults. About 60 per cent are estimated to be illiterate, although the government is investing billions of riyals in educational schemes ranging from university construction to establishing provincial vocational training centres. Training in turn involves at least 150,000 young Saudis in full-time education, further reducing the number who can participate in productive work. Women are, of course, forbidden from taking jobs in most sectors. The result is that as few as 750,000 Saudis may be actively involved in the economy, half the number of foreigners.

The implications of this phenomenon are more than simply economic. The government views the influx of foreigners and the shortage of nationals as one of the adverse effects of development. Strict limits on the numbers of foreigners allowed to work in Saudi Arabia are being applied, and even senior western expatriates may not be given permission to bring their families in.

But limiting the number of expatriates will have its own effect: Saudis will have to work harder and more productively than ever before.

Edmund O'Sullivan

Oil and gas

The kingdom's oil reserves are the world's largest: total proven reserves at the end of 1981 were officially reported to be 116,700 million barrels, equivalent to just over 33 years' production at 1980's record level. Probable reserves, however, could be 70 per cent higher, with Aramco each year discovering more oil than it extracts.

The existence of such riches under the sands of Eastern province was only guessed at little more than 50 years ago. Oil had been discovered earlier in the century in Iran, and in 1932 Standard Oil Company of California (Socal) identified oil in Bahrain. This was the first time the Gulf appeared to be a possible source of crude, and the discovery sparked off a wave of new exploration from Kuwait to the south of the peninsula.

The kingdom's oil story began in May 1933, a year almost to the day after crude was discovered in Bahrain. August 1933 saw the arrival of two US geologists, and the next five years were devoted to a largely fruitless search across Eastern province. The first exploratory well was sunk in April 1935. Oil was found, but in insufficient quantity to justify commercial development. The second well was sunk in February 1936 — again producing insufficient oil, but enough to encourage more exploration.

A further four wells were started in the Dammam area, and a wildcat northwest of Jebel Dhahran, an area of rocky ground rising inland from the coast. In December 1936, Dammam well number 7 was spudded, planned as the deepest exploratory well so far. The following 15 months were highly frustrating for the small team of geologists working there, and morale hit a new low on 31 December 1937 — more than one year after drilling

The days when it all began. A bedouin and his camel gaze across an Aramco pipeline

started — when the well was put out of action by a gas blowout.

Lucky strike

But the message from Socal's San Francisco head office was to continue, and on 3 March — an historic date in the world oil story — Dammam number 7 started producing crude at a faster rate than any previous exploratory well. Three weeks later, the well's output was a respectable 3,810 barrels a day (b/d), and by the autumn Socal could formally tell the Saudi government that Dammam was a commercially viable field. Forty-five years later, Dammam number 7 is still producing more than 1,000 b/d of crude, and its carefully maintained valves and pipework glisten silver in the sun, a monument in the centre of Dhahran to a turning point in the kingdom's history.

News of the Dammam discovery flashed across the world, and offers flooded in from firms eager to win a place in the fledgling Saudi oil industry. King Abdel-Aziz was pleased with the achievements of Casoc — the partnership between Socal and Texaco founded in 1937 to handle the two companies' work in the Middle and Far East — and the firms were confident they could keep their exclusive concession. However, with the start of negotiations about the rights to develop the fields in the neutral zones between Saudi Arabia and Kuwait and Iraq, they could not afford to be complacent.

This underlined the importance of making a good impression on the king when he first visited the oil facilities in spring 1939. The fishing villages of Dammam and Al-Khobar had probably never experienced anything like the royal tour. Accompanied by a caravan of 2,000 people in 500 cars, the king arrived at the end of April and set up a city of tents near Dhahran. After two days of feasting and celebrations, on 1 May 1939 the king opened the valve which let the first barrel of oil flow into the first tanker at Ras Tanura. At the end of the same month, Casoc signed a supplementary agreement extending the companies' exploration rights to the west and into the two neutral zones.

The second world war had a big impact on the oilfields, as the conflict at sea slowed ship-borne oil exports. But exploration continued, and in March 1940 the giant Abqaiq field was discovered. Three years later, work started on a 50,000 b/d refinery at Ras Tanura to replace the original tiny plant. Contractor for this work was Bechtel, a company which continues to play a key role in the kingdom's development. The project included an underwater pipeline to Bahrain's Bapco refinery.

1945 marks start of expansion

The war's end in 1945 marked the start of uninterrupted expansion of the Saudi oil industry. Casoc had in 1944 been renamed the Arabian American Oil Company (Aramco), and four years later the original shareholders gained two new partners — Standard Oil Company (New Jersey — Exxon) and Socony-Vacuum Oil Company (Mobil). This laid the basis for rapid production increases in the 1950s.

Preceding this development was the implementation of one of the most ambitious schemes ever conceived in the oil industry. During the war, plans had been suggested for a major pipeline running between the oil fields and the Mediterranean. In 1945, Aramco set up the Trans-Arabian Pipe Line Company (Tapline) to build the line. However, before work could start on what was then the world's largest privately financed construction project, the US Congress had to be persuaded to approve the oil companies' plans. This was made harder by growing political tension in Palestine caused by mass Jewish immigration.

In January work began, under Bechtel's direction, on the first section of the pipeline. The line quickly lengthened westward, and, after a delay during the first Arab/Israeli war in spring 1948, was completed in September 1950. Today, Tapline embodies the mixture of achievement and tragedy which has characterised the region in the past three decades.

Israel's invasion of Lebanon in June 1982 again interrupted the flow of Saudi crude to the Mediterranean, leaving Tapline largely unused and increasingly unwanted by its owners, the four Aramco partners.

However, at the time, the Tapline project marked the peak in Aramco's early growth. The company's labour force rose to 24,000 in 1952 because of the pipeline and other construction work, although it has since declined slowly. Nevertheless, production continued apace, increasing by an annual average of 19 per cent between 1945-74.

Moves into gas

The early 1960s saw the first moves into the gas industry. A gas plant was built at Abqaiq to produce the kingdom's first liquefied petroleum gas (LPG) for export. Production of natural gas liquids (NGL), the feedstock for Abqaiq and other gas plants, rose to more than 300,000 b/d in 1979, making Aramco the world's largest NGL producer.

Matching these developments has been a major investment programme in the Bahrain pipeline, Tapline and Gulf export terminals. These last took the lion's share of the budget. Four sea islands were built to accept tankers of up to 500,000 dwt, and offshore gas/oil separation plants (GOSPS) constructed to serve tankers directly.

In 1974, an export terminal complex was built at Juaymah, 25 kilometres north of Ras Tanura, which now rivals in size and importance Aramco's original oil terminal. This development was accompanied by major efforts to prolong the productive life of Saudi Arabia's older fields.

However, even this drive was dwarfed by the programme introduced in the 1970s. Between 1972-75, the company built more than 1,300 kilometres of pipeline, drilled 1,000 deep wells, built 24 GOSPS and installed more than $1,000 million worth of power turbines across its network. This provided the physical infrastructure for an extraordinary increase in production — from less than 3 million b/d at the start of the decade to 10 million b/d in 1978.

The sharp rise in energy prices in 1973/74 made further processing of Saudi Arabia's associated gas economically feasible. In 1975, Aramco was asked to design, develop and operate a nationwide system to gather and process gas to produce fuel, and the feedstock for the kingdom's planned petrochemicals industry. Eight years and $15,000 million worth of project spending later, the system's first phase is virtually complete. It comprises an enormous network of pipelines and GOSPS across onshore fields, and two major gas processing centres. The first, at Jubail, and the second, at Yanbu, on the Red Sea, are linked to the oil fields by a pipeline completed in 1981.

Manpower needs soar

Manpower needs have soared as Aramco's work increased. By the beginning of 1982 the company had more than 50,000 employees, about half of them Saudi nationals. The rest, recruited from around the world, have helped make Aramco a cosmopolitan company. The influx of staff has led to major investment in housing and community facilities. Dhahran continues as the firm's headquarters, but major towns have been built at Abqaiq, Udhailiyah and Ras Tanura, while smaller settlements are scattered across the concession.

These programmes have combined to make Aramco the world's largest oil exploration and development company. But its position in the Saudi oil industry is being challenged by Petromin, a wholly state-owned entity set up in 1962 to handle domestic marketing. In the succeeding two decades, Petromin has become active

Bringing power to the Kingdom

MANUFACTURERS OF ELECTRICAL WIRES AND CABLES FOR SAUDI ARABIA'S RURAL AREAS, INDUSTRIAL COMPLEXES, HOUSING PROGRAMMES, AIRPORTS AND SEAPORTS.

Head Office :
P.O. Box 4403
Jeddah
Tel: 638-0080
Telex: 402567 SAUCAB SJ

AL-QAHTANI MARITIME

GENERAL AGENTS OF

AL-QAHTANI MARITIME

AL-QAHTANI MARINE & OIL FIELD SERVICE CO. CR 2583
P.O. BOX 2224 - DAMMAM 31451 - SAUDI ARABIA
CABLE MARITIME - TEL: 8576754, 8576883
TLX: 601776 AQM SJ / 602219 AQMAR SJ

Laying the Trans-Arabian pipeline

in most downstream work. This ranges from refining — it has built three domestic refineries and lube plants in Riyadh and Jeddah — to international marketing and oil transport. It owns the transpeninsular pipeline linking Abqaiq with Yanbu, and is a joint-venture partner in three planned export refineries and one export lube plant. Petromin is now a significant member of the world oil industry in its own right.

Two other firms are involved in extracting oil in Saudi territory. The Kuwaiti-Saudi-Japanese Arabian Oil Company has the offshore concession in the neutral zone, and the US' Getty Oil Company the onshore concession. Neither is an important source of crude, and output is declining rapidly.

Price uncertainty dampens enthusiasm
Although uncertainty about short-term world price trends has tended to dampen enthusiasm for further oil developments, the kingdom's long-term strategy is to extend its oil and gas-gathering and processing system. The second phase of the master gas-gathering programme began recently, as did a major oil gathering programme in northern offshore fields. This scheme also entails construction of a major operations and community complex at Ras Tanajib, north of Juaymah. Work on the centre and on new offshore facilities for the Zuluf and Marjan fields is now under way.

However, recent political developments in the Gulf have underlined Saudi Arabia's vulnerability to potential external threats. One of the most worrying possibilities is an interruption to oil output, which would be disastrous both for the kingdom and the West. Rising production and low oil prices have resulted in non-communist countries becoming increasingly dependent on Saudi supplies. Even the US — for so long self-sufficient in oil — uses Saudi crude to meet about one-fifth of its total petroleum needs.

This vulnerability has helped accelerate the new transpeninsular projects and resulted in cancellation of Aramco's plans to build a refinery at Juaymah. It may be built inland instead. Concern about threats to Gulf routes is also behind possible new pipeline schemes — most notably the proposed link between Basra and Yanbu, although this is still in the early planning stage. Other projects reportedly being considered include a major oil storage system in the west.

These developments have helped make oil a truly national activity. The government takeover of the industry was completed in spring 1980 with the purchase of the oil companies' outstanding 40 per cent share in most Aramco facilities. This has cleared the way for the future creation of an integrated national oil company encompassing both Petromin and Aramco.

The peaceful and generally smooth transfer to the state of oil industry control is in marked contrast to the turbulence which surrounded similar moves in other Middle East countries. But the final result will be almost identical: a diminution in the oil majors' ability to determine the price and output of Arab oil. Saudi Arabia's confident handling of its oil strategy — however controversial it may be within OPEC — is a measure of the kingdom's progress in the past decade. But the new rulers of Saudi oil are not reluctant to acknowledge their debt to the oil companies' early efforts and to the endeavours of the intrepid band of geologists who helped change the course of history in Eastern province 50 years ago.

Construction

Despite the slump in oil revenues, Saudi Arabia remains one of the world's most active construction markets. The building industry is the second largest component of gross domestic product (GDP) after oil, and the principal employer of expatriate staff.

Because government accounts for about 75 per cent of construction spending, the oil cutback — to less than 5 million barrels a day at the start of 1983 — will have important implications. There are already clear signs that the market is in decline because of the reduction in public expenditure.

Nevertheless, the volume of business is still considerable. Total spending on construction in 1980 was a little under SR 130,000 million ($ 37,676 million), according to estimates produced by Aramco. This figure is believed to have risen sharply in 1981 before dropping in 1982. Activity was reasonably evenly spread throughout the kingdom, with the western region accounting for about 37 per cent and the central and eastern regions for about 30 per cent each.

Foreign companies now account for less than 50 per cent of the market, with local companies accounting for 27 per cent and the remainder going to joint ventures. The share of local and joint-venture companies is likely to have risen in 1981/82, reflecting the government's policy of favouring such firms, coupled with their increasing competence.

Korean contractors

During the late 1970s, Korean contractors established themselves as the most important participants in the industry, accounting for almost 25 per cent of all business, according to some estimates. Making use of low-cost, highly-productive labour, economies of scale, and government assistance, they became a powerful force in Saudi contracting.

However, recent events have shown them to be far from invincible. Since 1981, the Koreans have occasionally — though with increasing regularity — failed to secure important contracts, and they are expected to account for less than 20 per cent of the market in 1983. The reasons for this include higher wage costs, the use by competitors of low-cost Far East labour, and the Koreans' technical deficiencies. These generally disqualify them from bidding for the new wave of refinery and petrochemicals projects.

Aramco's 1980 survey figures suggest how the Koreans managed to penetrate the market so quickly. In the late 1970s, almost exactly 50 per cent of all spending on construction was on buildings requiring comparatively low-level skills. Civil work accounted for about another 25 per cent, with mechanical and electrical engineering contributing the remainder.

The most successful of the Koreans is Hyundai Engineering & Construction Company. The company was banned in 1979 because of an attempt by an executive to bribe a government official. However, it had returned forcefully to the market by the end of 1981, and has since secured a series of major contracts, mainly in power and water desalination schemes.

US contractors

There are comparatively few successful US contractors. Among the leaders is Bechtel Corporation — which has been working in the kingdom since the late 1940s — and its local affiliate, Saudi Arabian Bechtel Company. The corporation's contracts currently include management services on Madinat al-Jubail al-Sinaiyah (Jubail industrial city), and providing procurement, engineering, construction and management services for the King Khaled international airport in Riyadh.

Managing contractor for another major project, Madinat al-Yanbu al-Sinaiyah (Yanbu industrial city) is

King Abdel-Aziz international airport Hajji terminal has the tents of the bedu as its motif

Saudi Arabian Parsons, local affiliate of Ralph M Parsons. Developments at Jubail and Yanbu have slowed recently, though both cities will be sources of major contracting opportunities for at least two decades.

European contractors

Among the successful European contractors is France's Bouygues, now well into its shared contract for the King Saud university campus in Riyadh. It is working on the $1,700 million-plus scheme with Blount International of the US. Bouygues has also been highly successful in bidding for new hospital contracts throughout the kingdom.

West Germany's Philipp Holzmann has been working in Saudi Arabia since the mid-1960s and maintains a strong position. Its largest contract so far was for the $1,400 million Dammam port expansion, completed in partnership with Greek and Dutch companies in 1980. Dyckerhoff & Widman, another West German contractor, has gained prominence because of the important landmarks it has erected in Riyadh. The first were the water towers, while in 1982 it completed the beautiful, marble-clad television tower that dominates the city.

Japanese contractors

Japanese companies have been selectively successful, particularly in electrical and mechanical engineering projects.

Chiyoda Chemical Engineering & Construction Company is probably the leading Japanese contractor. Between September 1982 and January 1983, it won three major contracts in downstream hydrocarbons industries, all from the Saudi Basic Industries Corporation (Sabic). Since 1967, the group has won more than $3,000 million worth of building contracts from Sabic, Petromin and the Royal Commission for Jubail & Yanbu.

The system employed to fulfil large-scale projects is based on a model tried and tested by Aramco over four decades. A management contractor of international status is appointed to supervise construction work by local and more specialised foreign contractors. The Jubail and Yanbu projects provide the most substantial examples of this system, but it is also used by Sabic, among others.

A variation on this theme is pursued by the Defence & Aviation Ministry (MODA), the most active customer in the construction business. Most of its very large projects are supervised by the US Army Corps of Engineers. These include the Saudi Naval Expansion Programme; the Peace Hawk and Peace Sun programmes, which provided ground facilities for the air force's Northrop Corporation F-5 E and McDonnell Douglas F-15 aircraft and the King Khaled Military City (KKMC) near Hafr al-Batin in the far northeast.

The corps' grip on MODA construction work has slipped recently as the ministry has developed its own capacity for planning and supervision. The most significant example of such independent work is the National Guard's five-complex housing programme. Masterplanned by the corps, the scheme is being carried out by the National Guard itself.

The bidding phase was marred by the cancellation of turnkey bids for the first — and largest — Riyadh complex because they were too expensive. This led to a review of the contracting policy with the result that each of the five projects was broken into sections and put out to open bidding. All are now well under way.

Competition from Saudi companies

The deployment of indigenous construction and engineering expertise is now a feature of the Saudi market. All spending departments, including the municipal offices of smaller towns, have resident engineers capable of reviewing plans drafted by their foreign counterparts. In addition, the

The new Al-Khairia building in Riyadh houses the King Faisal Foundation headquarters

law now favours local engineering consultancies over foreign partnerships. Today, a link with a local engineering office is a prerequisite for success in most of the public-sector construction market.

The most visible change in the industry has been the emergence of highly competent local contractors. Most notable have been Saudi Oger, a specialist in high-speed, high-quality construction work; El-Seif Engineering & Contracting, a partner with Dragages & Travaux Publics in five hospitals in a major Health Ministry programme launched in 1980; and the Mohammad Binladen Organisation, one of the oldest-established local contractors, which recently bid successfully for major new Public Works & Housing Ministry projects in Makkah.

The advent of highly qualified local contractors has been accompanied by the emergence of a larger volume of business outside the three major conurbations. Efforts to lay a social infrastructure in populous though remote regions are creating new opportunities for contractors capable of mobilising quickly anywhere in the kingdom. This tends to favour local contractors and foreign companies familiar with local conditions. Recent examples of such projects include the Health Ministry's hospital construction programme, the Interior Ministry's housing schemes and power generation and distribution being carried out by the Saudi Consolidated Electric Company (Sceco) and the Saudi Electricity Corporation. Smaller-scale opportunities are available in the road construction programme, now almost totally dominated by local contractors.

Decentralisation is making new demands on established participants in the Saudi market. But prestige projects in the heartlands are still going ahead, including the new airport at Riyadh.

In addition, work is expected to start soon on construction of the

King's Office, Council of Ministers and Majlis al-Shoura (Kocomas) in Riyadh, one of the most lavish projects ever. In Jeddah, major plans are being drafted for the development of the old international airport site. And in Eastern province, Aramco continues to be a major source of business in all sectors: it accounted for about 6 per cent of all construction spending in 1980.

With the slump in demand for OPEC oil, the second great construction boom which started in 1979 appears to be coming to an end. Nevertheless, the opportunities for skilled contractors which can operate in the kingdom's unique environment will continue to be substantial for the remainder of the 1980s at least.

Manufacturing

Few could have imagined Saudi Arabia aspiring to, let alone winning, a place among the ranks of the world's industrialising nations before the 1973/74 oil price rises. A country apparently so ill-suited to any but the most limited productive activities seemed destined to remain a rentier economy, with its people well-provided for out of the proceeds of the sale of unprocessed crude oil.

So when King Faisal's government announced a strategy of creating major industries to compete with the best in the world, and confirmed this in the second development plan (1975-80), many were sceptical as to the programme's viability.

It remains difficult to determine whether manufacturing has a long-term future, but the kingdom has confounded some of the doubts expressed a decade ago. More than 1,000 factory units have been established, producing a wide range of intermediate and finished goods. The most recent plants to come on stream include factories making ball-point pens and breakfast cereals.

The overwhelming majority of the new factories are small businesses, though they are dwarfed by the gigantic petrochemicals and metallurgical schemes coming on stream in the industrial cities of Jubail and Yanbu (see Oil and Gas, and Regions). All told, the industrial sector is a small but rapidly expanding component of the economy.

The sudden emergence of manufacturing has little to do with the "invisible hand" of free market economic theory, as government planners freely admit. On the contrary, it is the result of a calculated strategy to create new sources of income and employment outside the oil industry, which has dominated the economy for half a century.

Investment in manufacturing plants had taken place before the preparation of the second plan, though on a limited scale and highly selectively. Easily the most important was Aramco's Ras Tanura refinery, the first units of which were built in the early 1940s. Now with capacity to process about 500,000 barrels a day of crude oil, it remains one of the kingdom's most significant industries.

The pace of investment in manufacturing quickened with the creation of Petromin in 1962 (see Petromin) Among its objectives was the establishment of hydrocarbons-related industries. This marked the beginning of the first serious attempt to establish large-scale industries. The first domestic refineries and the highly successful Saudi Arabian Fertiliser Company (Safco) plant in Dammam date from this period.

However, the strategy outlined by King Faisal in the 1970s called for industrial investment on a much grander scale. The government believed it had the key to success — huge sums of money to be invested in domestic industries — after the first oil price rises. New executive agencies were created, staffed by some of Saudi Arabia's most capable specialists, to cut through bureaucratic red tape and establish operating plants as quickly as possible.

Two categories of project were to be identified, and treated separately by these government agencies. The first — light industries and smaller plants — was to get low-cost, long-term capital plus general support, but was to be the product of essentially private initiatives, involving capital subscribed by domestic and foreign companies. The second category was to be an entirely new generation of strategic industries, managed and mainly funded by the public sector.

SIDF and Sabic

The Saudi Industrial Development Fund (SIDF), founded in 1974 and

Abdel-Aziz al-Zamil,
Sabic chief executive

accountable to the Finance & National Economy Ministry, deals with the first category identified above — light industries and smaller plants. The second category — of strategic industries representing many of the hopes for the future — is handled by the Saudi Basic Industries Corporation (Sabic), founded in 1976 and reporting to the Industry & Electricity Ministry.

SIDF

SIDF responded actively to the demand for funds from enthusiastic local entrepreneurs. It approved loans worth SR 150 million ($43.7 million) for more than 20 projects in the first year of operation. The next year, the value of loans approved rose dramatically to more than SR 1,000 million ($289.8 million) for 65 projects in 1977/78, SIDF agreed to lend more than SR 2,000 million ($579.6 million) for 136 schemes.

This was the peak year for SIDF. Fiscal 1978/79 saw the emergence of balance-of-payments and budget problems which provoked emergency austerity measures affecting all sectors of government. The 1979 oil price rises removed this budget restraint, but for SIDF the boom was over. The agency has since adopted a much more cautious lending programme and agreed loans worth SR 1,260 million ($ 365 million) in 1980/81 for little more than half the number of projects backed three years earlier.

The change in policy reflected three factors. First, SIDF simply did not have the capacity to monitor all its loans effectively. This constraint has become more important as efforts are made to increase the number of Saudi nationals holding senior posts and with the expiry of Chase Manhattan Bank's management contract with the fund.

Second, a significant proportion of borrowers failed to meet repayment schedules despite the very favourable terms attached to loans provided by the fund. There was a tendency, SIDF officials now admit, for any reasonable project to get support in the early days. Today, a much more conservative approach to new schemes is pursued.

Third, projects backed by SIDF did not always meet development objectives, even though most were successful. Almost a quarter of loans up to the end of 1980/81 went into projects supplying the construction industry. The difficulty is that the construction sector has been artificially stimulated by the government's rush modernisation programme and is expected to decline quite rapidly during the latter part of the 1980s. This would squeeze the market for construction material and put at least some of the plants supplying such goods out of business.

This is why SIDF is promoting other sectors, notably plastics and consumer goods. However, the Saudi market for these products is much more like a normal one in that local producers face intense competition from well-established and well-known foreign manufacturers. The number of entrepreneurs prepared to put up money for such projects is considerably smaller as a result.

Sabic

While SIDF's programme has slowed, the opposite is true of Sabic's. The early years were frustrating for the corporation, whose target was at least 10 large-scale plants producing petrochemicals, iron and steel, and aluminium for the world market. But to establish well-managed plants, producing high-quality products at competitive prices, Sabic needed help and turned to foreign companies to provide it.

Companies approached by the Saudis were understandably cautious about investing considerable sums of money and management time in Saudi Arabia. Nevertheless, Sabic eventually managed to compile a shortlist of potential partners. It had then to assemble a package of incentives which would make foreign companies want to get involved.

Early in the negotiations, Saudi Arabia suggested that companies backing heavy industries might be provided with supplies of crude over a period of years in quantities proportional to their investment. The sharp rise in oil prices in 1979 and the uncertainties about supply made this an extremely attractive component of the package, particularly to those oil companies interested in participating in the heavy industries. From the end of 1978, nine agreements committing foreign companies to invest in Sabic projects were concluded in quick succession.

The ownership structure of the various plants is almost identical. They are locally incorporated and owned equally by Sabic on the one hand, and the foreign partner or partners on the other. Equity accounts for about 30 per cent of each plant's total cost, with 60 per cent to be provided on very easy terms by the government's Public Investment Fund. The remainder will be raised in the form of commercial loans.

Jubail and Yanbu plants

The first of these, owned by the Jubail Fertiliser Company (Samad) and with capacity to produce 500,000 tonnes a year (t/y) of urea, was due to start

Lorries stirring up the dust alongside the Jubail-Yanbu pipeline

operating in the first quarter of 1983. Plants owned by the Saudi Methanol Company -- with capacity of 600,000 t/y of chemical-grade methanol — and the Saudi Iron & Steel Company — with capacity of 800,000 t/y — are due to come on stream at the same time. Six other plants are due to begin production by the end of 1985. Eight of the nine plants are located in Yanbu and the other in Jubail.

With the construction phase largely complete, Sabic can claim success in overcoming its first major obstacle. However, it has still to prove it can operate such sophisticated plants efficiently and find export markets for their output. This has been made more difficult by the recession and is now a major issue. When Dow Chemical Company of the US suddenly withdrew from the Arabian Petrochemical Company (Petrokemya) project in Jubail in December 1982, the company cited its unwillingness to accept responsibility for marketing the high and low-density polyethylene as the principal cause. This was a morale-shaking development for Sabic.

Nevertheless, Sabic's other partners seem to be secure. The majority are oil companies with a long-term interest in maintaining a close relationship with the kingdom because of the privileged access to crude supplies this guarantees.

The government itself is determined to press on with the heavy industry projects in which it has already invested massively. Analysts tend to support this approach because the plants provide a way for Saudi Arabia to cash in on its extra-low-cost gas supplies without greatly increasing its manpower requirements.

These recent developments have combined to produce a more hard-headed approach to the challenge of industrialisation. The present philosophy was defined concisely in summer 1982 by Industry & Electricity Minister Ghazi Abdel-Rahman al-Gosaibi. Industrial development, he said, is based on making use of the kingdom's abundant capital and energy, and the attributes to be sought in new projects are that they should "add value to human and material resources, supplement traditional oil exports, introduce new technologies, and provide basic linkages backwards to the raw material sectors and forwards to a wide variety of potential industries." A new generation of Sabic projects that will make use of the output of the Jubail and Yanbu petrochemicals plants have been approved because they satisfy these criteria. Others will undoubtedly follow, but the message is that haste will be made more slowly from now on.

Banking

There are few places in the world where banks are still growing by 20 or 30 per cent a year: Saudi Arabia is one of them. The Saudi government is still a big spender on development projects, pouring out billions of riyals annually to meet the local costs of building roads, hospitals and factories — and then paying people to maintain them. This money can go through the banking system several times. Local banks also do their share of arranging finance and guarantees for local and foreign contractors.

For the 11 licensed commercial banks it is a fantastic opportunity to make money. The fierce demand for bank shares on the infant local stock market shows that Saudi investors are also bullish about the banks. Yet, like shareholders in a gold mine, few are prepared to go and work at the pithead. Saudis are not keen to become bankers. They do not like institutions and they prefer to make money for themselves. The unofficial banking sector — the world of the money changers — is much more attractive.

To anyone who bought a piece of land in 1975 for SR 50,000, sold it six months later for SR 1 million, bought another plot for SR 300,000 and sold it nine months later for SR 9 million, the prospect of a directorship in an institution such as a bank is not enticing. A Saudi is unlikely to make banking his first choice of career.

Yet the process of Saudi-ising the banks, begun in 1975, aims to bring banking skills to a large number of nationals, eventually giving Saudis practical as well as theoretical control. Since 1975 the 10 banks which were 100 per cent foreign-owned have been transformed into joint-stock companies, owned either 60 or 65 per cent by Saudi interests, with the rest taken by the foreign parent banks.

The foreign parent also has a management contract with the Saudi bank on the understanding that it recruits and trains an appropriate number of nationals. Recruit and train it does, but there is no guarantee that these people will always turn up to work. In many cases the Saudi banker has an understudy to do the real work.

At a higher level, the Saudi founding directors of the newly Saudi-ised banks are there because of familiarity with the local business community and their desire to see a competent Saudi banking sector. They are generally recognised as dedicated men who, apart from the prestige they gain, are putting in more than they get out.

They have brought a subtle change to the banks — the ability to operate in a business society where a good name counts for more than a well-presented balance sheet or a watertight project. But at the same time, there is the danger that they will favour their friends.

On the other side of the counter, dealing with retail customers will be chaotic for years to come, and western banking practices have to be adapted to local conditions. At branches throughout the country, one-to-one appointments with a bank manager are rare. It is more likely that the bank officer will hold his own majlis, offering tea to waiting customers while in the same room doing some hard bargaining with a client. Appointments are often not kept. Clients will come and visit, but refuse for days to discuss business. The bank officer then has to stay late into the night to catch up on his paperwork.

Unorthodox paperwork

That paperwork can be fairly unorthodox. Many depositors refuse on religious grounds to accept interest. They are even more reluctant to pay interest on loans. Net depositors who run the occasional overdraft can be accommodated, but net borrowers will be asked to pay a service charge. On balance the banks do very well out of

Abdel-Aziz al-Quraishi, former SAMA governor

this system, particularly the two fully Saudi banks, National Commercial Bank (NCB) and Riyad Bank, which have a wide and traditional customer base. Their average cost of funds was probably less than 8 per cent while the riyal interbank rate was more than 10 per cent.

Saudi banks have two limitations which they are striving to overcome as fast as possible. One is lack of middle management; the other is poor capitalisation, which prevents them taking a large share of really big contract financing. For years, offshore banks have been able to scoop up this business. Now, with an eye to the future and to possible controls that the Saudi Arabian Monetary Agency (SAMA — central bank authority) could introduce, the offshore banks are favouring co-operation with local institutions. Big loan and guarantee syndications

Riyadh's SAMA buildings

now tend to include a fair spread of local names. Bahrain offshore banking units (OBUs) which sprang up after 1975 with a view to serving the entire Gulf region, have been forced to focus increasingly on investment banking business within Saudi Arabia. Most other Gulf states have come to discourage offshore intrusions into their market, and have imposed currency restrictions. Nor has Bahrain become the big centre for money placement by oil-rich governments that was once predicted. These governments have tended to fill the bigger pools of London, New York and Tokyo. Offshore banks operating in the kingdom know their presence is tolerated only because it has helped the Saudi economy cope with rapid evolution, and has encouraged the local banking sector to compete. They plan to keep ahead by being innovative, offering services and fee-earning advice more sophisticated than that offered by Saudi banks. At the same time the newly Saudi-ised banks are developing the same weapons to compete with their cash-rich big brothers, NCB and Riyad. At present, there is more than enough business for all. SAMA has proved a tolerant regulating authority, except in cases of offshore speculation with the Saudi currency.

Solving the financial paradoxes

But SAMA has yet to solve two paradoxes which prevail in the financial sector. One is the existence of para-banking — the money-changers, many of whom have branches all over the kingdom, take deposits, give overdrafts and carry out short-term trade transactions, yet have no legal reserve requirements and no answerability to SAMA. The other is that, in possibly the most Islamic country in the world, there is no licensed commercial Islamic bank.

A decree to limit money-changers' activities has been passed. In December 1981 they were given three years to revert to a purely money-changing function. However, that does not solve the problem. One of the money-changing houses, Al-Rajhi Company for Currency Exchange & Commerce, is extremely large. It has more branches than any of the licensed banks and, what is more, is performing a useful retail job, has more Saudi staff than any of the banks and is 100 per cent Saudi-owned. Its liquid funds are so great that, in a moment of crisis in 1979, when there was a muddle with SAMA's accounts, it was able to pump much-needed Saudi riyal liquidity into the banking system. Some of the other houses, although not as big, are also professionally run and cannot simply be told to disappear. An alternative may be to give one or more a banking licence, perhaps an Islamic banking licence.

But to inject an Islamic element into the Saudi banking system is an extremely risky business. Substituting other instruments for charging interest and other guaranteed return on investment — which is un-Islamic — could severely disrupt relations with the international banking system. SAMA, one of the world's major investors in interest-bearing deposits and securities, could not afford to change its status without considerable leadtime — decades rather than years. That is why the first step towards Islamic banking is taking so long.

SAMA is also reluctant to add more banks to the system. There are 11 commercial ones: NCB; Riyad Bank (34 per cent owned by SAMA); Saudi American Bank (40 per cent Citibank); Saudi French Bank (40 per cent Banque de l'Indochine & de Suez); Saudi British Bank (40 per cent British Bank of the Middle East); Albank Alsaudi Alhollandi (40 per cent Algemene Bank Nederland); Arab National Bank (40 per cent Arab Bank); Saudi Cairo Bank (40 per cent Banque du Caire); Bank al-Jazira (35 per cent National Bank of Pakistan); United Saudi Commercial Bank (small Iranian, Lebanese and Pakistani shareholdings, managed by Saudi Inter-

The Saudi and UAE finance ministers in Dubai in February 1982

national Bank), and the Saudi Investment Banking Corporation (SIBC — 20 per cent owned and managed by Chase Manhattan Bank, with small shareholdings by three other international banks). SIBC is a development bank, committed to a medium-term lending portfolio. The lion's share of medium-term development lending comes from the Saudi Industrial Development Fund, the Real Estate Development Fund and the Agricultural Bank. The Arab Investment Company and the Saudi Hotels & Resort Areas Company are other institutions set up with government help to encourage investment. Many other private investment companies operate in Jeddah and Riyadh but they are not licensed deposit takers. SAMA appears to regard the 11 banking licences as enough for the moment, while Bahrain can handle the overflow.

Under such severe constraints the Saudi banking sector remains small but highly profitable. SAMA's prudence may have seemed excessive a few years ago, but after the shock administered to banking confidence worldwide after August 1982 that prudence may indeed have been far-sighted.

Telecommunications

The telephone plays an important, even essential, role in contemporary Saudi society. It has become vital to efficient government and business in a country the size of western Europe, where major population centres are divided by hundreds of kilometres of different terrain only recently crossed by high-quality roads. Establishing telecommunication links with the outside world has also helped bind Saudi Arabia into the world economy.

The telephone plays an unusually large part in social affairs. It has sustained family life, one of the foundations of Saudi society, and helps women maintain contact with the world outside the home.

These are some of the reasons why creating a comprehensive, low-tariff domestic telephone system plus telecommunications links to other parts of the world has been one of the development priorities of the past decade. The achievements, though costly, have been considerable.

More than 650,000 telephones had been installed by the end of 1982, a figure that should rise to 1.2 million by the end of the present development plan in spring 1985. By then about 400 towns and villages throughout the kingdom should have direct dialling connections within it. Little more than eight years after the first telex was installed more than 13,500 subscribers have such links.

Telephones have a very short history in Saudi Arabia. The first automatic system was installed in 1969, serving Jeddah, Al-Madinah, Makkah, Taif, Riyadh, Hofuf and Dammam. But the pace of change really started to accelerate after the 1973-74 oil price rises. In 1974, work started on what is known as the "backbone project," a high-volume coaxial cable and microwave link running between the Al-Khobar-Dammam-Dhahran conurbation and the royal summer capital of Taif, via Riyadh and Jeddah.

The project allowed, for the first time, instant communication among the kingdom's most important cities. But it also laid the basis of a truly national telephone system. The "backbone" was expanded in 1978-80 to cater for rapidly rising demand for telecommunications across the country's strategic corridor.

Taking telecommunications into the hinterland is a microwave system installed in the late 1970s. The first phase has been completed and another 70,000 voice-frequency channels for subscribers in the regions are to be installed in a second phase started in summer 1982.

Philips telecommunications

Telephone users deal with the national telephone company, Saudi Telephone, now improving its performance and services with the help of Bell Telephone of Canada. One of the results is that the kingdom probably has the most efficient directory inquiries service in the Middle East. Taking the telephone link into the home is a partnership between Philips of the Netherlands and Sweden's Ericsson, which, by the end of 1982, had secured almost $5,000 million worth of contracts from Saudi Telephone. This includes supplying a national automatic mobile telephone system calling for 18,000 units and 866 channels.

The infrastructure supporting the kingdom's links with the outside world is probably the most impressive element of the entire programme. The medium is coaxial cable and microwave, for communications with neighbouring Arab states, plus major earth satellite stations for international calls in Riyadh, Taif and, by 1984, Jeddah.

Though the pace of telecommunications development is beginning to slow, reflecting the success of the past five years' efforts, major business opportunities can be expected to continue to emerge in this sector of the economy. The single most important project in the present plan — the new coaxial link between Riyadh and the Jordanian border via Taif, Makkah, Jeddah and Al-Madinah — was being tendered as this book went to press. The bulk of the work is expected to go to foreign companies in partnership with local contractors.

Saudi Arabia is playing an important part in helping to develop pan-Arab telecommunications. Riyadh is to be the site of the principal control-station employed by Arabsat, the agency developing an Arab satellite. This is to be launched by the start of 1984.

All these developments will help nurture the love-affair between Saudi Arabians and the telephone. The kingdom has set few limits on the amount it is prepared to spend in sustaining and developing this relationship.

Trade with the UK

The UK has failed to convert its long involvement with the Arabian peninsula into a leading share of the Saudi export market, one of the largest outside the industrialised world. Nevertheless, it continues to secure a respectable volume of the kingdom's new business.

UK exports in 1982 totalled £1,361.4 million ($2,133 million), up on the £1,134.9 million ($1,778 million) recorded the previous year. These were made up mainly of manufactured goods, machinery, food and beverages. Imports, however, were £1,447.8 million ($2,268 million), leaving the UK with one of the smallest visible trade deficits of all countries trading with the kingdom. Imports in 1981 totalled £1,841.1 million ($2,884 million).

Although details of the invisible trade balance are not available, the UK is almost certainly recording a substantial surplus on this account — reflecting its success in penetrating service markets, notably in consulting engineering.

Offsetting this good news is the fact that the UK takes only a small part of the total export market and has performed less successfully in the kingdom than in the Gulf emirates. In 1981, the UK accounted for just 6.2 per cent of Saudi imports, well behind the US and Japan, and significantly less than West Germany. This, however, was slightly up on the 1981 share of 6.1 per cent.

Despite the pattern of Saudi trade, the UK is unlikely to lose interest in the kingdom. It is by far the largest Middle East export market and the source of thousands of jobs. The government — while working hard to boost the volume of exports — can derive some satisfaction from the fact that the UK has managed to maintain its stake in the Saudi market despite intense competition and a grossly overvalued sterling/riyal exchange rate.

The achievement becomes more impressive when considered in the light of three difficult years in the Saudi-UK political relationship. In 1980, the UK was publicly rebuked for allowing the screening of a controversial television film about the kingdom. In an unprecedented move, Saudi Arabia asked the UK to withdraw its ambassador and refused to appoint its own ambassador to London. This led to almost six months of uncertainty, only ended by a visit by the then secretary of state for foreign and commonwealth affairs Lord Carrington in August that year.

Intense diplomatic efforts resulted in a swift revival in relations. This lasted until the end of 1982, when a new crisis emerged — provoked by Prime Minister Margaret Thatcher's refusal to meet an Arab League mission, including Arab heads of state plus a representative of the Palestine Liberation Organisation (PLO). The dramatic cooling in relations which resulted raised the prospect of reduced trade between the two countries.

The effect on UK exports of this latest development will not be apparent until the end of 1983. However, exporters can take heart from the fact that trade actually rose during the 1980 dispute. So far, business seems to have been immune to politics.

An important component of the UK's export effort is a revival in vehicle sales. The financial troubles at BL, the UK's only high-volume car manufacturer, meant sales were minimal in the late 1970s. However, since 1981 BL has made new efforts in the kingdom.

The company is concentrating on the luxury end of the market, particularly Jaguars and Range Rovers. Although sales of Land-Rovers have increased, this sector of the market has unquestionably been lost to the Japanese. Rolls-Royce has had a considerable impact, and has also been successful in supplying aero engines. An order from national airline Saudia for 100 engines for its fleet of jets led to a major contract for a maintenance facility to service Saudia engines.

The UK has the dubious distinction of being the kingdom's main supplier of tobacco. This has been a rapidly growing market, although the buoyancy may start diminishing following government anti-smoking campaigns.

The construction business has produced few rewards. The UK's share of the market is little more than 1 per cent, and British companies have been significantly less successful than their European, US and Japanese counterparts. Contractors which have made an impact include Laing Wimpey Alireza, a tripartite Saudi-UK joint venture which has won a series of hospital construction contracts, and Wimpey ME & C, working through its own Saudi joint venture on a £60 million ($ 98 million) sulphur handling plant in Jubail. Costain also won an important contract from the Saudi Ports Authority (SPA) in 1982 for work on Farasan island in the Red Sea.

Al-Esayi Saif Noman Douglas (Asad), a Jeddah-based joint venture involving RM Douglas, has been quietly successful. Among its present contracts is responsibility for building a housing complex in Jeddah for Arabian Cleaning Enterprise.

Construction companies generally are having a thin time. The same cannot be said of British consultants. Civil engineers, quantity surveyors and project supervisors have secured a disproportionate volume of Saudi work. Among the most successful are Sir Bruce White Wolfe Barry & Partners, consultant for most of Dammam port, and Sir William Halcrow & Partners, consultant for Jeddah port.

The UK's long experience of water engineering has also been used to good effect in the kingdom. John Taylor & Sons has been particularly active in designing and managing water and sewerage projects, while Ewbank & Partners has designed several small seawater desalination plants.

Queen Elizabeth II is greeted by King Khaled at Riyadh airport during her 1979 Gulf tour. Despite periods of misunderstanding, relations between the two kingdoms are developing in a friendly and positive manner

But it is in providing skilled labour that the UK is among the leaders in Saudi Arabia. One of the biggest UK contracts is held by BAC, a subsidiary of British Aerospace, for training Saudi pilots and providing technical assistance for the air force.

UK nationals are also well represented in health care. Recent major contracts — whether awarded to British or non-British firms — have led to a substantial increase in the number of UK medical staff in the kingdom. Two prestige health care contracts have already been secured by the UK: for Defence Ministry hospitals in Riyadh and Al-Kharj, being handled by Allied Medical Group, and for the new National Guard hospital in Jeddah, managed by International Hospital Group.

US companies providing health care services recruit heavily from the UK. The most notable is Whittaker, probably the most active in the kingdom. With more than 30 hospitals being built countrywide, the scene looks set for a major new recruitment wave in the UK during the 1980s.

UK defence, health and engineering specialists adopt the highest profile in the kingdom. However, they make up only a fraction of the total British expatriate population. Aramco, long the exponent of the American way in Saudi Arabia, now has as many UK as US employees. And throughout the kingdom, Britons are playing important roles in managing Saudi companies.

The provision of services is now the market with the greatest long-term potential for the UK. Despite the British economy's failings, the UK still manages to produce a surplus of high-quality professionals willing to work in the demanding Middle East environment for less than the salaries asked by US and other European nationals. In addition, the emergence of English as the kingdom's business language gives Britons another competitive advantage. The combination of these factors should ensure an enduring British presence in the kingdom.

US-Saudi relations

President Reagan's declaration on 1 October 1981 that the US would not "permit" Saudi Arabia to "be an Iran" marked the beginning of a year of extraordinary events in US-Saudi relations.

On 28 October, the Reagan administration won a bitter battle against Israel's Congressional supporters for approval of an $8,500 million military aircraft sale to Saudi Arabia, including five airborne warning and control system (AWACS) aircraft.

With this, the US anticipated heightened Saudi co-operation with US political and strategic aims in the region. The Saudis had been instrumental in helping US envoy Philip Habib to effect a ceasefire in southern Lebanon in July 1981 and in ensuring Palestinian adherence to it. The Saudis, however, were disappointed at the lack of a coherent US response to the then Crown Prince Fahd's enunciation in August of an eight-point Middle East peace plan which included implicit acceptance of Israel's "right to live in peace" — a longstanding US requirement. When, after the AWACS victory, Reagan said the Fahd plan would "recognise Israel as a nation to be negotiated with," it was dismissed as a presidential slip-of-the-tongue. The lukewarm US response undoubtedly did much to ensure the Fahd plan's failure to gain acceptance at the Arab summit in Fes, Morocco, in November.

The Saudis continued to resist US requests for military basing rights in the kingdom, while agreeing, in talks with Defence Secretary Caspar Weinberger in February 1982, to expand military co-operation by setting up a "joint committee for military projects."

If anything, Saudi sensitivity about military ties with the US will have been heightened following the brutal Israeli rampage through Lebanon beginning in June 1982; the widespread Arab perception was that the US had acquiesced in the invasion and failed to act to stop Israel's deadly siege of Beirut.

Acknowledging the oil threat
The Saudis have acknowledged the possibility of an outside threat to their oil fields, although, in more than 40 years, the flow of oil from those fields has never once been stopped by military or terrorist action. The US has failed to make a credible case for a Soviet threat to the oil fields. The Saudis have historically shown greater concern about the Iranians: in the first phase of the Iran/Iraq war, which began in September 1980, US analysts believed the Saudis and their partners in the Gulf Co-operation Council (GCC) would turn to the US for military assistance or even military intervention if the Iranians should push down into the Gulf. However, after the Iranian counter-invasion of Iraq in June 1982 — which coincided with the Israeli onslaught in Lebanon — the Gulf states saw a greater risk of exposure to Iranian pressure as the likely result of too close an identification with US military aims.

According to former US National Security Council Middle East specialist William Quandt, in his book Saudi Arabia in the 1980s: Foreign Policy, Security and Oil, the Saudis are likely to continue to resist US requests for an enlarged military presence, arguing that a sustained flow of the latest US military technology will be enough to deter outside threats. ("You are just arms salesmen, and we pay cash," a Saudi general has been quoted as saying to US officials.)

The US is likely to continue the flow of weapons — although it is debatable whether the AWACS struggle enhanced or depleted the political capital the administration has to spend in Congress on the kingdom's behalf — and will maintain a military position in the kingdom through its military training mission and National Guard advisers, through the US Army Corps of Engineers, manager of many of the kingdom's huge civil works programmes, and through the AWACS aircraft themselves, whether or not they have US operators.

The AWACS battle brought to the fore the extent of the US-Saudi economic relationship. Top executives from many of the 700-plus US companies with contracts in Saudi Arabia lobbied in Congress in favour of the aircraft sale. In a newspaper advertising campaign, oil giant Mobil, one of the original Aramco partners, noted that US firms held $35,000 million in Saudi contracts — excluding the Aramco investment. "The Saudi involvement with US industry covers virtually the entire spectrum of US commerce — from weather stations to chains of supermarkets, construction of petrochemical complexes and tyre-manufacturing plants, shipbuilding and hospitals," the Mobil advertisement pointed out.

US — the largest supplier
The US is Saudi Arabia's largest supplier, with a 25 per cent market share, and Saudi Arabia is by far the US' major Middle East trading partner, taking nearly 40 per cent of US exports to the region and providing up to half the value of US imports from the region.

US exports to Saudi Arabia in 1982 were valued at $9,026 million, 23 per cent more than in the previous year.

In 1981, the US imported $14,391 million worth of Saudi oil and petroleum products, a 13 per cent increase over the previous year. However, these imports declined by nearly half to $7,443.1 million in 1982, giving the US a favourable trade balance with the kingdom for the first time in nearly a decade.

The US economic imprint on Saudi Arabia is unmistakeable. US companies first developed the oil wealth, and the original Aramco partners maintain an active role in the Saudi-ised company (and most recently have sustained huge financial losses by lifting Saudi oil at above-market prices). Mobil, Exxon, Chevron, Texaco and Shell/USA are active partners in the huge gas-gathering schemes at Jubail and Yanbu. US contractors, led by the construction giants Bechtel, Fluor and Ralph M Parsons, are overseeing construction of the two industrial cities. Saudi hospitals are managed by US companies and run according to US medical standards. US high-technology goods and services are widely in evidence in telecommunications, computer centres, electricity supply, agriculture and water projects, education and training programmes.

This involvement means about 40,000 US nationals — including 4,000 employees and 9,000 dependants in the Aramco community — live and work in Saudi Arabia. Thousands more businessmen and top US executives visit the kingdom regularly. The familiarity and knowledge these Americans have acquired about Saudi history, culture and customs have begun to have an effect in countering the facile, distorted and unfair image of Saudi Arabia found in the US news and entertainment media. Without specific prodding from Saudi Arabia,

Saudi American Bank headquarters

major US corporations — particularly the oil companies, construction firms and health-care concerns — have produced or underwritten lavish films, exhibitions, books and information kits about the kingdom and its people.

Saudi investment in the US

The other side of the Saudi-US economic relationship is the $50,000 million or more worth of Saudi financial investment in the US. This is an issue that has generated controversy in the US, despite the obvious benefits of that huge investment in bolstering the flagging economy.

In spite of the tradition of expatriate ownership established by their own globe-girdling multinational companies, Americans tend to oppose the notion of foreigners "buying up" their own country. The widespread antipathy to Arabs in general, and to the Saudis in particular, which is encouraged and nurtured by pro-Israeli forces in the US, has wilfully overdramatised the issue of Arab investment.

For their part, the Saudis, while appreciating the capacity, diversity and security of the US as a market for their investments, have watched unhappily as much of their invested wealth has been eroded by US inflation and declines in the value of the dollar.

They have also reacted negatively to the hostile manner in which they are portrayed in the US media, to the attempts of some pro-Zionist congressmen to force the US Treasury to disclose details about Saudi and other Arab investments, and to the precedent of the Carter administration's freeze of Iranian assets in the US at the time of the Tehran hostage crisis.

Unlike the Kuwaitis, with their penchant for bold corporate acquisitions, equity purchases and real estate deals, the Saudis have tended to keep their investments in Treasury bills or short-term certificates of deposit. To the extent that Saudi capital is invested in commercial acquisitions, equity shares in companies or real estate, it tends to be done by a few individual entrepreneurs, such as Sulaiman Olayan, Ghaith Pharaon and Adnan Khashogji.

In the past two years, these investments have included the purchase of a 19 per cent share in New York stockbroker Donaldson, Lufkin & Jenrette; the acquisition by Pharaon of Hyatt International Hotels; the purchase of a Washington, DC, bank holding company, Financial General Bankshares, by Saudi, Kuwaiti and UAE businessmen, and the acquisition of interests in silver mines in Idaho and Texas. While such purchases attract the glare of publicity, they are insignificant compared with European, Canadian and Japanese investments in US companies.

Ironically, while some in the US show considerable hostility to Saudi investment, Saudi investors have faced some criticism at home for placing too much of the nation's "birthright" in US holdings without return gestures of friendship and confidence from the US.

Capital flows to Japan and Europe

The result, increasingly, is that Saudi surplus capital has begun to flow more towards Japan and Europe, and the implicit Saudi option of withdrawing assets from the US for political reasons has become more credible.

The Lebanon crisis of mid-1982 brought new calls in the Arab world for deployment of the oil "weapon" against the US and for the withdrawal of Arab investments from the US because of Washington's failure to restrain Israel. As the Saudis saw it, the Israeli assault on Lebanon and the Palestinians, with the simultaneous Iranian attack on Iraq, had changed the Arab strategic picture dramatically.

The fact that the US — despite the mediating efforts of Philip Habib — had failed to use its unique power and influence over Israel to stop the bloodbath in Beirut, and the fact that

US officials and commentators continued to assert with disarming frankness that, despite the coolest conceivable relations with Ayatollah Khomeini's regime, Iran ultimately remained the focal point of US interests in the Gulf region, gave the Saudis cause to reconsider their relationship with the US.

Once willing to assist the US in countering Soviet and "radical" influences in the region, the Saudis now felt that those hostile forces had been greatly enhanced by the frailty and clumsiness of the US response to the very real crises of the moment.

To the Saudis and other "moderate" Arabs, the US — through its complicity in aggressive Israeli expansionism and because of the hardening of Palestinian attitudes resulting from the siege of Beirut and the sustained Israeli repression in the occupied territories — has become the main "destabilising" factor in the Middle East. This puts US friends in the region at great risk.

The Saudis hope to use their influence in Washington — enhanced, they believe, since the AWACS battle and with the appointment of former Bechtel executive George Shultz as secretary of state to persuade the US to adjust its course, particularly on the question of Palestinian rights, before it is too late. If such an approach does not work — or, worse still, is rebuffed — the consequences for US and Saudi interests alike could be dire indeed.

US government agencies in Saudi Arabia

Jeddah	Telephone
US Embassy	6670080, telex 401459 amemb sj
US Commercial Centre	6670040
Federal Aviation (FAA)	6673664/6673624
Joint Economic Commission (Jecor)	6655687/6659135
US Army Corps of Engineers	6670077
US Geological Survey (USGS)	6674188
US Military Training Mission (USMTM)	6422329/6447368/ 6449718
Riyadh	
US Liaison Office	4640012
Jecor	4040544/4042336
USICA	4023251/4030367/ 4022061
USMTM	4778066/4765850
Taif	
USMTM	7322518
Dhahran	
US Consulate-General	8643200/8643452/ 8746500/8643616/ 8746400/8743977

The US Army Corps of Engineers

The US Army Corps of Engineers (USACE), with a workforce including about 40,000 civilian employees in the US and abroad, is the world's largest engineering and construction organisation.

With more than 200 years' experience, the corps has also developed the most extensive engineering capability in the world. In Saudi Arabia, more than $1,000 million in construction work is being placed annually in the corps' largest military construction programme ever.

USACE's involvement in overseas work began in the late 1950s with jobs in Europe, Africa and elsewhere.

Construction in Saudi Arabia is directed by the Middle East Division (MED), commanded by a general officer. The division is organised in much the same way as other corps field organisations, but is unique in that it is split into a division (forward) in Riyadh and a division (rear) near Berryville, Virginia.

To ensure better liaison during construction and for operational support, four field elements have been set up by the Saudi division. There are two districts — Riyadh and Al-Batin — to provide on-site construction supervision and maintain links between customer, contractor and corps. There is also an ordnance programme division responsible for working with the Saudi army ordnance corps in developing and managing an ordnance logistics system, and an engineer logistics command responsible for countrywide support services.

The entire project involves almost 1,600 employees, 1,200 of them in Saudi

Arabia. With work scheduled to extend into the late 1980s, its expected $20,000 million cost is fully funded and prepaid by the Saudis.

USACE has been in Saudi Arabia since 1951, when construction began on a US air force base at Dhahran. Additional US-funded projects followed, of which the most notable was the Dhahran civil air terminal at the same airfield. The terminal, completed in 1961, was financed under the sponsorship of the US State Department with funds from the US Agency for International Development.

A series of formal government-to-government agreements followed. The first involved setting up a countrywide black-and-white television system, as well as training Saudi operators. According to the agreement, construction began in 1964 and was completed in 1971 at a cost of $28 million. The same agreement also provided for design, construction and equipping of a radio station in Riyadh at a cost of $14 million.

By mid-1981, MED had completed $5,000 million of construction in the kingdom and was involved in five major programmes, all wholly funded by the Saudi government.

Engineer Assistance Agreement

The Engineer Assistance Agreement (EAA), sponsored by the State Department, is the result of an agreement calling on the US to provide advice and help in building military facilities for the Defence & Aviation Ministry. The programme began in 1964, initially involving construction of three military cantonments for the army.

The first cantonment, at Khamis Mushait near the Yemen border, was completed in 1971 at a cost of $81.4 million; the second, at Tabuk just south of the Jordanian border, was completed in 1973 for $81 million; and the third, a massive military city for 70,000 people, is at Al-Batin, a barren stretch of desert south of the Iraqi border. This last cantonment, King Khaled Military City (KKMC), will cost about $7,000 million. The undertaking is so huge that it is not due for completion until the mid-1980s.

To carry it out, most corps contractors have to bring in all their workers and provide them with housing and food. Most of the construction machinery and material also has to be imported. In addition, it has been necessary to build a port at Ras al-Mishab on the Arabian Gulf to handle the immense quantity of material needed to build KKMC and other schemes. The port has seven general cargo berths, one bulk cement berth, onshore stores and related facilities.

EAA's work has also included an air force headquarters in Riyadh and the airborne and physical training school at Tabuk. Still being built are headquarters for the Defence & Aviation Ministry in Riyadh, and the $1,500 million King Abdul-Aziz military academy outside the city. An engineer centre and school are also to be built for KKMC.

Since 1972, work for the navy has been proceeding under a memorandum of understanding between the US Defence Department and the Saudi Defence & Aviation Ministry. Overall manager for the project, the Saudi naval expansion programme (SNEP), is the US navy, and design is to US navy criteria. The corps manages the design and construction part of the work.

Two naval bases with deep-water facilities are being built at Jubail and Jeddah, while a naval headquarters has been built in Riyadh. There are plans to maintain an interim repair facility in operation on the Arabian Gulf at Dammam as a permanent installation.

Each naval base is essentially a miniature city with family housing, schools, shops and recreational facilities, as well as training and maintenance, and support facilities for vessels. Most of the facilities yet to be completed are associated with command and control, equipment maintenance and calibration, training and engineering facilities.

The navy is growing, with several ships recently bought from the US. The construction programme is expanding to accommodate new equipment and concepts and — while not yet a part of the construction programme — a naval academy is being designed.

The basic SNEP programme is for completion by the end of December 1984. However, more recently planned support facilities and possible additions to the family housing may extend work beyond then. The whole programme is costed at about $5,200 million — nearly one-third of MED's total.

The royal Saudi air force programme

MED is also helping to provide contracting and construction management support for the Saudi air force. Overall programme manager is the US air force logistics command, through its subordinate in Saudi Arabia, the logistics support group. The scheme involves upgrading Saudi aircraft and support facilities in two separate programmes.

The first is the Peace Hawk Programme for which the US air force is supplying F-5 fighters, and support facilities at Taif, Khamis Mushait, Tabuk and Dhahran. MED provided design review and quality assurance inspections. In the new Peace Sun programme, support for more advanced F-15s, MED is not only doing design review, but also full construction management.

The facilities needed for Peace Sun include aircraft shelters, an avionics maintenance building, a maintenance hangar, an engine repair workshop, and flight simulator and squadron operation buildings. Taxiway parking, apron expansions, roads, drainage, security fencing, and staff housing at Khamis Mushait and Taif are included.

Work is under way at both these sites, as well as Dhahran, with construction expected to be completed by June 1983.

The corps' work on these two programmes together totals $545.6 million.

The Ordnance Corps programme

Under the Saudi ordnance corps programme, USACE has been working since 1967 on a series of one and two-year agreements to modernise the Saudi Arabian Army Ordnance Corps (SAAOC). MED's ordnance programme division acts as contract administrator for maintaining and supplying ordnance and engineering equipment, and in training SAAOC cadets, and as disbursing agent for equipment purchases. The programme totals $2,900 million.

Its other major work is for the National Guard, the kingdom's internal security force. Since a memorandum of understanding was signed in 1973, the corps has been responsible for designing and building all facilities. These include a headquarters complex in Riyadh for 3,500 people costing nearly $300 million. Also complete are training facilities – including classrooms – shops, and warehouses at Khashm al-An, near Riyadh. Eighteen kinds of firing range have been built there.

Trade with France

The kingdom's relationship with France has grown closer and more complex since the start of the decade. Previous links, which centred almost exclusively on oil, have broadened to cover politics, diplomacy and major contract work. Since French President Mitterrand's accession to power in May 1981, Saudi Arabia has quickly become France's prime diplomatic discussion partner in the Arab world. There is still a strong feeling in Paris that Riyadh is likely to be the source of any real programme to settle the region's basic tensions.

Business and diplomacy traditionally go hand in hand in France. Former foreign trade minister Michel Jobert, must be included, as must such in 1973-74, regards them as complementary aspects of international relations. So it is not surprising that the growing diplomatic relationship between Riyadh and Paris has coincided with French attempts to make greater inroads into the Saudi market. Companies have had some notable contract successes, but the general feeling is that more needs to be done, particularly in establishing a wide-ranging and permanent presence.

Imports of Saudi oil, which increased rapidly in 1981 as Iraq's supplies dried up, ensured a huge adverse trade balance with the kingdom. The gap that year rose to FF 55,408 million ($8,124 million) following the 78 per cent increase in oil purchases. In the same period French exports to the kingdom rose by a highly respectable 64 per cent to FF 10,149 million ($1,488 million). But French dependence on imported oil means the trade relationship will remain lopsided for many years – however well French firms perform.

The oil link stems from a 1973 supply agreement concluded by Jobert during the presidency of Georges Pompidou. The deal — in which France had to take 12 million tonnes of oil a year — was criticised by Societe Nationale Elf Aquitaine chairman Albin Chalandon among others. In spring 1982, Chalandon told the government that France was in a position "bordering on the absurd" because of its commitment to take the oil at prices well above the world market rate. Chalandon and his supporters believed that to link the price France paid for oil, and the quantities it was obliged to buy, with broader political and diplomatic aims had proved a mistake. Given the oil glut, they wanted to be able to buy at the most advantageous rate, rather than being in a position where French companies had to buy a specified quantity of oil each year — and were making a loss at the same time.

Although the French government is naturally keen to cut its energy import bill, the problem with Chalandon's argument was that any attempt to change the terms of the 1973 agreement, or to end it completely, ran the risk of two potentially unpleasant consequences. If the oil glut dried up, it could mean problems in ensuring regular, fixed-price supplies, while it could also damage the relationship which France is anxious to develop with Saudi Arabia across the whole economic spectrum.

As a result, the agreement was renewed at the end of 1982, but for 3 million tonnes a year at the then official price of $34 a barrel. At the same time, Saudi Arabia agreed to help support the franc, which was under pressure. In an accord reported by reliable sources, although not announced by either government, the kingdom put $2,000 million at France's disposal, with the possibility of a credit line of up to $4,000 million.

The deepening relationship has been manifested in a series of construction contracts recently awarded to some of France's major firms.

The Saudi-French Bank

The contracts have both established a French presence in the kingdom, and also put Saudi Arabia in a top place in French order books. Most spectacular was the $1,717 million Riyadh university contract awarded in April 1981 to France's Bouygues and the US' Blount. Additional work decided since the contract signing is expected to take the total value to about $2,000 million. Bouygues hails the project as the "greatest the world has ever seen."

As Bouygues' team of experts and subcontracted workers moves into top gear on the Riyadh project, a second big French construction firm, Dumez, has started work on another landmark in the French move into the kingdom: a SR 3,300 million ($956 million) order for 4,576 National Guard villas at Khashm al-Aan. Another French concern, Societe Auxiliare d'Entreprise (SAE), has meanwhile taken a further big National Guard housing project at Taif.

French firms have also established themselves in the kingdom's hospital development programme. Bouygues won work on three 100-bed hospitals in autumn 1981, and followed this with a SR 493 million ($143 million) contract for a 574-bed hospital at Buraydah. Dragages & Travaux Publics has joined with Riyadh's El-Seif Engineering Contracting and South Korea's Samsung Construction Company in successful bids for five Saudi hospitals, the most recent being a SR 350 million ($102 million) establishment at Qatif, Eastern province.

French companies are tending to approach the Saudi market as part of an international consortium. Most French firms are aware of their individual limitations — whether size, resources, manpower or specialisation — and believe international link-ups make sense when faced with projects of the size of those in Saudi Arabia. Spie-Batignolles has joined West Germany's Mannesmann as co-leader of an international group building the pipelines and pumping station for the Jubail-Riyadh water supply system, a $910 million project for completion in 1983. It is also bidding with Japan's Hitachi Shipbuilding & Engineering Company for desalination work and — like several other French concerns — is setting up a local joint venture.

Another firm which has benefited from the international consortium approach to Saudi projects is engineering and plant construction contractor Compagnie Francaise d'Etudes & de Construction Technip. In 1981, a consortium in which the French company held a one-third stake secured a $1,000 million contract for refinery engineering, procurement and construction work at Jubail. And working on its own, Technip has secured an impressive range of Saudi orders, including a $175 million contract for multiflash distillation units at the Al-Khobar desalination plant, and extensive work for the Saline Water Conversion Corporation at Jubail. Through its Agrotechnip subsidiary, the company's work in the kingdom even stretches to supplying a trout farm as part of a $10 million contract for the Taif agro-industrial complex.

At the same time, French agro-food firms have been developing their own exports. Cereal exports nearly doubled between 1980 and 1981, from 382,783 tonnes to 697,121 tonnes, while the kingdom has also proved a booming market for sales of poultry and milk products. Total French agro-food sales to the kingdom rose from FF 1,352 million ($184 million) in 1980 to FF 1,911 million ($260 million) in 1981, and French officials hope for substantially bigger increases as French firms adapt their products to local needs.

France is also becoming known as a supplier of high technology and communications equipment. Thomson-CSF has provided television transmitters and installations in

Riyadh, Abha, Qassim and Al-Madinah, has handled the switch to colour of stations in Dammam, Riyadh and Jeddah, and has installed the closed circuit television system in Al-Madinah mosque.

Another French pacemaker in the communications field is CIT-Alcatel. In 1980 it dented Ericsson of Sweden's dominance of the Saudi telephone market when its E10 digital switching system was ordered for Jubail.

Exports of a different kind — in human form — go to the kingdom from France's Compagnie pour Outillages & Materiaux Speciales pour les Industries de Petrole (COMSIP), which has developed a strong line in supplying advisers to set up and operate sophisticated electronic systems. Its breakthrough came in 1969, when Aramco awarded it a major contract, and the links continue: 25 COMSIP engineers and technicians were working for Aramco at the West Side Yanbu installation in early 1982 and the total there is expected to reach 100. This will bring the number of COMSIP staff operating for Aramco to 180 by 1983.

Military co-operation has also strengthened since 1980 — notably with two major naval equipment and training agreements — while Saudi Arabia has become France's major Middle East market for engineering and metal goods. Exports increased by 55 per cent between mid-1980 and mid-1981.

And the banking relationship seems to be thriving. Fears that the socialist government's nationalisation programme — which covers private banks as well as big industrial groups — would antagonise Saudi interests appear to have been unfounded. Joint-venture discussions continue between Saudi private investors and French banks following the nationalisation legislation. The nationalised Banque de l'Indochine & de Suez (Indosuez) has a much prized 40 per cent stake in The Saudi-French Bank.

Agriculture

A massive government support programme is largely responsible for the revival in agriculture, which was sadly neglected after the 1973-74 oil price rises. Today, the kingdom enjoys self-sufficiency in wheat and, in some areas, plentiful supplies of chickens, locally produced eggs and dairy products. Without this support, agriculture's contribution to gross domestic product (GDP) would probably be even less than the 6 per cent recorded in 1980/81.

The government plans to spend SR 72,000 million ($20,867 million) on agriculture and water resources during the 1980-85 third plan. By mid-1982, one-third of this had already been allocated. Although the development of groundwater supplies and laying the necessary infrastructure accounted for a substantial proportion, an increasing amount will be devoted to developing production. The constraints on farmers

Saudi markets burst with local produce

remain considerable, however. These include the small size of most holdings, limited water, outmoded irrigation systems and increasing soil salinity in long-established farming centres.

Among the major projects are the Al-Hasa irrigation and drainage scheme and the National Agricultural Development Company (Nadec) — formerly the Haradh Agriculture & Animal Production Company (Hapco). Aramco has a well developed farming programme in Hasa, while Riyadh's King Saud university has an experimental farming project in Deirab, 25 kilometres from Riyadh on the Makkah road.

The most important agency involved is the Riyadh-based Saudi Arabian Agricultural Bank (SAAB), an independent entity responsible for disbursing most of the state's financial support to farmers and farming projects. Set up in 1963, the bank began to make a significant contribution to national development in the mid-1970s. But it was only as the third plan got under way that it started to disburse its annual budget in full — reflecting the general lack of enthusiasm about farming until then.

The bank's 1982/83 budget calls for project loans of more than SR 3,000 million ($869 million), and about half this again in subsidies. This compares with the SR 2,530.9 million ($734 million) lent in 1980/81 and the SR 1,128 million ($327 million) in 1979/80.

The government controls the price of much farm equipment, including tractors, combine harvesters, sowing machines, and milking equipment and accessories. Although prices are reviewed, they have recently failed to keep pace with international inflation.

Subsidies include:

☐ 50 per cent of the cost of fertilisers;
☐ 50 per cent of the cost of animal feed, or 50 per cent of the selling price from the state-owned Grain Silos & Flour Mills Organisation (GSFMO);
☐ 100 per cent of the cost of pesticides;
☐ 30 per cent of the cost of poultry

Comfortable transport for goats

equipment, provided it satisfies the requirements of the Agriculture & Water Ministry,
☐ 30 per cent of dairy equipment;
☐ 50 per cent of all other agricultural machinery, including pumps and irrigation equipment;
☐ five tonnes of seed potatoes free;
☐ free transport for 50 cows.

One trend emerging is the establishment of joint-stock companies involving local businessmen. The largest is Nadec, most of whose shares are owned by the founders and the public. Nadec is expanding its original Haradh project and developing new programmes in Qassim and Wadi al-Dawasir. Similar companies have been set up in Hail and Tabuk.

The government has also intervened to revive the declining national fishing industry; the Saudi Fisheries Company is already beginning to satisfy some of the kingdom's needs.

Foreign companies and businessmen have previously been reluctant to invest in Saudi agriculture, regarding it as dicey. While beginning to show more interest, they are likely to concentrate on management and equipment supply, rather than on becoming entrepreneurs in their own right.

Education

The huge increase in spending on human resources in the 1982/83 budget underlines the importance attached by the government to education. The SR 13,239 million ($3,848 million) budget allocation, 21 per cent more than in the previous year, makes education one of the biggest priorities after defence, and transport and communications.

The 1980-85 third five-year development plan envisages spending SR 122,500 million ($35,610 million) on education — 16 per cent of the total. Aims include free education for all, and the eradication of illiteracy. About 1.5 million pupils were enrolled in academic institutions in the 1980/81 school year, according to the Saudi Arabian Monetary Agency's (SAMA — central bank authority's) 1981 report — 6 per cent more than in the previous year. The number of teachers increased by 8 per cent to 82,786, while more than 600 schools opened. According to the report, the number of female pupils rose in the year to 569,887, making up 37 per cent of the total, compared with 35 per cent in 1979/80. At the same time the number of women teachers increased from 27,717 to 31,292.

The report adds that there are about 10,000 students on government scholarships abroad. Of these, 6,896 are studying in the US; the number in the UK has recently declined considerably.

The country has 16 universities and colleges. The major ones are King Faisal, King Saud and Imam Muhammad Ibn Saud Islamic universities in Riyadh; King Abdul-Aziz university in Jeddah and Makkah; King Faisal university in Eastern province; the University of Petroleum & Minerals, Dhahran, and the Islamic university in Al-Madinah.

Vocational training
The General Organisation for Technical

Education & Vocational Training (GOTEVT) was set up in 1981 as the result of the merger of the Education Ministry's technical education department and the vocational training division of the Labour & Social Affairs Ministry. Its aim is to attract non-academic Saudis into vocational courses, such as carpentry and brick-laying, to alleviate the shortage of craftsmen. It received an allocation of SR 1,663 million ($483 million) for fiscal 1982, of which SR 966 million ($280 million) was for capital projects. A team from the US Department of Labour is helping with vocational training, while a West German team is providing technical advice.

The basic provision offered by GOTEVT is a course at one of its six pre-vocational training centres. More than 3,000 students completed the 10-month pre-vocational course in mid-1982. The students, aged from 14-17, are each paid SR 500 ($145) a month, and given clothing and food allowances. On graduation each receives a basic SR 3,000 ($872); students deemed "excellent" get an extra SR 1,000 ($290).

At the top of GOTEVT's network are its eight technical high schools, which can train 8,000-plus students aged 15-20. One of the major incentives they offer graduating students wanting to open their own business is a SR 100,000 ($29,069) government grant. Responsibility for allocating these lies with the Saudi Credit Bank.

University of Petroleum and Minerals in Dhahran

PART 5 DOING BUSINESS

The Business Setting*

Commerce in Saudi Arabia is centuries old. The methods used by the people may have been different to those of the West, but their experience is considerable and you should have no illusions as to their shrewdness.

Many of today's businessmen, who have been educated in Europe or the US, have the advantage of experiencing life and business procedures in both East and West, and are therefore more able to assess the strengths and weaknesses of both.

If visitors sometimes seem to be mistrusted, you must remember that over-selling played a part in much western sales practice in the early 1970s. Pride in the quality as well as the price was not always evident and, all too often, you heard: "I won't be here when it goes wrong, so why should I worry?"

A major contributing factor in the recent halving to 10 per cent of advance payments made on award of government contracts was because, in some cases, the money was being transferred out of the kingdom and not solely used for the purpose intended. Elsewhere in the world, firms are expected to be self-financing from the start. So why abuse a bonus?

Similar avaricious approaches by a few have had adverse effects on several overseas suppliers, which many still regard as parasites.

Understanding the key

The major factor when setting up in the kingdom is thus to develop mutual trust and understanding. This will not happen overnight, but is essential for doing business. Sincerity has to be proved before acceptance is given.

Trading in the kingdom is basically the same as in any country with opportunities, provided you are prepared to get up and sell. However, its potential has to be greater because it is one of the few countries in the world with an expanding economy, and a growth rate among the world's highest. But despite the 20 per cent growth in imports in 1981, the boom will not last for ever. Companies which have yet to establish themselves will face greater problems, as their more farsighted competitors consolidate their existing position, and the established policy favouring local manufacturers gains strength. It is no longer an "order takers" market and, to compensate for decreasing margins, properly organised selling is the way to success, with hard work the key.

The kingdom's development programme is unique, unlikely to be repeated on such a scale elsewhere. To be involved in it is exciting as well as educational. You are competing with a myriad of suppliers from all over the world, selling to a galaxy of nationalities from an office with staff from half-a-dozen ethnic backgrounds. It is challenging, interesting and sometimes frustrating — inevitable when dealing with such a variety of people and methods, especially when the language

* See Riyadh Group of British Businessmen

barrier has sometimes to be overcome. But the tenacious succeed, as proved by many company balance sheets.

Customs, culture and environment may seem strange, but it is a great advantage to experience, at first hand, the traditions of other ethnic groups. The westerner is rarely always correct and an exchange of ideas and techniques can only be beneficial. It is important that whoever is doing the selling has — as well as expertise — previous knowledge and understanding of other peoples' customs, idiosyncrasies, strengths and weaknesses. Failure is certain for those who adopt "a better than thou" attitude from the beginning.

Flexibility is essential, as is adaptability to those methods which bring results. One simple example is bargaining, an integral part of any deal. You never offer the best price first; you must allow time for comparison and counterquote, and not expect instant acceptance. The expression "closed tender" is generally replaced by "open negotiation." You should also work to the customer's schedule and can ill-afford to be irritated if appointments are not kept or decisions delayed. Perseverance conquers all and one of the advantages of having a man on the spot is that he can always go back tomorrow. Someone who identifies with the kingdom and is not in and out on the first plane in an attempt to make a quick killing will receive a much warmer welcome and more solid response.

The groundwork

A basic requirement before deciding on any strategy is an in-depth market survey of the area to be tackled. It is amazing how many foreign manu-

ICL stand at the April 1981 Saudi Business Show

In Saudi Arabia — hospitality with a French accent at the Gulf Meridien Al Khobar.

Situated on the coast of the Eastern Province of Saudi Arabia, the Gulf Hotel Meridien is five minutes from the downtown commercial area and only fifteen minutes from Dhahran International Airport.

In the De Luxe 5-Star category it offers impeccable service in luxurious surroundings, with the needs of the business traveller being given particular attention.

Our excellent restaurants offer a variety of International, Arabic and Oriental menus to cater for all tastes.

* Royal suite with private swimming pool
* 2 Diplomatic suites
* 18 De Luxe suites
* 350 rooms
* All rooms air-conditioned and sound-proofed
* Direct dial telephones in all rooms
* Regular shuttle bus service downtown, and to airport
* Executive business service. Telex. Translations. Secretarial assistance.
* Conference and banquet services catering for up to 900
* Audio visual aids and simultaneous translation facility
* Private meeting and dining rooms
* 24 hour laundry/valet service
* 6 restaurants and lounges
* Shopping arcade
* Floodlit tennis courts
* Squash courts
* Recreation rooms
* Sauna
* Swimming pool, heated in winter cooled in summer
* Private beach.

For further information or reservations contact the hotel or your nearest Meridien, Air France or Travel Agent.

Hospitality with a french accent

Gulf Meridien Hotel. Corniche Boulevard – 28th Street, P.O. Box 1266 Al Khobar, Saudi Arabia
Telephone: 8646000. Telex: 670505 HOMER SJ or 670524 MERHOT SJ.

GULF MERIDIEN

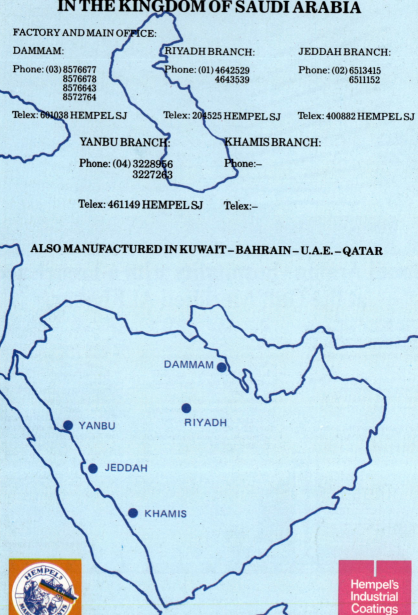

facturers fail to do their homework on Saudi Arabia — although whether this results from the size of the country, the strangeness of the environment or problems in obtaining information is a moot point. It is one of the world's largest potential markets — whether selling consumer products or services — yet many fail to obtain the maximum returns, or attempt to make a proper market plan.

One problem is that too few companies allow enough time to cover the whole country. Few realise there is potential in Buraydah and Khamis Mushait, as well as in the traditional regional centres of Jeddah, Riyadh and Al-Khobar. There is a tendency to "do" Saudi Arabia in a week or 10 days; barely enough time for even one place. The market's size can be illustrated by one construction statistic: money spent on the three-year programme at the new Riyadh university equals each week what it would take to build London's Charing Cross hospital in its entirety. And the university scheme is only one of many projects under way throughout the kingdom, being built to a scale that far exceeds anything seen in most manufacturers' country of origin.

Perhaps the market seems so huge that, not knowing where to start, the bewildered surveyor gives up too easily when confronted with apparently ambiguous answers to his questions. More often, it is simply the wrong choice of person to do the survey. He is neither senior enough to carry through recommendations nor experienced enough to extract the requisite information. This is compounded by the fact that people at the right level rarely visit themselves. Directors should have first-hand experience of the market so that when ambitious proposals are put forward, they are received with a sympathetic ear by someone in authority.

Once the approach is decided and the plan made, it is essential to have someone at the point of export who

Honour — the essence of Saudi business

is familiar with the day-to-day difficulties experienced at the point of sale.

Choosing your agent

Whether a survey reveals that money is to be made by exporting the finished product, or whether manufacturing or a combination of both is feasible, the key to success lies in correct choice of agent or partner (sponsor) in the kingdom. The most suitable company obviously varies according to commodity, and choosing the right one requires a virtual survey of its own. This is extremely important as, once having chosen, it is not easy to change. Help with this is available from embassies, banks, chambers of commerce and government agencies such as the Saudi Industrial Development Fund (SIDF) and the Saudi Basic Industries Corporation (Sabic). It is also useful to get information from those already in the market, while members of groups such as the Riyadh Group of British Businessmen are prepared to assist wherever possible.

While collectors of brass plates

abound, finding the right agent is more difficult. It is often hard to find a company with kingdomwide representation and this can prove a stumbling block. At the same time there is the problem of firms with fragmented agencies. The latter can lead to overlap and consequent in-house competition as well as disagreement on agency commissions due from direct sales. To find a partner or agent with sufficient coverage of the kingdom but no overlap of products in its existing range will not be easy. However, some share of the market is better than none.

The alternative is to concentrate on specific regions, in which case it is wise to define the area and towns involved clearly at the outset, to avoid later misunderstanding. This provides scope for the introduction of a sub-distribution network — used extensively in Europe and the Far East, but only as yet on a limited scale in the kingdom.

It is possible to find companies with their own offices in Europe and elsewhere. This is not only an indication of their financial resources and entrepreneurial initiative, but also enables valuable contact to be maintained outside the kingdom, close to the point of supply.

No-one can sell a product as well as its manufacturer and no-one should expect an agent to replace him entirely in his own country. For a market the size of Saudi Arabia's the producer would have a double-figure sales force with in-depth product knowledge and full scale back-up. It is unreasonable to expect to find an agent with more than a limited number of salesmen, all of whom will be selling a range of products including yours.

It is not possible for foreigners to hold equity in a trading company so you have to rely on your agent. Having made your choice, it is vital to identify completely with your agent to potential customers both in the kingdom and outside. With legislation being enforced that requires importing and buying to be done through Saudi trading companies it is more important than ever to pick the right partner and then back him to the hilt. You must build up mutual trust and understanding, as well as give adequate training and back-up service in selling the commodity.

Back-up and support

Your agent's efficiency is limited by the strength of your partnership with him in the same way as your return is likely to be in direct proportion to the amount you put into it. Having assessed the market, make a total commitment and do not be half-hearted in your approach.

Whether it is in stock, staff, premises, accommodation or cars, in terms of investment who takes the major risk — the Saudi trader or the overseas supplier? But who lays down the rules for the privilege of representing the manufacturer? Western firms are not the only ones with cash-flow problems, and realistic credit terms are essential. The local trader, who is expected to rely on guidance from the "export" supplier, does not have the benefit of a government-backed insurance scheme if the goods do not sell or his customers do not pay. Nor, when he has such heavy one-sided overheads, can he be expected to sell at the price often necessary to compete with manufacturers who attempt to supply direct to the consumer.

There was a time when domestic traders priced suppliers out of the market by exploiting the advantage of local availability. However, competition is now too fierce and common sense prevails. The ideal solution is a joint approach to the market with supplier and trader working closely together — not at arm's length — to achieve mutually satisfactory targets.

Too often, deliveries and credit terms indicate that the supplier only "makes to order." Yet it is an accepted fact that local availability of stock is a key to successful business. Is it not reasonable for suppliers to assist with financing, to increase stock to a level which ensures a continuous on-the-spot delivery service? Would it be outrageous for the supplier to keep stock of his own in the kingdom?

Local in-depth product expertise is not easy to find, nor is it reasonable to expect it. It makes sense for manufacturers to supply their own qualified employees by arrangement or secondment, but always working through the agent and enhancing the identity of the two in clients' eyes. The additional expenditure — over and above hotel bills and airline tickets — is limited, but the benefits considerable. There is no substitute for on-the-spot experts who will absorb the local atmosphere. Apart from their constant presence, which indicates commitment, they are able to keep abreast of changes in legislation as well as market developments, and not learn half the story during their next visit.

They are also able to boost the agent's confidence and help with training sales representatives, thus increasing general effectiveness and efficiency with on-the-spot customer service. They will become familiar faces, which gives added strength in a part of the world where clients prefer to deal with the same person regularly.

Choosing your man

Whether you decide on a resident or pursue the market with visitors, choosing your man is as important as selection of the agent. You either try to find people who know their way round the market, with a view to teaching them the product, or choose an expert and try to teach him the country. If the latter, it is worth sending him to visit the kingdom before making a final commitment. Above all you must find an expert who is prepared to learn, accept and adjust to the environment in which he is working.

Legislation does not make it easy to find a combination of the two, as it is not possible to transfer from one company to another without the previous employer's agreement.

A man who knows the products can be effective immediately and it should be possible to find someone in "home sales" who can adapt to the local environment. However, it is not always possible for a resident to begin with married status.

The most effective results will come from hungry young sales representatives who know their product, see the potential, and will get on with selling it alongside their Arab colleagues. It is perhaps worthwhile, therefore, for suppliers with companies around the world to consider candidates from these, as well as the product's point of supply.

Whether or not a resident is appointed or seconded, it is sensible to run training courses for your agent's sales staff. This applies particularly where equipment servicing is involved, for only in this way will you obtain the user's full confidence in your distributor's product knowledge. The most successful suppliers are those who show local customers that their agents are an extension of themselves, and that they can get as much information and back-up locally as by going direct.

At the same time it is essential that the supplier gives support through visits to the kingdom. Again, it is best to use the same person regularly as it enables him to become self-sufficient, in that he can find his own way round the market and, in effect, becomes an additional selling arm, rather than having to go everywhere with a local salesman. However, his visits must be co-ordinated and he must identify himself with the agent. All quotations to the market — whether fob, cif or ex-local stock — should only be presented by or through the agent.

One complaint often made by suppliers against their agents is that they are spread too thin, with too many lines being handled by not enough staff. It is easy to blame lack of success on the agent's apparent inefficiency, but an understaffed export department can have worse repercussions — especially when dealing with the world — if the left hand seems unaware of what the right one is doing.

Proper understanding of the market and its potential is essential. Suppliers are there to help or give constructive criticism, but they should recognise their own limitations. Irregular brief and breezy visits by someone demanding full attention and in a hurry to move on to the next port of call are not appreciated and are often counterproductive.

On the paperwork side it is helpful — and avoids duplication — if a two-way feedback or reporting system is established. Again, however, you must recognise probable local staff limitations. If everything is directed through the Saudi agent with a seconded resident this helps reduce unnecessary repetition.

Keeping standards in mind

In terms of technical back-up, you must remember that US standards and specifications predominate in Saudi Arabia, as do those of the UK, West Germany and Japan. These are in addition to an increasing number of Saudi standards, which are based on a combination of them all.

Too few manufacturers seem to recognise the importance of producing certificates and evidence proving their goods do meet specifications other than those of the country of origin. Those who make the effort, and the investment, have a far easier opening into the market. Users simply do not want the time-consuming problem of trying to show one specification is as good as another, and a manufacturer who can prove the product meets both is usually on to a winner. Suppliers from the Far East are generally more flexible in this than those from the West. Equally, some of the most successful companies are those who have produced a product not usually in their standard range specifically to

Abdullah al-Hudaithi, Deputy General Manager, MABCO Prefabricated Building Co

Middle East requirements. This is in contrast to those who believe that because a product sells in Europe it must sell in Saudi Arabia. Research and development should stretch beyond home shores.

The same principle can apply to packaging. It is all very well to sell by the container load, but suppliers must also consider handling and storage at the Saudi end. A product's appearance is important, and suppliers must recognise the problems involved in handling goods, often with limited equipment, which have to be distributed around the kingdom before sale to the consumer. This is in addition to the compulsory removal of the container at the port of entry.

The way ahead

Although free trade, rather than import substitution, is still the basis of business, increasing emphasis is being placed on local manufacture. This is particularly true of the construction industry, where many government contracts stipulate that priority must be given to locally produced materials.

Saudi Cement Company

22 Years in Production & Marketing

A new Extension to Boost Production
to
2.3 MILLION TONS A YEAR
Reflects SCC's increasing contribution
to
National Economy Towards
SELF SUFFICIENCY

TYPES OF QUALITY CEMENT PRODUCED:
- High sulphate resisting type V
- High sulphate resisting with high compressive strength type I/V
- Moderate sulphate resisting and moderate heat of hydration type II
- Moderate sulphate resisting and low heat of hydration type IV
- Rapid hardening ASTM type III
- Oil well cement

For further information and enquiries from Saudi Arabia & GCC States, please contact:
Saudi Cement Company's Head Office (Marketing Department) Dammam/Saudi Arabia.
Telephone: 83-25177 or 83-25179. Telex: 601068 CEMENT SJ. P.O. Box 306

مصنع لوحات التوزيع الكهربائية (حوا)

(المنطقة الصناعية ـ الدمام) الخبر ص.ب: 398 ـ المملكة العربية السعودية
تلكس: 602200 EPBF SJ   تلفون: 8570612/8573720 /8571196

ELECTRIC PANEL BOARD FACTORY (HAWA)

BRANCH
(INDUSTRIAL AREA-DAMMAM) P.O. BOX 398, AL-KHOBAR
KINGDOM OF SAUDI ARABIA. TELEPHONE: 8573720, 8571196 and 8570612
Telex: 602200 EPBF SJ

Import duties are levied on foreign-made goods and, while not punitive at present, the machinery exists to give greater protection to local industry. So it is worthwhile for foreign manufacturers to consider some form of "break bulk" operation. It will also be found that Saudi traders will want increasingly to identify themselves with locally made products. Should manufacture be decided on, the ideal is to choose a partner who has his own distribution network, to avoid possible conflict on where the profit is made.

After materials produced in the kingdom, priority is given to purchasing through a local company. Direct buying is openly discouraged and will eventually be stamped out — it is only a matter of time before existing legislation is enforced. The equipment and machinery sectors are particular targets: the government is determined to remove suppliers whose products do not have adequate spare parts and proper servicing facilities.

The main areas for development will probably be in high technology and downstream petrochemicals. Emphasis is also being placed on agriculture. Maintenance and services will always be needed while there is also considerable scope in the world of advertising and promotion, previously surprisingly limited. As in all countries with emphasis on fitness and youth welfare, there are wide opportunities in the sports industry; these range from coaching and equipment to building playing surfaces. There is also a sizable demand for medical and dental equipment for many hospitals being built or just completed.

Once established, doing business in Saudi Arabia is really no different from doing it anywhere else. The right product, at the right price, with the best customer service, rarely fails. Hard work always pays dividends and the secret of success lies in proper and in-depth preparation.

However, because of the scale of potential business, the cultural and environmental differences, and the country's geography, it may take longer than elsewhere to establish the correct approach. Having chosen your partner, it is vital to work together and give thorough back-up in all aspects of the business to ensure absolute trust and consequent mutual success. To quote an eminent government minister: "Commitment has to be in the heart; if you wish to, you can find a way. If intention is there, you will succeed."

But to do this you must identify yourself with your Saudi partner — you cannot do it alone.

Courier services

SNAS Worldwide Courier in association with **DHL**

Worldwide courier service for door-to-door shipment of documents and small parcels (150 locations in 60 countries). Overnight service to and from Europe; 48 hours between Saudi Arabia and the US. Service includes pick-up, transport, customs clearance and delivery at destination.

Charges: handling fee — SR 1,000 a month maximum or SR 200 a shipment; weight rates from Saudi Arabia: Gulf locations — SR 50 per half kilo; London — SR 50; Europe/Near East — SR 60; all other DHL locations — SR 70. SPX surcharge per shipment — SR 135 (see regions for local details).

Skypak

Worldwide courier service for shipment of documents and parcels.

Charges: handling fee — SR 875 a month membership fee and SR 175 maximum per consignment; weight rates from Saudi Arabia per half kilo: Middle East — SR 43; London — SR 43; Europe — SR 53; US/Australasia/Far East — SR 63 (see regions for local details).

World Courier Service Contact Bandar Agencies, tel: 6655647. PO Box 2682, Jeddah, telex: 401480 khaldi.

Provides 24 to 48-hour desk-to-desk delivery to nearly every part of Europe and the US. Material is collected at end of business day and forwarded on first available direct flight; also en route shipments. Guarantees delivery time and confirmation of delivery. Represented in more than 100 countries. Also industrial courier for spare parts, tools, samples, and so on (see regions for local details).

Exporter's checklist

To export goods to Saudi Arabia the following documents are required: commercial invoice, certificate of origin, bill of lading (or airway bill), packing list, insurance certificate (if applicable), shipping certificate. Much of the following will be undertaken by your clearing agent in the kingdom.

Commercial invoice — five copies required. Three must be certified by a chamber of commerce as to current prices; two must be certified by a Saudi consular office in the country of origin; three more copies of invoices are required in Arabic. Exports from the UK must also be certified by the Arab-British Chamber of Commerce and from the US by the Arab Chamber of Commerce, Washington.

The commercial invoice must include a complete description of all merchandise, trademarks, volume, weight and price of each item. It must also list contents of each container, all relevant expenses and discounts, the names and addresses of consignors and consignees and a statement that each product was manufactured in, or originated in, the country from which it is being exported.

Certificate of origin — five copies are required; they must be certified by a chamber of commerce and legalised by a Saudi consular office. Both will retain a copy.

The certificate must describe the place of origin of the goods, the name and address of the manufacturer and, if relevant, the name of the ship and its sailing schedule. If foreign components are included in the product to be shipped, the certificate must specify the name, address and country of origin of the components' manufacturers.

Bill of lading — take care to see this is complete. The name, address and telephone number of the consignee must be included, as must such information as weight, volume, and measurement. A certificate is essential to prove that the ship carrying the goods is not on the Arab Boycott of Israel list.

Packing list — must be included in the consignment. It must give accurate descriptions of the contents, with full dimensions, gross and net weights, and cif value. All measurements must be metric and signatures handwritten.

Insurance certificate — must contain the name, office address and country of incorporation of the insurance carrier. It must also include the name and address of the company's Saudi agent or representative. This must be in notarised form.

Shipping certificate — showing the nationality of the vessel and its owner must accompany the bill of lading. It must also contain a notarised declaration stating that the ship is not owned by Israeli nationals or residents; it is neither registered in, nor in passage for Israel; the ship is in every way eligible to enter Saudi ports in conformity with all relevant laws.

Letters of credit — a new memorandum concerning the opening of letters of credit (LCs) was endorsed by the then Crown Prince Fahd in 1978 (corresponding to 14.8.1397 AH). Complaints from merchants and Saudi corporations over ambiguities in opening LCs and lack of agreement when translating the original LC decision (28.8.1386 AH) into English led to new procedures being laid down.

A copy of this agreement was published in Middle East Executive Reports (see Bibliography) vol 1 number 2, November 1978.

Doing business

Price quotations

Prices are usually quoted cif Jeddah, Dammam or Riyadh (dry port), although an increasing number of Saudi firms are appointing their own shipping managers and buying fob. Business visitors are often asked for off-the-cuff quotations and should be in a position to provide firm offers.

Payment terms

It is advisable to conduct business with new customers on letter of credit terms, although cash against document terms are also used.

Credit

Sight draft terms are common, but with payment being postponed until the arrival of the goods, this often amounts to 90 days or so. Many better known firms obtain 90, 180, or occasionally, 300 days' sight terms. Demands for two-year credit are growing.

Debt collection

There is no procedure for protesting bills in Sharia (Islamic) law. Disputes on default must be submitted to the Committee for the Settlement of Commercial Disputes but the procedures can be costly and time-consuming.

Commercial agencies decree and regulations

The Commercial Agencies Decree issued on 22 July 1962 stated that only a Saudi individual or 100 per cent Saudi-owned corporations could act as commercial agents. All agents and agency agreements must be registered with the Commerce Ministry.

A royal decree issued in January 1978 governs the relationship between foreign contractors and Saudi agents, while Commerce Ministry resolution no 1987 of 30 March 1981 regulates the relationship between agents and distributors and their principles (excluding contractors).

The Commerce Ministry has issued a specimen contract for the conclusion of a commercial agency agreement. The format is not compulsory. (There are also specimen contracts for service agency and joint-venture agreements.)

Buying seasons

For exporters of consumer goods, the best time for a visit is well ahead of each of the following peak buying seasons:

☐ the pilgrimage (Hajj) season, which lasts about two months beginning about a month before the Eid al-Adha. This is the peak season for merchants in Jeddah, Al-Madinah and Makkah;

☐ Ramadan, the Muslim fasting month, which ends with the Eid al-Fitr holiday. This is the time when Muslims buy new clothes for their families, toys for their children, and furniture for their homes;

☐ the school summer holidays, which begin in June, when thousands of Arab expatriate school teachers leave for their homes, taking with them all kinds of gifts, particularly textiles, small household appliances, and radios and stereo centres.

Civilian employment in Saudi Arabia ('000)

Nationality/sex	1979/80	1984/85*	Net change	Annual growth rate (%)
Saudi men	1,308.4	1,437.4	+129.0	1.9
Non-Saudi men	1,014.9	1,023.9	+9.0	0.2
Total men	*2,323.3*	*2,461.3*	*+138.0*	*1.2*
Saudi women	103.0	120.0	+17.0	3.1
Non-Saudi women	44.9	44.9	—	—
Total women	*147.9*	*164.9*	*+17.0*	*2.2*
Total Saudis	1,411.4	1,557.4	+146.0	1.9
Total non-Saudis	1,059.8	1,068.8	+9.0	0.2
Grand total	**2,471.2**	**2,626.2**	**+155.0**	**1.2**

* Projected

Source: Third Development Plan (1980-85), Ministry of Planning, Saudi Arabia

Saudi Arabia: estimated employment by occupational category

Category	1979/80		1984/85*	
	Employment ('000)	Distribution (%)	Employment ('000)	Distribution (%)
Professional †	240.4	9.7	270.8	10.3
Clerical	231.7	9.4	266.8	10.2
Sales and manual ††	1,076.9	43.6	1,184.9	45.1
Farming and fishing	622.2	25.2	558.0	21.3
Services	300.0	12.1	345.7	13.2
Total	**2,471.2**	**100.0**	**2,626.2**	**100.0**

* Projected

† Including technical, managerial and administrative

†† Including crafts, operators and labourers

Source: Third Development Plan (1980-85), Ministry of Planning, Saudi Arabia

Allkem
ALLKEM CHEMICAL INDUSTRIES CO. LTD,

Offers you the best solution for all your problems in Coating, Painting or Decorating.

ALLKEM manufactures skim coating, fillers and thin plasters delivered in ready-to-use paste form that does not require mixing on site. ALLKEM manufactures as well a full range of textured coatings. By using ALTEK it would be possible for a team of 3 persons with a spray machine to coat 500 square metres of single coat in one day!

FOR MORE DETAILS PLEASE CONTACT:

ALLKEM CHEMICAL INDUSTRIES CO. LTD.

P.O. BOX: 7422, JEDDAH -TEL: 636-1285/637-9029 · TLX: 400574 ALLKEM SJ
P.O. BOX: 6233, RIYADH · TEL: 478-3701 · TLX: 201792.

FOR ITS PROTECTION

THE PEARL HAS ITS SHELL

FOR YOUR PROTECTION

SAUDI PEARL INSURANCE CO. LTD.

GENERAL AGENTS IN SAUDI ARABIA

*KHOBAR	: Tel. (03) 8946616 - 8946828	Telex : 671449 SJ - P.O. Box 809
*RIYADH	: Tel. (01) 4789329 - 4789381	Telex : 202619 SJ - P.O. Box 40997
*JEDDAH	: Tel. (02) 6531084 - 6531628	Telex : 403024 SJ - P.O. Box 742
*JUBAIL	: Tel. (03) 3610308 - 3613524	Telex : 631024 SJ - P.O. Box 30

(Jubail Representatives : KHONAINI INT'L CORP.)

ALL CLASSES OF INSURANCE

Use of Arabic

In 1978 all foreign companies and organisations operating in the kingdom were ordered to correspond with government agencies in Arabic. Companies that repeatedly violate the order can be refused government business for a year and may face heavy fines. The Commerce Ministry has powers to prosecute offenders before the Board for the Settlement of Commercial Disputes.

The Saudi Labour Law

The labour and social insurance legislation (royal decree M-21) issued on 15 November 1969 covers all workers employed under written or oral contracts. Its main provisions are:

☐ Probation periods — three months for monthly paid employees; one month for others.

☐ Working hours — eight hours a day or 48 hours a week except during Ramadan when the maximum is six hours a day or 36 hours a week.

☐ Minimum wages are established by the Labour Office.

☐ Overtime — payable at 150 per cent of the standard rate.

☐ Holidays — 15 days after one year's service, 21 days after three years' service.

☐ Public holidays — these, prescribed by the Labour Ministry, may not exceed 10 days a year.

☐ Sick leave — paid at the full rate for 30 days and at 75 per cent for the next 60 days, if the company employs at least 20 people.

☐ Maternity leave — half pay if the mother has been with the employer one year or more, and full pay if the service period is three years or more.

Incentives for industrial investment

1 Licensing of all new industrial plants, after ensuring the present and projected market is large enough to support the output of a new plant in addition to existing capacity.

2 Once a proposed new industrial plant is licensed, it becomes eligible for:

☐ land in a government industrial estate at an annual cost of SR 0.08 a square metre, with road access, power, water and sewerage installed to the boundaries of the land provided;

☐ financing of up to 50 per cent of total capital, fixed and working, needed to build the plant and put it into operation at an annual service fee of 2 per cent;

☐ duty-free import of necessary equipment and raw materials;

☐ repatriation, at any time, of earnings of a foreign partner participating in the venture or of his original capital invested in that venture, and

☐ a 10-year income tax holiday on earnings by foreign partners in joint ventures.

3 For all licensed industrial plants producing products which are not priced more than 10 per cent higher than similar imported products, and which perform at least 90 per cent as well as similar imports, their products are to be specified for purchase in government purchasing schemes and on government-financed projects where contractors selected to carry out the projects make purchases.

The significance of these investment incentives can be seen in the following example:

Product to be made *small-diameter steel pipe*

Annual capacity *40,000 tons*

Capital investment:
    foreign partner *40 per cent*
    Saudi partner *60 per cent*

Annual return on equity at full capacity:
    with full incentives *46.4 per cent*
    if 50 per cent SIDF funding at 2 per cent is eliminated *34.2 per cent*
    if land had to be bought at SR 50 a square metre *39.8 per cent*
    if duties had to be paid on equipment and raw materials *37.6 per cent*

if taxes had to be paid on foreign partner's income foreign partner *25.5 per cent*
Saudi partner *37.6 per cent*
if all four above incentives were not offered: foreign partners *10.8 per cent*
Saudi partner *46.4 per cent*

Source: Ministry of Industry & Electricity, Riyadh

Qassim Chamber of Commerce in Buraydah

Chambers of commerce and industry

Council of Saudi Chambers of Commerce & Industry Tel: 4054277, 4040044. PO Box 16683, Riyadh Chamber's Building, Al-Dhabab Street, Riyadh. Telex: 201054 tjaryh.

Abha Chamber of Commerce & Industry Tel: 2249480, 2249488. PO Box 722. Telex: 901125. President: Eid Said Abu Milha.

Al-Hasa Chamber of Commerce & Industry Tel: 20458. PO Box 1519, Al-Hofuf. Telex: 661140. President: Nasser Bin Hamad Bin Zaraa.

Dammam Chamber of Commerce & Industry Tel: 8325217-8. PO Box 719, Al-Bureid Street, beside Passport Department. Telex: 601086 ghurfa. President: Fahael Muhammad al-Muajil.

Jeddah Chamber of Commerce & Industry Tel: 6423535, 6424824. PO Box 1264, King Khaled (Al-Mina) Street. Telex: 401069 ghurfa. President: Shaikh Ismail Abu Daoud.

Al-Madinah Chamber of Commerce & Industry Tel: 8225190, 8225380. PO Box 443, Airport Street. Telex: 470009 iccmd. President: Habeeb Mahmoud Ahmad.

Makkah Chamber of Commerce & Industry Tel: 5744202, 5745775. PO Box 1086, Al-Ghazzah Street. Telex: 440011 chamec. President: Salih M Jamal.

Qassim Chamber of Commerce & Industry Tel: 3235436, 3236104. PO Box 444, Buraydah. Intersection of Alwehda and Alamarah streets. Telex: 801060 sinaia. President: Abdullah Yahya al-Shouraida.

Riyadh Chamber of Commerce & Industry Tel: 4040044, 4040300. PO Box 596, Al-Dhabab Street. Telex 201054 tjaryh. President: Mohammad al-Fraih.

Tabuk Chamber of Commerce & Industry PO Box 567. Telex: 881173. President: Abdul-Aziz Muhammad al-Awdah.

Taif Chamber of Commerce & Industry Tel: 7364624. PO Box 1005, Al-Sadad Street. Telex: 451009 ghurfa. President: Awad Bin Sahou al-Otaibi.

Yanbu Chamber of Commerce & Industry Tel: 3224257-8. PO Box 58, King Abdul-Aziz Street. Telex: 461036 ghurfa. President: Abdullah M A Saeidi.

Freight forwarding

A vast number of services are available from steam ship companies to organisations sending goods to and from Saudi Arabia. However, the fact remains that a far higher percentage of freight is moved to the kingdom through forwarding agents than directly through shipping firms.

The most likely reason is that it requires considerable expertise to overcome the problems which arise when dealing with this market. New regulations concerning documents, customs clearance and container loading can all confuse the inexperienced, as can the fluctuation in freight rates. Transport within the kingdom can sometimes prove an even greater complication.

Because of the ever-changing situation, it is essential that anyone who intends dealing with the Saudi market should get expert advice. Several UK forwarding agents employ Europeans based in offices in the kingdom, and have also set up joint ventures with local transport companies and freight forwarders, which can provide a constant flow of information. In general, forwarders are able to spend more time than shipping companies in analysing this information and keeping up to date — a clear benefit to exporters who decide to use a forwarder.

Freight prices are undoubtedly exporters' main concern. Experienced freight forwarders should be aware of virtually every shipping company's services to the area and conversant with available rates, enabling them to negotiate on customers' behalf for the best possible price. The fact

Giant industrial steam generator built by Foster Wheeler Power Products en route for Ras Tanura

that freight forwarders often have bulk purchasing powers also benefits exporters.

It is possible for exporters to expedite their contract through a forwarder, taking advantage of the latter's experience in documentation and knowledge of the market, and to find they are paying little or no more than if they had dealt directly with a shipping company.

Problems in moving freight within the kingdom have largely disappeared in recent years — partly the result of improved infrastructure, and partly because more forwarders and shipping firms have gained the necessary expertise and facilities.

Most well-established forwarders operating services to and from Saudi Arabia can deal with all types of cargo, ranging from suitcases of personal effects to complete factory projects.

Choosing the right forwarder is very important — incorrect selection can prove catastrophic, resulting in delays, demurrage, high storage charges and the penalties which result from late delivery. The cheapest rate is not necessarily the best. A saving on freight charges can prove a false economy when weighed up against the problems that can result from delays.

A large proportion of freight being shipped into Saudi Arabia is containerised. Recent decrees by port authorities allowing in less-than-container loads have increased the benefits of containerisation. However, excellent conventional freight services do exist and may prove advantageous when rules on packing and storing containers are taken into account.

Problems with airfreight have also virtually disappeared in the past few years, with the introduction of new, more sophisticated methods of handling the freight. It is important, however, that you find an airfreight service which will transport the goods direct to destination — if possible without transhipment.

Business events 1983-84

Date	Location	Subject
1983		
February		
February	Al-Gosaibi hotel	Fourth annual motor show
5-9	Jeddah	Middle East electricity and electronics exhibition
6-11	Jeddah	Middle East aviation and ground support exhibition
13-17	Riyadh	Saudi food '83
27-3 March	Jeddah	Water and sewage technology exhibition
March		
March	Al-Gosaibi	Second annual holiday show
16-25	Jeddah	Ideal home and consumer goods show
April		
April	Al-Gosaibi	Fourth annual electric and electronic home appliances show
24-28	Riyadh	Saudi education '83
24-28	Riyadh	Saudi business '83
May		
May	Al-Gosaibi	British health care
October		
October	Al-Gosaibi	Third annual industrial vehicle show
23-27	Riyadh	Saudi build '83
23-27	Jeddah	Saudi safety, security and fire equipment exhibition
November		
November	Al-Gosaibi	Second annual office equipment show

December

December	Al-Gosaibi	Third annual cosmetics exhibition
1-9	Jeddah	Motor show

1984

February

February	Jeddah	Arab Health '84
24-28	Jeddah	Middle East construction exhibition

March

14-23	Jeddah	Ideal home and consumer goods show

October

22-26	Jeddah	Saudi agriculture and fishing exhibition

November

29-7 December	Jeddah	Motor show

For further information contact Al-Dhiafa Exhibition Centre, tel Riyadh 4644475, PO Box 7633, Riyadh, telex 20079

British Pavilion, First Middle East Electricity Exhibition, Jeddah Expo Centre, March 1981

Saudi Arabia: budget allocations
(SR million)

	1983/84	1982/83	1981/82
Defence and security	75,733	92,889	82,533
Transport and communications	24,950	32,532	35,343
Human resources	27,791	31,864	26,248
Municipal facilities	19,070	26,224	26,292
Internal credits	20,000	23,382	24,850
Economic resources	13,209	22,045	22,679
Public administration	(1)	9,480	21,844
Health and social services	13,591	17,010	13,716
Infrastructure	9,583	11,705	14,126
Local subsidies	9,020	11,162	9,100
Miscellaneous	47,053	35,107	21,269
Total	**260,000**	**313,400**	**298,000**
Actual spending		243,652	288,174
Revenue	**225,000**	243,676	na

(1) Figure for public administration amalgamated with all miscellaneous items

Source: Saudi Press Agency

Allocations for development of human resources in 1982/83 budget
(SR million)

	1982/83	1981/82	% change
Education	13,239	9,835	+34.6
General Presidency of Girls' Education	6,738	4,867	+38.4
King Saud university	3,810	3,386	+12.5
King Abdel-Aziz university	1,501	1,392	+7.5
University of Petroleum & Minerals	814	931	−21.6
King Faisal university	834	730	+14.2
Imam Mohammad Ibn-Saud Islamic university	1,139	1,148	−0.8
Al-Madinah Islamic university	382	314	+21.7
Umm al-Qura Islamic university	523	432	+21.1
General Organisation of Education & Vocational Training	1,663	1,701	−2.2
Others	1,221	1,512	−19.2
Total	**31,864**	**26,248**	**+21.4**

Source: Ministry of Finance & National Economy, Riyadh

PART 6   THE REGIONS

THE HEJAZ
(THE WESTERN REGION)

Makkah al-Mukarama

"In the West you see us as an oil state; the country that exists to keep your gas tanks filled. But that is a very modern way of looking at Arabia. It is not how we see ourselves, and it is not how our country is seen by millions of people who share our religion.

"If you want to understand the kingdom you must understand that 1,400 years ago God revealed His Word to the Prophet Muhammad in the Holy Cities of Makkah and Al-Madinah. They are on the other side of Arabia from the oil fields, but they are part of the same country and in our eyes they matter more than anything else. So, if I have to say one thing that this kingdom stands for above all others, it is not oil. It is Islam. One day even we will run out of oil. But we will never run out of Makkah and Al-Madinah."

Ahmad Zaki Yamani

Makkah al-Mukarama, known to believers as Umm al-Qura — Mother of the Villages — is the spiritual centre of the Islamic world, which groups an estimated 800 million people. Five times every day Muslims turn their faces towards this sacred city wherein lies the Ka'aba — a stone house, empty on the inside and covered on the outside by an enormous black cloth with the names of God woven into it and adorned with bands of calligraphy sewn with silk thread dipped in gold. The Ka'aba is now surrounded by an enormous multi-level mosque which can hold about 1 million people. Throughout the day and night pilgrims move around the house, constantly touching the Yamani corner and kissing the black stone. The latter is said to have been white when it fell from heaven but was turned black by the sins of the millions of pilgrims who have touched it through the ages.

According to Islamic tradition, Makkah was founded and established by the Prophet Abraham at the command of God. He was ordered to take his slave woman, Haggar, and their infant son, Ishmael, into the wilderness of the desert. Having done this, he committed them to God's protection. This was one of the many tests imposed by God upon Abraham. In desperation, Haggar ran between the two mountains of Safa and Marwah in search of water for her son. After seven times, she abandoned her search, imploring God to help her. Then from beneath her feet water began to flow. Thus the well of Zam Zam appeared.

The tribe of Jurhum, who lived close to the valley of Makkah, made an oath with Haggar on account of the water which God had provided for Ishmael. From this it seems likely that the place where Haggar lived is the area around Zam Zam. This was formerly called Beer-Sheba, or the Well of the Oath, mentioned in Genesis (chapter 21, verse 14).

After Haggar and Ishmael became established in Makkah, Abraham returned and was commanded by God to build the first House of Unitarian Worship on the earth — the holy Ka'aba. His footprints, worn into the stone from constant standing, have been preserved and can be seen today encased in crystal at the Station of Abraham where he used to pray.

"And when We settled for Abraham the place of the House: 'Thou shall not associate with Me anything. And do thou purify My House for those that shall go about it and those that stand, for those that bow and prostrate themselves; and proclaim among men the Pilgrimage, and they shall come unto thee on foot and upon every lean beast, they shall come from every deep ravine that they may witness things profitable to them and mention God's Name on days well-known over such beasts of the flocks as He has provided them: "So eat thereof, and feed the wretched poor." Let them then finish with their self-neglect and let them fulfil their vows, and go about the Ancient House."

(Quran: XXII)

The Hajj

The sons of Ishmael continued to worship one God and follow the teaching of Abraham and the rites of worship established by him, and Makkah became a place of pilgrimage (hajj). The procession around the house, the prayer at the Station of Abraham, the standing on Arafat and Muzdalafah, and the stoning of the devils in Muna — all parts of the modern Muslim pilgrimage — were established in ancient times by Abraham. As generations passed the people of Makkah forgot the teachings and fell into idolatry. By the time of the birth of Muhammad, the citizens of Makkah — the tribe of Quraysh — had become a thoroughly idolatrous people.

Nevertheless, the rites of pilgrimage established by Abraham were never abandoned, but transformed into vehicles for idolatry. Makkah remained a spiritual centre and a point of pilgrimage for Arabs of the Hejaz. It also became a major trading outpost in the Arabian peninsula. This made the citizens of Makkah a prosperous merchant class, trading with the Yemens, Byzantium and Persia.

The Prophet Muhammad was born the son of Amina and Abdullah Bin-Abdul Muttalib in Makkah in 571 AD.

Aerial view of Makkah

He lived there for about 53 years until his migration to Al-Madinah. At the age of 40 he received a revelation from God establishing him as a prophet for his people and a messenger for the whole of creation. He continued his mission in Makkah until he and his followers were driven out and took refuge in Yathrib, which became known as Al-Madinah. After a series of battles between the Muslims and the Makkan armies, the Quraysh surrendered Makkah to the Muslims without a struggle and all its inhabitants converted to Islam. Makkah has since been an entirely Muslim city, with non-Muslims prohibited from entering. Today, non-Muslims caught within the precincts of Makkah face heavy penalties and deportation.

Pilgrimage to Makkah is the fifth pillar of Islam incumbent once in life upon every adult Muslim who has the means for the journey (see Introduction to Islam). The lesser pilgrimage, Umrah, is also considered of tremendous benefit and blessing, especially during the holy month of Ramadan. The Prophet Muhammad said: "To perform the Umrah in Ramadan is like performing the Hajj with me."

Makkah as a modern city

With the tremendous increase in trade with the outside world, many international companies have found it advantageous to send Muslims, whenever possible, as their representatives to the kingdom. These Muslim businessmen and technicians usually take advantage of their time in Saudi Arabia to visit Makkah and perform the Umrah or — if their timing is right — the Hajj. Many simply take one of the Saptco buses which connect all the cities in the western region with Makkah, while others hire a taxi to take them directly from their hotel to the Holy Mosque. Others, who can spare the time, remain for the weekend — Thursday and Friday — or for a few days after they have completed their business in the kingdom.

The best time to perform the Umrah is between the late evening prayer and the dawn prayer (see Prayer times). Then it is cool and uncrowded and, outside the sacred months, easy to kiss the black stone and to stand at the Door of Multazim.

Late autumn and winter are the best times to visit Makkah. In these months the weather is outstanding — cool in the evenings and early mornings, with a gentle wind rising at daybreak to freshen the air. The days are warm but not hot, occasionally shaded by passing clouds. The Holy Mosque is uncrowded, allowing pilgrims to perform their prayers in a relaxed atmosphere and to appreciate the sublimity of the sacred place. The crowds and pressures of Hajj make this experience more difficult.

There is no way to describe adequately the beauty of the Ka'aba, which has been a centre of worship and pilgrimage for 5,000 years. One non-Muslim expatriate reflecting on this said: "Makkah sure must have good vibrations." When you enter the Mother of the Villages you can feel these vibrations, despite the city's modern appearance. This blessing is what makes Muslims wish to return there again and again.

Like Jeddah in the past decade, Makkah has become a city in the process of massive transformation, although the reasons for Makkah's change are somewhat different from Jeddah's. While Jeddah has become a major international business centre and port city, Makkah has essentially remained the same — the religious centre of Islam and the place of pilgrimage. But with the advent of international air travel, the number of pilgrims has increased dramatically in the past 30 years. At present, the number stands at about 2 million, with unofficial estimates putting the figure at 5 million-plus in the next 20 years. As a result, the city and the surrounding area is subject to increasing strain — strain which exceeds the limits of its infrastructure.

The government has undertaken projects to meet the city's most urgent needs, and to cope with the intense pressure on it and to upgrade existing facilities. An ambitious road and tunnel building project is under way to help relieve the Hajj traffic congestion and ease access to Muna, Muzdalafah and Arafat. A stormwater project has successfully diverted the flood waters which used to plague the city, and by 1984 a SR 1,575 million project to supply drinking water to Makkah by converting saline water is due for completion. Medical facilities, public transport and telephone services are also being upgraded. As a result, aesthetic considerations have, temporarily, become of secondary importance. Tentative attempts have been made to beautify the city by building fountains and shaded sitting and play areas, but these will probably remain on a small scale until the infrastructure has been comprehensively upgraded.

Despite Makkah's small-town feel and the appellation Mother of the Villages, the city has a substantial permanent population of around 500,000. The radical measures necessary to remedy the problems of the Hajj have changed its face dramatically, at the same time affecting those living there.

Thirty years ago Makkah was a homogeneous cluster of white Hejazi-style homes — tall and whitewashed, with ornate wood facades — filling the valley and covering the lower hills around the Holy Mosque. These homes were unusually large to accommodate pilgrims during the months of the Hajj — there were no hotels until recently — which provided residents of Makkah with a source of income. Even in the 1950s these buildings were between 70 and 150 years old, and as the number of pilgrims increased, they were put under more and more strain.

In more usual circumstances, such buildings could be preserved and restored, but the annual punishment they underwent as pilgrims competed for every square metre of space made this impractical, and even dangerous. The owners of many of these homes found that rather than commit themselves to costly repairs, it was easier and far less expensive to demolish their old houses and build new homes with modern plumbing, electrical wiring, spaces for airconditioners, and so on. However, 25 years ago the building materials, labour, and technology available in the kingdom were limited, and many of the buildings constructed then are as structurally unsound as the old Hejazi houses they replaced.

The government has therefore embarked on a programme of demolition that will, on completion, have razed more than 3,000 homes which are considered unsafe or which lie in the path of the tunnel and road systems now being built. Large sections of Shubaikah, Masfalah and most of Ajyad have already been demolished to make way for these road systems or to clear structurally weak buildings.

The Ka'aba

The government has paid property owners handsomely for the land appropriated, which has allowed many residents and businesses to move into outlying districts. As a result of this exodus, the city is becoming decentralised and the perimeters of Makkah are expanding rapidly in all directions.

Air communications
Saudia Tel: reservations 5433333; Bab al-Umrah 5433522; Al-Balad office 5743200, 5743211, 5743222; university office 5589184; Al-Nuzhah office 5433522.
Kuwait Airways Ajyad Street, Ajyad.

Hajjis arriving at Jeddah Airport

Hotels

Hotels are a relatively new phenomenon. Before the dramatic rise in the number of pilgrims in the past 25 years there were none, as pilgrims stayed in the spacious private houses built especially for the purpose.

The pilgrimage is a time when worldly comforts are eschewed and religious observances increased, so visitors are primarily concerned that their accommodation be near the Holy Mosque. Other comforts and services are secondary. The older hotels around the Holy Mosque have all taken a tremendous beating over the years. Still they are — for the most part — pleasant and comfortable enough, although not of five-star quality. They provide relatively inexpensive accommodation in the off-season, decent food and service, and, most important, easy access to the Holy Mosque.

The schedule for hotel restaurants revolves around the prayer timetable. Breakfast is usually served after the dawn prayer, lunch after the noon prayer and supper after the night prayer.

Makkah Intercontinental Tel: 5434455. PO Box 1496, Jeddah Street, Umm al-Joud, seven kilometres from the city centre and 100 kilometres from the new King Abdul-Aziz airport. Telex: 440006, cable: inhotelcor.

Surrounded by lush gardens, the spectacular complex has won the Aga Khan architectural prize. Has 215 air-conditioned rooms and five villas with full room service, laundry and valet.

Shops include news-stand, barbers shop, gift shop and jeweller; has a doctor in residence. It also has a ladies lobby, airline desk, offices and businessman's lounge. In addition, there is a starkly beautiful mosque where all prayers are performed, including the Friday congregational prayer. The conference centre has a main auditorium seating 1,400 and three seminar rooms each holding 150. Simultaneous translation, secretarial services and projection facilities are available. Parking for 300 cars.

In the off season — other than the months of Hajj and Ramadan — a shuttle service is provided between the hotel and the Holy Mosque for all prayers. Special tours are also arranged to holy sites and the Keswa factory, as is a one-day shopping tour of Jeddah. Pilgrims who have pre-booked rooms off-season are met at the airport and are guided through airport formalities by hotel staff. Porterage is

Makkah Intercontinental Hotel

provided, guests are driven directly by bus or limousine from the airport to the hotel, and driven back again at the end of their stay, with all services free.

Savoury international dishes are served in the Tihama restaurant (open 0630-1000, 1230-1500, 1900-2300) and in the family dining room. International specialities are also served in the Al-Zaher Coffee Shop (open 0600-0200) and in the quiet lobby lounge.

Rates: (off season) single SR 345, double SR 448, suite SR 517.50; (in season — 20 Ramadan to 5 Shawwal, and 15 Dhul Qida to end of Dhul Hijjah) add 75 per cent. During this period a 15-day stay is mandatory and must be pre-paid.

Credit cards: American Express, Diners Club, Carte Blanche, Visa, Eurocard, Masterchage.

Khogeer hotel group

Abdul-Aziz Khogeer is one of the most successful of mutawwefs (pilgrim guides). So successful in fact that he is now one of the main hoteliers in the sacred areas, with three large hotels in Makkah (Al-Fateh, Abdul-Aziz Khogeer, Africa) and three in Al-Madinah (Dar As-Salaam, Aqeeq and Abdul-Aziz Khogeer).

Catering mainly for pilgrims from Europe, America and South Africa, he manages to provide an almost completely airconditioned Hajj for his clientele. Only in Arafat do pilgrims need to suffer the heat.

The group's hotels are divided in three classes: A, B and Economy. The one characteristic they share is proximity to the Holy Mosques.

A *Al-Fateh Hotel* Tel: 5431353, 5431242, 5431464. PO Box 274, Al-Malak Street. Telex: 440083 khogeer sj, cable: alfateh hotel.

Charming oriental decor. 111 comfortable airconditioned rooms with private bath, refrigerator, telephone and 24-hour room service.

Barber shop, downstairs meeting room/salon, spacious upstairs lounge and dining room. Restaurant serves continental, Arab and eastern food. Cafeteria open 24 hours for snacks.

Rates: (off season) single SR 150, double SR 195; plus 10% service.

B *Abdul-Aziz Khogeer hotel* Tel: 5435020, 5436331, 5434919. Ajyad Street. Telex: 440083 khogeer sj, cable: khogeer hotel.

286 airconditioned rooms with refrigerator, telephone and 24-hour room service. Directly across from King Abdul-Aziz Gate, the hotel commands a stunning view of the Holy Mosque. Basement restaurant serves continental, Arab and eastern food. Coffee shop has an excellent patisserie, as well as a regular menu.

Rates: (off season) single SR 80, double SR 120; plus 10% service.

Economy
Hotel Africa Tel: 5744166, 5746738. PO Box 501, Bab al-Umrah. Telex: 440083 khogeer sj, cable: aziz khogeer.

128 airconditioned rooms with telephone and refrigerator, 24-hour room service. Cafeteria and dining room.

Rates: (off season) with private bath single SR 55, double SR 85, three-bed SR 95, four-bed SR 110; with shared bath single SR 45, double SR 70, three-bed SR 80, four-bed SR 90.

Seasonal rates are not listed because most hotel space is taken by government-assigned pilgrims in the months of Hajj and by groups during Ramadan. Otherwise add 100%.

The Khogeer group also offers group package tours of Makkah and Al-Madinah at big discounts during the off-season. Tours include all transport, food and accommodation. All UK bookings must be made through the London-based International Travel Company, an affiliate of the Bank of Credit & Commerce International.

Hotel Shobra Tel: 5428240-2. Ajyad Street. Telex: 440112 shobra sj, cable: shobrad.

220 airconditioned rooms with refrigerator, telephone and 24-hour room service. Upstairs restaurant serving continental, Arab and eastern food, and cafeteria serving snacks. Translators available.

Rates: (off season) single SR 115, double SR 150; (in season) SR 350 a room. Rooms must be pre-paid and booked for a 45-day minimum stay during the Hajj.

Makkah Hotel Tel: 5747177. PO Box 372, Bab al-Umrah. Telex: 440111 makkah sj, cable: rizk.

220 airconditioned rooms with refrigerator, telephone, TV and 24-hour room service. Restaurant serving continental, Arab and eastern food. Cafeteria. Comfortable upstairs lounge with view of Holy Mosque. Translators available.

Rates: (off season) single SR 137, double SR 181, suites available (in season) single SR 274, double SR 362. Hajj minimum 45 days prepaid. Ramadan pre-paid reservation must be from 15 Ramadan to 5 Shawwal.

Kaaki Hotel Tel: 5427604-5. Ajyad Street.

145 airconditioned rooms (450 beds) with telephone, refrigerator, and 24-hour room service. Laundry. Information desk and travel service with reservation facilities. Restaurant serving continental, Arab and Turkish food. Four meeting rooms each with a capacity of 150.

Rates: (off season) single SR 80, double SR 120, three-room SR 140, four-room SR 160; (in season) single SR 180, double SR 270, three-room SR 315, four-room SR 360; plus 10% service. Reservations for Hajj and Ramadan must be made two months in advance with a 25% deposit. Hajj minimum 45 days.

Al-Ansar Hotel Tel: 5746634, 5746166, 5742658, 5746725.

5748821. Bab al-Umrah, Shubaikah.
All rooms airconditioned with telephone and refrigerator.

Rates: (off season) with private bath, single SR 80, double SR 120, three-room SR 140, four-room SR 160; shared bath single SR 70, double SR 105, three-room SR 120, four-room SR 140; (in season) add 120%.

Zahrat Makkah Tel: 5749724. Bab al-Umrah.

Al-Safaa Hotel Tel: 5740042. Bab al-Ziyadah.

The Mosque Hotel Tel: 5427720. Al-Hajilah.

Hotel al-Ameen Tel: 5438394. Jayal Street, Ajyad.

Ajyad Forum Hotel (for completion by the time of the Hajj in 1983) Ajyad Street, next to Mount Masafi. When finished, it will be the second five-star hotel in Makkah. Designed with the help of the Intercontinental Hotel Corporation, it will have 400 rooms, including royal suites. Facilities will include TV, radio and close-circuit video, secretarial and translation service, telex and telephone. It will have several restaurants offering international menus, a shopping arcade, a special area for performing ablutions before prayer in every bathroom, facilities for the handicapped, and banqueting rooms seating 400.

Courier service

SNAS-DHL Tel Jeddah 6825826, telex 402559 snascr sj.

Banks

The National Commercial Bank Tel: 5422639. Shaab Ali, Almawlad; Al-Ghazzah branch, tel: 5741404; Otaybiah branch, tel: 5434708; Al-Joumizah branch, tel: 5740646; Shubaikah branch, tel: 5741177.

Arab Bank Tel: 5743455. Al-Ghazzah.

Bank Al-Jazira Tel: 5741649. Al-Ghazzah.

The Saudi French Bank Tel: 5738647, 5738519. Al-Ghazzah.

Albank Alsaudi Alhollandi Tel: 5736379, 5730250. Al-Ghazzah.

Saudi Cairo Bank Tel: 5737153.

Eating out

Al-Lail Mansour Street, Hindawiyyah. Serves Lebanese-style food, chicken and meats cooked over charcoal. Outdoor garden and tables in the rear for men only. Family dining upstairs.

Al-Yusr Jeddah Street, Al-Nuzhah. Directly across from Shopping Centre Establishment. Opened in October 1982, a Thai/Saudi venture run by Muslims from Thailand. Serves continental and Arabic food, Thai dishes and varied ice creams. Excellent service in pleasant wood-panelled dining rooms in a converted mansion. Separate family dining rooms. Prices reasonable with no main course more than SR 35.

Qahwa Umm al-Qura Corner of New and Malak streets, Shubaikah. Possibly one of the best-patronised eating establishments in the world. Directly across from the Holy Mosque in front of the site of the House of the Khalif Uthman. Serves all the traditional Arab pavement food — roast chicken, red rice, shawarma, mattabaq, tea and Indian sweets. Open almost 24 hours a day — very much part of Makkah.

Shopping

"My Lord! Make this (Makkah) a secure region, and provide for its people fruits, for such of them as believe in God and the Last Day"
(Prayer of Abraham. Quran 11:126)

In Makkah, commerce and religion have been intertwined from earliest times, and the marketplace has always surrounded the Holy Mosque. The old market in Makkah has possibly been one of the most consistently prosperous shopping areas in the world.

The high season is — obviously — the months of Hajj and Ramadan. The huge influx of pilgrims during the Hajj creates great demand for the cheap items necessary for performing the pilgrimage and for the stay in Makkah — prayer carpets, blankets, water containers, tea flasks, ready-made Islamic robes, head-coverings, plastic sandals, white towels for ihram — as well as basic foods, bottled water, juices, soft drinks and medicine. And as most of the poorer Muslim states have imposed extremely high import tariffs on luxury and consumer goods, many of the pilgrims from these countries take advantage of the low prices in the kingdom, buying jewellery, watches, clothes and electrical goods which are cheap even by European and US standards.

Ramadan is a time when the spirit of generosity prevails. Enormous sums of money pass into the hands of the poor and disabled and lavish gifts are exchanged. New clothes are traditionally made for the Eid, and during the months preceding the fast tailors do a roaring trade, as do gold merchants and parfumiers. Food shops remain open and full throughout the nights of Ramadan, and the rest of the stores close sometime after midnight.

Much of the immediate area around the Holy Mosque has been taken over by the government for its road and tunnel projects. Consequently, the marketplace is gradually receding and moving out to other parts of the city. The four major shopping areas in the centre are:

Mudaa Market The main shopping area. A honeycomb of shops and stalls, and the last remaining part of the Night Market (Souq al-Lail) where the companions of the Prophet Muhammad had their shops. It extends from the Sa'y (running path between Safa and Marwah), separated from the Holy Mosque by a ring road and flyover along Ghazza Street, to the main post office building.

Almost all basic commodities are sold here — clothes, appliances, watches, household and kitchen goods, perfumes and cosmetics, cloth, toys and foods. There are also major banks and money changers here. The gold market is now moving to new premises across the street, the start of a transformation that will completely alter the large covered market in the next few years. Most of the buildings making up the market are very old. Demolition has begun and will most likely continue until the whole market has been replaced by modern buildings.

Ajyad Market Most of the market disappeared in 1981-82 to make way for the tunnel to Muna and Muzdalafah. The rest is confined to the Ashraf Buildings on Ajyad Street, across from Ajyad hospital.

Most of the shops are cloth, clothing and shoe stores, where prices and styles range from cheap indoor wear from the Far East to very elegant and expensive American and European party clothes. Other shops include a parfumerie, a watchseller, a news-stand, a photographer and three pharmacies.

Little Market (Al-Souq al-Saghir) Shubaikah.

The main food shopping area. A wide footpath winds through tall buildings and wraps its way through two city blocks. It sells grains, fresh and frozen meat and poultry, fresh fruit and vegetables, spices and packaged foods. However, demolition has already begun, and the entire market will probably be razed to the ground.

Marwah Market A ring of shops surrounding the Holy Mosque from just before Bab al-Umrah to Marwah, parallel to Bab Abdul-Salaam Street. The last that remains of the market right next to the Holy Mosque.

These are mostly old-style parfumiers selling essential oils and incense, cloth stalls, gold merchants and religious booksellers.

Other shopping areas

The exodus from the city centre has created new growth areas and also increased the business of others.

Rusaifah A few years ago Rusaifah was a stony wilderness on the outskirts of Makkah, scattered with shanties, and primitive potters' workshops and furnaces. Government development around the Holy Mosque has changed all that. Between Ibn Khaldoon and Jeddah streets, Rusaifah Street is lined on both sides with new shops and showrooms selling mostly luxury items — clothes, shoes, jewellery and perfumes. Several toy stores have recently opened and more shopping centres are near completion. The residential area is behind both sides of the street and extends to the other side of Ibn Khaldoon Street. Several new shopping centres are being built in that area.

Nuzhah Jeddah Street, between the highly visible Bougari mansion and Rusaifah Street. For many years the wealthier district of Makkah, with large villas and mansions along quiet streets. Shopping centres and showrooms are now being opened or are being built along much of the street.

Aziziyah Parallel to Muna and Muzdalafah. It was formerly used by affluent pilgrims who wanted to be near the holy sites and has become the site of Umm al-Qura university. Now many families are building homes in Al-Haud, the new residential area next to Aziziyah, the latter is likely to become the main commercial area in this part of Makkah. A large shopping centre is near completion beyond the university, and several high-rise blocks, including the Fakieh office building, are also under construction.

Umrah On the old Al-Madinah Road. The number of residential buildings is expanding rapidly here, and the area beyond Umrah Mosque, just outside the sacred precincts, is becoming the main industrial and warehousing area near Makkah. Commercial expansion is beginning to follow.

Otaybiah Hejoun Has a wide variety of shops on either side of this busy street. The first mini-shopping mall — the Beyari Centre — opened in December 1982, a charming complex of shops around a fountain. Lifts and a spiral staircase in the centre give access to upper level shops and a roof-top car park. There is also a large market in the basement.

Supermarkets

Shopping Centre Establishment Al-Nuzhah. Opened in December 1982. Spacious well-stocked market with a large delicatessen and meat department. Also has a parfumerie.

At the start of 1983 this was the only establishment which could be termed a supermarket in the American or European sense. However, there are other smaller markets providing a variety of food and other goods. These include:

Ibnul Wadi Shopping Centre Hejoun Street, Otaybiah.
Al-Ghamdi Market Otaybiah Street, Otaybiah.
Beyari Centre Market Otaybiah Street, Otaybiah.
Al-Nakhla Shopping Centre Aziziyah Street, Aziziyah.
Central Aziziyah Market Aziziyah Street, Aziziyah.
Family Centre Market Aziziyah Street, Aziziyah.
Yathrib Mini-Market Corner Ibn Khaldoon and Rusaifah streets.
Bin Goubous for Supplies Rusaifah Street, Rusaifah.
Beiban Stores Beiban Square, Beiban and Al-Rawda Street, Shisha.
Umm al-Qura Market Mansour Street, Hindawiyya.
Marwan's Market Andaluz Street, Otaybiah.

Fruit and vegetables

Vegetable Market (the halaqa) Behind and beside maternity hospital, Jarwal. Offers wide variety of fresh fruit and vegetables in bulk or by the kilo, at low prices. Surrounded by wholesalers selling canned and packaged food and other goods in bulk.

Bread and cakes

Badr Electrical Bakeries Hejoun Street, Otaybiah.

The House of Bread & Sweets Rusaifah Street Rusaifah. Also has a mini-market and delicatessen. Delicious shawarma served at night.

Hanaa-Irianon Al-Rawda Street, Shisha. Jeddah-based patisserie offering excellent biscuits and pastries, and decorated ice cream cakes. Tables and chairs inside.

Hotel Abdul-Aziz Khogeer Coffee Shop Ajyad Street, Ajyad. Excellent cakes served. Special party cakes made to order.

Meat

Meat is available in all markets and some corner grocers. The best place to buy it is still the *Little Market* near the Holy Mosque. European cuts of meat are not available in Makkah. Beef usually sells for SR 20 a kilo (22 in some markets) and lamb at SR 25. Imported meat from Turkey, when available, is SR 14 a kilo.

Bulk frozen meat and poultry can be bought from *Modern Cold Stores* on Hejoun Street, Otaybiah and Umrah Street, Umrah, or from *Nawari Cold Stores* on the Al-Madinah Road in Umrah.

Dry cleaners

Zuhour Cleaners Mansour Street, Hindawiyya.

Al-Faten Automatic Cleaners Hejoun Street, Otaybiah. Both companies' service includes carpet cleaning. Service usually takes three to five days.

Medical

King Abdul-Aziz Hospital. Tel: 5421633. Al-Zahir Street.

Ajyad Hospital Tel: 5426166. In front of Holy Mosque on Ajyad Street.

King Faisal Hospital Tel: 5566470. Shisha.

Emergency Hospital Tel: 5564378. Muna.

Maternity Hospital Tel: 5424802. Jarwal, Abdul-Wahhab Street.

Saudi National Hospital Tel: 5562170. Aziziyah.

Doctor Ahmad Zahir Hospital Tel: 5436569. Al-Nuzhah. Private.

Entertainment

Makkah's religious character means public entertainment is discouraged. Weddings, a favourite form of socialising, are held either in hotels or private homes decorated with strings of lights. The Inter-Continental hotel is often used on these occasions, as is Al-Zahir gardens, a favourite amusement park.

Amusement parks

Al-Zahir Gardens Zahir Street, Al-Zahir. A wonderful amusement park surrounded by trees, and dotted with hedges and coloured lights. Many rides including a ferris wheel, roller coaster and merry-go-round. Cafeteria and snack bar. Admission SR 2; rides SR 2-3. Open all week from 1600-2130 (women Wednesday, Thursday and Friday; men Saturday, Sunday, Monday and Tuesday).

Ahmad M Baqadir Park End of Mansour Street, Masfalah. Has an enormous illuminated ferris wheel which can be seen miles away. Many rides. Cafeteria and ice cream parlour. Admission SR 2; rides SR 2-3. Open all week from 1600-2130 (women Wednesday, Thursday and Friday; men Saturday, Sunday, Monday and Tuesday).

Places of interest

Makkah's entire history has been bound up with religion, centred around the Holy Ka'aba. There are other sites which are of historic and contemporary interest to visitors, if only to let them find their historical bearings in a city which is much changed. Most historic sites are not marked and must be discovered with a map and the help of local residents.

Mountain of Light (Jabal al-Nur) The mountain where the Prophet Muhammad would retreat during the sacred month of Ramadan for fasting and contemplative prayer and where, in the cave of Hira, he received his first revelation from God through the angel Gabriel. It can be reached either from Al-Sail or Al-Ashure roads.

The striking peak is visible from afar but it is best to ask for directions from the main roads. While the climb to the top is arduous and takes about two hours, the view is spectacular. The Holy Mosque is clearly visible and, when illuminated in the early morning and at dusk, looks like a majestic ship at sea. A surprising number of pilgrims undertake the rigours of the climb, especially during the months of Hajj and Ramadan.

Plain of Arafat The plain where all pilgrims gather for the most important day of the pilgrimage. The Prophet Muhammad said: "Hajj *is* Arafat," and if you have stood on Arafat on that day, then you have made the Hajj. The area includes the Mountain of Mercy (Jabal al-Rahma), where the Prophet Muhammad delivered his sermon during the last pilgrimage. The extensive and well-marked roadways provide easy access to Arafat, and the entire area is well-lit. Off season many local residents picnic there, or simply go out to enjoy the desert air.

House of Abdullah Bin Abdul Muttalib The house where the Prophet Muhammad was born, and now the modest Makkah library. On the circular road just beyond the parking structure on the Safa-Marwah side of the Holy Mosque.

Hajjis and tents on the Plain of Arafat

House of Khadija Bint Khuwailid The house of the first and most beloved wife of Muhammad. It is where he spent the first 20 years of his married life and from where the teaching of Islam was intially spread. Amid the Mudaa Market in Al-Qushashiyyah.

House of Uthman Bin Affan The house of the third Khalifa of Islam. Directly behind the Umm al-Qura hotel in Shubaikah. Now the Algerian pilgrims' hostel.

House of Ali Bin Abu Talib The house of the nephew and son-in-law of Muhammad — he was married to his favourite daughter, Fatima Zahra — and the fourth Khalifa of Islam. In the historic Souq al-Lail (Night Market) area.

House of Argam The house where Muhammad taught many of the early Muslims and where the second Khalifa, Omar Bin al-Khattab, became a Muslim. On the Mount of Safa across from the new tunnels beneath the royal palace and now incorporated into the Holy Mosque.

House of Abu Sufyan One of the greatest enemies of Islam who, on the conquest of Makkah, became a Muslim and was thereafter one of its strongest supporters. Between the site of Khadija Bint Khuwailid's house and the Farouk Kogir hotel near Mount Marwah.

Ain Zubaydah The well dug under the supervision of Zubaydah, the wife of the Khalifa of Baghdad, Harun al-Rashid, who undertook to supply the pilgrims with water along the routes from Baghdad to Makkah. Still in use. On Rusaifah Street near Jeddah Street.

Royal palace Newly built on the Mount of Safa overlooking the Holy Mosque. Its massive marble facade can be seen from every part of the city centre.

Ajyad castle The Turkish fort is one of the oldest buildings in Makkah, a reminder of a bygone era. Perched on a mountain overlooking Ajyad Street, directly above the circular road tunnels now being built.

Holy Mosque Library An ornate building, in the architectural style of the Holy Mosque, which, when completed, will be the home of the enormous mosque library. Directly across from the main King Abdul-Aziz Gate.

Keswa Factory This is where the covering for the Ka'aba is handwoven and embroidered. On Jeddah Street. Visits must be pre-arranged.

Maps
These are very useful to have around when visiting Makkah. The cartography improves with each new one.
1982-83 map By Zaki Farsi, published by Tihama, and the best so far. Tel: 6659871, 6675441. PO Box 7114, Jeddah. Telex: 402949 zfarsi sj.
1981 map by Hussain Bindagi, cartography by Oxford University Press. Tel: 6674375. PO Box 8003, Jeddah.
Ministry of Information map by Saudimap/Hassam Establishment, Boogaerts & Associates Architects & Engineers. PO Box 5002, Riyadh.

Al-Madinah (Al-Madinah al-Munawwara — The Illuminated City)

Al-Madinah, the second holiest city in Islam after Makkah, played a role in early Islamic history of almost as great a significance as Makkah itself. It was to Al-Madinah that the Prophet Muhammad and his Ansar (followers) made the Hijra or Migration in July to September of the year 622 AD.

At that time Al-Madinah was enduring inter-tribal conflict. When the Al-Madinans heard of the Prophet's call to the pagan Makkans to submit to the One True God and of the persecution that he and his followers were suffering at the hands of the Makkan merchants, they decided to ask Muhammad to live in Al-Madinah to arbitrate in their affairs. Their request implied their own agreement to submit (Islam) and to replace their paganism with recognition of the Unity of God.

The Islamic era (see Islamic calendar) begins on the first day of the year in which the Hijra took place, 16 July 622 AD. When the Prophet, in pursuance of the Ansar, arrived in Al-Madinah in September of that year, there was a symbolic incident when he selected his abode in such a way so as to avoid suggestions of favouritism. The Prophet's camel was let loose and at the house before which it crouched, there the Prophet made his home.

Al-Madinah is about 425 kilometres from Jeddah and 447 kilometres from Makkah. The trip the pilgrim makes to Al-Madinah takes him through the history of early Islam. As he approaches from the Red Sea he comes to Badr, a village where the Muslims won their first battle against the pagan Makkans.

After Badr he winds through wind-weathered hills to Kuba on Al-Madinah's outskirts where the Prophet's Mosque, a simple white-washed building, stands. On the far side of Al-Madinah opposite Kuba is the red rock of Mount Uhud dominating the palm groves which stretch along the watercourse at the foot of the mountains. It was at the Battle of Uhud that the tiny Muslim army was defeated by the Makkans but survived to defeat them at the Battle of the Khandaq (Ditch) two years later. On the outskirts of Al-Madinah stands the Mosque of Victory (Masjid al-Fatah) built to mark the place where the Prophet prayed for victory.

The Prophet's Mosque inside Al-Madinah is a low brick enclosure with elegant minarets, pointed arches and a bright courtyard. It was here that Abu Bakr, the Prophet's closest companion and the first of the Khalifas after his death, announced to the grieving Muslims on Muhammad's death: "Oh men, if anyone worships Muhammad, let him know that Muhammad is dead. But he who worships God let him know that God is living and undying." In the mosque — where the pilgrim intones the Unity sura of the Quran — lie the tomb chambers of the Prophet and of the first two Khalifas, Abu Bakr and Omar.

Access to non-Muslims

Access to the city of Al-Madinah, as to Makkah, is forbidden to non-Muslims. However, both Al-Madinah airport, 20 kilometres outside the city limits, and the Sheraton (see Hotels) are accessible. Meetings between Madinan businessmen and non-Muslim foreigners regularly take place in both.

Hotels

Al-Madinah Sheraton Hotel Tel 8230240. PO Box 1735, Sultanah Road, Sultanah, on the outskirts of the city near the airport. Telex 470076.

192 rooms including eight royal suites and 24 deluxe suites with fridge, colour TV, video and direct-dial telephone; 24-hour room service.

Built as four square wings connecting to a central dome with inside gardens, fountains and a mosque. Business facilities include conference room, two function rooms, banqueting hall and meeting rooms. Shopping arcade, sauna, health club, terrace and lounges.

The Sultanah and Alrouchan restaurants serve Arab and international food, and are open all day.

Rates: single SR 300, double SR 390, suite SR 450, royal suite SR 2,200; plus 15% service.

Credit cards: American Express, Diners Club, Visa.

Al-Nakheel Hotel Tel: 8232135; Telex: 470245 naksm sj.
Rates: single SR 200, double SR 260, suite SR 300; plus 15% service.

Al-Rihab Tel: 8235600. Telex: 470025 marheb sj.
Rates: single SR 200, double SR 260, suite SR 300; plus 15% service.

Bahauddin New Hotel Tel: 8233051. Telex: 470029 bhamed sj.
Rates: single SR 80, double SR 120; plus 10% service.

Al-Haram Hotel Tel: 8223201. Telex: 470050 haram sj.
Rates: single SR 137, double SR 181; plus 15% service.

Air communications (domestic)

The airport is to be expanded to cope with more pilgrims. Direct daily flights to Jeddah, Riyadh, Abha and Gizan; direct twice-weekly flights to most other cities.

Saudia Tel: reservations 8233333; passenger services 8231463; cargo services 8235572. PO Box 6710, King Abdul-Aziz Street.

Local transport

The city is accessible from the airport either by public transport, limousine or taxi service. However, the public transport bus does not serve the Sheraton hotel.

Chamber of Commerce

Al-Madinah Chamber of Commerce &
Industry Tel: 8225190, 8225380. PO Box 443, Al-Madinah. Telex: 470009 iccmed sj.

Medical

Hospitals

Al-Malek Hospital Tel: 25737, 25221, 25226. Bab Ashami. Director: Ibrahim Hussain Zalli. 256 beds. 45 GPs, 41 specialists, 128 nurses.

Inpatients' department: general surgery, intensive care, emergency care, blood bank, pharmacy, orthopaedic surgery, internal medicine, radiology and laboratory. Outpatients: surgery, pharmacy, cardiology, orthopaedics, diabetes, dermatology, urology, ear, nose and throat and dental.

Maternity & Paediatrics Hospital Tel: 29122, 25406, 28122. Bab Alkomah. Director: Mohammed Hassan Kafi. 195 beds. 46 doctors, 90 nurses.

Inpatients: accident and emergency, gynaecology and obstetrics, major and minor surgery, paediatrics, incubators and laboratory. Outpatients: accident and emergency, gynaecology and obstetrics, paediatrics, dental, radiology and ultrasound.

Psychiatric Hospital & Clinic Tel: 27509. Sultan Street. Director: Jamaliddin Abdul-Aziz Hassan Bilal. 36 beds. 4 GPs, 25 nurses.

Inpatients: pharmacy, shock therapy, radiology, EEG and laboratory. Outpatients: social and psychological research, emergency.

Pakistani Hospital Tel: 34884. PO Box 221, Sihaimi Street. 4 beds. 1 doctor, 2 nurses.

Inpatients: clinic.

Jeddah

The beautification programme which got under way in 1980 has utterly transformed Jeddah. In addition, the naming of streets and the application of address zip codes in late 1982 have made communications easier. With the opening of the massive and exquisite King Abdul-Aziz international airport in 1981, and the introduction of courtesy buses between the airport and most major hotels, visiting Jeddah is no longer the battle many visiting businessmen will remember from the early and mid-1970s.

For residents, particularly women, the problem of shopping has been considerably eased by the proliferation of huge shopping malls. These are now a feature of modern Jeddah. The Jeddah International Market beyond the Tahliyah flyover on Al-Madinah Road and the immense Middle East Centre on Palestine Road which was opened in mid-1983 have made it possible for expatriates to cocoon themselves from the social constraints of Saudi Arabian life, if they so wish.

"After their wearing time among the hostile Arabs in Egypt, they encountered to their astonishment in Djidda a population disposed to be friendly to them. For the first time they were able to walk about the streets and visit the coffee houses as they felt inclined without being in any way molested. The Arabs did not regard the presence of Europeans in Djidda as an insult, as they had done in Egypt, even though they did not know them so well. Highborn and lowly were equally courteous, equally curious" (Arabia Felix, by Thorkild Hasen — an account of a journey made to Arabia in 1861).

Dramatic urban expansion

Sprawling across 350 square kilometres in the narrow coastal plain between the Red Sea and the Hejaz mountains, Jeddah's growth has exceeded expectations. By mid-1982 the population had risen to about 1.2 million from little more than 300,000 at the beginning of the 1970s. This compares with an original 1982 target of 1 million. A revised masterplan for the city prepared by Sert Jackson of the US estimates a population of about 1.6 million by 1990 and 2.5 million by 2000.

Pressures

Many of the newcomers have come from the countryside, lured by the prospects of well-paid government jobs and better services. However, the majority of Jeddah's inhabitants — at least 60 per cent — are foreigners, as a casual examination of the main streets at rush hour will confirm.

This phenomenal increase in population has put massive pressure on Jeddah's infrastructure, despite heroic efforts by the municipality to keep pace with the spread of the city's boundaries. A skeleton of roads has been laid, but mains water and connections with the central sewerage system have lagged behind Jeddah's growth. For at least the next five years, new roads will be torn up to install such essential services.

The municipality's first task is to improve the city's road network which is frequently overloaded and congested. About 75 per cent of the SR 1,900 million ($550 million) of the municipality's 1982/83 project budget was allocated to road-building, new flyovers, pavements and street-lighting.

Figuring prominently in the 1982/83 budget are improvements in stormwater drainage, shore protection, urban beautification and new municipality buildings to replace the overcrowded office complex in the city's northeast. The programme to make the city attractive, including a massive tree-planting scheme, will

Jeddah is now a bustling city wreathed with ring roads and flyovers

absorb about SR 1,000 million ($ 290 million) in 1982 and 1983.

One of the biggest projects will be the development of the site of the former Jeddah international airport. Plans are being drafted for a comprehensive programme, including major commercial projects. No new public housing programmes are in the pipeline. The massive tower block completed for the Public Works & Housing Ministry close to the old airport in the late 1970s remains unoccupied because the locals prefer villa-style housing. Jeddah does not have a shortage of homes, but the quality is generally poor.

Jeddah should continue to be one of the biggest consumers of state funds allocated to municipal development throughout the 1980s. In May 1982 municipal officials were awaiting government reaction to Jeddah's request for approval of a spending programme of SR 14,000 million ($ 4,057 million) at constant prices for 1985/86-1989/90. This would represent a substantial increase in disbursements in the city over the previous two five-year plan periods.

Preserving old Jeddah

The municipality's overall objective for the 1980s is to turn Jeddah into one of the Arabian peninsula's most attractive cities and the government is prepared for massive investment to meet this objective. One of the priorities is the preservation of ancient Jeddah — once enclosed by a city wall and now hemmed in by the tower blocks of the Corniche commercial district.

Early in 1982 Jeddah's outspoken and ambitious mayor, Mohammad Said Farsi, gave the city's landlords 18 months to paint all their buildings white or clad them in white marble. To provide a splash of colour, all the city's public cleaning vehicles are painted turquoise, reflecting the colour of the Red Sea.

The area of central Jeddah containing beautiful, coral-ragged Ottoman buildings such as the famous Nassif House with its latticed balconies has been immaculately renovated. Some of the buildings have been whitewashed and the streets are neatly paved, giving the air of a tourist town in southern Spain. This gives access to the area to all, including clients for the many small shops and westerners seeking the exotic and the calm after a hard day's work. With its benches, pretty street lamps and small flower gardens, it is an exciting place to wander at night.

Developing leisure facilities

Jeddah is to get more leisure facilities. Early in 1982, the then Crown Prince Fahd approved a project for two artificial islands, which would include restaurants and a racetrack. A water tower with a revolving section containing a restaurant and other leisure facilities has been designed for the Corniche.

The private sector has contributed to Jeddah's development primarily by building villas, hotels and large commercial centres. By early 1983 three new first-class hotels — an Inter-Continental, Marriott and Holiday Inn — had opened in Jeddah, adding an extra 1,200-1,300 hotel rooms to a market showing signs of overcapacity. Jeddah already has four first-class hotels: Hyatt Regency, Sheraton, Meridien and Nova Park.

Part of the impetus behind the municipality's ambitious plans stems from the growing competition between Jeddah and Riyadh for the unofficial title of Saudi Arabia's leading city. The capital's growing importance will be underlined in the mid-1980s when Jeddah's huge community of diplomats moves to Riyadh. Nevertheless, the port and dockyard, the new international airport, the university and other prestige projects should sustain Jeddah's key role in the kingdom's economy. "Competition among different municipalities is very intense," says one senior Jeddah official. "But we feel we will continue to be a priority for the government because of our activities, new projects and forward-thinking."

Jeddah's Geneva Fountain

Jeddah's Corniche area

The Saudis aim to make the Corniche one of the most glamorous in the world. Between the Manaqabah lagoon opposite the Foreign Affairs Ministry and Palestine Road, the coastal area has been dredged. Trees have been planted and a low wall and lamps now dominate the shoreline. Driving along the Corniche by night is a stimulating experience. Coming from the lagoon you pass on your left the famous "Geneva" fountain which soars from a mabkharah (incense-burner), a massive sheet of water like a hazy white broom switch spreading into the night sky. The two ships anchored nearby are owned by Greek Petrola, which donated the fountain to the kingdom. In the evenings the Corniche has the air of England's Brighton with families sitting along the shore and brightly-painted ice cream vans doing a lively trade. Three of the kingdom's most magnificent hotels (see above) — the Inter-Continental, the Holiday Inn and the Ramada — as well as the famous Dolfin fish restaurant are located on the other side of Corniche Road from the fountain and the boats.

Jeddah's fairgrounds

Jeddah's first amusement park, the Luna park on Palestine Road near the Nova Park hotel, contains a giant wheel for adults, swings, bomber cars, baby karts and video games. The company is now preparing another such park between Obhur and Al-Hamra on the lines of Disney Land. Total investment is expected to be about SR 20 million ($5.8 million), according to Luna Park's managing director Adnan Doughan. Another park opened in July 1982 near the Hamra Guest Palace at Jezirat al-Afra on the Corniche. This offers a water sport known as "Bum Bum Boats," imported from the US. Other facilities include a giant wheel, autoscooters, aeroplanes, jostlers and a mirror house.

The Creek (see also below)

The route to the Creek has been made somewhat complicated by all the dredging work — which has absorbed some 50 yards of the water for much of the way — and by the fact that the road, which was well-surfaced in places, petered out into track elsewhere (July 1982). You can still see beach villas with their small piers isolated on the right-hand side of the road. On the northern side of the Creek you pass the Attas hotel and a little further the Movenpick al-Bilad hotel. Soon you reach the wooden villas of the Creek which, on Fridays, is the social centre of expatriate society and an environment in which sea-sports skills can be practised. All sports enthusiasts head there. Small sailing boats, Lasers and Sunfish, and hundreds of sail-boards tack around the blue waters desperately making way for the big, noisy motor boats that roar through the waters. Some of the speed boats pull water-skiers behind them.

Snorkellers mill with bathers on the small pier heads at the end of each group of chalets. Enough of the reef is close to the surface to make snorkelling exciting and pleasurable but Scuba divers maintain that the real delights of underwater and coral life can only be enjoyed with the help of air tanks and at depths of more than 100 feet (see Sea Sports).

Sailing race in Jeddah's North Creek

Ministries in Jeddah

Foreign Affairs Tel 6690900. Baghdadiyah, at the southern end of Al-Madinah Road, telex 401104 khasji.

Regional offices:

Agriculture & Water Tel 6876022, 6876238, 6874128. Telex 401632 westag.

Commerce Tel 6873400, 6873613. Telex 401019 tijara.

Communications Tel 6518280, 6515468, 6511880, 6654586.

Defence & Aviation Tel 6673664, 6673624, 6673708, 6553552.

Education Tel 6426248, 6422144, 6422546.

Finance & National Economy Tel: 6431033, 6431429, 6655874.

Health Tel 6512108, 6654066. Telex 401296 health.

Industry & Electricity Tel 6420433, 6871784. PO Box 3784, telex 401355 indest.

Information Tel 6446222, 6445222. PO Box 373, telex 401184 moijed.

Interior Tel 6692050, 6692002, 6872322.

Passport & Civil Affairs Tel 6317188.

Justice Tel 6650857, 6650214, 6674233, 6672931.

Labour & Social Affairs Tel 6438272, 6424945.

Municipal & Rural Affairs Tel 6874303, 6875011, 6674387, 6875195. Telex 400707 moder.

Petroleum & Mineral Resources Directorate-general, tel 6310355, 6310371-2, 6310756. Telex 401157 dgmr.

Pilgrimage & Endowments Tel 6673844. Telex 401494 awqaf.

Planning Tel 6510974, 6651366. PO Box 1221.

Posts, Telegraphs & Telecommunications Tel 6440055, 6516956, 6551323.

Public Works & Housing Tel 6670471, 6670483, 6559502. Telex 402368 ashgal.

Embassies

Algeria Chancery Tel: 6670688, 6670732. PO Box 1613. Consulate Tel: 6653202-3. PO Box 8132, Al-Madinah Road.

Argentina Chancery Tel: 6652666. PO Box 5888, Villa Bakr Khomais, south of UK embassy. Commercial Tel: 6602626. PO Box 7797, Al-Harithy Centre, Palestine Square. Telex: 401466 embarg.

Australia Tel: 6651303, 6652329, 6671107. PO Box 4876, off Al-Hamra Road, west of Al-Madinah Road. Telex: 401016 austem.

Austria Chancery Tel: 6652573, 6652548, 6657005. Off Al-Hamra Road, opposite Planning Ministry. Commercial Tel: 6512304, 6511816, Fitaihi Building, near Caravan Shopping Centre.

Bahrain Tel: 6692095, 6692087. PO Box 5954, Ruwais, near Old Royal Palace. Telex: 401436 bahrni.

Bangladesh Tel: 6878465, 6894712, 6894416. PO Box 6215, Kilo 3, Makkah Road. Telex: 401443 bangd.

Belgium Tel: 651352, 6513856, 6513860. PO Box 290, Kilo 2, Al-Madinah Road, Shaikh Amawi Building. Telex: 401456 ambel sj.

Brazil Tel: 6515124, 6514876, 6514872. Al-Hada Centre, Sharafiya. Telex: 401028 braemb.

Burundi Tel: 6653716. PO Box 9684, Madrassat Bin Kathir Street, Mushrefah. Telex: 403778.

Cameroon Tel: 6871780, 6871782. PO Box 1140, Kilo 4, Makkah Road. Telex: 401234 amcash.

Canada Tel: 6434900, 6434597-8, 6434587. PO Box 5050, 6th floor, Queen's Building, King Abdul-Aziz Street. Telex: 401060 domcan.

Chad Tel: 6674035. PO Box 3057, Palestine Road, near Japanese embassy.

Denmark Tel: 6659349, 6657743, 6659183. PO Box 5333, Al-Hamra. Telex: 401034 ambdk.

Djibouti Tel: 6887140, 6891520, 6886070. PO Box 7142, Makkah Road.

Egypt (see Sudan)

Ethiopia Tel: 6653443-4, 6653622. PO Box 495, Al-Hamra, Musaidiyah Square.

Finland Tel: 6515660, 6515664, 6515668. PO Box 5382, Villa Zogheibi, Khalid Ibn Waleed Street, Sharafiya. Telex: 401109 finamb.

France Chancery Tel: 6421233, 6421447. PO Box 145, Mohammed Abdul-Wahhab Street. Telex: 401151 fradja. Commercial Tel: 6653357, 6652375, 6654031, 6650824. Off Palestine Road, behind Nova Park hotel. Telex: 400177 comfra.

Gabon Tel: 6651364, PO Box 5442, Palestine Road. Telex: 401460 agadas.

Gambia Tel: 6654173. Khalid Ibn Waleed Street, Sharafiya.

Germany (West) Tel: 6653344, 6653545, 6657225-7. PO Box 126, Al-Hamra. Telex: 401013 aadjid.

Ghana Tel: 6652779. PO Box 1657, Al-Madinah Road, off Palestine Road.

Greece Tel: 6674064, 6674088. Al-Hamra. Telex: 401891 grem.

Guinea Tel: 6653718, 6652730. Ruwais.

India Chancery Tel: 6421602, 6510211. PO Box 952, Al-Madinah Road, Baghdadiya. Telex: 401261 india. Commercial Tel: 6421985. Shaikh Mohammed Ibrahim Masoud Building, Al-Madinah Road, Baghdadiya. Consular Tel: 6434190.

Indonesia Tel: 6653740, 6602735. PO Box 10, Khalid Ibn Waleed Street, Baghdadiya. Telex: 400081. Commercial Tel: 6510868.

Iran Tel: 6514291, 6514287. PO Box 1438, Abu Tayeb Street, Al-Madinah Road. Telex: 401146 iransa.

Iraq Chancery Tel: 6513092, 6513116. PO Box 212, Al-Madinah Road, Amar Ibn Yassir Street. Telex: 401021 iraqia. Commercial Tel: 6604888. Al-Asfahani Building, Al-Madinah Road.

Ireland Tel: 6658972, 6655481. PO Box 5134, Al-Madinah Road, Al-Musaidiyah Street. Telex: 401410 iverna.

Italy Chancery Tel: 6447344, 6447016. PO Box 215, Ahmed Abdullah Amoudi Building, Sharafiya. Telex: 400508 itdisa. Commercial Tel: 6517184, 6517452. PO Box 1193, Khalid Ibn Waleed Street. Telex: 401439 itce.

Japan Tel: 6652412, 6653421, 6604933. PO Box 1260, between Palestine and Al-Hamra roads, near US embassy. Telex: 401159 taishi.

Jordan Tel: 6715779, 6715829, 6715812. King Fahd Street, near Crown Prince's Palace. Telex: 400847.

Kenya Tel: 6656718, 6601885. PO Box 6347, Al-Madinah Road, near Juffali.

Korea (South) Chancery Tel: 6690050, 6690073, 6690031, 6657666. PO Box 4322, near Globe Square. Telex: 401174 gksaud. Commercial Tel: 6654844, 6656277. PO Box 4323. Telex: 400066 kotra.

Kuwait Tel: 6604914, 6653237, 6604898, 6654103, 6601845. PO Box 5374, Al-Madinah Road, behind Jeddah Shopping Centre. Telex: 401531.

Lebanon Tel: 6515688, 6511308. PO Box 987, Al-Madinah Road. Telex: 401455 amlib.

Libya Tel: 6651273, 6651037. Al-Madinah Road.

Malaysia Tel: 6519443, 6519447. PO Box 593, off Khalid Ibn Waleed Street, Sharafiya. Commercial Tel: 6424481. Queen's Building, King Abdul-Aziz Street.

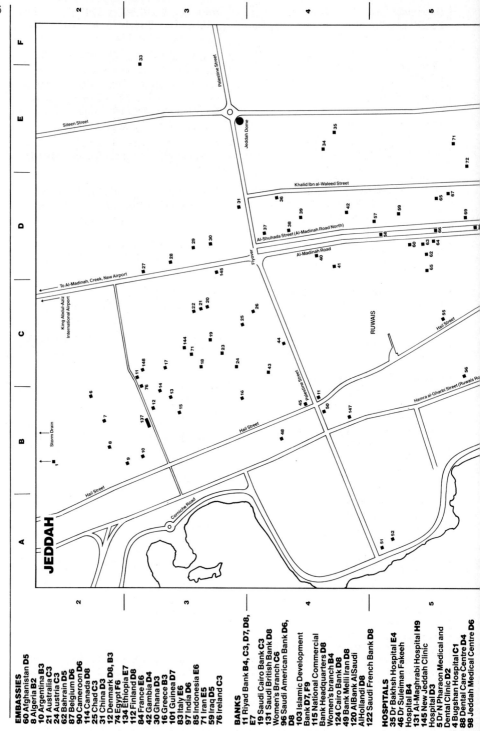

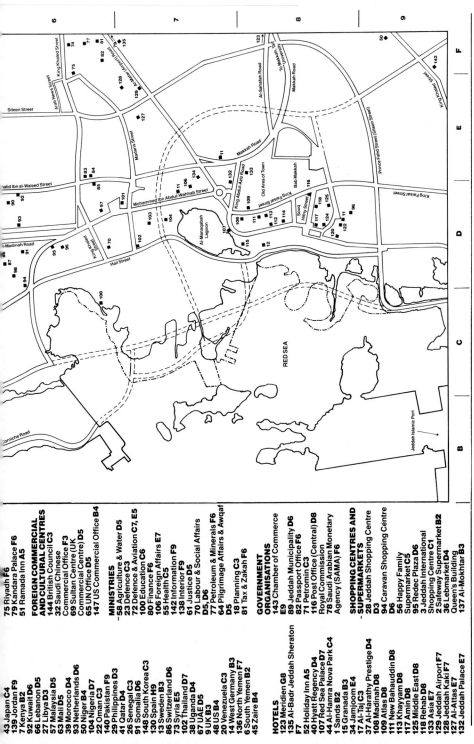

Mali Tel: 6515712. Al-Madinah Road, near Al-Mira Building. Telex: 400011 ammlij.

Mauritania Tel: 6878171, 6879694, 6881788. PO Box 1784, south Madain al-Fahd, near New Okaz school.

Mexico Tel: 6517550. PO Box 3665, Al-Hada Centre, Sharafiya. Telex: 401951 embmex.

Morocco Tel: 6605013. PO Box 498, Al-Madinah Road, near Bugshan Mosque. Telex: 401098 sifmar.

Nepal Tel: 6658161. Al-Hamra. PO Box 7358.

Netherlands Tel: 6519272, 6519024, 6511844, 6513644. PO Box 1776, Al-Madinah Road. Telex: 401463 nedjee.

Niger Tel: 6534811. PO Box 1709, Sharafiya. Telex: 401247.

Nigeria Tel: 6432835-6, 6432773. Baghdadiya. Telex: 401079 embang.

Norway Tel: 6604394, 6650638. PO Box 6251, Al-Madinah Road. Telex: 401471 noramb.

Oman Tel: 6653618-9. Al-Hamra, near Ministry of Interior. Telex: 401089 omanem.

Pakistan Tel: 6692371, 6691051, 6691046, 6691047. PO Box 182, off Al-Madinah Road.

Philippines Chancery Tel: 6656611, 6659233, 6656811. PO Box 4794, Al-Hamra. Consular Tel: 6653343, 6653266, 6653255. Kilo 5, Al-Madinah Road. Commercial Tel: 6601524. PO Box 9113, Al-Hamra.

Portugal Tel: 6674402. PO Box 9075, Al-Hamra, north of UK embassy.

Qatar Tel: 6653973, 6652538. PO Box 313, Al-Madinah Road, north of Ministry of Communications. Telex 401088 qatar.

Senegal Tel: 6654465. PO Box 1394, behind New Jeddah Clinic hospital. Telex: 400680.

Sierra Leone Tel: 6650146. PO Ł 7028, Mushrefah, off Al-Baladiya Street.

Singapore Tel: 6672806, 6691573. PO Box 9296, near Sands hotel.

Somalia Chancery Tel: 6673903, 6673915, 6773891. PO Box 729, Anaikish. Consular Tel: 6451419, 6453025. Kilo 2, Al-Madinah Road. Commercial Tel: 6422633. Queen's Building.

Spain Chancery Tel: 6602916. PO Box 453, off King Fahd Street, opposite Prince Abdullah's Palace. Telex: 401313 embspa. Commercial Tel: 6673628. PO Box 6388, Al-Harithy Centre, Palestine Square. Telex: 402371 ofcom.

Sri Lanka Tel: 6729475, 6729714. 10 Alkefah Street, Mushrefah. Telex: 403366 lanka sj.

Sudan Tel: 6470560, 6476003. PO Box 480, Sea Port Street. Egyptian affairs Tel: 6311940, 6311957. PO Box 1669, Airport Road, Sharafiya. Consulate Tel: 6447874, 6447766. PO Box 9137, Madaris Street, Baghdadiya.

Sweden Tel: 6654735, 6654833, 6659850. PO Box 2005, Al-Musaidiyah, west of Al-Madinah Road. Telex: 401464 svensk. Commercial Tel: 6659687, 6674195. Al-Hamra, west of US embassy. Telex: 402066 swtrof.

Switzerland Tel: 6510772, 6510776, 6511032. PO Box 1016, Kilo 2, Al-Madinah Road. Telex: 401470 amswis.

Syria Tel: 6513100, 6511560, 6510947. Sharafiya, north of Al-Askan Buildings.

Taiwan Tel: 6659161, 6671123, 6602264, 6602316. PO Box 114, north of Palestine Road, east of Al-Madinah Road, near Palestine Square. Telex: 401061 sinoem. Commercial Tel: 6653072, 6601445. PO Box 580, Kaki Building, Al-Madinah Road.

Thailand Chancery Tel: 6720211. PO Box 2224, Macarona Road. Commercial Tel: 6672954. PO Box 8014, Ibrahim al-Shaker Building, near Caravan Shopping Centre.

Tunisia Tel: 6872121, 6873590. Kilo 3, Makkah Road.

Turkey Tel: 6601607, 6654873. PO Box 70, Kilo 6, Al-Madinah Road, Al-Musaidiyya Street. Telex: 402631 cibmen.

Uganda Tel: 6656016. PO Box 4838, Khalid Ibn Waleed Street, opposite Madrassat Manara. Telex: 401092 ugemjd.

United Arab Emirates (UAE) Tel: 6518207, 6515436, 6530928. PO Box 5451, Othman Bin Affan Street, Sharafiya. Telex: 401458 emarat.

UK Tel: 6604430, 6604871, 6652544, 6652849, 6652974, 6658412. PO Box 393, Hail Street. Telex: 402399 britem. Commercial Tel: 6531983, 6531727. Sultan Centre, Kilo 2, Al-Madinah Road. Telex: 401043 prodrm.

US Tel: 6670080. PO Box 149, Palestine Road, Ruwais. Telex: 401459 amemb s. Commercial Tel: 6670040. Opposite embassy compound.

Upper Volta Tel: 6715757. PO Box 8009, Al-Sahafa Street. Telex: 400744 ahvd.

Uruguay Tel: 6653880, 6654457. PO Box 8186, behind Jeddah Shopping Centre. Telex: 402695 urujed.

Venezuela Tel: 6651124. Al-Hamra Street, near Interior Ministry Office. Telex: 401445 embave.

Yemen (North) Tel: 6874291, 6881771, 6873934. Madain al-Fahd, Kilo 4, Makkah Road.

Yemen (South) Tel: 6601627, 6656592. PO Box 6346, Al-Madinah Road, west of Juffali.

Consulates
Afghanistan Tel: 6653142. PO Box 6349, Al-Madinah Road.

Zaire Tel: 6652973, 6652979. PO Box 5204, Hail Street. Telex: 401462 zairem.

Getting around
Airport
With the summer 1981 opening of King Abdul-Aziz international, Jeddah now boasts one of the world's newest airports. With an area of 105 square kilometres-plus, it is also one of the biggest. It lies on the flat desert plain between the Red Sea and the foothills of the Hejaz mountains and, with its own nursery growing plants to landscape the surrounding area, is beginning to look more like a huge oasis than an airport.

The future operational area of the airforce is not yet much in evidence. It is the airport's commercial section with its three runways, south and north commercial terminals, royal pavilion and — most of all — spectacular Hajj terminal which catch the eye. From this complex it is possible to fly direct to 92 foreign destinations by one of the 42 airlines which operate regularly, including the national airline Saudia.

The large south terminal, with its six pointed glass arches, is used exclusively by Saudia. Its facilities include restaurants, banks, car hire desks, hotel representatives and mosque. It has extensive car parks and its own exit on the south side of the airport. As a result, it takes 15 minutes less to travel downtown from there than from the north terminal, which is smaller and at the other end of the runways.

This terminal, which echoes the south terminal architecturally, serves the international flag carriers. It has a bank, cafeteria, car hire desks and a large open-air car park. Like the south terminal it is kept spotlessly clean, while baggage handling is equally efficient.

The customs men are brisk but thorough, and suitcases are usually searched. Flight information is given in both Arabic and English. Porters are available, charging SR 1.50 for each piece of luggage. There is also an ample supply of luggage trolleys which can be wheeled easily to the car park. Buses, taxis and limousines serve both terminals; the last offer a particularly good service, at a competitive rate of SR 30-50, depending on destination.

Travellers leaving the north terminal on the 30-minute journey into Jeddah have an unparalleled view of the Hajj terminal — which lies north towards the exit — as the road plunges between the two halves of the massive white building. On either side of the road stretches a 750 by 340 metre area with open sides, roofed in by 105 tent-like units suspended from pillars. These fibre-glass "tents" are six storeys above ground at the lowest point and 10 storeys above at the peak. Under these covered halves are five modules, each with two aircraft gates and an airconditioned passenger building, through which about 600,000 pilgrims pass during the Hajj. Every conceivable facility, ranging from mosque to post office, is housed within the enormous edifice.

Halfway along the airport perimeter visitors pass the last major airport building, which has its own entrance and palm-lined approach. This is the royal pavilion. Beneath its gold roof lie elaborately decorated reception rooms hung with Aubusson tapestries and paintings by Arab artists. These rooms have special facilities for King Fahd, as well as for visiting heads of state, ministers and VIPs.

Airlines

Air Algerie Tel: 6422233, 6422454. Ali Reza Building, King Abdul-Aziz Street.

Air Djibouti Tel: 6446475, 6447197, 6434828. Ibrahim Shaker Building, Caravan Shopping Centre.

Air France Tel: 6518504, 6518252, 6518772; air cargo 6603821. Near Hyatt Regency hotel, Al-Madinah Road.

Air Iberia Tel: 6311295, 6311235. Hassan Bin Ladin Centre, Al-Madinah Road.

Air India Tel: 6600500, 6675080. Al-Harithy Centre, Palestine Square.

Air Maroc Tel: 6472643, 6446475, 6447197, 6434828. Ibrahim Shaker Building, Caravan Shopping Centre.

Alia, the Royal Jordanian Airline Tel: 6444814, 6433414. Al-Madinah Road.

Alitalia Tel: 6600640, 6600856. Al-Harithy Building, Al-Madinah Road.

Alyemda Tel: 6433125-6. Al-Jauhara Building, Al-Madinah Road.

Austrian Airlines Tel: 6655611, 6602356. Fourth floor, Jeddah Shopping Centre, Al-Madinah Road.

Biman (Bangladesh airlines) Tel: 6433125-6. Al-Jauhara Building, Al-Madinah Road.

British Airways Tel: 6693464, 6673544, 6693269, 6693273. Jeddah Shopping Centre, Al-Madinah Road.

Cathay Pacific Airways Tel: 6670224, 6602953, 6438381. Alfaki Building, Near Jeddah Palace Hotel, Al-Madinah Road.

China Airlines Tel: 6437675, 6432020. Al-Faisaliya Centre, King Abdul-Aziz Street.

Cyprus Airways Tel: 6513541, 6514268. Opposite Riyad Bank, King Abdul-Aziz Street.

EgyptAir Tel: 6600616, 6600624, 6423493. Kaki Building, Al-Madinah Road.

Ethiopian Airlines Tel: 6433125-6. Al-Jauhara Building, Al-Madinah Road.

Garuda Indonesian Airlines Tel: 6674689, 6674693, 6672592. Jeddah Shopping Centre, Al-Madinah Road.

Gulf Air Tel: 6517496, 6511962. Al-Qitmi Building, Al-Madinah Road.

Iraqi Airways Tel: 6515144, 6515136. Al-Amri Centre, Al-Madinah Road.

Iran Air Tel: 6516496, 6421172, 6672013. Khouja Building, Al-Madinah Road.

Japan Airlines Tel: 6447000, 6442845. Al-Faisaliya Centre, King Abdul-Aziz Street.

Kenya Airways Tel: 6470853. Al-Maghrabi Building, near King Abdul-Aziz Street.

KLM/Royal Dutch Airlines Tel: 6670888, 6673744. PO Box 1080, Jeddah Shopping Centre, Al-Madinah Road.

Korean Airlines Tel: 6443440, 6426354, 6440106. Al-Jauhara Building, Al-Madinah Road.

Kuwait Airways Tel: 6691044, 6691088. Jeddah Shopping Centre, Al-Madinah Road.

Libyan Arab Airlines Tel: 6435111, 6433777. Al-Faisaliya Centre, King Abdul-Aziz Street.

Lufthansa Tel: 6428714, 6423324, 6447839, 6448880, 6448742. PO Box 1713, Al-Jauhara Building, Al-Madinah Road.

Malaysian Airline System Tel: 6447839, 6448880, 6448742. PO Box 1935, Redec Centre, Al-Madinah Road.

Middle East Airlines Tel: 6512720, 6512364, 6512748, 6512756, 6512752. Jeddah Palace Hotel, Al-Baya Square.

Nigeria Airways Tel: 6433125-6, 6425437. Al-Jauhara Building, Al-Madinah Road.

Olympic Airways Tel: 6510828, 6515030, 6517076. Opposite Hyatt Hotel, Al-Madinah Road (north).

Pakistan International Airlines Tel: 6312777, 6313777, 6444110. Tihama Building, King Abdul-Aziz Street.

Pan-American World Airways Tel: 6431151, 6533102, 6533106. Near Jeddah Medical Centre, Ruwais.

Philippine Airlines Tel: 6519516, 6516192. Al-Madinah Road (south).

Sabena Tel: 6534928, 6534936. Near King Fahd Palace, Sharafiya.

Scandinavian Airline System Tel: 6693376, 6693352, 6693792. Jeddah Shopping Centre, Al-Madinah Road.

Singapore Airlines Tel: 6674345, 6671813, 6671690.

Somali Airlines Tel: 6672758. Al-Harithy Building, Al-Madinah Road.

Sudan Airways Tel: 6423142, 642687. Opposite Asia Hotel, Bab Makkah.

Swissair Tel: 6519780, 6519544, 6519784; air cargo 6603821. Near Air France, Al-Madinah Road.

Syrian Arab Airlines Tel: 6532708, 6532712, 6433419, 6532716. Statco Building, near Bank al-Jazira, King Abdul-Aziz Street.

Thai International Tel: 6693376, 6693356. Jeddah Shopping Centre, Al-Madinah Road.

Trans Mediterranean Airways Tel: 6428446. Al-Attar Building, King Abdul-Aziz Street.

Trans World Airlines (TWA) Tel: 6510828, 6448397. Al-Madinah Road.

Tunis Air Tel: 6422448, 6422474. Al-Maghrabi Building, opposite King Abdul-Aziz Street.

Turkish Airlines Tel: 6447274, 6444380. Bab Makkah.

Yemen Airways (Yemenia) Tel: 6440043, 6433169, 6510192. Al-Maghrabi Building, opposite King Abdul-Aziz Street.

Air communications (domestic)

Direct daily flights to Abha, Bisha, Dhahran, Hail, Jizan, Al-Madinah, Qassim, Riyadh, Tabuk, Taif and Yanbu. Direct flights to Jauf and Wedjh.

Saudia Tel airport information 6851234; reservations 6433333.

Head office tel 6864268, 6864384, Abu Algadail Building, Airport Road.

Main sales office tel 6863074, 6863420.

Queen's Building tel 6864201, 6864225, King Abdul-Aziz Street.

Kandara Palace hotel tel 6864235-6, Airport Road.

Sheraton hotel tel 6310309, 6312010, Airport Road.

King Abul-Aziz university campus tel 6879033, 6879202.

Petromin tel 6367411.

Bin-Ladin Plaza tel 6864241-2.
Al-Madinah Road office tel 6653755, 6653765.

Public transport

Saudi Arabian Public Transport Company (Saptco) Provides bus services within the city, and to Makkah, Al-Madinah, Yanbu and Riyadh.

Fares:
Within Jeddah — SR 1; regular services every five or 15 minutes depending on route.
Jeddah Corniche to Makkah — SR 15; 35 journeys a day each way, extra on Friday.
Corniche to Al-Madinah — SR 50; 11 journeys a day each way.
Corniche to Taif — SR 30; seven journeys a day each way, two via bypass.
Corniche to King Abdul-Aziz international airport; 18 journeys a day each way.
Corniche to Yanbu — SR 60; three journeys a day each way.
Bab Makkah to Makkah — SR 15; 16 journeys a day each way.
To Yanbu — SR 20; two journeys a day each way.
To Riyadh — SR 130.
To Dammam — SR 190.

Car hire

Abu Diyab Rent-a-Car Tel: 6716787. Siteen Street, near King Fahd's Palace. Rates on request.

Arabian Car Rental (Europcar/National Car Rental/Tilden) Head Office: Okaz Souq, Meridien hotel, tel: 6317274, 6317231. Branches: airport (south terminal), tel: 6855540; Siteen Street, tel: 6710480, 6719126; Airport Road, opposite Kandara Palace hotel, tel: 6313718; Hyatt hotel tel: 6519800 ext 1133.

Avis Tel: 6511668, 6518152. PO Box 1271, Al-Hada Centre. Telex: 401384 best. Branches: Kandara Palace hotel, tel: 6423155; Al-Waha hotel, tel: 6600900; Red Sea Palace hotel, tel: 6428555; Jeddah international airport, tel: 6855542 (south terminal). 6853008 (north terminal) — open 0800-1400, 1630-2400.
Credit cards: most major cards accepted.

Budget Rent-a-Car Tel: 6516196, 6532440. PO Box 3612. Telex: 402818 budjed. Branches: Jeddah international airport, tel: 6855543; Sheraton hotel, tel: 6310000; Hyatt Regency hotel, tel: 6690401.
Conditions: driving licence (local or international) held for at least one year; minimum age 21.
Credit cards: American Express, Budget International.

Godfrey Davis/Hanco Rent-a-car Tel: 6433965. Airport Square opposite Kandara Palace hotel. Branches: Al-Attas Oasis hotel, tel: 6448171; Meridien hotel, tel: 6314000, ext 1123; Jeddah international airport.

Hala Car Rental Head Office: Tel: 6517643, 6511779, 6532670. Khalid Ibn Waleed Street. Telex: 404039 halaco. Branches: Jeddah international airport, tel: 6855544 (south terminal), 6853004 (north terminal).

Sahary Rent-a-Car (Inter Rent) Tel: 6602089, 6603217. Mushrefah Street. Branches: Jeddah international airport, tel: 6855541, 6853006; Nova Park hotel, tel: 6602000; Al-Attas hotel, tel: 6420211.
Conditions: delivery and collection free to hotels, offices, airports; any valid licence held for at least one year; minimum age 22.

Saudi Car Tel: 6318087, 6312950. PO Box 4235, opposite Kandara Palace hotel, Airport Road. Telex: 400647 sdicar. Rates on request.

Unique Car Rental Company Tel: 6517651, 6517680. PO Box 6160. Telex: 401737. Branches: Jeddah international airport, tel: 6855545 (south terminal), 6530276 (north terminal). Rates on request.

ARABIAN CAR RENTAL

Model	Daily rate (SR)	Weekly rate	
		limited (SR)	unlimited (SR)
Datsun Sunny/Mazda 323	85	535	835
Datsun 200B/Galant	120	755	1,055
Datsun SW/Buick Regal	140	950	1,250
Buick PA/Chevrolet Caprice	170	1,070	1,370

AVIS

Model	Daily rate (SR)	Weekly rate (SR)	Per km (SR)
Honda Civic/Datsun 140 Y and 150 Y/Pony	85	510	0.25
Datsun 180 B/Toyota Cressida/ Mazda 929/Galant 2000	120	720	0.35
Buick Century/Toyota Crown/ Datsun 280	140	840	0.50
Chevrolet Impala/Chevrolet Caprice/ Buick Park Avenue	170	1,020	0.50

BUDGET RENT-a-CAR

Model	Daily rate (SR)	Weekly rate (SR)	Per km (SR)
Gemini	80	550	0.25
Mazda 323	85	575	0.25
Mazda 626	105	710	0.35
Mazda 929	120	810	0.35
Chevrolet Impala/Caprice	170	1,150	0.50

GODFREY DAVIS/HANCO RENT-a-CAR

Model	Daily rate* (SR)	Weekly rate (SR)	Per km (SR)
Honda Civic/Toyota Corolla	85	595	0.25
Datsun 180/Honda Accord	120	840	0.35
Buick Skylark/Pontiac Phoenix	140	980	0.50
Chevrolet Impala (auto)/Chevrolet Caprice	170	1,190	0.50

*100 kilometres free a day
All cars are airconditioned

HALA CAR RENTAL

Model	Daily rate (SR)	Weekly rate (SR)	Per km (SR)
Honda Civic Corolla/Lancer	85	595	0.25
Cressida/Galant	120	840	0.35
Crown	140	980	0.50
Chevrolet Impala Chevrolet Caprice	170	1,190	0.50

SAHARY RENT-a-CAR (INTER RENT)

Model	Daily rate (SR)	Weekly rate (SR)	Per km (SR)
Honda Civic	85	535	0.25
Mazda 626	105	661	0.35
Toyota Cressida	120	756	0.35
Buick Century	140	882	0.50
Chevrolet Caprice	170	1,071	0.50
Buick Lesabre	180	1,134	0.50

Hotels

Al-Badr Jeddah Sheraton Tel: 6310000. PO Box 6719, Airport Road. Telex: 401512 sher.

563 rooms including 10 executive suites, four royal suites and five function rooms for groups of 20-500. All airconditioned with colour TV, two-channel video, fridge, direct-dial telephone, private bathroom.

Three restaurants and lounges; coffee shop open 24 hours. Shopping arcade, bank, car hire, news-stand, airline reservations, car park, patisserie, outside laundry, barber shop. Telex and secretarial services. Swimming pool, sauna, gymnasium, massage parlour and sundeck.

Rates: single SR 300, double SR 390, executive suite SR 450, royal suite SR 2,000, plus 15% service.

Credit cards: American Express, Diners Club, Mastercharge, Visa.

Meridien Hotel (Hotel al-Salam Meridien) Tel: 6314000. PO Box 6582, King Khaled Street. Telex: 401276 mersal. The curvilinear facade is fronted with attractive solar reflecting glass.

400 rooms, each with video, TV, minifridge, and individually controlled airconditioning. Barber shop, beauty salon, shopping arcade with patisserie, gift and bookshop, news-stand, florist, parfumerie, jeweller, travel agency, car hire; dry cleaning and laundry; babysitting service; photocopying. Banqueting and conference facilities include cinema, video, simultaneous translation and speaker systems. Swimming pool open to guests and club members only.

Al-Bustan poolside bar serves snacks and drinks. Oasis coffee shop (ground floor) open 24 hours and serves continental and Arab food. Often busy at lunchtime but pleasant decor and good food — excellent home-baked croissants, French bread, Lebanese honey cakes. Buffet lunch SR 50 for three courses, breakfast SR 30, dinner SR 60. Also Arab restaurant Al-Badiya,

Jeddah's Meridien Hotel

on first floor. Le Vendome restaurant serves French dishes; pianist entertains in the evenings. Al-Diwania tea lounge (ground floor) serves pastries, ice cream and soft drinks.

Rates: single SR 300-330, double SR 390-430, suite prices on request; plus 15% service.

Credit cards: American Express, Diners Club, Carte Blanche, Mastercharge, Eurocard, Access, Visa.

Atlas Hotel Tel: 6423361. Sharia al-Jadid. Telex: 401721 habib.

70 rooms. Restaurant serving set lunch and dinner at SR 30 a head. Rates: single SR 105, double SR 149. Prices include breakfast and service.

Al-Bilad Hotel Tel: 6822276, 6828088. PO Box 6788, Corniche Road. Telex: 403010 biladh.

Arabian barbeque, restaurant, cafe. Bowling, tennis, swimming, squash, health centre.

Rates: on request.

Red Sea Palace Hotel Tel: 6428555. PO Box 824, at the north end of King Abdul-Aziz Street. Telex: 401014 rsph.

275 rooms with private bath, direct-dial telephone, TV and video, 24-hour room service.

Al-Bouharia restaurant and Al-Gahwa coffee shop; pizzeria opening soon. Barber shop, laundry, dry cleaning. Tennis court, swimming pool.

Rates: single SR 250, double SR 325, suites SR 375-500; plus 15% service. Children up to six free in parents' room.

China Centre and China Rose Apartments Tel: 6714133, 6714261, 6713715. PO Box 1567. Telex: 400856 sauchi. Apply at China Rose Restaurant, Macarona Road.

Furnished rooms with kitchenette, fridge and telephone.

Rates: daily — for one person SR 230, for two SR 276, for three SR 322, for four SR 373; weekly — one SR 1,610, two SR 1,932, three SR 2,254, four SR 2,576; monthly — one SR 5,850, two SR 6,900, three SR 7,950, four SR 8,850, service included.

Royal Hotel Tel: 6428137, 6442048. In street parallel to King Abdul-Aziz Street at back entrance to main souq. Telex: 400326 ryljed.

240 rooms, of which about one in three is used as a single.

Two restaurants, one serving Chinese and Filipino meals, the other European and Arab food.

Rates: single SR 152, double SR 210 including breakfast and 10% service. Check-out 1400.

Al-Rehab Hotel Tel: 6432216, 6432303. PO Box 6206, Sharia al-Jadid. Telex: 401091 alrehab.

88 rooms with TV. Restaurant serves Arab and European food.

Rates: single SR 132, double SR 185, including service.

Sands Hotel Tel: 6692020. PO Box 7030, Al-Hamra district. Telex: 400789 sands.

Nearest first-class hotel to Jeddah international airport. 230 rooms, 10 apartments, two royal suites, all with airconditioning, international direct-dial telephone, colour TV, three-channel video, mini-fridge.

Maxim restaurant serves continental cuisine in warm, attractive atmosphere; poolside Sahary coffee shop, open 24 hours, for oriental and continental food. Shopping arcade, travel agency, barber shop, car rental, gift shop. Banquet and meeting rooms, 24-hour secretarial and telex service. Two swimming pools, recreation centre. Transport to and from the airport is free; airconditioned private limousine service is also available for transport within Jeddah.

Rates: single SR 240, double SR 290, suite SR 480.

Credit cards: American Express, Diners Club, Carte Blanche.

Asia Hotel Tel: 6425111, 6429814, 6447009. King Abdul-Aziz Street, Bab Makkah. Telex: 401517 amoudi, cable: asia palace.

112 rooms and suites with telephone. Roof-top garden restaurant; cafeteria open 24 hours.

Rates: single SR 121, double SR 167, suite SR 242, including service and breakfast.

Taj Palace Hotel Tel: 6313203, 6313075. Airport Road. Telex: 401637 tajco, cable: taj palace hotel.

65 rooms and suites with telephone, mini-fridge, colour TV and video.

Restaurant open 1600-1000, 1200-1500, 1700-2300; coffee shop open 24 hours. Breakfast SR 16, lunch SR 30, dinner SR 35. Laundry service, valet, deposit vaults, 24-hour room service. Cable and telex office, secretarial and translation service.

Rates: single SR 125, double SR 165, suite SR 450; plus 10% service.

Hotel Alhamra Nova-Park Tel: 6602000. PO Box 7375. Palestine Road, 10 minutes from the heart of Jeddah and seven minutes from the airport. Telex: 400749 nova.

300 rooms and suites, all with balconies overlooking the Red Sea,

private bath, telephone, radio, video, colour TV, fridge.

Royal Tent restaurant for lunch and dinner with Arab and international food; Swiss Chalet serves Swiss food at breakfast, lunch and dinner; International Grill serves grills for lunch and dinner; poolside barbeque restaurant open for dinner except in summer; coffee shop open 24 hours for business meals. Outside catering, with prices negotiated according to menu and numbers.

Travel agent, shopping arcade, car hire, parking for 150 cars, cinema, video theatre, hairdressers. Banqueting and conference rooms with audio-visual facilities. Swimming pool, health club, sauna and massage.

Rates: single SR 280, double SR 365, suites SR 420-1,000; plus 15% service. Nova Park Residence — three-room apartments: daily SR 650, monthly SR 10,000-15,000.

Credit cards: American Express, Diners Club, Visa, Eurocard, Mastercharge, Access.

Hyatt Regency Tel: 6519800. PO Box 8483, Al-Madinah Road. Telex: 402688 hyatt sj.

265 rooms and 33 suites, all with radio, TV, video, direct-dial telephone, fridge.

Gourmet restaurant, coffee shop open 24 hours; Chinese, Japanese and Italian restaurants; lobby terrace.

Car hire and limousine service, travel agency, clinic. Business centre, conference and banqueting facilities, secretarial service. Swimming pool, health club, sauna. The Regency class, on one floor, offers an exclusive service to guests who seek privacy and special attention.

Rates: standard single SR 330, double SR 390, superior single SR 340, double SR 410, deluxe single SR 360, double SR 430, junior suite SR 600, executive suite (one bed) SR 800, (two bed) SR 1,100, princely suite (one bed) SR 1,100, (two bed) SR 1,500, royal suite from SR 2,200; plus 15% service.

Credit cards: American Express, Diners Club, Eurocard, Mastercharge, Visa.

Amin Hotel Tel: 6433191, 6439118. PO Box 3785, King Abdul-Aziz Street. No restaurant.

Rates: single SR 55-66, double SR 75-82, including service.

Jeddah Airport Hotel Tel: 6313571. PO Box 2012, Airport Road. Telex: 401115 apht.

86 rooms. Travel office, photocopying and telex, laundry. Restaurant offers oriental and European food; coffee shop open 24 hours.

Rates: single SR 100, double SR 130, suite (for two) SR 190, (three) SR 245, (four) SR 300; plus 10% service.

Jeddah Kaki Hotel Tel: 6312201, PO Box 2559, Airport Road. Telex: 401739 khotel.

One of the newest and liveliest medium-price hotels with 216 rooms. Has a good restaurant with excellent Arab food, as well as the Ming Court Chinese restaurant. News-stand, shopping arcade, barber shop. Conference and banqueting facilities. Swimming pool (morning for women and afternoon for men).

Rates: single SR 200, double SR 260, suites on application.

Kandara Palace Tel: 6312177, 6312944. PO Box 473, Airport Road. Telex: 401095 kph.

435 rooms. Restaurant serving Indonesian food on Monday evenings. Barber shop, gift shop, Saudia ticket office. Tennis court, swimming pool open to non-residents (four days for men and three for women — SR 15).

Rates: on request.

Jeddah Palace Hotel Tel: 6446117-8. PO Box 473, Bab Jadid. Telex: 401095.

120 rooms. Restaurant, banqueting facilities for 600, complimentary airport service.

Rates: on request.

New Bahauddin Hotel Tel: 6423511. PO Box 2130, King Abdul-Aziz Street. Telex: 401174 bahajed.

70 rooms. Restaurant, laundry service, 24 hour cafeteria.

Rates: single SR 120, double SR 150, suites SR 330-550.

Al-Attas Hotel Tel: 6420211, 6420400. PO Box 1789. Telex: 401158.
  250 rooms. Al-Rawshan restaurant, Al-Arouss coffee shop, shopping arcade, swimming pool, courtesy airport bus.
  Rates: on request.

Al-Harathy Prestige Hotel Tel: 6670540, 6670520, Palestine Road. Telex: 400687.
  40 single rooms, 44 double. Candlelight grill, coffee shop.
  Rates: single SR 250, double SR 350.

Al Waha Hotel Tel: 6710003. PO Box 2300. King Fahd Street. Telex: 401892 alwaha si.
  100 rooms, 35 suites. Al-Kheimah restaurant, Al-Patra restaurant, Masfrahiah coffee shop. Banqueting facilities, swimming pool, leisure centre, courtesy bus service to airport and souq.
  Rates: single SR 150, double SR 180, suites SR 300.

Al-Attas Holiday Beach Hotel Tel: 6562921-2, Obhur beach. Telex: 401158.
  100 rooms, 15 suites. Restaurant serving continental and oriental food, coffee shop, swimming pool, courtesy airport bus.
  Rates: on request.

Obhur Beach Hotel Tel: 6562100, Obhur beach. Telex: 402527 shobak.
  36 rooms, three suites, five villas, 26 apartments. Two restaurants, swimming pool.
  Rates: on request.

Al-Haramain Modern Hotel Tel: 6426655, 6434167. PO Box 85, King Abdul-Aziz Street. Telex: 401619.
  84 rooms. Restaurant.
  Rates: single and double SR 105.

Al-Haramain Palace Hotel Tel: 6448044, 6448055. Madaris Street, Baghdadiya.
  165 rooms with 24-hour room service. Oriental and European restaurants. Telex, transport to and from airport, and coffee shop.
  Rates: on application.

Al-Jazierah Hotel Tel: 6422365. King Abdul-Aziz Street. 24 rooms.
  Rates: single SR 40, double SR 80.

Al-Nasr Hotel Tel: 6428137, 6442048. Al-Jadid Street, behind Queen's Building. Telex: 400326 ryljed sj.
  129 rooms. Restaurant.
  Rates: single SR 120, double SR 155, special suites SR 180.

Al-Riyadh Hotel Tel: 6313860, 6312819, 6312820. PO Box 4211, Airport Road, Sharafiya. Telex: 401154 ziadsj.
  113 rooms. Restaurant. Free postage, video and TV.
  Rates: single SR 24, double SR 89, special suites SR 250, breakfast included.

Al-Sharafiya Hotel Tel: 6447998. Khalf Gahwa Shabab, behind Stones Garden, Sharafiya.
  20 rooms with TV and fridge. Chinese restaurant. Television lounge.
  Rates: single SR 66, double SR 100.

Arafat Hotel Tel: 6432248. King Abdul-Aziz Street. 86 rooms.
  Rates: single SR 66, double SR 88.

Granada Hotel Tel: 6690062, 6657543. PO Box 531, Al-Hamra. Telex: 401281 honada sj.
  34 rooms. Lebanese restaurant.
  Rates: on request.

Jamjoom Hotel Tel: 6533587-8. PO Box 7828, Altouba Road.
  45 rooms with telephone. Fridges and TV available on request. Oriental and continental restaurants.
  Rates: single SR 80, double SR 105.

Khayyam Hotel Tel: 6433560, 6425759. King Faisal Street. Telex: 401708 sj.
  89 rooms. Restaurant.
  Rates: single SR 110, double SR 154.

Al-Madinah Hotel Tel: 6432650, 6438148. King Faisal Street.
  45 rooms. Restaurant.
  Rates: on request.

Middle East Hotel Tel: 6433837, 6430515. King Abdul-Aziz Street. Telex: 401734 qhar sj.
  58 rooms. Restaurant.
  Rates: on request.

Under construction

Holiday Inn To be opened in mid-1983 on Corniche, about eight kilometres from the business centre. 530 rooms, all with airconditioning, private bath, radio, colour TV and in-house video. It will have a Polynesian restaurant, coffee shop, outdoor swimming pool, squash court, shopping arcade and banqueting facilities for 400.

Ramada Inn To be opened in 1983-84. On Corniche, west end of Palestine Road.

Communications

Telex and telegrams

Telexes and telegrams can be sent from the public offices at the Post, Telegraphs & Telecommunications Ministry building on Mina Road, telex 401001 pbtx. The average waiting time for transmission is 15 minutes, while the minimum advance for sending telexes is SR 50, with change given if the transmission costs less. Replies can also be received at this office, but unclaimed telex messages are destroyed after 10 days.

Charge a minute: UK SR 14; US SR 18; most European countries and Japan SR 14. Identification must be produced.

Telegrams can also be sent from several offices around the city. All telegrams delivered to these are sent to the ministry building for dispatch.

General post office

The main office is off Hail Street, north of the Caravan Shopping Centre. Hours: 0700-1400; 1600-2200. There are sub-post offices throughout Jeddah.

Telephone

A major expansion and reorganisation of Jeddah's telephone system is under way, with many seven-digit numbers being changed. The operator will either interrupt to give the new number, or a recorded voice will advise in English and Arabic that the number dialled is incorrect.

From the UK dial 010-966 and Jeddah code 2. To phone London from Jeddah dial 00-44 and London code 1.

The central exchange is on Al-Madinah Road (north), virtually opposite the Kaki Building and just before the Palestine Road flyover.

Rates for a three-minute call handled by operator (double for urgent calls): UK SR 42; US SR 36 (+ SR 12 person-to-person); France SR 42; West Germany SR 39 (+ SR 13 person-to-person); South Korea SR 39; Italy SR 42; Switzerland SR 39; Greece SR 39; Belgium SR 42. Rates for calls dialled direct to Europe and the US about SR 14 a minute.

International calls can be made from the Posts, Telegraphs & Telecommunications Ministry on Mina Road. Telephone booths all over the city take 10, 50 and 100 halalah pieces. Local calls of up to six minutes from phone booths cost 10 halalahs; from private numbers local calls are free.

Useful numbers
Fire 998
Police 999
Ambulance 997
Traffic accidents 993
Operator 900
Directory enquiries 904

Courier services

SNAS-DHL Tel: 6825826-7, 6828143, 6822886, 6821303. PO Box 7977, East of Al-Madinah Road, off second and third flyovers. Telex: 402559.

To get there travel north along Al-Madinah Road, past the Palestine Road flyover and past the second flyover to Airport Road. Leave main road and go through "traffic lights in the sky," keeping right on descent, on to the slip road. Passing East West Express, Gray Mackenzie and the yellow warehouse of GRC, turn right before AQ Sports Store, and then left to the SNAS-DHL compound, immediately behind Wavin Plastics.

Skypak Tel: 6600034, 6600038, 6659801. PO Box 5604, Brothers Commercial Company Building, King Fahd Street. Telex: 401510.

World Courier Service Tel: 6655622, 6655647. PO Box 2682, seven blocks north of Palestine Road. Telex: 401480 khaldi.

Travel agents

ACE Travel Tel: 6533102, 6533106. PO Box 6152, Prince Abdullah Faisal Building, King Abdul-Aziz Street. Telex: 403094 acetvl. Next to Jeddah Medical Centre, behind Caravan Shopping Centre.

Al-Anhar Travel Agency Tel: 6313751, 6311985. PO Box 4572, Old Airport Square. Telex: 401652 anhar.

Arab Wings Tel: 6671690, 6671813. PO Box 1620, Kaki Centre, Al-Madinah Road. King Abdul-Aziz Street, tel: 6429610, 6429782.

Areen Travel Tel: 6512964 6516524, 6516528, 6515248. Al-Mabani Building, Hail Street. Al-Ruwais.

Attar, Mohammed & Saddik Tel: 6447229, 6423244, 6693464. PO Box 439, King Abdul-Aziz Street. Telex: 401075. Jeddah Shopping Centre, Al-Madinah Road, tel: 6600508.

Azco Travel Tel: 6652304. PO Box 5700. Telex: 401062.

Eastern Travel & Tourism Tel: 6604310, 6654264. PO Box 1800, Kaki Centre, Al-Madinah Road.

Fahad Travel Tel: 6477861, 6423901, 6476001. PO Box 1135, King Abdul-Aziz Street, near Riyad Bank. Telex: 401605, cable: unitouragency. Al-Madinah Road, by Palestine Road flyover, tel: 6659592, 6674127, 6659466, 6892230-1.

Kanoo Travel Agency Tel: 6824432, 6823751. Regional headquarters, Al-Madinah Road. Al-Faiha branch, Al-Faiha Building, tel: 6534176, 6531743, 6534835.

Kurban Travel Tel: 6531135, 6532391, 6532159. PO Box 5039, Airport Road, Sharafiya. Telex: 401808-9 kurban.

Misr Travel Tel: 6438797, 6443662. PO Box 5274, Mufti Building, King Abdul-Aziz Street. Telex: 401708 khayam, cable: misship.

Mohsen Travel & Tourism Tel: 6310151. PO Box 3498, Airport Road, opposite Sheraton hotel. Telex: 401513 mohsen.

Samara International Tel: 6442061. PO Box 4457, Al-Madinah Road, by Indian embassy, Baghdadiya. Telex: 400235. Offers receptions for businessmen, hotel reservations.

Saudi Tourist & Travel Bureau (STTB) Tel: 6437048, 6428466. PO Box 4693, Al-Jauhara Building, Al-Madinah Road, Baghdadiya. Hyatt Regency hotel, tel: 6519800, ext 1193. Al-Faisaliya Centre, King Abdul-Aziz Street, tel: 6439111, 6437647. Several other branches, including one in the Sarawat market.

Sultan Travel Agency Tel: 6444988, 6444867. PO Box 7325, Hail Street, next to Caravan Shopping Centre. Telex: 402550 benia.

Wabel Travel Tel: 6448724, 6448880. PO Box 1935, Redec Plaza. Telex: 401122.

Zahid Travel Agency Tel: 6510828, 6515030, 6515966. PO Box 4754, King Abdul-Aziz Street. Telex: 403276 zhdtvl.

Eating out

Dynasty Tel: 6653065, PO Box 163, immediately northeast of Palestine Road flyover; well-marked. Continental cuisine with specialities from the Philippines. Open 1230-1530; 1830-2130; closed Friday.

Jakarta Oriental Restaurant Tel: 6651179. Close to Steak House butcher — turn left off Siteen Street at the metal palm tree. Takeaway and catering service, bakery and gift shop. Indonesian food with a European speciality every night. Recommended: nasi goreng and satay with peanut sauce. Open 1130-1500; 1900-2400; closed first Saturday in each month.

Royal Chinese Restaurant Tel: 6442048, 6428137. Second floor of Royal hotel, behind Queen's Building. Open every day.

Il Castello Tel: 6652281. West of Khalid Ibn Waleed Street, close to post office and Rolls-Royce dealer. Delicious pizzas and a selection of pasta and grills, and attentive service in trattoria-style restaurant. Recommended: pizza "Il Castello," grilled lamb chops and Coquilles Saint Jacques. Open daily 1230-1500; 1900-2400.

Sil Ra Korean Restaurant Tel: 6714640, 6720115. Off Siteen Street close to flyover beside Sony sign. Recommended: Ghengis Khan, a Korean version of Fondue Bourguignonne served with a very hot sauce. Open daily 1200-1600; 1800-2300.

Kentucky Fried Chicken Next to Al-Mohktar supermarket in Al-Hamra, near the British embassy. Takeaway service and limited dining facilities.

Shehrezade Restaurant Tel: 6824929, 6827944. Al-Madinah Road, near Kodak factory. Middle East and international dishes. Recommended: sizzling lamb chops and mezze. Party facilities.

Granada Restaurant Tel: 6657543. At Granada hotel, near Al-Mohktar supermarket in Al-Hamra, opposite the Swedish embassy. Telex: 401281 honada. Open 1200-1500; 1800-2100.

Leila wa Leila Tel: 6675193. Al-Dakhil Building, Palestine Square. On top floor of block next to Palestine Road flyover. Live music and view over Jeddah. Middle East food. Open daily 1200-2400.

Arabian Nights Restaurant

Arabian Nights Restaurant Tel: 6428770, 6420109. West of Al-Madinah Road in north Jeddah, one kilometre north of Kodak factory. Exotic Arabian decor in large tent — low tables and substantial cushions, Syrian antiques and candelight. Outdoor garden dining and smaller tents for private parties. Middle East, Lebanese and some Persian specialities. Good mezze. Recommended: fish, and lamb served with honey. Open daily 1300-1530; 1900-0100.

Pizza House Macarona Road, opposite China Rose Restaurant and Chinese commercial centre. Fast takeaway with good pizzas and hamburgers. Limited dining facilities.

Hollywood Restaurant Tel: 6671392. Macarona Road. Indian, Pakistani and continental food.

Jasmine Restaurant Tel: 6656858. Al-Madinah Road, near Palestine Square. Chinese food. Open daily 1200-1530; 1800-2300.

Kilo Ten Restaurant 10 kilometres out on Makkah Road. Arab food.

Saudi China Commercial Centre Tel: 6657059, 6657054. Macarona Road.

Restaurant & Cafeteria Aimen Oriental and western meals, refreshments and sweets; takeaway food for parties.

China Rose Restaurant Tel: 6714133, 6713715, 6714261. At junction of Palestine and Macarona roads. Chinese food, Manchurian barbecue and buffet at lunch. Open daily 1300-1500; 1900-2400.

Chinese Gardens Restaurant Tel: 6716846. East of Siteen Street beside Sony sign. Open 1300-1500 (except Monday); 1900-2330.

The Char-coal Grill Tel: 6650816. South of Palestine Road just after flyover if going east. American-style menu. Open daily 1200-2400.

Satay House Last turning right off Palestine Road before flyover going west. Indonesian food. Open daily 1230-1530; 1900-2300.

Arirang Restaurant Tel: 6311363, 6311431. New Taj hotel, Passport Street, near Sheraton hotel. Korean food. Open daily 1200-1500; 1800-2400.

Formosa Restaurant Tel: 6658193. North off Palestine Road, last turning right before flyover going west. Chinese food. Open daily 1300-1500; 1800-2300.

Shopping

The number of large shops and shopping complexes in Jeddah has grown to match the city's expansion since the late 1970s. The days of travelling miles to one shop for one particular item are gone, and most people now have a European-style supermarket or complex in — or at least very near — their neighbourhood. This is as well as the local corner shops, bakeries and cafes selling takeaway kebabs and grilled chicken.

Even those without a car can take heart. Buses run daily from most compounds to different areas, and improved public transport schedules mean King Abdul-Aziz Street and the souqs are available to all.

With the various souqs (see Souqs) and the new Afghani quarter for local purchases, maps and antiques, the "Bond Street" shops of Khalid Ibn Waleed Street and Al-Madinah Road, and the neighbourhood shopping centres, Jeddah can fairly be described as a shoppers' paradise.

A well-stocked Jeddah vegetable market

Shopping centres and department stores

Redec Plaza Tel: 6448880. West of Al-Madinah Road (south) and near the Caravan Shopping Centre; opened in 1979. Concentrates on luxury shopping.

Two shopping levels are arranged around a central indoor garden with fountain and a sail board on display. On the first level shoppers sit at white trellis tables of the Cafe de Faubourg which serves good coffee and cold drinks; the second level is L'Oriental Restaurant.

Shops in the centre include: MAS Travel and Wabel Travel; Nina Ricci, Carven and Ted Lapidus; Porcelaine for quality china; the Saudi Book Centre (see Bookshops). There is also a toy shop; a clothes shop with segregated departments for men and women; an interior design shop; a tobacconist and an art gallery which mounts regular exhibitions.

Jeddah Shopping Centre Tel: 6604199, 6651878. On Al-Madinah Road, just north of the Palestine Road flyover beyond the new Jeddah Clinic. Free parking.

One of Jeddah's best known shopping centres, with a well-stocked, spacious supermarket selling a good selection of western food including fresh meat, bread and cakes, fruit and vegetables; a perfumery; a cassette tape department and a good coffee shop which sells fresh roast and ground coffees, and serves cappuccino coffee, croissants and cakes.

Other units include: British Airways, KLM, SAS, and Kuwait Airways; Ahmed Fitaihi jewellery; Lord John menswear; a barber; two toy shops; an artificial flower shop; a pharmacy; a stationery and office equipment shop; two camera shops; Sony showroom; jeans and casual wear; children's clothes and a souq arcade including local clothes and footwear.

Caravan Shopping Centre On Corniche Road (Hail Street), west of Al-Madinah Road and south of Ruwais.

One of the country's largest and most popular centres. The excellent supermarket has a fast turnover and is therefore good for perishable goods; a good range of dairy products, tinned foods, household goods, soft drinks, meat, fruit and vegetables.

Other units are: the Caravan Restaurant; the Cup of Coffee coffee bar; Concord children's toys; Dayvilles Original American Ice Cream; Nussy Shoes; Nataly Mother and Baby Care; the Lens camera shop; a pharmacy; Indian souvenir shop; newsagent; a Snoopy shop, and several small shops ranging from a T-shirt printers to a shawarma stall. There is also Okaz Bookshop and a branch of the Saudi British Bank, which has a separate women's branch.

Jeddah International Shopping Centre Tel: 6830033. On west side of Al-Madinah Road opposite Pepsi-Cola factory. Extensive car park. American-style centre, Jeddah's newest and largest, with more than 100 shops.

Completely enclosed and fully airconditioned, it is designed with "outdoor" cafes with an international theme — a Paris street corner, a Japanese garden, and so on. It gets very crowded, especially at weekends. The largest unit is the Sarawat superstore, selling all the usual range of goods found in a supermarket, and more.

Also has branches of stationery and office equipment supplier Al-Maktaba; Tihama Bookshop; Sporty House sports equipment; Wedgewood china; Saudi British Bank; a Computerland showroom, and small Honda and Daihatsu showrooms. There is also a pet shop; flower and plant shop; barber shop; displays of most makes of hi-fi equipment; Turkish rug and antique shop; travel bureau, and one-hour dry cleaning service.

Supermarkets stock every kind of food

The Queen's Building In the centre of King Abdul-Aziz Street downtown. Among the first high-rise commercial and shopping centres to be built in Jeddah.

Saudia's main ticket office is on the ground floor; to the left and behind the high-rise building are two floors of shops selling mainly clothing, perfumes, watches and jewellery, cassettes and electronic goods, and cameras. On the first floor a large Gazzaz store sells cosmetics, jewellery and toilet goods (American Express and Diners Club cards accepted); Shamsan has toys and cameras; plus a Saudi National Shipping Lines office (see Shipping). At the rear of the first floor is a supermarket selling food and drugstore items.

To the right of and behind the building spreads the large modern souq, shaded by a roof of plastic moulded domes. At the centre of the souq is Gabel Street, for pedestrians only. This runs from King Abdul-Aziz Street under King Faisal Street and up to the Bedouin souq, and the houses and mosques of old Jeddah. Alleys lead off both sides with small shops selling material, rugs, electrical goods, gold, dresses, shoes and luggage. In the evenings especially, it is thronged with shoppers of all nationalities.

Al-Sawani Department Store Tel: 6531328. Near old airport, next to Arab News Building on the edge of Sharafiyah. Supermarket on ground floor. Other departments: stationery, handicraft, gifts, men and women's clothes.

The Middle East Centre Due to open in 1983. It will be one of the biggest shopping malls in the kingdom, with banks, restaurants, supermarkets, reception rooms, offices and — eventually — a residential tower.

Al-Mohktar Department Store Tel: 6650780. In Al-Hamra district, close to British embassy and Hail Street. The nearest thing Jeddah has to a department store.

Basement: hardware and building section; ground floor: supermarket selling fresh meat, other food and household goods, pet department with various exotic birds, animals and fish; first floor: stationery, books and newspapers, toys and sports equipment, garden furniture, clothes and shoes; second floor: TV, radio and cassettes, gifts, furniture and pharmacy. Excellent bakery and Kentucky Fried Chicken outside.

Sands Shopping Centre Tel: 6512112, 6511092. Between Khalid Ibn Waleed Street and Al-Madinah Road in Sharafiya.

Good range of food, fruit and vegetables, and some household appliances. Units in first floor include parfumerie, stationers and clothes shops.

Supermarkets

Jeddah has many supermarkets selling good quality, well-packaged European and American food, as well as fresh fruit and vegetables, fresh and frozen meat, and often a wide range of household goods, including china and glass. Prices are fairly high, but the quality and choice of food is generally good.

Most supermarkets have a noticeboard, which is a good source of community information — advertisements can be posted concerning articles for sale, local events, lost and found pets, services and jobs vacant, language tuition, and so on.

Lebmarket East of Al-Madinah Road (north) and west of Khalid Ibn Waleed Street, near the Al-Madinah Road fruit and vegetable shops and the large mosque.

One of Jeddah's first supermarkets, with a wide range of products. Good for packaged products and milk. Upstairs is a household goods department selling inexpensive china, glass and kitchen equipment, as well as toiletries, perfume, women's shoes and some furniture.

Happy Family Supermarket Tel: 6513360, 6513364. Near the Corniche on Andalus Street, south of Palestine Road. Run by the Halwani group.

Excellent but expensive meat, Lebanese delicacies, and very good delicatessen with some high-quality imported cheeses; good bakery; high-quality glass, china and kitchenware department, plus food and household staples. Also sells newspapers and perfume.

Safeway Supermarket Large new store opposite the Sands hotel, off Tahlia Street.

Good but expensive fresh and frozen American meat; bakery; household and electrical goods; children's clothes; houseplant section, and large fruit and vegetable counter. Ample parking space and well-designed check-out counters.

Al-Wadi Supermarket Prison Street, close to Jeddah Towers apartment blocks.

Smaller supermarket but fresh meat, range of dairy products, and fruit and vegetables available. Good for Lebanese cheese and olives, bread and savoury products.

Jumbo Market Siteen Street, close to ice-cream parlour.

A smaller supermarket useful for packaged goods and household items. Discounts for bulk purchases.

Mohsen Supermarket Siteen Street, near flyover. Sells a wide range of goods from all over the world. Car park.

Sahary Centre Palestine Road near Luna park. Opened at the end of 1982. A large supermarket, with many other shops nearby. Ample car parking.

Al-Fao Superstore East end of Prince Abdullah Street, near Bicycle roundabout, in Shaker centre. Wide selection of food with first-floor department store. Ample car park.

Al-Fanous Al-Baladiya Street, east of Jeddah Dental Clinic. Well-stocked local supermarket with other shops in complex. Limited parking.

Meat
Most supermarkets have a meat counter, but quality varies and particular cuts are often difficult to get.

The Steak House Butcher. West off Siteen Street; turn left at the metal palm tree. Good selection and is familiar with the popular European and American cuts. Sells a range of poultry, veal and beef ham. The meat is imported from Europe and Australia.

Abbar & Zainy US Beef Northeast of the Caravan Centre. Sells freezer packs of excellent American meat and frozen fish. Rather expensive. New branch in north Jeddah near Samir Colour laboratory west of Al-Madinah Road.

Meat Market Al-Madinah Road, near the fruit and vegetable souq.

Halwani Al-Madinah Road. Expensive but excellent imported and local meat.

Fish
Fresh fish, locally caught, is sold at the fish souq on Corniche Road near King Abdul-Aziz Street. An interesting selection, but get there very early in the morning. On Fridays fish can often be bought from fish sellers in Palestine Road — or try to catch your own over the reef!

Supermarkets stock frozen fish — including fish fingers — while lobsters and crab are also available.

Nuwaylati Fish Market Tel: 6673621, 6673657. Al-Hamra, on the corner of street parallel to the Palestine Road/US embassy junction and near Al-Hamra park. Probably the best place for fresh fish.

Eggs
The supply of eggs fluctuates but supermarkets are the best source, as freshness is more reliable. Small local grocers' shops have only intermittent supplies.

Fruit and vegetables
Fruit and vegetable souq On Al-Madinah Road (south) towards the Palestine flyover. The best place for

Jeddah supermarket shopping list (1983) (SR)

	Sarawat	Safeway	Al-Mohktar	Jeddah shopping centre	Al-Fao	Sand	Caravan
Jar peanut butter	8.45	8.45	8.00	8.95	7.50	8.95	8.00
Jar jam	4.60	4.95	7.50	5.00	4.50	4.85	4.40
4 cans soup	10.80	11.00	10.80	11.00	12.00	11.00	10.80
3 cans ravioli	12.00	12.75	12.00	12.00	12.00	11.25	12.00
4 cans baked beans	9.80	11.00	10.00	11.00	10.50	11.00	11.80
2 cans corn	5.60	5.50	6.00	5.70	5.00	5.70	5.40
½lb tin tea	8.20	8.25	9.75	8.40	8.00	8.40	8.40
4oz instant coffee	10.00	9.45	9.00	8.75	9.00	9.50	8.75
2 boxes cookies	9.40	9.10	9.10	8.90	9.50	4.65	9.20
Can peaches	2.90	3.75	3.30	3.45	5.50	3.75	3.50
Can pears	3.60	3.45	3.75	3.35	3.50	3.95	3.75
3 kilos oranges	12.00	12.00	15.00	21.00	12.00	12.00	12.00
2 kilos apples	8.00	11.00	10.00	12.00	10.00	10.00	10.00
1 kilo margarine	11.80	11.80	12.00	11.20	12.00	12.50	10.00
500gm butter	9.50	9.25	10.00	10.00	9.50	10.00	9.70
500gm frozen peas	6.25	6.25	6.50	5.50	6.95	6.25	6.20
Kilo frozen mixed vegetables	11.75	11.50	11.70	11.75	11.75	13.00	11.60
2 lettuces	15.00	36.00	12.00	16.00	14.50	9.50	10.00
3 kilos tomatoes	15.00	24.00	18.00	18.00	24.00	21.00	18.00
1 box water	24.00	24.00	24.00	24.00	22.00	24.00	24.00
Box tide	12.50	12.50	20.50	12.50	12.50	25.00	12.50
Tray of eggs	14.00	13.00	12.00	11.00	10.00	12.00	11.00
2 kilos steak	56.00	72.00	50.00	44.00	50.00	50.00	50.00
2 kilos minced beef	40.00	48.00	40.00	44.00	40.00	40.00	44.00
Frozen chicken	7.60	4.95	8.50	7.00	7.00	6.00	7.60
Kilo stewing beef	24.00	31.00	40.00	22.00	25.00	25.00	25.00
Pkt frozen fish	8.25	8.25	8.75	10.50	7.50	7.95	7.50
Pkt hot dogs	4.50	4.45	4.25	4.45	4.50	4.50	4.00
Pkt paper towels	7.70	8.45	9.50	7.65	7.50	8.25	7.35
Pkt toilet paper	7.00	8.75	7.80	6.65	7.25	10.00	7.80
2 box kleenex	7.50	7.50	7.50	7.30	6.50	6.70	7.20
Cleanser	8.00	8.00	7.00	6.90	7.00	7.15	8.50
3 loaves bread	6.00	6.00	6.00	6.00	6.00	6.00	6.00
2 kilos flour	7.45	7.55	7.20	6.60	5.50	7.75	7.20
2 kilos sugar	3.00	3.00	3.00	3.00	3.50	3.25	3.00
2 kilos potatoes	7.85	8.00	8.00	8.00	8.00	7.00	6.00
2 kilos onions	10.00	5.00	6.00	10.00	6.00	5.00	4.00
6 cartons milk	18.00	18.00	18.00	18.00	18.00	18.00	18.00
2 cake mixes	10.80	10.50	11.10	11.30	11.00	11.30	10.40
3lb rice	7.05	4.45	7.75	8.00	7.00	7.65	7.70
Large mayonnaise	5.20	7.25	5.50	7.10	4.75	5.25	5.00
2 pkts sliced cheese	10.90	10.90	9.80	11.20	10.00	10.50	11.50
Total	**481.95**	**540.95**	**506.55**	**489.10**	**474.20**	**485.50**	**468.75**

fruit and vegetables — a row of small shops with a good choice of quality produce. Much better value than the supermarkets as goods can be hand-selected. Nearby are a well-stocked pharmacy, grocer's shop and Lebanese butcher.

Vegetable souq Roadside market run by Yemenis on the extension of Tahlia Street heading east. Very good for wholesale purchase of fruit and vegetables.

Dairy produce
As well as the local "long-life" Saudia Dairy reconstituted products, there is now an extensive range of fresh dairy produce — milk, cream, labneh, laban, buttermilk and cottage cheese. All can be found in big supermarkets.

Ice cream parlours
Dayvilles Caravan Shopping Centre and Jeddah International Shopping Centre.

Svensen's Airport Road, east of junction with Khalid Ibn Waleed Street.

Houseplants and flowers
Golden Rose Tel: 6600680. Siteen Street, just north of flyover.

Florina Tel: 6670719. Khalid Ibn Waleed Street, near King Fahd's palace. Good for houseplants and cut flowers; will make bouquets and arrangements. Interflora service. Branches: Palestine Road tel: 6659669; Khalidiya tel: 6823023.

House & Garden Tel: 6659927. PO Box 4734, continuation of Palestine Road, west of US embassy.

Green House West side of Siteen Street, south of the metal palm tree. Houseplants only.

Meridien Hotel Sells houseplants in the shopping centre.

New 'Al-Mohktar' Al-Hamra. Limited selection of cheap houseplants.

Reem Flowers Tel: 6658195.

Safeway Supermarket Opposite Sands hotel. Good selection of houseplants.

Plants are also available at outdoor nurseries on Al-Madinah Road (south) near the Palestine Road flyover, on the Palestine Road near the Jeddah Dome, and at the Jeddah International Shopping Centre. School and embassy bazaars are another excellent source of plants and cuttings — and much cheaper than the shops!

Cakes and bread
Supermarkets sell packaged bread of varying quality and freshness, and many have bakeries nearby.

Patisserie Venecia Khalid Ibn Waleed Street, next to the pharmacy. Sells excellent rolls, cakes and savoury pasties at lunchtime.

Patisserie Suisse Opposite Lebanese embassy. Cakes and pastries.

Le Vendome Al-Madinah Road (south). Particularly good for cakes and pastries; Arabic savouries to order; ice cream cakes.

Alafandi Siteen Street, virtually opposite airport entrance. Arab pastries, sweets and nuts, hot savoury takeaway food. First-floor restaurant serves Middle Eastern and continental food, open 1200-1500; 1700-2330.

Sarabia Good bakery opposite Dr G Pharaon clinic near Steak House.

Patisserie Francaise North of Nova Park hotel on street immediately east of hotel. Very good cakes, pastries and bread.

Sports shops
Al-Quraishi Tel: 6431402, 6431364. Al-Madinah Road, one kilometre south of Pepsi-Cola factory. Sells boats, sailing accessories, games, Mistral surf sailers, toys, sports clothing and leisure goods.

Sports & Camping Centre Tel: 6650551. PO Box 4745, Palestine Street near Jeddah Dome. Sells boats, tents, sporting and camping goods.

Mickey Sports Shop Al-Madinah Road, virtually opposite Jauhara Building.

Marine Equipment Beside Caravan Shopping Centre.

Sporty House Al-Madinah Road, near Pepsi-Cola factory. Wide range of sports equipment, clothes and footwear. Branch in Jeddah International Shopping Centre.

Women's hairdressers
Simone Mahler Beauty Institute Tel: 6443214. Near Wedding Palace, villa behind Redec Plaza. Hairdressing and beauty treatments.

Miss Monde Binzert Street, next to Lebmarket. Branch in Meridien hotel.

Dry cleaners
Sheraton hotel, Hyatt Regency, Jeddah International Shopping Centre, Al-Mohktar.

Bookshops
Al-Khazindar Distributing Tel: 6871869. Bookshops on Al-Madinah Road and in Meridien hotel.

Head office: PO Box 157, Jeddah; subsidiary offices: Riyadh tel: 4024502, 4024853, telex: 201319; Al-Khobar tel: 8641746, PO Box 1036; branch offices: Makkah, Taif, Khamis Mushait, Yanbu, Al-Madinah, Tabuk, Jubail and Buraydah.

The most comprehensive distributor of books, newspapers and periodicals; acts as sole agent for material from English, Arab, French, German and Italian distributors. Distributors for Hachette Gotch, Comag, Hachette International, World Wide Media, Luchelle, International Herald Tribune, Time, OUP, Newsweek, International Communications, Middle East Economic Digest (MEED), Burda, Bush Hansa, Agenzie Internazionale Italiana, Rizzoli Editore, Rusconi Editore, Corriere della Sera, Transworld, CBS, Feffer Symonds, Dell.

Saudi Publishing and Distributing House Tel: 6424043, 6432821. PO Box 3029, Datsun Building near Foreign Affairs Ministry, Al-Jauhara Building, flats 7 and 12. Telex: 404351 nashra, cable: meccalan. Manager Muhammad al-Wazir, can also be contacted at Marwa Advertising, tel: 6675100.

Bookshop is on corner of King Abdul-Aziz Street, soon after the Queen's Building.

A good selection of books in English and Arabic with emphasis on English as a Foreign Language textbooks and reference books.

Dar al-Shorouq Bookshop Tel: 6426610. PO Box 4146, next to Kaymak Glace Cake Shop near Foreign Affairs Ministry, Al-Madinah Road. Head office: tel: 6432166, PO Box 5941, telex: 401360. Owned by Mohsin A Baroum.

Saudi Book Centre Tel: 6448880. First Floor, Redec Plaza, off Al-Madinah Road.

Bright, well-stocked comprehensive, but expensive bookshop. Range of English, French and German paperbacks. Magazine and newspaper subscription service.

Tihama Bookshops Tel: 6440000. Head office, Ministry of Foreign Affairs Circle (contains small bookshop).

Main bookshop beyond Dutch Embassy, Al-Madinah Road (north). Bookshop branches: Saudia head office, Airport Road; Saptco bus terminal, Corniche Road; Saudia terminal bookshop, Jeddah international airport; Tihama outdoor advertising branch bookshop, Hassan Ibn Thabit Street, Baghdadiya; Macarona Road bookshop, opposite Saudi Chinese Commercial Centre by Dutch embassy; Shahba Advertising bookshop, Palestine Road, opposite Chinese embassy; Jeddah International Shopping Centre.

Okaz Bookshop Tel: 6601590, 6607574, 6601612. Head office: Okaz Street. PO Box 5941, telex 401360 okaz.

In the Caravan Shopping Centre on Hail Street. Sells paperbacks, hardbacks, academic books, newspapers and stationery.

Meridien Hotel Bookshop Sells newspapers, magazines, paperbacks, hardbacks and greeting cards.

International Bookshop Al-Madinah Road (north). Mostly Arabic books and magazines.

Saleh Bookshop Al-Madinah Road (north). Mostly Arabic books and newspapers.

Supermarkets such as Al-Mokhtar (see shops) sell foreign newspapers and magazines.

Antiques

The export of various antiques is controlled by the Department of Antiquities, to prevent fine examples of Saudi art and workmanship leaving the country. Before attempting to export these items — which include swords, daggers and firearms — a certificate must be obtained from the department. In cases where the item is deemed an important part of the national heritage, a certificate will not be granted, and the item will be bought by the department for museum display.

Prince Nawaf Ibn Abdul-Aziz antique shops The airport souq, opposite the old airport building.

This row of shops and stalls is one of Jeddah's main tourist attractions. Most sell Oriental rugs and carpets, ranging from the finest Persian and Turkish silk carpets to modestly priced items from Afghanistan and Pakistan. Persian Qum, Isfahan, Nain and Shiraz rugs and carpets are sold, as are Afghan and Afghan Baluch prayer mats.

Almost all the shops sell a range of Arab and bedu antiques and bric-a-brac. These include carved silver-mounted Saudi and Yemeni daggers (khanjar or janbiya) and swords (sayf); bedu bracelets, anklets, bells and other jewellery; bedouin women's veils (burga), often decorated with silver or metal embroidery, old coins and beadwork, and "Kuwaiti" chests — of wood decorated with brasswork and occasionally carving — most of which are imported from India.

Also sold are pieces of decorative woodwork from the balconies of old houses in Jeddah and Yemen; relics of the bedu way of life — long-handled coffee roasting spoons, tent-strips, and so on; finely enamelled silver boxes said to be from Makkah, but probably from India, and various items from Sudan and elsewhere in Africa. Prices are often extremely high, with fierce, prolonged bargaining necessary to bring them down to a reasonable level.

The Gold Souq Behind the Queen's Building.

Various shops selling Oriental rugs and bedu bric-a-brac. Although there is usually not as much choice as in the airport souq, prices are lower.

The souq groups a collection of stalls selling a remarkable variety of mainly second-hand goods. These include domestic and electrical appliances, furniture, clothes and old brass and copper — Arab coffee pots, hubble-bubble pipes (shisha) and large copper bedu cooking pots. "Kuwaiti" chests and bedu items can be found, as can low and medium quality rugs. One stall imports Yemeni woodwork and often has magnificent pairs of heavily carved doors, decorative items from rawshan balconies, and intricately worked furniture.

Coffee pots are just one of the many types of antique to be found

Nasir al-Haidari On the lower ground floor of the Nova Park hotel, on Palestine Road.

Sells a wide variety of mainly Oriental antiques and objets d'art, although some are from Arabia. Sells Syrian mirror frames and furniture inlaid with mother-of-pearl; "Kuwaiti" chests; copper and brassware; fine silverwork from Turkey; Indian antiques including painted windows and shutters; boxes and chests, and silver jewellery.

Oriental Antiques On the north side of Sharafiya, just east of the junction with Al-Madinah Road.

The Iranian manager travels widely in Asia, and imports antiques and objets d'art ranging from small brass, silver and ivory trinkets to rare, extremely fine pieces. The stock is variable, as better pieces are often sold within a few days of arrival. It can include fine Indian furniture and wood sculptures; Tibetan mandala paintings; Indian and Persian miniatures; a small selection of Oriental rugs, and brass items, including hanging lamps and Turkish coffee mills.

Abu Zaid King Abdul-Aziz Street, next to the Saudi Cairo Bank. There is a second, smaller branch in the Caravan Shopping Centre.

A well-established dealer selling high-quality Oriental carpets, objets d'art and antiques from the top end of the market. Excellent Persian rugs, including fine silk Qums, Isfahans, Nains and Tabriz, as well as Turkish Hereke silk rugs, at prices ranging up to SR 1 million. Also a wide choice of finely crafted metal pieces from Iran, including trays, silver coffee pots and cups, and a range of antique objects, many from Turkey.

Turkish carpet shop Next to the bakery beside Happy Family supermarket.

A large, new store — as yet unnamed — selling Turkish rugs and carpets. Most of the stock consists of silk rugs, although there are some modern items in wool. Also a small number of older pieces.

Turkish Carpets & Antiques Jeddah International Shopping Centre.

This new shop has an excellent range of Turkish rugs, from modestly priced wool Bergmas and Yahyalis to fine silk Herekes and several larger, older pieces. Also some Turkish brass and copperware.

Fine art

TAG Art Gallery In street parallel to Al-Madinah Road, one block west of Hyatt Regency hotel.

Exhibitions of paintings, prints and sculptures. Framing also done.

Medical

Hospitals

Dr Bakhsh Hospital Tel: 6510666, 6510222, 6510111, 6533310. PO Box 6940. About 25 metres west of Siteen Street, opposite old airport. Telex: 402060 medica. Opened in 1978.

Has about 122 beds. The nursing staff are predominantly British and all doctors are British-trained.

Forty private deluxe rooms with 20 beds and separate salons; 60 first class private rooms with one bed; 60 second class rooms, each with two beds. Visiting 1600-2100.

Emergency room open 24 hours. Basic consultation fee SR 100; ambulance available on call; comprehensive dental treatment by British dentist; hospital will screen company employees and arrange treatment; no vaccinations; outpatients' clinics from Saturday-Thursday; pharmacy.

Specialities: internal medicine; general surgery; ENT; orthopaedics; paediatrics; physiotherapy, obstetrics and gynaecology; urology; ophthalmology; dermatology; plus X-ray and pathology departments.

Dr Suleiman Fakeeh Hospital Tel: 6655000, 6671451-5. Palestine Road, close to Nova Park hotel. Telex: 401433 fakeeh.

Has 170 beds and Filipino nursing staff with British matron. The medical staff is Egyptian.

Bed rates: deluxe SR 800, first class SR 400, second class SR 200. Visiting 1000-2100.

Vaccinations for travellers and infants; check-ups SR 900; two ambulances on call; pharmacy.

Specialities: internal medicine; surgery; paediatrics; ENT; gynaecology; dermatology; opthalmology; cardiology; dentistry; plus X-ray department, laboratory, physiotherapy, and renal dialysis and intensive care units.

Al-Maghrabi Hospital Tel: 6369822, 6368076. PO Box 7344. By Old Palace off Makkah Road. Telex: 400646.

120 beds. Specialist ear, nose and throat hospital also offering dental care. Staffed by American, British and Egyptian staff, backed up by local professors.

Bed rates: on request.

Optical department can provide and fit soft contact lenses, and hard lenses ordered from the US.

Dr M Erfan Hospital Tel: 6825857, 6825959. PO Box 6519. King Fahd Street, north of Tahlia Street roundabout and near vegetable market. Telex: 400981 erfan. Opened in 1982.

Has 150 beds. The nursing staff are mainly Filipino with British head nurses. Has Arab consultants trained in the US and UK.

Bed rates: single SR 300, double SR 400, suite SR 600.

Emergency room open 24 hours; ambulance available on call; dental clinic for orthodentistry and surgery; medical and surgical intensive care units; two fully equipped operating rooms for micro-neurosurgery, plastic and general surgery; pharmacy; gift shop.

Specialities: adult and child psychiatry; addiction centre; neurosurgery; radiology; fully automated hormonal, biochemical and histopathological services.

Bugshan Hospital for Women & Children Tel: 6691222, 6690356, 6690244, 6690876, 6691292. PO Box 5860. Tahlia Street, just off Al-Madinah Road (north) by Pepsi-Cola factory. Telex: 402519 helthy. Opened 1980.

Has 120 beds. Indian and Filipino nurses with British senior nursing staff. All midwives are British-trained.

Bed rates: rooms SR 350-450, suites SR 650.

Specialities: baby care unit; intensive care unit; ENT microsurgery; casualty department with separate

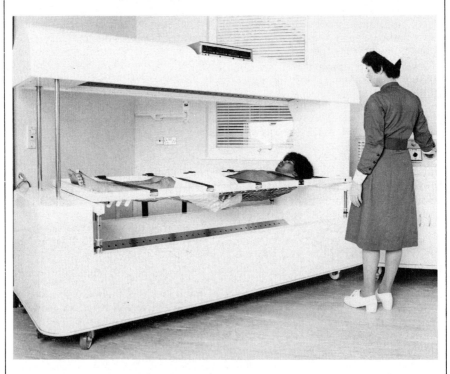

New form of relief for heat stroke victims in the kingdom

Visitor's palace, Riyadh

Yemeni stonemason, Abha

Eating a kabsa in Yanbu

Village south of Abha

Terraced fields in the Asir

entrance; two operating theatres for minor operations and resuscitation. In polyclinic: ENT; paediatric surgery; dental clinic; general surgery; internal medicine; cardiology; outpatients; laboratory.

New Jeddah Clinic Hospital Tel: 6675888. PO Box 7692. On west side of Al-Madinah Road, near Jeddah Shopping Centre. Telex: 401266 shark. Opened June 1979.

Has 100 beds. The medical and nursing staff are mainly Chinese, Filipino and Arab.

Bed rates: shared ward SR 250, single room SR 400, single room with extra bed for relative SR 450, suite SR 700. Visiting 1000-1200, 1600-2100.

Emergency room open 24 hours; one ambulance on call; vaccinations for infants only.

Specialities: surgery; cardiology; paediatrics; dentistry; acupuncture; orthopaedics; ENT; obstetrics and gynaecology; physiotherapy; laboratories providing histopathology, hormonal assay, serology and bacteriology services.

Jeddah Medical Centre Tel: 6515935, 6515939, 6515943, 6515947. PO Box 7360. Immediately northeast of Caravan Shopping Centre. Telex: 401025 zinada. Opened 1979.

Has 110 beds. Staff include Americans, Europeans and Arabs.

Bed rates: third class SR 200, second class SR 300, first class SR 400, apartment SR 600, extra bed for visitors SR 150.

Emergency room open 24 hours; ambulance on call; check-ups.

Specialities: oriental medicine — acupuncture and acupressure; surgery; cardiology; paediatrics; urology; obstetrics and gynaecology; nephrology; gastroenterology; neurology; infectious diseases; dentistry; pharmacy; radiology departments with mammography and ultrasound equipment, and renal dialysis unit.

Dr Siddiqa Maternity Hospital. To be opened in 1983. Bani Malik Road.

Has 30 beds. All the doctors are female. Staff include two consultants, a child specialist, general physicians, radiologist, pathologist and pharmacist, matron with 15 nurses and 20 junior nurses or nursing aides.

Clinic

Dr Ghassan N Pharaon Medical & Dental Clinic Tel: dental 6658784, 6658516; medical and emergency 6692904. Al-Baladiya Street opposite Steak House and behind Juffali showroom. Telex: 402476 pharo.

Open Saturday-Thursday 0900-1000, 1630-2000. 24-hour emergency service.

Medical section: five doctors, mainly British and Arab, with clinic run on appointment system. Specialities include diabetes; ENT and all other general practice; laboratory; X-ray, physiotherapy department; minor operations. Day beds available.

Dental section: 12 British and Arab dentists; American orthodontist; British peridontists; dental laboratory. Appointment system but prompt emergency service.

Dentists

Most hospitals have out-patient dental clinics (see Hospitals).

Dental Care Centre Tel: 6653676. East of Khalid Ibn Waleed Street, behind King Fahd's palace. Open 0900-1300, 1630-2000. Four dentists; laboratory.

General practitioner

Alan Homay Tel: office 6675045, home 6657370. PO Box 5723. Al-Sayed Abdul-Wahab Street, near Al-Mokhtar and Bahrain embassy. Open Saturday-Thursday 0900-1200, 1700-2000.

Vet

Dr Ian McLaren Tel: 6824614. Near Samir Colour factory and old Arabian Homes compound on the left side of

Al-Madinah Road (north). All veterinary services, plus boarding for dogs, cats and birds. Open 0900-1000, 1700-2000.

Pharmacies

There are good ones in the Caravan and Jeddah shopping centres, on Khalid Ibn Waleed Street and Al-Madinah Road (close to vegetable souq).

A list of pharmacies open in the evening is posted in the English language newspapers and include, on a rota basis, the following:

Al-Shati Drug Store Tel: 6654835. Al-Madinah Road (north).

Al-Batterji Pharmacy Tel: 6423259. King Abdul-Aziz Street.

Al-Jazirah Drug Store Tel: 6425715. Opposite Al-Jazirah hotel.

Al-Madinah Pharmacy Tel: 6658052. Al-Madinah Road (north).

Ehsan Pharmacy Nuzlah Bani Malek.

Al-Ahlia Pharmacy Tel: 6422689. King Abdul-Aziz Street.

Nazih Drug Store Tel: 6422441. Bab Makkah.

Ashraf Drug Store Tel: 6431952. Sharafiya.

Al-Hayat Drug Store Tel: 6420032. Bab Makkah, Mousli Building.

Khalid Ibn Waleed Pharmacy Tel: 6651480. Khalid Ibn Waleed Street.

Hamra Pharmacy Tel: 6655135. Al-Madinah Road, near vegetable souq.

Tamer Pharmacy Tel: 6422313. Queen's Building.

Dr Al-Madhoun Tel: 6675447. Jeddah Shopping Centre.

Many supermarkets sell aspirin products, indigestion tablets, shampoo, soap, toothpaste and deodorants.

Estate agent

Saudi International Properties Tel: 6672098-9. Telex: 400577 sirop. Division of Binladin Brothers. Handles real estate in Jeddah, Riyadh and Yanbu, and arranges acquisition of overseas properties.

Pest control

Ciba-Geigy Tel: 6824561, 6821066. PO Box 5513. Telex: 403433.

Pestokil Tel: 6829606. Offers regular maintenance of property against all kinds of pest.

Arab Cleaning Enterprise Contracted to the municipality for cleaning the city. Provides a free pest control service.

Jeddah for the expatriate

Jeddah has long been one of the most sophisticated and cosmopolitan cities in the Arabian peninsula, retaining its unique character despite vast expansion and the enormous increase in the number of Saudi and expatriate citizens.

Most expatriates prefer to live in compounds and, indeed, companies have been encouraged to house their workers this way. The residential area of the city has expanded northwards, and it is here that most of the new compounds, villas, supermarkets and shopping centres are found. Most of the compounds have swimming pools, and gardens are rapidly being developed to bring a touch of green to the dusty areas of new building. Most compounds also provide their own morning bus service to take children to school and shoppers to the stores. Those who live near bus routes can also take airconditioned local buses to King Abdul-Aziz Street and the souqs (see Souqs).

There is plenty to see in Jeddah. After visits to the souqs and new shopping centres have palled, the city and its surroundings can be examined more closely. The architecture of the old town with its white walls and brown woodwork can be compared with that of the modern villas which have sprung up in the fashionable districts of Al-Hamra or the area west of Hail Street. Some have been built in the traditional style with white crenellated walls and mashrabiya windows, some are uncompromisingly modern, gleaming with marble and glass, while others have incorporated the Islamic arch and dome into surprisingly unconventional backgrounds. Everywhere are new monuments and statues commissioned by Mayor Farsi — a Henry Moore figure, a flight of metal birds, an enormous stone thumb, stranded ships, metal flowers, bronze coffee pots, and so on. And rivalling these is the increasing profusion of trees and plants.

The city is not short of leisure activities. Although home entertainment comes high on the list, the more physically active have the bonus of the Red Sea — miles of sandy beaches, the reef for diving and snorkelling, lagoons and creeks for sailing and waterskiing. This is in addition to the tennis, squash, cricket, rugger and even ten-pin bowling which are available. For the culturally minded there is no shortage of concerts and plays, while, with a little patient research, natural historians will find a wealth of plants, insects and birds in the nearby desert wadis.

And children are not forgotten — for them there is football, brownies, cubs and even the Duke of Edinburgh award scheme.

Education

Schools

All schools contacted insisted that parents should think very carefully before sending *older* children to school in Jeddah. Some facilities exist, but the general environment is rarely thought appropriate for teenagers.

The Jeddah Preparatory School Tel: 6823509. C/o British embassy, PO Box 393, in northeast part of the city in a new building. Set up in 1967 and managed by the British and Dutch communities.

Educational standards match those of the better UK primary schools. The infant and junior schools take 480 British and Dutch children from the ages of 4-12, and prepare them for entrance examinations, including Common Entrance to UK schools. Many of the teachers, including the headmaster, are on contract from the UK. Classes average 20-25 children. A new reception department for children aged at least 4 on 1 September of each year opened in January 1983. All children attending reception classes are guaranteed a place in the main school when they are old enough.

Hours: 0800-1330.

Fees: SR 3,600 a term payable at the start of each term: SR 1,800 deposit; SR 100 registration fee.

Facilities include assembly hall and gymnasium, sports and games area, and swimming pool. Also a range of recreational pursuits including ballet, brownies and guides, cubs and scouts, field study trips and hobbies.

Parents are advised to register as soon as they can because of the shortage of places.

Continental School Tel: 6690515; secondary school tel: 6608965; primary school tel: 6652470. PO Box 6453, southwest of British embassy. Telex 401319 kinico. Opened October 1977.

Has 1,100 children in its early primary (3½-6 years), junior (6-11) and secondary schools. Open to children of all nationalities except Arab Muslims. The curriculum is based on the UK syllabus with up to 11 subjects offered at 'O' level for older children. Six-form entry into the secondary school — students are accepted if they are able to follow a programme meeting the requirements of the overseas board of London university. Most of the 80 staff are UK-trained.

Hours: 0815-1325.

Fees: SR 3,000-5,000 a term;

SR 100 registration fee; SR 1,000 entrance fee; SR 100 termly book fee.

Facilities include two swimming pools, laboratories, music rooms, secondary school common room, and two computer workshops for the secondary and junior schools. Recreational pursuits include sport, culture, brownies and guides.

Parents are advised to contact the school before they arrive as there is often a long waiting list.

Manaret International School Tel: 6719732, 6710832, 6710610. PO Box 3446, off Macarona Road, behind China Rose Restaurant.

Provides an Islamic education in either English or Arabic for children from nursery age upwards. Boys and girls are segregated from grade one on. The English section is open to non-Arab children, although there is occasionally a waiting list for the lower grades. An American syllabus is followed, although provision is made for 'O' level preparation in the secondary division. Most teachers in the English section are British-trained.

Fees: English section SR 12,500 a year; Arab section, primary SR 4,500 a year, secondary SR 6,500.

Activities include afternoon sports and weekend trips.

Korean School Tel: 6673704. Near Korean embassy. Opened in 1976.

Has 100 children aged 6-11, and a small kindergarten. Both Arabic and English are taught.

Hours: 0900-1500.

Fees: $35 a month.

French School Tel: 6671274-5. PO Box 7077, in French embassy annex, in road opposite Turkish embassy.

Has a kindergarten and primary and secondary school sections. English and Spanish are taught at secondary level, and English and Arabic at primary.

Hours: 0800-1330.

Fees: SR 1,000 a year admission; SR 2,000 a term for French nationals and SR 2,500 for others; deposit of up to SR 1,500 also payable.

During school holidays, enquiries should be made to French embassy.

Indian School Tel: 6421602. PO Box 852, Al-Madinah Road (south), in grounds of Indian embassy. Opened in 1969.

Junior school and kindergarten for Indian children only.

Hours: Junior school 0730-1315; kindergarten 1330-1630.

Fees: up to SR 200 a term.

Japanese School Tel: 6823182. Close to Al-Madinah Road/Thalia Street. Set up in 1975 for Japanese children only.

Has a kindergarten taking up to 44 children and a junior school taking up to 80.

Fees: up to SR 450 a term, although a third child goes free.

For enquiries, telephone the school or write to the Japanese embassy.

Italian School For Italian children only. For information contact Italian embassy, tel: 6421541.

German School In north Jeddah, close to vegetable market and Jeddah Prep School.

Takes 120 mainly German children although non-German speakers are admitted.

Fees: SR 11,000 a year.

For further information contact Deutscher Schulverein, PO Box 7510, Jeddah, or Deutsche Schule Jeddah, c/o Botschaft der Bundesrepublik Deutschland in Jeddah, PF 1500, 5300 Bonn, West Germany.

Nursery schools

There are several nursery schools for children aged 2-4. These operate from private homes, where the children benefit from supervised play, handicrafts, singing and storytelling. The hours are usually from 0830-1200.

Parents should, however, first satisfy themselves as to the experience and ability of the staff, who may not always be trained teachers.

Fees usually range from SR 800-1,400 a term.

Adult education
Private classes are held in activities such as yoga, keep-fit, handicrafts and painting; details of these can be obtained from embassies. Language classes are also held.

British Council Tel: 6672867. C/o British embassy, PO Box 393. Promotes educational and cultural co-operation with the UK, and provides information, advisory and recruitment services in education and training.

Jeddah French Saudi Centre Tel: 6602628, 6602476. Offers French language courses.

German embassy course Nova Park hotel, Al-Hamra. Ten to 12-week course in German language held twice weekly by the German embassy.

Larsen & Nielsen Saudi Arabia Tel: 6692090. Twelve-week course in English language held daily from 0900-1500.

Ahmed Abdul-Qassim Tel: office 6719041, home 6825879. Offers spoken Arabic course, in four grades, familiarising students with the Arabic spoken in Jeddah — simple conversation, instructions to employees, counting, asking questions, and so on. The vocabulary of each course is about 300 words. A written Arabic course teaches the alphabet and elementary grammar, reading of city and commercial signs, and simple written dialogue.

Al-Faisalya Women's Welfare Society Tel: 6655887 and ***Jamaiya Khayeriya: The Women's Welfare Society*** Tel: 6365351. Both offer various courses, including Arabic.

Homelly C 1 Programme Tel: 6475924, 6475762. PO Box 2797. Three-month course (60 hours) with cassettes and books for home learning.

Housing

In Jeddah at the end of 1982 about 70,000 homes were believed to be empty. Even so, finding suitable accommodation is not easy. Rents vary from about SR 30,000 a year for a two-bedroom flat around Macarona Road (east of King Fahd Street and north of Palestine Road), to SR 150,000-200,000 in Al-Hamra (west of Al-Madinah Road and north of Palestine Road). Expatriates may not, by law, buy real estate.

Jeddah is progressively moving north and most expatriates now live north of Palestine Road. Although there are a substantial number of private flats and villas available, many expatriates prefer to live in compounds. Most of these are also north of Palestine Road.

Finding somewhere to live can be exceptionally time-consuming and you will be lucky to find your precise requirements quickly. To find a villa or flat try:
☐ notice boards at supermarkets;
☐ advertisements in local newspapers;
☐ local estate agents;
☐ expatriates resident in Jeddah for some time, including embassy officials, and
☐ driving around residential areas looking for rental signs or for buildings with no airconditioners in evidence. While this is time-consuming and frustrating, it is generally considered the most productive.

Accommodation on compounds is not always easy to get. This is partly because the facilities offered — swimming pools, squash and tennis courts, maintenance services — are so good and, therefore, popular, and partly because many companies rent accommodation for extended periods and use it for successive employees.

Residential areas
The prime residential area is Al-Hamra, the location of many embassies and ambassadorial residences. Nearly all accommodation in this area is in villas and very expensive. Mushrefah, east of Al-Madinah Road and north of Palestine Road, is a well-established area with both villas and flats. The Macarona Road area is full of apartment blocks with rents of between SR 30,000-35,000 a year. Further

north of Jeddah, on both sides of Al-Madinah Road, are several areas — including Hay al-Rowdah and Hay al-Salama — with a substantial number of apartment blocks. Most of the compounds are also in this area.

Prices

Prices vary greatly and care should be exercised. Flats are available for SR 30,000-100,000 a year, depending on area, size and quality. Villas are likely to be available from about SR 80,000 for three bedrooms and a small garden, up to SR 200,000 a year or more for larger villas with a reasonable garden and swimming pool.

Compounds, which usually have a selection of villas and flats, tend to be more expensive than equivalent private villas because of the facilities provided. On top of the rent must be paid a quarterly maintenance charge which should be taken into account in initial costings as it can be quite considerable.

Advice

Expatriates should, where possible, ensure accommodation is part of the package being offered by the employer. Specific details of the accommodation should be ascertained in advance and incorporated into the employment contract. High rents and inadequate housing in the past have probably been responsible for a substantial number of resignations.

Sport

Tennis Tournaments are held in compounds such as that of Armaska and Rayville in Jeddah. The Jeddah open ladies doubles tennis tournament and the Armaska open are held at the former, and the Raytheon ladies doubles American tournament at the latter.

The Jeddah Squash League Founded in 1978, had 100 players in early 1983 and 16 teams. Games are played in compound squash courts.

Jeddah Euro Motorcross Association Sponsors international motorcycle races. In 1980 the race was held in the grounds of the National Guard hospital, where Saudi riders competed against contestants from Sweden, the UK, West Germany and Switzerland. Regular races are held.

The Dunes Club Beside the US embassy, offers tennis, swimming, golf, cricket, squash and handball to individuals and families. Runs a full league and cup programme throughout winter. For Jeddah residents only. Managers: Mrs Williams and Mrs Hadley.

Al-Hamra Fitness Club At the top of Jeddah Shopping Centre, Al-Madinah Road.

Sea sports

A warning should precede any discussion about the opportunities for swimming, snorkelling or scuba diving — never swim or dive alone; always maintain visual contact with your companion, wear shoes against stonefish, and protective clothing such as a T-shirt (some advise wearing gloves as it is easy to cut yourself on the coral).

Scuba (self-contained underwater breathing apparatus) diving should only be attempted by those who are properly trained. The few tragic accidents have almost always befallen those who have not attended the BSAC or PADI courses (see below). It is also advisable to get a professional manual such as the BSAC manual (from BSAC, 76 Upper Woburn Place, London WC1H OQW); the US Navy diving manual NAVASHIPS 250-538 (from the Superintendent of Documents, USG Printing Office in the US)

Jeddah is largely built on coral which has been accumulating along the coast for hundreds of thousands of years. Jeddah's reef stretches on either side of the city — the port developed in one of the few natural breaks in the chain of coral.

The water is shallow enough for the snorkeller to study the beauties of underwater life; the coral's need for sunlight encourages it to grow as close to the surface as possible. Even at the cliff at the reef's edge, where the sea floor descends suddenly from two to 30 metres, the clarity of the water enables the snorkeller to see a great deal from the surface.

Diving
To dive in Saudi Arabia you should be a member of the BSAC or its US equivalent, PADI (see also Eastern province), or possess an international diving certificate. The rule is sound as it is extremely dangerous for untrained people to attempt scuba diving. The BSAC claims that no member has ever had a serious accident. However, several have occurred among non-members.

Jeddah BSAC has two branches: one is open to all; the other is restricted to employees of Whittaker Corporation.

The BSAC Training Course, considered the most rigorous in the kingdom, has run for about nine years. There are about 40 members. Instructors are not paid. At weekends the BSAC takes members to the Twenty-nine Palms, a series of reefs 60 kilometres north of Jeddah, and an area a little north of the Jeddah desalination plant.

Types of sailing
Dinghy sailing is pursued at the Red Sea Sailing Association (RSSA) which has a compound on the lagoon north of Obhur Creek. Membership is open to those interested in sailing and who own an RSSA-class boat — 470s, lasers, sunfish. The lagoon provides an extensive area of water with ideal sailing conditions. Organised class and handicap racing, and also sail training, take place throughout the year.

The Red Sea Board Sailors' Association caters for board enthusiasts. Organised sailing and racing facilities are available at Silver Beach on the Red Sea north of Obhur Creek, Jeddah.

Keel boat sailing is generally limited to pleasure cruising. The relevant regulations permit non-Saudis to bring their own vessels into the kingdom for their personal use, subject to customs clearance formalities and provided the vessel does not exceed 10 grt and does not have an engine exceeding 150 hp. At present, vessels can be moored at Obhur Creek.

Before any vessel (whether a keel boat or dinghy) can be used, it is necessary to obtain a registration certificate, issued by the Ministry of Communications, and an annual licence to operate the vessel, issued by the Ministry of Communications in conjunction with the coastguard authority.

Windsurfing
It takes about five hours of practice to be able to get the sailboard to go the way the beginner wants and then he is ready for further practice away from the nursery shallows. Once the basic skills of windsurfing are mastered the next stage is usually racing and in Jeddah some expatriates have got together and race their Mistrals every week-end of the year. Even in December nobody wears wet suits.

For the past three years, expatriates from Saudi Arabia have gone to the Mistral windsurfer world championships and hope to attend this year's event in Barbados. The Saudis themselves are not a swimming people — even the local fishermen rarely swim and consequently have not yet taken to the sport in large numbers but one or two western-educated Saudis are starting to show interest.

A Mistral board will cost about SR 4,500 new, but they hold their value very well and after two years of constant use can often be re-sold for at least SR 3,500, giving a good return in fun and cash for the original outlay. However, apart from the cash consideration, the relaxation and sheer escape from the hectic and arduous life of the expatriate must be worth some inroads into his capital.

Recreation

Social interest groups
For information on social events in Jeddah, Riyadh and Eastern province see Arab News (Community News) and the Saudi Gazette (Who, What, Where and When).

Theatre
Jeddah has several masterly theatrical troupes, of which the *Jeddah Players* and the *Saudi Equity Theatre (SET)* are pre-eminent. Auditions are held at the USGS Recreation Centre or the Players Playhouse. Some performances are put on at the British embassy.

Smaller groups include *One-Off Productions,* sponsored by the British embassy, and the *Off-Runway Players* at the New Jeddah International Airport Theatre at the Hochtief Camp.

Music
The Jeddah Concert Committee was set up in 1978 to provide a wide range of music. It attracts artists from all over the world.

The Hejaz Choral Society performs throughout the year traditional, folk, classical and oratorio works from different countries. Singers of any nationality are welcome.

The Jeddah Light Opera Society holds regular Monday rehearsals for its productions.

The Classical Musical Circle meets twice a month in private villas.

Other groups
Scottish dancing group meets at the Jeddah Prep School on Monday evenings. Contact through embassy.

The Saudi Arabian Natural History Society meets on the first Saturday of the month at the Al-Hamra Nova Park hotel. Talks are given and members receive details of trips to make themselves.

The Saudi Arabian Philatelic Society (SAPS) holds annual stamp shows and auctions. It was set up after 16 stamp collectors met at the Riyadh Inter-Continental in April 1979 and the Youth Ministry provided them with a centre off Siteen Street.

The British Wives Association meets on the first Monday in the month at the British embassy.

The British Airport Circle Wives of the Hochtief camp at Jeddah's new international airport began meeting in early 1980. The group, which is bilingual in German and English, arranges trips within Jeddah and abroad, and publishes a newsletter.

Saudi Women's Welfare Society On Makkah Road. Started by the late king Faisal's wife, Iffat. Runs an orphanage, 17 day care centres for children of working mothers, nursery and kindergarten classes, and free health clinic. Women attend literacy, sewing and language classes and take part in social evenings.

Bridge clubs
Several hold regular meetings, usually on company premises. The largest is attached to the Dunes Club. Most clubs have teams in the Jeddah bridge league. Visitors are welcome.

Other interest groups in Jeddah include brownies and guides, chess, cricket, darts, Duke of Edinburgh award scheme, rugby football, scouts and cubs.

Banks

Commercial banks
The Saudi French Bank Tel: 6605863 (10 lines). PO Box 1, 16 Om al-Muomenin Street 147, Sharafiyah. Telex: 403879 sfgm sj, cable: safbank djeddah. Managing director: Raymond Bravard.

Albank Alsaudi Alhollandi Tel: 6652690, 6690536. PO Box 6677, Al-

Madinah Road. Telex: 400324 bsho sj, cable: saudilanda. Managing director: W J van der Mei.

Arab National Bank Tel: 6422896, 6423579, 6423349. PO Box 344. Telex: 401099 arabank, cable: bank arabi.

Bank al-Jazira Tel: 6313968, 6312289. PO Box 6277, Kaki Building, Airport Road. Telex: 401574 hjaz, cable: raeesy. General manager: Athar Husain.

Bank Melli Iran Tel: 6431687-8, 6429749, 6423808. PO Box 1686, King Abdul-Aziz Street. Telex: 401188 jedmel sj, cable: bankmelli. General manager: Mohammad Hossein Hosseini Ghenani.

International Commercial Bank of China C/o Office of Economic Counsel or embassy, PO Box 580, Telex: 401061 sinoems sj. Representative: C S Lee.

Korea Exchange Bank Tel: 6427905. PO Box 6221.

Lebanese Arab Bank Tel: 6658327-8. PO Box 2581. Telex: 401124. Representative: Ilyas Ansari.

The National Commercial Bank Tel: 6423794, 6443404. PO Box 3555, King Abdul-Aziz Street. Telex: 401102, 401086 ncb, cable: banksaudi (head office), mowafak (branches). General manager: Salim Bin Ahmad Bin Mahfouz.

Riyad Bank Tel: 6474777. PO Box 1047, King Abdul-Aziz Street. Telex: 400619 (dealers), 401006 rydx sj, cable: riyadbank jeddah. Managing director: Ahmad Abdel-Latif, general manager: Ibrahim M S Shams.

Saudi Cairo Bank Tel: 6534140, 6534144, 6534148, 6534392. PO Box 496, Al-Faiha Building, Al-Madinah Road. Telex: 400205 scho sj, 402524 (dealers), 402189 scdc sj, cable: saudicairba jeddah saudi arabia. Managing director: Hamid M Henaidy.

United Saudi Commercial Bank PO Box 1686, King Abdul-Aziz Street. Chairman: Mahsoun Jalal. *Moving to Riyadh 1983.*

Specialised banks
Islamic Development Bank Tel: 6360011. PO Box 5925, Khuzam Gardens. Telex: 401137, cable: bankislami. Chairman: Ahmad Mohammad Ali.

Islamic Investment Company Tel: 6512496, 6512728. PO Box 9707, Pearl of Jeddah Building, 3rd Floor, Hail Street. Telex: 403763 darmac sj. General manager: Samir A Shaikh.

Other financial institutions
Al-Rajhi Company for Currency Exchange & Commerce Tel: 4054244 (20 lines), 4013947, 4013153, 4040875, 4039117, 4035644. PO Box 28. Telex: 201073, 201630 rajhi sj. General manager and managing director: Sulaiman al-Abdel-Aziz al-Rajhi.

Arab European Investment Corporation Tel: 6870361, 6885786. PO Box 1588. Telex: 401042. Managing director: John A Gould. *Name to be changed to Arabian Business Services.*

The First Saudi Investment Corporation Tel: 6603882, 6673233. PO Box 6540. Telex: 400282 fsic sj. Managing director: G Colin Davies.

Injaz Financial Services Bahlas Building, Moquf Khat, Bab Makkah.

Islamic Banks' International Association Tel: 6897341, 6448364. PO Box 4992. Telex: 401430 focus sj. Secretary-general: Ahmad al-Naggar.

Saudi Arabian Investment Company Tel: 6656193. PO Box 2096, Al-Madinah Road. Telex: 410211 saico. Chief executive: Ahmad A al-Maghrabi, managing director: Michael Palmer.

Saudi Arabian Investment Company (Overseas) Tel: 6656193, 6653380. PO Box 2096, Al-Madinah Road. Telex: 401211, 401823.

Saudi International Investment Company Tel: 6532511-6. PO Box 1716, Abraj (Citibank) Building, Fifth Floor, Towers A & C, Ali Bin Abi Talib Road. Telex: 401214 emam sj, cable: myhome jeddah. President: Hani S Emam.

Saudi Investment Group Company (SIG) PO Box 7805, Shaikh Ibrahim Shaker Building, Had Street, Al-Roweis. Manager: Ziad Zaghloul.

Saudi Research & Development Corporation (Redec) PO Box 1935. Telex: 401122-1.

Lawyers

Arabian Law Office (Abdul-Aziz A al-Ghamdi) Tel: 6530811. PO Box 3983, King Fahd Street, north of Jeddah Towers.

A Yehia Dannaoui Tel: 6429344. PO Box 4386, Abdulfattah Building, behind Redec Plaza, off Al-Madinah Road. Telex: 403708 denawi.

Mohamed A Mugraby Tel: 6651992, 6652628. PO Box 6500, Kaki Building, Al-Madinah Road. Telex: 402972 avocat sj.

Ahmed Bin Khaled al-Sudairy Tel: 6651842, 6657233. PO Box 3674, Palestine Road, in front of US embassy.

Hassan M Abu-Azmah Tel: 6519044, 6519624. PO Box 6808, Alshohada Street, Al-Krimly Building. Telex: 402467 azmah sj. Languages: Arabic, English.

Mohammad Said al-Awadi Tel: 6425032, 6423329. PO Box 590, King Abdul-Aziz Street, 4th floor, Prince Abdullah al-Faisal Building. Telex: 401850 minhad sj. Open 0900-1400, 1700-2000. Languages: Arabic, English.

Sami Bakr Saem al-Dahr Tel: 6691427, 6673619. PO Box 2477, Al-Madinah Road, Jeddah Shopping Centre, Office 302. Telex: 402064 sirwl. Languages: Arabic, English.

Wahib I Allami Tel: 6534740. PO Box 8796, Sharafiya, Allami Centre. Languages: Arabic, English.

Hasan al-Maheseeni Tel: 6671862, 6658170, 6690938. PO Box 2256, Al-Hamra, near Al-Mohktar Supermarket. Telex: 401793 libra sj. Open 0900-1330, 1700-2000. Languages: Arabic, English, French. Associate firm: Burlingham, Underwood & Lord, New York.

Mohamed A Elkhereiji Tel: 6601423, 6655458. PO Box 8632, Alhamra. Telex: 400534 incent sj. Languages: Arabic, English, French.

Abbas Faiq Ghazzawi Tel: 6600095, 6600087, 6659143, 6659155. PO Box 2335, Fitaihi Building, West Palestine Street. Telex: 400961 faig sj. Languages: Arabic, English, French, Italian.

Ahmad Mohammad Muzhar Tel: 6530955, 6532763. PO Box 5052, Sharafiyah, Faiha Building. Telex: 400067 mazhar sj. Languages: Arabic, English.

Hussein Shukry & Mahmoud el-Ayouti Tel: 6433385, 6420927, 6442708, 6433543. PO Box 667, King Abdul-Aziz Street, Commercial & Residential Centre. Telex: 401707 shoukr sj. Open 0830-1330, 1700-2000. Languages: Arabic, English.

Ahmed Zaki Yamani Tel: 6429559, 6429557, 6429550-1. PO Box 1351, Bakhashab Building, near Foreign Affairs Ministry. Telex: 401015 baship. Open 0900-1400, 1730-2100. Languages: Arabic, English, French. Associate firms: Surrey & Morse, Washington; Cameron Markby, London.

Almihdar Law Firm Tel: 6877326, 6874791, 6873403. PO Box 1180, Makkah Road. Telex: 402713. Open 0900-1330, 1600-1700. Associate firm: Lovell, White & King, tel: London 2366011, 21 Holborn Viaduct, EC1.

Dr Mujahid M al-Sawwaf Tel: 6690751, 6690753. PO Box 5840, Al-Musaidiyah Street, Al-Hamra. Telex: 402262 furat sj.

Trips to make in the Jeddah region

The following are based on trips made by the Saudi Arabian Natural History Society incorporating updated material from Shirley Kay's Travels in Saudi Arabia (see Bibliography).

Warning: every precaution should be taken before embarking on these trips, particularly where they involve desert tracks (see Desert Driving Survival Checklist). Although the editor has every confidence in the accuracy of the information, neither he nor the publishers can take any responsibility in this respect.

Introductory tour

This introductory tour shows the various land forms around Jeddah plus some places of interest to break the monotony of driving.

Starting at the southwest corner of Saudia city — the compound in Jeddah for Saudia staff — head north along the coast road to join the Al-Madinah Road south of the north terminal flyover. Continuing north, pass the turning to the North Creek and almost immediately bear right before the flyover and follow the signs for Usfan. You are now heading northeast, leaving the coastal plain, or Tihama, and going into the foothills of the Hejaz mountains. These stretch for almost the whole length of Saudi Arabia and rise to 3,000 metres-plus near Abha, in the south. The landscape now becomes more barren, with hills of volcanic rock lying loosely over sand. Continue until you reach a slight crest in the road. To your left you will see a group of palm trees, providing some shade for a picnic. A little further on is an old Turkish fort with round towers and a room with two chambers in the centre — but beware the snakes and bats which live there!

Introductory tour*

Km	
Start	southwest corner of Saudia city
20.6	foreign airlines (north terminal) turnoff
18.2	North Creek turn
29.8	flyover; follow signs to Usfan
56.2	Usfan on left; palm trees
58.9	Turkish fort on left
60.8	flyover; follow signs to Makkah
73.1	signpost Sedco farm project; turn left
76.1	Sedco hydroponic farm
84.2	brickworks
117.0	Al-Jumum crossroads; turn right to Jeddah
112.2	chicken farm on left
141.5	Makkah to Jeddah road; turn right
160.5	Turkish fort on left
167.6	Al-Oboor service station
168.7	turn left to Jeddah
174.5	kilometre 10 flyover

* All distances for these tours are approximate
Average driving time 2¼ hours

Usfan

From the fort is a good view of Usfan, which has grown considerably in the past few years. Beside the road are ploughed fields and many wells with diesel pumps and small block cisterns alongside. If you have four-wheel-drive it is possible to trace the route of the old water channel from Usfan to the palm grove in front of the fort; the channel was still being used a few years ago but is now blocked. Taking the road to Makkah you see on your left a small escarpment of volcanic rock known locally as Harrat.

Wadi Fatima

If you have four-wheel-drive it is possible to reach the top of the escarpment via Wadi Fatima. The area, Harrat Rahat, is uninhabited and completely barren. At the signpost Taif 160/Makkah 70, you see on your left the roof of the Sedco hydroponic farm. The farm, which grows cucumbers, tomatoes and lettuce, can be reached along a bumpy, well signposted track. Visitors are welcome, especially on Fridays, and the resident horticulturalist is usually glad to show people round.

Returning to the asphalt road, turn left towards Makkah and continue to Al-Jumum, set on the crossroads formed by the Wadi Fatima and the main Al-Madinah to Makkah roads. Wadi Fatima is to the left and Jeddah to the right.

The drive to Wadi Fatima is pleasant, along a new asphalt road passing small farms and the pumping stations which provide Jeddah with some of its water. The road to Jeddah passes two new industries — the Bitter Soda bottling plant on the right and a chicken farm on the left — while there are many small farms, surrounded by low pink hills. You join the old Jeddah to Makkah highway at Haddad, before turning right on the last stage of your trip. After Bahrah the road passes through a built-up area, and you can see a well-preserved cistern on top of a small hill, and directly ahead another Turkish fort, built to provide shelter for pilgrims on their way to Makkah.

At Al-Oboor service station, turn left onto a track alongside a high wall. A little further on is a traditional pottery selling clay pots made by hand and fired in a large kiln. Returning to the main road turn left and return to Jeddah, either by continuing along Makkah Road or by bearing right at the flyover to north and central Jeddah via the new expressway.

Hanakiyah

Kilometres

Start	southwest corner of Saudia city
18.2	North Creek turn-off
29.8	flyover; follow signs to Al-Madinah
408.7	Police check at Al-Madinah
409.5	Bear right to overpass leading to bypass; follow signs to Qassim and Riyadh
540.3	Hanakiyah village
561.4	Hanakiyah rock visible on left about two kilometres away

It takes about 5½ hours to reach the red sandstone rock of Hanakiyah by car from Jeddah. You get there by heading north along the coast road to the Al-Madinah Road and continuing north past the North Creek turning until you reach the flyover. Take the turning for Al-Madinah and continue along it for nearly 400 kilometres. After the Al-Madinah police check and bypass, follow the Qassim road until 20 kilometres east of Hanakiyah village, when it runs over the edge of a lava flow and immediately over a bridge. At the east end of the bridge a track, indicated by a blue arrow on a round white board, turns off to the north. Hanakiyah rock can be seen two kilometres to the north, jutting out from the sandy plain.

The rock is covered with ancient engravings; some, in Arabic and even European script, are pale, almost white, while others depicting camels, ostriches and palm trees and with an older version of Arabic script, are deep pink. Near these are writings, deep pink in colour, in a script older than Arabic. Most of these engravings are carved only three or four metres above the ground on relatively soft rock.

Higher up is a vertical face of hard smooth rock, the mound's original surface. Dotted on this are quite different rock carvings, mostly dark grey, showing scenes unknown in the peninsula today. They depict processions of cattle with huge curving horns

— similar to the long-horned cattle of sub-Saharan Africa — which are thought to have roamed western Arabia 5,000 or 6,000 years ago. Shown with the cattle are tall, thin men wearing strange head dresses and jerkins, and carrying unidentifiable tools. The tools are also depicted on their own.

As no writing accompanies the drawings, it suggests they were made before people became literate. The engravings' colour has faded so much it is clear they were carved long before those with Islamic and pre-Islamic script. They are, however, the most carefully carved: the animals' outlines are carefully detailed and the rock surface has been first pecked out by hammering with a hard stone, and then polished with stone to give a smooth finish. Later engravings are simply pecked, not polished.

A few of the old engravings were made on sections of cliff face which have fallen, and can be seen on the ground. Oxen, the dominant figures in the oldest carvings, are shown from the side, but with the heads and horns carved as if seen from above. Square patches on the animals' backs and sides may indicate piebald colouring, or some kind of saddle. As the men are drawn in close association with the oxen, it seems the animals were domesticated.

Alongside the men and oxen are smaller animals with pointed ears and curling tails. Looking very like some modern dogs, they almost certainly represent domesticated dogs. Other animals depicted include ibex, with large, curved black horns, while there is a particularly fine frieze of large gazelles.

The large red Hanakiyah rock is shaped rather like a Y with an elongated base. The oldest carvings are on the base of the Y, and along the inner side of the opening's northern arm.

The foothills east of Jeddah airport
(see introductory tour)

An ideal trip for those who want a journey that will not take too long — it can be done in a day.

Leave Jeddah by the Palestine Road flyover and turn north along the Makkah to Al-Madinah Expressway. After about 18 kilometres you reach exit 28 (signposted air force). Just after this exit turn right on to a dirt track leading to Hochtief labour camp 1-3. Fork left at the end of labour camp 1 and soon after you will see the quarry. Before you get there, turn left along a well-surfaced road running through low brown hills.

After about eight kilometres bear left, taking the route through Wadi B, which should be signposted. About four kilometres further on, take the right fork and immediately bear right on to a single-lane ungraded track. Although the ride now becomes rougher, it is not uncomfortable.

The drive now is through stony desert between the foothills, which are dotted with low acacia trees and several varieties of shrub. The area is full of sites suitable for camping, and it is safe to camp out here alone.

If you intend to take the track all the way to Usfan, it is best to go with at least one other vehicle — preferably four-wheel-drive — as the ground tends to be soft where small wadis cross the track. Passing through the wadi you see some fenced-off areas where water melons are grown in season.

If you have a dirt bike or dune buggy you can leave the main track and drive off to find other tracks hidden in the hills. After about 17 kilometres on the single-lane track, you suddenly descend a very steep sand dune, which it was previously impossible to drive back up because of the soft sand. However, with the increase in traffic the track has become quite firm and it is just possible to climb up if you want to go back by the same route.

If you go on about five kilometres

further, though, you reach the village of Usfan, on the Makkah to Al-Madinah highway. The track joins the asphalt road opposite the Turkish fort and you can return to Jeddah either via the Creek or via Al-Jumum. The former trip takes about 45 minutes and the latter double this. The round trip going via the Creek is about 117 kilometres and via Al-Jumum 174 kilometres.

Taif rock carvings

Kilometres

Start	East Palestine Road/Expressway
11	flyover; Makkah Road
47	turn left to Al-Jumum (signposted Taif)
69	Al-Jumum; straight over crossroads
88	asphalt road on left into Wadi Fatima
130	turn left to Taif (straight over bridge into Makkah)
169	Sayl al-Kabir
194	Taif to Riyadh road; turn left
200	Taif airport on left
215	Turkish forts on right; rock carvings on left
329	Jeddah (via escarpment)

Although not as spectacular as the carvings on the Hanakiyah rock, east of Al-Madinah, the Taif rock carvings are well worth a visit. And with the road through Wadi Fatima now complete, the drive is quite pleasant.

The new road leaves the wadi bed about 88 kilometres from Jeddah and rises up towards Taif. Then take the Taif to Riyadh road, which runs northeast past Taif airport. About 10 kilometres beyond the airport (33 kilometres from Taif) the road cuts through a prominent rock ridge running almost at right angles to it. To the east you can see a series of Turkish forts, some reasonably well-preserved. The ridge divides the desert from the town; north is barren, open desert, while south the land is quite densely covered with large acacia trees, which provide a good picnic area.

The rock carvings lie along the ridge's crest, nearly two kilometres left of the main road. To reach them turn left along a good track soon before the ridge. Follow the track running along the base of the ridge until you reach a waste dump.

The carvings cover rocks near the ridge's summit, and extend for hundreds of metres in each direction. Individual carvings, hammered out of the rock surface with a small hard stone, were clearly made over thousands of years, as the amount of patina on them varies greatly. The rocks are black on the surface but orange inside, and newer carvings show bright orange or almost white. They include scenes of camels and horses, bedouin tribal marks and some recent Arabic script.

Older carvings range from darker orange to virtually black. The oldest and most interesting are quite difficult to see as their colour blends in with the rock surface. They depict various animals — ostriches, dogs, gazelles, ibex and lions — and, occasionally, people. Alongside them are a few inscriptions in the ancient scripts of the peninsula.

They resemble the animal carvings at Hanakiyah in some ways — the bodies are always drawn with patches on them — but the representations are more naturalistic. The same kind of tool — possibly the flint axe-head often found in the deserts of Arabia — is also shown.

Al-Wabah and Al-Birkah

Kilometres

Start	Jeddah; take old Makkah Road
47	Haddad; turn left to Al-Jumum (signposted Taif)
69	Al-Jumum; straight over crossroads
88	asphalt road left to Wadi Fatima
130	turn left to Taif
169	Sayl al-Kabir
194	Taif to Riyadh road; turn left
200	Taif airport on left
215	Turkish forts on right
297	Radwan; turn due north on to desert track at east end of town
385	Al-Hofr (the pit); petrol, repairs
401	Al-Wabah; head due west (many tracks)
461	Intersect with Darb Zubaydah; turn south
521	Al-Birkah (the wells)
571	Ushayrah
646	Riyadh to Taif road; turn right
666	Taif airport
830	Jeddah (via escarpment)

The massive Al-Wabah crater is the largest of its kind in western Arabia. In the Harrat Kishb, it is now accessible to anyone in a car with good ground clearance. The crater is about two kilometres wide and 260 metres deep, while the salt flat at the bottom is half a kilometre in diameter.

Although the surrounding area resembles a sandy plain, it is, in fact, a bed of volcanic ash, which rises towards the crater's lip. On the crater's northwest side is an older volcano, cut through by the massive subterranean explosion which caused the formation of Al-Wabah.

About one-third of the way down the crater's north side is an abandoned palm grove, with a brackish spring and several man-made cisterns among the palms. As it takes about 30 minutes to reach the bottom of the crater, it is best to do this before it gets too hot.

The large area of harrat — lava — northeast of the crater is ideal for camping, as many secluded "inlets" give both shelter and privacy.

About 60 kilometres due west of Al-Wabah, the Darb Zubaydah — an ancient pilgrim and trade route — runs from the south of the Arabian peninsula up into Iran. Alongside were built large water systems, established under the direction of Queen Zubaydah, wife of Harun al-Rashid, the Khalifa of Baghdad from 768-809 AD.

The route from Al-Wabah to the Darb Zubaydah crosses very soft, sandy wadis and four-wheel-drive is advisable (see Desert Travel). Ignore the many other tracks, and continue due west for about 60 kilometres until the main track appears. Turn south and go on for about 60 kilometres, when you will see the two water systems of Al-Birkah, probably the best-preserved on the whole route. From Al-Birkah to Ushayrah is a further 50 kilometres, and from there to the asphalted Riyadh to Taif road a further 75 kilometres along a road which was still being built at the time of writing. You can get to Jeddah either by going through Taif and taking the escarpment road, or by turning off after the airport through Sayl al-Kabir.

The dams at Khaybar

Kilometres

Start	Jeddah — creek flyover
383	Al-Madinah; flyover
423	ruined mansion on right
506	Silsilah; mosque at north end of town
520	microwave towers
528	track to right (opposite truck wreck)
531	Khaybar dam
679	Al-Madinah
1,063	Jeddah

Time needed **two days**

One of the largest pre-Islamic dams in the kingdom is the Sudd al-Qasaibah, known locally as Qasr al-Bint (the maiden's castle), hidden in the Harrat Khaybar north of Al-Madinah.

The dam, one of several in the area, is a good starting point for further exploration in the region. A local guide will probably be needed for trips to the other dams, though, as they are harder to find.

The dams' history is rather vague, although they are generally attributed to the great dam-builders of the kingdom of Saba, now modern Yemen.

The Sudd al-Qasaibah has been breached for about one-third of its length, but the remaining structure is still substantial, and on first sight quite breathtaking. It is about 135 metres long and 20 metres high, with the upstream face plastered with yellow/orange mortar, and the downstream face with bare stone. The breached cross-section shows the successive layers added to the dam to strengthen it.

Along the top of the dam is a walkway with a series of steps on the downstream side, purpose unknown. There is also evidence that a large structure was built on the western end of the downstream face. This is thought to have been part of a sluice system or an additional reservoir, but there is no sign of channels leading to it.

The dam itself sits in what is now a dry wadi bed, but the date palms on either side make it a pleasant place to picnic or camp overnight.

Part of the Sudd al-Qasaibah or Maiden's Castle

Khaybar town, about 25 kilometres north of the dam, is well worth a visit. There is an ancient citadel in the old part of the city, but before taking photographs or exploring, get permission either from the guard or the local amir's office.

If a guide is available, the two other dams in the area to visit are Sudd al-Khasid, which has now been modernised and is used as a flood barrier, and Sudd Hashquq, a much smaller, though nonetheless impressive, structure.

The Hejaz railway

Kilometres

Start	Jeddah; creek flyover
383	Al-Madinah; flyover
401	Tabuk road, petrol station (railway on left)
419	1st station (Hafirah)
443	turn-off to Al-Ayn
459	2nd station (Buwatah)
478	3rd station (Al-Silk)
498	4th station (Al-Buwayr — train)
520	5th station (Istabl Antar)
536	6th station (Abu al-Na'm)
554	7th station (Jada'ah)
576	8th station (Hadiyah — two trains)
596	9th station (Al-Mudarraj)
609	train blown off track
625	10th station (Wayban)
638	11th station (Tuwayrah)
655	12th station (Al-Sawrah)
680	13th station (Zumurrud)
687	Al-Ula/Tabuk road
797	Al-Ula/Khaybar junction
1,003	Al-Madinah
1,386	Jeddah

Comfortable time needed **four days**

The Hejaz railway is perhaps more famous for the manner of its destruction than for its achievements while operating. It was opened in 1908 to take pilgrims between Damascus, Amman and Al-Madinah, but in 1917 was put out of action by T E Lawrence and a small band of Arab companions. Despite periodic attempts to reconstruct the Saudi section of the line, it has been idle ever since.

Derelict shed of the old Hejaz railway

In his book Seven Pillars of Wisdom, Lawrence describes how he mined the line:

"It was a complicated mine, with a central trigger to fire simultaneous charges thirty yards apart... Burying the mine took four hours, for the rain had caked the surface and rutted it. Our feet made huge tracks on the flat and on the bank as though a school of elephants had been dancing there.

"To hide these marks was out of the question, so we did the other thing, trampling about, even bringing up our camels to help, until it looked as though half an army had crossed the valley."

The first glimpse of the railway comes in Al-Madinah as you pass a large park on your left marked By-Road Pilgrims, immediately after the new stadium on the Al-Madinah bypass. Don't try to join the railway here as there are several police checks which may cause delays if they are missed.

Taking the road north to Tabuk, you see the first railway station on the left, about 20 kilometres from the bypass. Again, don't join the line here as it passes through barren country with little of note.

Twenty-three kilometres further north, turn left at the junction signposted Al-Ayn. If you go on to a T-junction and then turn right, the railway can be seen running parallel with the road. It is easily distinguished by the telegraph poles and neat piles of rails, and the sleepers now serving as fence posts for the well-cultivated fields.

On arriving at Al-Buwayr, you can see a station on the left with what is left of a goods train in the nearby siding. The station buildings are well-preserved, with the southernmost one now a police post. It is as well to ask permission before taking photographs or exploring.

Taking the asphalt road out of Al-Buwayr the track is on the left. After eight kilometres the asphalt finishes and from here to Zumurrud — about 100 kilometres — there is no petrol or water and very little habitation. However, the drive is one of the most pleasant in the kingdom: the hills and sand dunes defy description and the peace and tranquillity are unrivalled. There are eight stations between Al-Buwayr and Zumurrud and, although all are similar, each has a character of its own. The line itself is badly pot-holed and difficult to drive on, but tracks on either side are followed easily. Four-wheel-drive is essential now: in some areas sand dunes have covered the railway and the number of rocks and stones make high clearance a must.

Taif

This cool hill-town, the traditional summer resort of the citizens of Jeddah and Makkah, sits above soaring crags at 1,800 metres above sea level. Despite its pockets of fertility, its cool breezes and misty views of mountain ranges, the change of altitude may cause headaches and lassitude when you arrive.

The 155-kilometre journey from Jeddah via the Christian bypass around Makkah takes about two-and-a-half hours along superb, metalled roads. There is a control point at an intersection 53 kilometres from Jeddah. A signpost pointing ahead reads "Makkah road — Muslims only" and another pointing to the right reads "Makkah bypass — all non-Muslims." At the former cars are searched and passengers checked by police. Always carry your passport as you may be asked for it at an earlier police checkpoint.

The bypass takes you swiftly through barren, dusty hills within a few kilometres of Makkah, although the road is built so you never glimpse the Holy City. An approaching mountain range appears impassable, but you soon see the beautifully sculptured modern road which at the peak hangs delicately on huge concrete stilts towering over the valley. Drive carefully — crumpled car bodies lie as a warning in the rocks.

The journey offers a wealth of natural history to the discerning traveller. Ironically, some of the best flora is found along the sides of the road, because the goats, whose grazing easily destroys natural cultivation, have been moved away from the road where the number run over was extremely high.

On rare occasions porcupine quills have been found on the Taif escarpment where the porcupine's main nourishment, the gladiolus, flourishes. Baboons can often be seen on the extreme lip of the Hada escarpment on which the Sheraton sits. Acacias grow in the desert areas; dutchman's cup vine is found in the foothills of the escarpment and violets higher up. Most plants have been grazed out at the top of the escarpment, except species such as juniper, which goats will not touch. Thyme and similar herbs also grow there.

Climbing the mountain towards the top of the escarpment that dominates Taif on the other side, you can dimly make out the Sheraton hotel at the top. The Sheraton, flanked on both sides by palaces, is about 20 kilometres from Taif.

From the Sheraton you continue driving through black rocks interspersed with clumps of grass and dazzling flowers until you reach the prefabs of modern Taif — an initial disappointment.

To reach the Inter-Continental you drive across and beyond the town. The hotel had to be built in a hurry, so was airlifted brick by brick to the mountain. It is impressive, with four corridor wings and open plan decor with scattered plants, and a fountain playing outside.

The prize of Taif is its souq, behind and to the southeast of the Aziziyah, a large hotel facing you as you arrive from Jeddah. At the Aziziyah the road forks to the right and left of the hotel. Between these two streets are countless alleys lined with shops. Park your car alongside the tall raffia benches where the locals will be smoking their narguileh pipes, then walk into the souq via one of the alleys. Along the left side of the Aziziyah are the tent shops which sell the white tents with coloured linings popular with the bedouin today. Beyond that is a shop which sells the long strips of traditional black tent-cloth. All along the western side is a clothing market. On the other side of the road, opposite the market, is a series of alleys running south into a maze of narrow alleys which form the main souq. In one of these alleys is the bedouin dress souq — row after row of little shops filled with dresses, brightly coloured and heavily embroidered. In front, men sit with sewing machines using velvet, cotton or synthetic fabric.

Moving south you come to the gold souqs and then to a wider area where spices, grain and incense are sold.

Sadly, much of old Taif was destroyed in 1924 when it was captured by Ibn Saud's religious warriors, the Ikhwan, in an incident deeply regretted by Ibn Saud. It has remained surprisingly cosmopolitan, with a population of a mere 70,000. After he took the city, Ibn Saud treated it as his summer capital and today, during the summer months, the king and the princes and most of the government move to Taif from the heat of Riyadh and burning humidity of Jeddah.

Over the centuries pilgrims have settled in Taif. Two thousand Chinese Muslim infantrymen, fleeing from defeat by Mao Tse-tung's forces in a battle in China's Hunan province, took refuge in the Hejaz in 1930 and, after making the Hajj, settled in Taif. Today you see many Chinese faces beneath thobe and gutra, and the older ones still speak Chinese. Turcomans fleeing from repression in Soviet Central Asia settled in Taif in the 1930s. Many of them still speak Turkish and send their children to school in Istanbul.

Hotels

Al-Hada Sheraton Hotel Tel: 7541400. PO Box 999, Al-Hada, near Taif. Telex: 451092 sherid.

The hotel was designed for security, catering as it does for kings, presidents and visiting diplomats. The building is quadrangular with an open centre so the lobby can be seen from each of the six floors. The hotel is full in summer, but rooms are usually available in winter.

The Al-Ghadir restaurant has Swiss, German, Egyptian and Lebanese chefs, and serves continental and oriental food. The Palms coffee shop is open from 0600-2400.

Facilities include a Saudia travel agent, Rent-a-car desk, swimming pool (mornings for women, evenings for men), sauna, and banqueting facilities for 100-150 people.

Rates: October-May single SR 320, double SR 415, suites SR 640-1,500; June-September single SR 400, double SR 510, suites SR 800-1,875.

Credit cards: American Express, Diners Club, Eurocard, Mastercharge.

Massarrah Inter-Continental Hotel Tel: 7328333. PO Box 827, halfway between the airport and city centre.

Al-Hada Sheraton, Taif

Telex: 450055 masara, cable: inhotelcor. Promoted as "the most luxurious hotel in Saudi Arabia."

205 rooms. It is a complex of 36 self-catering, VIP villas, three swimming pools, a health club, three tennis courts, a banquet hall for up to 1,200 people and a mosque.

The Hawazen restaurant, which serves a good selection of Arab, Lebanese and European cuisine, and the Okaz coffee shop, are both open between 0700-1000, 1230-1500 and 1930-2200. There is also an elegant garden.

The hotel has a news-stand, barber, gift and bookshop, in-house physician, businessmen's lounge and parking.

Rates: package tours — SR 275 per person for twin room for one night with full board and sight-seeing tour of the area, SR 450 for two nights, service included; children between four and 14 staying in their parents' room get three meals a day for SR 75.

Rates: normal — single SR 400, double SR 519, suite SR 600; plus 15% service.

Credit cards: American Express, Diners Club, Visa and Carte Blanche.

Communications

Air communications (domestic)
Direct daily flights to Abha, Jeddah and Riyadh; direct flights to Al-Madinah, Bisha, Dhahran, Najran, Sharoura and Tabuk.

Saudia Tel: reservations 7320333, 7366666; information 7251200; airport cargo services 7252328.

Post office and telex
East of central souq. To make a trunk call to Taif from within the kingdom dial 02 plus number.

Courier service
SNAS/DHL Tel: 7361946, 7334970. Al-Mathna Road, two kilometres west of New Ministry Building, Taif. Telex: 402559 snascr sj.

Travel agent
ACE Travel Tel: 7363040, 7328333. PO Box 827.

Restaurants
China Restaurant Tel: 7324698. Shehar Sadad Street, behind National Guard Headquarters.

Shangri-La Tel: 7360835. Chinese food.

Shops
Taif Marketing Centre Tel: 7361579. Taif Hawia Road, Benzaid Building, in front of Saptco. Car park. Sells a wide range of goods — food, fresh and frozen meat, vegetables, cosmetics, perfumes, books, all household utensils and electrical fittings.

Tihama Bookstall Saptco terminal, Airport Road.

Hospitals
King Faisal Hospital Tel: 7322645, 73233433, 7323838, 7322838. Al-Malek Street. Director: Dr Musa Ahmed Bayameen. 706 beds. 133 doctors, 160 nurses.

Inpatients: surgery, dermatology, gynaecology, obstetrics, paediatrics, urology, opthalmology, ear, nose and throat, neurosurgery, dental, orthopaedics and incubators. Outpatients: surgery.

Psychiatric Hospital Tel: 7325640, 7321880, 7326844. Director: Usamah Mohammed Al Radi. 1,000 beds. 56 doctors, 230 nurses, 14 social workers, 3 psychiatrists.

Pharmacies
These are open on a rota basis — see English-language press.

Al-Hikmah Drug Store Barha al-Abbas.
Al-Najah Pharmacy Barha-al-Qazzaz.
Okaz Drug Store Okaz Street, Sharquiah.
Salam Drug Store King's Street.
Al-Hayat Pharmacy Mina Road, Shehar.
Al-Burj Pharmacy Al-Burj Building.

Yanbu

Planners' dreams to turn 188 square kilometres of sand along the Red Sea into a major crude oil, gas processing, refining and petrochemicals complex, housing 135,000 people by 2006, are fast becoming reality. In one of the most ambitious urban and industrial development schemes ever conceived, the Royal Commission for Jubail & Yanbu was in 1975 charged with setting up basic infrastructure for heavy petrochemicals plants and for associated secondary service industries at Madinat Yanbu al-Sinaiyah (Yanbu industrial city) and at its twin city of Jubail, in the east.

Yanbu, about 350 kilometres northeast of Jeddah and 10 kilometres south of the old town of Yanbu al-Bahr, lies at the western end of two 1,200-kilometre oil and gas pipelines. The completion of the transpeninsula lines in 1981 — the Petroline oil line in July and the gas line in December — is what makes the city's development possible. Petroline will supply both the export terminal and local refineries, while the gas line will carry previously wasted natural gas liquids (NGL) from east coast processing plants for separation into export products and feedstock for the petroleum complex now being built.

In the 30-year masterplan for Yanbu, a three-phase programme was envisaged and work is now proceeding apace, with more than 30,000 labourers from 40 countries in the city by February 1982. In the first phase, which ends in 1986, heavy and light industry facilities with homes and infrastructure for a population of 55,000 are to be built. Much interim construction — management housing, workers' camps, services and support roads — is already complete, in only four years. Designs for some permanent features, such as homes, public facilities and landscaping, are nearly ready. Several construction contracts have been awarded, while more are being tendered each week.

Large areas have been set aside for the private sector. Once they have been provided with the necessary infrastructure, they will be offered to Saudi investors.

The city's new port and seawater inlet is said to be the world's largest. The crude oil export terminal started supplying supertankers in 1981. In its first six months of operation, 126 tankers of up to 440,000 dwt docked there, taking on more than 1 million barrels a day (b/d) of crude. In the same period, 48 cargo vessels docked at the nearby construction support port, unloading goods totalling 33,000 tonnes-plus.

An industrial port is being developed separately. One of the first parts of Yanbu to be completed, it is now to be expanded in stages, and will soon include dry cargo berths and roll-on, roll-off (ro-ro) facilities.

Light and heavy industries are being developed in different areas of the city, divided by the main highway to Jeddah. More than 30 licences have been issued for the 400-hectare light industry zone — on the inland side of the highway — mainly for construction-based businesses. The most recent annual plan calls for construction of a second, similar-size zone. The heavy industry areas are on the seaward side of the city. Buildings in this zone will include a petrochemicals complex, an export refinery, a crude terminal, an NGL plant, a domestic refinery and a lube oil refinery.

More basic infrastructure has also been completed. About 200 kilometres of water pipeline, and 130 kilometres of primary sewage and industrial waste collection lines have been laid; 150 kilometres of primary power cable completed; an earth satellite station and an electronic switching system for 3,000 telephone lines installed, and 3,210 metres of runway built to allow daily commercial flights by Saudia. At the same time, there are plans to install more than 400 kilometres of telecommunications and power lines.

Education and health also figure on the list of priorities — three schools have been built, two for Arab children and one for expatriates' children, with plans drawn up for a further 140. A design contract has also been awarded for a 330-bed hospital and medical centre to add to the existing 68-bed hospital and clinics.

The planned communities will be self-sufficient, complete with shopping centres, mosques, and recreation parks and halls. And as part of a bid to foster greater self-reliance among Saudis, a vocational training and management development centre has been designed to take up to 1,000 students.

Government department
Chamber of Commerce Tel: 3224121. Ali Bin Abitaleb Street. Telex: 461042 tegari (Arabic only).

Getting around

Air communications
The airport is north of the old town of Yanbu al-Bahr. It has a comfortable departure terminal with snack bar and news-stand. Customs agents are on duty. Tickets must be bought before arrival at the airport. The Royal Commission provides transport to and from the airport for its workers, as does the Hyatt hotel for its guests. Direct daily flight to Jeddah; flights on Saturday and Monday to Riyadh and Dhahran.
Saudia Tel: 3212333. PO Box 500. Building no 3335. Closed Thursday. There is also a city ticket office in Yanbu al-Bahr.

Taxis
These are available in the centre of town.

Buses
Royal Commission Tel: 3211121. Operates a community bus service for which there is a modest charge. A daily service to Jeddah is available to all Royal Commission employees although others may use it with permission. Reservations must be made in person at the Transport Office, Building no 3445, and must be accompanied by a travel authorisation.

Saudi Public Transport Company Saptco runs daily coach services between Yanbu, Jeddah and Al-Madinah. The trip to Jeddah takes 6½ hours and costs SR 60 one way. The Al-Madinah trip takes about 3½ hours and costs SR 35. The office is near the inter-city taxi stand and across from the Royal Commission.

Car hire
Budget Rent-a-Car Tel: 3211191, 3212179. Telex: 430313. Hyatt hotel, tel: 3223888. Open Monday to Thursday 0800-1200, 1500-1900; Friday 1000-1200, 1700-1900.

For models/rates see Jeddah section.

Hotels
Business visitors are advised to make hotel reservations well in advance of their trip.

Hyatt Yanbu Hotel Tel: 3223887, 3224111, 3223851. PO Box 300. By the Red Sea, four kilometres from the town centre. Signposted left off main road to Yanbu. Telex: 461053 hyatt.

179 rooms and suites. All are fully airconditioned with two-channel in-house video and mini-bar.

Cafe restaurant serves international dishes. Drugstore, travel agent, and two meeting rooms for conferences and group seminars. Airport transport — hotel meets all incoming flights. Two swimming pools with terrace and sun lounges, two tennis courts, boating and access to coral reef for snorkelling and Scuba diving.

Rates: single SR 275, double SR 330, suite SR 560; plus 15% service. Reservations recommended.

Credit cards: American Express, Diners Club, Eurocard.

Middle East Hotel Tel: 3221281. In the centre of town. Restaurant.

Holiday Inn The hotel has been leased by a major company and no longer accepts guests.

Communications

Telephone and telex
A 24-hour communications centre in Building no 3427 is available to all residents for business and personal telephone calls and telexes. It is possible to dial most areas of the world direct. Cash payment is required at the time of service, unless alternative arrangements have been made.

There are two other centres, for telephone calls only, in Al-Nawa village (B-13) and in Camp (haii) 12.

Post
The Royal Commission has a mail distribution centre in Building no 3397. As it is not a government post office, services are limited to selling stamps, weighing letters and small packages, and receiving and sending mail. Many companies have postboxes in the centre for distributing inter-city mail. The centre is open on Saturday to Thursday from 0630-1730, although closed for lunch from 1130-1230.

The government post office is in Yanbu al-Bahr on Umar Ibn al-Aziz Road.

Courier services
SNAS-DHL Tel: 3213099, (homeward bound) 3228396. Camp 3, Building no 3335. Telex: 402559 snascr sj (Jeddah).

Skypak Tel: 3225443, 3225467. Telex: 461027 kanoo.

Travel agents
It is best to contact travel agents well in advance of departure.

Attar Travel Agency Tel: 3211211, Building no 6090.

Kurban Travel Service Tel: 3222616, 3221759. M Abdul-Wahab Street. Telex: 461021 kurban. Also does car and bus rental.

Sultan Travel Agency Tel: 3211228. Building no 6090. Telex: 430307 sultan.

Restaurants

There are two restaurants operated by Rolaco in Al-Nawa village. The two — in Camp 2 (tel: 3211904) and Camp 5 (tel: 3212963) — offer breakfast, lunch and dinner. Visitors can also eat in the B diner in Camp 1.

The restaurants in the Hyatt and Middle East hotels are available to residents, and there is also the Al-Ariche restaurant in Yanbu al-Bahr.

Shopping

An ample and varied supply of food, clothing, and personal and household goods can be found in the Yanbu area. The commissaries in camps 2 and 5 have a wide variety of fresh vegetables, meat, eggs, canned goods, bread, juices, soft drinks, and toiletries. Consumer goods such as furniture, jewellery and watches, televisions, radios, video recorders, cameras, books and stationery, toys, sports equipment, home appliances and musical instruments are sold in the stores in camps 1 and 3. There are also bakeries, patisseries, florists and shops selling shoes, clothes, gold and silver, as well as many industrial supply shops.

Shops usually close in the afternoon and reopen in the evening. There are daily shopping buses to Yanbu al-Bahr for women, and an evening service for men and families.

The souq
The old souq is opposite the port entrance. In this older section of town there are several very attractive Ottoman houses with intricately carved balconies and screens. Some are built of coral blocks cut from the reef.

Education

School
International School Tel: 3211089. Staffed and operated by International School Services, Princeton, New Jersey, US. Superintendent: William P Davidson.

500 children of all nationalities attend the school in grades 3 to 9. Teaching is in English; children with no or little English are given special coaching. The academic programme is combined with physical education, handicrafts, music, business studies and industrial arts. Buses are available for transport.

Fees: SR 21,000 a year.

For further information contact the admissions office.

Libraries
These are in the recreation halls of camps 1, 2 and 5. All have newspapers and magazines, while that in Camp 2 has a travel corner with literature on resorts and holiday areas. The libraries welcome gifts of English and Arabic books.

Housing

Employers and employees rent their homes from the Royal Commission at fixed rents. Many are furnished, and equipped with household appliances and utensils for which the occupants become responsible. An inventory of the property is made before departure, when repairs and replacement of missing articles must be paid for.

Household repairs and maintenance
Exterior and interior repairs are carried out by the Royal Commission's contractors, although tenants are responsible for routine interior maintenance. Applications for the repair of electrical systems, plumbing and appliances should be made to the camp manager.

Water
All homes have piped water which comes from desalination plants and is drinkable. It should not be wasted!

Electricity
The electrical supply is 115 V.

Rubbish collection
Rubbish is collected three times a week throughout Al-Nawa village. Bins are provided and new liners delivered at every pick-up.

Pets
Residents are discouraged from keeping pets because of the harsh environment and lack of veterinary care. Pets will, however, be allowed in residential areas provided they have the necessary inoculations and health certificates, wear a tag issued by the manager's office, are supervised in public areas and placed in a suitable home when owners leave.

Medical

The Royal Commission operates an emergency hospital and a health care clinic. Both are open 24 hours, seven days a week for emergency care, although not to the public. Employers usually arrange medical care for staff and their dependants.

Hospitals
Al-Nawa Hospital Tel: 3212971; emergency ambulance 997.

Facilities include surgeries, laboratory, X-ray, oral surgery, intensive care unit and isolation rooms. The medical staff include a paediatrician and obstetrician.

Hours: outpatient Saturday to Wednesday 0730-1200, 1300-1700; Thursday 0730-1200.

Industrial Medical Clinic Tel: 3210202. Telex: 200805 gamma sj.

Facilities include laboratory, X-ray, pharmacy, outpatient clinics, 24-hour casualty section.

Medicine
Medicine on prescription and medical supplies are issued by the Al-Nawa hospital and the Industrial Medical Clinic at the time of treatment. Those not immediately available can be ordered by a doctor from other sources.

Pharmacies
Ahmadi Pharmacy At the last roundabout.
Red Sea Pharmacy Umar Ibn Abdul-Aziz Road.
Alkhiwa Pharmacy On Abu Bakr Road near the Seiko shop and the Friday Mosque.
Bin-Hamdan Pharmacy By the PTT building near the central commercial district.

Dental care
Al-Nawa Dental Clinic Tel: 3212554. Building no 6001, behind the hospital.
Provides general dental care by appointment, as well as emergency treatment. Orthodontist and peridontist visit regularly. Fees are payable at the time of treatment.
Hours: Saturday and Monday 0800-1200, 1400-1800; Sunday, Tuesday, Wednesday 0800-1200, 1600-1900; Thursday 1800-1200, 1400-1700.

Other services

Banks
The banks issue travellers cheques but do not exchange currency. This may be done at the two Al-Rajhi currency exchanges in the commercial district, which deal in dollars and other major currencies.
The National Commercial Bank Building no 6090.
Riyad Bank Tel: 3221125. PO Box 107, Building no 6090. Telex: 461009.

Catering
Private catering can be arranged through:
Greyhound Services Saudi Arabia Tel: 3211111.
Rolaco Catering Tel: 3211904.
Al-Tawil Food Services Tel: 3211258.
Dallah Avco Saudi Arabia Company Tel: 3211448.

Men's hairdressers
There are barber shops in Camp 1 (no 1997), Camp 5 commissary building (no 5995) and in the bachelor recreation building in Al-Awaell village.

Car service/repair
Both the Chevrolet and Toyota dealers in Yanbu al-Bahr sell new cars and provide a repair service. The Chevrolet dealer services all General Motors cars, trucks and buses. There are also several smaller, specialist shops for mechanical, electrical, engine and body repair services. Spare parts for all makes of European, US and Japanese cars are available in several shops in Yanbu al-Bahr.

Petrol
There is a 24-hour petrol station in the central service area by the "bird tank."

Gardening supplies
Garden Centre Tel: 3213223. In buffer-zone next to Camp 5 in Al-Nawa village. The centre, operated by the Urban & Rural Development Company, sells plants, seeds, garden equipment and furniture. Open Saturday to Wednesday 0930-1200, 1300-1830; Thursday 1200-1830; Friday 0730-1130.

Recreation

Social life
There is no shortage of activities for men, women and children in Yanbu, and newcomers are always welcome. Clubs and organisations cater for devotees of bridge, yoga, mah jong, handicrafts, art, music, cribbage, photography, gardening and even dieting. Older children can join guides

and scouts, while younger children can join in the story-telling group. Parents have banded together to form a babysitting co-operative to enable participation in these activities. A Women's Activities Co-ordinating Committee helps to plan and organise activities solely for women, as well as some general community events. The clubs and organisations are usually self-financed and manage their own affairs. For details of clubs see Al-Nawa News.

Recreation centres
Several recreation halls have been set up in Al-Nawa village and equipped with pool tables, games and televisions. Family recreation halls are in camps 2 and 5; bachelor recreation halls in camps 1 and 2.

Women's service centres
The centres, in camps 2, 5 and Haii al-Marjan, organise women's programmes, classes and parties.

Sports
Sports enthusiasts are well catered for. The scope is wide, with clubs and company-sponsored teams for softball, basketball, soccer, rugby, tennis, racquetball, karate, and squash, which compete in regional and national sports tournaments. For water enthusiasts there is fishing, sailing and Red Sea diving. Royal Commission sports facilities — including the Saudi Turf field — are available free to residents and clubs, but equipment is not provided. Many clubs organise community events such as sailing regattas and "fun runs."

Swimming pools
Each camp has one or more swimming pools manned by a lifeguard.
Family pools — camps 2 and 5, and Al-Marjan camp.
Women's pools — camps 2 and 5, and Al-Marjan camp.
Bachelors' pools — camps 1, 2, 3, 4 and 5.

The Media
Al-Nawa News Weekly community newsletter, published in both English and Arabic. Information on recreational and community activities distributed to residents free.

Television
A community cable television service, at present being expanded, transmits programmes on sport, music, news and entertainment in English and Arabic to many areas of the city. Residents have to buy their own sets, preferably one with all four major systems. Applications for connection should be made to the contractor's office in the communications centre building (Building no 3427). The cost of connection is SR 150, plus a quarterly service charge of SR 150 payable in advance.

Places to visit

Yanbu al-Nakhl
A 50-kilometre drive with numerous farms en route. Take the turn-off to the foothills between the Hyatt hotel and the first roundabout. Yanbu al-Nakhl is an agricultural village with a very picturesque souq, selling many bedouin artefacts at high prices.

Yanbu al-Bekkah
Thirty kilometres from Yanbu al-Bahr. Just before reaching Yanbu al-Nakhl, turn off to Yanbu al-Bekkah, an abandoned village with an old crumbling Turkish fort. Park at the foot of the hill and climb to inspect it.

Useful telephone numbers
Royal Commission for Jubail & Yanbu Tel: 3216000.
Vendor Relations Department Tel: 3212209.
Public Relations Department Tel: 3216000.

THE NAJD
(THE CENTRAL REGION)
Riyadh

No roads led to Riyadh at the beginning of the century; it was as isolated as Tibet. Until the early 1950s it was still a desert city with clay palaces and surrounded by heavy mud walls. Then came the boom years and this city, the very symbol of Najdi culture and the puritan reformation of the followers of Ibn abd al-Wahhab and Muhammad Ibn Saud (see Historical Introduction), began to mutate.

The early manifestations of development were unfortunate. In the early 1970s the old and new cohabited in frenzy. The cars and packed jeeps of Batha Street moved in a cacophony of horns, stirring up dust from the broken pavements. Dust coated villas and sickly trees.

It was a city seeking a new identity. Down came the old buildings. Down came the new to be replaced quickly by the newer. By the early 1970s it was hurtling into the limelight. During the 1980s the move of the entire diplomatic quarter in stages from Jeddah will mean the end of Riyadh's traditional isolation; it will take on the role which it has sought since the early eighteenth century, that of the pivot of the Arabian peninsula. Today, all roads lead to Riyadh.

Riyadh's age-old raison d'etre was its vast palm plantation — hence its name ar-Riyadh, "the Gardens." Now the capital of the kingdom and of the administrative division of Riyadh, the city lies in the heart of Central Najd. It sits on a sedimentary plateau 600 metres above sea level at the confluence of the Wadi Hanifa and its tributaries Wadi Aysan and Wadi Batha.

When the name Riyadh was first used by Ibn Bishr in 1636 it referred to the ancient city of Hajr and its gardens. In 422 the town was deserted by its inhabitants and the tribe of Bani Hanifa moved to it with their chief, and took and defended 30 houses. Thus the early city took on the name of Hajr or "defended."

In 1901 the city was probably at its widest not more than a few hundred metres across. A thick mud wall about seven metres high surrounded it, in which immense north, south, east and west gates were set. Inside it was a maze of twisting streets, not unlike the casbah of Fes in Morocco today. Some streets were so narrow that it was difficult for two men to walk abreast.

The only open space was the central market. On one side was a large mosque and on the other the palace which Ibn Rashid had seized from the House of Saud. Nearby was a tiny market place reserved for the women.

Riyadh's subsequent history is closely associated with the rise of the Muwahidun (the Wahhabis) and that of the House of Saud (see Historical Introduction). Its recapture by Ibn Saud from the Rashid in 1902 was a watershed for the House of Saud and the beginning of the city's rise to becoming one of the world's major capitals.

The city is trying to preserve its Najdi, desert identity — both the charming simplicity of the Musmak fort and the elegant lines of the modern SAMA building suggest this — and to absorb what is best from the Hejaz, and in particular from its cosmopolitan port of Jeddah.

The interaction between nomadic, sedentary and urban populations cannot be seen more effectively than in Riyadh today. This and the climate have influenced Riyadh's architecture. During the day in summer the desert burns with a fierce heat. There is an intolerable glare and frequent sandstorms. The traditional Riyadh building had a courtyard exposing the house to the sky's coolness at night —

Aerial view of Riyadh with the television station in the middle

this idea is being incorporated into modern buildings.

With its new dual-carriageways and ultra-modern flyovers, its first-class hotels and an incipient era of fine architecture influenced by local traditions, Riyadh is coming into its own. It is no longer the "secret city" which the romantic travellers of the nineteenth century expected. Today it is developing into a sophisticated world capital and inheriting the manners and mores that this implies.

Population figures tell Riyadh's expansion tale. From an estimated 19,000 in 1920 the population had reached about 62,000 in 1945 and 666,000 by 1974. Today Riyadh has a population of about 1 million.

Guide to Riyadh

From the airport the road ahead leads to the Petromin roundabout and onwards down Airport Road (King Abdul-Aziz Street), also known as Ministry Row. Along its right side are the ministries of commerce and industry, education, agriculture and water, communications, interior, and defence and aviation. On the other side is a line of modern shops including the University Bookshop, Qahtani's Furniture Store and the Romana restaurant.

Further, opposite the ministries, are

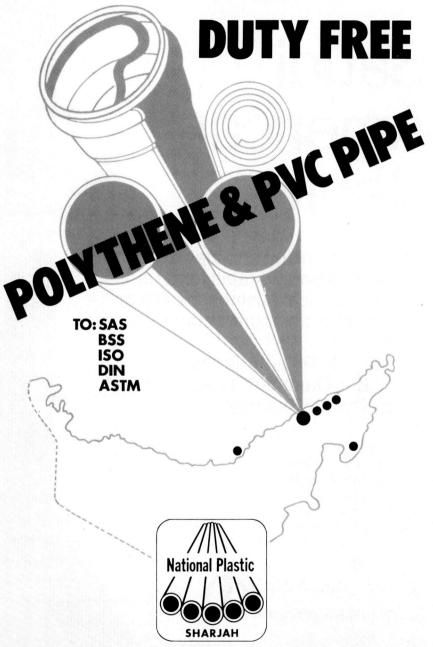

Saudi American Bank

Complete banking services in the kingdom of Saudi Arabia for personal customers, local businesses, major corporations and correspondent banks.
Branches in Riyadh, Jeddah, Al-Khobar, Dammam, Hofuf, Oneizah, Abha, Khamis Mushayt.

Head Office:
Adil Kashoggi Building
Airport Road, Riyadh
P.O. Box 833
Tel: (Riyadh) 477 4770
Telex: 200195 Samba SJ

the Yamamah (now closed) and Zahret al-Sharq hotels. Between these hotels is the Saudi American Bank in the Khashogji Building, which also houses the ultra-modern Danish Centre for Modern Design. The Movenpick Restaurant stands behind it. To the left of it are the marble towers of the elegant SAMA buildings.

The Zahret al-Sharq hotel stands on the edge of Ministry of Commerce Square and opposite the ministry. The complex roundabout and criss-crossing flyovers were completed in 1982. If, from the airport, you turn left at Petromin on to the Khurais Road this will lead you to the Marriott Khurais hotel.

If you turn right, you are on Maather Street (the ring road that passes the Inter-Continental hotel). Taking this road you see soon after the Petromin roundabout bend the new military hospital for employees of the Defence Ministry and their families. Just beyond, down a road to the right, is the International Medical Services office (see Medical).

Continuing, you will see on your right a turning to Riyadh's fast-developing residential and shopping area, Olaya. Further right is the Inter-Continental hotel and Convention Centre, both opened in 1975. The road continues through Nasiriyah.

If you turn right before reaching the centre of Nasiriyah you reach the King Faisal Specialist hospital, the modern referral hospital designed to treat people with special problems that could not previously be treated locally.

Most of the palaces of the royal family are in Nasiriyah. Beyond is the old Diwan, now the Natural History museum, formerly the palace in which official receptions were held.

Further, on your right, is the new Conference Centre and beyond that, in a date garden, Riyadh's first public swimming pool (for men only). Bab Nasiriyah stands at the intersection of King Saud and Muhammad Ibn Faisal Ibn Turki streets. Opposite is the Ministry of Foreign Affairs Guest House and the Saudi Press Agency. The street leading south crosses one of Riyadh's most important streets, Umar Ibn al-As Street, but better known as Television Street because it houses Riyadh's television station, which first went on the air in 1965. The university's engineering college is in nearby Muhammad Ibn Faisal Ibn Turki Street.

Continue straight down Imam Saud Ibn Abdul-Aziz Ibn Muhammad Street. You pass the Ministry of Foreign Affairs on your right and, soon after the Imam Faisal Ibn Turki crossing, you come to the Department of Antiquities on your left (see Museum). At Tibb Square you reach the Shumaisi General hospital to which every victim of a traffic accident is taken (see Medical).

Turning left down Al-Imam Turki Ibn Abdullah Street (better known as Shumaisi al-Jadeed Street) you reach the souq area.

The old town

Several years ago demolition seemed the likely fate of the old areas of central Riyadh, built as they were of adobe (sun-dried mud brick made with straw and sometimes manure), to give way to high-rise concrete buildings. However, ideals of conservation prevailed at the eleventh hour and certain buildings of historical interest have preservation orders on them. Of these, the most important is the Musmak (from musmaq — lofty) fort which Ibn Saud scaled with seven companions in 1902 when he seized power in Riyadh from the rival Rashid family (see Historical Background).

Riyadh's principal street until the 1950s was Thumairi Street, named after a companion of Ibn Saud who died in the struggle for Riyadh. Thumairi Street (known by foreigners as Seiko Street because of the proliferation of watch shops) lies west of and half way down Wazir (King Faisal)

Faisal) Street. Today it is the best place to buy cameras and other electronic equipment at bargain prices.

The Musmak fort, built in 1865 by the Amir Abdullah as an inner defence for the town, lies off a small street on the right of Thumairi Street. It is the oldest important building. The door through which you enter within the great gate is so small that you must stoop. The diminutive door ensured that defenders inside armed with swords might hold the advantage over any would-be attackers. You can still see in the door the point of the spear which Ibn Jiluwi thrust at the governor, Ajilan (see Historical section), during Ibn Saud's recapture of the fort.

Thumairi Street leads into Deera (the bedouin word for homeland) Square, otherwise known as Safa (purity) or Adl (justice) Square. Riyadh's High Court, the Palace of Justice, is to the left shortly before the Riyadh Governorate. The open space in the centre of the square is a car park. It is also the place where penalties for crime are carried out according to Sharia law (see Sharia law), usually after the Friday midday prayer.

Deera (Safa) Square

On Thursdays the king often holds a majlis (meeting) with tribal shaikhs and ulema (religious leaders) in the Governorate building, which controls one of the four principal regional governorates headed by the king.

Riyadh's Musmak Fort

Television tower, Riyadh

National Guard in Riyadh

School children in Jeddah

Cement works, Jeddah

Villages and terraced fields north of Abha

The two buildings stand on the site of the royal castle (qasr) built in 1824 by Turki Ibn Abdullah Ibn Muhammad, the founder of the second Saudi state and direct ancestor of all the Saudi kings of the twentieth century.

To the far right of Deera Square, bordering Al-Suwaylim Street on the other side, stands the concrete Great Mosque (as-Masjid as-Jaami' al-Kabir) built in the 1950s. It was built on the site of the mosque in which the Amir Turki Ibn Abdullah was assassinated as he left Friday prayers in 1834.

Beyond the square to the left is the gold souq, behind it, the Mgheibra fruit and vegetable market and beyond that the Souq al-Hareem (women's souq) where only women sell, and where filigree silver jewellery and other bedouin handicrafts can be bought. In this area some of the lovely old Najdi buildings clustered in winding alleys can still be seen. South of Deera Square lies Dokhna Square, the site of the city's southern gate.

Deera Square leads on, through Shumaisi al-Jadeed Street on the left of the Musmak fort and through Thumairi Street on the right, into King Faisal (Wazir Street) which, with Batha Street, is the principal artery of the city. It has many smart clothes shops as well as low price restaurants such as Kentucky Fried Chicken.

The Kuwaiti souq is an important feature of Batha Street but the sudden profusion of new flyovers has suddenly altered the fabric of this once antiquated street. Wazir Street leads on to Aziziyah Square, on the edge of which are exotic shops such as the Gazzaz perfumery.

Glancing westwards into Khazzan Street you can see the immense King's Building, completed in 1980. Nearly opposite Gazzaz is the Riyadh National Book Palace. This opened in 1964 with more than 4,000 books and is one of the main exhibition halls for special art and literary shows.

Continuing up King Faisal Street you pass the palaces of Princess Sara Ibn Abdul-Aziz and then that of Princess Nura, Ibn Saud's favourite sister. The road leads into a large gardened square in the centre of which is the Riyadh water tower. The tower, disc-shaped and resembling a flying saucer, has a large reception room at the top with a magnificent view. Visitors must first get permission to go there from the Agriculture & Water Ministry.

Ministries in Riyadh

Agriculture & Water Tel: 4012777, 4012184, 4011796, 4015084, 4014780. Airport Road. Telex: 201108 agrwat sj, 201692 agrirs sj. Minister, tel: 4022939.

Commerce Tel: 4012229, 4014708, 4014684. PO Box 1774. Airport Road. Telex: 201057 tijara sj. Minister, tel: 4035567.

Communications Tel: 4043000, 4043440, 4043648, 4043036, 4042928. Airport Road. Telex: 201616 hiway sj.

Defence & Aviation Tel: 4785900. Airport Road. Telex: 201188 mdat sj; military works, telex: 201506 dwm sj; medical services, telex: 201178 saafms sj; projects, telex: 202798 spdmsd sj; signals, telex: 201110, 201621 modar sj. Minister, tel: 4777313, 4776623.

Education Tel: 4042888, 4042952, 4043678, 4043744. Airport Road. Telex: 201673 maaref sj. Department of Antiquities & Museums, telex: 202650 archeo sj. Minister, tel: 4024066.

Finance & National Economy Tel: 4012666, 4015000, 4015112, 4012988, 4050080. Temporarily in GOSI Building, Airport Road. Telex: 201021, 201669 finans sj. Zakat and income tax, tel: 4041495, 4044386, 4044378; customs, tel: 4013334, 4014284.

Health Tel: 4012220, 4012392, 4012696. Airport Road. Telex: 201628 health sj, 201157 dhelth sj. Minister, tel: 4026394.

Higher Education Tel: 4412408. King Faisal Hospital Road. Telex: 201481 ali sj.

Industry & Electricity Tel: 4772722, 4776400. PO Box 5729, Riyadh Industrial Estate. Telex: 201154 indel sj.

Information Tel: 4014440, 4013440. Nasiriyah Street. Telex: Minister 202640 minmoi sj; deputies 200186 moi fi sj; technical affairs 201461 rinfor sj.

Interior Tel: 4011944, 4011872, 4030800, 4030955. Telex: 201622 mors sj.

Justice Tel: 4351155, 4351167, 4351511.

Labour & Social Affairs Tel: 4771480, 4787166. Dhahran Road. Telex: 201043 labour sj.

Municipal & Rural Affairs Tel: 4021500, 4021512, 4021333, 4021534. Nasiriyah Street. Telex: 201063 doma sj. Minister, tel: 4035111.

Petroleum & Minerals Tel: 4781661, 4781133, 4788981. Airport Road. Telex: 201058 ptromn sj.

Pilgrimage Affairs & Awqaf (Religious Endowments) Tel: 4022200, 4022212. Telex: 201603 awqaf sj. Minister, tel: 4024844.

Planning Tel: 4013292, 4014572, 4023800, 4023026. PO Box 358, University Street. Telex: 201075 plan sj.

Posts, Telegraphs & Telecommunications Tel: 4040288. Airport Road. Telex: 201220 telcom sj, 201020 gentel sj. Minister, tel: 4012233.

Public Works & Housing Tel: 4022268, 4022036. Washm Street. Telex: 201141 ashghal sj. Public works, tel: 4022255; housing, tel: 4037132. Minister, tel: 4764979.

Diplomatic services

British Liaison Office (BLO) Tel: 4760607. PO Box 487. Telex: 201334 ecbrit. Director: R J S Muir. From town centre take Airport Road towards Petromin roundabout. Turn left opposite the Nejd hotel. You have to backtrack a little to reach the Sabreen Store opposite the hotel; turn right here. Turn right at the end of the block around Riyadh Continental School. Turn left at the end, and second left down a narrow street. The BLO is in a brown villa with arches on the upper storey to your left.

The consular office is open on Saturday-Wednesday 0830-1230, and on Tuesday from 1400-1700. It will help people in serious difficulty but cannot give legal advice. A consular official is always on call, although the only matters he will usually handle outside office hours are genuine emergencies. The vice-consul is available on Tuesdays from 0800-1200 and 1400-1700.

US embassy liaison office and *US International Communications Agency (USICA)* Tel: 4640012. Beside the Bustan hotel off the Dabbab Street extension in Sulaymaniyah. To reach the offices take the road from the airport past the Sahary al-Riyadh hotel on your left and Riyadh customs on your right until you reach a set of traffic lights. Turn left here into Dabbab Street, a dual carriageway. Drive past two sets of traffic lights and turn first left, then first right. The USICA entrance is on the corner.

Embassy liaison office open Saturday-Wednesday 0900-1200, 1400-1600; USICA open 0800-1700.

West German economic liaison office Tel: 4777455. PO Box 8974. Telex: 202297 aariad.

Provides business help and limited consular services.

Other liaison offices

Australia Tel: 4777944-5, 4777951.

Canada Tel: 4769486.

Egypt Tel: 4034065, 4014428.

France Tel: 4774794, 4774803.

Japan Tel: 4780136, 4762937.

Jordan Tel: 4761883.

Kuwait Tel: 4787163.

Netherlands Tel: 4068016.

Pakistan Tel: 4761042.

Switzerland Tel: 4643326.

Transfer of the diplomatic quarter

In 1975 the government decided to transfer the Foreign Affairs Ministry — now in Jeddah — to the capital. The decision entailed transferring all embassies from Jeddah to Riyadh — to be done during the 1980s and 1990s. The first stage has begun. The second stage will last from 1990 to 2000.

In its first phase the bulk of public facilities and residential and non-residential buildings will be put up for diplomatic missions expected to move to Riyadh this year. Between 1983-90 buildings and amenities are expected to expand to house 90 diplomatic missions and 15,000 people. By the end of the second stage, the quarter should accommodate 120 missions and 25,000 inhabitants.

Planners expect 80 per cent of the quarter's inhabitants to be from Arab countries. When it is complete the diplomatic community will make up only half its residents. The site of the quarter is on a hill dominating the green Wadi Hanifa and Riyadh to the southeast. To the northwest of Riyadh, the site covers 5.8 million square metres and is about eight kilometres from the centre of Riyadh on the Dir'iya road.

Getting around

Airport
Lying to the north of Riyadh opposite the Sahary al-Riyadh hotel (see Hotels), the airport and its international and domestic lounges stand side by side. International arrivals has a branch of The National Commercial Bank and an Al-Rajhi money exchange. There is a large cafeteria in both the arrival and departure lounges, and a women's waiting room in the arrivals section. There are also nine automatic phone booths. Porters come at a negotiable price.

The arrivals section of the domestic lounge has a Godfrey Davis car hire desk and there is a cafeteria. An

Prince Salman with the British Prime Minister, Margaret Thatcher, in London

Prince Salman Bin Abdel-Aziz
Born in 1937, Prince Salman has been governor of Riyadh since 1962. He is a member of the so-called Sudairi Seven correctly known as the Al-Fahd, the seven sons of Ibn Saud by his wife Hassa Bint Ahmed al-Sudairi. Educated almost entirely in Saudi Arabia, the prince is respected for his hard work.

Arabian Express office desk covers domestic travel (see Arabian Express).

In 1982 the Riyadh-Dhahran single flight cost SR 170 first class, and SR 120 second. Riyadh to Jeddah single was SR 360 and SR 240.

It is possible, but chancy, to get a flight without having obtained a boarding pass (for economy and first class) from Arabian Express the previous day. Hotel travel agencies make a charge for this service. Flights within the kingdom are very congested and a long wait in the airport can be tedious. Taxis at night are sometimes

RIYADH

HOTELS
Hyatt Regency **E5 46**
Intercontinental **C5 41**
Al-Khozama **B3 16**
Marriott Riyadh **E3 28**
Minhal **E3 20**
Riyadh Palace **D6 63**
Saudi **C7 68**

PLACES OF INTEREST
Al-Dhiafa Exhibition Centre **B5 40**
Al-Khairiya **B3 15**
King Faisal Conference Centre **C5 42**
King Faisal Foundation **G5 52**
Al-Musmak Fortress **E9 92**
National Museum **C9 86**
University of Riyadh **G6 53**
Zoo **G4 32**

TRAVEL
Railway station **G7 79**
Riyadh airport **F1 6**
Arab National Bank **F3 31**
Banque de Caire **E9 88**
Al-Jazirah Bank **E9 87**
National Commercial Bank **F4, G8, E9, C1 O 90**
Riyad Bank **E9 91**
Saudi British Bank **E6, D6 62**
Saudi French Bank **E3 26**

SHOPPING AREAS
Batha Souq **E9 89**
Deera Souq **E9 95**
Fish Souq **D7 72**
Greenhouse Supermarket **E4 37**
Johar Supermarket **B3 17**
Kuwait Souq **E9 82**
New Gold Souq **E9 93**
Panda Supermarket **D6, F3, C3 18**
Al-Swaka Souq **E9 94**

HOSPITALS
King Faisal Specialist Hospital **A5 39**
Obeid Hospital **F5 49**
Riyadh Military Hospital **E3 19**

FOREIGN AND INTERNATIONAL INSTITUTIONS AND CENTRES
British Council **E7 74**
British Liaison Office **E3 66**
French Consulate & Language Institute **F7 77**

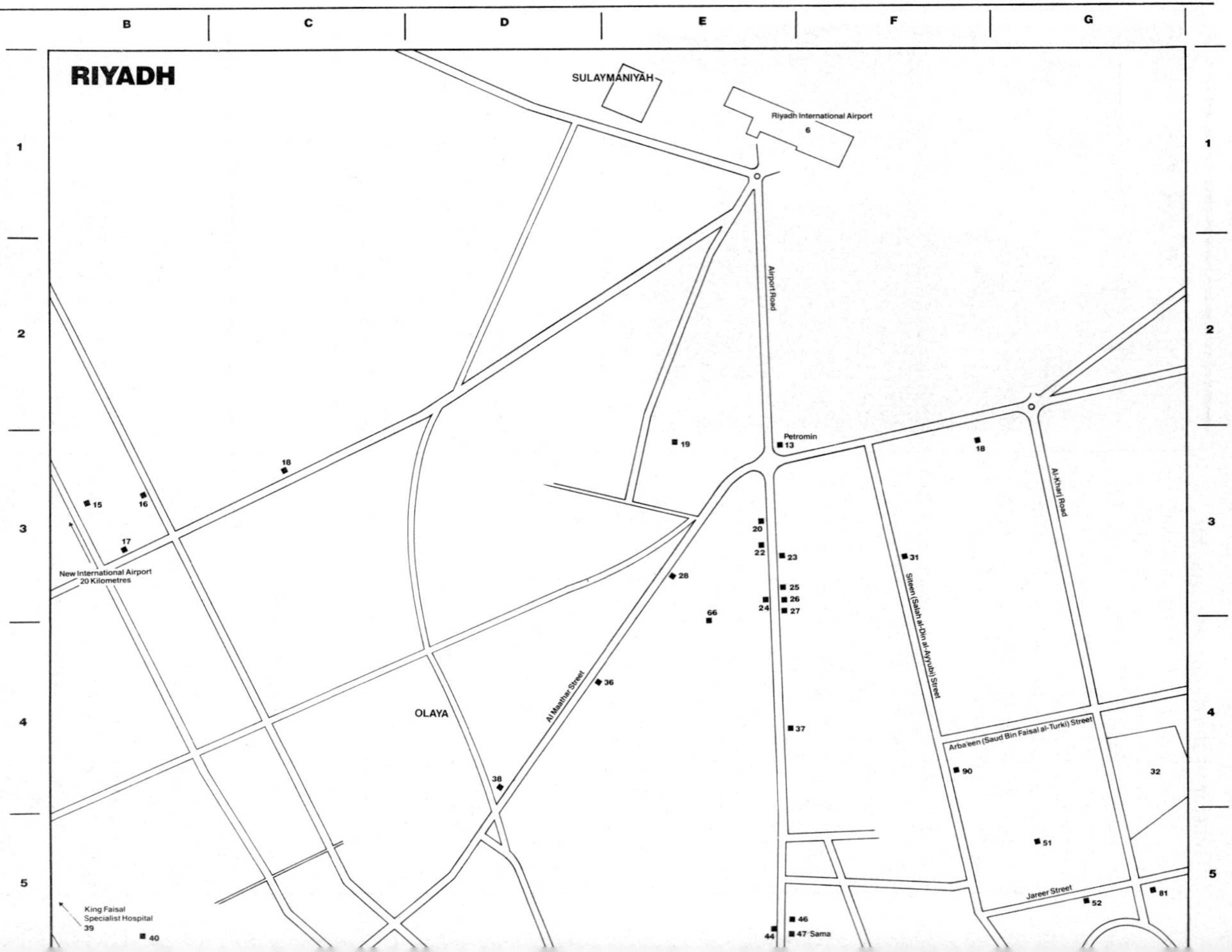

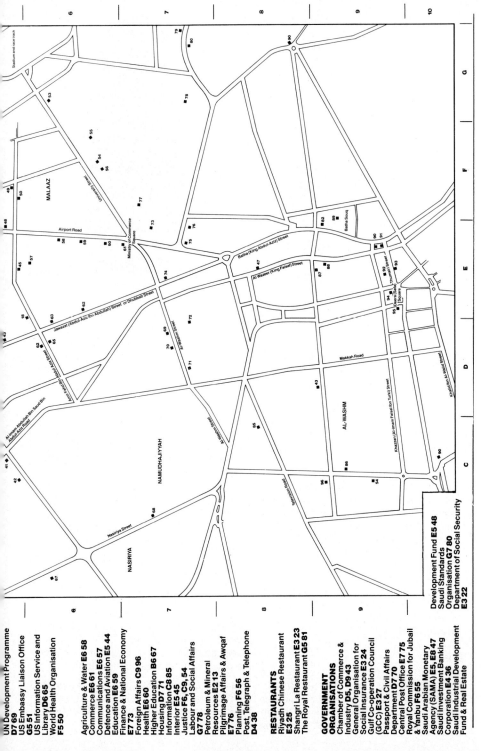

difficult to obtain. As there are no international scheduled flights from Riyadh the airport is used less than Jeddah and some taxi drivers obviously feel it is not worth working the night shift.

The new airport
Because of expansion and increasing air traffic, a new airport is being built to replace the present one about 35 kilometres to the north. It is scheduled to open in 1984. With a total area of 300 square kilometres, it is designed to expand to accommodate the forecast 15 million passengers a year by 2000.

One and, later, two terminals will service domestic and international routes. These will be at the north end of the roads which approach the airport. At the south end the royal terminal will dominate the ceremonial mall leading to the mosque at the far end. The airport's control tower will be one of the largest in the world. Beside the airport will be a community housing the 3,000 or so people employed at the airport — 390 villas or apartments, schools for 600 students, a 500-room hotel, a community mosque, a recreation complex, a golf course, a sports field and a lecture theatre.

Air communications (domestic)
Direct daily flights to Abha, Al-Madinah, Dhahran, Qassim, Jizan, Hail, Hofuf, Jeddah, Najran, Tabuk and Taif. Direct flights to Arar, Bisha, Jouf, Qaisumah, Turaif and Yanbu.

Saudia Tel: reservations 47722221, 4773333, 4774444; airport passenger services 4769480; airport cargo services 4761044.

Buses
Saptco runs a daily non-stop service between Riyadh and Taif, tel: Riyadh 4545000, Taif 7384648. It leaves Riyadh airport at 1800, arriving at the Taif Saptco terminal at 1430. It leaves

Saptco bus-stop

the Taif terminal at 1800, arriving at Riyadh airport at 0430.

Reservations must be made at least 48 hours in advance; fare: SR 100.

All buses are airconditioned and have washing facilities and drinking water.

Car hire

Avis Al-Malez Tel: 4763909, 165 Salman al-Farsi Street, PO Box 40280; Riyadh Palace hotel, tel: 4012644, ext 248-9; airport, open seven days a week. All branches open 0800-1400, 1630-2100.

For rates/models see Jeddah section.

PTS Rental Cars Tel: 4657224. PO Box 731. Telex: 41076 rabbit. Offices in Malaz and Sulaymaniyah.

Conditions: current national or Saudi licence; temporary visa holders may use international driving licence or any valid licence held for at least a year; minimum age 21. Deposit, deducted from final account, SR 500 a day. Long-term rates negotiable.

Saudi Limousine Central Province (Riyadh) Tel: 4657224. A chauffeur-driven service operated by PTS Rental. Rates start at SR 60 an hour.

Abu-Diyab Tel: 4762575, 4768092. Airport Road. From Petromin crossing, second right towards airport. Open 24 hours, seven days a week.

Model	Daily rate (SR)*
Toyota Corolla	120
Mazda 929	140
Chevrolet Caprice/ Toyota Hilux	170
Buick	270
GMC Suburban	320

*Free mileage within Riyadh, 10% discount on monthly rates

Arabian Hala Company Tel: 4789986-7. PO Box 6164. Telex: 201969 hala. From airport take Airport Road. Turn right at officers' club and company is 200 metres down.

Conditions: must carry current national or Saudi licence; temporary visa holders may use international driving licence or any valid licence held for at least one year; minimum age 25.

For rates/models see Jeddah section.

Shary Rent-a-Car PO Box 10681. Telex: 203428 shary sj. Sulaymaniyah, behind officers' club, tel: 4766968; Minhal hotel, Airport Road, tel: 4782500, ext 103; airport desk, tel: 4777313; Zahret al-Sharq hotel, tel: 4038800, ext 197.

Model	Daily rate (SR)*
Toyota Corolla	69
Toyota Carina	85
Toyota Cressida	100
Toyota Crown	125
Chevrolet Impala	155
Buick	200
Cadillac Fleetwood	385

*plus daily insurance of SR 30. Rates available on unlimited mileage basis

Chauffeur-driven service, tel: 4766968. Rate: SR 60 an hour.

Sahary Rent-a-Car Airport, tel: 4764200, 4764166; Sahary al-Riyadh hotel, tel: 4766707.

For rates/models see Jeddah section.

Hotels

Hyatt Regency Tel: 4771111. PO Box 18006. Redec Plaza centre about 10 minutes from the airport. Telex: 202963. Opened April 1982.

350 rooms, all with direct-dial telephone, colour TV and in-house video.

Travel agency, car hire, barber, courier and valet service. Business centre with local business information library, secretarial services. Outdoor heated swimming pool, billiards and games room, sauna, massage, gymnasium and indoor jogging track.

Le Dome restaurant serves Middle East and international cuisine; Cafe Louloua, open 24 hours, serves breakfast, lunch and dinner.

Hotel Inter-Continental Tel: 4655000. PO Box 3636. Maather Street (the ring road west of the Petromin roundabout on Airport Road). Telex: 201076 ihchot, cable: inhotel.

All rooms have a terrace, bathroom, airconditioning, local direct-dial telephone, fridge stocked with non-alcoholic drinks, colour TV with video, 24-hour room service.

Laundry and dry cleaning six days a week, secretarial and translation services, telex facilities between 0600-2400, news-stand, barber shop, gift shop, boutique, jewellery shop, taxi service, travel agency, Saudia desk.

The Oasis restaurant has a German chef, and serves oriental and international cuisine. Refreshment lounge has a pianist every Friday from 1700-1900. Twice weekly barbecue evenings from mid-April to mid-November, usually on Wednesday and Thursday, cost SR 80 a person.

Recreation and fitness centre, swimming pool, sauna, floodlit tennis courts, billiards, bowling alley and gymnasium. Membership available to non-residents. Tennis and swimming lessons also available — coaching SR 40 an hour. Swimming lessons for seven to 12 year olds, SR 400 a course. For further information, contact club manager, ext 7938.

Rates: single SR 300, studio single SR 300, double SR 390, studio double SR 430, junior suite SR 450, suite SR 600, pool cabana SR 300, pool cabana twin SR 390; plus 15% service.

Credit cards: American Express, Diners Club, Carte Blanche, Visa, Barclaycard.

The Inter-Continental also has 17 fully furnished two and three-bedroom villas in Malaz, between the airport and the city centre. Services include reception office, housekeeping, switchboard and message service; laundry and dry cleaning, 24-hour room service, in-house video, private gardens, telex, direct-dial telephones, fully equipped kitchens and private parking. Tel: 4787000.

Marriott Riyadh Hotel Tel: 4779300. PO Box 2066. Maather Street (Inter-Continental hotel road), minutes from airport, near Petromin flyover. Telex: 200983 marr.

New luxury hotel but less imaginative in design than its sister hotel, the Marriott Khurais. Restaurant, coffee shop, news-stand, travel agency, barber, car rental, in-house videos and gift shop. Outdoor swimming pool, games room, gymnasium and sauna. The fitness centre is available to non-resident members for SR 1,200 a person annually.

Rates: single SR 330, double SR 390; plus 15% service.

Credit cards: American Express, Mastercard, Diners Club, Carte Blanche.

Al-Khozama Hotel Tel: 4654650. PO Box 4148. Telex: 200100 khoz sj. In Olaya, four kilometres from airport and minutes from Riyadh's commercial centre and King Faisal Hall; off the ring road to the Inter-Continental.

175 rooms and 15 suites, all with bathroom, international direct-dial telephone, colour TV and video, mini-fridge; 24-hour room service.

Convention and banqueting facilities for up to 100. Business executive services (including translations and Arabic typing). Boutique, drugstore, photo-studio, car hire (limousine service), travel desk, hairdresser and barber; swimming pool and fitness equipment — membership for the swimming pool open to non-residents (men only) at SR 600 a year.

The Windrose Restaurant employs 11 Swiss chefs so the food is excellent. The meals are international, Arabic or "nouvelle cuisine" (foods that are all fresh — never frozen — cooked lightly in non-rich sauces). Dinner in elegant atmosphere with piano music.

The Gourmet Club is open to men only, although women are invited to the dinners. New members must be proposed by two current members. The club holds three or four dinners a year, with each course introduced by one of the club's officers. The seven or eight courses take about five hours to eat. The club has table rules: no smoking throughout the meal, no political or religious discussions, and no-one but the "taster" may leave the table during the meal.

The national branch of the french culinary association "La Chaine des Rotisseurs" was founded at the Al-Khozama on 17 December 1981. Informal gatherings over a light lunch take place eight times a year.

Farmers' brunch on Friday (1000-1500) is popular and very much a family affair — children are welcome. Barbecues every Sunday and Tuesday in the garden.

The Caravan Stop coffee shop (open 1000-2400) serves light meals and Italian pasta. Excellent pastries, homemade chocolates and bread are sold at the patisserie in the lobby.

Rates: single studio SR 275, twin room SR 325, suites from SR 375, bungalows from SR 600; baby cots SR 60, extra bed SR 60; plus 15% service.

Credit cards: American Express, Diners Club, Visa/Barclaycard, Eurocard.

HOTEL
AL KHOZAMA
RIYADH

Enjoy Swiss hospitality in Riyadh

The Hotel Al Khozama features:
- 175 rooms, 15 suites
- 2 Restaurants, meeting facilities
- Business Center, car rental
- Swimming pool, shops
- Colour TV, in-house video
- Air-conditioning
- Direct dial telephone

The Windrose Restaurant for fine dining.

"The Caravan Stop" Coffee Shop for light meals and snacks.

HOTEL AL KHOZAMA
P O Box 4148, Riyadh, Kingdom of Saudi Arabia. Telex 200100
Telephone (01) 465 4650

HRI The Leading Hotels of the World

STEIGENBERGER RESERVATION SERVICE

SWISS INTERNATIONAL HOTELS

Service means you [get all the perks] of business class [on our] Golden Economy.®

A choice of International and Middle Eastern cuisine honoured by La Chaine des Rôtisseurs.

All you need for a good night's sleep…

Cause for celebration. Let us know in advance and we'll bake a cake for you.

Complimentary fruit and refreshments.

The movie comes free and cards or chess or backgammon set are yours for the asking.

As you can see, you get a great deal when you fly Golden Economy® on one of our Golden Falcon® TriStars from the Gulf.

All the extras you'd expect flying the best business class, in fact.

Plus one or two that are uniquely ours.

The movie, refreshments, the pick of the days papers, the freshest of fresh fruit – they're yours, with our compliments.

A choice of International and Middle Eastern meals prepared to a standard honoured by La Chaine des Rôtisseurs – they're a standard feature of our Golden Falcon® Service.

Chess, cards, backgammon sets – they're yours to use just for the asking.

Seats that let you really stretch out and relax, our slipperette and eyeshades nightflight kit – we care for your every comfort.

Gulf Air Golden Economy.®

Twenty one flights from the Gulf to London Heathrow with daylight flights every day of the week.

No wonder that, last year, the readers of Executive Travel Magazine voted us the businessman's No 1 choice to the Middle East.

For more information contact your travel agent or Gulf Air.

طيران الخليج

GULF AIR
Spread your wings

ABU DHABI AMMAN ATHENS BAHRAIN BANGKOK BEIRUT BOMBAY CAIRO COLOMBO DELHI DHAHRAN DOHA DUBAI HONG KONG JEDDAH KARACHI KUWAIT LARNACA LONDON MANILA MUSCAT PARIS RAS AL KHAIMAH SALALAH SHARJAH TUNIS

FOR ALL YOUR WORLD – WIDE TRAVEL NEEDS

ZAHID TRAVEL AGENCIES CO. LTD

JEDDAH	RIYADH	AL-KHOBAR	YANBU
6607539	4028875	8644416	3222945
6612340			

Universal Travel Agencies CO. LTD.
Member of the Zahid Group of Companies

JEDDAH	RIYADH	AL-KHOBAR	YANBU
6422228	4778016	8646282	3224385
6612360			
6612364			

Riyadh Palace Hotel Tel: 4012644, 4054444. PO Box 2691. In ministerial quarter off King Fahd Street. Telex: 200312 rph sj.

306 double rooms, 36 executive suites, six deluxe suites, all with international direct-dial, colour TV with video, radio, message indicator, air-conditioning, circular bath, shower and bidet.

Laundry, dry cleaning, bookstall, boutique, barber shop, bureau de change. Outdoor heated swimming pool and sun terrace. Secretarial services, information centre with data on embassies, chambers of commerce and ministries, conference and banqueting rooms and taxi service.

La Fontaine restaurant serves French, Arab and international dishes. Cafe Bleu Coffee Shop has a la carte menu with grills and light refreshments, open 1630-2400.

Rates: single SR 322, double SR 408, executive suite SR 488, deluxe suite SR 1,150; plus 15% service.

Credit cards: American Express, Diners Club, Trust Houses Forte.

Sahary al-Riyadh Hotel Tel: 4761500. PO Box 10574. Telex: 201027 sahary.

One of Riyadh's older hotels; not first class, but conveniently sited just opposite the airport.

Rates: single SR 160, double SR 240, suites SR 320-400, villa SR 500. Breakfast SR 12, lunch SR 35, dinner SR 40; plus 10% service.

Oasis Airport Mutlaq Hotel Tel: 4762193, 4763483. PO Box 506. Airport Road. Telex: 201802.

Very modern, a few minutes from the airport. All rooms have colour TV and bathroom; 24-hour room service.

Coffee shop open 0700-2300 has German chef and serves international dishes. Swimming pool and sun terrace. Reception and banquet rooms, business centre. Car hire, travel desk valet service, barber shop, bookstall, boutiques.

Rates: single SR 260, double SR 310, suite SR 390-520.

Al-Diyar Residence Tel: 4780183, 4781774, 4789764. East of Airport Road, behind King Abdul-Aziz hospital, same street as Agency of Industrial & Electrical Affairs. Telex: 201665 reside.

Ideal for visiting businessmen staying several weeks to conclude their business or as temporary accommodation; as company guest apartments; or for diplomats and businessmen making frequent visits to Riyadh. Sauna and small recreation room.

There are three types of apartment: 70 type A, six type B, 17 type C (15% service added to all rates).

Type A (1-2 people) SR 8,260 (4 weeks); living/dining room screened from bedroom area which has 2 beds, kitchenette, bathroom.

Type B (2-4 people) SR 13,860 (4 weeks); living/dining room, sofa converts into double bed, bedroom with two beds, full kitchen, bathroom.

Type C (2-4 people) SR 16,660 (4 weeks); spacious living/dining room — sofa converts into double bed, bedroom area with 2 beds and a second sitting area, full kitchen, bathroom.

La Residence is luxuriously furnished and has central airconditioning. Every apartment has colour TV with local and three video channels, and three programmes of music; telephones in every room (not direct dial). Telex service 24 hours. Laundry service and arrangements for dry cleaning. Swimming pool (men only), TV room, ample parking. Restaurant Orangerie and news-stand with confectionery and toiletries.

Embassies and companies are invited to open accounts and send their guests accompanied by a letter. Discounts on long stays.

Minhal Tel: 4782500. PO Box 17058. Airport Road, minutes from airport. Telex: 203088 minal sj.

255 rooms, all fully airconditioned,

with local direct-dial telephone, radio, colour TV and in-house movies.

L'Aigle restaurant serves French and oriental food, and Shalimar coffee shop offers 24-hour service. Conference facilities for 200, bureau de change, laundry and drycleaning, nursery and baby-sitting service, car rental, drugstore, boutique, French take-away bakery with delicious cakes and bread.

Rates: single SR 288, double SR 374, suite SR 431, apartment SR 690.

Al Yamama Tel: 4774048, 4774043. PO Box 1210. Airport Road opposite ministries. Telex: 201056 yamtel sj. Under new management.

184 rooms and 10 suites, most reserved for government staff. All have fridge, telephone, TV and radio.

Restaurant, coffee shop, swimming pool, gardens, library, banqueting room, barber shop.

Riyadh Hala House Tel: 4782333, 4782316, 782444. PO Box 7400. Telex: 201651 haltil, cable hala house.

Five minutes from the airport and centre. All rooms are airconditioned with private phone, TV and radio.

Rates: single SR 110, double SR 130, apartment SR 400.

Saudi Hotel Tel: 4024051, 4035051, 4037141. PO Box 244. Nasariyah Street. Telex: 201069 saudin.

100 rooms, 12 suites; 24-hour room service and cafeteria, swimming pool, barber, telex, car rental. Terrace serving hot and cold drinks and sandwiches.

Rates: single SR 160, double SR 210, suite SR 240; plus 10% service.

Al-Boustan Hotel Tel: 4650023, 4657094. PO Box 5868. Telex: 201555 bostan. Minutes from the airport. Al-Khaima restaurant serves European and oriental food. Swimming pool.

Al-Bata Hotel Tel: 4039913, 4039973. PO Box 17199. Telex: 203132 203133 mansor sj. Centrally located close to ministries and financial centres. 336 rooms and suites. Business and executive services, conference and banquet facilities, 24-hour room service. Al-Shaikh Restaurant serves international food; coffee shop open 24 hours.

Rates: single SR 120, double SR 170, suite SR 220.

Credit cards: Diners Club, American Express.

Zahret al-Sharq Hotel Tel: 4028216, 4023978. PO Box 3615. Corner of Airport Road and University Street, opposite the Ministry of Commerce. Telex: 201017.

116 rooms, 30 suites, 16 villas. Once one of Riyadh's best hotels but has been superseded by luxury hotels built over the past two years. Fully airconditioned, all rooms have bathroom, telephone and TV. Telex facilities. Restaurant with Egyptian chef (open to the public for lunch 1300-1500 and dinner 2000-2200); coffee shop; swimming pool open to the public, mornings for women and afternoon for men (free for guests). Conference hall seating 700; Areen Travel Agency in courtyard (see Travel Agencies); barber shop; newsstand.

Rates: single SR 160 (rarely available), double SR 200, double (two guests) SR 240, small suite SR 320, deluxe suite SR 400, villa SR 400; plus 15% service.

Communications

Telex and telegrams

Public telex and telegram offices are at the airport, in King Faisal Street just off Water Tower Square, in Nasiriyah, Deera and Manfouha. Prices are about half hotel prices (see Jeddah for prices).

Post

The new postal centre is opposite Spinney's supermarket at the lower end of Airport Road. Post takes about five days to reach most parts of

Europe. Parcel post goes from an office to the left of the airport in Sulaymaniyah Road. Each district has its own post office.

Courier services
SNAS-DHL Tel: 4778059, 4779668, 4779653, homeward 4771970. PO Box 5641. Off Airport Road. Telex: 203272 snascr.

Travelling from the city towards the airport along Airport Road turn right immediately after the Najd Hotel (BAC private hotel). This is opposite the Sabreen building, before reaching the Dammam Road (Petromin flyover). Then first left, first right and the SNAS-DHL office is the second building on the right. It is signposted from Airport Road to the office.

Skypak Tel: 4648874, 4658160, 4649810, 4649127. PO Box 5895. Olaya Street, near City supermarket. Telex 203923 brothr.

Travel agents
Ace Travel Tel: 4648810. PO Box 667.
Areen Travel Tel: 4027685, 4028876, 4027670. PO Box 2953. Zahret al-Sharq hotel, University Street, Airport Road. Telex: 201699. Agent for Bangladesh Airways, British Caledonian, Iberia, Sabena, Tunis Air and Ethiopian Airways.
Attar Travel Tel: 4787208, 4787210-2. PO Box 364. Khurais Road, behind Panda supermarket. Agent for SAS, Thai Airways, Kenya Airways, Cyprus Airways, Iraqi Airways and Qantas.
Ewan Travel Tel: 4785120. Alhassa Avenue.
Fahad Travel Tel: 4480865, 4480738. Abercrombie & Kent, c/o Tanhat, PO Box 648. Telex: 201950 tanhat.
Falcon Wings for Travel & Tourism Tel: 4775429, 4774553-4. PO Box 1343, Najd Building, Airport Road. Telex: 202464.
Kanoo Offices Pepsi-Cola Street, tel: 4789528. PO Box 753; Khurais Road, tel: 4914620.

Red Sea for Tourism & Aviation Tel: 4029225. Nimer Building, Airport Road. Telex: 200316; Khereiji hotel, 1st floor, Al-Rajhi Building, Batha, tel: 4039919, 4039913, ext 390.
Riyadh Tours & Travel Services Tel: 4774433, 4774455, 4773279. PO Box 753. Airport Road. Telex: 201038, cable: rytours.
Saddik & Mohammed Attar Tel: 4787225, 4787212. Behind Panda supermarket, Khurais Road.
Saudi Tourist & Travel Bureau Tel: 4013346, 4774115, 4774382. Arba'en Street. Agent for Korean Airways, Cathay Pacific, Japan Airlines, Singapore Airways, Malaysian Airways, Sudan Air, Air Lanka, PIA, Turkish Airlines, Garuda and Iran Air.
Saudi Travel & Tourist Agency Tel: 4022820, 4031752. PO Box 215. King Faisal Street, Aziziyah Building. Telex: 201125.

Eating out

There are almost too many restaurants to mention. For a good meal, expatriates go to restaurants in the first-class hotels. Almost all serve evening poolside barbecues which are very popular, as the climate is ideal for them. Most offer an exciting selection of non-alcoholic cocktails; in restaurants most people choose a drink which is half apple juice and half Perrier water.

Movenpick Restaurant Orangerie Tel: 4780183. "La Residence" building, in Mocha area, one block off Airport Road facing the ministries. Telex: 201665 reside.

Charming atmosphere with both privacy and space, comfortably seating 160; Tiffany lamps and soft background music. Different specialities are offered every two to three weeks, based on a theme (eg shrimp). Distinctive Swiss cooking which, as chief chef Verner Seewald explains, is "not disguised in heavy sauces or hot spices, but is appreciated for its true flavour." A hearty "Swiss Farmers' Breakfast" is served every morning from 0700-1330.

The restaurant is open seven days a week from 0700-2400. Make reservations, particularly on Thursday, Friday and Saturday evenings.

Oriental Food Restaurant Tel: 4767838. PO Box 733. On the right, off Jareer Street, fourth street right after Siteen Street crossing. Serves Korean food.

La Romana Tel: 4762347. PO Box 4171. Opposite King Abdul-Aziz Military School, Airport Road. Cable: martoz. General manager: Marwan al-Fawaz.

Exotic decor, friendly service. Lebanese chef — wide selection of food, from Chateaubriand steak (SR 45) to Iranian caviar (SR 65).

Shangri-La Tel: 4762432. Chinese restaurant behind The Saudi French Bank, Airport Road.

Al-Khaima Tel: 4650023, 4657094. Next to Al-Boustan Hotel. Dim lights. Lebanese cuisine.

Al-Ajami Restaurant Tel: 4785045-6. Siteen Street, behind Al-Aamer Furniture. Established in 1920, winner of the Lebanese Award. Takeaway foods, ice cream, Lebanese sweets such as qatayef, kenafah, esmaliyah. Western daily dish. Parties catered for.

Riyadh Chinese Restaurant (formerly the Pagoda) Tel: 4761056. Airport Road. Good Chinese food in an attractive setting. Takeaway service.

Green Valley Oriental Restaurant Tel: 4027627. Airport Road, above Spinney's. Tea rooms. One of Riyadh's oldest western-style restaurants.

Al-Tannour Tel: 4761565, 4764724. East of Airport Road. Completely renovated in 1980. Lebanese and European cooking. Home baked bread. Takeaway service. Monthly memberships.

Al-Aqwass Restaurant and Cafeteria (self-service) Tel: 4642892. PO Box 244, Sahara Towers, Olaya Road. Open seven days a week, 0700-2300.

Japanese Steak House Tel: 4761659.

PO Box 3504. Near Petromin crossing at Khurais Road and Airport Road intersection. Specialises in steak or prawn dishes. Good service. Set meal SR 50-85.

Atta Restaurant Beside Al-Zahra'a Hotel, Airport Road. Food includes steam roast, karahi tikka, haleem mince-meat nan, mince-chicken nan, roghni nan.

Sinbad Restaurant Tel: 4026557. Jamaa Street. Steak specialities.

Semiramis Tel: 4023841. Wazir Street. Specialises in Lebanese cuisine.

Broasted Chicken First block to the left off Jareer Street. Takeaway service.

60 Restaurant Tel: 4760706. Near Petromin roundabout. Attracts sophisticated diners.

Massis Airport Road. Small restaurant specialising in Lebanese cuisine. Good takeaway service.

Mocca Airport Road, next to University Bookstore. Snacks.

Palms Arba'en Street. Lebanese snacks and takeaway pizzas.

Restaurant International House Tel: 4763936. In Malaz, off Jareer Street. Serves Korean, Chinese and Japanese food. Good takeaway service. Restaurant has a small garden, with a water garden and fountain. An aviary with parrots and budgies adds to the entertainment for children. Closed Saturdays.

Bamboo Restaurant Tel: 4658019. Aroub Street, Olaya. Buffet on Fridays with food from Italy and the Middle East; adults SR 60, children SR 30.

Chinese Gardens Restaurant Tel: 4761056. Airport Road, behind Hyatt Regency Hotel.

Indian Gardens Restaurant Tel: 4761218. In Malaz, off Siteen Street behind Saudi-British Bank and Sony Agency. Takeaway service.

The Royal Tel: 4765129. Pepsi-Cola Street, near racecourse and Sadhan stadium in Malaz.

Takeaway food

Kentucky Fried Chicken Siteen Street, between the Arba'en and Jareer Street roundabouts.

Hardees American hamburger chain with two shops, one on Siteen Street near the Kentucky Fried Chicken, and one in Olaya near the supermarket.

The Golden Fry In Olaya, near the Circle Supermarket, almost opposite Hardees. Genuine English fish and chip shop.

Wimpy House Wazir Street. Not used much by expats.

Freezer Foods
Home-cooked freezer food or complete meals are very popular with Riyadh's bachelor population. Food is made to order, frozen and delivered. For further information, tel: 4653600.

Shopping

Hours of business vary slightly; some shops open all afternoon, while those in downtown areas open from 0900-1200 and 1600-2100. During Ramadan, most shops are closed during the day but stay open until 0200.

Supermarkets
Almost too many to mention. All sell imported foods, local bread, local milk, cream, yogurt and dairy produce. Most of the larger ones now sell chilled meat, while imported meat is available in all. Food is more expensive than in the UK.

Many supermarkets are run on a departmental basis, as in the US, selling everything from clothes to televisions.

Panda Supermarket Khurais Road, on Petromin side of Pepsi-Cola factory. Specialises in fresh meats (beef, lamb, baby camel). Competitive prices. Open daily 0830-2300 except for prayers. A chain of 16 shops is planned.

Stadium Supermarket Opposite stadium in Malaz.

City Supermarket Olaya. Ground floor sells fresh fruit, vegetables, bread, cheese; first floor sells watches, cosmetics, sports goods, televisions and videos. Cash and carry, and wholesale services.

City Supermarket Sulaymaniyah.

Golden Shopping Centre Pepsi-Cola Street, Malaz (near Golden Bakery).

Greenhouse Supermarket Airport Road. Sells good fresh meat.

Riyadh Supermarket Airport Road.

Johar Supermarket Jareer Street, Olaya. Large department store with boutiques, jewellery, newsagents, ladies tailor, shoe shop and refreshment stall. Also sells birds, indoor plants and garden equipment.

Najd Centre Supermarket Jareer Street, Olaya.

Circle Supermarket Arba'en Street, Sulaymaniyah.

Hussaim Stores Khurais Road. Food store on ground floor, shoes and household goods on first floor.

Le Gourmet Olaya Road. A superb selection of Canadian and Scotch smoked salmon, French cheeses, pates, lobster and other luxury items. Also homemade and imported chocolate and confectionery counter, a patisserie counter and a humidified room where cigars can be bought.

Euromarche A hypermarket, opened in 1981, which sells French-made children's and adults' clothes, and French food. Fresh fruit and vegetables arrive from Paris every Sunday. It also sells household goods, toys, garden equipment, birds, fish and small animals, tapes and records and freshly baked cakes and biscuits.

Patisseries
Al-Khozama Hotel Has an excellent patisserie selling homemade cakes, chocolates and bread. The bread is fairly expensive at SR 3 a medium-size loaf but well worth it. Cakes can be ordered in advance.

The Movenpick Restaurant Another excellent patisserie which has fresh cream cakes. It is best to order in advance.

Children's shops

The quantity and quality of all children's toys and equipment is excellent. Fisher-Price toys, Chicco equipment, games, puzzles and clothes are all readily available.

There are three large shops which sell everything for children: *Ahmed Jamal Toys,* half-way down Jareer Street on the left; *Al-Arabi Assaghir,* turn into University Street from Siteen Street, left at lights and fourth on the left; *Chicco Shop* which is almost opposite the Panda supermarket. There are also plenty of smaller shops and a new Chicco shop on Olaya Road, which sells a wide range of equipment including push chairs and camping cots.

Dry cleaning

Marriott Khurais Hotel Dry cleaning facilities are available to non-residents — open 0800-1130, 1600-1930, Saturday to Thursday.

Hotel Inter-Continental Shop next to hotel. Open to non-residents.

Shopping areas

Airport Road (King Abdul-Aziz Street) One of the principal shopping areas and the most well-established, apart from the central shopping areas of Wazir Street and Batha Street.

Al-Qahtani Furniture (tel: 4762573) opposite King Abdul-Aziz Military College sells high-quality furniture. *Christian Dior* is alongside, its plush windows fronting a shop of the utmost elegance — one door for men and the other for women. *Sabreen,* the elegant women's clothes shop, stands opposite the Najd hotel. Beside Citibank is *Danish Centre for Modern Design* (tel: 4786940, 4786938), one of the most sophisticated shops selling a variety of modern furniture.

Other shops include the *Golden Rose Florist* behind Citibank (roses SR 10 each, carnations SR 8 each, tulips SR 50 a bunch); *University Bookshop* (see bookshops); *Spinneys Supermarket,* lower (town) end of Airport Road opposite new Post Office building; *Al-Samhar Supermarket,* between Romana Restaurant (see restaurants) and University Bookshop.

Redec Plaza also on Airport Road, tel: 4761349, 4761359. Contact: Muhammad al-Ali, PO Box 611. Parking on ground floor. 252 deluxe offices on eight floors, six meeting halls (one on each floor of the office block), 146 showrooms on three floors. The centre has 10 lifts, escalators, 250 telephone lines, and telex lines. Redec Plaza also incorporates the five-star Hyatt Regency hotel (see hotels).

Malaz One of the main residential areas, although new areas such as Olaya are beginning to compete. Most shops are either in Siteen Street, the principal street, or in smaller streets running off it such as Jareer Street which is the best place to find roast chicken, fruit and vegetables. The main supermarket in Siteen Street is near the roundabout.

Pierre Cardin is at the end of Siteen Street on the corner of Abdul-Aziz Ibn Muhammad Street (Khurais Road). *Sports Shop* in Siteen Street is probably the best sports shop in town. Horse riders can buy excellent riding equipment — saddles, bridles, and so on. Other shops include *Mutlaq Furniture,* on Siteen Street; *Ahmad Jamal Toy Shop* and *Jareer Bookshop.*

Pepsi-Cola Street (otherwise known as Zoo Street because the Riyadh zoo stands on it — real name Al-Ahsa Street). There is a good supermarket on 8th Street to the right heading for the Khurais Road. Next door is one of the best bakeries in town — the *Golden Bakery* — which sells every kind of oriental and European bread (including garlic bread).

Olaya One of Riyadh's newest residential areas and already contains some of the city's best shops. It has the *City Supermarket* (see supermarkets), and *Le Cicogna* (tel: 4654010) beyond Sahara Towers on the right, a shop for babies and children. *Toyshop* on Al-Olaya Street stocks toys from Hamleys (opposite the Al-Khozama hotel). There are several good shops on the corner of TV Street (Umar Ibn al-As Street): *Bajsair* for scent, watches and jewellery; *Happy Home* for household effects; *Chic Baby* for babies' clothes; *Dar Okaz Bookshop* (see bookshops) and *Al-Jazeerah Store* for food, shoes and toiletries.

Gardening shops and nurseries
Many supermarkets also have garden and nursery departments.

Nursery On the right of lower Airport Road, next to Spinneys supermarket.
Fantastic World On the right going towards the airport on Olaya Road, near the Panda supermarket.
The Golden Rose At the south end of the airport on the left.
Chicken Street 30 metres in on the right hand side, coming from Jareer Street.

Other shopping
Hajji camp Each year during the Hajj, Muslims flood in from all over the world. Many come overland and those from Pakistan, Afghanistan, Iran and countries east of Riyadh pass through and set up camp for several days, selling their wares to pay for the trip. The camp is on the right of the Dhahran road, just before the amusement park. Although many of the goods are imported, some traditional and tribal wares are sold, particularly oriental rugs and carpets.
Fish Souq A few hundreds yards down on the right hand side of a small road leading off left from Washm Street. The turn is just before the Washm Street fire station.
  The souq is open all week during normal shopping hours; the best time to buy is fresh from the trucks on Monday or Thursday afternoon. It stocks dairy goods, frozen meat and vegetables, and has huge freezers full of local fish, brought up by truck from Eastern province. Most of the fish has been caught in the early morning off the east coast and is very fresh. The souq also has excellent prawns and, occasionally, crab.

Bookshops
The Modern Commercial University Bookshop Tel: 4786617, 4790261. PO Box 394 Airport Road. Opposite Abdul-Aziz Military College. Manager: Tawfik A Baamer.
  Although small, it is one of the most efficient and best-stocked bookshops in the kingdom. It has two floors: the ground floor sells magazines, books on the Middle East, and stationery, and the first floor reference books, children's books, novels and posters. Also sells English and other European language books.

Dar Okaz Bookshop Tel: 4040814. PO Box 2934, Umar Ibn al-As Street, near Al-Asarat flyover. Cable: darkaz. General manager: Farouq Salaam.
  Two floors of English and Arabic books, magazines and stationery. A good bookshop, although not very central. Dar Okaz has a branch in Jeddah's Caravan Shopping Centre (see Jeddah). One of the main participants in Riyadh university's annual book fair in February. Open 0900-1500.

Al-Khazindar Distributing Establishment Tel: 4024853, 4022341. PO Box 457, Wazir Street, Aziziyah Building, Flat 212. Main office in Jeddah.
  One of the main distributors of magazines. Well stocked with periodicals, stationery, and English and Arabic books. Branches in Dhahran, Al-Khobar, Dammam, Jubail, Makkah, Taif and Khamis Mushait.

Mars Publishing Tel: 4034600, ext 276. PO Box 10720, Dar al-Marikh,

Stall in the gold souq

Al-Khereiji Building, Al-Batha. Telex: 200102 kabchar.

Mars Publishing has no bookshop but is a major distributor and runs a large stand at Riyadh university's annual book fair, where it represents foreign publishers.

Dar al-Uloum Siteen Street.

Jareer Bookshop Jareer Street.

Tihama Bookshop Tel: 4012969. Dhabab Street behind Saudi Real Estate Company Building, Al-Wazrat.

The old souqs (see map)

The Antiques Souq

As you reach the clock tower at the end of Thumairi Street, turn very sharp left into Othman Ibn Affan Street. Passing a few metres of shops repairing broken radios and televisions, turn right into a series of concrete alleys in grid pattern full of stalls selling Arabian clothing (thobes, gutras and agals, and the embroidered black synthetic silk dresses of bedu women). Behind these is the carpet souq and beyond that an open area of antique souqs. You will see a profusion of bedu artefacts, from immense wooden water wheels to houdaj's (the covered wooden canopy in which women may ride in seclusion in the camel train).

An old man accompanied by his small son runs the main stall on the left. If you have a smattering of Arabic and a smile he may offer you a bench and innumerable cups of tea.

The stalls inside are bursting with khanjars (daggers), mabkharas (incense burners), dillis (Turkish-style coffee pots), shatts (brass coffee containers), and copper-studded Zanzibar chests. There are also leather bedu bags covered with bright embroidered cloth. You will also see chains of armour which sell for up to $1,000 and countless muskets and battered Lee Enfields. The Swiss explorer John Burchardt saw some chain mail vests in use when he visited Arabia in 1816.

Average prices today are: khanjar SR 300; dilli SR 65; mabkhara SR 60; musket SR 800. Camel saddles range from about SR 400 to about SR 900. Among the most interesting memorabilia are the carved and garishly painted Najdi doors with their massive locks.

Gold Souq

There are two gold souqs, one on Makkah Road in the Deera Square region, and the other off Batha Street. All jewellery is valued by the gram. Items are weighed at the time of purchase and prices vary daily according to the world gold price. Some of the gold is worked in Florence. Some very beautiful jewellery can be bought here, generally for much less than in the UK.

Makkah Road Souq

The old covered souq, in Deera Square, an alley filled with people, shops and smells, has given way to a purpose-built souq on the Makkah Road. Although the shops sell the same clothing, pots and pans, fabrics and gold, the new market lacks the character and interest of the old souq. To get there, take the flyover road that crosses the Inter-Continental Hotel Road, almost at the level of the hotel. Go south over six flyovers and then you will see the many white arches of the new souq on the right.

Batha Souq

Also known as the Kuwaiti Souq it is to be found east of Batha Street. The main souq area has a variety of items for sale, mostly imported, though the silver souq has small shops where craftsmen can be seen making, repairing and re-modelling traditional silver jewellery. Wood working, household and engineering tools are frequently sold along the souq's pavements.

Outside the main areas there are several interesting souqs.

Hubble-Bubble or Pottery Souq

To get there go south down Wazir Street and turn left into the street after Thumairi Street, under the flyover. Shops can be seen on either side selling hubble-bubble pipes (narguilehs). Take the first right turn into a narrower street where there is a mosque on the right — here you will see the coiled mouthpieces of the narguilehs being made. Further up the street you will find glazed pots of all shapes and sizes and also locally made metal barbecues. A shop opposite the mosque sells traditional Arab musical instruments and, in the alleys behind this shop, there are similar small shops.

Tent Souq (Souq al-Khaimah)

This is off Batha Street about 400 metres north of Khazzan Street. Facing north there is a Peugeot agency (Al-Saleem) on the left of Batha Street and a small street going off to the right with a shop on the corner called Al-Shehetan.

A short way along this street are the shops where men work with canvas, making awnings and patio screens to order, and doing repairs. Articles of bedu weaving can also be found here.

Camel Souq (Souq al-Jamal)

To get there go south down Wazir Street to the T-junction (Pepsi-Cola Street), turn left past the fire station and left again to Batha Street (take the right-hand lane). A grey wall about 500 metres long is on the right enclosing a cemetery. Turn right at the end of the wall into a narrow lane (point 328 painted on the wall) which winds along for about 400 metres before reaching the open area of the camel souq. Earth ramparts allow the camels to walk up into trucks and there are some wooden hoists for the reluctant ones.

Medical

There are many qualified doctors and dentists in Riyadh, most of whom speak English. Most expatriates prefer to choose a doctor or dentist of their own nationality because of language difficulties.

Many larger companies have their own clinics with doctors and nurses — the Saudi labour law now contains certain provisions on the subject. These are a few new private clinics in Riyadh which are open to members on an individual or company basis. Most have expatriate doctors and nurses, and some have inpatient facilities. None has maternity facilities.

Clinics

Transad Medical Service Tel: 4650840, 4650828. PO Box 42911. In Sulaymaniyah, behind the Grand Festival Palace.

The only licensed expatriate clinic in Riyadh, it provides a 24-hour emergency service; routine outpatient care, including X-rays and minor surgery; obstetric and gynaecological care; paediatrics; preventive medicine; immunisation, examinations and dental care. It does not provide in-patient nursing, specialised X-rays, major surgery or a maternity service.

Fee: individual dental care SR 250

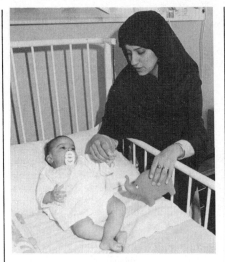
Maternity and baby care is very advanced

a person a month; company rates SR 130-200 a month.

Hours: Saturday-Wednesday 0800-1200, 1300-1700; Thursday 0800-1200; Friday closed.

The Allied Medical Clinic Tel: 4769287, 4768757, 4784691, 4789707 (night). PO Box 2816. In north Malaz behind the Golden Loaf Bakery, off Pepsi-Cola Street. Telex 201758.

Staffed by expatriate, mainly British, doctors and nurses, it offers primary care in most fields; observation beds, facilities for minor operations; X-rays; a laboratory; physiotherapy; immunisations; ante-natal and gynaecological care; paediatrics; preventive medicine; industrial health examinations. Also offers routine and emergency dental care.

Fees: company rates, full medical plan minimum SR 150 a person a month; dental plan add SR 20 a month.

The Saudi Medical Clinic Tel: 4646961. PO Box 9, Olaya. Staffed by expatriate doctors and nurses.

Green Crescent Health Service Tel: 4644434. PO Box 292. In Olaya, near City supermarket.

It provides general practice in most fields of medicine; physiotherapy; radiology; laboratory; home visits; routine and emergency dental care. Support services include 24-hour emergency cover; day surgery, recovery beds, ambulances including Lear jet air ambulance.

Fees: personal membership SR 1,200 a year; family plan SR 1,200 plus SR 1,000 for wife, SR 900 for children and SR 1,000 for additional adults; visitors' plan SR 450 a quarter. Reductions for companies.

Hospitals

There are two excellent expatriate-staffed hospitals which are among the finest in the world — unfortunately they are not open to the public.

The King Faisal Specialist Hospital Tel: 4647272. Off Maather Street. Open to Saudis only.

As it is a specialist hospital all cases must be referred. The emergency department will accept any patient in danger of losing life, sight or limbs, but any other expatriate wishing to be treated here must have a letter personally signed by King Fahd.

The Obeid Hospital Tel: 4778939. PO Box 3484. Farazdak Street.

It is the only privately run hospital and has been open for about nine years. Open to any nationality. The hospital has 40 beds with about 10 resident doctors and a team of specialists for consultations or for surgery.

Departments include: gynaecology and obstetrics — including a full maternity unit with premature baby unit; general surgery; orthopaedics; ear, nose and throat; opthalmology; emergency/casualty; laboratory; X-ray.

For inpatient care there are three classes of rooms: suite; first class with single room and bathroom; second class with shared room and bathroom.

The cost of treatment varies but, as an example, three days in hospital and all medical care for a mother and new-born baby would be: suite SR 1,500, first class SR 900, second class SR 700.

Hours: outpatients 0800-1200,

1600-2000; inpatients 0900-1100, 1700-1900.

Riyadh/Al-Kharj hospital programme

Two military hospitals are run by the programme — the Riyadh Military Hospital and the Al-Kharj Hospital. The UK's Allied Medical Group (AMG) is responsible for supplies, computing, finance and recruitment, and advises the programme on running them. All employees, although recruited by AMG, while working in Saudi Arabia are employees of the Riyadh/Al-Kharj hospital programme and governed by the medical services department of the Ministry of Defence & Aviation.

Riyadh Military Hospital Tel: 4777714. PO Box 7897. Telex: 201645 rkhpa.

It has 500 beds and the Al-Kharj 56. Mainly for military personnel and their dependants, Defence Ministry employees and their dependants, and renal transplant and cardiac surgery patients. It is occasionally possible to be referred for treatment by listed sponsors authorised by the Defence & Aviation Ministry or the armed forces chief-of-staff.

The main hospital provides high-quality medical services in primary care; accident and emergency services; general medicine and surgery; cardiology and cardiac surgery; dietetics; dentistry and oral surgery; obstetrics and gynaecology; paediatrics; pathology; physiology; psychiatry; opthalmology; orthopaedics; urology; ear, nose and throat surgery; oncology; dermatology; renal, X-ray and nuclear medicine.

Shumaisi Hospital (Central Hospital) Tel: 4351900. Shumaisi Street.

The largest of Riyadh's hospitals. All traffic victims are brought here so there is a large intensive care unit and orthopaedic department; also all other medical and surgical departments, laboratories and X-ray units, and the city's only blood bank.

Open to all nationalities and has a few expatriate doctors. It is also the only place in Riyadh which inoculates against yellow fever.

Al-Mubarak Hospital Tel: 4015282. PO Box 15563. In the Muraba'a area, near the junction of Wazir and Washm streets.

This small hospital was opened in 1981 for Saudis and expatriates. It has about 20 doctors, some of whom are expatriate. Departments include outpatients; emergency; general medicine; general surgery; gynaecology and obstetrics; full dental unit; paediatrics; dermatology; ear, nose and throat; X-ray; orthopaedics; physiotherapy; pharmacy; intensive care; maternity and premature baby unit. 24-hour emergency service.

Rooms are either first or second class, or suites — maximum number of beds to a room is two.

Major operating room in the King Faisal Specialist Hospital

Hours: 0800-1200, 1600-2000; visiting 1000-1400, 1800-2100.

Company clinics

All are staffed by expatriate doctors and nurses, with services provided solely for company employees and their families.

Ballast-Nedam Tel: 4647647. PO Box 5898. In the Ballast-Nedam village about 25 minutes' drive from the centre of Riyadh. Turn left off Dammam Road past the Marriott Khurais hotel and follow the signs to the village. The clinic, run by Dr Ganswyk, has both dental and medical facilities.

Bechtel Tel: 4647647. Complete hospital for workers on the new airport site.

Bell Canada Tel: 4543336. Dr Michael Denton.

Bendix-Siyanco Tel: 4762088, ext 175. PO Box 3453. In Sulaymaniyah, right of the airport. The clinic, run by Dr Taylor, offers both dental and medical facilities.

British Aerospace Tel: 4785288, 4766566, ext 4377. Dr John Nokes.

Lockheed Aircraft Corporation Tel: 4420240. In Nasiriyah, behind traffic office. Dr Alan Parry.

Philips-Ericsson. Tel: 4782314, 4787880. Dr Stort.

Specialists

Dr Ishaque Qureshi Tel: 4654211 (clinic), 4033759 (home). Abdul-Khalil Building beside city supermarket, Olaya Road. Dr Qureshi, a senior ear, nose and throat specialist, speaks excellent English. Although specialising in ENT he also does general practice. It is advisable to register with him in advance, but he does accept emergencies and will make home visits. Hours: 0900-1200, 1700-2100; Friday by appointment.

Dr Gabr Tel: 4028555. Specialises in obstetrics and gynaecology at King Abdul-Aziz university hospital. Holds clinics on Sunday and Tuesday.

Dr Ghazi Hannun Tel: 4766019. PO Box 3213. Surgery a few hundred metres from the Obeid hospital and well marked. Specialises in obstetrics and gynaecology. As Dr Hannun trained in Germany he speaks good German and some English. Hours: 0900-1300, 1500-2100.

Dr Salah Taha Tel: 4028555 (clinic), 4775761 (home). Paediatrician at King Abdul-Aziz university hospital.

Dr Mehar Bano Tel: 4646907. Abdul-Rahman Mossa Building, Flat 1, opposite Al-Khozama hotel. Specialises in gynaecology. Hours: 0900-1200, 1500-2000.

Dentists

Most expatriates join one of the new health centres. These provide both routine and emergency dental care and are often more reliable than downtown dentists.

Dr G Pharaon Tel: 4774970. Well-equipped surgery on the first floor of the building behind the flower shop on the right of Chicken Street Appointments are not absolutely necessary but should be made where possible.

Dr Dikran Yeranassian Tel: 4022221, 4022232. Dentist at the Al-Ahli Hospital, Khazzan Street. Hours: 0800-1200, 1600-2000.

Opthalmologists

Dr Sharif A Khalifa No telephone. The professor of opthalmology at the Nasiriyah eye hospital; also has a surgery on Nasiriyah street next to the traffic office.

Dr Abdul-Razak Saleh Tel: 4028420 (clinic), 4761460 (home). Clinic in Alwohana Building, Flat 11, 2nd floor. Few hundred yards north of Khazzan Street crossroads with Wazir Street, on right of road.

Dr Ghoury Tel: 4024661.

Opticians

Riyadh is a good place to get yourself some spectacles. Most opticians will make them in one to three days and for less than they would cost in, for example, the UK. Plastic and glass lenses are available as well as graded coloured plastic lenses. A new pair of spectacles costs an average SR 70-100 for lenses and SR 70-250 for frames.

Al-Koblan Optics Tel: 4766142. On Siteen Street between Jareer Street and Arba'en Street roundabouts. Offers good selection of French-designed frames.

Al-Arabi Optics On Wazir Street between Khazzan Street traffic lights and Thumairi Street on the left, next to the Tamer Pharmacy.

Pharmacies

There are plenty of well-stocked pharmacies. Most medicines are available over the counter without a doctor's prescription. Prices are government controlled.

Two pharmacies widely used by expatriates are the Jareer Street, Pharmacy and the Tamer Pharmacy. Both have English-speaking pharmacists.

Jareer Pharmacy Tel: 4767252. Good selection of baby products. Hours: 0900-1400, 1500-2200.

Tamer Phamacy On Wazir Street next to Al-Arabi Optics and a few hundred metres before the Thumairi Street crossroads. Has a well-stocked pharmaceutical section downstairs, and a perfume and cosmetic department upstairs.

Al-Olaya Pharmacy Olaya, main road.

Arafat Drug Store King Faisal Street.

Al-Saad Drug Store Opposite Maternity Hospital.

Al-Karnak Drug Store Khazzan Street.

Red Sea Drug Store Hejaz Road, Salam Circle.

Al-Khayyam Pharmacy King Faisal Street.

Tareq Pharmacy Thalathin Street Sulavmaniyah.

Al-Rahma Pharmacy Manfouha, Main Road.

Teaching hospital

King Abdul-Aziz University Hospital At the southern end of Airport Road, next to the Citibank building. Teaching hospital and part of Riyadh university, 100 beds.

Open to Saudis and non-Saudis. Some expatriates on the medical dental and nursing staff. Fees are nominal and good plain food is provided for all patients.

No orthopaedic department; most orthopaedic cases are treated at the Shumaisi central hospital. All patients are admitted through outpatients as there is no casualty/emergency department. The hospital has the following departments: dentistry, medicine, surgery, ENT, opthalmology, and obstetrics and gynaecology.

Several expatriates have had their babies delivered in this teaching hospital. The maternity section is small with the delivery room next to the operating theatre in case of emergencies. Although there is no premature baby unit, the hospital has an isolette in which any baby can be maintained until transfer. Most babies are delivered by natural childbirth.

Vets

Betsy De Marino Tel: 4658494 (pm). Surgery in Sulaymaniyah, near the Panda supermarket. A very reliable vet, dealing with small animals. Small animal surgery 1200-1800 by appointment. Equine and house calls by appointments, with the owner providing transport. Gives clinics at company compounds by arrangement.

KING SAUD UNIVERSITY

The present campus   Model of the new King Saud university

IN early 1982 Riyadh university changed its name to King Saud university, in honour of Saudi Arabia's second king, Saud Ibn Abdul-Aziz.

When the university opened in 1957 it was the kingdom's first higher education institute. Since then seven colleges have been added to the original two, King Khaled University hospital, a teaching hospital, has been opened, and the College of Engineering's research centre, set up in 1974, has become the kingdom's leading engineering research establishment. In addition, a college of allied medical sciences was set up in 1976.

A new campus, on the outskirts of Riyadh near the ruins of Dir'iya, is due to open on 9 August 1984 at a cost of $5,000 million. "We want it to be the best university in the Arab region," says its president, Mansour al-Turki. "We have no excuse not to be the best because we have the financial backing." The new campus will be able to take 21,000 students, compared with the present 18,000.

About one in five students is foreign. Most come from Arab countries such as Sudan and Somalia, although some come from the UK and the US to study Arabic. In all, 70 nationalities are represented. Of the university's 1,000 professors, one-quarter are Saudi; including lecturers, the figure rises to 50 per cent. Forty-three of the Saudi professors are UK-trained.

The university is entitled to send 10 per cent of its graduating class overseas to get masters' degrees and doctorates. In 1981, 97 students went abroad — 20 to the UK and the rest to the US.

By late 1982, the university had 76 departments, most offering a two-year masters' degree. In 1983 courses leading to doctorates in Arabic and history also began.

Of the 18,000 students, 4,000 are women, for whom a new campus is being planned. Women can attend the colleges of business and pharmacy, medicine, dentistry and nursing. Arts courses for women include English and social work.

Every student gets a monthly allowance of $300; those who come from outside Riyadh also get free accommodation. In addition, there is an 80 per cent food subsidy in the five canteens, and a 75 per cent book subsidy. A fund to which each student contributes SR 10 ($2.91) a month enables all students to borrow money to further their studies or help out at home.

Libraries and museums

British Council Library Tel: 4021650, 4043286, 404795. Off Washm Street. Telex: 200565 brtcon.

The library is open to all and has a good range of fiction and non-fiction books for children and adults. There is also a good selection of newspapers and magazines. Open Saturday-Wednesday 0800-1400 men and women; 1700-1930 men only; Thursday 0900-1200 men only.

Information and reference services are free, but there is an annual subscription for borrowing books: single SR 100, family SR 130, students SR 60.

US International Communications Agency Tel: 4640012. In US liaison office building, opposite the Al-Boustan hotel in Sulaymaniyah.

A basic reference library including atlases, encyclopaedias, American university prospectuses and telephone directories of major US cities. Open Saturday-Wednesday 0800-1700.

Museum of Archaeology & Ethnography Sharia Imam Abdul-Aziz Bin-Mohammad, north of the Shumaisi hospital.

The museum, part of the department of antiquities, is well worth a visit. It has excellent displays on almost all aspects of Saudi Arabia, ranging from artefacts from the Stone Age and rock carvings, to the history and impact of overland trade and expansion. The curator and his staff are eager to help, and there is a bookstall selling posters and books. A new folklore heritage wing is to be opened. Open daily except Friday from 0800-1400, 1700-2000; Monday evenings and Thursday mornings women only.

Shada Art Gallery Tel: 4042176. PO Box 1749, King Fahd Street, opposite Riyadh Palace hotel. Display of local and international art.

Riyadh international book fair

Now one of the most important such fairs in the Middle East after the Cairo book fair. The Riyadh international book fair is held each year at the gymnasium of Riyadh university's new campus, nine kilometres from the city centre in Dir'iya.

The fair aims to provide a forum in which international publishers of academic and educational books and materials can display, sell and discuss their publishing programmes with the deans of libraries and colleges, faculty staff, educational and cultural organisations, and government departments. In 1980 about 300 leading publishers from Arab and Islamic countries with American, European and Afro-Asian publishers displayed about 25,000 titles in Arabic and English. Subjects included Islam, history, arts and literature, geography, topography, science, technology and medicine. The university publishes a catalogue of books displayed with names and addresses of all publishers taking part. The fair lasts 10 days. Participants should contact the Dean, Riyadh university library.

The university undertakes to arrange entry visas for participants and make hotel reservations.

Education

The Education Ministry's long-term aim is understood to be to provide all non-Muslim children with appropriate educational facilities on the site now occupied by the Riyadh International Community School. The curriculum would take into account the differing needs of children who come from and are likely to return to schools which do not use the US system. The way this will be achieved and details of the facilities to be provided are still being considered.

By law non-Muslim schools cannot accept children whose parents are, or whose father is, Muslim. Such children must attend the International Islamic School, which has a section for non-Arab children with teaching in English.

Although there are several non-Muslim schools in Riyadh, forward planning is essential as, at present, they are barely meeting demand; several schools have a waiting list.

Schools

Riyadh International School (British Section) Tel: 4542748. PO Box 2907.

The school, one of the best in the kingdom, accepts children from four to 12. Children must be four on or before the date on which term begins and no older than 12 when enrolled for their last school year. About 700 children are divided between the reception department (four to five year olds) in the Olaya annex; infants (five to seven) in the main school; juniors (seven to nine) and preparatory (nine to 12), both in the Malaz annex.

Although run on British lines with about 80 per cent British pupils, up to 29 nationalities are represented. Maximum 15-20 children in one class. Those whose first language is not English must be able to understand it well enough to allow them to benefit from lessons before they are admitted.

In the senior school, various activities, including tennis, cricket, gymnastics, soccer, volleyball, swimming, chess, rollerskating, and arts and crafts take place in the afternoon. There is a swimming pool in each building.

Staff are all qualified teachers, most recruited locally but some on contract from the UK. Transport is not provided by the school.

Hours: 0815-1315 (infants) and 0800-1530 (senior).

Fees: registration SR 1,100 (non-refundable); tuition SR 13,000 a year payable in advance at the beginning of the academic year. A deposit of SR 2,000 a child, payable on acceptance of offer of a place, is refunded when the child leaves school. Where a company is paying, the loan will be refunded direct to the firm following a written request. A full term's notice of intention to leave is required.

French School Tel: 4030892. PO Box 1392. Centrally sited in front of the Riyadh Palace hotel. Headmistress: Annick Abita.

Has 400 children ranging from four to 15 years, with nursery, primary and secondary departments. The curriculum is French; English is taught in all primary groups and Arabic for Arab children. The school has cultural, arts and sports facilities.

Fees: SR 8,000-10,000 a year. There is usually no waiting list.

German School Tel: 4761454. PO Box 8974. Deutsche Schule der Riyadh, no 14, 28th Street, Malaz. Between Farazdaq and 16th streets (third street behind the Institute of Public Administration). Telex: 202297 aariad.

Co-educational with 200 pupils ranging from three to 16, divided into kindergarten (three to five) and grades 1 to 10 (six to 16). All non-Muslim children are accepted, provided they have a good command of German. Waiting list for the kindergarten.

The curriculum is based on that of Baden-Wuerttemberg (Grundschule, Hauptschule, Realschule, Gymnasium up to grade 10). English and French are taught, and examinations taken at the end of grade 10. Sports facilities include a swimming pool, and gymnastics and hardball. There is a small choir, small orchestra and theatre group.

The school is run by the Deutscher Schulverein der Riyadh whose members are parents from German companies in Saudi Arabia. The headmaster and several teachers are government officials supplied by the Bundesverwaltungsamt, Cologne.

Terms (approximate): 1 September-10 June, with holidays of one week during the Hajj, three weeks at Christmas and one week at Easter.

Fees: SR 1,500 a month; no deposit. Subject to annual changes made by the directors.

No transport is provided. Most children live in company compounds and are taken to and from school by company buses.

Riyadh International Community School (US section) Tel: 4915932, 4915936. PO Box 990. A few kilometres beyond the Marriott Khurais hotel.

The oldest and largest co-educational school with 2,200 pupils ranging from four to 15. The curriculum is American with a strong English as a second language bias, as there are many nationalities at the school. At present there is no waiting list.

The sports programme is extensive, with outdoor facilities for tennis and ball games, and a swimming pool. Art lessons, foreign languages, computer science, music, photography and drama are also offered.

Terms: mid-September to January, January to mid-June. Two weeks' holiday at Christmas and one at Easter.

Fees: SR 7,000 a term or SR 14,000 a year; SR 5,000 non-refundable deposit payable on registration.

BAC School Dutch School — Ballast Nedam. Tel: 4420224. For further details contact company.

Bechtel School Tel: 4647647. For further details contact company.

Playschools and nurseries

For pre-school children there are plenty of good playschools and nurseries in most areas. These are advertised on the bulletin boards of supermarkets and bookshops. Childminders also advertise on these noticeboards.

Housing

Finding a place to live

Insist that accommodation is included in your contract. Rent for villas is high (SR 80,000-175,000 a year). Most companies provide well-equipped villas or villa compounds for employees.

If you are on a short contract, or waiting to move into permanent accommodation, there are a few residential hotels which are cheaper than the main hotels. They are centrally located, modern and well equipped with restaurant and video (see hotels).

To find a villa or apartment try:
☐ bulletin boards in all the large supermarkets and bookshops
☐ local newspaper advertisements
☐ contact the estate agents

There are numerous estate agents; service is variable but one should use them. Usually they are small offices, signs usually read "Real Estate." Agents tend to deal with property in their area, so if you want to live in Malaz, try the Malaz agents first. Because few streets have English signs, the estate agent will shut up shop and, with the key from the landlord, will take you himself to visit the accommodation. This means two things — first, that you may visit the estate agent at normal opening hours and find it closed and, second, it is not easy to synchronise your visit so that the agent is in his office and the landlord can be contacted for the villa key. However, with perseverance, this is often the best way of finding a house.

Residential areas

Malaz is the largest and oldest of the three main residential areas and is nearest to downtown Riyadh. It has an excellent shopping centre for fresh fruit and vegetables, and delicatessens. The houses are among the oldest in Riyadh and you are more likely to find a villa with trees and a garden in this area. Houses built 15-20 years ago are considered old and, although they may need a little renovation or rewiring, they usually have more garden. Trees are almost a luxury.

Sulaymaniyah is nearer the airport and houses are a mixture of old and new.

Olaya, the newest housing area, is developing rapidly. Almost all the houses are new; new shops and supermarkets open almost daily.

It is wise to choose a house on slightly higher ground because flooding can be bad in the rainy season.

Swimming pools

Many houses have swimming pools but various companies will install a pool within several weeks. Once you have installed one, however, it becomes the property of the landlord.

Leases

Remember that estate agents are purely middlemen. They have no responsibilities to either the owner or the lessee. Most estate agents expect a 3 per cent fee for each year's rental. The landlord may ask you to pay one, two or even three years' rent in advance — this is usually open to discussion but one or two years in advance is normal.

When leasing a property, estate agents often have a standard lease agreement. This will not have any special conditions incorporated and will usually be in Arabic. Get a translation before signing, and ensure any special conditions are included.

The contract between the landlord and client must be written clearly using either the Hijra or the Gregorian calendar. This is important: the Hijra calendar is 11 days shorter and you may find yourself without a home earlier than you anticipated if you do not pay careful attention. It must also be clear who is to be responsible for maintenance — the landlord or the client. Usually any improvements to a house, such as repainting, rewiring, replumbing or installing swimming pools, equipment or fittings such as kitchen cabinets and water heaters, become the landlord's property on expiry of the lease. You must, therefore, add a clause giving you possession of such effects. Otherwise, anything attached to the house belongs to the owner of the house. Many people have learned this the hard way.

In addition, make sure the property has been completed, or will be on the date agreed. Check that all mains services are available; also check all fixtures and fittings and if they do not work get them fixed before payment. Septic tanks can be a problem if the water table is high. Confirm who is responsible for its emptying and if necessary negotiate a reduction, taking into account that landlords can be elusive when it comes to paying bills.

Electricity

Most houses are connected to 110V and 220V which can be confusing for the newcomer. As a general rule most sockets are 110V, airconditioners run off the 220-V supply and there are usually one or two 220-V sockets for electrical appliances. Sockets are sometimes clearly marked but, if in doubt, test each socket with a voltmeter and then label it accordingly.

Transformers for 110V and 220V are available from electrical shops — there are several on Jareer Street and in the Deera Square area.

Electricity lines are not grounded or earthed in Riyadh and so great care must be taken when plugging or unplugging electrical appliances — always avoid having wet hands, feet or shoes.

In many houses the state of electrical confusion can be alarming to a newcomer. When moving into a new house, have the electricity supply checked, not only for safety but also to see if supply is sufficient for the needs of the house. The supply is sometimes inadequate to cope with several airconditioners running constantly and cutouts may occur. If this happens you may ask the electricity company for further supply lines or, more simply, remember to turn off all non-essential airconditioners during the summer.

Bills are monthly and delivered by the meter reader, who may leave it beneath the meter or hand it to the person responsible. Electricity is supplied by Riyadh Electric Company & Suburbs (RECS); the bill can be paid at any of its offices. Electricity costs SR 0.08 a kWh, while the meter rental is SR 1 a month.

For properties on the outskirts of the city, investigate the practicality and costs of having a generator.

Gas
There is no piped gas supply. Butane is supplied in cylinders, each costing SR 5, by many small depots. However, it is on an exchange basis and you have first to buy empty cylinders to exchange. You can get these from the Gas Supply Store in Semiramis Square, at the south end of Airport Road, for SR 100.

Always have a spare full cylinder as shortages do occur, especially over holidays. As a precaution check the gas system for leaks at regular intervals.

Some villas are equipped with large gas storage cylinders either inside the front wall or at the roadside. These are filled by gas tanker on request.

Water
Mains water is metered and supplied for a token charge by the municipality. However, its salinity makes it undrinkable.

In areas where there are no house connections, you can buy water in tankers, usually of 2,000 gallons, which last a normal house five to seven days. Good quality water costs SR 200-300 a tanker and saline water SR 70. Many people prefer not to drink either, while use of the latter for any length of time will result in the corrosion of plumbing systems.

Drinking water can be bought at shops and supermarkets, or at Healthy Water factories.

Domestic help
Most homes are built with small servants' quarters next to the main house. A servant is almost a necessity because houses are large, and dust is an endless problem.

There are two kinds of domestic help:

☐ the live-in maid, usually of Eritrean origin. A maid would expect accommodation and food plus SR 1,800-2,500 a month salary;

☐ Help-by-the-hour — many of the Indian, Pakistani and Bangladeshi workers like to supplement their salaries by doing a few hours' domestic work a week. Average pay is SR 15 an hour, and hours can be negotiated.

The only way to find domestic help is by word of mouth, but with the rapid turnover of residents in Riyadh, it is not hard to find. Check on your employee's visa and passport as you are liable to a heavy fine if you employ someone who is not in the country legally, who does not have a sponsor or whose documents are not in order.

All servants should have a routine medical examination including chest X-ray, blood, urine and stool checks, to see that they are in good health and free from infectious diseases. The Obeid Hospital will do this for a small fee. The Shumaisi Central Hospital will provide free facilities, but may take a little longer to produce the results.

Servants, who are almost always Muslim, will expect time off for the Hajj and also at the end of Ramadan for the Eid al-Fitr festivities. A small bonus or gift is usually given at this time.

Many catering companies, such as Algosaibi Grandmet and Poon (Saudi), offer package deals including catering, cleaning and laundry services. These are ideal for companies with large numbers of unaccompanied staff. Charges are on a work-day basis.

Drivers
These are provided by the company for most wives. They are easy to find but check they have the necessary Saudi driving licence. Salary approximately SR 2,500-3,500 a month.

Cost of houses
This depends on the location, supply

and demand, and the size of accommodation, but the following is a guide to approximate annual costs in Riyadh (1982 prices).

House	2 bedrooms, garden, no pool	SR 80,000
House	3 bedrooms, garden, pool	SR 140,000
House	5-6 bedrooms, garden, pool	SR 175,000
Apartment	3 bedrooms	SR 40,000

No non-Saudi can own property or land in Saudi Arabia, except in certain instances, so leasing is the only option.

Lease agreements do not have to be certified, registered or translated to be binding, and the Arabic will take precedence in court over an English translation. It should also be noted that rent increases are controlled by decree, and it is wise to familiarise yourself with your legal position.

Not all accommodation has a telephone, although installation is much faster now than several years ago.

Maintenance

Maintenance firms run a comprehensive service for all types of domestic maintenance and are very convenient. However, it may be cheaper to hire a private tradesman — they usually charge about SR 50 an hour. If the workman has an accident on your property — no matter whose fault it was — you will be held liable, so check your insurance covers this.

Cooling systems

Some form of cooling — other than fans — is essential in Riyadh in the summer. There are two methods of cooling your house:

The desert cooler is larger and more cumbersome than an airconditioner but simpler in design, therefore cheaper to buy and easier to service — it uses less electricity.

A desert cooler is a rotating chamber which passes through a tray of water and through which air is blown. The air is therefore cooled and moistened by the water. They are fitted into the walls, so the bulk of the machine is outside. Approximate price: SR 1,000.

Airconditioners are more efficient at providing colder air but all moisture is removed from the air — an important consideration in an already very dry atmosphere. Approximate price: SR 1,600.

The best system is a combination. The airconditioner will provide the cooler temperature and the desert cooler will provide the humidity.

Maintenance is highly efficient

Humidifiers It is essential to humidify your house somehow. Many newcomers suffer from the dryness until they are acclimatised, and sinusitis and dry skin are common.

Humidifiers are available from Algosaibi Engineering, by the Post Office in Farazdak Street. Approximate price: SR 400. However, many people simply place bowls of water unobtrusively round the house and these evaporate surprisingly fast. Alternatively, buy a small plastic water fountain from a flower shop. These are almost unbreakable and more efficient than bowls of water. At SR 120 they are considerably cheaper than conventional humidifiers.

Gardening

With a little effort the sandy soil can be transformed into an attractive garden. It is wise first to cover the garden area with top soil and manure, and to water daily during the summer.

The best times for planting are September-November (autumn); February-March (spring). Flood the area with water before and after planting.

There are plant shops and nurseries, and seeds are readily available (see Shops).

Gardeners are available on a full or part-time basis. Most gardeners are Yemeni and, for a monthly fee of SR 200, will keep your garedn in order.

Pest control

Ciba-Geigy Tel: 4918225, 4760179. PO Box 5770. Telex: 201588.

Recreation

There are countless social and recreation groups for resident expatriates.

Music and drama

The Riyadh Players

This group put on plays every six weeks. Performances are surprisingly good and sometimes include professional actors. Now in its fifteenth year. Highlights have included the Pirates of Penzance, the Mikado and HMS Pinafore. One of the highlights in 1980 was Rodgers and Hammerstein's Carousel, which played in the US Military Mission Community Centre. In the same year an adaptation of the Agatha Christie novel Ten Little Indians was also performed. Membership is open to all.

The Choral Society Tel: 4769364. Secretary: A Wynniat-Husey. PO Box 1290.

The society, which meets every Sunday in Malaz, performs large scale choral works to a high standard. Formed in 1980 by developing a choir from the ranks of the amateur and not-so-amateur singers of Riyadh. Any nationality and any voice is welcome; members do not have to be highly trained or qualified, nor need they read music — enthusiasm is more important. Future programmes will aim to cater for all tastes and will include traditional and popular music, choral and oratorio, opera and operetta, and international folk songs.

The Riyadh Concert Band Tel: 4780880.

Mainly a brass and woodwind band which gives private and occasional public concerts, sometimes with the Choral Society. Meets every Monday evening. Although most players are experienced and have their own instruments, the band also hires some.

Travel

Travel Interest Group Tel: 4788520. Martin Wale. Meets informally to see slides on different countries with a view to future holidays.

Desert Ramblers The best source of information on desert travel, particularly in the Riyadh region. As this group does not seek publicity, it should be contacted via the local expatriate grapevine.

Expatriate family's recreation room

Other groups

Riyadh International Women's Group (RIWG)

As most companies sending staff to the kingdom know, it is an important that the candidate's wife understands the ambience in which she will live as it is for the employer himself. Many a job has been tarnished by family misunderstandings when a couple go to work in a country that has been improperly introduced. Saudi Arabia is a traditional Islamic country in which women enjoy a status that is often misunderstood in the West. In fact, women who have studied social conditions in the kingdom properly have often found living in it a creative and exciting experience.

RIWG, like its sister group in Eastern province, exists to introduce women coming to live in the kingdom to the ambience. The group's sensitivity to life in Saudi Arabia and their energetic work in setting up countless activities have done much to achieve this. The group also produces a book called Welcome to Riyadh.

Any resident wishing to participate in the RIWG's activities must become a member. The fee is SR 50 a month for the morning programme. Non-members may attend meetings as guests. The club meets on the first Tuesday of every month at the Grand Festival Palace in Sulaymaniyah. It is best to enquire about the group through organisations such as the Saudi-British Office of Economic Co-operation (tel: 4760607) or the British embassy in Jeddah.

The group organises a Newcomers Tour, open to all new members. It takes place on the second Monday of the month and costs SR 100. There is room for 45 women — the buses are lent by two Swedish companies and are always full.

The tour takes about two hours and covers the souqs, the ministries, the zoo, the museum, the downtown shopping area, university, king's palace, the old city of Riyadh and the King Faisal specialist hospital, as well as other places of interest.

After the tour everyone is invited back for refreshments, which allows people to meet one another in a more informal way than at the monthly meetings.

The RIWG also offers other interests — bridge, mah jong, yoga, cooking, handicrafts, drama classes, batik making, keep-fit and a music group, to name but a few.

The group's monthly newsletter, the Desert Digest, gives information on these groups and has a useful advertisement section for domestic items.

Riyadh Arts & Crafts Tel: Viv Sutcliffe, 4771863. Meets monthly.

Riyadh Round Table Tel: Gordon Howly, 4783466 ext 118, 4750784.

Videos

With no cinemas in Riyadh, videos are very popular. Almost everybody has one, while companies provide them in all recreation rooms. Video libraries abound, and the cost of joining them varies greatly, as does the quality of films. It is best to join a library recommended by a friend, as some libraries tape their own film and the reproduction is very bad. Video machines are widely available, with a top-quality machine costing SR 6,000.

Video Technical Services Tel: 4657224. PO Box 731. In Sulaymaniyah, near the Circle supermarket. Telex: 41076 rabbit.

Supplies, installs, services and maintains video systems for individuals and companies. It also installs closed-circuit video systems for compounds or hotels, and has a video film production unit.

Sport

Running

Hash House Harriers Tel: Mike Reeve 4787880. For those interested in non-competitive running. It aims to combine exercise with camaraderie and socialising, and now has 300 members. Meetings are family affairs, open to all, and are held on Thursday at 1630 in the summer — although sometimes earlier in winter.

Runs takes place at different venues — sometimes in the desert, the wadis or the escarpment. They take about one hour in winter and 40 minutes in summer, and are strictly non-competitive — members can walk the course if they want. More serious runners, however, can take part in international events.

Other activities include curry suppers, social evenings and a monthly barbecue. Transport can be arranged.

Footprint magazine is produced weekly with light-hearted news and views, and details of future runs.

Road runners Tel: Philip Bannan, 4043696. PO Box 43069. Road and cross-country running.

Golf

The Desert Golf Club Tel: Don Gander, 4645858. In the desert 15 kilometres outside Riyadh in the precincts of the new international airport. It is run by Bechtel under the patronage of the Defence & Aviation Ministry.

An 18-hole golf course with more than 600 members who can invite non-members to play. The annual subscription is SR 200 with a green fee of SR 10. As the ground is very stony most members carry a small square of artificial grass so they don't damage their clubs.

Squash

Riyadh Squash League Various compounds have courts. There are three sections to the league. Contact 1) Peter and Mandy Todd, tel: 4762519, 4767130, 4766135; 2) John Muldoon, tel: 4918695; 3) Pete and Sue Johnson, tel: 4042882 ext 589, 4780033.

Riyadh Bowling Centre Tel: 4640552. Manager: David Bradbury. A new centre with excellent squash and tennis courts, and a 24-lane bowling alley, with snack and coffee bar. Membership is on a subscription basis.

Rugby and soccer

After squash, soccer and rugby are the two most popular games. Details about each can be had from John Melville, tel: 4765528 (work) and 4647747 (home).

Cricket

The most recently established sport, with about 21 teams now competing in the Riyadh league.

Harlequins Tel: Chris Syer, 4654980, 4654764 (home). Comprises various

Diving

Oasis Sub-Aqua Club PO Box 7892. Secretary: Delcy Wells.

Supreme Diver C/o Saudi Tarmac, PO Box 4880. Secretary: Alison Ayres.

Riding

Al-Hari Riding Stables Tel: Mr Knight, 4649482 ext 1341. This is a stables rather than a riding school, providing facilities for desert riding. Most of the horses kept here are owned by members of the Riyadh community, so lessons for beginners are not available. The stables are for experienced riders and have stalls for 12 horses.

Jacoub's Stables At the beginning of Al-Kharj Road. The horses here are owned by the stables, and riding lessons are given. It concentrates on riding in the area rather than desert riding.

The king's camel race

The camel race held in the king's honour each April or May is run at the Al-Janadriyah race track, 20 kilometres north of Riyadh. A nine-year-old jockey won the first prize of SR 35,000 and a 2,000-gallon water truck in 1980 at the sixth annual race, with Abu Dhabi and Qatar as runners-up. The 22-kilometre race takes about an hour — it is the longest such course — and is organised by the Al-Ferrousiyah Equestrian Club in Riyadh. Up to 3,000 camels take part, some of which race regularly at Riyadh's Malaz race course from October to April.

Sudanese camels usually compete in the morning races. Smaller, faster and thinner-legged than the Arabian camels, they are usually female and mostly white. At a gallop they average 16 kilometres an hour.

Arabian camels transported by truck from Qatar, Kuwait, Abu Dhabi and other Gulf states usually compete in the afternoons. They are larger, slower and

National guardsman at the camel race

bigger-boned, and black or brown. Sadly, fewer camels compete each year. They are being replaced by the pickup and are no longer vital to the bedu.

Most of the camels arrive at the stables one month before the race for training. During this period they are fed, groomed and ridden by their jockeys, who are aged between eight and 55. Hobbled, they are allowed to wander freely. As the bedu say: "Any nomad can recognise his camel's foot-print from another's."

Racing camels are between five and 12 years old and never older than 15. The first 200 riders to finish get prizes. When the first rider finishes, a National Guardsman dashes to him and gives him a wooden mallet with a number one which is later exchanged for a prize. Admission is free.

A spectator's view...

The Dammam road from Riyadh cuts through barren desert, broken only by scattered buildings, settlements and the occasional small hill. Slipping into the queue of Cadillacs, Mercedes and electric-coloured, fur-trimmed Toyotas, confronted by a stream of supply trucks from the Eastern province, we aim for the Al-Janadriyah race track, for the annual camel race.

Ahead, thick dust billows where cars

pull off the road into the desert, and large, black tents sprout from the sand, beside them shiny limousines. In the distance, the marquee housing King Khaled's entourage in grandstand formation shimmers in the afternoon heat.

We reach a good vantage point; around us are voluble expatriates standing on the roofs of their cars in true grand prix fashion, while sedate Arab families spread rugs on the sand and exchange opinions on the outcome of the race. Overhead, air force helicopters patrol the skies, while Land Rovers and Jeeps throw up clouds of dust as they monitor the track, separating the crowds from the course. Soldiers carrying automatic rifles with fixed bayonets stand guard at intervals.

A ripple of excitement passes through the spectators, and on the horizon appears a line of camels. Reminiscent of Custer's last stand at Little Big Horn, the line approaches and now the vibrating thump of more than 2,000 galloping camels can be heard. Suddenly, they draw level with us and the riders, faces swathed in dust-protective gutras, cling to the swaying humps, miraculously balancing behind the camels' outstretched, horizontal necks. The cheers and encouraging shouts reach a deafening pitch and a roar follows the thundering herd as they cross the finishing line by the king's tent.

David and Liz Tricker

Riyadh racecourse

Next to Malaz football stadium (see Riyadh map), at the junction of University and Siteen streets.

Riyadh's racecourse is a microcosm of Ascot and, for those who know India, it has the hallmark of one of the sumptuous, green racecourses of Empire days. Its tiers of open-air seats are surrounded by immaculately kept flower gardens.

The course is 3,000 metres — races are usually 1,000-2,000 metres. They are held on Mondays at 1530, except during the Hajj, Ramadan and the summer months. The first race is a camel race which is usually followed by three to five horse races.

Camel racing is usually cancelled when the ground is wet. Between 10 and 16 camels compete. They are usually white and slightly built with long, thin legs for speed and can run at 14-18 kilometres an hour.

The jockeys who come from in and around Riyadh are usually between eight and 15 years old, both professional and amateur. Until 1968 jockeys wore the traditional thobe but have since taken to wearing western-style racing silks.

The horse races have attractive prizes, although betting is forbidden and condemned by Islam. In 1980 prizes ranged from the SR 9,000 Guriat prize to the SR 13,000 Kharj prize. Admission is SR 15. Tickets are available at the door.

The Riyadh-Dammam railway

Although there has been talk of building a new line from Jeddah to Riyadh, the kingdom's only railway at present is that between Riyadh and Dammam.

Trains leave Riyadh at 1430 Wednesday to Friday, and 0830 Saturday to Tuesday. There is one stop, at Hofuf. The return journey from Dammam leaves at 1525 Wednesday to Friday, and 0900 Saturday to Tuesday. There is a restaurant car on the train. Riyadh railway station, opposite the Saudi Consulting Centre, is south of the Malaz football stadium and west of the Industry & Electricity Ministry building.

The first-class fare is SR 60 and second-class SR 40, with half fares for children under 10.

Each passenger may travel with two pieces of hand luggage. Additional baggage is considered "Express Passenger Shipment" and 50-100 kilos cost an extra SR 4. Tickets should be bought a day in advance and passengers are advised to reach the station half an hour before the train is due to depart. Muslim women must be accompanied by their husbands or a male relative aged 17 or over. Western women should be escorted by a male, preferably the husband, or by a female friend.

The new train is airconditioned, with wall-to-wall carpets, soft seats and reading lights. There is a ladies' wash-room and lavatory. A meal costs SR 30 in the restaurant.

The 480-kilometre journey takes the passenger through varied country. Just outside Riyadh, the train passes through several attractive villages. After about half an hour, it reaches the agricultural region of Al-Kharj, with its vegetable and alfalfa fields, dairy and poultry farms, and plant nurseries. After Al-Kharj, waterholes — some of them 100 metres deep — can be seen. The line then branches east, through more farmland. Next stop on the old train is Atawdayia station, shaded by trees and smelling of sweet herbs from the nearby gardens. The journey continues across the beautiful orange sands of the Dahna dunes to Haradh, the sheep-rearing centre of Eastern province. Between Haradh and Hofuf the countryside is flat, barren and sparsely populated, but as the train approaches Hofuf, strangely contorted rock formations can be seen. Northeast of Hofuf, burnt-off gas from the oil wells flares in the distance and at Abqaiq the line passes close to large oil installations. As the train approaches Dammam station, the traveller will be able to catch sight of the sea.

Banking

Central bank authority
Saudi Arabian Monetary Agency (SAMA) Tel: 4787400. PO Box 2992, Airport Road. Telex: 201734-7 markzy sj, cable: markazi riyadh. Governor: Hamid al-Sayari.

Commercial banks
Saudi American Bank Tel: PO Box 833. Telex: 200195. Managing director: Robert D Botjer.
The Saudi British Bank Tel: 4050677 (15 lines). PO Box 9084, King Fahd Street. Telex: 202349, 202350-1, 204081 sabb sj, cable: sbrit riyadh. Managing director: John Paton.

Specialised banks
Saudi Arabian Agricultural Bank Tel: 4023934, 4023911. Oman Bin al-Khatab Street. General manager: Abdel-Aziz Mohammad al-Manqur.
Saudi Credit Bank Tel: 4029128, 4029625. Cable: taslef. For details contact SAMA.

Other financial institutions
The Arab Investment Company Tel: 4823444 (10 lines). PO Box 4009, Telex: 201011 arbvst, 201236 taic st, cable: amwal riyadh. Chief executive: Jad A Suidan.
Contractors' Financing Programme C/o General Investment Fund. For details contact SAMA.
Credit Fund for Contractors For details contact SAMA.
The General Investment Fund Tel: 4012666, 4012988, 4015208, 4014904. C/o Ministry of Finance & National Economy, Airport Road.
Gulf Investment Corporation For details contact SAMA.
Public Investment Fund Tel: 4058673. PO Box 6847, Ministry of Finance, Airport Road. Telex: 201021 finans sj, cable: ministry of finance. Secretary-general: Sulaiman al-Mandil.
Saudi Fund for Development Tel: 4640292. PO Box 1887. Telex: 201145, 201744 sundoq. Managing director: Mohammad A al-Sugair.
Saudi Industrial Development Fund Tel: 4774002. PO Box 4143, Airport Road. Telex: 201065, 202583 sidfnd sj, cable: banksinaie. Director-general: Saleh al-Naim.
Saudi Investment Banking Corporation Tel: 4778433. PO Box 3533. Telex: 201170 sibcor sj, cable: sibcorp riyadh. General manager: Richard F Stacks.
Saudi-Pakistani Investment Company For details contact SAMA.
Saudi-Philippine Islamic Development Bank (Spidbank) For details contact SAMA.
Saudi-Tunisian Investment Company For details contact SAMA.

Lawyers

Salah Hejailan Tel: 4650723, 4656721. PO Box 1454. Telex: 200486, 201109 hejlan, cable: al-hejailan. Associated with Clifford Turner (London, Paris, etc).

Saud M A Shawwaf Tel: 4782510, 4039618. PO Box 2700, Siteen Street. Telex: 201831, cable: cable: saudconsult. Other offices: Houston, Texas and Beirut.

Tawfiq al-Emboagh Tel: 4025058. PO Box 582, King Faisal Street, Mohammad Ibn Saud Building.

Tarek Murad King Faisal Street, Al-Rosais Building.

Ibrahim Nour Eddeen & Zein Eddeen Fatany Tel: 4763870. PO Box 1216.

Muhammad Abdul-Aziz Ibn Zarah Tel: 4027031. PO Box 870, Site 28 Tower Building.

Abdullah Emran Khazzan Street, Al-Reef Building.

Fathi Hussain Khalil Tel: c/o Petromin 4761113. PO Box 757.

Dr Muhammad H Hoshan Tel: 4648353, 4648363. PO Box 2626, Al-Musa Building, 4th floor, Olaya Road, directly across from the Al-Khozama hotel. Telex: 200877 delphi.

Hassan al-Mansour Tel: 4024742. Wazir Street.

Ahmed A Audhali Tel: 4657849, 4649948. PO Box 10851. Telex: 202588 audhli sj. Associated with Fox & Gibbins & Company (London, Cairo, Abu Dhabi and Dubai).

Ahmed Zaki Yamani Tel: 4762685, 4762511. PO Box 7159, near Al-Hayek market, Sulaymaniyah. Telex: 203609 lawyer. Associated with Surrey & Morse, Washington.

Peter T James Law Office Tel: 4642702. PO Box 4838. Telex: 203441 mohami sj. Open 0900-1300, 1700-2000. London office, tel: London 4998921. 2 Carlos Place, Mount Street, W1.

Abdul-Aziz A al-Mohaimeed Tel: 4053274, 4058288, ext 331. PO Box 16545, Yamama Cement Company Building, Suite 605, opposite Rahj Buildings. Telex: 202076 ouda sj.

Doing business

Riyadh Group of British Businessmen (RGBB) Tel: 4760607. PO Box 487. Telex: 201344 ecbrit.

The group began to meet informally in 1978, and its first annual general meeting in October 1981 was attended by 150 members. Its aims are to boost British trade and services exports and, where applicable, to encourage investment; to develop Anglo-Saudi links, and to help British businessmen and their families adjust to their new environment. These aims can be achieved in several ways. Some of the most important are to identify areas where British products and expertise are lacking, and to advise the UK government and industry; to set up a London-based group of people who have recently left the kingdom who can help would-be exporters; to compile a trade directory of UK companies, products and services available in the kingdom; to help trade missions, especially those which are new to the kingdom, and to link up with business groups from the US, Sweden, West Germany and France.

Meetings are held on the second Monday of every month at 1700 in the Inter-Continental hotel. Women are generally welcome at a lunch given every third meeting. For further information contact Christopher Syer, RGBB chairman.

View of central Riyadh, the heart of the kingdom

Trips in the Najd region

The following trips are closely based on a book, Day Drives around Riyadh, published privately in Riyadh by Peter Shurville. It costs SR 10 and can be obtained from Peter Shurville, Government Liaison Manager, British Aircraft Corporation, PO Box 1732, Riyadh, tel: 4783466.

Warning: **every precaution should be taken before embarking on many of these trips, particularly where they involve desert tracks (see Desert Driving Survival Checklist). Although the editor has every confidence in the accuracy of this detailed information, neither he nor the publishers can take responsibility for it.**

All the drives below can be done in a day, although on many there are suitable places for camping. They can nearly all be tackled in an ordinary car, although some people may prefer to use a four-wheel-drive vehicle for off-the-road tracks. Simple precautions are, however, necessary.

Travel is best restricted to the cooler winter months. Always take plenty of water with you, plus a shovel and some sort of matting or sheeting to provide cover. Should you bog your vehicle in sand or gravel *don't* try to get it out by constant revving — that just digs it in deeper. Stop immediately. Then try reversing the car out, with a helping push from passengers. If this doesn't work dig out around the tyres and put down some large stones, and preferably cloth or nearby brushwood. Let half the air out of the tyres and then *ease* the car out with plenty of pushing by your passengers. Keep repeating this until you reach hard ground. Always tell someone where you are going so a search party can be sent out if the worst happens.

Many of the sites are of historic and archaeological interest, so treat them accordingly. Don't leave litter around and don't deface the area.

Main routes out of Riyadh

At the time of writing extensive roadworks were under way in Riyadh, with new diversions being introduced every few weeks. The best thing to do is to buy a local map and seek the guidance of friends. The following may, however, help.

Airport Road

From the airport, the main route into Riyadh is down Airport Road, which runs roughly north to south. Coming from the airport you soon reach a major diversion, where a complex flyover is being built next to the military hospital and the main Petromin office. The road east goes to Dammam and Dhahran, the roads west to the Escarpments and Jeddah Road, and eventually north to Dir'iya and Buraydah. At the southern end of Airport Road is a major flyover leading to Batha Street. Soon after going under the flyover there is a left turn, clearly signposted Al-Kharj. This leads to the only main road south of Riyadh.

Dir'iya

Dir'iya, about 18 kilometres from Riyadh city centre, is the most important historic site in the area. First settled in 1446, its importance derives from its position as the capital of the first Saudi state from the mid-eighteenth century until 1818. The surrounding land was originally owned by Ibn Dir, who gave his name to the whole oasis settlement.

In the early eighteenth century the towns in the Najd were not unified under a national government. From 1744 on, the religious teacher Mohammad Ibn Abdul Wahhab, based in Dir'iya, promoted religious reforms and by the end of the century most of the Arabian peninsula was united under one leadership from Dir'iya (see Historical Introduction).

The Ottoman Empire viewed the Arab challenge with alarm — especially after the loss of Makkah and Al-Madinah, and the deletion of the Ottoman emperor's name from Friday prayers — and an Egyptian army under

Best to travel in convoy

Ibrahim Pasha was sent to recover lost territory. In 1818 the army entered Dir'iya and after a six-month siege penetrated the defences on the Turaif, totally destroyed the houses and cut down every tree in the palm groves. The Egyptians were estimated to have lost 10,000 men in the siege and the defending Saudi forces 1,800.

The route to Dir'iya is a confusing complex of new roads and half-finished flyovers. If possible, make your first trip with someone who has been before. If you do go alone, drive out of Riyadh on the Buraydah road. Soon after the new Riyadh university you see the ruins of Dir'iya on your left and come to a road on the left marked Dir'iya. Follow this to a T-junction, turn left and second on the right over a bridge crossing the Wadi Hanifa. Park just over the bridge. You can then either walk up the hill ahead or to the right through the palm trees to the "citadel" of Al-Turaif. A walk to the top affords a good general view of the area destroyed by Ibrahim Pasha. Photographs are allowed.

Making your way back to the T-junction takes you on past the new part of town, with the Social Development Centre on the right. Just past the centre the road leads to the right. A few kilometres further, you reach a "percolating" dam. The Wadi Hanifa floods several times each year and the dam, built in 1958, holds back the waters until they seep into the ground.

First camel trail

Before the asphalt road was built in the early 1960s, the route to Riyadh from the west was either through the Wadi Hanifa or up one of the camel trails to the top of the Tuwayq escarpment. These trails were on the trade routes from Yemen to Kuwait, and were also used by pilgrims on their way to Makkah.

The first trail after the escarpment's descent is winding, wide and carefully constructed. To reach it, take the old route to the Escarpments and the Jeddah Road, and descend the escarpment. About 65 kilometres from Petromin is a small adobe village with a large asphalt parking area on the right. Go on two kilometres then take the track to the right. Follow this for three kilometres and park in front of the trail, which winds to the top of the escarpment. The climb to the top takes about 15 minutes and once there you can enjoy the superb views across to the red sands and Shaib Awsat.

There is much to see for the skilled and cautious driver

Second camel trail

The second camel trail is not, like the first, an engineering feat — it is narrow, not so winding and more like a footpath. Four-wheel-drive is essential. However, it is in a beautiful setting, following the course of a deep river bed and up an escarpment to a superb waterfall. Although the trip can be made in a day, it is wiser to camp at the foot of the hill overnight and climb the escarpment in the early morning.

To get there, take the old route to the Escarpments and the Jeddah road, and descend the escarpment. Seventy-seven kilometres from Petromin you pass a water tower on the right with a telephone soon after. Less than one kilometre on turn right onto a track leading towards a line of low hills and head for the right hand end of the hills. Pass over the hills, watching out for a tall isolated pinnacle, to be kept on your left; a large, thick-trunked tree, to be kept in front of you and then to your right; a small green crane on top of the cliffs, which is to the left of the wadi where the camel trail is, and a small pinnacle at the end of the wadi which marks the start of the trail.

One word of warning though: it is about 12 kilometres from the road to the trail. The area is criss-crossed with tracks and it is very easy to head down the wrong one. The going can be very soft and the journey over the stone quarry quite hair-raising. Four-wheel-drive and a bold and skilful driver are therefore essential.

Round trip to Wadi Hanifa

Wadi Hanifa starts at the top of the Tuwayq escarpment, about 70 kilometres north of Riyadh, and runs southeast down through Riyadh and on into the fertile farming area of Al-Kharj. There have always been farms and villages in the valley as shallow wells provided enough water for irrigation.

The Darb al-Hejaz — the old caravan route from the Najd to the Hejaz — followed the winding Wadi Hanifa up to a natural pass in the Tuwayq range, past Khasm Hisyan and on down the other side of the escarpment following Wadi Hisyan.

Many years ago towns and villages flourished in Wadi Hanifa, particularly in the area between Riyadh and Al-Ayenah. High walls were built round all the settlements and look-out towers constructed on the tops of the nearby hills. Parts of the walls can still be seen around Al-Ayenah, while tower ruins stand sentinel over nearly all the villages in the valley.

In the early eighteenth century Al-Ayenah was one of the most important agricultural centres in the Najd and was the birthplace of Mohammad Ibn-Abdul-Wahhab in 1703 (see Historical Introduction).

As the villages are left behind the trees become larger and more plentiful. It is a serious offence to damage or cut them so there are some fine specimens of acacia — ideal to picnic under. In the cooler winter you can see many different flowering plants and if there is heavy rainfall, the whole ground is soon covered with a huge variety of flowers.

To get to Wadi Hanifa take the Buraydah road out of Riyadh, past Dir'iya. Keep on the main road until you reach large communication dishes, and then take the left fork to Al-Jubaylah. At present, a dual carriageway is under construction on this route, with a flyover being built at the Al-Jubaylah junction, so turning into the Jubaylah road requires considerable care and eagle eyes for the temporary signposts. After a few kilometres take the right fork to Sadus.

At 68 kilometres a good track leads to the left. This runs into the wadi, following the old Hejaz way. The wadi stretches for 43 kilometres, with plenty of camping and picnicking areas. As the wadi breaks through the escarpment you have a choice of two routes. The first is the main graded track following the new east-west oil pipeline (Petroline), which cuts through the Tuwayq range here. If you follow the track you come out on the main Makkah road about 35 kilometres north of Durma. Driving along the new track you will come to the original track going off to the left — keep a close watch, as it is easily missed. The main landmark is a small radio mast opposite the track. This second route takes you down through green trees, ideal for picnicking. However, the going gets soft in places and it is not for the faint-hearted. Like the first route it comes out on the Makkah road, but nearer Durma.

Shaib Awsat

Shaib Awsat is a dry water course — wide, with room for a ridge of sand dunes down the middle, separated from the towering cliffs on either side by a stretch of sandy gravel. It runs parallel to Wadi Durma but is separated from it by a ridge of mountains which in places have been worn away to leave isolated towers and pinnacles resembling the scenery in a Western. There are little villages and farms in the valley, including an experimental Agriculture Ministry farm.

Just past the first camel trail turn-off on the right is a new paved road on the left leading to Wadi Nisaa. The road passes across a wide stretch of flat sandy ground covered with small bushes to a small gap in the mountains. From the top of the gap is a breathtaking view across the orange dunes to the sheer cliffs the other side of Shaib Awsat. The paved road cuts straight across the valley through the dunes and on towards Wadi Nisaa, with several tracks leading off on both sides and plenty of picnic spots.

Shaib Laha and Al-Hair

This is a short trip — about 80 kilometres — ideal for a "lazy" day in the desert, with a great variety of scenery and plenty of picnic spots. There are green date palm groves, wadis with smooth rock pools — some containing water all year round — sandy slopes on some of the cliffs and many large acacia trees to sit under. The cliff faces on either side of the wadis are worn into strange shapes, with caves and holes affording hiding and resting places for foxes and birds.

Al-Hair is a small village with a river flowing past it. The river originates in Riyadh, meandering down Wadi Hanifa and giving life to much vegetation. There are several watchtowers still standing on the cliffs overlooking the village. At the top of the paved road leading out of the village is a large pumping station supplying water to Riyadh. For the first part of the trip, four-wheel-drive is advisable.

To get there, take the old route to the Escarpments and the Jeddah Road. Twenty kilometres from the Hanifa bridge is a Red Crescent first aid post on the left. Two kilometres further the road descends the Escarpments. At the bottom take the paved road to the left and round into the valley. At the bottom turn left. Six kilometres on is a wide valley leading off to the left with a track eventually reaching a permanent water pool which attracts water beetles, water scorpions, frogs, dragonflies, mice and birds.

The paved road continues along the bottom of Shaib Laha, with a few farms on the right. At the end of the paved road a good track, suitable for all types of vehicle, continues down the valley. At the point where the paving ends is a wide wadi — Wadi Hesham — off to the right. A track suitable for four-wheel-drive leads up it for about seven kilometres. The main track continues along Shaib Laha passing several wadis until it becomes narrower. The paved road resumes at Al-Hair; follow it across the bridge and up the hill. It is then a straightforward run back to Riyadh across flat, open ground.

Check the route with the local people

Ayn Hit and Al-Kharj

The trip to Ayn Hit can be done in a morning, although continuing on to Al-Kharj makes it a full-day outing. The waterhole of Ayn Hit has always been known to the bedu; Ibn Saud is said to have watered his camels here in 1902 on his way to capture Riyadh. And it was here in 1936 that American geologists discovered strata near the water level which encouraged them to return to Dhahran and drill deeper for oil, resulting in the great oil strike soon after.

To reach Ayn Hit take the Al-Kharj road out of Riyadh. About 35 kilometres from the first flyover take the broad track across the railway and veer right at the junction just over the crossing. This track runs straight to the Ayn Hit cavern, which can be identified from a distance by a small hut standing alone at the foot of the escarpment. Drive past the hut to a parking area and descend about 100 metres.

If you miss the turning, another track crosses the railway after a further three kilometres. This leads to a village. Follow the track, taking the left-hand route just before the village and follow the track to the cavern. Although this route involves travelling over soft sands, it is suitable for a car provided you don't slow down. If you drive past the radio masts you have gone too far — so go back and try again.

There is now a fast dual carriageway between Riyadh and Al-Kharj, while Ayn Hit is on the old single carriage road. At the point where the two roads meet you can drive off the dual carriageway on to the old road — but as the area is being developed at present, you may have to use your own initiative in doing this.

Leaving the water hole you can continue on to Al-Kharj. The government started using water for agriculture here back in 1937, and it is now a well-developed farming area. Driving into the town you can see a derelict palace and barracks on the right, built by Ibn Saud in the 1920s. It is well worth a visit, but be careful about taking photographs. The old town is on the left, a few hundred metres past the palace. The second paved road leads through the main souq area to a family park and, five kilometres further on, to the palm groves of experimental dairy and poultry farms.

The water holes of Ayn Semha and Ayn Dhila can be reached by turning right at the main crossroads in the town. They are worth a visit but, being at ground level, are not as spectacular as Ayn Hit.

Wadi al-Jafi

Wadi al-Jafi is one of many wadis leading off a small escarpment running parallel to the Tuwayq range but about 70 kilometres further east, towards the Dahna dunes. When it rains these wadis become raging torrents, rushing down towards the dunes to form large shallow pools, which are soon surrounded by small plants, grass and bushes.

Wadi Atshanat al-Jafi used to be part of an old route leading to wells on the edge of the Dahna dunes, and was thus frequented by bedu and camels. It is also good fossil-hunting ground: it is possible to find oysters, small sea urchins and ammonites in the cliffs on either side of the wadi. These cliffs have in places been worn into strange mushroom-like shapes, providing shade for the goats and sheep usually in the area.

In the past few years, much heavy plant has ploughed up some of the wadi, so four-wheel-drive is recommended. If you want a weekend away from it all, this is the place to go. Take your car about 12 or 15 kilometres into the wadi, following the tracks close to the trees, and you will be rewarded with pleasant views and complete peace.

To get there take the Dhahran road and drive 75 kilometres from Petromin. On the right of the road you will then see a small green sidr (lotus) tree directly opposite a paved road leading off to the left towards some low hills. Take the road, which leads to a construction camp, in front of which a good track bears right into the wadi.

Quwayah and the graffiti site

Throughout the Arabian peninsula you can find rock carvings, many perfectly preserved. They were made by hammering on the cliff face with a hard stone. Most show animals — either domesticated, or those hunted by the artists, and also herds of long-horned cattle. As these were unable to survive in Arabia after 3000 BC as the deserts became progressively drier, the carvings are thought to have been made between 4,000 and 6,000 years ago.

Fine examples of carved ostriches, camels, horses, donkeys, foxes, cattle, dogs, a scorpion — and even humans — can be seen on a hill near Quwayah. To get there take the old Jeddah road. About 71 kilometres from Petromin turn left at the cloverleaf flyover to Muzahimiyah and Ghat Ghat (signposted Taif). Along this part of the route you get fine views of the escarpments to the left and right. From the Ghat Ghat turn, clock a further 80 kilometres, driving through beautiful red sand dunes, ideal for photographs.

Desert hospitality

You will then see a signpost showing 50 kilometres to Quwayah. A few hundred metres further is a lay-by on the left and a track leading off to the right. Take this track, keeping a small hillock to your right. Follow the track slightly to the right behind the hillock and then on across the plain. The graffiti rock can be seen clearly in the distance, a small flat hill standing by itself, just to the left of a line of hills at the point where they slope down to the plain. Having explored the rock it is worth climbing the hill to the right to look at a fine stone ring.

If you want to turn this trip into a weekend outing you can camp either at the graffiti site or beyond Quwayah. Off to the sides of the main road you can see old mudbrick farms and unspoilt villages. Numerous tracks running off into the wild, craggy black hills bordering the road present immediate invitations to eager campers.

Wadi Horaymilah

This is a very pleasant wadi, suitable for a day trip or overnight camp. Although the going gets soft in places, the whole route can be travelled by car.

To get there take the Buraydah road out of Riyadh. Keep on the main road passing large communications dishes at 39 kilometres. A left fork is marked to Al-Jubaylah and Sadus, but keep to the main road signposted Salbukh and Horaymilah. At 61 kilometres there is a petrol station; take the left fork marked Salbukh and Horaymilah. At 64 kilometres take the right fork signposted Horaymilah — Salbukh is the village and oasis on the left.

At 85 kilometres the road starts to wind down into the wadi. This is a good place to park; walk over to the left and you will get a good general view of the area.

After 91 kilometres you reach Horaymilah. Watch out for the 90° left turn into the town, then follow the road through to a flash flood dam at 98 kilometres. The road ends here and a track runs through the wadi.

It is a good idea to stop at 116 kilometres. To the right is an extensive exposed reef with excellent sea and coral fossils. Soon after, you break through the escarpments and the track winds across the flat. At 133 kilometres you pass the small town of Barrah, enclosed within adobe walls, and at 147 kilometres you hit the main Jeddah road at a T-junction. Turn left here and follow the road back to Riyadh.

Tumair and the Valley of the Iris

The Valley of the Iris earned its name in 1976, an exceptional year for rain. There were showers and storms on and off from December until April, all the wadis were running and large shallow pools of water appeared everywhere. A huge variety of plants flowered in the valley, as well as the iris. There hasn't been another really wet winter since, so there haven't been as many flowers, but it is still an attractive valley even when only a few plants bloom.

Tumair, an old village set against the side of the wadi, used to blend into the scenery. However, it is expanding on to the surrounding hills with new cement block houses and accompanying construction paraphernalia, while a new highway passes straight through the centre of the village.

To reach Tumair, take the Buraydah road and stay on the main Riyadh to Majma'ah road. About 40 kilometres from the Intercontinental hotel, just pass the dish antenna, is a turning to Al-Jubaylah and Sadus — but keep straight on. A further nine kilometres on is a right turn to the village of Ban-Ban. Watch out for the Y fork 14 kilometres past the Ban-Ban turn-off and bear right towards Majma'ah (the left fork goes to Salbukh). Continue on the Majma'ah road until you see a large new petrol station and restaurant on the right, 148 kilometres from Riyadh. A few hundred metres further is a paved road to the right signposted Tumair. Follow this for 18 kilometres until you reach a bend in the road skirting a small hill on the right. On the left is a graded track at the beginning of the curve leading into the Iris valley. The village of Tumair is at the end of the paved road, seven or eight kilometres past the valley.

Towqi

The completion in 1978 of a new route bypassing Riyadh and linking the Dhahran and Majma'ah roads opened up new territory to those who enjoy spending their weekends in the desert.

To get to these away-from-it-all areas, leave Riyadh on the Dhahran road and about 20 kilometres from Petromin turn left near the communications masts on to the road signposted Majma'ah.

Follow the road past the site of the annual camel race, the Buwayb junction and the king's farm, all on the right. After about 81 kilometres turn right on to the road marked Towqi and follow this for 11 kilometres to the end of the tarmac, by when you will have ascended the escarpment. One kilometre further the track divides, with both branches leading to pleasant picnic spots. The Darb Towqi was an old track to Rumah wells, one of the best-known watering holes on the ancient route between Kuwait and Riyadh. The area provides homes for many varieties of bird, presumably because of its trees and water. There are also many fossils on the surrounding hills.

Warning: If you intend going to Rumah you should only attempt the trip if you go with someone who really knows the way — all routes to Rumah are criss-crossed with a great variety of tracks heading off in different directions. It is very easy to become lost, and you are more likely to end up on the edge of the treacherous Dahna sands than at the little settlement itself.

Qassim Province

By Rosalind Ingrams

"We were now in Kasim, the populous (and religious) nefud country of the caravaners. . . .the inhabitants are become as townsmen: their deep sand country, in the midst of high Arabia, is hardly less settled than Syria. The Kusman are prudent and adventurous."

Charles Doughty rode into Qassim from the northwest from Hail, and spent several weeks in Buraydah and Anayzah, the twin cities of the province. Palgrave had preceded him some 20 years earlier, in 1860, and in 1918 Philby wrote a detailed description of his sojourn here. Although times have changed, the careful records of these travellers greatly help a contemporary visitor to this most interesting region.

Bounded to the north, east and west by immense and lifeless desert, Qassim astonishes the traveller by its fertility and its unexpected air of old-established civilisation. The source of its prosperity has been its fertility and, historically, its position at a major crossroads for traffic crossing from the Red Sea and the Gulf. Iraq and Persia sent their pilgrim caravans via Buraydah and Anayzah and on to Al-Madinah and Makkah, and this in turn fostered the trading links with the eastern coast which have always characterised the area. Today, the province is one of the most advanced and highly developed in the kingdom. Huge glittering silos proclaim modern farming methods, great electrical generating stations are being built, and schools are within reach of every village. Buraydah is the home of Saudi Arabia's first agricultural institute while Anayzah boasts a technical training institute with courses in mechanical and automotive engineering, metal working and electronics. An industrial estate has been established between the two towns and licences for about 30 factories have been issued. Traditionally the home of resourceful, independent people, Qassim is the birthplace of many of the younger men now prominent in business and government in Riyadh.

The green settlements and stately palm gardens of Qassim, which are now the subject of intensive agricultural development, owe their existence to an abundance of ground water. The great Wadi Rima rises in the lava highlands of Khaybar, some 400 miles to the west, and flows eastwards, finally spending itself in the Dhana dunes which separate Buraydah from the adjoining populated district of Sudair. The wadi divides Buraydah, to the north, from Anayzah 15 miles to the southwest. It is famous for its occasional tremendous spates *(seyls):* the writer witnessed one in May 1982, and can confirm local stories which Doughty and Philby could scarcely believe. They, of course, were both there in high summer. I crossed the stoney-dry wadi in October 1978, and would never have believed it could become the broad brown torrent that surged before us in 1982. A most necessary bridge has recently been built across it — there was previously an ancient stone causeway. Ground water is easily obtainable within a wide radius of this area. Beyond, wells are sunk to very deep levels.

We visited a typical farm 70 kilometres northwest of Buraydah on a journey from Al-Madinah across pebbly white desert of frightening monotony. After hours of stupefying heat and tedium, a slight roll or swell to the land took the place of the dead-level plain. Trees smudged the horizon; they were the closely-planted *ithil* (tamarisk) trees, of a smokey greenish-blue, which every traveller has noticed in these parts. Planted as windbreaks to enclose fields, they handsomely demarcate the squares of alfalfa and vegetables.

The farm turned out to be an agricultural marvel, or so it seemed after the long wilderness. There were not only the usual green crops, but tomatoes, vines, olives, figs and pomegranates. The wells pumped up water from a depth of 1,500 metres and sent it bubbling along a system of raised channels. Most pleasing of all, the owner had a fancy for gazelles, and kept a small herd which was allowed to roam freely.

As you turn south towards the city the eastern horizon is bounded by a low cliff or scarp, dotted at long intervals by stone-built cylindrical watch towers. These are now mostly ruined, but they were once vital to the security of the farming people of Qassim. Barclay Raunkiauer, the young Danish traveller who visited in 1912, described a watchman in one of these towers. The watchman stood all day, turning his gaze steadily through the 360 degrees of the compass, screwing his eyes into the glare to scan for strangers and marauders. The office was paid for by common subscription, and the work faithfully fulfilled.

Buraydah

"And from hence appeared a dreamlike spectacle! — a great clay town built in this waste sand with enclosing walls and towers and streets and houses! and there beside a bluish dark wood of ethel-trees upon high dunes! This is Buraydah! and that square minaret, in the town, is of their great *mesjid*. It was, as it were, Jerusalem in the desert. The last upshot sunbeams enlightened the dim clay city in glorious manner...."

How true Doughty's well-known words are, even to us moderns driving a Blazer along an asphalt road towards a modernised town. The situation of the town is very striking, for it lies in the lap of great encircling dunes. Their smooth golden slopes almost spill into the town on the western side, and it seems that only a straggling plantation of *ithils* holds them back. Neither a bucket and spade not five thousand bulldozers could remove those majestic sandhills.

Since 1978 Buraydah has expanded and developed rapidly. The walled city described by the old travellers and photographed by Philby is only very partially recognisable now. The walls have gone, and with them the imposing and thoroughly grim fortress in which both Doughty and Raunkiauer were detained in alarming circumstances. The townspeople have always had a reputation for religious austerity, and the atmosphere remains markedly conservative. The masons and builders of Buraydah are famous: this was one of the best-built of the old mud towns of Najd, with wide streets and stately houses. Local men have traditionally been summoned by Riyadh when work on or repairs to the traditional palaces was needed. The work on the recently restored Musmak fort in Riyadh, for instance, was thus supervised.

The old town

The old town lies to the west of a north-south depression which used to be just outside the walls. Most of the new development has taken place across and eastwards from this depression. There is a large open souq on the bank just above the slope within

The road to Buraydah

the Zilfi gate. On our first visit we noticed a large pair of weighing scales in the middle, for the corn market which was in full swing, but we could not see them on our last visit. At one time both cotton and barley were staple crops here. Wheat and barley rather than rice were the staples in Najd until Ibn Saud introduced imported rice on a large scale because he thought wheat **burghul** too "heating."

On the north side of the square coloured umbrellas shade the melon sellers, while lining the open space on the east are a number of tentmakers' shops. Here you can find all the requirements for nomadic home-making, including the woven woollen strips, in brown, black and white, of the traditional **bait sha'ar** (house of hair). Gaily-painted tin trunks from Pakistan will take your goods, and you will choose heavy black iron tent pegs, rather than the oryx horns which Doughty found. On the opposite side a low arcade shelters the open stalls selling clothes, and opening off it is one of the high cool avenues of the covered souq. This covers several acres, in a somewhat haphazard way, crossing one or two main streets as it goes. As always, the souq is divided into sections for spices, clothes, carpets, gold, bedding, and so on. The atmosphere is noticeably quiet and dignified. The bearded merchants may be in business, but they let no vulgar emotion or commotion ruffle their reserve, or their ruminative conversation. Two or three shopkeepers often sit in the booth of one, exchanging news and slow gossip, and this, one feels, is their preferred occupation. Westerners are more out of place here than in Jeddah or Riyadh, and a grave **mutawwa** may take a husband aside and advise him, in a paternal fashion, to take his womenfolk back to the privacy of his car. In 1978 we were asked whether we were Turkish or Syrian hajjis. However, development has brought a number of westerners to live in Qassim, and in 1982 several Europeans could be seen.

At the western extremity of the town is an enormous open space containing the fruit and vegetable souq. If you are there in the season, buy some of the delicious big black grapes grown here and marketed as far as Riyadh. Standing in this wide circumference you get something of an impression of the place as it once was. To the east the sands rise beyond a mosque with a tall tapering minaret. Close by the market is busy, and far across the square the mud houses lie close together, their low roofs decorated with crenellations and the skyline marked here and there with tall minarets.

Walking through the unpaved streets of this old quarter (and there are one or two other districts which have survived too), you will notice the wonderful wooden doors of Buraydah. More handsome here than in any other part of the kingdom, they are built of thick tamarisk wood, with a decorated, iron-studded crosspiece. The wood is frequently painted with decorative patterns, usually of triangles made up of circles, looking something like a bunch of grapes. Generally brown and yellow, the pattern can sometimes be blue and red, which is most attractive. Above and below the crossbar is the highly elaborate lock **(mislaq)**, a system of latches and wards which must make going out and coming in rather lengthy. These locks are raised, embossed and decorated. The doors are set into the house or courtyard wall, with a step down on the other side. The mud surround, especially above the door, is generally decorated with a shallow triangular "sharkstooth" pattern.

Aneyzah

The doors in Anayzah are not so handsome, though made in a similar manner. Nor perhaps are the houses and streets quite so fine, though there remains much that is very attractive. The two towns, though so near, are quite distinct in character, the Wadi Rima seeming to effect a real divide between them. In the past they have often been at war, both on their own account and as parties to the struggles between the Al-Rashid, rulers of Hail, and the Al-Saud (see History). While Buraydah impresses, Anayzah charms. The old town must be seen with the eye of faith, for it too has been disappearing fast under modernisation programmes, but although in 1978 it looked as though it was on the point of vanishing for good, a visit in 1982 showed that the destruction had been arrested and that everything remained just as it was.

The old town

If you want to glimpse the old town, turn west off the main north-south road, and be guided by the tall clay minarets. You should arrive at what was once the main square or *menzil*, which is not in fact square but more of a lozenge shape, and now somewhat neglected and underused. In Philby's time the houses fronting this *menzil* had curved fronts to fit the sweep of the lozenge, like Regency houses in a crescent in England's Bath. This was the idea of one man, Ibrahim Ibn-Salih, who was 70 years old in 1918. He built all the best houses in Anayzah, and was responsible for the remarkable, lofty minaret of the chief mosque, the Jami'a Masjid, built about 1890. It still stands, one of the finest examples of a peculiar form which characterises a region of Najd running north from Washm, through Es-Sirr and ending in Anayzah-Buraydah. Elsewhere, minarets are square, or dumpy "thimble" shapes, but in this region tall cylinders (reminiscent of factory chimneys) taper high above the towns and villages. They are built on a lower stone base, and then in sections, creating a "lampshade-upon-lampshade" effect.

The old architect told Philby the minaret was 80 feet high, and he could have built twice as high, only his base would have had to be much wider. He was paid $40 by the citizens. None of his buildings had ever collapsed, he boasted, yet he was quite untrained and relied entirely on his

Traditional architecture in Anayzah

eye. He used neither plans nor plumblines. Philby does not record that the architect was nicknamed Abu Sitta, or Father of Six, because he had six fingers on one hand.

Afternoon prayers were called from the minaret while we were there, and the male citizens of the locality came hurrying along. Their glances in our direction were civil and benign despite their preoccupation, and verified the town's reputation for courtesy and good breeding. Doughty found friendship and hospitality here (for a period) after he had been expelled from Buraydah, and Philby was so astonished by his warm welcome that he rhapsodised — "It seemed to me that I had stepped suddenly out of barbarism into a highly civilised, even cultured society. . . .in this gem among Arabian cities. . . ." — and reflected on its historical independence and central commercial importance. However, Buraydah, with its airport and major development plans, now surpasses it in importance.

Reduced to ruins by the Egyptian Ibrahim Pasha in 1819 (as noticed by Captain Sadleir, a British agent sent by the Governor of Bombay to parley with Ibrahim), Anayzah had sufficiently recovered half a century later to be called the principal city of Qassim. While Buraydah engaged actively in caravanning and livestock trade (camels, cows, and especially purebred horses), the citizens of Anayzah promoted this and other commerce much further afield, setting out for the Gulf, Basra, Baghdad and India, as well as Damascus, and establishing strong footholds there. The merchant Abdullah el-Bessam, for example, had in the course of his successful career gone first to Baghdad, then traded slaves to Zanzibar and sugar to Mauritius. He later shipped rice from Bombay and finally settled at Basra where he was a corn merchant. Doughty found among "the best younger spirits of the (foreign) merchants. . .readers in the Encyclopaedia, and of the spirituous poets of the Arabian antiquity," who "leaned to the new studies" and some of whom could speak Hindustani, and even a little English. They dreamed of sending their sons to school in Baghdad or Beirut, with a final polish in Turkey and Europe. Inside their homes they spoke freely on religion and world affairs, and even smoked at a time when tobacco was abominated by strict Wahhabis. Forty years on, Philby found the same outlook and manners, and was delighted to be able to trace old men who had known "Khalil" (Doughty).

A sense of the local hospitality can be obtained by a stroll along the unpaved alleys around the Jami'a Masjid. Almost deserted in 1978, the once-fine houses have recently found a new lease of life in providing shelter for the families of Pakistani and other immigrant workers. Tiny children play in the dust, and run shrieking with laughter round corners if a camera is raised; sturdy white donkeys stand patiently in courtyards while they are loaded up with sacks, and voices and the clatter of saucepans can be heard from deep within the houses, repeating timeless domestic patterns.

Examples of Najdi architecture

Courtyards and upper pillared porticoes are principal features of the best Najdi mud architecture, in addition to the fine incised plasterwood *(jiss)* and painted window shutters which decorate the reception rooms. Good examples of plasterwork can often be seen in the gaping ruins of torn-down buildings — the effect is light, delicate and airy. It is usually in the main *majlis,* around the coffee-hearth and along the walls above where guests sat on rugs, against cushions. Doughty wondered if this "pargetting of jis," this "gypsum fretwork. . . .all-adorned and unenclosed" originated from India. However, the Najdi work seems very different from that seen in the Eastern province and Oman, which are linked with Indian traditions, and rather resembles the motifs and patterns found in ancient Mesopotamia. The rosette, the star, the triangle and the stepped-pinnacle pattern of dadoes are all ancient patterns, and can be found all over the Middle East of antiquity. Qassim seems to be the home of the art, and there it is normally worked in hard white plaster (though what you see is usually begrimed with the smoke of the coffee-hearth). In Riyadh, examples can be seen in unadorned clay.

Wandering on down the quiet lanes, which are maze-like in Anayzah, you will soon emerge in the palm gardens which still flourish. In the past these were the glory of the town, and the perimeter wall ran outside them. They were famous for every sort of fruit and vegetable — especially melons and dates — and travellers were often feasted with grapes, pomegranates, peaches, apricots and figs, and also cow's milk. All the travellers were surprised and delighted to find cattle and cow's milk in Qassim. The citizens of Anayzah keenly appreciated good cooking and good housekeeping, and wives originating from Al-Madinah, or even Armenia, were boasted of for their domestic refinement.

Picnics in the groves were once a common entertainment, though less so now, it seems. Every orchard owner questioned the foreigners closely on how best they might increase the draught of their wells. One well might water 10 acres, and there were often as many as eight or 10 beasts (donkeys, cattle and camels) working the wells. Modern methods have now answered their prayers and made Qassim a green garden.

The Rabadi'yah Oasis

We did not have time to explore the many settlements around Anayzah, nor to visit Ar-Rass, a large and old-established town (with an airport) to the west, but turned for Riyadh by way of Zilfi. Leaving Anayzah, we passed the cemetery at the northern end of the town and the palm groves of El-Wadi, and soon crossed the full torrent of Wadi Rimah. We skirted Buraydah this time, just passing through its busy new suburbs, filled with shops and real estate dealers and the offices of the Al-Rajhi brothers, and made for the northeast, for the oasis of Rabadi'yah.

Sand country takes over on the outskirts of the town and soon you find yourself on a ribbon of asphalt running through golden, crested dunes. What astonished us on our second visit was the apparition of an immense shallow lake among the dunes! It was no mirage, but a real watery lake, marking the final home of the flooding Wadi Rimah. The huge dunes, 200-300 feet high, block all passage for the water which spreads itself out for at least a mile, and can remain standing for many months. Several crashed cars lay marooned up to their windows, and, as it was a Thursday, a good many family picnics were being enjoyed at the water's edge, with much wading and splashing. At the edge of the water were some grain plots, well soaked, and it looked as though someone had thought of profiting from the flooding and was growing rice. The great sheet of water reflected the crested sand dunes and the reddening sky.

Once up and over the sand bar, the country is higher, and before long, rocky cliffs run along the horizon ahead and green strips of cultivation appear at their foot.

This is the oasis of Rabadi'yah, and, of a fine early morning, before the great heat of the day, it presents a scene as peaceful and rural as any to be found in Europe. Green fields stretch in orderly rectangles, sheltered by tall tamarisk rows, pumps thud like quietly droning insects, and now and then a cock crows from one of the prosperous-looking farmsteads. As far as the eye can see the landscape is nurtured and blooming.

Nevertheless, as the road runs east the sand country returns and the journey is a delightful switchback ride over the surge and billow of the dunes.

Hail

"It is like a dream to be sitting here, writing a journal on a rock in Jabal Shammar. When I remember how, years ago, I read that romantic account by Mr Palgrave, which nobody believed, of an ideal state in the heart of Arabia... and how impossibly remote and unreal it all appeared; and how, later during our travels, we heard Hail and this very Jabal Shammar spoken of with a kind of awe by all who knew the name... I feel that we have achieved something which is not given to everyone to do" (Lady Anne Blunt: A Pilgrimage to Najd).

Modern Hail, 700 kilometres north of Riyadh, lies between the Jabal Shammar in the north and the volcanic mass of the Jabal Selma to the south. A huge plain, now made fertile by agricultural development, stretches away to Qassim south of Jabal Selma while stretching north beyond Jabal Shammar is the contrasting aridity of the Nafud which affected Palgrave with horror during his summer passage and Anne Blunt with ecstasy.

Today, your first sight of Hail is of tree-bordered dual carriageways and gleaming white houses — a sign in English says "Welcome to Hail." The Koreans are there in force, as a neighbouring sign directing the visitor to a construction camp suggests.

Since 1976 the town has seen dramatic development symbolised by a 60-metre tower in its centre. In early 1980 a sports centre with playgrounds, swimming pools and housing was opened by President of Youth Welfare Prince Faisal Ibn Fahd. Hail has a new hotel, the Hail, which serves excellent Arabian food.

Hail was traditionally one of the great capitals of Arabia, in the heartland of the hegemony of the Rashid, long the opponents of the House of Saud. It was one of the prizes of every western visitor to Arabia — Guarmani in 1864, Wilfred and Anne Blunt in 1878, Gertrude Bell in 1914. From the earliest days of Saudi dominion in the eighteenth century, Hail was governed by a viceroy originally chosen from the Ali branch of the Abda, the main clan of the Shammar tribe. It had always been a pragmatic custom of the Sauds to reinstate local rulers rather than substitute them with strangers who would be unable to win the allegiance of the local people.

Hail's history up to the end of the nineteenth century was bloody. Eight of the nine Rashid rulers who had governed died at the hands of relatives. A great battle between the Sauds of Riyadh and the Rashids of Hail took place at Judi in 1885. The Sauds were defeated and the Rashids became rulers of Central Arabia while the divided family of Saud fled to Hejaz and Kuwait.

In 1901 the head of the family of Saud, Abdul-Rahman Ibn Saud, with the ruler of Kuwait and his protector, Shaikh Mubarak, made a full-scale attack on Shammar. A ghastly battle ensued which ended in a Pyrrhic victory for the Rashids and a bloody defeat for the Sauds who fled to Kuwait. To avenge this, Abdul-Aziz led a group of followers to Riyadh the following year and took Riyadh (see Historical Introduction).

A visit to Hail is ideal for a long weekend. The journey along the fast road from Riyadh can be made easily in one day. If you want to make a camping halt, you can leave Riyadh in the evening and camp near the beautiful iris fields in the Tumair area.

Leave Riyadh on the Dir'iya road. After about 200 kilometres you reach the Sudairi villages named after the family of the Sudairi Seven who include King Fahd and Prince Sultan Ibn Abdul-Aziz. You then pass through Zilfi whose modern mosques are patterned with coloured stones.

From Zilfi to Buraydah you cross the magnificent dunes of the great Nafud desert which so captivated the imagination of Anne Blunt: "The Nafud... is better wooded and richer in pasture than any part of the desert we have passed in leaving Damascus. It is tufted all over with ghada bushes, and bushes of another kind called yerta."

Palgrave, crossing the Nafud in the burning July of 1862, was reminded of a passage from Dante's Inferno in which one of the circles of hell is conceived as a plain of burning sand.

Today, the Nafud has tarmac roads which lead to the small communities among those red dunes. Soon you reach Buraydah (see Buraydah), capital of Qassim province. Continue north.

The main road divides, the left fork continuing to Al-Madinah and a fork slightly to the right to Hail. Some cultivated areas border the road and then you cross a plain. Nearby, on the Darb Zubaydah is the historic village of Fayd. Some date the original settlement back 3,000 years.

About 75 kilometres before Hail you enter imposing mountain ranges — the Jabal Shammar, the Jabal Aja and the Jabal Selma. Ancient graffiti can be seen in the rocks.

Hail retains the atmosphere of tribal Arabia, although it is a developed, modern city. You can still see the black, goat-hair tents of the bedu on the outskirts.

The area is fertile with huge palm groves and vegetable gardens. Agriculture has been enhanced by the construction of the Silf and Agda dams which block off the deep wadis of the Jabal Shammar some kilometres to the north of the town.

Hail was once a city of great buildings. Guarmani describes his attendance at the court of Talal, the amir of Hail, in the great mosque. "He ordered death for assassins, cut off the hand of those who wounded another. . . imprisonment was the punishment for thieves; rebels had their goods confiscated. His sentences were just and his generosity excessive. . . ."

Today many of the great buildings have disappeared. Even in 1914 Gertrude Bell found Ibn Rashid's castle's population sharply depleted by fratricidal killings. Four old buildings which had survived until recently were the Kishla, the eight-towered former barracks, the Ibn Rashid and Ibn Jiluwi castles and the Aarif fort (now the police headquarters). Between Hail and the village of Qufar about 10 kilometres to the east, the Ministry of Agriculture has developed immense olive groves. Shirley Kay writes of green tamarisks and beige mud ruins of Qufar scattered among the olive groves.

The old town of Ghofar, once larger than Hail itself, lies in ruins to the west of Hail, beyond the airport.

It was abandoned about 180 years ago after most of the inhabitants were said to have died of plague. However, the villagers told one correspondent in 1978 that lack of water was the reason.

Air communications (domestic)
Direct daily flights to Al-Madinah, Jeddah, Riyadh; direct flights to Arar, Qassim, Jauf, Rafha, Tabuk, Turayf.
Saudia Tel: reservations 5320105; airport passenger services 5320013. Airport Road.

THE NORTH

Tabuk

A desert town in the northwest, 750 metres above sea level, Tabuk is the first main town travellers reach coming south from Jordan. It lies about 1,110 kilometres north of Jeddah and 450 kilometres south of Amman. It is the administrative capital of Tabuk province which, with an estimated total population of 250,000, is one of Saudi Arabia's less populous provinces. The town is the site of a major military cantonment guarding the northwest frontier and only minutes by jet from Israeli airspace.

The town's dramatic growth in the past decade has resulted partly from an influx from the surrounding villages and partly from the increase in the number of people working on government projects, particularly the cantonment itself. In 1974 Tabuk's population was estimated at about 18,000; by 1979 it had risen to 90,000-plus, and today some 120,000 people live there, making it the most populated city of the northern provinces.

Its expansion, however, has been at the expense of the province's other main centres — Umm Lajj, Al-Wejh and Dubba (all on the Red Sea coast) and Tayma (see Tayma). Each of these towns has more than 10,000 inhabitants. Tabuk's 42-year-old provincial governor, Prince Abdel-Majid Ibn Abdul-Aziz, a son of Ibn Saud, has encouraged injections of central government funds. "However, we don't want to make the area as congested as Riyadh and Jeddah so that it absorbs all the small neighbouring villages. We will try to develop Tabuk but not at the expense of other areas in the region," he says.

The great hope for the province in the coming decade is agriculture. Projects which have attracted private investment include a dairy farm near Tabuk town with a herd of 1,000 cattle, and poultry and wheat schemes. The biggest investment is represented by the Tabuk Agricultural Development Company (TADC), which was set up with capital of SR 200 million in late 1982. Its first programme was to grow winter wheat and Sudanese peanuts over 8,000 hectares near the town.

Massive recent development has all but swamped old Tabuk. One of the traditional stopping places for tribes migrating between Yemen and summer pastures in Jordan and Syria, the town has played a strategic role for at least 2,000 years. The Prophet Muhammad is said to have found a freshwater spring there during one of his early campaigns in the north of the Arabian peninsula. The town lies on the site of the biggest station of the obsolete Hejaz railway, built by the Turks but destroyed in 1917 by the Sharif of Makkah's son, Faisal, and T E Lawrence (see Hejaz Railway).

Tabuk's busy main streets are modern dual carriageways taking a lot of heavy traffic — large container trucks bringing goods overland from Europe come through on their way south to Al-Madinah, Jeddah and Riyadh.

The general impression is of heat, dust and noise. What little greenery there is, is covered with a grey film of fine sand. The wind blows across the town almost constantly, bringing the desert with it. Temperatures are extreme: in summer the maximum is 42°C, but in winter it drops to 2.5°C.

There are plenty of small shops, coffee houses and petrol stations in the main streets, and a souq in the older part of town. There are luxury and first-class hotels. Business visitors usually stay in the guest houses of companies stationed there.

Graceful eucalyptus trees grow in Tabuk, an unusual sight in Saudi Arabia. A Turkish fort dating back to 1064 AH (1694 AD) stands in a high palm grove on the edge of the old part of the town.

Air communications (domestic)

Tabuk airport, seven kilometres from the town, can take medium-size aircraft. Direct daily flights to Jeddah and Riyadh; direct flights to Al-Madinah, Gurayat, Hail, Jouf and Al-Wejh.

Saudia Tel: reservations 4233333; airport cargo services 4221417. Main Street, cable tuumsmsv.

Courier services

SNAS/DHL Tel: 4227522. PO Box 771, Bank Street. Telex: 402559 snascr (Jeddah).

Sport

British Sub-Aqua Club C/o BAC, PO Box 2. Secretary: K P Sills.

The road south

From Riyadh to Najran, via Leyla Aflaj and Qaryat al-Fau

It is now possible to make the journey to Najran, the most southerly and beguiling of Saudi cities, by road from Riyadh. Until 1981, much of the road was track, to be undertaken only by the brave and experienced, as the route crosses vast, inhospitable wastes bordering the Rub al-Khali.

The journey is a long one, nearly 1,000 kilometres, but well worth making, for not only does it traverse the heart of Arabia, but it passes close by ancient sites — reminders that, for all its brand new asphalt, this route has been used since time immemorial.

From Riyadh, take the road east to Al-Kharj, and turn south on the new turn-off before the town. It is marked to The South, Al-Junub, as well as to Dilam and other local places. The Al-Kharj oasis is ever widening with increasing agriculture and the use of circular-pivot irrigating machines. The green fields of wheat, barley, and alfalfa which have sprung up recently give a dreamlike impression. With the windbreaks of slim blue-green tamarisks, ithil, set around the plantations you could be forgiven for imagining yourself, for a moment, in France or Lombardy.

Yamama, as this fertile district is commonly known, has always been an important centre of settled life in the heart of Najd. It stands at a crossroads of traditional trade and movement from the south, and of east-west traffic to the Gulf. William Gifford Palgrave, making his way to the east coast in the mid-nineteenth century, noted how fertile and rich the land was, then bearing crops of cotton. The royal horses were pastured there, and indeed still are: it was, he thought, the "paradise of Najd."

The journey south from Al-Kharj is conveniently broken at the oasis of Leyla Aflaj, 335 kilometres directly south. On the way you pass the "ghost town" of Hauta. It stands on top of a ridge, just after a settlement of mechanics' workshops, petrol pumps and tea houses. A bewildering variety of road signs, pedestrian crossings, lamp-posts, car parks and municipal flowers and bushes have been laid out in the middle of nothing. Baffling — until you turn right (west) off the main road, and follow a route lined with palms and oleanders in wire cages down to the real Hauta. This is an old-established mud village; the mechanics' shops at the top are to catch the main body of passing traffic, while the surrealist lamp-posts and one-way signs are perhaps a touch of wishful thinking, a planner's dream for a future, expanded Hauta. The village is at the eastern end of the Wadi Hariq, a fertile and picturesque valley. The men of this region took part in an uprising against Ibn Saud in 1912, led by the king's cousin, Saud Ibn Abdul-Aziz. Those from Hariq suffered awful punishment, but the men of Hauta were more fortunate, for they had wisely refused to shelter the rebels.

In 1918 Harry St John Philby made a journey from Riyadh to Wadi Dawasir and back, and his detailed description remains the most valuable account of the area. Before him only W G Palgrave had been there, and Philby gives Palgrave a rigorous cross-examination in his book The Heart of Arabia. He

A new road to Najran

finds Palgrave's descriptions seriously wanting, and suggests that, while Palgrave certainly was in central and eastern Arabia, he exaggerated and falsified much of his narrative. In particular, Philby takes Palgrave to task for his account of Leyla.

Leyla Aflaj

Leyla Aflaj is a remarkable and still little-known spot. Aflaj is the plural of falaj — also known as qanat — an ingenious subterranean canal system of irrigation. Stone-lined channels carry the water from its source to destinations perhaps 24 or 30 kilometres away. The source is always higher than the destination with the watercourse built on a very gradual downward incline. The watercourse will be roofed over to a height of one metre or so, and access shafts, looking like mole hills, are built all along the length. These let in maintenance experts and light them along the intervening tunnels. The system was devised in ancient Persia, where its widespread use enabled many tracts far from a water source to be fertilised. They are common in Eastern province and even in Al-Kharj.

Leyla and Al-Kharj share several features. Some are also found in Al-Hasa, to the east, which has led many to class the three together as a group, a triangle connected subterraneously, despite the great arid distances dividing them above ground. Deep aquifers connect them, and make their appearance in strange "pits" or small, deep lakes. There are three such pits at Al-Kharj, and a chain of seven or eight just south of Leyla.

Expatriates call these the Leyla lakes and many make the long journey from Riyadh for the sake of water-skiing and bathing (see Journeys from Riyadh). A body of water in central Arabia seems an impossibility, until you actually see those rather mysterious deep blue, almost black waters.

Leyla

The town itself is straggling and unremarkable, although the surrounding palm groves are lush, and shady, pleasant places for a picnic. About seven kilometres beyond the big water tower at the southern edge of the town is a curve in the road with a track going off to the left marked by two poles. The lakes lie five kilometres east of the main road, and somewhat north — to the left. They are not easy to find because they are quite invisible until you are almost upon them. Near them the land drops suddenly and the water level is well below that of the banks. We got hopelessly lost the last time we were there, and grew anxious because the sun was setting and darkness would be upon us before we could set up camp. There seemed no-one to guide us until suddenly we saw an old man sitting quite still by his Toyota. We stumbled towards him, and when we reached him he forestalled our inquiries by saying impassively: *"Weyn el ayun?"* (where are the lakes?).

We must have been the umpteenth lost Europeans to accost him. With maddening slowness he raised himself and slowly spoke and pointed, rather blind, rather deaf, unexpectedly finishing with: "Hurry up! It's sunset!"

We fled on our way, thankfully, and found the lakes. The first, Umm al-Jibal, is the largest and the one on which both Saudis and Europeans ski and boat at week-ends. But if you are looking for peace and quiet, you are likely to find it further on, by the banks of one of the smaller, remoter pools.

Here and there you can make out the process which brought the lakes into existence. The steep banks crumble and erode inwards, often overhanging dangerously; sometimes an inner pool is about to join the main pool as the thin wall between them flakes away. The water is thought originally to have been all underground, and the shell, or ceiling, that covered them to have broken through gradually, thus revealing the water. The process can be seen more clearly at the Al-Kharj pits.

The ground is fine pale sand, supporting low bush-tamarisk and reedy grasses. Tall, feathered reeds grow thick near the water, and you might see a kingfisher. You have to dive into the lakes, as the banks fall sheer into them. Reputed to be bottomless, like Scottish lochs, they are perhaps 100 metres deep, hence the blackness of the water. It has a slightly mineral tang, and has not led to more than marginal vegetation nearby. The water is not entirely free of bilharzia, according to recent tests.

All around are clear indications of past efforts at irrigation and cultivation. The long straggly bumps criss-crossing the area are extensive qanat systems, now ruined, leading from the lakes. There are ruined qasrs and forts on the edges of the distant palm groves, and numerous traces of ancient activity. Philby was convinced there were clear signs of ancient civilisation, emanating from the Gulf area, parallel to what is known in Oman. Both Dr Abdullah Masri, of the Department of Antiquities in Riyadh, and Professor Abdul-Rahman al-Ansary of Riyadh university's archaeological department emphasise the site's importance for future excavation.

Leyla is not only fascinating on account of its strange water system, but it is also a key staging post on a route otherwise dangerously close to the Rub al-Khali. Leyla and its water wells were on the road which led from Najran to the Gulf, originally a branch of the incense route, but which continued to be used by people from the more populated south searching for opportunities in Iraq and on the coast. A proverb expresses that movement: *"Al-Yaman rihm w'al-Iraq qabr al-'Arab"* (Yemen — the south — is the womb, and Iraq the grave of the Arabs).

Many stopped en route and made a life for themselves in Leyla or Kharj. From Leyla to Sulaiyil, the next place of any size, is 210 kilometres of almost unrelieved desert. Immense salt flats and low dunes stretch away to the east beyond which lies the yet greater desolation of the Rub al-Khali. If, now and then, some acacia bushes or camels appear, it seems an event to be celebrated. About 68 kilometres beyond Leyla is a sudden patch of green, a brilliant field of alfalfa, a house or two, and some luxuriant trees. This spot, Himam, sells petrol. The cultivation has been allowed by a well, which is almost certainly a last outpost of the subterranean aquifer running between Hasa, Kharj and Leyla. A curious domed rock formation visible near the fields is the same type of formation that has caved in and revealed water in the other places.

Sulaiyil

Sulaiyil is an oasis town set in Wadi Dawasir, the great valley that runs east through a gap in the Tuwaiq escarpment, which stretches north-south for the greater part of central Arabia. The road swings west through a great gap where the chain momentarily breaks, said to be the result of the massive pressure — much greater in earlier times — of seasonal torrents rolling east along the Wadi Dawasir and spending themselves in the sands. The water ran off the steep mountains of Asir and collected in a huge seasonal river. The wide silted valley supports waving palm groves, while the mountains look as though they had been ripped apart, two great spurs separated by the four or five kilometre wide wadi. The rains of spring 1982 left no illusions as to the colossally destructive powers of flash floods in Arabia: the wrecked roads, bridges and property in the Asir have cost millions of riyals in insurance claims, while many people died.

At Sulaiyil the cliffs stand on either side. To the north are an airport and military installations, and all the paraphernalia of a growing modern town. The southern end is green with palms, dotted with the mud houses seen by Philby. He was highly excited by his visit here, for he was the first European ever to have reached this "heart of Arabia." He had long been anxious to see for himself the geography of the then only vaguely known Wadi Dawasir. He found at Sulaiyil a modest half-way house of commerce: coffee from Yemen being exchanged for Indian cloth and goods from Basra.

From the first narrowing of the cliffs on the approach to Sulaiyil to the gap and the start of the Wadi Dawasir to the west is about 45 kilometres. Ahead lie the green of the wadi, and broad tracts of crops irrigated by the spindle-legged circular-pivot machines which are now everywhere. As our route, however, lay to the south, we turned left on to the fine new highway which stretched ahead into a blank, perfectly level horizon.

The Tuwaiq escarpment resumed its march, parallel with the road, but now to the left or east of it. It was a dramatic sight. There is ample time to appreciate the striations and crumplings of the rock, its dull dark grey lightened with streaks of pink or lilac, the upper parts growing tawny, and ever-changing in the altering light of the lengthening afternoon. At its foot, the sands are level and golden, whitened occasionally with a glaze of salt, or turning purplish nearer the rock. Suddenly you notice the cliff has receded on the left, a vast bay of sand has opened out, and the road is swinging a little to the west to rejoin the further arc of the bay. At 122 kilometres from Sulaiyil, near two petrol stations, is the site of the astonishing archaeological discovery of Qaryat al-Fau, an ancient caravan city.

Qaryat al-Fau

Its existence was first suspected by Aramco engineers and geologists flying over the desert wastes in the 1940s; its importance was then predicted by Philby. To Philby fell the honour of reporting almost everything of interest that lay in his path, but he had the attendant frustration of never disturbing the soil, out of respect for the inhabitants' strongly held beliefs. It was Professor Al-Ansary who followed up Philby's lead and started digging at Al-Fau in 1972.

Ten years later, the professor has just published a book showing the results of his digging, while a film has also been made. The book, Qarayat al-Fau: a Portrait of Pre-Islamic Civilisation in Saudi Arabia, tells the story of the excavations in both Arabic and English, pointing out the significance of the most interesting finds.

The site's physical layout has been established. From north to south it is more than two kilometres, and from west to east about one kilometre. In addition, there were wide strips of cultivated land. Staring at the lunar sterility of the landscape now, it is difficult to imagine how such a great city could have supported itself. The climate was undoubtedly kinder than it is now. Seventeen wells have been uncovered in the course of the excavations, as well as cisterns and underground canals. Wild animals and domestic animals abounded, borne witness to by hunting scenes and heaps of bones. Agriculture was practised, with date palms, vines, olibanum trees and grain grown.

Al-Fau's main features seem to have been those of all pre-industrial cities: temple, marketplace and palace, or — as Professor Al-Ansary puts it — religion, commerce and politics. The temple does not appear to have been of overwhelming size and importance, while the souq seems to have been the most active part of town. This ties in with the basic assumption that Al-Fau was a merchant or caravan city, like most other cities in the peninsula — outside south Arabia — in the period leading up to the birth of the Prophet.

The souq has a striking appearance. A tell, or mound, eight metres high, it has been carefully uncovered during the 10 seasons' digging, and is now the most complete of the discoveries so far. The most curious feature is the immensely thick ramparts which surround the inner courtyard or marketplace. Professor Al-Ansary believes the ramparts were the first parts to be built and that the inner area came to be used as a souq later. It was then that it was divided into the shops and dwellings now visible. It therefore seems that the high thick ramparts were part of an earlier, citadel, where the inhabitants could take refuge in times of danger. As the city prospered, it outgrew this primitive stage and set up buildings beyond the citadel.

The inner souq is fascinating in the completeness of its arrangements. It has an enormous, deep stone-lined well, and a stone-cut channel to lead water off. The well is at the eastern end of the small central court, surrounded on three sides by houses, shops, workshops and storage chambers. Many of these had two storeys above ground and cellars with steps leading down. Buildings on the southern sides of the court are finely constructed, of squared and trimmed stone, and still stand more than two metres high. The excellence of this masonry can be compared with the fine ashlar masonry of the south Arabian cities, such as Marib and Timna, and also Ukhdud in Najran. This fine work may also belong to the earliest citadel stage. The citadel seems to have had only one narrow gate on the western side, although seven towers built around the walls further strengthened and buttressed it.

A somewhat unusual feature is the apparent existence of numerous lavatories, with arrangements for removing waste, probably for agriculture.

Outside the ramparts are several additional souq areas to the north, west and south, as yet only partly excavated. Further west and south lies the residential area, also not fully explored, but already offering many clues to the life of the city. Particularly interesting is the discovery of several large caravanserais, each measuring 28 by 18 metres. These great resthouses for travelling caravans confirm the city's basic function. Further evidence lies in the quantity of weights and measures yielded, some large and striking objects.

Discoveries of fine linen

The houses, too, seem to have been substantial, with plenty of storage area. Corn was ground in every big house, store channels provided water, and weaving, in particular, was widespread. Professor Al-Ansary and his team were able to deduce this by careful examination of the walls. In some walls there were two holes at the bottom, with corresponding holes in the opposite wall. On either side of these were two smaller cavities "allowing the insertion of a wooden or iron bar to which wool or linen could be fastened from a square or rectangular shape in accordance with the size required for weaving." Similar arrangements noted in other parts of the town make it certain weaving was a major activity — then as later.

The fragments of material which have been found are pieces of fine linen with worked patterns, rather than rugs. The linen is very beautiful, rather similar to the fragments of Coptic manufacture from Egypt seen in the British Museum and elsewhere.

The weaving of fine linen is also depicted in one of the most exciting discoveries of all, the painted wall frescoes from the palace. So far, the palace consists of two main chambers, one larger and more important than the other. Its roof was supported by two pillars, and a bench ran round the internal walls. Archaeologists have found a mass of fallen debris in the middle. It was this which yielded up the frescoes. Covered in a layer of plaster, the fragments are painted in red, black and ochre, superbly preserved by the sand. So far, about six scenes have been assembled; each is about 50 by 40 centimetres and must have formed a series of panels round the palace chambers. One scene depicts the legs and hooves of horses splashing through water in which large goldfish are swimming merrily. Another shows part of a Cupid-like figure holding the reins of an invisible chariot, with pennants fluttering, while yet another shows camels and vines. The most striking fragment depicts a man's head, wreathed and adorned by two smaller female figures. It is probably a portrait head: huge dark eyes glow intently out of the picture, eyebrows and moustache are firmly delineated, as is a small stubble of beard. A mass of dark curls surrounds the broad, ruddy face, and a kind of diadem surmounts the whole. Huge bunches of grapes dangle from an accompanying decorative motif, while two charmingly grave young women extend their hands on either side of the man. His name, Zky, is inscribed in black in the proto-Arabic script known by the Arabs as Musnad.

Restoring the paintings
These wall-paintings are being restored by the Department of Archaeology in Riyadh university. Restoration is a complex and delicate business, and to witness the process is to be filled with respect for the meticulous care and training needed. For all the cracks the frescoes have suffered, you can admire the strong, glowing colours and the freshness and assurance of the painter's handling. A touch of white on every grape highlights its bloom, and each one stands out in relief from the dark shadow behind it. Vine leaf and tendril curl elegantly, and while the human figures are somewhat stiff, they are still treated in an assured way which renders lips, noses and eyes in the classical style.

Here you come up against one of the many questions which face the visitor to Al-Fau: To what extent was this city in touch with the contemporary culture of the outer world? What sort of era was this? Did the citizens import their craftsmen or were they native? Were the numerous artefacts imported or home-made?

These questions grow even more urgent when you turn from the frescoes to the remarkable sculptures found in the area of the temple. The finest examples are in bronze. Two glaring lion's heads with rings between their teeth were probably the ends of throne arms. Two sinuous sea creatures, one a dolphin, are in the form of statuettes. A small, decorated tripod bears the image of the goddess Kahl with upraised arms and crowned head. This goddess, whose name is found repeatedly at Al-Fau, served to identify the previously unknown site. Inscriptions found in south Arabia, at Saba and elsewhere, referred to Dhat Kahl in the state of Kinda, mentioning expeditions and raids against the "city of Kahl." Nobody knew where it was until the discovery of Al-Fau showed the innumerable inscriptions to the goddess.

Several fragments of large statues in the form of bronze hands, fingers and feet have been found. These are hollow, and of excellent workmanship. Most striking of all are two statuettes discovered recently. One is a Hercules of the highest Greco-Roman workmanship. About 19 centimetres high, of classical realism, the hero stands with his club and the pelt of the Nemean lion hanging over his arm. Muscular, alert, this figure is probably the closest to the mainstream of Mediterranean culture yet found in Saudi Arabia. Parallels are the boy riding a lion from Timna, and the superb bronze horse from Yemen, now in Washington.

The other figure is an enchanting statuette of a winged boy, Horus, or Harpocrates, as the young Horus was known. Delightful in his easy pose — finger to his lips — he carries a cornucopia in his left arm. He is crowned with the double crown of Upper and Lower Egypt as befits the child of Isis and Osiris. In this figure can be seen a current from the Helleno-Oriental civilisation which spread from Alexandria in the time of the Ptolemies, and influenced Rome from the second century AD. The cult of Isis, and of Harpocrates, became widespread throughout the eastern Mediterranean and beyond. While innumerable figures of the boy god have been found elsewhere, the example from Al-Fau — now in Riyadh — has certain features, notably the pendant around the neck, which are distinctly Arabian. There are also small, charming bronze figurines of camels and ibexes, very like the little bronzes from Luristan and Parthia, of the contemporary Persian culture.

To list all the finds — the dice made of bone, patterned with black dots, the silver cups, the bronze shields, alabaster vessels and wooden combs — is impossible, but mention must be made of one of the most significant. These are the inscribed fragments of bone, mostly shoulder blades of camel and ox. Large bold Musnad script, generally in reddish ink, covers quantities of these bones, which were cleaned and prepared for the purpose. So far, parchment or papyrus has not been found for writing on. We know from the hadith that verses of the Quran were written down on the shoulder blades of camels or the spines of palm fronds, but never before had such examples been found.

It also seems that Al-Fau must have had some connections with the Nabataeans, as some Nabataean pottery and an inscription have been found there.

Writing is all over the site, not only in ink on bone or wall, but chipped into the cliff rocks close by, or carefully engraved on stone. Most important are the funerary inscriptions, which tell something of the notable dead. Not a great deal has been yielded at tombs at Al-Fau, as they were robbed in antiquity. The tombs of a king, Muawiya Bin Rabia, and of two noblemen have so far been found. Precious fragments remained in some of the chambers, left behind by the robbers. These included pieces of painted wood, presumably from the coffins, and small items such as exquisite glass and crystal scent phials and bottles. Of special interest is the inscription on the tomb of a nobleman, dire and menacing in tone:

"Ijl Bin Hafam has built for his brother Rabil Bin Hafam a tomb, for himself and his son and his wife and grandsons, and great grandsons and their lawful free women of Al-Ghalwan and asked for them the protection of Kahl, Lah and Athar-Ashraq to preserve them from all distress and weakness and the wickedness, and their wives likewise, for ever from all losses, otherwise may heaven rain blood and the earth be a blaze."

The same sort of threats are made on tombs in Medain Salih. The extraordinary brick towers at Al-Fau may be connected with the tombs. Huge but eroded, rearing like stranded boles above the plain, they are the most immediately striking objects on the site. Funerary towers are a feature of many other ancient sites in the Middle East, and future seasons may uncover more about the burial customs of Al-Fau.

In his book, Professor Al-Ansary considers the question of the era of Al-Fau's prosperity. From the evidence of coins and scientific tests, the period of occupation was between the second century BC and the fifth century AD. This fits in with the already established period of the pre-Islamic incense trade culture, already in decline before the rise of Islam, as paganism — with its elaborate temple rites — waned with Constantine's official acceptance of Christianity by 325. The demand for incense fell dramatically, and it was never again a major commodity.

If you want to visit Al-Fau, first get

permission either from Professor Al-Ansary at the Department of Archaeology, Riyadh university, or from Dr Abdullah Masri, Department of Antiquities, Riyadh. After you have seen the site, go and look at the finds displayed in the Department of Archaeology, but ring first as a courtesy, as the display is not generally public.

Leaving Al-Fau, you continue south. Although the desert appears as barren as ever, change is on the way. Thirty kilometres after Al-Fau we noticed a faint green sheen over the dark golden dunes stretching west, and a wide sprinkling of acacias where camels browse. Eighty kilometres south is a petrol station, and 40 kilometres further mountains can be seen to the west. The immense level monotony of the central desert gradually gives way to the fertile mountainous country of the southwest, and the traveller's spirits rise accordingly.

We camped about 150 kilometres beyond Al-Fau and not long before we stopped we passed a road sign promising only 171 kilometres to Najran. Of the many camps we have made in Saudi Arabia this was one of the most perfect. It was April and signs of spring were everywhere. The green sheen had been growing ever more noticeable as we proceeded south, and when we got out of our vehicles we saw the source of it. A tiny yellow flower, a member of the Cassia family, dotted the sands, and it was this which was providing rich herbiage for the many camel herds pasturing the steppes. Steppe seemed the appropriate word for those cleanly rolling uplands, touched with delicate green, and punctuated here and there by the low black horizontals of bedouin tents. Throughout the journey the intense activity of the bedouin was very evident. It is often said in the cities that little remains of this kind of life. Such remarks could only be made by stay-at-homes. We saw innumerable tents, flocks, herds, and frequent moves by pick-up truck of families and animals to fresh pastures.

After a cool, refreshing night, spent under the solemn splendour of a full moon, we were eager and ready for our goal, Najran.

Najran

The Romans called it Negrana reflecting pronunciation in the south, where "j" is always pronounced "g." They came here, the only known occasion of a Roman presence in the peninsula, on a military expedition led by Aeius Gallius in 24BC. Their object was to discover the mysterious incense country and so control trade, but they failed, defeated by thirst and exhaustion, although they had come within two days' march of the Wadi

The exquisite buildings of Najran

Hadhramaut, gateway to the incense country.

Long before the rise of Rome Najran was a city of importance. Culturally and geographically it belonged to the civilisation that grew up in Arabia Felix, now Yemen. Although knowledge of this civilisation is incomplete, its broad outlines have long been deduced from the splendid monuments and inscriptions that remain. The great dam and temple at Marib, and the ruins at Timna and Shibam testify to the high level of a culture whose legendary example was the Queen of Sheba.

Najran was probably the most northerly outpost of the city states of Arabia Felix. Wadi Najran describes a broad, gentle southwest to northeast curve, 40 kilometres long, and five or six kilometres wide. To the south it is barred by a sheer wall of mountains. In one cleft the Wadi Madhiq, a dam, has been built to control the flood waters which might otherwise pour turbulently down into the valley. Built by a consortium of mostly French engineers it was officially opened on 10 May 1982 by Interior Minister Prince Nayef Ibn-Abdul-Aziz. It is 73 metres high and 274 metres long, while the reservoir can hold 85 million cubic metres of water.

When Philby spent a month in Wadi Najran 50 years ago, he discovered extensive traces of an ancient dam, and signs of cisterns, aqueducts, and canalisation in the same spot. He urged restoration of these works then, for despite the area's natural fertility the population was far from prosperous.

The sight as you approach the valley from the northeast is memorable: waving palm fronds, scarlet blossomed pomegranate orchards, trailing vines, lime-green banana trees, level patches of dense alfalfa and scattered, stately houses, all stretching into a blue distance ringed by mountains. Beautiful in any circumstances, it is even more so for the traveller who has crossed 1,000 kilometres of parched desert. The journey we made in two days once took three weeks by camel: for those travellers, the oasis of Najran must have been a sweet sight indeed.

Today, it is a bustling city. We first visited it in 1977, and again in 1978. In the space of four years the town appears to have doubled in size. At first we were unable to find what we regarded as the real town — the area round the old governor's palace, Qasr Aba al-Saud, which on maps is often all that is marked by way of settlement in Wadi Najran.

Yemeni traditions and colour

Qasr Aba al-Saud must be one of the finest examples of mud architecture in the kingdom. An immense construction, it resembles a sandcastle, with turrets, curtain-walls and crumbling round towers grandly dominating its surroundings. Philby stayed here and grew to regard it as "home" after his extended explorations of the area. It seems now to be abandoned to time and decay, but it would be a great pity if it should crumble away from neglect.

Philby was officially here on a mission from King Abdul-Aziz to establish the frontiers with Yemen. Yemen relinquished its claims to the territory in 1934 and this was the last province to be added to the new and vast kingdom of Saudi Arabia. Not surprisingly, there is a great deal to remind the visitor of the proximity of Yemen, especially in the dress and manner of the inhabitants. Bandoliers and weapons are commonly worn by men, reminders of the unsafe days of not so long ago, while women are much less formally veiled than in Najd. The people are extremely relaxed and friendly.

Judging by the ruins, Aelius Gallus would have found Negrana a city of great splendour. The site of the ancient city, known in Arabic as Ukhdud, lies south of the broad sandy torrent bed on whose northern shore present-day Najran is built. To visit the ruins it is necessary to get a letter of permission from the Department of Antiquities in

Riyadh, which must be presented to the Governor of Najran. The site is carefully guarded.

Philby estimated it covered about 28 hectares. Plain bumpy ground denotes the area of the town, whose buildings would probably have been made of mud, while a mass of masonry reveals the citadel. You can clearly see the defensive moat, and the town walls and the main gate, with its enormous granite lintel. Within the citadel, the scene looks confused, because of the tumbled ruin of masonry caused by an earthquake in the eight century AD. The finest masonry however, withstood the quake and still stands, with one building having walls about four metres high. The masonry here is superb: squarely cut and dressed, tight-fitting and even, and compares with the excellent masonry at Timna. On several of the stone faces incised "drawings" — now familiar through photographs — have been found. There is a horse, in classical Hellenistic style, two intertwined snakes, a foot and several outstretched hands. Some of the stones have been carefully bevelled, and some bear a curious chess-board pattern.

Ukhdud — the historic city

The palaces, canals, gates and walls of ancient Ukhdud are referred to in a near-contemporary account of an incident also recorded in the Quran. In about AD 522 most of the city's inhabitants, being Christians, were massacred by an invading neighbour, the Jewish King Dhu Nawas. The verse in the Quran (sura 85) refers to "the trenches" in which the martyrs were thought to have been burnt alive. The name Ukhdud, meaning trenches, came to be given to the spot. When the site is fully excavated, there can be no doubt that a confused period of early Arabian history will be illuminated. A beginning has been made on this task, and revelations and discoveries can certainly be expected.

On the three occasions we have visited the oasis we have been invited into people's homes and have enjoyed their hospitality. Najran has traditionally been made up of homes scattered throughout the cultivated oasis, with only a very small urban huddle near Qasr Aba al-Saud. There are a few streets there of adjoining houses, but generally homes are set apart and surrounded by their own orchards and plots.

There are two main types of building: one is the family home, the other is the qasr, or tall fortified stonehouse. We once watched a mud house being built in the oasis, and stayed in another, only two or three years old, but of a traditional pattern. The mud is laid in courses about 50 centimetres thick, mixed with chopped straw and sometimes crumbled mortar. The builders form a team or chain, mixing, tossing, catching, laying on and smoothing. This teamwork continues unbroken, held together by a work-chant which all sing. The chant of each corresponds to his job, with the "I mix, I toss, I catch," producing a rhythmic harmonious whole.

From the base, the walls taper gradually towards the top, and the corners of the mud courses tilt upwards, so the four top corners are like spurs. The roof, or roofs — for there are several with the different wings — are always finished with a crenellated parapet, whitewashed and highly decorative. These lacy white encrustations on the tops of the houses, and the white surrounds to the small square windows, make them look extraordinarily festive — almost like white sugar houses. The houses have two or three storeys, with wooden beams supporting the ceilings. The layouts vary: some are L or E-shaped, others are hollow squares with courtyards within. On our way out to the dam we passed a very fine example of a fortified farmhouse, with round towers at each corner of its walls. Generally, however, the homes of Najran are not bristling with defences — as so often elsewhere — but are gracious peacetime houses.

Within, they are light and airy, although the staircase in the centre of the house may be steep and dark. The windows have no glass, but wooden shutters.

The preference is for rooms with windows on three sides, which explains the many narrow E and F-shaped wings. On warm summer evenings, the family gathers on the flat roof under the stars, leaning on cushions against the parapet, while the evening meal is prepared on the embers on a small adjoining roof.

Qasrs are built to a different plan. They are generally narrow lofty buildings, on the skyscraper model, often protected by outer walls. They usually have a stone foundation, extending above ground for about one metre. The mud courses are above that, their horizontal bands decorating the towers whose tops culminate in parapets, which are not, however, crenellated or whitewashed. There is often an extra, smaller storey at the top where the guardian of the storehouse sleeps.

I explored a disused qasr in a quiet palm grove. It proved to have eight storeys, with the lower ones clearly storage rooms. Many little low clay-built walls divided the floors into areas for different purposes, with built-up platforms used for threshing or kneading. Light was almost non-existent on the lower floors, but the small windows increased as I went up, until at last I came out on to the platform surrounding the small top chamber. From here there was a magnificent view over the palm-tops, across the valley to the mountain walls a few kilometres to the south which bar access to Yemen. Modern Najran lay to the north, and to the northwest the way to Asir, the traditional path to Makkah and Syria. To the northeast was the way we had come, the harsher road to Iraq and the Gulf. Due east, the valley spread out for 20 kilometres or so until the groundwater failed, and straight ahead unrolled the silent expanses of the Rub al-Khali. Skirting the southern edge of those sands the ancient caravans had come from Dhofar and Hadhramaut, bearing their goods to Najran and then parting, some to Syria, some to Mesopotamia.

Turning back from the absorbing panorama, I saw in front of me the little chamber of the haris, the guardian of the barn-fortress. His mat lay in front of one of the two low shuttered windows, and there were two arched and pointed niches in the walls to hold a lamp. The room was about three metres high, whitewashed, and with a crow's nest view of the world from the low windows. Above this room was a look-out point, reached by wooden rungs.

In Najran you sense a flow, a satisfying historic continuity. Young married couples are proud to build their new homes in the style of their fathers and grandfathers, and builders still sign their artefacts as their ancestors did thousands of years ago.

Rosalind Ingrams

HASA
(EASTERN PROVINCE)

Five years ago a young Saudi graduate, returning home with a foreign bride, sought a place to live. Muhammad chose Dhahran because he felt Jane would feel most at home there. It is still true that of all the regions of Saudi Arabia, the Dhahran-Al-Khobar-Dammam triangle presents westerners with the mildest culture shock.

Since the 1930s Americans have spread their influence throughout Eastern province. American programmes are shown on local television, American food lines the shelves of supermarkets, and American cars career over the speed bumps in the roads.

This is the oil-producing region of a country whose economy rests on oil — 90 per cent of output comes from about 800 producing wells here.

Dhahran grew up as a company town beside oil well number 7, the first to gush in 1938. Aramco, the corporation formed by four big US oil companies to extract and export oil, is now 100 per cent owned by the Saudi government (see Oil).

Aramco's Dhahran camp is like a hermetically sealed town which looks and smells like an affluent suburb of Phoenix, Arizona. Kids on bikes and skateboards play on the tree-lined avenues, neighbours chat over the backyard fence, or run errands to the commissary, post office, or library.

The effect of Aramco's 25,000 employees has been out of proportion to their number. Historically, Aramco policy has been to promote a strong local economy. It has instituted employee training programmes; given technical and financial assistance to business and industry; built many of the schools in the province, and offered scholarships for college training.

Aramco has assisted the Al-Sharq and Al-Salamah hospitals, and its own modern health centre has spearheaded better health care. Malaria was stamped out in the province after intensive DDT spraying by Aramco in the 1950s.

Egg production, too, began in 1960 thanks to Aramco. Before 1958, no vegetables grew except dates, watermelons, and squash. To help oasis farmers, Aramco hired agriculturalists whose goal was to provide fresh vegetables for Aramco employees. Everyone benefited, however, when carrots and ripe tomatoes appeared in the souqs.

Newcomers to Dammam and Al-Khobar are startled by the jumble of humanity in the souqs. At weekends, the streets swarm with the Koreans, Filipinos and Pakistanis employed on massive construction projects. It sometimes feels like the Far East, rather than the Middle East.

Clusters of modern high-rise apartments contrast with the walled-in houses of the past two decades. Sandy streets and honking motor horns previously drove most westerners to live in smaller, more westernised Al-Khobar. However, extensive building and a massive clean-up in Dammam may reverse the trend.

Daily life

"Early to bed, and early to rise," is the fate of many expatriates. Those who expect an easy life are quickly disillusioned: 12-hour days, six days a week is the normal work pattern, with few siestas. Work continues without let-up in all seasons, yet expats learn to live as if the climate didn't count. As most buildings are airconditioned, temperatures of 43ºC (100ºF) seem trifling to all but those who work outside.

Religion

Here, as elsewhere in Saudi Arabia, the rhythm of life is dominated by the call to prayer. Shops close and drivers park by the roadside to face Makkah for prayers five times a

Street scene in old Jubail

day. Prayer times, which vary according to the position of the sun, are announced daily in the English-language and Arabic press. After the noon prayer comes the main meal of the day. The tempo of business life picks up again after afternoon prayers (about 1500), pauses for evening prayers, then resumes until about 2100 when most shops close. Foreigners get used to the routine, just as they come to accept Friday as the weekend.

Dress

Islam dictates clothing too, at least for women. Western women should bring several wraparound skirts or long dresses. Bare arms and legs arouse unpleasant stares and possible censure from the police. Trouser suits are often worn for casual dress but shorts only on all-western compounds. Bikinis are frowned on, and most pools are segregated.

Cotton is the best fabric for the climate although polyester blends are suitable from December to late March. There are few shops for women in the area, and a woman cannot always try on the clothes as the sales staff are men.

Dress for men is informal — open-necked shirts and lightweight trousers. Most Saudi men wear the thobe — white cotton for summer, dark coloured and heavier for winter. It can be made to measure for about SR 60 by many of the small tailors in and around the souqs. Western women often choose the thobe style for long dresses in bright prints. To complement the thobe, Saudi men wear the ghutra, a red-checked or pure white headdress known further west as the keffiyeh. Worn over the tagiyya, a white crocheted skull cap, it costs about SR 45. Leather bedouin sandals are sold in the souq for about SR 50.

Climate

The climate in eastern Arabia is cool and bright from early December to mid-March with occasional rainstorms that flood the streets. A few hardy souls swim all year round, and many compound pools are heated for the less vigorous.

Late March and early April are like perfect British summer days. All too soon in May it gets hot and stays hot until mid-October. Summer daylight temperatures often exceed 43°C at midday, and humidity often hovers around 90 per cent in August and September.

Shopping

Five years ago, there was little to tempt expats to spend their hard-earned cash. Now it is different. Lobster, grouse, pheasant, and mallard duck lie claw by wing in the deep freezers of the local supermarkets; couture dresses by Cardin hang above shoes by Bally and Charles Jourdan; Omega and Piaget watches nestle beside tapes and records of country, jazz, and classical music; scents abound, as do electronic gimmicks of all sorts; even Dutch tulips are flown in.

Language is not a problem as most shopkeepers know English. But prices do go down when you speak a little Arabic. Bargaining is expected in the fruit and vegetable souq and the fish market. A 5-10% discount is the norm. The government fixes daily prices for the fruit and vegetables, which are posted in Arabic outside the shops.

Food costs more than in the US or UK because of transport costs. Food and household supplies for a family of four can easily reach SR 600 a week. Most families stock up on clothes during home leave. Inflation runs at about 15 per cent, but there are frequent government checks on stores.

Electronic goods — TVs, radios, and tape recorders — are good value. Luxury items are cheaper than in their heavily taxed points of origin. Scent, in fact, is cheaper in the souqs of Al-Khobar than duty-free on aircraft.

For food bargains, many families patronise wholesale distributors, and share cases of chicken, oranges, crabmeat and peanut butter with neighbours. In Al-Khobar, Family Food Supply is another wholesaler popular with western shoppers.

And there are a few expats who keep their savings in gold. The gold souqs in Dammam — one near the main mosque and the other near the fabrics souq — are cheaper than the shops in Al-Khobar.

Few traditional handicrafts have been for sale until recently, although bedouin women sell their silver jewellery and narrow hand-woven carpets in the village squares in Qatif and Hofuf. New antique shops such as that of Nabila Bassam now cater for the increasing market.

Because of the high mobility in the area, lots of secondhand goods are on sale through the year. Announcements of garage and "Leaving Saudi" sales are posted in the large supermarkets. The post office at Aramco has several bulletin boards filled with sale notices for everything from boats to furniture — an especially good place to look for a used car.

Servants

Most servants employed by westerners are Yemenis. They charge from SR 10-15 an hour and will do most household chores. These men send most of their meagre earnings to their families. Bakshish is given them at the religious holidays, the two Eids. The usual way of finding a houseboy is by word of mouth. Live-in servants are unusual among western families, but many Saudi families employ female Filipino or Sri Lankan housekeepers.

Compound living

This is a striking feature of life: most compounds are walled, and even the smallest have guards and gates, partly to prevent young children from wandering into the desert. Facilities within each compound are generally reserved for the residents; badge numbers and ID cards are required to get into most recreation centres. Although this leads to close relations within groups who have to live, eat, work and play together, it also spawns an insular, claustrophobic atmosphere. In larger communities such as the Royal Commission at Jubail, Aramco, or the University of Petroleum & Minerals in Dhahran, a conscious effort is made to promote international harmony by mixing various national groups. Nonetheless, socialising generally tends to be with one's own national group. Bachelors are often segregated from family areas.

To give the system its due, compound living alleviates some of the stresses of keeping house. Usually there is no worry about repairing the stove, painting the ceiling, or unclogging the lavatory.

Living in town

In the town, rubbish is collected daily. Gas cylinders are sold at all small grocery stores. Private telephones are less hard to come by in private villas and there are public telephones on the main streets.

Transport

Most compounds have buses which take children to school and women to market. These range from Aramco's fleet of airconditioned Greyhounds to the more common minibus.

Saptco (Saudi Arabian Public Transport Company) buses, which have a special rear partition for women only, have given both local and western women far greater mobility. Routes now cover most of Al-Khobar, Dammam and Dhahran airport. Buses run every 20-30 minutes, and are clean and airconditioned. The fare is SR 1 on all routes except route No 15 linking Dammam to Dhahran airport, which costs SR 5 a trip. There is also a new limousine service from the airport.

Taxis can be hailed on the street in both Al-Khobar and Dammam. The main ranks are by the fountain in Al-Khobar and near the central mosque in Dammam. Taxis are now metered in town. It should cost SR 5-10 to take you anywhere in town, and about SR 15-20 to go from one town to the other. Women should not go in taxis alone.

Driving is less hazardous here than elsewhere in the kingdom, but be alert for dicey situations and roads in need of or under repair. Drivers must always carry a Saudi driver's licence, car registration, safety triangle and fire extinguisher. Car insurance is advisable — accidents can result in legal nightmares. Women are forbidden to drive (see Hints to Motorists).

Leisure

There is a lot to do in Eastern province, especially in the cities. Social life often centres around the hotels with their private sports clubs; motor and ideal home shows, and food festivals. Plays are performed regularly by groups at the Dhahran air base, Jubail, and Aramco camp, as well as the Dhahran Academy.

The waters of the Arabian Gulf are never more than a few kilometres away. More than 200 species of fish swim here, among them schools of dolphins. Game fish include hamour, a dark-coloured grouper whose flesh is like that of sea bass. The hamour — the biggest weigh nearly 14 kilos — live under rock ledges near the coast. Another favourite is the kan'ad, a silver-coloured king mackerel weighing about nine kilos. For those who don't enjoy fishing, beachcombing can be as attractive as swimming in the clear waters.

Sailing is taken up by many people for the first time when they come here, but they must have a licence. The sandy beaches of Half Moon Bay, where the water drops rapidly to about seven or eight metres, is good for boating. Winds are sometimes strong, but the sea never becomes turbulent because there is no open stretch of water in which the wind can pile up waves (see Sea Sports).

Be careful when exploring the desert. Apart from five types of harmless snake, there is the venomous sand viper and the common scorpion. Four-wheel-drive vehicles are essential for those who want to go off the beaten track. When travelling, take food, extra petrol, and lots of water, and wear a head covering. If your car gets stuck in the sand, stay with it. Lone stragglers are less noticeable in the desert than a stricken car (see Desert Travel).

Gardening

Gardening enthusiasts find that where there is water almost anything can be grown — from maidenhair fern to eucalyptus. December and January is the planting season. Seeds and peat are sold at the supermarkets and florists. Manure is available at Hobby

Farm nurseries in Qatif, Saihat, and at Dammam which will also supply sweet sand and fertiliser. Bulbs such as tulips, narcissus, scilla and daffodil do not do well, but carnations, sunflowers, hollyhocks and periwinkle will thrive. Suitable shrubs include frangipani, bougainvillaea, and oleander.

Hydroponic farming experiments at Aramco produce mouth-watering tomatoes which have never touched the soil. Polythene greenhouses protect plants from the heat of the sun and from fierce sandstorms.

Social

A few professional groups combine business with pleasure. The Society of Petroleum Engineers sponsors lecturers at its monthly meetings at Aramco which are open to the public (tel: 8743249). There is also an Arabian Gulf section of the American Association of Cost Engineers which meets at Aramco. The Arabian National History Association has two branches, one in ARAMCO and one in Al-Khobar. Lectures range from subjects such as Arabian archaeology to bird watching.

Bridge addicts can play daily at one compound or another. There is also a bridge tournament for players from all over the kingdom.

The universities provide some social life. The University of Petroleum & Minerals has a distinguished lecturers series

In sports, the Dhahran rugby club, the Al-Khobar tennis tournament, the Al-Khobar open table tennis tournament, fencing and squash tournaments break the monotony of the working week.

For the adventurous or those feeling wanderlust, the Dhahran Outing Group is a non-profit organisation open to all Aramco employees, although non-members can attend meetings. The group started 24 years ago with 22 members — now there are more than 1,300, and branches in Ras Tanura and Abqaiq. Monthly meetings are held in Dhahran, and members come from as far as Riyadh, Taif and Jeddah to attend meetings and take part in group outings. The group sponsors several trips throughout the peninsula, to Bahrain by dhow, and to points east.

Local dining

Westerners are often surprised to find that Saudis traditionally eat seated on the floor around a clean cloth. Eat with the right hand only; dip it into the communal platter, squeeze some rice into a firm ball, and pop it into the mouth. Kabsa is the speciality of Eastern province. Sambousik, m'tabbel, and stuffed chicken are popular imports from Lebanon. Pavement vendors on the main street of Dammam sell falafel (deep-fried pastry filled with hummus), shawarmas (broiled lamb with tomatoes and onions) and grilled chicken.

Chairs are rarely used in the family room; guests and family sit propped up against the wall on cushions. The sexes are strictly segregated. If a woman receives an invitation from a girlfriend, she should assume it is for her alone. Women do not usually call when the husband's car can be seen parked outside.

At Saudi ladies' parties everyone is dressed up to the nines, and there is an air of innocent merriment. First the pale-green Arabic coffee and sweets are passed around, then a glass of Pepsi. An hour or so later guests feast on whole lamb, huge platters of rice, and salad.

After dinner the dancing begins. The hostess or one of her daughters will start, pulling to her feet first one, then another seemingly reluctant friend. As the party gets going, ladies ululate and clap to encourage their dancing friends.

Men arriving to collect their wives wait outside in the fresh air under strings of naked light bulbs hoisted from tree to roof for the occasion. Inside, incense is passed around in a smoking silver brazier for each guest to waft into her hair and garments.

Women

Few western women can get work permits. Those who do are often surprised by the benefits accorded them by Saudi labour law. Extensive maternity leave before and after birth, nursery care at work, and time off to breast feed the baby make motherhood easier to combine with work than in many western countries.

The Al-Salama hospital in Al-Khobar has two obstetricians, Dr Saleh and Dr Marzouk, both British-trained and well thought of. The usual 48-hour stay costs SR 1,500-2,000. Babies stay in their mothers' room so feeding is on demand. Medical care is adequate but not lavish.

The Abdullah Fouad hospital in Dammam, opened in 1979, offers ante-natal classes for eight weeks preceding delivery (about SR 40 each). The maternity wing has 10 double rooms. Babies are kept in the nursery, except for scheduled feeding times. The cost for a normal delivery is SR 1,200, plus about SR 400 a day for room, board, and medical care.

At the smaller Dr Fakhri hospital in Al-Khobar, the consultant is assisted by a midwife during delivery. Babies are brought to their mothers three times a day, and a consultant visits twice a day.

Whatever the hospital chosen, the parents must get from the hospital business office both an Arabic and an English certificate of live birth. These documents are important if there is any delay in obtaining the official Saudi birth certificate.

Pets

It is difficult to bring in pets — and almost impossible to import dogs. Only the saluki, the famed hunting dog, is considered clean. Veterinary services are available at the Arabian Kennel Club, PO Box 2418, Dhahran Mail Centre (tel: 8743517 for emergency). Vets see pets between 0800-0900 and 1100-1300 at Building 1941 in Aramco on a first-come, first-served basis. The service is open to non-Aramco employees.

Vets visit Abqaiq on Sunday afternoon (tel: 8724236 for appointment) and Ras Tanura on Tuesday afternoon (tel: 8735106).

Diplomatic services

US Tel: 8913200, 8913452, 8913613.

The US consulate-general is in its own compound, just off the road leading to the University of Petroleum & Minerals, opposite the Petroleum Ministry. It is the only foreign government office in Eastern province to offer complete consular services to Americans and non-Americans alike. Open Saturday-Wednesday 0800-1230, 1400-1530.

UK Tel: 8948011, ext 1443. Al-Khobar.

A British consular official is now resident in Al-Khobar. 0800-1400 Sat-Wed, 0800-1200 Thurs.

West Germany Tel: 8643586. Al-Khobar.

A West German consular official comes every three months to the Lufthansa office on King Fahd Street. He will renew or issue passports and help nationals fill out tax exemption forms. Three weeks before the visit, West German companies in the area are informed; Lufthansa informs smaller subcontractors. The airline helps its own passengers with visas and will ensure customers' passports are returned from Jeddah after issue of the visa.

France Tel: 8649129. Abdullah Fouad Centre.

There is a full-time French trade commissioner, Herve Thenot, who serves the interests of the 2,500-strong French community working in the province.

Italy Tel: 8649480. Al-Khobar.

Pakistan Tel: 8645777. Pakistani School, off King Abdul-Aziz Street, one block behind Maxim's Restaurant.

The Pakistani community is visited every two months by consular officials from Jeddah who stay for two weeks to complete necessary business.

Getting around

Air travel

Dhahran international airport
The new international airport is used by about 2,000 people an hour. It has a telex and international telephone centre with six international telephones, and a post office as well as a telex system. In the arrivals section are an Al-Rajhi hotel information office, five telephone booths and a cafeteria, while the departures section has a pharmacy, an Al-Rajhi money exchange, seven telephone booths, a mosque, a shop selling electronic equipment and suitcases, and a 250-seat restaurant. A Hanco bus system connects the international and domestic terminals, which are several hundred metres apart. Public buses operated by Saptco run every 60 minutes between the airport and Dammam and Al-Khobar (SR 10 and SR 5 respectively).

Domestic terminal
The new domestic terminal is separate from the main airport. Hanco car hire is near the entrance and there is a small bookshop on the way to the departure lounge which has a cafeteria, an Al-Rajhi money exchange, two freephones for calls to Aramco, Dammam and Al-Khobar, and several telephone booths for long-distance calls. The single fare Riyadh-Dhahran is SR 120 and Jeddah-Dhahran SR 680. Flight information, tel: 8792600.

Air communications
International From Dhahran daily to Bahrain, London and New York; regular flights to Athens, Bombay, Cairo, Frankfurt, Karachi, Paris and Rome. Also flights to Abu Dhabi, Aden, Amman, Baghdad, Bangkok, Beirut, Damascus, Geneva, Hongkong, Istanbul, Kuwait, Muscat, Seoul, Shiraz, Singapore and Zurich (some international flights are via Riyadh).

Domestic Direct daily flights to Al-Madinah, Hofuf, Jeddah, Riyadh; direct flights to Qassim, Jizan, Najran and Taif.

Saudia Tel: reservations 8943333; airport cargo services 8647340. PO Box 126, Dhahran airport.

Airlines in Al-Khobar
See also general sales agents listed under Travel Agencies.
Air France Tel: 8947474, 8947701. PO Box 171, Dhahran airport. Al-Tahlawi Building, 4th Street, opposite Gazzaz Cosmetics.
Air India Tel: 8943358, 8943953. Airlines Centre.
Alia, the Royal Jordanian Airline Tel: 8641238, 8641231. King Khaled Street.
Alitalia Tel: 8641867, 8645239, 8645924. Kanoo Centre, near intersection of King Abdul-Aziz Street and 28th Street.
Cathay Pacific Tel: 8942727. PO Box 1004. Abdullah Fouad Centre, King Abdul-Aziz Street.
China Airways Tel: 8649733, 8649740, 8644051.
Cyprus Airways Tel: 8947476.
EgyptAir Tel: 864207, 8644051. PO Box 561. King Khaled Street and Airport Road.
Gulf Air Tel: 8648473, 8643670, 8646161. PO Box 189. King Khaled Street.
Iran Air Tel: 8642076.
Iraqi Airways Tel: 8795284.
Japan Airlines Tel: 8642076.

AL-KHOBAR

HOTELS
Al-Gosaibi **E1 5**
Al-Khaja **D2 16**
Al-Khobar Palace **D2 12**
Al-Mana **E2 10**
Meridien **E1 8**
Al-Nimrah **D1 3**
Royal Hotel **D1 4**

King's Palace **E1 9**
Al-Nimran Consulting Office **D2 13**

Pepsi-Cola factory/fountain **E1 7**
Saudi British Bank **E1 6**

RESTAURANTS
Shahrazad Restaurant **D2 11**

HOSPITALS
Dr Fakhri Hospital **D3 17**
Al-Salamah Hospital **E3 23**
Al-Sharq Hospital **D3 21**

TRAVEL
International Travel Agency **D1 2**

GOVERNMENT ORGANISATIONS AND DEPARTMENTS
Al-Khobar Municipality **D3 19**
Al-Khobar Police Station **E3 25**

Al-Khobar Post & Telegraph Office **D3 18**
Labour Office **D2 15**
Ministry of Justice **D3 22**
Ministry of Labour & Social Affairs **D2 14**
Passport Office **E3 24**
Telephone Exchange **D3 20**
Al-Thuqbah Police Station **D4 26**

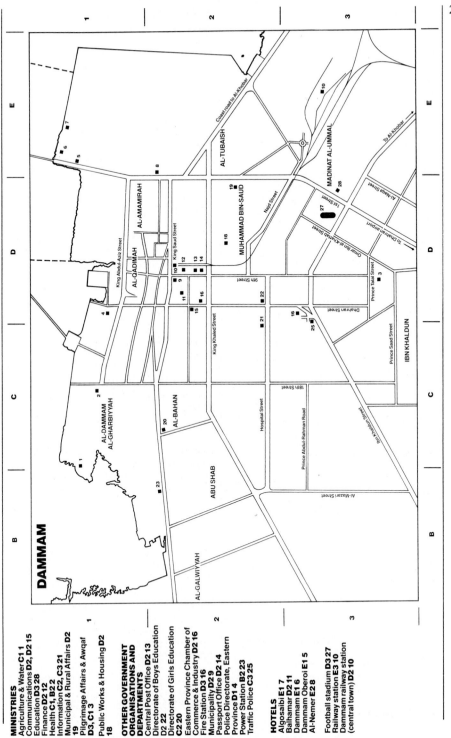

KLM/Royal Dutch Airlines Tel: 8951234. Kanoo Centre, King Abdul-Aziz Street.
Korean Airlines Tel: 8645233. PO Box 179.
Kuwait Airways Tel: 8947240, 8642102. PO Box 115. King Abdul-Aziz Street.
Lufthansa Tel: 8943586, 8947800. PO Box 7. Near intersection of King Fahd and First streets.
Middle East Airlines Tel: 8641648, 8646118; airport tel: 8792365. Intersection of Alef and Prince Nasir streets.
Nigeria Airways Tel: 8647624, 8648065.
Olympic Airways Tel: 8644416, 8646282. General agent: Zahid Travel Agencies, Al-Qahtani Building, Airport Road. Telex: 671376 zatrvl.
Pakistan International Airlines Tel: 8643033, 8642591. PO Box 392. Amir Nasir Street.
Pan Am Tel: 8942977, 8943144; airport tel: 8795289. Open 1500-0200.
Royal Air Maroc Tel: 8649726. In Riyadh Tower Building, intersection of King Abdu-Aziz and 28th streets.
Sabena Tel: 8646601, 8946601. Al-Qahtani Building, Airport Road.
Saudia Tel: 8943333 reservations; ticket office 8645555; airport cargo services 8645555, ext 250. PO Box 126, Dhahran airport.
Singapore Airlines Tel: 8646025, 8951515, 8645545. PO Box 1760. Intersection of Alef and Prince Nasir streets, above MEA building.
Swissair Tel: 8951212. PO Box 122. Kanoo Centre, near intersection of King Abdul-Aziz and 28th streets.
Syrian Arab Airlines Tel: 8641930.
Thai Airways Tel: 8648065, 8647624.
TWA Tel: 8641034. Agent: Ameco Travel Agencies, PO Box 1785. Airport Road, by the Al-Sharq hospital.
Turkish Airlines Tel: 8646308.

Car hire

Avis Tel: 8646085. PO Box 2169, Water Tower Road, Dhahran. Telex: 401384 best sj. Other branches: Al-Nimran hotel, tel: 8645861; airport office, tel: 8792202; Al-Hamra Ambassador hotel, tel: 8327877. For models and rates see Jeddah section.

Arabian Hala Company Al-Khobar: Tel: 8641376, PO Box 1663, King Abdul-Aziz Street, Dhahran: Dhahran airport, tel: 8649488, 8792930; Dhahran Marriott hotel, tel: 8948222. Dammam: Al-Nemer hotel, tel: 8320546, 8320641.

Godfrey Davis/Hanco Rent-a-Car Al-Khobar: Algosaibi hotel, tel: 8942466; Meridien hotel, tel: 8646000; Marriott hotel, tel: 8948222; Ramada hotel, tel: 8645444. Dammam: tel: 8325517, PO Box 2284, telex: 601295; Dammam hotel, tel: 8329000; Dammam Oberoi hotel, tel: 8345555. Dhahran: domestic airport terminal, tel: 8649813; international terminal, tel: 8792290.

Codeco Tel: 8642126. PO Box 266, Codeco Building, Airport Road, Al-Khobar. Telex: 670037. Also offers van and pick-up rentals.

Model	Daily rate (SR)*
Volkswagen Beetle	60

* unlimited mileage. Weekly rental 10 per cent discount, monthly rental 20 per cent discount.

BCR Tel: 8642217. Prince Hamood Street, Al-Khobar. Telex: 670169 fatin.

Model	Daily rate (SR)*
Toyota Corolla	95
Buick Park Avenue	230

* 100 kilometres free a day. Weekly rental 15 per cent discount.

Sahary Rent-a-Car Tel: 8948555. PO Box 428, Dhahran airport.

Hotels

Al-Khobar

Carlton al-Moaibed Hotel Tel: 8575455, 8575429. PO Box 1235. Nine kilometres from Dhahran airport between Al-Khobar, Dammam and Dhahran. Telex: 670064 carlton.

All rooms have individually controlled airconditioning, TV, video, radio and mini-fridge.

Coffee shop open 24 hours, international restaurant, barbecue. Outdoor swimming pool, tennis court, billiards, bowling alley, sauna, judo and karate. Barber shop, gift shop and travel agency. Secretarial, typing and translation services.

Rates: single SR 281, double SR 338, suite SR 563, cabana SR 225; plus 15% service.

Cards: American Express, Visa, Mastercharge and Eurocard.

Al-Khaja Hotel Tel: 8643122, 8643538, PO Box 45, First Street. Telex: 670025.

Chinese restaurant.

Rates: (old building) single SR 125, single (two guests) SR 140, double (one guest) SR 156, double (two guests) SR 188; (new building) single SR 150, double SR 175, twin SR 225.

Al-Nimran Tel: 8645618. PO Box 340, Pepsi-Cola Street. Telex: 670147 nimran.

50 rooms, including two three-bedroom penthouse apartments with cooking facilities. Each has individually controlled airconditioning, bathroom, TV and radio.

Cafeteria open 24 hours, Italian restaurant. Conference rooms, telex facilities, library. Hairdresser and barber shop.

Rates: single SR 185, double SR 210, suites SR 250-700; plus 15% service.

Credit card: American Express.

Rezayat Apartments Tel: 8576829. PO Box 90, five kilometres north of city centre. Telex: 670006 rezyat sj.

263 bachelor service apartments, each with bathroom, airconditioning and fridge. All receive daily servicing. Self-service restaurant, recreation centre, swimming pool, squash and tennis courts.

Rates: on request.

Algosaibi Hotel Tel: 8942466, 8946466. PO Box 51, Dhahran airport. Talal Avenue, extension of Pepsi-Cola Street, behind Pepsi-Cola factory. Telex: 670008 gostel. Managed by Grand Metropolitan Hotels.

Opened in 1973, the oldest first-class hotel in Eastern province. Elegantly decorated by New York interior designers Stylist/Durrell. Has its own sweet water supply and a back-up system for generating electricity should the public current fail. All rooms have bathroom and video showing three films a day.

It has an immaculate kitchen where it bakes its own bread and croissants. Prime beef is imported from the US. Its superb coffee brew comes from the local Bayoumi Stores. The restaurant's buffet lunch is a large display of hors d'oeuvres, cold meats, giant prawns and sweets.

Caters for weddings of up to 1,000 guests. Kabsas, sheep feasts ("mutton grabs" to expatriates) can be arranged at short notice. Seminars by major companies and airlines are regularly held at the hotel. During Queen Elizabeth's visit in 1979, the Algosaibi

Al-Khobar's oldest 5-star hotel

was used as a press centre for journalists covering the event.

Has a business centre, bank, car hire offices, Olympic-size swimming pool, three tennis courts, 12-lane bowling alley, and hairdresser and courier service.

Rates: single (not usually available) SR 282, double SR 338, suite SR 390, small suite SR 450, deluxe suite SR 563, small villa SR 900, large villa with three bedrooms SR 1,200, poolside cabana room SR 360; plus 15% service.

Credit cards: American Express, Diners Club, Access, Mastercharge, Visa.

Royal Hotel Tel: 8644076, 8646664, 8647917. PO Box 673, Prince Hamood Street. Telex: 670056.

140 rooms, with private bath, TV and fridge.

Family-style restaurant featuring French and Lebanese food. Hamour, its fish speciality, costs SR 35 and a plat du jour lunch, including crudites, is SR 28; plus 10% service. Offers secretarial services in French and English; 24-hour restaurant and room service. 200-seat conference room available free to guests.

Rates: single SR 125, double SR 156; plus 10% service.

Al-Khobar Palace Tel: 8648671. PO Box 25, Dhahran airport. 10th Street, near intersection with Prince Hamood Street. Telex: 670169 ashraf.

50 rooms; six suites.

Al-Diwan Restaurant on first floor serves Lebanese and American dishes. In-house video. Conference room seating 150. Barber shop, coffee shop.

Rates: single SR 150, double SR 180, SR 240 suite (single occupancy); plus 10% service.

Gulf Meridien Tel: 8646000. PO Box 1266. Corniche Boulevard, 28th Street. Telex: 670505 homer.

351 rooms, including 20 suites and royal suite. All have balcony with sea view, airconditioning, telephone, TV and video, private bathroom, mini-bar and fridge.

Cafe de Paris serves evening buffet costing SR 70; Hatem al-Tai specialises in Middle East food and serves a few Chinese and Japanese dishes; also bar, tea lounge and beach terrace snack bar. Bank, car hire, bookshop, gift shop, jewellery store, travel agent, barber shop. Business centre with four conference, banquet and exhibition rooms with 29-900 seats. Sports facilities include swimming pool, two squash and tennis courts, sauna, recreation room and private beach.

Rates: single SR 300, double SR 360, suite SR 450-600; corporate discount SR 45; plus 15% service.

Credit cards: Amexco, Visa, Eurocard, Diners Club, Mastercharge, Access.

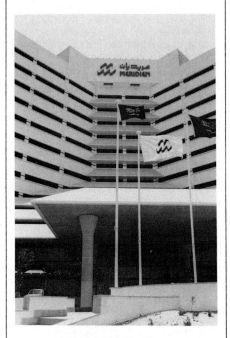

Al-Khobar's Meridien

Dammam

Balhamar Hotel Tel: 8320117, 8320181, 8320484. PO Box 2259. Facing National Commercial Bank near Finance Ministry. Telex: 601167 baotel.

All rooms have a music system,

video programmes, telephone, TV and mini-fridge.

Coffee shop and restaurant offer oriental and continental dishes, plus buffet. Facilities for outside catering and wedding parties. Airconditioned and insured American cars available for hire.

Rates: double SR 188, double (two guests) SR 225, one-bedroom suite with drawing room SR 300; also deluxe villas and suites; plus 15% service.

Credit card: American Express.

Al-Hamra Hotel Tel: 8333444, 8334002. PO Box 1411. King Khaled Street, between 10th and 11th streets. Telex: 601449, cable: shihotel.

160 rooms, all airconditioned with bath, telephone, TV and radio.

Grill Room serves international haute cuisine; Chinese restaurant and coffee shop. Party and banqueting facilities for 120 people. Secretarial services, limousine service. Billiards, table tennis, squash court and gymnasium.

Rates: single SR 185-230, double SR 250, double (two guests) SR 290-350, junior suite SR 400, executive suite SR 600; inclusive of service.

Credit cards: Access, Intercard, Mastercharge.

Dammam Hotel Tel: 8329000. PO Box 1928, First Street, 25 minutes' drive from Dhahran airport. Telex: 601108 dhotel; cable: dammamtel.

All rooms have private bath and telephone; suites have colour TV, telephone and fridge. Private villas — each with two bedrooms, bath, kitchen and lounge — are equipped with colour TV, telephone and fridge.

Restaurant serves Middle East, international and Indian dishes — at SR 45, its buffet is one of the best buys in town. Coffee shop serves informal meals and snacks. Private room for seminars and conferences, secretarial service, photocopying. Same-day laundry and dry-cleaning, car hire,

courtesy airport pick-up. Swimming pool.

Rates: single SR 140, double SR 165, suite SR 190, villa SR 500; plus 10% service.

Dammam Oberoi Hotel Tel: 8345555. PO Box 5397. Telex: 602071 obhotel.

277 rooms. All are airconditioned, with TV and fridge.

Al-Gazelle Restaurant serves French and Lebanese food; Al-Bustan coffee shop opens 24 hours and features a daily lunch buffet; roof-top Le Chinois restaurant with traditional lamp, red carpet and beaded curtains. Limousine for airport and downtown transfers, travel desk, banqueting and conference facilities for 1,000. Health club, gymnasium, swimming pool, flood-lit tennis courts.

Rates: single SR 300, double SR 360, suites SR 450-600, royal suite SR 2,500; plus 10% service.

Al-Kadi Hotel Tel: 8327235-6. PO Box 2151. Telex: 601151.

Alarifi Tel: 8334444. PO Box 1448. One block north of railway station, at the corner of King Faisal and 9th streets. Telex: 601249.

80 well-decorated rooms, with colour TV.

Caravanserai Restaurant serves English, French and Arab food. Conference room suite for large meetings.

Rates: single from SR 200; plus 15% service.

Al-Nemer Hotel Tel: 8320641, 8320111. PO Box 4997, First Street, facing public garden. Telex: 601149 nemtel.

Andalusia Restaurant serves Lebanese and French specialities. Continental breakfast SR 15, lunch SR 35, dinner SR 40.

Rates: single SR 160, double SR 200, double (two guests) SR 240; travel agents and airlines get special prices, and terms can be quoted for long stays; plus 15% service.

Credit card: American Express.

Dhahran

Dhahran International Hotel Tel: 8948555. PO Box 428. Four minutes from Dhahran airport. Telex: 601272 diah.

The shining blue and marble facade, which incorporates an ancient Arab arch in modern form, catches the eye of visitors as they leave the airport a few yards away. The lobby is exotic, with open spaces and greenery, a trickling pool and rock garden.

All rooms have a luxury bathroom, colour TV, direct-dial telephone and message waiting signal.

Restaurant with international cuisine and 24-hour coffee shop. Offices with secretarial and translation services, telex and Reuter services. Conference and banqueting facilities for up to 1,000 people. Shopping arcade. Swimming pool.

Rates: twin SR 300, twin (two guests) SR 360, executive suite SR 450, presidential suite SR 600, royal suite SR 1,000; plus 15% service.

Credit card: American Express.

Dhahran Palace Hotel Ramada Tel: 8645444, 8645333. PO Box 381, Dhahran airport. Near Aramco, 10 minutes from Dhahran airport on the crossroads to Riyadh to the west, and Ras Tanura and Kuwait to the north. Telex: 601227 ramada.

All rooms have private bathroom, closed-circuit films, individual airconditioning, telephone and mini-fridge, 24-hour room service.

The Falcon and Al-Bustan restaurants serve international food with fish a speciality; light snacks also available at recreation centre. Telex and secretarial service; bank/exchange bureau. Doctor on 24-hour call. Poolside cafe, 25-metre swimming pool, billiards, pool, four-lane automatic bowling alley, gym and sauna.

"Breakaway" weekends cost SR 300 for one and SR 470 for a couple; children under 18 may book individual rooms at half price or share parents' room for an extra SR 100. The price includes a candelight dinner at the Falcon Restaurant, a four-course buffet lunch and continental breakfast. Special reduced rates for children's menus; babysitting; playground with swings, seesaws, roundabouts and rocking boats. For parties of 10 or more a guided tour of nearby Qatif oasis can be arranged, with shopping in the old souq.

Rates: single SR 220, double SR 286; plus 15% service.

Communications

Post office

Dammam has several: post office No 2 on 9th Street is perhaps the most convenient. All sell postage stamps and accept registered mail; No 2 also has a public telex. The main post office is at the intersection of 23rd Street and Qatif Road, opposite the Girls' Education Building. Branches include one beside the Al-Adana hospital and another east of the Red Crescent hospital.

Al-Khobar Post Office No 1, Airport Road, near the municipality building. Open daily 0800-1330. Provides only postal services. Trunk calls can be made in the building behind No 1, open 24 hours.

Telex and telegram

Al-Khobar Opposite Mazda showroom, King Saud Street. The ground floor cable office is open six days a week from 0730-2400, with interruptions from 1230-1300 and 2030-2100. The telex office upstairs is open seven days a week, 24 hours a day.

Many businesses prefer to telex from the large hotels. These are usually open to non-residents with a three-minute minimum, as at the Algosaibi and the Dhahran Marriott.

Courier services

Al-Khobar
SNAS-DHL Tel: 8645522, 8640471. PO Box 2136. Off King Abdul-Aziz Street. Telex: 670404 snascr. Travelling along King Abdul-Aziz Street away from Dammam turn right at the Peugeot dealer's showroom. Immediately past the showroom turn right on to a vacant block of land. You will then see the office.

Skypak Tel: 8643472. PO Box 481. Ground floor, NAJD Trading Building, near Jazeera Clinic. Telex: 671206 najd.

IML Couriers Tel: 8942466, ext 119. PO Box 51, Dhahran airport. Algosaibi hotel. Telex: 670008 gostel.

Dammam
SNAS-DHL Telex: 670494 snascr sj. (Dhahran).

Skypak Tel: 8340293, 8340349. PO Box 2284. First floor, Ibrahim Establishment Building, opposite King Faisal Street mosque. Telex: 601295 hanco.

Hofuf
SNAS-DHL Tel: 5864174. Telex: 670494 snascr sj (Dhahran).

Travel agents

Kanoo Travel Agency
This is a name which has been synonymous with travel in Saudi Arabia and the Gulf for 32 years. Kanoo has 14 offices in Riyadh, Jeddah and Eastern province, and covers group travel (special bookings for social or sports club travel); incentive schemes for employees; booking services for conference and exhibition travel; local holiday travel in the Gulf; business travel (air travel, hotel and reservations) and car hire. There is a computerised booking system at Dhahran for general travel; also insurance cover for personal accident, medical expenses and baggage. Its brochure gives full details of package tours to most parts of the world.

Al-Khobar
International Travel Agency Tel: 8641993, 8645968. Kaki Building, Prince Nasir Street. Also King Abdul-Aziz Street, tel: 8946577, 8942424, 8945924.

Kanoo Travel Agency Tel: 8641992, 8647471, 8643755. King Khaled Street.

Kanoo Holidays Tel: 8442020-1, 8447718, 8646879. Kanoo Centre.

Dammam
Kanoo Travel Agency Tel: 8322499, 8323789. PO Box 37, King Faisal Street. Telex: 601011 kanoo. Also Dammam Oberoi hotel, tel: 8345555, ext 2404.

Dhahran
International Travel Agency Tel: 8792436-7, 8792663. Dhahran airport.

Kanoo Travel Agency Tel: 8948222. Dhahran Marriott hotel.

Ras Tanura
Kanoo Travel Agency Tel: 6670388, 6737147, 6735159, ext 38.

Ras al-Khafji
Kanoo Travel Agency Tel: 7660045.

Jubail
Kanoo Travel Agency Tel: 3611069, 3611337.

Other travel agencies
The International Women's Group (see Recreation) and Aramco's Dhahran

Outing Group arrange tours for newcomers to Eastern province.

Al-Khobar

Areen Travel Tel: 8948411, 8946601. King Abdul-Aziz Street; tel: 8643221, Airport Road, Al-Qahtani Building.

Ocean Travel Tel: 8648349; 8648543; 8648593, 8648577. PO Box 250, Dhahran airport. Telex: 671451 falkho. On ground floor of the Fluor Arabia Building on the Dammam to Al-Khobar highway. Friendly and comprehensive service; recommended for company patronage.

National Agency Tel: 8646752. King Khaled Street, next to Air France office. Should be consulted by the economy-minded.

Atlas Travel Tel: 8647176, 8642703. PO Box 650. Prince Talal Street, opposite the Saudi British Bank. Is helpful in working out itineraries for those suffering from travel shock.

ACE Travel Agents Tel: 8944400. Pan Am agent.

International Travel Agency Tel: 8946577. Kanoo Centre.

Globe Travel Tel: 8645472. PO Box 40, Prince Nasir Street, Telex: 671429 world.

Kurban Travel Agents Tel: 8649824, 8649835. Telex: 670576 kurban.

The Travellers' Travel & Services Tel: 8646167; 8641436, 8646717. PO Box 321, King Khaled Street, Suwaiket Building. Telex: 670193 aziz.

Saudi Travel & Tourist Agency (Statco) Tel: 8643670, 8644390. PO Box 189, Dhahran airport.

Jet Travel Agency Tel: 8644613, 8644849. PO Box 373, Kaki Building, Airport Road.

Yousuf al-Gosaibi Travel Agency Tel: 8641916, 8641922. PO Box 106, off King Khaled Street.

Misr Travel Tel: 6849449. Almutlaq Commercial Centre.

Space Travel Agency Tel: 8649122, 8946780. King Abdul-Aziz Street.

Saudi Tourist & Travel Bureau Tel: 8642076, 8644051. Airport Road.

Pan Arab Travel Agency Tel: 8641715, 8648079. King Khaled Street.

Sahara Travel Tel: 8641986. Algahtani Building, Airport Road. Telex: 670031 hakirm.

Ewan Travel Tel: 8944414, PO Box 344, Dhahran airport. Telex: 671415, cable: ewan. Group excursions to Bangkok.

Dammam

Saudi Tourist & Travel Bureau Tel: 8325249. Dhahran airport, tel. 8792565, 8795151.

Pan Arab Travel Agency PO Box 131, King Khaled Street. Telex: 601030.

Al-Dabal Travels Tel: 8326095. PO Box 1102, Prince Mansour Street. Telex: 60124 aldabai.

Bassam Travel & Tourism Tel: 8326835, 8325247, 8322881. PO Box 285, King Saud Street. Telex: 601021 alfahad, cable: alfahad.

Dossary Travel & Shipping Agency Tel: 8328217, 8325786. PO Box 990, Airport Road. Telex: 601580 bnbate, cable: benbete.

Intercontinental Travel Company Tel: 8647637. PO Box 2093, 28th Street.

Almojil Travel Agency Tel: 8647264, 8648065, 28th Street. Agent for Thai Airways.

Dhahran

Pan Arab Travel Agency Tel: 8645720, 8645921. Ramada hotel.

Abqaiq

Saudi Tourist & Travel Bureau Tel: 5661845.

REAL ESTATE BROKERS

JEDDAH – YANBU – RIYADH
FOR RENT/SALE

FURNISHED FLATS, APARTMENTS, VILLAS, COMPOUNDS, OFFICE SPACE AND LAND SUITABLE FOR DEVELOPMENT. COMPOUND DEVELOPMENT A SPECIALITY

ALSO

INTERIOR DECORATING, MAINTENANCE, AND SWIMMING POOL CONSTRUCTION SERVICES

INTERNATIONAL PROPERTY FOR SALE

APARTMENTS, VILLAS, CHALETS, LAND AND COMMERCIAL PROPERTY IN SPAIN, CYPRUS, SWITZERLAND, FRANCE AND THE UNITED STATES
FOR FURTHER DETAILS PLEASE CONTACT: SIP

الشركة السعودية الدولية للعقارات

Saudi International Properties
P.O. Box 2734, Jeddah, Saudi Arabia
Tel: 6672098/6672099 Telex: 400577 SIPROP SJ

General Sales Agents

Asia's first Airline.
5 times weekly Dhahran – Manila non stop

Canadian Pacific

Reservations:
Alkhobar 8944360, 8642510
Dammam 8266858, 8266954

PO Box 654 Dhahran Airport

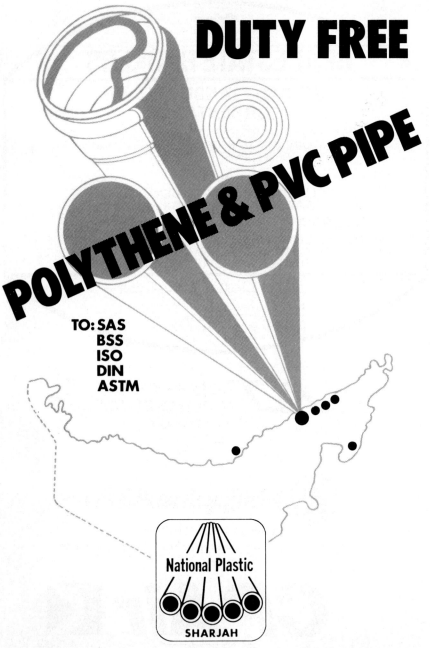

Riyadh – looking southeast

Vegetable market, Riyadh

Primary school, Jeddah

Luxury homes, Jeddah

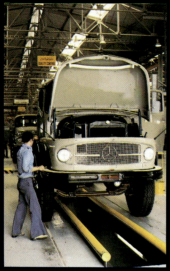

Saudi Mercedes factory

SAPTCO double-deck bus, Jeddah

Jubail – Yanbu pipeline

Jaramax 17 dropping anchors

Eating out

The China Palace Tel: 8947604. First floor of a new building in Abdul-Aziz Street, next to the Thomas Cook Travel Agency and near the crossroads with 16th Street.

It has two public dining rooms and three private dining rooms, richly decorated in red and gold. An extensive menu offers dishes from all parts of China, prepared and served to the strains of piped Chinese popular music. Paper-wrapped chicken, at SR 26, is a starter to be recommended.

The Vienna Woods Tel: 8648257. Just off 28th (Pepsi-Cola) Street, five blocks east of the intersection with King Abdul-Aziz Street, Al-Khobar.

Five years ago, Herr Blum's 380-year-old farmhouse nestled in the hills above Lake Constance. It has since been dismantled, containerised, and reassembled to make the interior decor of Al-Khobar's most popular restaurant. Patrons dine on their favourite schnitzels by the light of converted egg baskets and wheel axles. Apple juice is served in inverted carafes. Two rooms, one downstairs with places for 60 and one recently completed upstairs with capacity for 30; open for lunch 1200-1500 and dinner 1900-2300. Meal for one about SR 115.

The Rendezvous Owned by Souq Company; same shopping complex as the main Souq supermarket, on the Military Trunk Road nearly two kilometres north of the intersection of that road and the Riyadh to Al-Khobar road. A bright, biggish room seating 100.

Specialises in short order food, modestly priced, such as haricot beef for SR 20 and sausage 'n mash for SR 18. Managed by Taylorplan Catering, it will soon offer oriental cuisine in a more restaurant-like atmosphere. Open 0900-2200; no service charge, tipping discouraged.

Kentucky Fried Chicken/Pizza Hut/ Mr Sizzler Al-Khobar, in the Al-Ahlia Company's building at the corner of Airport Road and Amir Hamoud Ibn Abdul-Aziz Street.

Kentucky Fried Chicken lost part of its floor space to the Wimpey chain's Pizza Hut, which opened in 1980. Colonel Sanders' secret recipe is imported along with the chicken for this 50-seater restaurant — two-piece chicken snacks SR 8, dinner of three pieces plus French fries SR 12.

Upstairs Mr Sizzler Family Steak House serves Canadian T-bone steaks at SR 29 to a predominantly American clientele. Salad costs SR 6 with a steak, or SR 10 by itself.

Open from 1130-2400; seats 80. Has parquet walls and its window overlooks the traffic which flows continuously along Airport Road. More of a restaurant than its fast food neighbours downstairs; offers, like them, a takeaway service.

Kentucky Fried Chicken has branches in Dammam, in Khazan Street near the central vegetable and fruit market (tel: 8347075), and Jubail in Jeddah Street.

Pizzeria Portofino Tel: 8951796. One block behind the Khashoggi building on Airport Road.

Some of Al-Khobar's tiniest pizzas and cappuccino coffee. The tiny cafe seats only 12 on tall stools; principally takeaway service. Pizzas cost SR 12.50-18. Chef Hussain Asfour is in business from 1100-1400 and 1700-2230 every day.

New Seoul Restaurant Tel: 8327235. In Kadi Hotel, Dammam (see hotels). Korean food.

Maxim Tel: 8642004. In the same building as the Saudi Investment Banking Corporation, on King Abdul-Aziz Street.

Local adaptation of famous French restaurant. Redecorated early 1980 and sub-divided into a quick-service snack bar, seating 60, and a proper dining room with the same capacity.

Both serve the same food, but the snack bar's decor is Italian tile-and-glass while the restaurant half is swathed in Richelieu red velvet with a marbled mirror ceiling. The Lebanese staff specialise, of course, in Lebanese cuisine — the traditional mezze at SR 30 for two is recommended. Standard French fare from Chateaubriand steak down is available. Open daily except Friday, from 1000-2400.

Broasted Abu-Nawas Tel: 8326363. One of Dammam's modest landmarks, at the corner of Prince Mansour and 9th streets.

Snack bar and takeaway open 1130-0300 for hungry night owls. This Syrian-run eatery specialises in fish and chicken, done in Damascene style. A full chicken is SR 20 and fish ranges from SR 12-21, for small to extra-large portions. Recently redecorated; seats 24 at tables and half as many at a counter which wraps around the room.

Dhahran Airport Restaurant In international arrivals and departures building.

Quick service guaranteed, 24-hour service, seven days a week; seats 400. Indian, continental and Lebanese food — hamburger SR 7, filet mignon SR 40, both appropriately garnished; plus 15% service.

Jade Garden Restaurant Tel: 8949092. 16th Street, two blocks west of King Abdul-Aziz Street, Al-Khobar.

New Chinese restaurant, on the first floor of the building, offers a businessman's lunch at SR 40. Cantonese seafood dishes are recommended. Open 1130-1400 and 1730-2230.

La Fonda Desierta Tel: 8943228. PO Box 533, Al-Khobar. Corner of 16th and Prince Miqrin Streets.

Sombreros on the wall and piped Mexican music set the tone of this delightful four-room restaurant. Serves sour cream enchiladas (SR 27) and tacos al carbon (SR 39) with luncheon specials and barbecue. Empenada for two (dessert of Mexican pastry filled with banana, pecans, raisins and honey) SR 18; plus 10% service. Not cheap but the food is excellent. Takeaway service; caters for parties on or off the premises.

Shahrazad Tel: 8640110. On Al-Khobar's King Abdul-Aziz Street next to La Boutique.

Middle East and Moghul cooking as well as traditional French food. Chateaubriand steak for two at SR 100 is recommended, as well as mutton and chicken curries and biryanis. The restaurant seats 72, the snack bar 10. Restaurant open 1000-1430 for lunch, and 1730-2300 for dinner; snack bar open continuously from 0900-2300.

Sahara Drive-In Cafe and *Ice Cream Shop* Tel: 8646149, 8646940. Seven blocks apart on 16th Street; Drive-in Cafe is at the corner of 16th and Prince Hamood streets.

Open daily 1100-2300, closed weekdays 1400-1600, these related establishments dish up American fare with Filipino flair. Despite its name, the cafe is not a drive-in. It specialises in takeaway food, which can be ordered by phone, but is big enough for a handful of tables where patrons devour hamburgers, pizzas, and Texas fried chicken, washed down with ice-cold Dr Peppers or three-flavour milkshakes. Expensive but popular and the garnish is authentically, mouth-wateringly US Grade A.

The ice cream is made with local ingredients and can be ordered by the cup, cone, or two-litre package, in ordinary as well as gourmet flavours. Ice cream buffs consider it the best west of Bahrain.

Picnic A shawarma-serving quick-food dispensary on Airport Road, Al-Khobar, at the city limits — enormously popular, especially with students.

Silver Tower Tel: 8649191, 8640860. 1st floor, Riyadh Tower Building, King Abdul-Aziz Street, Al-Khobar. Korean and Chinese cuisine in exotic surroundings. Expensive.

Kwik Food Restaurant In the Safeway shopping complex in Al-Khobar and Dammam.

Offers pizzas (SR 14-19), hamburgers, milkshakes and ice cream to those who need a break before heading home with the groceries; takeaway service. Open 1100-1400 and 1700-2200; Thursday and Friday from 1000-2200.

National Restaurant Tel: 8642351. Centrally placed in Al-Khobar on Amir Muhammad Street near the popular meeting spot, the International Book Shop. Mainly Arabic food.

Shangri-La Tel: 8943122. In Al-Khobar's Al-Kharja hotel.

Deservedly one of the best-known of Eastern province's restaurants, serving Szechuan food at reasonable prices. Americans and Europeans flock here for the spring rolls and the sweet and sour dishes. A typical meal might consist of spring rolls, fried wonton, soup — both the abalone and the chicken with corn are delicious — gingery hot beef with garlic, chicken with cashews, and giant prawns in hot sauce. For dessert try the ice cream with fried bananas or the lungan, Chinese for dragon eyes. Don't let the name put you off — these tiny fruit are fresh and cool, and a pleasant contrast to the Szechuan food, which can be as hot as it is delicious.

Seats 60 in oriental-style room with phoenix and dragon ceiling squares, and the occasional tinkle of piped Chinese string instrument music. Open daily except Friday; lunch 1130-1400, dinner 1800-2230.

Arirang Tel: 8643221. Algahtani Building, Airport Road, Al-Khobar.

Offers Korean, Japanese and Chinese dishes. The Japanese like the bean mash soup and the sliced raw fish (sashimi); the Koreans choose bulboki — barbecued beef with Korean cabbage pickle to go with the ginseng tea. Fans of Chinese food can have tasty titbits such as fried shrimp with asparagus for SR 30. There is little concession to sweet-toothed westerners; fruit cocktail and ice cream are the only desserts.

Thai Restaurant King Khaled Street, south of the fountain past the new library.

The 28 items on the menu include serpent fish soup, sukiyaki Thai-style, cuttlefish with basil and chilli, and deep-fried mackerel seasoned with peppers. The SR 10 lunch of noodles is delicious; dinner for two costs about SR 50. Filipinos, Thais and a few westerners are regular customers. Thai music available on request.

Galaxy Just round the corner from the Thai Restaurant.

Dishes include chicken tikka masala, shrimp biryani — with almost as much shrimp as rice — and a foot-long pancake stuffed with onions, green chillis and potatoes. Good value at about SR 60 for two.

Green Belt Prince Sultan Street, a few blocks west of King Khaled Street.

Al-Khobar's first Filipino restaurant, serving pizzas as well as kare kare, a blend of oxtripe, oxtail, eggplant and string beans in a peanut sauce. Most westerners pass it up in favour of the noodle dishes pansit canton and pansit bihon — sauteed noodles flavoured with cabbage, chicken, celery and spring onions — priced very reasonably at about SR 12. The premises are clean and well-lit.

Bayouni Express Two doors down from the Green Belt. Offers Indonesian dishes — jado-jado (a green salad with peanut sauce), julai kambing (curried mutton), nasi goreng (barbecued meat with satay sauce) and, especially for the weekend, rist-tafel.

Shopping

Shopping centres
Gulf Centre At the end of Airport Road, Al-Khobar.

Swish residential and commercial building boasting some of the city's most prestigious shops, including Radio Shack, with the latest in microcomputers, computer publications, children's science kits, TV antennae and home burglar alarms. Also in the lapis lazuli-coloured cube of the centre are an optician, EgyptAir office, several video and cassette stores, parfumerie, gift and curio shops, and French clothes for both men and women. At Al-Rabei Store you can find clothes by Cartier, Lanvin, Laroche, Dior and Cardin at the same prices as in France.

Prince Mishal Centre Airport Road, near the fountain, Al-Khobar.

Sells various consumer goods.

Al-Khobar Commercial Complex South side of Airport Road, Al-Khobar.

Has a honky-tonk flavour with pop music blaring and suitcases piled up along shop fronts.

Suwaiket Shopping Area Three blocks west of King Khaled Street, 1½ kilometres north of Airport Road, Al-Khobar.

Local market for consumer perishables, clothes and novelties, with prices generally cheaper than elsewhere.

Groceries
There's a corner shop on every other block in Dammam and Al-Khobar, and plenty of supermarkets for those who want to do their week's shopping under one roof. Bulk buying at wholesale prices is possible at several places along the Dammam to Al-Khobar dual carriageway.

Al-Swani Tel: 8646383. King Abdul-Aziz Street, Al-Khobar. Open daily from 0830-2130, closing for prayers.

On the ground floor are 6,500 items of American, European and Arab food. Upstairs is a hardware store selling toys, plants, bathroom accessories, and arts and crafts supplies.

Al-Khobar Family Shopping Centre Tel: 8646364. Just behind Babtain Building, near Albank Alsaudi Alhollandi, Al-Khobar.

It has unusual items not found elsewhere, plus delicious US beef. Upstairs are novelties and household goods.

Tamimi & Fouad Safeway Two branches in Eastern province: on Al-Khobar corniche and Dammam to Al-Khobar dual carriageway, about 12 blocks west of the Dammam sports stadium.

These shops stock 8,000 items, and import fresh produce from Greece and Lebanon to supplement seasonal local produce. The Al-Khobar store is somewhat larger than the one in Dammam. Open daily 0800-2200.

Souq Supermarkets Three branches in the area: main branch — northwest of Al-Khobar on the military trunk road, near Ballast-Nedam; Dammam — behind the Toyota showroom on the Qatif road; Al-Khobar — Al-Aziziyah

Street, one block south of Airport Road.

Each centre stocks about 6,000 items and is open daily from 0900-2100.

Dammam Shopping Centre Tel: 8326748. PO Box 1309, 10th Street, Dammam.

Green Centre 10th Street, Dammam.

Fobeco Al-Khobar.

Dhahran Shopping Centre Airport Road, on the perimeter of Dhahran's main shopping area.

Meat
Fresh and frozen meat is also sold in all supermarkets.

Steak House Butchery Round the corner from Fobeco supermarket on Prince Bandar Street, Al-Khobar. Meat can be ordered in advance. Closed Saturday morning.

Vita Meat King Abdul-Aziz Street, opposite Al-Swani supermarket, Al-Khobar.

Fish
Saudi Fisheries Tel: 8269671, 8262805. Opposite the Riyadh Towers, Dammam. Top quality and freshness.

Soft drinks
Ahmed al-Gosaibi Brothers Tel: 8642865-7, 8641478. On Pepsi-Cola Street, Al-Khobar, along from the Al-Gosaibi hotel. Supplies crates of Teem, Pepsi and Mirinda.

Saudi Refreshments & Industries Tel: 8323523. On the lower Al-Khobar/Dammam coast road. Supplies crates of Kaki-cola and Orangina.

Electrical equipment
Many stores in Dammam, Hofuf and Al-Khobar stock radio, cassette and stereo equipment made by Sony, Sanyo, Pioneer, Akai, Grundig and other well-known manufacturers.

An excellent selection of electrical appliances is available, including General Electric, Kelvinator, Hoover and Westinghouse.

Haberdashery
Al-Zamil Store Tel: 8641919. On the seafront road, Al-Khobar. Stocks every sewing notion required — macrame, cushion filling, zips, wools, thread, fancy braiding and binding. Excellent selection.

Gardening shops
Many of the new supermarkets now stock potting soil, pots, supports, plants and cut flowers.

Landscape Gardening Tel: 8643483. Near the Royal hotel on Hamood Street, Al-Khobar.

Saihar Nursery Dammam to Ras Tanura road. Sells soil, fertiliser and outdoor plants, shrubs and trees.

Golden Rose Flower Shop Tel: 8644360. In the Al-Mutlaq Centre, 28th Street, Al-Khobar. Fresh flowers and plants, potting soil, pots and other garden accessories.

The Modern Agricultural Corporation Tel: 8644221. Prince Muhammad Street, Al-Khobar.

Agricultural Centre Tel: 8326276. Main Street, Dammam, in the Seiko building.

Cosmetics and hair care
Gazzaz Tel: 8641324. On King Khaled Street, Al-Khobar. Stockist of Estee Lauder, Clinique, Germaine Monteil, Orlane, Stendhal, Mary Quant, Charles of the Ritz, Lancome — to name a few. All perfumes and an excellent selection of general beauty products.

Paris House Prince Muhammad Street, Al-Khobar.

Bureau Tamer Tel: 8642115. King Abdul-Aziz Street. Sole distributor of Orlane and Rochas perfumes; sells bath luxuries. Closed Thursday afternoon and Friday.

Zahraini Main Street, Dammam.

Al-Karnak Beauty King Khaled Street.

Ready-to-wear clothing
Most of the stores listed below stock Italian, French, Swiss, English and Middle East garments and accessories.

Fashion House King Khaled Street, Al-Khobar.

Select Shop King Khaled Street, Al-Khobar.

Batik Third street off King Khaled Street, Al-Khobar. Specialist in Indonesian batiks.

Tiring 1843 Tel: 8642028. King Abdul-Aziz Street. Sells men's and women's clothes by Ted Lapidus, Frank Olivier, Christian Dior and Eminence, as well as Holland & Sherry materials. Open 0930-1230, 1600-2100.

La Boutique Al-Khobar.

Kismet Dhahran Road, Al-Khobar.

Deema's Boutique Prince Sultan Street. Offers a wide selection of cotton dresses from Thailand. Open daily 0830-1200, 1600-2100; Friday open in afternoon.

Furniture stores
These stores, which import furniture from Italy, West Germany, the UK and the US, have an excellent selection.

Al-Mutlaq Dammam, tel: 8322393; Al-Khobar, tel: 3646080.

Sleep Comfort Tel: 8644893, 8644446. 28th Street, Al-Khobar.

Cado Decor Tel: 8644797. King Abdul-Aziz Street.

Al-Khobar Furniture King Abdul-Aziz Street.

Crown Furniture Dammam Road, past Juffali compound.

Luxury household items/gift shops
Port Store Tel: 8641109. King Khaled Street, Al-Khobar. Specialists in fondue dishes, silver and gold-plated giftware.

The New Store Tel: 8642184. Corner of Prince Faisal and 3rd streets, Al-Khobar. Lego and many other well-known brands of toys. Excellent selection of Waterford crystal.

Decor Home King Abdul-Aziz Street, Al-Khobar. Stocks Italian, French and other crystal, and ornaments.

Marvels King Abdul-Aziz Street, Al-Khobar. A delightful gift shop.

Al-Kauser Store Tel: 8641116. King Khaled Street, Al-Khobar. Stocks Limoges, Baccarat, Lalique, Stuart Crystal and other items in crystal, china and wood.

Shamsuddin Ashraf Tel: 8651104. First Street, Al-Khobar. Noritake specialists.

Household goods
Everything you need to set up house can be found in the following stores.

Jamil Store Tel: 8642948. Prince Muhammad Street, Al-Khobar.

Saleh Saeed Batook Tel: 8641084. Prince Nasir Street, Al-Khobar.

In addition the supermarkets and souqs all stock household and kitchen equipment.

Stationers and office equipment
Al-Maktaba Tel: 8646437. King Abdul-Aziz Street, Al-Khobar. For all stationery and office supplies.

Al-Nahdah Stationers Tel: 8642269. PO Box 353, Prince Muhammad Street, Al-Khobar.

Greetings cards of all kinds are sold by stationery shops, souqs and Safeway and Al-Swani supermarkets.

Caterers
Several companies offer catering facilities to your home or company offices. All the main hotels will also cater to order to your home.

Taylorplan Tel: 8641902. PO Box 1470. Talal Street and 22nd Street, Al-Khobar.

Al-Suwaiket Catering Services Tel: 8641436. Al-Khobar.

Rezata Catering Services Tel: 8646829. Al-Khobar.

Al-Gosaibi Grand Metropolitan Services Tel: 8324555, 8324630. Dammam.

Removals

Global Movers Saudia Tel: 8640489, 8643519. PO Box 1858, Al-Khobar. International packers and freight movers.

North American Van Lines Tel: 8644272, 8641583. PO Box 612, Al-Khobar. Corner of Prince Nawaf and Seventh streets. Telex: 670063 ict, cable: ict alkhobar.

Dry cleaning

All the large hotels have dry cleaning facilities open to non-residents. There are several dry cleaners in the towns.

Northern Laundry Intersection of Prince Bandar and 17th streets, Al-Khobar. Open 1800-1200, 1400-2100 six days a week.

Najd Automatic Laundry Prince Miqrin Street, Al-Khobar. Open daily except Friday 0700-1300, 1400-1900.

Amro Cleaners Dhahran Road, opposite the Green Shopping Centre, Dammam. Open six days a week 0730-1200, 1530-2100. Also next to Riyadh Towers, King Abdul-Aziz Street, Al-Khobar.

General shops (Al-Khobar)

Bayouni Coffee Stores Tel: 8642014. Prince Sultan Street, behind Fobeco's. Good-natured service and fine Ethiopian coffee, ground or beans. Dammam branch (tel: 8324179) is opposite the Balhamar hotel. Open daily except Friday 0700-1200, 1500-2000.

Saadeddin's and *Madka* Prince Bandar Street. Their Arab and Western pastries will satisfy those with a sweet tooth.

Miss Batik Prince Bandar Street. Supplies Indonesian, Indian and Thai batik.

Kismet Airport Road. Sells moderately priced men's and women's clothes imported from Turkey and Germany. Open 0900-1200, 1600-2030 daily.

Shamsuddin Ashraf. First Street. Has a lavish display of Noritake china, Pentax and Nikon photographic equipment.

The Sanyo Agency Tel: 8641480. King Khaled Street. Just to the rear of the showrooms.

Lego First Street at the intersection of King Saud Street. Sells more than toys, despite its name. Sole distributor for Waterford Crystal. Open daily except Friday 0830-1200, 1600-2100.

Omega Tel: 8631105, 8633666, 8625666. Corner of First and King Fahd streets. General agent for Omega and Patek Philippe watches. Open daily 0900-1200, 1600-2100.

Al-Khobar Furniture Centre Telex: 670043 unitra. The one shop in Eastern province which stocks American brand name furniture such as Simmons and Schweiger. Open daily except Friday 0800-1200, 1500-2000.

Modern Living Tel: 8648110, 8647897, ext 49. 28th Street. Agent for General Electric. Open 0830-1200, 1530-2030.

Modern Agricultural Corporation Tel: 8644221. Specialist in indoor plants and cut flowers. Near Airport Road in Prince Muhammad Street. Open six days a week 0800-1200, 1600-2000.

Studio Samir Tel: 8649639. Prince Muhammad Street. Distributes Kodak products and offers 24-hour film developing service — not for slides or movies. Open 0800-1200, 1600-2030.

Bohaimed Antique Shop Tel: 8644189. Prince Mansour Street. Still the best place to buy Kuwaiti and Al-Madinah chests and antique muskets. Ask to see the warehouse.

General shops (Dammam)

Muhammad Ali Trading Establishment Tel: 8327304. Prince Mansour Street between Broasted Abu Nawas and Dhahran Shopping Centre. Open 0900-1200, 1600-2100; Friday 0900-1100, 1600-1800. Agent for Acoustic Research; distributor of hi-fi stereos for Kenwood, DBX, Koss, Phase Linear, and ADC.

Al-Zahrani's King Saud Street. Sells a wide range of French perfumes and is agent for Molinard, Charles Blair and Eric Dorian. Products by Givenchy, Hermes and Lancome also available. Open 0830-1200, 1530-2130.

Juffali Group Tel: 8323333. A large store in 9th Street, opposite Eastern Province branch of the Ministry of Finance & National Economy. Agent for Kelvinator, Mercedes Benz, IBM, and York Air Conditioning. Open daily except Friday 0800-1300, 1530-1830. IBM workshop, which offers house service, can be contacted on ext 43.

Services

Car repair

Toyota Establishment Tel: 8577645. On the coast road between Al-Khobar and Dammam. It is equipped to handle body and mechanical repairs on Toyotas. The showroom, on Qatif Road, Dammam (tel: 8321004) carries out mechanical work.

Volvo Tel: 8571900. PO Box 579, Dammam. Half days Tuesday and Thursday; closed Friday.

General Machinery Agencies Tel: 8644184. PO Box 287, King Khaled Street, Al-Khobar. Services General Motors vehicles.

Codeco Tel: 8642126. Airport Road, Al-Khobar. Agent for VW and Audi, and sole importer for Porsche. Open Saturday-Thursday 0800-1200, 1400-1800.

Arabian Motors & Engineering Company (Ameco) Tel: 8322626, 8322411, ext 41. PO Box 166, Dhahran Road, Dammam. Agent for Cadillac, Chevrolet and Oldsmobile. Open Saturday-Thursday 0700-1200, 1400-1700.

Mercedes-Benz Tel: 8322444. Just off King Saud Street, Dammam. The garage is run by the Juffali group.

Alesayi Trading Corporation Tel: 8322565, 8327369. Prince Mansour Street, Dammam. Sells Mitsubishi cars and trucks (Galant and Sigma).

Olayan GCC Tel: 8642733, 8642036. PO Box 356, intersection of Prince Bandar and 16th streets, Al-Khobar. Supplies and services and BL vehicles (telex: 670019 olayan).

Books and stationery

International Book Shop Tel: 861784, 8641393-4. PO Box 307, Dhahran airport. Telex: 6171229 salah. Owned by International Publications Agencies. Owner Said Salah. Two branches in Al-Khobar; the main one is at the corner of Alef and Prince Muhammad streets, and the other just off 28th (Pepsi-Cola) Street at the intersection with King Fahd Street.

Distributes Bantam, Fawcet, Dell, NAL books as well as the coffee-table illustrated books which it publishes in Singapore. The store stocks as many as 2,000 paperback titles, with a wide assortment of UK dailies, the International Herald Tribune, French and German magazines. Open daily 0830-1200, 1530-2100 (closes one hour earlier both morning and evening on Friday).

The New International Bookstore Tel: 8644470. Prince Muhammad Street, Al-Khobar. PO Box 349, cable: arabia. Manager Abdul-Aziz Hassan al-Jabre.

Stocks about 1,500 titles in paperback, encyclopaedias, dictionaries, medical and language texts, guides, engineering books and best sellers. Office supplies are also sold, as well as children's books. A wide selection of Indian, Pakistani, Thai and Filipino newspapers and magazines. Open daily 0830-1200, 1530-2100 (closes one hour earlier both morning and evening on Friday).

Saudi Publishing & Distributing House Tel: 832515. Main Street near Seiko

Building and beside British Bank of the Middle East, Dammam. Small branch; main office in Jeddah.

Khazindar Establishment Tel: 8645805. 28th Street, Al-Khobar. Has possibly the widest selection of English, French, German, Italian and Lebanese newspapers and magazines Open daily 0900-2100.

Dammam Tower Bookshop Tel: 8272077, ext 44. Dammam Tower shopping centre. Open 0900-1200, 1500-2000.

Al-Khobar National Library Prince Muhammad Street, Al-Khobar. A good selection of office supplies with Arabic language publications including dailies such as Al-Ahram.

Printers

East Press Tel: 8641706. PO Box 232, Al-Khobar. Telex: 670175 rima.

Modern Printing Press Tel: 8641739, 8643170. PO Box 496, Faisal Street, Al-Khobar. Offset and letterpress printing, book binding and rubber stamps.

Al-Traiki Press Tel: 8323753. Dammam's industrial site.

Al-Mutawa Press Tel: 8321123, 8321127, 8326080. PO Box 343, 11th Street, Dhahran. Telex: 601486 mutawa. Designs and prints litho offset all kinds of books and annual reports. Partners Sulaiman al-Ghuneim and Ibrahim al-Mutawa. Open Saturday-Wednesday 0700-1200, 1330-1630; half-day Thursday; closed Friday.

Housing

There are several estate agents' offices in Al-Khobar and Dammam which have lists of available apartments and villas. Accommodation is usually unfurnished.

Most families prefer compound living as with it come recreational facilities such as a swimming pool, tennis courts and recreation hall. There are now more compounds, making more villas available for rental to those families now placed in their company compound.

Agents include:

Al-Bustan Tel: 8578011, ext 1221-2, facilities office.

Al-Hada Tel: 8578011.

Juffali Tel: 8643417, Dick Ford.

Dammam Towers Tel: 8332102, 8332121.

Carlton Hotel Villas & Apartments Tel: 8665455, 8645214.

Forwarding, clearing and shipping agents

Yusef Bin Ahmed Kanoo Tel: 8323011. PO Box 37, Dammam. Telex: 601011 kanoo.

A A Turki Company Tel: 8329963. King Khaled Street, Dammam.

Electricity

Voltages in Al-Khobar and Dammam vary between 110V and 220V.

Pest control

Ciba-Geigy Tel: 8429586. If you have a pest problem this is the expert in the control of rats, mice, cockroaches, flies, mosquitoes and termites.

Medical

Hospitals

Al-Mana Hospital & Research Centre Tel: 8642330 (eye clinic); 8644281 (dental clinic); 8645376 (accounting); 8645869 (administration). PO Box 311. In Al-Khobar at the intersection of Talal and 16th streets. Telex: 6700967 almana, cable: mana.

200 beds. Specialises in eye and dental care; has 30 nurses. Dental clinic is staffed by six dental surgeons,

two hygienists and two ordinary dentists. A dentist is available 24 hours a day for emergencies. The eye clinic, which employs four ophthalmologists, has an operating room. About 100 eye operations are done a month.

Mohammed Dossary Tel: 8945524, PO Box 124, Dhahran airport. Behind a square of trees and bushes, just off Airport Road, one block west of the municipality. Telex: 670125 ramzi, cable: mostashrek alkhobar.

120 beds. Expansion has given 10 more beds, and a modern ENT clinic and surgery, and two new X-ray rooms, equipped with radiography and fluoroscopy instruments. Staffed by 27 doctors, most of whom are US and European-trained. Provides treatment in surgery, medicine, paediatrics, obstetrics and gynaecology, ENT, urology, and ophthalmology — dental and eye specialists are expected soon. Specialist back-up is available 24 hours a day for emergencies. The nursing staff of 85 is recruited mostly from India, Egypt and Pakistan. The 12 deluxe rooms have electric beds.

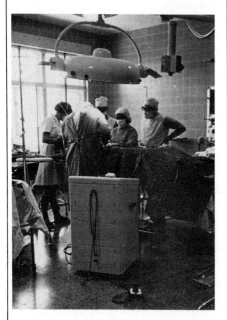

Modern surgical techniques in action

Dr Fakhri Hospital Tel: 8641977, 8642322, 8641728, 8641960, 8641732. PO Box 251, Al-Khobar. At intersection of Prince Bandar and Second streets. Telex: 670126 fkh, cable: fakhry.

Private hospital with 250 beds. Staff of 38 specialists and 14 general practitioners, 185 staff nurses and 14 practical nurses with 11 ward aides. Doctors are mostly Egyptian, many on long-term loan from the universities of Cairo, Al-Azhar and Alexandria.

Has a new cardiology department and the only physiotherapy department outside the Aramco camp at Dhahran. The intensive care unit has four beds.

Specialities: internal medicine, paediatrics, dermatology, physical medicine, general surgery, gynaecology and obstetrics, ENT, dentistry, ophthalmology, orthopaedics, clinical pathology and radiology.

Private hospital costs are subject to government control — a bed costs SR 180 a day; private rooms with colour TV, telephone and fridge are SR 300.

Abdullah Fouad Hospital Tel: 8262111. PO Box 560, Dammam. On the outskirts of the city. Telex: 601636 afhosp, cable: fouad.

310 beds. Will admit any private patient. Two patients usually share a room.

Specialities: ENT, orthopaedics, paediatrics, dermatology, dentistry, psychiatry, general medicine and surgery, physiology, obstetrics and gynaecology.

Average cost of check-up SR 70; maternity unit SR 2,500 for delivery and three-day stay.

Al-Salama Hospital Tel: 8641025. PO Box 296, Al-Khobar, PO Box 96, Dhahran airport. Telex: 670128.

175 beds, 50 of them for paediatrics. Established in 1958 as a paediatric and maternity hospital, it was completed in 1965. Central call system links all wards and can call physicians

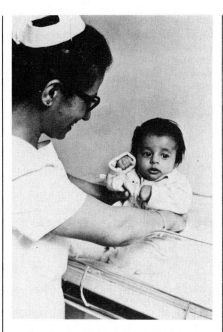

Excellent maternity and post-natal care

in an emergency. Separate dental clinic, the Al-Mana, across the road.

Departments: general medicine (intestinal, chest and cardiac diseases, physiotherapy, and isolation of contagious diseases), private rooms, semi-private and ward services, obstetrics and gynaecology, paediatrics, surgery, ENT, outpatient services, radiology, laboratory services, pharmacy; emergency receiving room on 24-hour call.

Cost of charges can be obtained from the hospital. Sample fees: delivery room SR 125, surgeon's fee for normal delivery SR 500, chest X-ray SR 65; chloera, smallpox, typhoid innoculation SR 15.

Al-Khobar Teaching Hospital Tel: 8943600, 8645800. In the Agrabia district of Al-Khobar.

The 381-bed hospital, a teaching hospital for King Faisal university, provides free care for all Saudis and those working for the government. It has a 24-hour emergency room, with facilities open to all.

Ministry of Defence Hospital Dhahran airport.

Excellent, but limited to Defence Ministry employees.

Dentist

Al-Moaibed Dental Clinic Tel: 8572600, 8573112. Al-Khobar Road, Dammam, behind Carlton al-Moaibed hotel. General dentistry. Open 1800-1200, 1500-1900.

Education

Schools
Abqaiq

Abqaiq Academy On the northern edge of the Ghawar oil field, the world's largest onshore oil reserve. Principal: Don Jeanroy. 40 pupils from 11 countries, mainly the US and UK.

Rahima Academy Tel: 8332982, 8332797. Principal: Joe Gestaut. 82 pupils.

Al-Batin

Al-Batin Academy Tel: 8334131, 8336513, ext 4513-4. King Khaled Military City in the northeast, about 1½ hours by small aircraft from Dhahran or 6-8 hours by road. Principal: Gary Cullen.

American-style education for children of men involved in construction of the military city. The academy, which opened in March 1978, now has 15 teachers and two buildings, one for elementary pupils and the other for junior high. Pre-school classes are held three half-days a week. School facilities are also used for meetings and adult education classes in subjects from Arabic to advanced education.

Al-Khobar

The British School Tel: 8951404. PO Box 269. Headmistress: S Howley. In two villas on the corner of 28th and Ras Tanura streets, about five minutes' drive from the city centre.

The school is a non profit-making organisation supported entirely by tuition fees and run by a board of governors. There are 10 classes with a maximum 16 pupils in each. Pupils range in age from five to 11½. Priority in admission is given first to siblings of children already there and then to British passport holders. The waiting period for entry can be quite long.

Out-of-school activities include football, rugby, gymnastics, ballet, cubs, scouts and brownies.

Fees: registration fee of SR 1,000 payable on placing child's name on waiting list — half is offset against the first term's tuition fees; tuition fee SR 9,000 a term payable in advance.

French School On sea road between Al-Khobar and Dammam just past the Saudi French Bank compound. 350 pupils.

Open only to French-speaking students from 3 1/3 to 13. The curriculum is run on Lycee Francais lines. Extra music and Arabic lessons can be arranged. For further information write to Ecole Francaise, Saudi-French Bank, PO Box 2792, Dammam.

The Italian School Al-Madinah area near the Al-Firdaus compound behind the Jeddah Towers building. Director: Roberto Noferini. 48 pupils.

The school follows an Italian curriculum and is recognised by the Italian Education Ministry. Five elementary classes and three junior high classes.

Fees: SR 300 a month for elementary and SR 500 for junior high.

The Pakistani Community School Tel: 8645777. Off King Abdul-Aziz Street, one block behind Maxim's restaurant. Headmistress: Rathnore Butt. 4,000-5,000 pupils.

The school follows the Federal Board of Islamabad curriculum and exams are sent out from Islamabad. Separate classes for boys and girls.

Hours: 0730-1230, 1500-1900.

Fees: SR 100 a month plus SR 400 to cover library and other expenses.

Dhahran

The Dhahran Academy Tel: 8643842. C/o US consulate-general. Inside the US consulate-general, about one kilometre from Dhahran airport. Principal: 1982/83 Lee Teeples.

The school accepts children between the ages of five and 16 (grades 1-9). About 60 per cent of elementary pupils and 62 per cent of junior high school pupils are American, as are the teaching methods and system. There are not usually more than 25 pupils in a class. Despite the American emphasis, efforts are made to ensure children transfer back easily to schools in their home countries.

The school has expanded to more than 80 classrooms, with a new centre, a gymnasium and three office buildings. Divided into two schools — Dhahran Academy Elementary School (1-6) and Junior High School (grades 7-9). Courses include languages, arts, social studies, science, maths, physical education, reading, health, Arabic, French, Spanish, typing and also English as a Foreign Language.

Hours: grades 1-9 0800-1425; kindergarten 0800-1050, 1130-1425.

Fees: SR 18,000 a year; kindergarten SR 11,250.

Ras Tanura

Korean School This has 40 pupils who follow the Korean curriculum. Several of the children commute from Al-Khobar and Dammam.

Higher education

University of Petroleum & Minerals About one kilometre from Dhahran airport. 3,000 students.

On a hill about one kilometre from the airport, the campus, with a 75,000-gallon water tower soaring above, has become one of the main tourist attractions in Eastern province.

UPM's central library contains 150,000 books and 3,400 journals, mainly for use by the university although some private companies and government agencies are allowed to borrow.

As its name indicates, it is a science and engineering school which awards both undergraduate and postgraduate degrees, most in civil engineering. The students are overwhelmingly Saudi although some from the US, Europe and other Arab countries are enrolled. The language of instruction is English.

King Faisal University Has two campuses in Eastern province. One near Dammam, about eight kilometres south on the coast road, houses the faculties of architecture and medicine. The other — at Al-Hasa oasis, about 170 kilometres away — contains the faculties of agricultural science and veterinary medicine.

Newer than UPM — it opened to students in 1975 — KFU is housed in a collection of spacious prefabs while its permanent campuses, being built in two phases, are completed. There are about 1,000 students of both sexes; women study medicine in Dammam and home economics in Al-Hasa in facilities reserved for them. The university graduated its first batch of medical students — 19 men and 13 women — in December 1981.

Women's College Dammam. Opened recently for general education and business administration classes.

Language classes

University of Petroleum & Minerals Continuing education department, tel: 8643000, telex: 601060. Offers Arabic courses for foreigners at beginner, intermediate and advanced levels. The course includes texts and three hours' instruction a week for about SR 250. The university also offers classes for men, tel: 8602149.

Dammam Language Institute Tel: 8261334. Dhahran Street, in the PIA Building near Bank al-Jazira.

Courses for men in English and Arabic as second languages. The Arabic is a three-month course for six hours a week — on Saturday, Monday and Wednesday from 1930-2130. Cost is SR 2,300 for 72 hours. Classes are limited to 12 and the Saudi colloquial dialect is taught. English classes are held three times a week with a maximum of 15 to a class. The fee for 36 hours' instruction is SR 850.

Translation

Dr Saudi Shawwaf Authorised Translation Tel: 8647816, 8648608. For translations into Arabic or English by professionals.

Ismail Nazer Tel: 8643083, 8649651. Prince Hamood Street, Al-Khobar.

Recreation

Women's groups
Al-Khobar International Women's Group (IWG)
Started in September 1975 with 18 women seeking ways of occupying themselves and meeting people, the IWG arranged lessons in mah jong, international cooking, Arabic and Spanish, and bridge.

By February 1976, 80 women were meeting each month and within two months a nominating committee had been formed. In the early days meetings were held in private houses but today they are held in the compounds of foreign companies.

General meetings are held on the second Tuesday of the month at the Al-Gosaibi hotel from 0830-1130. Newcomers may join on the third Tuesday of the month — same time, same place. Open to those living in the area south of the Carlton hotel, to include Dhahran, Al-Khobar, Abqaiq, Udhaliyah, Hofuf and further south.

From early 1977 the group began to arrange tours for members, initially to Qatif, Hofuf and the University of Petroleum & Minerals (UPM), and later to Riyadh and Bahrain. In 1980 the group held its first fashion show in the Al-Gosaibi hotel. A group newsletter started in 1977 and soon became known as the Sand Paper — describing group activities and events in Eastern province.

Speakers at its functions have given talks on members' visits to Pakistan, Kashmir and Kenya, bedouin crafts; health problems and solutions; oriental and Iranian carpets; archaeology in Saudi Arabia; falconry; Marianne Alireza's life in Saudi Arabia, teaching medicine in Saudi Arabia, and Indonesian cooking. Social functions have included a "crazy hat brunch," fashion shows, an around the world in Al-Khobar lunch, a barbecue and newcomers' coffee morning.

Activities organised by the IWG include mah jong, garden club, handicrafts, needlepoint, international cookery, bridge, book discussion group, tennis, cake decoration classes, dress pattern exchange, magazine exchange, beginner's bridge.

Dammam International Women's Group Set up in January 1979. Includes women in and around cities north of the Carlton hotel—Dammam, Qatif, Ras Tanura, Juaymah, Rahimah and Jubail. Meetings are held on the first Tuesday of the month at the Al-Nemer hotel, Dammam, from 0930-1130. Newcomers meet at the Al-Nemer on the second Monday of the month.

Gulf Women's Association Tel: 8642425. The main social service group in the area. President Badriyya al-Dulaijan leads about 100 prominent Saudi women. Some British and American women have started offering classes in English in exchange for tuition in Arabic. There are also classes in typing and sewing. The group spearheaded pre-school education in Eastern province and has a nursery school.

It is a good way of making contact with Saudi women. Although a new building should be completed soon, at present the group meets at the 13th Street intersection with Prince Mansour Street.

Drama groups

British Aerospace has a group which welcomes anyone interested in drama and is always looking for more talent. For further information, tel: John Wiggins 8792520.

Tours

Many compounds run their own residents' groups and produce their own news-sheet. This details tours both within the kingdom and out, and all activities available to residents.

Aramco produces monthly "Travel News" which details many tours to all parts of the world, plus a list of telephone numbers of the various travel agencies and tour leaders. The news-sheet can be obtained from the Aramco post office in Dhahran.

Museums

The Oil Exhibit Theatre at Aramco, Dhahran, and the Jubail Exhibition Centre can be seen by appointment. The University of Petroleum & Minerals, Dhahran, also has a small geology museum.

Arab Heritage Gallery For details contact Nabila Bassam, tel: 8647225. Prince Saud Street, between 27th and 28th streets, Al-Khobar.

Opened in May 1979, the gallery features traditional and modern arts and crafts from Saudi Arabia and the Middle East. Open 0900-1300, 1600-1900; Friday 1000-1200.

Business groups

British Businessmen's Lunch Group Meets on the third Wednesday of the month at 1230 for lunch at the Al-Gosaibi hotel. Talks are given by prominent businessmen in the area, as well as visiting guests. Membership:

SR 100. Open to all British businessmen. For further information tel: Alan Holmes 8948011, ext 1482.

American Businessmen's Association Passes on business information of interest to all members. Meets on the third Monday of the month at the Meridien hotel at 1200 for lunch. The association represents more than 120 US firms in Eastern province. Membership: SR 200 a year. For further information contact US consulate.

Sports

Recreational facilities are offered through compounds. Sports include tennis, sailing, squash, badminton, swimming and billiards. In addition, the Al-Gosaibi, Dhahran International, Ramada, Marriott, Carlton, Dammam and Oberoi hotels all offer recreational facilities for an annual fee.

Private Beach Club For details about membership, contact: Public Relations Department, tel: 8647499. PO Box 272, Al-Khobar. Telex: 671294 sete sj.

Floodlit tennis courts and swimming pool. Sailing club and storage facilities for the boats with coast guard; sports marina for power boats. Lock-up boat sheds. Children's playground and playroom; coffee shop and restaurant. One, two and three-bedroom chalets for rent. Special children's activities arranged over weekends. Courtesy bus service during the week for members.

(All boats have to be registered with the Saudi Coast Guard).

Rugby
There are several local teams in Eastern province which play against each other during the winter. Training is twice a week. The Gulf rugby union, affiliated to the UK union, also arranges matches between the eight major teams in the Gulf — home and away. Opportunities too to join a touring rugby team — to date, tours have been to Thailand, Sri Lanka and Singapore. Tel: 8642043, 8756981.

Cricket
The cricket league groups 24 teams and about 350 players from Commonwealth countries, with Pakistanis, Indians and Sri Lankans predominating. It has 16 pitches throughout Eastern province.

Sports clubs
These three clubs are private, but government supported. Their aim is to develop Saudi sports. Most members are Saudi but membership — restricted to males — is open to all nationalities.

Qadisiyah Club Tel: 861518. In Al-Khobar, on 10th Street, just off King Abdul-Aziz Street. 600 members.

Instruction in football, running, basketball, volleyball, or swimming. The club owns a 60,000-gallon L-shaped swimming pool, and organises competitions in gymnastics, karate and taekwondo.

Ettifaq Club Tel: 8323347. 13th Street, near the Education Department. Similar facilities to above.

Nahda Club Tel: 8321698. Near the Gulf Secondary School. Similar facilities.

Riding
Aramcons have access to Hobby Farm, a few kilometres from the main camp where they can canter in the beautiful Imhof gardens whose fields and meadows make one forget the desert. Non-Aramcons are admitted as spectators to the twice-monthly gymkhanas on the race track. Once a year there is the Spring Show and Horse Trials when horses and riders come from all over the country to participate in more than 10 classes of events. Non-Aramcons are welcome.

Sea sports

Going to the beach and boating are two of the main leisure activities, both in summer and winter, in Eastern province. The coast was once famous for sailing dhows carrying dates and other products to and from Tarut, Al-Khobar and Uqair. Today pleasure boats ply between Jubail and Half Moon Bay, about 15 kilometres south of Al-Khobar on the Abqaiq road. At weekends windsurfers, Sunfish, Lasers, single and double-sail Hobie Cats and even a few bigger keel boats can be seen on the green waters of the Gulf. Saudi Arabia has one of the smallest registered Hobie Cat fleets — sailors who accumulate the best point scores during the season on Half Moon Bay become official entries in the world Hobie Cat championship.

There are two main sailing clubs in Eastern province: the Aramco Yacht Club, which meets each Friday, and the Sunset Sailing Club at Aziziyah beach at the end of King Abdul-Aziz Street.

The British Sub-Aqua Club (BSAC)
Branches: Arabian Divers, Secretary: Valerie Johnson; PO Box 8350, Aramco; BSAC Abqaiq, Secretary: Darcy Campbell, PO Box 1113; Ras Tanura Divers, Secretary: I Griffiths, PO Box 760, Aramco; Juaymah Diving Club, Secretary: C Roberts, PO Box 713, Ras Tanura.

BSAC activities are divided equally between trips and diving in Half Moon Bay. Groups also go on novelty dives to the artesian wells near Qatif where the water is fresh and 91°F constant. The most common fish to be seen around the reefs are moray eels, lion fish, stonefish, octopus, clown fish, anemones, sea snakes, sponges, lobsters and crabs.

New members are trained right through from snorkel diver to 3rd class and 2nd class qualifications based on a comprehensive practical and theoretical training. For experienced divers the club is a forum, offering them the opportunity to go on regular diving trips. Further training is available enabling 3rd class divers to proceed to 2nd class. The club urges experienced divers to repay their training by assisting in the training of newcomers.

BSAC encourages members to use the Al-Gosaibi Diving Equipment Stores in the centre of Al-Khobar: PO Box 133, tel: 8641171, telex 670137 dska Dhahran Airport.

Media

Television stations

There are more than a dozen TV stations within a radius of 250 kilometres. High humidity, especially in hot weather, allows the reception of the programmes in Dhahran; sand storms, dry weather and aircraft overhead sometimes reduce the clarity of reception. All the stations transmit in colour and black and white on the PAL European system. With a normal TV-top antenna you can tune into:

Channel 6 — Saudi Arabian TV from Dammam (1600-2330). Mostly in Arabic with daily English news and

Putting up a tent for a beach party

some American and British films dubbed or subtitled in Arabic.

Channel 2 — Aramco TV from Dhahran (1530-2230). The most popular station among expats; all programmes are in English. Sample viewing — Anna Karenina, The Voyage of the Beagle, Chico and the Man, All in the Family, Sesame Street.

Channel 4 — Bahrain TV. Mostly in Arabic with daily news in English at 2200.

Channels 5, 7, and 11 are transmitted from Abu Dhabi and cause interference with the stations above. Dubai TV transmits on *Channel 10*.

Arab News publishes Saudi and Dhahran (Aramco) programmes, while the weekly Gulf Mirror lists most others.

Radio

Aramco has four FM stations: the soft-music station plays round the clock,

with news at 1145, 1245 and 1745, the last two repeating the noon news. The other three stations broadcast music for the young, country and western, and classical. The BBC broadcasts from 0800-2200 with a short break at noon; see Arab News for details.

Radio Bahrain is popular with listeners in Eastern province. It has a disc jockey, regular hourly news, and advertisements, and is especially useful for airline information.

Medium and short-wave stations around the world can be picked up. Radios and TVs are relatively inexpensive.

Saudi television

Lawyers

Ismail S Nazer & William P Alexander Tel: 8649651. PO Box 154, Al-Khobar. Prince Hamood Street, near Royal hotel. Telex: 671315 randla. General law. Languages: Arabic and English.

Peter Shrubb, Ahmad Audhali Co., Tel: 8945837, 8643011. Telex: 671462 audhali.

Ahmed A Audhali Tel: 8643011, 8643783. PO Box 1158, Al-Khobar. Telex: 671462 audhli sj. Associated with Fox & Gibbons & Company (London, Cairo, Abu Dhabi and Dubai).

Shaun T Harrington Tel: 8943000, 8943322. PO Box 2105, Al-Khobar. Telex: 670404 law sj.

Talal Amin Ghazzawi Tel: 8332576, 8322935, 8328550; home 8323780. PO Box 381. Imara Street (Coast Road) near Dammam. Telex: 601533 lawyer, 601102 amin. General law with commercial registration and authorised translation. Languages: Arabic and English.

Marwan Muhammad al-Fahoon PO Box 69, Dammam.

Aramco

Aramco is based in Eastern province with its main communities at Dhahran, Abqaiq and Ras Tanura, and two smaller communities at Udhailiyah and Safaniya. Much of the information in this section is based on the Aramco booklet Welcome to Aramco.

Communications

Telex and telegrams
All area telegram offices provide a 24-hour service. Employees have to show proof of identity and a fee is then deducted from their salary. Outgoing telegrams will usually be delivered within 24 hours. Telegram enquiries, tel: 44313.

Telephones
Calls from Aramco may be made from any externally connected telephone using Aramco codes. International calls can usually be made at short notice outside peak hours on proof of identity. Dialling Aramco from the UK and US — international code 010 (UK) and 110 (US) + country code 966 + area code 3 + 87 + Aramco number.

Emergency telephone numbers
Dhahran: fire 44210, 53220; hospital 48056; ambulance 48278.
Dhahran north: fire 58202; ambulance 58191; security 58459, 58201.
Ras Tanura: fire 33110; hospital 38813; ambulance 33209.
Abqaiq: fire (working hours) 23166, (24 hours) 23175; hospital (emergencies) 23229, 27729; ambulance 27721, 23229.
Udhailiyah: fire (working hours) 77518, (24 hours) 77693; hospital 78169, 78232; ambulance 78232, 78212.

Getting around

Driving
Female employees are allowed to drive but only within Aramco compounds. All sites are linked by asphalt roads. Drivers must have either a temporary or permanent Saudi driving licence, which employees can apply for on Aramco form 7268 available from area driving licence offices.

Buses
Buses are provided for shopping outside Aramco sites.

Taxis
24-hour service.

Eating out

There are no restaurants on Aramco sites, although each compound has a cafe serving breakfast, lunch and dinner.

Aramco is a world of its own within the kingdom

Shopping

Aramco has its own on-site commissaries selling a wide variety of fresh fruit and vegetables, meat, poultry and tinned food. Also available are toiletries, household goods, and a selection of US and UK magazines and newspapers. Employees pay cash for purchases from the commissaries. Various food, clothes, household and luxury goods are available from shops and souqs in the nearby towns. Domestic appliances can also be bought through Aramco. On-site hairdressing, beauty salons, laundry, dry cleaning and shoe repairs are carried out by local contractors at reasonable rates.

Plants and flowers
Saihat Nursery Tel: Aramco 44514. Saihat Road, just off the Dhahran to Ras Tanura highway.

Petrol
Each of the main sites has its own service station.

Banking

National Commercial Bank Tel: 54165. Building 16, Dhahran. Cheques of up to £500 or $1,000 may be cashed freely, but cheques for larger amounts must be signed by a department manager and countersigned by the bank manager. All usual banking services are available. Open: Saturday to Wednesday 0730-1100, 1300-1530.

Medical

Hospitals and clinics
Aramco operates a 365-bed hospital at Dhahran, and clinics at Ras Tanura and Abqaiq. All are fully equipped and staffed by qualified European, US and Middle East workers. Aramco employees receive general medical care and hospital treatment free.

Dhahran hospital Tel: 48056. 24-hour service.

Dhahran North clinic Tel: 58191, 58967. Open 24 hours. Mainly out-patients and emergencies.

Ras Tanura clinic Tel: 38812. Open daily 0700-1130, 1230-1600.

Abqaiq clinic Tel: 27723, emergencies 27725. Open daily 0700-1130, 1230-1600.

Udhailiyah medical department Tel: 78232. Open Saturday to Wednesday 0700-1130.

Dental clinics
Only limited dental treatment is available and this is not free.

Dhahran clinic Tel: 43257, 48063.

Ras Tanura clinic Tel: 38818. Open daily 0700-1130, 1230-1600.

Abqaiq clinic Tel: 27740, 27723. Open daily 0700-1130, 1230-1600.

Udhailiyah clinic Tel: 77120.

Recreation

Dhahran Community Information Centre Tel: 45872. Provides information on all community activities in Dhahran. There are plans to expand the service to include Ras Tanura, Abqaiq and Udhailiyah but at present residents there must contact their local recreation offices. For information, tel: Ras Tanura 35221-2; Abqaiq 28136; Udhailiyah 77471.

Membership of all groups is open to every Aramco employee.

Dhahran
Bowling lanes Tel: 45518. Open daily 0900-2245.

Swimming pool Tel: 50563. Third Street. Open daily 0800-2245.

Tennis courts Tel: 45711-2. Third Street/Patio. Open daily 0700-2400.

Cinema Tel: 42112. Programmes 1600, 1830 and 2030; 1400 Thursday; 2045 Sunday.

Library Tel: 45738. Open daily 0900-2245.

Dhahran North

Cinema Building 611. Programmes 1930 daily; Friday 1400.
Library Recreation Building. Open daily 0600-2200.
Swimming pool Near Recreation Building. Open daily 0900-2100 summer; 0900-1800 winter.
Tennis courts East and Seventh streets. Open 24 hours.

Ras Tanura

Bowling lanes Tel: 35221. Open daily 1300-2230.
Swimming pool Tel: 33144. Open daily 0900-2230.
Cinema Tel: 32852. Open daily 1615-1930.
Library Tel: 34514. Open daily 0900-2230.
Tennis courts Tel: 33233. Open daily 0700-2300.

Abqaiq

Bowling lanes Tel: 23113. Open daily 1100-2200.
Swimming pool Tel: 25118. Open daily 0900-2230.
Cinema Tel: 28218. Open daily 1615-1930.
Library Tel: 28106. Open daily 0900-2230.
Tennis courts Tel: 25134. Open 24 hours.

Udhailiyah

Swimming pool Tel: 78427. Open daily 0700-2100.
Cinema Tel: 71833. Open daily 1630-1900.
Library Tel: 78569. Open daily 0800-2300.
Tennis courts Open daily 0600-2100.

Housing

Expatriate employees accompanied by families, single female staff and single senior male staff are housed on main sites; junior male staff live in contractor camps.

Housing offices

Dhahran main office Tel: 43073.
Dhahran North family housing Tel: 58484, 58447, between 0700-1900; bachelor housing, tel: 58447 24 hours.
Ras Tanura Tel: 33103, 33195, between 0700-1130, 1230-1600 Saturday to Wednesday.
Abqaiq Tel: 22089, 28127 between 0700-1130, 1230-1600 Saturday to Wednesday.
Udhailiyah Tel: 78446 between 0600-1130, 1200-1630 Saturday to Wednesday.

Furniture for hire is available through the housing offices.
Linen is provided for employees living in Aramco accommodation for the first time.
Water and gas supplies are maintained by Aramco.
Electricity 110V, 60 cycles. Sockets take standard American flatpin plugs.
Car services Members of the Arabian Automobile Association can use the garages and equipment on community sites. Mechanics are also available.

Media

Television

Aramco has its own colour TV service, transmitting programmes on current affairs, sport and drama from four to six hours daily. At least five other local channels also transmit programmes. The service operates on the European system and American sets are incompatible (see Media).

Radio
Aramco provides music to suit all tastes for 24 hours a day; international news is broadcast three times a day. It is possible to listen to the BBC World Service and Voice of America broadcasts on suitable receivers, although frequencies for the latter may vary and are published in the Gulf Mirror. TV and radio programmes are listed in all the local newspapers.

News-sheet
Distributed daily throughout the Aramco communities.

Trips to make in Eastern province

Hofuf
Hofuf is the capital of Al-Hasa and a delightful town to visit. Its atmosphere is lively, with a bustling covered souq and an old mud fort. Surrounding the town is one of the largest date groves in the world. The area was occupied by the Turks until 1913 and Turkish-style arches and windows can still be seen, although they are fast disappearing.

As the town is 385 kilometres from Riyadh an overnight stop is recommended. Four-wheel-drive is not necessary. To get there take the Dammam route out of Riyadh. About 100 kilometres on, the road enters the rolling dunes of Dahna, a belt of red sand running north to the Nafud desert and south to the Rub al-Khali. At 160 kilometres you reach the small village of Khurays. Built largely of timber and corrugated iron, it grew up after the discovery of oil in 1957 and is the most westerly oil field in the kingdom. Khurays has the first petrol station after leaving Riyadh and is a sensible place to top up.

At 300 kilometres is a police checkpoint; here the road forks right to Hofuf. You are now in the heart of the oil country and the white sands are dotted with pipelines and gathering stations. After 35 kilometres you cross the railway and come immediately to crossroads. The left turn is to Jebel al-Qara and the right one to Hofuf.

The camel market
Hofuf is camel country and, while Dammam is now the capital of Eastern Province, remains one of the most popular spots for eager photographers and the gathering place for local tribes. One of the best times to visit is on Thursday from dawn to 0900, when the weekly camel market is held. Prospective buyers huddle around the camels which stand waiting to be sold and making a great commotion, groaning and grinding their teeth. Teenage entrepreneurs hawk rides to expatriates — SR 5 to mount and SR 10 to ride round the packed-sand marketplace.

To get to the market, pass the modern supermarket on the right, continue and turn right at the signs for the five hospitals project and the secondary vocational school. Follow the road past Hofuf railway station until you reach a yellow cement wall topped by an iron fence. This is the animal market, with the camel market in the extreme left corner.

From the market you can go to see the old Turkish fort in the centre of town near the Rawda hotel. Although closed to the public, you can glimpse above its walls the dome of the Mosque of Ibrahim, an outstanding example of traditional Muslim architecture.

The covered market is also worth visiting. Inside this single-storey whitewashed building is everything from frankincense and myrrh to shepherds' staffs, hand-crafted axes and sickles — you can see them being made — mattresses, bedouin carpets and antiques. All are sold under a roof of palm trunks and interwoven fronds, with shafts of sunlight piercing the gloom.

Beyond the covered market is the women's souq selling clothes, bedu jewellery and baskets. Although the women there are happy to talk to you, they don't want their pictures taken.

Jebel al-Qara

Just east of Hofuf are the potteries, worked by eight generations of the same family. Palm fronds fuel the kilns and each potter turns out about 40 pieces a day, including vases, jugs, flower pots and children's moneyboxes.

Nearby are the caves, a favourite picnic spot in the hot summer months. You enter through towering walls, down a passage which leads to 24 cement steps installed by Hofuf municipality in the early 1960s. A passage off to the left ends in a 30-metre-high vaulted chamber called, appropriately enough, the majlis. Casual gatherings of villagers are often held here.

To reach Jebel al-Qara, retrace your journey back to the junction with the railway crossing and carry straight on towards Dhahran. After a few kilometres you come to the railway lines; drive over and at about 5½ kilometres from the main crossing there is a turning to the right. Continue on this for 18 kilometres following the signs for Jebel al-Qara (or Gara). You will eventually reach an unsignposted T-junction; the right turn leads back to Hofuf and the left to the village of Al-Qara. Keep on through the village until you see some low rocks and caves on the left. Soon after passing some cattle pens there is a car park in front of the entrance to a small network of caves housing a pottery, which you can look round.

Abqaiq

Abqaiq offers tourists the chance to see a 5,000-year-old salt mine still in operation. Although the salt is now used in oil drilling and airconditioning, it is mined in the same way as it was centuries ago. Labourers shovel it up, tossing the salt on to mounds which gleam in the sun. Large chunks of the crystals make attractive natural sculptures. With a pick or even bare hands — though it does sting — it is easy to pry chunks of the salt loose. As it dries it hardens and, when spot-lit, makes an unusual and attractive table centrepiece. As soon as it gets dusty you can return to the salt pits to get another.

To get there, take the Hofuf to Riyadh road out of Abqaiq. About 15 kilometres outside town, turn left at power lines just before the Tradco-Vulcan blockmaking factory. Follow this road to the railway tracks and immediately after crossing them turn right. The salt pits are at the end of the road.

On a nearby escarpment are hundreds of burial mounds dating back 5,000 years. Shaped like Bahraini burial mounds, they bear witness to the life which once existed on the shores of a great lake, now dry. The mound has been excavated; tourists are warned that it is an offence to pick up pots or shards.

Beaches

The most popular Friday pastime is to go to the beach. The best beaches near Al-Khobar lie to the south, starting with Aziziyah and continuing along the northern edge of Half Moon Bay. If you are willing to make a longer trip, the beaches north are even better. At Ras al-Zawr, past Uqair, there is an especially good beach where a 20-metre cliff splits two bays. The water deepens quickly and is not too salty.

This coastal region is also a bird-watcher's paradise during the migration seasons in October and March. Then, thousands of shag — similar to cormorants — are often seen flying past.

Uqair

Once the chief port for Hasa oasis and the meeting point of caravans travelling to Hofuf and into the centre of the Arabian peninsula, Uqair is now just a small settlement of breezeblock houses.

The ruins of the old harbour town and the caravanserai are still visible, as is the old Turkish customs house. Hundreds of camels could be loaded with the sugar, coffee and copper to be hauled to Hofuf. Some carved doors, arches and staircases still remain.

Some believe that Uqair is the site of Gerrha, as chronicled by Ptolemy, Pliny and Strabo, a fabulous city on the incense routes between Mesopotamia and the Hadhramaut in South Yemen. Gold and silver are said to have encrusted the doors, walls and roofs of the houses of Gerrha, inlaid with ivory and dotted with precious stones.

Along the coastal route from Dhahran the Turks later built round stone watchtowers at frequent intervals to protect the camel caravans from marauding bedu. The port was last used commercially by Aramco for a brief period during its pioneering days.

To reach Uqair take the Riyadh road west out of Dhahran past a railway crossing and drive for about 18 kilometres. Then turn left at the crossing and take the coast road for about 95 kilometres.

Qatif

The quickest and perhaps best local excursion from the three-city area is the hour trip to Qatif. At the large Thursday market expatriates rub shoulders with locals, and buy fruit and vegetables at good prices. Local handicrafts such as weaving and basketry are also available — both made and sold by women.

The weavings are found under the arcades, conveniently near the municipal car park in the centre of town. The abaya-clad weavers huddle over the long strips of brightly coloured red, black and orange weavings or the contrasting natural brown and black stripes made of camel and goat hair. This handweaving, one of Arabia's most developed art forms, is threatened by modernisation and the sewing machine. Most weavers are already in their forties. For SR 250-500 you can buy a bedside carpet or a camel saddle; the price depends as much on the buyer's bargaining talents as on the quality of the weave.

In the souq one kilometre away are the shishas — water pipes — and the Omani and Yemeni dried tobacco leaves smoked in them. Here you can also find the miswak, the toothbrush which businessmen, merchants and students use to sweeten the breath and clean the teeth. At the far end of the souq nearly 40 women line up their plaited baskets, fans and mats for tourists. They drive a hard bargain — baskets cost from SR 10-50, while a large sufra (circular mat used as a tablecloth or wall decoration) costs up to SR 200.

The market gets congested soon after 0900, so it is best to arrive early. There are tasty nibbles for those who miss breakfast — Egyptian spicy falafel or sweet zalabiah.

There are also several nurseries near Qatif where plants and shrubs can be bought cheaply.

Tarut island

Archaeological evidence from Tarut and surrounding sites — including countless grave chambers — "firmly establishes the island as the oldest known town-site in Saudi Arabia" (Ahlan wa Sahlan vol 3 issue 3), according to the director-general of antiquities, Dr Abdullah Masri (see Antiquities and museums).

Tarut island, joined to Qatif by a causeway, has been shown by archaeologists to have been one of the main centres of Sumerian civilisation nearly 5,000 years ago. Dr Masri says written records of the Sumerian city-states including Uruk, Ur and Eridu have proved the importance of the eastern coast for channelling Sumerian trade. Strong links have been found as far back as 6000 BC between the Ubaid type pottery of eastern Arabia and southern Iraq.

The main barter was the pearls, minerals and stones of eastern Arabia, and the agricultural produce and developed pottery of south Iraq.

During this time (6000 BC and later) Tarut was probably one of the most important points in these trading connections. Others, north of Tarut, were the islands of Jinna and Musallamia, and the Ras az-Zor peninsula.

In time Tarut increased in importance as the centre of production of rare stones and raw materials such as copper, steatite (soap-stone), lapis lazuli and pearls. The traders, merchants and craftsmen of the island obtained their food supplies from neighbouring Qatif.

The island's most prominent remains, according to Dr Masri, are in the middle, forming a mound on top of which rests a seventeenth century citadel (Qala'at Tarut).

Tarut's commercial importance continued into the third millenium bringing it into contact with distant cultures such as one in Pakistan where pottery dating back to about 2400 BC has been found.

Tarut's port of Darin to the south is a favourite local picnic spot. Beside are the ruins of a nineteenth century mudbrick castle built by a wealthy pearling merchant. However, only women may approach the fort as it encloses springs used by women for bathing and laundry. On Thursdays musical sessions in which various Arabian instruments are used take place in a majlis on the outskirts of Darin.

Jubail

One hour's drive from Dammam, past the oasis towns of Saihat and Safwa, is the new industrial city of Jubail, 104 kilometres north of Dhahran. In 1976 there was no road to Jubail. Today a new six-lane highway with cloverleaf intersections and overpasses connects Safwa and Jubail.

Along the road camels graze and plantations of palm trees are fenced in by dead leaves. On the other side of the road the Gulf can be seen through a haze created by a temperature of 110°F and humidity of 100 per cent.

About 16 kilometres south of the city limits you begin to understand what the Jubail project really means. On the right is the Ghazlan power station, strobe-lit at night, the kingdom's biggest steam-generated power plant. Next on your right is the world's largest desalination plant, which will pipe in Riyadh's main water supply. Pass a mini-city springing from the sand and several flares until you reach the sign for Jubail industrial city.

In nine years, Jubail will be a city half the size of Amsterdam. Only four years ago, only a few hundred people lived there but it already has 50,000 inhabitants and, when complete, will be as large as the Al-Khobar-Dammam-Dhahran area with a population of 350,000.

By 2000, after investment that may reach $40,000 million, Jubail will have become an industrial metropolis with 20 industries, two large ports and an international airport. Jubail today is tens of thousands of neat blue and white houses arranged in rows as far as the eye can see. Expansion will take place primarily in the industrial city, some eight kilometres from Old Jubail along the Abu Ali Road.

Hotels

Al-Jubail International Hotel Tel: 3610167, 3610645. PO Box 215. Close to the new industrial complex of Jubail, 90 kilometres north of Dhahran. Easily reached by hire car from Dhahran international airport, while limousine pick-up service available on request. Telex: 631027 jubint sj.

196 rooms with 14 suites, all with bathroom, telephone, airconditioning, radio, colour TV, video and mini-fridge. Now under the same Swiss management as the Al-Khozama hotel in Riyadh and the Red Sea Palace in Jeddah.

Business service available with translations and Arabic typing, meeting and conference facilities for up to 280; gift shop, book shop, barber, gourmet boutique, swimming pool with poolside bar serving snacks and refreshments. 24-hour room service.

The Dhow room restaurant and the Garden Room coffee shop are two of the finest eating places in the city. The Garden Room seats 80 in its fresh green decor; you can read complimentary newspapers while eating a continental breakfast (SR 14), or a buffet breakfast (SR 24). For lunch you can choose between poached hamour (an excellent local fish) at SR 18, T-bone steak at SR 35, or veal escalope at SR 30. Open 0600-1100. The more formal International Room has gold and brown decor with chandeliers and a view of the pool. The hot and cold buffet at SR 45 is the main lunch offering in this 90-seat room. Lunch 1200-1430; a la carte dinner from 1900-2230.

Rates: single SR 250, double SR 300, suites SR 375-500; plus 15% service.

Rezayat Motel Tel: 3612636. PO Box 216. Four kilometres south of Jubail town centre. Telex: 631039 rezmot sj.

260 rooms, all with bathroom, airconditioning, telephone and fridge. A la carte restaurant, coffee shop, function rooms, recreation room, swimming pool, and tennis court.
Rates: on request.

Communications

Post offices

There are three post offices in the Jubail area. The two most used are the one in the industrial city, and the one on Safwa Road, one block south of Jeddah Street.

Safwa Road branch has telephone, telex, and telegram facilities open 24 hours a day. Numbers throughout the world can be dialled direct. To telephone, enter the first room off the corridor to your right (ground floor). Give the number to the man at the desk who will direct you to a booth as soon as the number has been dialled. Telex and telegram offices on the first floor. Postal services are available from 0700-1400, and 1630-2000.

Jubail can be dialled direct from Dhahran, Al-Khobar, and Dammam. The code is 833-3000, the number of the central switchboard for the Royal Commission, whose operator will transfer you to the required extension.

Courier services

Skypak Tel: 3612161. Al-Hajry Building, corner of Prince Muhammad Street. Telex: 631065 sahel.

SNAS/DHL Tel: 3416156, 3416136. Block S-7-002, Camp 7, Royal Commission. Telex: 670494 snascr sj (Dhahran).

Car hire

Godfrey Davis/Hanco Car Hire Tel: 3610167, 3612176. Al-Jubail International hotel. For models and rates, see Al-Khobar/Dammam/Dhahran section.

Travel agencies

Kanoo Travel Agency Tel: 8332012, 8331885, 8331877, ext 65.

International Travel Agency Tel: 8333000, 8320000, ext 4560-1.

Areen Travel Agency Main Street, Al-Shaiqi Building.

Kurban Travel Agency Tel: 3611900. Near International hotel.

Shopping

Old Jubail's three main shopping streets are Jeddah, Riyadh, and School Streets, all of which intersect Safwa Road, an oleander and tree-lined maidan. Shops usually open at 0830, close for noon prayers, and reopen at about 1500-1600 until 1900-2000. More shops tend to remain open on Friday mornings than in Dammam or Al-Khobar.

There is a fruit and vegetable souq at the corner of Jeddah Street and Safwa Road, and a novelties, linen, and clothing souq in the alley between School and Jeddah streets.

Shops in Jubail differ from those in more established commercial centres such as Al-Khobar and Dammam in that under one roof you can find a motley assortment of goods. Many of the shops mentioned are general stores. As the town grows, they are likely to develop specialities of their own.

Jubail Shopping Centre Riyadh Street. A main grocery outlet which has just added a second floor with toys, gifts, and men's and children's clothes.

The Coffee Grinder Riyadh Street. A delicatessen with nuts, cheeses, dairy products and, of course, freshly roasted coffee from Brazil and India.

The Lucky Centre Riyadh Street. An offshoot of the Al-Khobar store with the same name. Sells clothes, toys, and Clarks shoes.

Al-Nagah School Street. Tailor noted for his thobes.

Salva Clothes & Cosmetics and, next door, *Salwa Fabric Shop* stock clothes for the whole family. The fabric shop also has sandals.

Jamil Store Jeddah Street. Supplies most houseware needs.

Korean Gift Shop Just off Jeddah Street. Has a large selection of leather coats and jackets.

Al-Hadhban Trading & Contracting Riyadh Street. For cameras, watches, and electrical goods; Rollei, Canon, Olympus, and Minolta cameras as well as Omega watches. Develops colour film in one day.

Banks

There are branches of the following banks, with more being built all the time:

Riyad Bank Tel: 3613612, 3610388. PO Box 73; Riyadh Street. Telex: 631025.

Saudi British Bank Tel: 3613844, 3610789. Riyadh Street. Telex: 631024 sabb.

Albank Alsaudi Alhollandi Jeddah/Qatif streets. PO Box 110.

National Commercial Bank Jeddah Street.

Saudi-French Bank Jeddah Street, west of Safwa Road.

Banking hours are 0800-1130 and 1600-1800 Saturday to Wednesday; Thursdays 0800-1100.

Bookshops

Bookshops and stationers include *Al-Washm Bookshop* on Riyadh Street, and *Khazindar Stationery,* also on Riyadh Street, with Thai and English newspapers.

Malaz Book Shop In Jeddah Street, the largest bookshop, stocks 12 daily newspapers (Sunday Telegraph, Times, Observer, etc) and more than 200 book titles, as well as a large selection of international magazines. Its stationery department sells everything from typewriter ribbons to Lego and other educational toys. Open 0800-1200 and 1600-2100.

Eating out

Sheherazade Restaurant West of Safwa Road on School Street.

Offers Arab cooking at SR 10-15 a plate, for such Lebanese delicacies as kibbeh, kufta, and eggplant dishes. The 12-stool restaurant will do take-aways.

Kentucky Fried Chicken has a popular branch on Jeddah Street near the water storage tank.

Close by are ***Chicken Tikka, Wimpey,*** and ***Restaurant Try,*** all fast-food spots where you can get a quick bite for a reasonable price.

Alireza Hotel has a poolside barbecue (SR 45 a head) from 1830-2100 during the warm season.

"Hole in the wall" restaurants, where you can get broiled chicken and local cooking, include ***Farabi*** and ***Al-Shalimar.***

Residents of Jubail industrial city can eat at the Camp 6 cafeteria where they are served a choice of two set lunches or dinners. Menus are announced in the Jubail Jotter. They include such dishes as beef escalope and quiche lorraine for lunch, braised beef, chicken a la king, lasagne, beef chop suey, and fish portuguese.

Medical

Pharmacies

Three pharmacies maintain a rota so one is open 24 hours a day for emergency.

Al-Jurayied Pharmacy Jeddah Street. Open from 0800-2100, supplies medicines, cosmetics, perfumes, and baby needs.

Jubail Pharmacy Safwa Road.

Beach Pharmacy Near taxi station.

Hospitals

Al-Jubail Hospital on Safwa Road. A government hospital.

A 150-bed hospital is being built for the Royal Commission at Jubail industrial city.

Education

Jubail Academy Tel: Dixie McKay (elementary principal) and Jim McKay (junior high principal) 3417550.

Opened September 1978. In 1980 enrolment was 228 students in grades 1-9 with 27 staff. It plans a sizable increase in enrolment and may move.

Most students live within the industrial city, although some are from the King Abdul-Aziz naval base. The schools use community swimming pools and recreation facilities such as a library, tennis and basketball courts, softball and soccer fields, commissary and snack bar.

Fees: SR 24,000 a student.

Media

In the early morning Voice of America and the BBC can be received. Aramco broadcasts radio and TV from Dhahran, 104 kilometres away, and programmes can be picked up if your aerial points in the right direction.

Most companies in the industrial city have their own film showings and recreation centres.

The ***Jubail Jotter,*** the biweekly publication of Bechtel in Jubail, is read widely throughout the area. It lists items of interest to the community of the industrial city.

Recreation

Jubail Women's Group All women in the industrial city are eligible to join. Meets on the second Monday of the month in the recreation hall of Camp 8. About 400 members; no membership fee. Most activities such as the monthly lunch are social, but there are also craft and educational classes. The group sponsors outings to the beach and to collect sand roses. There is an annual bazaar in December. The group visits (and is visited by) other women's groups in Eastern province.

Jubail Repertory Theatre Had its first performance in autumn 1979 when "Arsenic and Old Lace" was seen by more than 1,000 people; the second production was equally successful — "My Three Angels" in spring 1980. About 80 members perform comedies suitable for family entertainment. Auditions are announced in the Jubail Jotter, and membership — as well as attendance at its productions — is open to all.

There are many social groups open to all camp dwellers. The **Jubail Travel Group** has frequent slide shows and trips to Taif and Hofuf. **Duplicate bridge** enthusiasts can play twice weekly in Camp 7's multipurpose building. A **Weaver's Guild** meets at members' homes the first and third Saturday of each month to weave, share ideas, and go on field trips. There is a stamp club, a photography club, boy and girl scout troops, a book club, which meets the first Tuesday of each month at members' homes, a quilting group and a film and video club. **Storytime,** a chance for mothers to have stories read to their children, is on Sundays in Camp 8 library from 1530-1600.

Sports

Organised sports include fencing, squash, basketball and tennis — for each there are tournaments or league fixtures. Five new tennis courts, four basketball courts, and a softball field are available on a first-come, first-served basis.

The **Whispering Sands golf club** holds a tournament on the last Friday of each month.

The four heated swimming pools are segregated. **Jubail Overground Group (JOG)** alleviates the loneliness of the long-distance runner. Fishing is a favourite activity at weekends. Sand roses can be found off the road to Ras Tanura on the edges of sabkhas by the coast. Many enjoy boat trips to nearby Jurayd island with its white shell beaches and coral forests under the calm surface. Crabbing is popular and scuba diving trips are often arranged to nearby islands.

Jubail Divers (BSAC) Secretary: Mr Paddon, PO Box 33, Dhahran airport.

Useful address: Royal Commission for Jubail & Yanbu. Tel: 3414171, 3413198. Telex: 632011 jabe.

THE SOUTH

Abha

A new coastal road, opened in 1979, connects Jeddah with Abha; the old road goes via Taif.

The first 200 kilometres of the old — more scenic — road passes through bare, rocky mountains and occasional wadis with scattered acacia trees and, in winter, pools of water. Houses in the modern villages are made of concrete, but brightly painted, following local tradition, with stripes and pictures in red, yellow, blue and green, emulating the beautiful stone fortress houses of the Asir proper.

The road then winds up through hair-raising bends on to a higher plain. On every hill stands one of the famous stone watchtowers built over the centuries to monitor the movements of potential invaders. On a clear day you can see over the ranges of the escarpment and down into the narrow coastal plain of the Tihama. Green terraces line the mountain sides and wild flowers abound in spring.

Baha

This small town, the gateway to the Asir, is surrounded by hillsides terraced thousands of years ago. About 220 kilometres from Taif, it has the usual collection of small shops, cafes and petrol stations.

Baha's lovely juniper woods, whose pine-like scent is a tonic to city dwellers, are the main attraction. To reach them turn right down a steep embankment at the end of the causeway which leads into Baha. Then take the asphalted track which doubles back initially to the north and keep left at further forks. After four kilometres vast woods appear on the left.

Terraces plummet down among the trees. The woods are at 2,000 metres so you must walk slowly because the air is thin. Here the days are hot and the nights cold. Rain and hail are not uncommon in April, according to Shirley Kay (see Bibliography).

Al-Baha Hotel Tel: 140. Ghamid Country, PO Box 13, Com Reg, cable: mohajjim. A small hotel. Rates: SR 120 for two; plus 10%.

The Asir

Abha is a good base from which to explore the most interesting parts of Asir. The climate is pleasant, you are within easy reach of attractive, contrasting countryside, and the villages are picturesque. The people are hospitable, and there is generally someone in the family who will have a smattering of English. The best time to visit is April-May when the almond blossom is out.

The most distinct physical feature is the escarpment, rising to some 2,000-3,000 metres above sea level. It is this, and the rugged terrain north and south, which has always made surface communication difficult and justified the name Asir (literally difficult country). Now getting there is easy by air, with frequent flights from Jeddah and Riyadh to the new Abha airport (see below). Getting out of the plane at Abha and feeling the crisp morning air is delightful after the sultry stickiness of Jeddah.

Regular rain is the other striking physical feature, although there have been droughts in the past few years. Asir has always been relatively densely populated because of the potential for rain-fed agriculture and the water supply in the fertile wadis. The extensive terracing that follows the contours and holds back the water run-off is vivid evidence of the immense effort and community organisation that must have been expended in the past. Every available inch of ground seems to be used on the slopes that catch the rain, and the terraces almost spill over the precipitous edge of the escarpment.

Without the escarpment the area would be extremely arid, as it causes the air masses from the Red Sea to rise and cool sufficiently to produce rain. To the north and east heavy erosion has carved out a jagged relief, and isolated lonely wadi valleys. Further inland the flat, gently sloping desert plateau takes over. The area's traditional isolation is being overcome by new roads linking it to Taif, Jizan and Najran. The strategic military centre being built at Khamis Mushait is bringing urbanisation.

The development of the air and army bases at Khamis Mushait has doubled its population in less than five years. Now it seems to be Abha's turn; it is attracting large numbers of government jobs, encouraged by an energetic new governor who has sited his palace at the edge of the town.

Despite all this rapid urban development, life in the countryside seems to be much the same. Dirt tracks now lead everywhere and electricity has been distributed to the villages above the escarpment. There are a few tractors, but it is like using a sledge hammer to crack a nut because the fields are so tiny. Most families still plough with oxen. Corn is threshed by dragging a heavy weight over it and flailed with heavy sticks on the threshing floor.

One of the lyrical valleys of the Asir

Local architecture

The Shaar Descent near Abha

Life in the country cannot be easy, but it is here that the people are most hospitable. Agricultural incomes are low and mostly supplemented by younger family members commuting into Abha to do some government clerical job. It is the next generation which could experience an uneasy transition away from the old livelihoods in search of better jobs and living conditions.

Many farms in the richer irrigated area are worked by Yemeni sharecroppers with the Saudi landowner as administrator. This is likely to become more prevalent in the drive to increase productivity with larger farms, some of them on virgin land irrigated with sewage effluent from the towns. However migrant labour is unlikely to want to sharecrop in the rain-fed areas so it is difficult to see in which direction the area will develop.

There are many small villages. Sometimes they look very impressive in the mountains and hills, with the houses seeming to buttress each other, making the group rise like a citadel above the fields. These villages are defensive in character, in contrast to some others in the wadis such as at Tindaha. An exceptionally closely clustered village can be seen at Al-Yanfa in the Tam'nia district. Here, the paths have become covered passageways running beneath the house extensions built above.

The villages are a classic example of architecture without architects. The form of the farmstead building is distinctive and is a response to social and climatic pressures.

The ordinary farmstead is like a tower, without any interior courtyard, but always with a terrace at the top. The thick walls are made either of mud or clover stone walling with small window openings. The staircase is massive and can take up a quarter of the floor area — possibly because it was used as a ramp during the building when a donkey would have carried up the materials for each course. Certain mud-built houses have a row of slates projecting from between each course like a stone plumage to protect the mud wall from the rain. Decoration is discreet but always effective with a few splashes of colour or rendered mud bands around the windows. Doors are often carved and the walls sometimes have vertical drains of lime plaster with strongly moulded patterns just below the roof.

Traditional houses are still being built and it is always difficult to decide just how old a house is. Most new houses, however, are of reinforced concrete with a cement block infill. It is surprising that the many people who say they prefer the old houses do not try to adapt the old. Their thick walls and small windows ensure coolness in summer and warm conditions in winter with a charcoal brazier alight on the hearth.

The largest houses are called qasr, Arabic for fort (or castle). A good example can be seen down the turning on the left, seven kilometres from Khamis Mushait centre on the road to Najran.

Apparently unique to Asir architecture are the qasaba towers. Controversy surrounds their function — some argue that they were built as lookouts, and others that they were keeps, or even granaries. Perhaps it is a combination, although the right position for a watchtower, on a hill top, is the wrong place for a keep or granary.

Most of the qasaba have a circular plan, although some are square. Sometimes they have a band of quartz stones just below the windows or framing the windows — one well preserved example is at the top of Wadi Ain. The remains of a martello-like stone structure are just off the dirt track north of Al-Masnah. It appears to be an interesting antecedent of the Asir farmhouse and perhaps closely related to the qasaba. It is in ruins now but was once a dwelling and is strongly defensive.

Local scenery

The rocks are sometimes very soft, which is perhaps why so many mountain tops have been bulldozed away around Abha. But in much of the interior granite and granidiorite have formed huge boulders and striking mountain peaks. A favourite picnic area is around Qara where the ground is strewn with boulders that have broken away from the rock outcrops.

Another scenic area, although isolated, is northwards along the escarpment from Habalah (see Habalah). Here three great pillars of rock stand away from the edge of the escarpment. One, with a top shaped like Cleopatra's needle, is supposed to make a poet of anyone who can stay there all night without becoming insane. The others are flat-topped with a green sward and on one are the remains of house foundations as well as many cairns arranged like sentinels on the edge of the sheer cliff.

The local people can be charming and helpful

Along the escarpment it is generally cloudier, and rain can be plentiful, especially over the mountainous area of Jabal Sawdah. Here you are high enough to be in the clouds as they race over the top and can watch the wind jetting them through clefts in the rock like geysers. The rainfall here has encouraged a sizable area of juniper forest. The undergrowth is sometimes dense and the local people scavenge the area for timber. A brisk trade in charcoal is carried on by people from Tihama below the escarpment. The area of forest cover is quite small and the view is almost primevally barren looking from the escarpment over all the wadis funnelling down to the Red Sea set in valleys with sides like shrivelled skin.

Visitor's palace, Riyadh

Jeddah Islamic port

Rock-cutting equipment, Najran

Jeddah fountain by night

Operating rock drill, quarry north of Najran

Airport Road roundabout, Jeddah

Madain Salih

Jeddah Islamic port — ro-ro terminal

The national park

The national park is designed with a series of visitor centres which are intended to provide both camping and picnic facilities and information on what can be seen. It has been modelled very closely on the US national parks.

Many feel that to succeed, the park would probably have to seem to be spectacular in a commercial way — which probably means zoos and commercial attractions, all anathema to the basic principle of safeguarding the natural habitat. But designating a national park is so farsighted that it is to be hoped that the aims of the creators will be achieved.

The best introduction to the Asir National Park is to see the visitor centre at Abha — just off the ring road where it climbs to its highest point.

Places to visit

Jabal Sawdah

Typical villages can be seen in the terraced area along the road to Jabal Sawdah from its junction with the Taif road. The junction for Jabal Sawdah is 17 kilometres along the Taif road from Abha. The road leaves the Taif road just beyond an electricity substation and passes through Wadi al-Atif where there are several typical stone-built Asir villages. The masonry work can be impressive with the large stones smoothed on the outside and the interstices jammed with small pieces of schist. At Jabal Sawdah there is a magnificent view from the road down to Wadi Hali and the descent to it from the top of the escarpment. The road along the top of the escarpment continues to Abha past the Al-Buhaira hotel — the whole round trip can be managed in two hours.

Sawdah mountains

Most of the typical wadi villages lie away from the asphalt roads. The dirt tracks connecting them can be tackled with a two-wheel-drive vehicle but the ride can be rough and dusty. The villages here lie in the middle of the Sawdah mountains.

Leave Abha ring road at the Friday Mosque and continue past the prince's palace. The road passes a school on the right and immediately afterwards reaches open country, passing the Abha sports centre on the left. Pick up the new feeder road being built and follow it along the edge of a wadi to Al-Masnah. The road continues and for a short time follows the bed of a wadi. Leaving the wadi there is a school on the right and on your left some intriguing ruins of a stone-built circular house. Then you can either continue west and eventually meet the Sawdah road near Al-Souk, or follow the line of wooden electricity poles north to a series of picturesque villages. These are strung along some tracks that thread north to the Sawdah and Taif roads.

The deep south is now easily accessible

Wadi Tindaha

This wadi has more than 20 villages in it; it is sometimes difficult to see where one ends and the next begins. The typical farmsteads are of mud but without the slates that are found in the areas where schist is common.

A round trip can be made through several villages by starting from Khamis Mushait, following the wadi south until you meet a road which leads back to the military cantonment and Khamis Mushait. Leave Khamis Mushait on the old airport road driving east. Soon after the road has crossed the wadi and before you reach Zinc City (a squatter settlement of zinc huts), turn left down a narrow lane to the local power station. An S bend takes you round the walls of the power station. It then heads east towards Tindaha; once there a track leads south along the wadi and through various villages.

On the way back the asphalt road passes a conical hill just before it joins the Khamis-Najran road. Legend associates it with the Queen of Sheba who was supposed to have stopped there on her way north. There are some interesting carvings at the top.

Al-Nesab

Within Abha there are also some villages that should not be missed, if only to wonder how they can continue in their present state with growing commercial pressure to develop. The best preserved one is Al-Nesab. To reach it take the Khamis road from the centre of Abha, but instead of going up the hill turn left immediately. This road leads to the village alongside the wadi.

Mahala, Qara, Al-Yanfa

Favourite picnic areas are at Mahala (leave the asphalt road opposite the new sports centre now being built); Qara with its rock paintings (23 kilometres on the left from Abha); the meadows nearby at the T-junction beyond; Tamania with the ancient mosque at Al-Yanfa — not to be missed — and the Sawdah mountains.

To reach some pleasant spots in the Sawdah mountains take the road past the Al-Bouhaira hotel. A short distance before the Sawdah visitor centre for the national park is a track on the left heading for the escarpment. Follow this track which leads to some pleasant green meadows. About three kilometres further back along the road to Abha near a bend in the road is another track which is worth following. It heads west towards the escarpment, where it finishes, but a mule track continues with some excellent views over the various wadis leading to the Red Sea.

Habalah

A popular outing is to Habalah, a village in an awesome setting at the foot of a sheer cliff. It can be reached easily by taking the asphalt road from Ahad Rafidah to Qara and at the first T-junction continuing straight ahead towards the radar domes. The road soon narrows and after climbing for five kilometres you leave it by a track on the left between some houses. Follow this track over the rocky plateau in the direction of the electricity transmission lines, but after four kilometres turn left away from the line of electricity poles down a wadi to the cliff face above Habalah (see above).

The Tihama coastal plain

Interesting day trips can also be taken down the escarpment to the Tihama. There are six descents, only one of which, the Jizan descent, can easily be made by a two-wheel-drive vehicle.

A pleasant way to get to know the escarpment around Abha is to take the turning from the ring road past the Sarawat hotel in Abha. After climbing for six kilometres there is a track on the right cut into the embankment. Follow this track over a wadi and then turn sharp left at the second junction. You are now on a track which follows

Traditional wattle huts of the Tihama

the edge of the escarpment, ending at the asphalt road to Sawdah.

Once down on the coastal plain the mountain chain's full effect as a cultural barrier in the past can be appreciated. Villages of circular brushwood houses with pointed roofs, the people's dress and lifestyle, the crops and domesticated animals all reflect the mixture of southern Arabia and Africa that is apparent all round the coasts of the southern Red Sea.

Jarash
The ancient city of Jarash, now in ruins, was once a flourishing staging point on the trading route which extended from Yemen through Arabia via Makkah to Damascus. Allegedly laid waste in the seventh century, little remains today. A hut on a low mound near the road marks an area where, at ground level, the outline of a few stone buildings can be seen, but there is little else.

To get there turn left at the southern end of King Faisal military cantonment and follow the road to Al-Rubba. One kilometre along, on the right, are the ruins.

Hamoma
One kilometre beyond Jarash, across the Wadi Bisha, is the black conical mound of Hamoma. It is also known locally as Jebel Shiba, deriving its latter name from the popular belief that the Queen of Sheba stayed here on her way to visit King Solomon. As it lies next to the main north-south highway it is possible there is some truth in the legend.

The hill can be scaled most easily from the south. At the summit are several weathered written etchings, plus an impression of a fertility maiden picked out in the rock. The scramble is further rewarded by an excellent view of the local surroundings.

Al-Dhana waterfall
The Al-Dhana waterfall is about 115 kilometres from Abha on the Taif road, near the village of Tanomah. It is well signposted and easy to find. The volume of water cascading from the rocks into a pool about 20 metres below varies, but the area is always green, well watered and an ideal spot for picknicking.

The road from Abha to Tanomah initially passes through barren country but this gives way to typical Asir villages with spectacular views across the escarpment and down about 700 metres to the Wadi Shaah and the new road to Mahayle. This stretch also provides birdwatchers with their best chance of seeing the relict species of magpie, pica pasirensis, which lives in the area and often breeds in the trees round the waterfall.

Wadi Dirs
This trip is recommended to those who admire the local architecture or want to bring back photographic souvenirs of their visit. To get there, take the road towards Najran for about 40 kilometres before turning left on to a clearly signposted asphalt road. Al-Dirs, 18 kilometres ahead, is where the road ends.

Once past the ribbon developments — whose fingers extend from Khamis Mushait to beyond King Faisal military cantonment — the scenery softens and the road passes through farming country with villages on the left and occasional watchtowers. The best architecture is, however, in the Wadi Dirs region. Heading towards Al-Dirs you pass well-preserved square and round watchtowers before reaching the Al-Nadir turn-off. Al-Nadir itself is a village of classical buildings, largely uncluttered by TV aerials, power lines and the like.

Turning back on to the Al-Dirs road you find the wadi about one kilometre ahead.

Wadi Shaah Turkish fort
The remains of Turkish fortifications are found throughout the Asir, often commanding superb views. This is certainly true of the Wadi Shaah fort, which lies just off the Abha to Taif road. Although the main fortification is in ruins, several towers still dot the area, while just below and to the right, officers' and other ranks' burial grounds are in good condition.

A new road to Jeddah is being built down the escarpment and should be finished in late 1983. The Chinese construction company carrying out the work has had to cope with exceptionally difficult terrain.

You reach the fort by travelling 28 kilometres from Abha towards Taif and turning left on to a broad dirt road for a further two kilometres. Several small towers on high ground to the left of the Taif road precede the turn-off.

Jabal Faifa
Jabal Faifa is a richly populated, highly cultivated, terraced massif forming part of the Tihama highlands. Faifa has five peaks, the highest nearly 2,000 metres above sea level. In summer it affords a welcome relief from the heat and humidity of the coastal plain. In winter, when the air is crisp and clear, it provides a panoramic view of an area which takes in the mountains of Yemen to the south, Jizan to the southwest and a broad expanse of the Tihama to the north and to the west.

On the lower terraces of Jabal Faifa

Villages on Jabal Faifa

barley and maize are the prime crops. Higher up these give way to bananas and coffee. The neatly cultivated rows of terraces, looking like giant steps ascending the massif, have a remarkable visual impact, and more so when seen from higher up against Faifa's panoramic backdrop. Adding further to the area's charm are the rounded, tower-form houses, looking like windmills without sails, which are a feature of this area.

Faifa is a must for travellers to the region, but potential visitors are advised to use four-wheel-drive.

From Abha travel 77 kilometres down the escarpment road to Al-Darb — a winding descent of about 2,000 metres. At Al-Darb turn left on to the Jizan road and continue for a further 85 kilometres (two kilometres short of Sabya and 32 from Jizan) before turning left again on the Id'abi road. Follow this for 37 kilometres before taking a good surface dirt road which cuts off to the right and climbs to the top of Jabal Faifa.

If your time is limited it is best that, once on top of Faifa, you drive to the first village and turn left at the tea house. From there descend to the plain via a steep but good dirt road. At the bottom turn left — the right hand track leads to Yemen — and follow a brief stretch of tarmac road past the police station and on into the wadi leading to Id'abi (also known by its old name of Souk 'Aiban). The village of Id'abi spills over the right hand bank of the wadi about two kilometres ahead. Turn left here and rejoin the tarmac road leading back past the Faifa turn and on to meet the Jizan to Al-Darb major road. But a word of warning: the stretch of road from Id'abi to just beyond the Faifa turn-off crosses and recrosses a wadi bed many times. After storms the road gets broken and rough, and running water may have to be traversed.

Khamis Mushait

Khamis Mushait is only 27 kilometres northeast of Abha, inland from the escarpment edge, but in many ways it is a very different town. It is flat and laid out in a grid pattern, the climate is hotter than Abha's and there are many more foreign companies and workers.

The name means literally the "Thursday (market) of the Mushayt (tribe)." The city has retained and is expanding its traditional commercial role. The 1974 census put the population at 48,200; now it is nearer to 60,000. The establishment of large army and air force bases a few kilometres south has been the catalyst which sparked the city's recent rapid expansion.

The most noticeable aspect of this growth is in the ribbon developments of shops and homes which creep steadily out from the town along the roads to Abha and Najran.

A dual-carriageway connects Abha and Khamis Mushait, with an off-shoot halfway leading to Abha airport. Traffic on the main road is increasing and travel time between the two city centres can vary, depending on conditions and accidents. However, on average, it takes 30 minutes.

A good road to the south leads to Najran, 255 kilometres away from where you can now join the recently completed highway to Riyadh.

Taxi fares to and from the airport are the same as for Abha. Hundreds of taxis ply the road between the two cities every day and, while it could cost a single passenger SR 50 or more, most travellers share a taxi.

Hotels

There are very few first-class hotels yet. Most of the existing hotels are very basic and not really recommended, although they are cheaper than similar places in Abha.

Al-Rehab Hotel Tel: 2239028. A couple of blocks south of the main Abha road, near the Saudia booking office, about 500 metres west of the main Friday Mosque. 34 rooms.

Al-Haramain Hotel Tel: 2237831. In the same neighbourhood as the Al-Rehab, a couple of blocks further west. 16 rooms.
   Rates: single SR 40.

Al-Mutlaq Hotel Tel: 2238018, 2222344. On the main Abha road, on the right going into Khamis, about 500 metres west of the main Friday Mosque, next to the new sports shop. 20 rooms.
   Rates: single about SR 63, double SR 72, three beds SR 93.

Hotel Zahrat al-Janoub Tel: 2230074. On the southern side of the main Abha road where one-way traffic leads out of the city centre, about 300 metres from the main Friday mosque. 19 rooms.
   Rates: single SR 40.

Hotel al-Khamis Frantel Tel: 2234436. Telex: 906618 arabi sj. Nearly 10 kilometres from the city centre and Abha airport, on the Khamis side of the Wadi Atwud bridge just off the King Faisal bypass to the town.
   175 double rooms and 10 suites, all with bathroom, balcony, radio, TV, closed-circuit video, telephone, automatic alarm call system, mini-bar, hair dryers. Pets are allowed in rooms only.
   French restaurant seating 120, coffee shop seating 110 and cocktail lounge for 60. Catering service, bureau de change, safe deposit boxes, telex, laundry, car hire, travel agent, shopping arcade, barber shop. Indoor swimming pool, bowling, sauna, gymnasium, tennis and squash. Conference and banqueting rooms with audio-visual equipment with capacity for 800-plus.

Bahes Village Tel: 2232900, 2232908. PO Box 824. Telex: 906088.
   Resident/guest complex eight kilometres from Khamis and 19 kilometres from Abha on the main dual carriageway linking the two towns. Eight villas, each divided into two apartments, all with master bedroom with bathroom en suite, two other bedrooms sharing bathroom, sitting room, dining room and fully equipped kitchen. Telephone, video and piped music.
   Restaurant and coffee shop, separate family and bachelor gardens, swimming pool and play area for children.
   Rates: SR 900 an apartment (summer), SR 400-600 (winter); plus 15% service.

Communications

Post office
The central post office is on a side street a couple of blocks south of the Abha road, about 800 metres west of the main Friday Mosque, just behind the new sports shop and the Al-Mutlaq hotel. As in Abha, all mail is delivered through post office boxes (tel: 2237184).

Telephone
The PTT Ministry has its main office in the centre of Khamis on the Old Airport road. It is a high, windowless building on the opposite side of the road to the main mosque. As in Abha, private telephone lines are in great demand and enquiries should be made to the subscription office (tel: 2237834).

Telex
The public telex office is a few blocks west of the main Friday mosque, close to the old post office building behind the Pakistani souvenir shop (tel: telex manager 2237182).

Telegraph
Difficult to find, tucked behind the main one-way street which leads east into the city centre. Turn right at the section of the street which includes several ironmongers and sanitaryware shops, and look for a red building (tel: 2237944 for telegraph registration).

Courier service
SNAS-DHL Tel: 2239842. Telex: 402559 snascr sj (Jeddah).

Restaurants

Few restaurants are recommended.

Al-Saadeh Tel: 2232836. A small Lebanese restaurant on the south side of the Abha road, 100 metres east of the bridge over the Wadi Atwud. Dinner costs about SR 30. A shop next door sells a good selection of sweet and savoury delicacies.

Al-Lega Siteen Street, 700 metres west of the traffic lights on Hospital Road. About SR 30 for a meal.

Al-Boustan One kilometre beyond the Wadi Atwud bridge on the Khamis to Abha dual carriageway, the end building of Al-Gharawi Trading & Tourist Centre. European and Arab food, and Lebanese specialities. A substantial meal costs about SR 70. Seating for 100. Open daily 0800-2200.

Genghis Khan A Chinese restaurant 10 kilometres from Khamis next to the Crown shopping centre at the junction of the Air Base and Najran roads. Serves a wide range of reasonably priced dishes. Open daily 1130-1430, 1730-2200.

Shopping

The growth of supermarkets in the area has led to keen competition and prices now vary little.

Shopping centres

Al-Gharawi Trading & Tourist Centre On the southwest of town, one kilometre beyond the Wadi Atwud bridge on the Khamis to Abha dual carriageway. It houses the largest and best-stocked supermarket in the area, selling food on the ground floor, and electrical goods, toiletries, perfume and clothes on the first.

There is also a precinct catering for a wide range of family and household needs.

New Supermarket Four kilometres south on the Khamis to Najran dual carriageway. Like the Al-Gharawi the ground floor has a well-stocked food market while the first floor sells a wide range of women's and children's clothes, dressmaking accessories, perfume, optical and photographic goods, toys and brassware.

Bin Choneim Commercial Centre Next to the New Supermarket and something of an Aladdin's cave. It stocks an exceptional range of outdoor and indoor leisure goods, garden furniture, picnic and barbecue sets, kitchenware, travel accessories, books and stationery. The stationery department is unique in the area for the number and quality of greeting cards.

Crown Shopping Centre 10 kilometres from Khamis Mushait at junction of Air Base and Najran roads. Sells a wide range of food, while other departments sell cosmetics, perfume, watches, photographic accessories, brassware and cassettes.

Cold store On Najran road, 1½ kilometres from the New Supermarket. The building has no name, nor does it advertise. It is made of concrete, looks like a warehouse, and stands next to a greetings arch spanning the road. The store is recommended for bulk purchases of tenderloin beef, chicken and frozen vegetables.

Fresh fruit and vegetables

Next to the New Supermarket are fruit and vegetable stalls and, of particular importance, a shop selling sweet water. There are also several shops and stalls opposite the King Faisal military cantonment, four kilometres from the Air Base to Najran road. You can buy pitta bread freshly baked in mud brick ovens, and fresh fruit and vegetables at some of the lowest prices in the area. Spit-roast chickens are a speciality and at SR 10 — pitta bread and lemon included — a bargain.

Car servicing
Industrial area At traffic lights next to Al-Gharawi centre. You can negotiate the recovery and repair of both light and heavy vehicles, with repairs to a high standard and reasonably priced. You can also buy an extensive range of car accessories.

Souqs
The covered souq is across the road from the open car park in the centre of town. It extends two blocks back with the blocks intersected by a road. You can buy gold and luxury goods, clothes, dress material, perfume, toiletries, hardware and various other goods.

The open souq, which long characterised Khamis Mushait, has disappeared. Gone are the fruit and vegetable stalls stacked high with produce, the leather workers and basket weavers, the brightly dressed women selling spices and bedu jewellery, and the men with their antique firearms, coffee pots and bric a brac. All that remains is a small area where local farmers sell their produce; the rest is now a car park.

Beyond this area and facing the market are two or three antique stalls whose quality and range of wares varies. Stocks are renewed periodically, with much coming from Yemen, and bargains can be found. However, as demand seems to exceed supply, the prices asked are invariably high but can be reduced by haggling.

There is also a third souq, housed in iron stalls. You get there by turning right at the traffic lights next to the main mosque when approaching the town from Najran and continuing along the road for two kilometres. The main goods sold are dates and hardware. However, with the closure of much of the original open market, this souq is expanding and the range of wares may well increase.

For those who want a traditional market and are prepared to get up early, Ahad Rufaida is well worth a visit. The market is held in the town square every Sunday from 0600-0900. Sheep, goats, vegetables, basketware, spices, dates and incense are all sold. Many of the vendors and buyers come from outlying areas and dress in the colourful garb of the Asir. The market is one of few which have changed little over the years. To reach Ahad Rufaida, 18 kilometres from Khamis, take the Najran road, go past the King Faisal military cantonment and turn left off the new bypass 2½ kilometres from the Al-Qara turn. One kilometre on, turn left again and follow the road for about 300 metres until it ends in the town square.

Banks
National Commercial Bank Tel: 2237323. On the north side of Abha road where it is one-way traffic east, about 400 metres from the main mosque. A new and easily distinguished building faced with bricks. Currency exchange and usual banking services.

Riyad Bank Tel: 2237354. A small office on the same side of Abha road as National Commercial Bank, but 200 metres nearer the city centre.

Al-Rajhi Bank Next to Riyad Bank. Often the best exchange rates — as all four banks are so close it is easy to compare prices.

Saudi-Cairo Bank Opposite National Commercial Bank.

Useful telephone numbers
All prefixed by 223, except where marked*

Saudia — sales and reservations manager 7293; reservations 7777, 7222; confirmations 7315

Emirate office — complaints 7655

Ministry of Defence & Aviation — King Khaled air base 7813-5; King Faisal military cantonment 8836, 8848, 8860, 8872

Ministry of the Interior — police 7614-6; police — emergency *999; traffic accidents *993; passport office — residency 7350; fire station *998

Ministry of Municipal & Rural Affairs — municipality, mayor 7187

Ministry of PTT — telephone manager 7755; maintenance *905

Medical

Khamis Civil Hospital Tel: 2237021; ambulance 2237020. Has improved recently but is still well below the standard expected in the West. It is about 1.5 kilometres south of the city centre on Hospital Road, a dual carriageway running parallel to Najran Road.

Al-Borg Dispensary Tel: gynaecology 2239930; cardiology and internal medicine 2239180; urology 2230413. Close to the Civil Hospital, a few blocks west of Hospital Road and 250 metres nearer the city centre.

Within the King Faisal military cantonment there is a military hospital administered and staffed by Whittaker Corporation of the US. The facilities and personnel are excellent. The hospital is restricted solely to military staff and their families and Whittaker employees, although in emergencies patients have been known to be admitted from outside.

Asir Dental Clinic South of Abha road three kilometres from Wadi Atud bridge.

Housing

Several very large companies are located in and around the city, mainly contracted to the Defence & Aviation Ministry either on the King Khaled air base or the King Faisal military cantonment. The companies have large, almost self-contained, compounds but they are mostly within the bases themselves. Access to them is subject to military regulations.

Elsewhere, houses and villas are available for rent and prices are comparable with Abha's. Houses of good quality are hard to find. A detached house, large enough for two families, could cost around SR 3,500 a month. A house divided into separate flats costs between SR 1,500-1,700 a month for each flat.

Water
Domestic water supply is not controlled by the municipality; private arrangements have to be made with local suppliers. Most suppliers congregate just off Siteen Street, near the traffic lights at the junction with Hospital Road, and contracts are usually made there. Prices are about SR 140 for 10 tonnes. As there is no dam in Khamis, prices fluctuate with the amount of rain.

Electricity
Electricity supply is at 220V, 60 cycles (Khamis Electricity Company, tel: 2237598).

Education

School
The Asir Academy The only school in the province for expatriate children. In the Northrop Corporation compound on the Asir Base road. Take the Najran road from Khamis and after about 10 kilometres turn left following sign for airport. The compound is on the left three kilometres on.

The school, run by the Saudi Arabian International School, only accepts children fluent in English. It follows an American curriculum with classes from kindergarten to ninth grade; maximum size of class 15.

Contact should be made by a personal visit as neither the compound nor the school is on the public telephone network. It is possible to walk into the compound but a gate pass is needed for a vehicle.

There is no public transport in Khamis or Abha so children attending the Asir

Academy will need to be driven there and back.

Playschool In the Northrop compound.

Fees are about SR 200 a month for two hours a day, five days a week.

Recreation

Leagues for different sports have been organised by expatriates in the area. Most are based around Khamis and use the facilities of the larger companies, although individuals and companies from Abha do participate.

Where a league includes a team living on either of the military bases, problems may be encountered by other teams trying to get on to the bases and procedures which have been developed to provide temporary passes should be followed.

Most leagues are run over the winter period. The sports include soccer, men's softball, ladies' softball, tennis (mixed teams), squash and darts. There is also a highly competitive bridge league.

One-off events, such as motocross meetings, are organised occasionally by enthusiasts, while sailing regattas have been held on the Red Sea.

Jizan

Jizan is the modern capital of Jizan province, but neighbouring Sabya and Abu Arish are both past capitals of the region. Domed mosques and carved decorative plasterwork show Ottoman and Yemeni influence. The fort of Dosariyah which commands Jizan is Ottoman. Sabya was the capital of the short-lived Idrisi domain at the beginning of the twentieth century, and the extensive remains of the Idarisah palace, with its outstanding decorative plasterwork, can be seen near the main road on the outskirts of the town. Similar plasterwork can be seen in the fort at Abu Arish. The new museum of the coastal Tihama will be in the planned new town of Jizan.

Historically, ports along this coast have risen and declined swiftly over the centuries. The remains of several, both pre-Islamic and Islamic, are known, but their surface features are not worthy of note. Some of these ports and towns were united in the tenth century AD and became famous collectively as the Mikhlaf al-Sulaymani.

Old and new live side by side in Jizan

Hotel

Hyatt Jizan Tel: 3220020, 3220024. PO Box 219, telex 911054 hyatt. At the entrance to harbour, 13 kilometres from Jizan, 16 kilometres from airport. 72 rooms.

All rooms have colour TV, in-house video, radio, telephone, refrigerator.

Restaurant serves continental, Middle East and Tunisian specialities; food also served at poolside terrace. Secretarial services, five-language translation, shuttle service to port, town and airport.

Rates: single SR 200, double SR 250.

Credit cards: American Express, Carte Blanche, Diners Club, Visa, Master Charge.

Places to visit

Farasan island

The island, a four-hour boat ride from Jizan, has perhaps the richest archaeological potential of the coastal region. There are three major pre-Islamic settlement sites and several minor ones. They are remote, and cannot be visited without a guide from the Education Department in Jizan; nor are there any roads.

Farasan town itself has more fine plasterwork buildings than any town on the coastal Tihama. Little recent building has taken place. The Farasan people take their name from a famous seafaring tribe of antiquity which once controlled the port of Al-Mukha in Yemen.

The colourful dress of the south

A warning to those travelling between Jizan and Jeddah, or Abha and Jeddah, via the coastal route

Both routes converge at Al-Darib, from where Makkah is signposted — **but incorrectly.** The traveller to Jeddah must turn right 38 kilometres past Al-Darib on to the Muhayle road, although Makkah is signposted straight on. The unwary who heed the sign will follow an excellent road through Al-Qahmah, Al-Birk and Amq only to find the road suddenly running out in deep, soft sand. There is no alternative but to retrace your steps back to the Muhayle turn — a time costly 200-kilometre diversion.

Mitsubishi gas production unit on the move

APPENDICES

THE ECONOMY

Crude oil production 1938-81

	Barrels a day	Total barrels
1981	9,623,828	3,512,697,344
1980	9,631,366	3,525,080,035
1979	9,251,079	3,376,643,747
1978	8,066,105	2,944,128,176
1977	9,016,952	3,291,187,434
1976	8,343,953	3,053,886,653
1975	6,826,942	2,491,833,893
1974	8,209,706	2,996,542,558
1973	7,334,647	2,677,146,337
1972	5,733,395	2,098,422,603
1971	4,497,576	1,641,615,332
1970	3,548,865	1,295,335,759
1969	2,992,662	1,092,321,543
1968	2,829,982	1,035,773,333
1967	2,597,563	948,110,468
1966	2,392,737	873,349,148
1965	2,024,870	739,077,565
1964	1,716,105	628,094,543
1963	1,629,018	594,591,671
1962	1,520,703	555,056,388
1961	1,392,518	508,269,201
1960	1,247,140	456,453,173
1959	1,095,399	399,820,590
1958	1,015,029	370,485,754
1957	992,114	362,121,478
1956	986,129	360,923,384
1955	965,041	352,239,912
1954	953,000	347,844,850
1953	844,642	308,294,245
1952	824,757	301,860,885
1951	761,541	277,962,605
1950	546,703	199,546,638
1949	476,736	174,008,629
1948	390,309	142,852,989
1947	246,169	89,851,646
1946	164,229	59,943,766
1945	58,386	21,310,996
1944	21,296	7,794,420
1943	13,337	4,868,184
1942	12,412	4,530,492
1941	11,809	4,310,110
1940	13,866	5,074,838
1939	10,778	3,933,903
1938	1,357	495,135

Producing oil wells

1981	1980	1979	1978	1977
646	748	706	763	782

Estimated Aramco oil reserves (million barrels)

	Proven reserves	Probable reserves*
1981	116,747	177,229
1980	113,491	178,729
1979	113,384	177,904
1978	113,284	177,758
1977	110,443	177,643

* Probable reserves include proven reserves

Estimated Aramco gas reserves* (billion cubic feet)

	Proven reserves	Probable reserves
1981	70,810	111,852
1980	68,779	114,572
1979	65,861	114,473
1978	66,715	112,912
1977	62,405	111,258

* Includes dissolved, associated and non-associated gas

Gross domestic product by sector
(SR million)

	Third plan 1980*	1979†	1978	Second plan 1977	1976	1975	First plan 1974
At current prices							
GDP	496,855	384,237	247,622	223,818	203,942	163,893	139,224
Oil section	339,835	254,342	140,384	133,935	136,248	116,570	111,101
Non-oil sector	157,020	129,238	107,238	89,883	67,694	47,323	28,123
private	89,658	74,223	61,335	50,884	40,219	28,382	18,252
government	67,362	55,672	45,903	38,999	27,475	18,941	9,871
At constant 1969 prices							
GDP	52,766	48,812	44,521	41,765	39,318	34,250	31,539
Oil sector	24,525	23,628	21,999	21,513	21,626	19,112	18,903
Non-oil sector	28,241	25,184	22,522	20,252	17,692	15,138	12,636
private	19,025	16,881	14,979	13,588	11,819	9,938	8,439
government	9,216	8,303	7,543	6,664	5,873	5,200	4,197
Implicit deflators (1969 = 100)							
GDP	942	787	556	536	519	479	441
Oil sector	1,385	1,076	638	623	630	610	588
Non-oil sector	556	516	476	444	383	313	223

* preliminary estimates
† revised estimates

Source: Finance & National Economy Ministry, Central Department of Statistics, National Accounts of Saudi Arabia, 1389/99 AH, dated 11 March 1981

Actual revenue and expenditure
(SR million)

	1982*	1981	1980	1979	1978	1977	1976	1975
Oil revenue	na	na	319,305	189,295	115,078	114,042	121,191	93,481
Other revenue	na	na	28,795	21,901	16,427	16,617	14,766	9,903
Total revenue	313,400	na	348,100	211,196	131,505	130,505	130,505	103,384
Total expenditure	313,400	288,174	236,570	188,363	147,971	138,048	128,273	81,784

* estimate

Source: Finance & National Economy Ministry

Markets for Aramco crude oil 1977-81
(%)

	1981	1980	1979	1978	1977
Europe	42.4	42.7	41.2	38.8	41.6
Asia	35.2	33.1	33.8	36.9	33.3
North America	15.5	18.2	19.5	18.0	20.3
South America	3.8	3.3	3.2	4.4	2.9
Africa	1.6	1.3	1.0	0.6	0.7
Australia	1.5	1.4	1.3	1.3	1.2

Aramco — workers in Saudi Arabia

	1981	1980	1979	1978	1977
Saudi Arabians	29,753	26,321	21,839	17,894	16,740
Americans	5,255	4,651	3,738	3,282	2,323
Other nationalities	18,429	15,898	12,666	9,277	6,464
Total	**53,437**	**46,870**	**38,243**	**30,453**	**25,527**

Aramco production at a glance

	1981	1980
Oil production	3,513 million barrels	3,525 million barrels
Natural gas liquids	163,582 million barrels	135,139 million barrels
Ras Tanura output	416,421 b/d	418,550 b/d
Total proven oil reserves	116,700 million barrels	113,500 million barrels
Total proven gas reserves	70,800,000 million c/f	68,800,000 million c/f

b/d = barrels a day
c/f = standard cubic feet

Source: Aramco

SIDF: value of approved industrial loans and disbursements
(SR million)

Year	Disbursements			Approved loans		
	Cement	Others	Total	Cement	Others	Total
1974/75	—	35	35	—	150	150
1975/76	95	195	290	360	668	1,028
1976/77	225	479	704	—	1,251	1,251
1977/78	260	1,008	1,268	863	1,228	2,091
1978/79	320	797	1,117	—	987	987
1979/80	580	719	1,299	400	939	1,339
1980/81	470	662	1,132	400	859	1,259
Total	**1,950**	**3,895**	**5,845**	**2,023**	**6,083**	**8,106**

Totals may be inexact because of rounding

Source: SIDF, Riyadh, May 1982

Saudi Arabia: passenger/cargo air traffic, 1981

	(million passengers)				(million kilos)	
	Domestic	International	Total	% change from 1980	Cargo	% change from 1980
Jeddah	3.6	3.7	7.3	−2.3	77.7	+24.2
Riyadh	4.1	1.2	5.3	+0.4	43.5	+43.0
Dhahran	1.8	1.9	3.7	+11.6	49.7	+30.1
Total	9.5	6.8	16.3	+1.5	170.9	+30.3

Source: International Airports Projects, Jeddah

King Khaled international airport, Riyadh
(million passengers)

	1975	1976	1977	1978	1979	1980	1981
Domestic	0.6	1.2	2.2	2.8	3.4	4.2	4.1
International	0.2	0.3	0.5	0.8	1.0	1.1	1.2
Total	0.8	1.5	2.7	3.6	4.4	5.3	5.3

Forecast, 1986-2001
(million passengers)

		1986	1991	2001
Domestic	max	6.4	8.8	11.0
	min	5.8	7.2	8.4
International	max	2.0	3.0	4.1
	min	1.6	2.2	3.0
Total	max	8.4	11.8	15.1
	min	7.4	9.4	11.4

Source: Data Systems Research & Development

Saudi Arabia: higher education

	Students			Teachers		
	1980/81	1979/80	% change	1980/81	1979/80	% change
King Saud university	14,238	13,124	+ 8.5	1,644	1,321	+24.5
King Abdul-Aziz university	21,745	19,287	+12.7	1,424	1,206	+18.1
University of Petroleum & Minerals	3,054	2,794	+ 9.3	621	552	+12.5
King Faisal university	1,430	1,158	+23.5	505	385	+31.2
Imam Mohammad Ibn-Saud Islamic university	5,870	5,919	−0.8	692	507	+36.5
Al-Madinah Islamic university	2,739	2,271	+20.6	350	239	+46.5
Women's colleges	5,321	3,437	+54.8	710	576	+23.3
Total	**54,397**	**47,990**	**13.4**	**5,946**	**4,786**	**24.2**

Source: Higher Education Ministry, Riyadh

Total number of graduates from vocational training centres (by profession)

	Regular programme			Evening programme		
	1978	1979	1980	1978	1979	1980
Airconditioning mechanics	343	422	437	194	428	675
Car mechanics	1,353	1,737	2,119	717	1,699	2,942
Carpenters and upholsterers	961	1,171	1,373	521	939	1,293
Construction workers	575	556	573	123	190	198
Electricians	1,216	1,592	1,970	794	1,548	2,394
General mechanics	523	582	644	—	17	—
Metalworkers	237	248	273	—	—	13
Office machine operatives	111	137	154	—	—	—
Plumbers	481	566	741	325	620	933
Printers and bookbinders	208	249	293	—	—	—
Radio and television mechanics	106	135	153	—	—	—
Welders	604	727	983	255	580	931
Others	198	293	11	27	27	63
Total	**6,916**	**8,415**	**9,724**	**2,956**	**6,048**	**9,442**

Source: Saudi Arabian Monetary Agency (SAMA), 1980/81 annual report (1401 AH)

BIBLIOGRAPHY

General

Colours of the Arab Fatherland by Angelo Pesce. Oleander Press, Cambridge, UK. 1975. 143 pages. Illustrated.

The kingdom of Saudi Arabia Stacey International, London, UK. 1977. 256 pages.

Saudi Arabia today — an introduction to the richest oil power by Peter Hobday. Macmillan Press, London, UK. 1978. 133 pages.

Who's who in Saudi Arabia 1978-79 Tihama/Europa, London, UK. 1978. 309 pages.

Saudi Arabia: past and present by Shirley Kay and Malin Basil. Namara Publications, London, UK. 1979. 149 pages.

The American in Saudi Arabia by Eve Lee. Intercultural Press, Chicago, US. 1980. 111 pages.

King Faisal and the modernisation of Saudi Arabia edited by Willard A Beling. Croom Helm, London, UK. 1980. 253 pages.

Colourful Saudi Arabian Red Sea by Hagen Schmid and Peter Vine. Privately published. 86 pages. illustrated.

Eternal Saudi Arabia by Rick Golt. Elk Publications, London, UK. 1980. 150 pages. Photographs and text.

Aramco and its world: Arabia and the Middle East edited by Ismail I Nawwab and others. Aramco, Dhahran. 1980. 275 pages. Illustrated.

The Kingdom by Robert Lacey. Hutchinson, London, UK. 1981. 630 pages.

State, society and economy in Saudi Arabia edited by Tim Niblock. Croom Helm, London, UK. 1982. 314 pages.

Guides

Medical handbook for living in Saudi Arabia International Medical Services, London, UK. 1978. 44 pages.

The green book: guide for living in Saudi Arabia Third edition, by Madge Pendleton and others. Middle East Editorial Associates, Washington DC, US. 1980. 178 pages.

A short guide for British personnel living and working in the Middle East Committee for Middle East Trade, London, UK. 1980.

The definitive guide to living in Saudi Arabia by Brian McMaster. Privately published. 1980. 95 pages.

Passport to Saudi Arabia by Saudia Public Relations Department, Jeddah. 1982. 221 pages.

ERI Guides: Salaries and living costs — Saudi Arabia: Jeddah; Salaries and living costs — Saudi Arabia: Riyadh; Salaries and living costs — Saudi Arabia: Eastern province. Executive Resources International. Available from MEED. Published annually with an update.

Maps and atlases

Atlas of Saudi Arabia Third edition, by Hussein Hamza Bindagji. Oxford University Press, UK. 1978. 61 pages.

Map with Gulf Shipping Routes Gulf Agency Company, GAC Shipping.

City map of Riyadh by Hussein Hamza Bindagji. Oxford University Press, UK.

Riyadh - map and guide Saudimap, Boogaerts & Associates, PO Box 5002, Riyadh.

City map of Jeddah by Hussein Hamza Bindagji. Oxford University Press, UK. 1981.

The new street map of Al-Khobar and Al-Thugbar published by Tac Advertising, PO Box 1717, Dammam.

The new street map of Dammam published by Tac Advertising (see above).

Oxford Map of Saudi Arabia Geoprojects, Beirut. Available in UK from Roger Lascelles, London, UK. 1981.

Bartholomew world travel map: the Middle East Bartholomew & Sons, Edinburgh. 1981. Scale: 1:4,000,000

The Hejaz

Hejaz before world war one by David George Hogarth. Oleander Press, Cambridge, UK. 1978. 155 pages.

Jeddah

Jeddah 68/69 University Press of Africa & University Press of Arabia, Nairobi, Kenya. 1968. 174 pages.

Jeddah: portrait of an Arabian city by Angelo Pesce. Oleander Press, Cambridge, UK. 1977. 254 pages. Illustrated, maps.

Jeddah old and new Stacey International, London, UK. 1980. 143 pages. Illustrated.

Jeddah today Saudi Advertising, Jeddah. 1982. 88 pages.

Al-Madinah

Medina, Saudi Arabia A geographic analysis of the city and region by M S Makki. Avebury Publishing Company, UK. 1982. 231 pages.

The Najd

Riyadh

Saudi Arabia: Riyadh master plan Doxiadis Associates Review, no 45, Vol 4 (1968).

Riyadh — history and guide by William A Pugh. Al-Mutair Press, Dammam. 1969. 112 pages. Maps.

Riyadh Citiguide (a guide with maps) Tihama, Riyadh. 1980. 128 pages.

Welcome to Riyadh, Saudi Arabia by International Women's Group, privately printed by Riyadh International Women's Group.

Hail

Ha'il: Saudi Arabian oasis city by Philip Ward. Oleander Press, Cambridge, UK. 1983.

Hasa (Eastern province)

The oasis of Al-Hasa by F S Vidal, Aramco, Dhahran. 1955.

Water resources and land use in the Qatif oasis of Saudi Arabia by C H V Ebert, Geographical Review 55 (Iv), 1965, 496-505.

The Al-Hasa irrigation and drainage schemes Wakuti, 1970, mimeo, 1970.

The South

Asir before world war one by Sir Kinahan Cornwallis. Oleander Press, Cambridge, UK. 1976. 155 pages.

History

The seven pillars of wisdom: a triumph by Thomas Edward Lawrence, Jonathan Cape, London, UK. 1935. 702 pages. Maps.

Lord of Arabia: Ibn Saud, an intimate study of a king by H C Armstrong. Penguin Books, UK. 1938. 247 pages.

Faisal, king of Saudi Arabia, 1906-1975. Prince Faisal speaks. Riyadh. 1963. 45 pages.

Arabian days by Shaikh Hafiz Wahba. London, UK. 1964. 184 pages.

Faisal: king of Saudi Arabia by Gerald De Gaury, Barker, London, UK 1966. 191 pages. Maps.

Saudi Arabia H St John B Philby. UK: Ben; US: International Book Centre, Detroit. 1968. 358 pages.

Faisal; the king and his kingdom by Vincent Sheean, Tavistock Publications, London, UK. 1975. 161 pages.

Faycal, roi d'Arabie: l'homme, le souverain, sa place dans le monde (1906-1975) Albain Michel, Paris, France. 1975. 302 pages.

The birth of Saudi Arabia: Britain and the rise of the house of Sa'ud by Gary G Troeller. Cass & Company, London, UK. 1976. 287 pages. Map.

Arabia in early maps by Gerald R Tibbetts. Oleander Press, Cambridge, UK. 1978. 175 pages. Illustrated.

Saudi Arabia: an artist's view of the past by Safeya Bin-Zagr. Three Continents Publishers, Switzerland. 1979. 139 pages.

Arabia United: A portrait of Ibn Saud Mohammed Al Mana. Hutchinson Benham, London, UK. 1980. 328 pages.

The desert king: a life of Ibn Saud by David Howarth. Quartet Books, London, UK. 1980. 213 pages.

Philby of Arabia by Elizabeth Monroe. Quartet Books, London, UK. 1980. 332 pages.

Qaryat al-Fau A portrait of pre-Islamic civilisation in Saudi Arabia by A R al-Ansary. Croom Helm, London, UK. 1982. 147 pages. Illustrated.

Travel and exploration

Travels in Arabia J L Burckhardt. 1829.

A Pilgrimage to Najd Lady Ann Blunt. 1881.

The heart of Arabia: a record of travel and exploration by H St John Philby. Putnam & Company, London, UK. 1923. 2 volumes. Maps.

Travels in Arabia deserta by Charles M Doughty, Jonathan Cape, London, UK. 1926. 690 pages. Maps.

The empty quarter, being a description of the great south desert of Arabia known as Rub' al-Khali by H St John B Philby. Constable, London, UK. Reprinted, Norwood, Pennsylvania: Norwood Editions.

Northern Najd: journey from Jerusalem to Anaiza in Qasim Gian Carlo Guarmani translated by Lady Capel-Cure. 1938.

Wanderings in Arabia by Charles M Doughty. Duckworth, London, UK. 1949. 607 pages. Maps.

Travellers in Arabia by Robin L Bidwell. Hamlyn Books, London, UK. 1976. 224 pages. Maps.

Arabian Sands by Wilfred Thesiger. Allen Lane, Middlesex, UK. 1977. 347 pages. Maps.

Diary of a journey across Arabia (1819) by George Forster Sadleir. Oleander Press, Cambridge, UK. 1977. 161 pages.

Far Arabia: explorers of the myth by Peter Brent. Weidenfeld & Nicholson, London, UK. 1977. 239 pages. Maps.

Explorers of Arabia by Zahra Freeth and Victor Winstone. George Allen & Unwin, London, UK. 1978. 308 pages.

Travels in Saudi Arabia by Shirley Kay; edited by Rosalind Ingrams. Published privately. 1978. 187 pages.

Captain Shakespear: a portrait by H V F Winstone. Quartet Books, London, UK. 1978. 240 pages.

Explorers of Arabia: from the Renaissance to the end of the Victorian era by Zahra Freeth H Victor F Winstone. Allen & Unwin, London, UK. 1978. 308 pages. Maps.

Report on a journey to Riyadh by Lewis Pelly (1865). Oleander Press, Cambridge, UK. 1978. 114 pages.

Desert, marsh and mountain by Wilfred Thesiger. Collins, London, UK. 1979. 304 pages.

Travels in Arabia (1845 and 1848) by George August Wallin. Oleander Press, Cambridge, UK. 1979. 187 pages.

Monarchy

A handbook of the Al-Saud ruling family of Saudi Arabia by Brian Less. Royal Genealogies, London, UK. 1980. 64 pages.

Burke's Royal Families of the World Vol Two: Africa & the Middle East. Burke's Peerage, 1980.

The House of Saud by David Holden and Richard Johns. Sidgwick & Jackson, London, UK. 1981. 569 pages.

Islam

Encyclopaedia of Islam edited by B Lewis, J Schact. Brill, Leiden. 1953.

The road to Mecca by Muhammad Asad. Simon & Schuster, New York, US. 1954. 380 pages.

Muhammad, Prophet & Statesman by W Montgomery Watt. Oxford University Press, London, UK. 1961.

Pilgrimage to Mecca by Mohamed Amin. MacDonald & Jane's Publishers, London, UK. 1978. 257 pages.

Mecca: the Muslim pilgrimage text by Ezzedine Guellouz; photographs by Abdulaziz Frikha. Paddington Press, London, UK. 1979. 124 pages. Photographs, maps.

Armies in the sand: the struggle for Mecca and Medina by John Sabini. Thames & Hudson, London, UK. 1981. 223 pages.

Politics and economics

A house built on sand: a political economy of Saudi Arabia by Helen Lackner. Ithaca Press, London, UK. 1978. 224 pages. Maps.

The cohesion of Saudi Arabia: evolution of political identity by Christine Moss Helms. Croom Helm, London, UK. 1981. 313 pages.

Saudi Arabia in the 1980s: foreign policy, security, and oil by William B Quandt. Brookings Institution, Washington DC, US. 1981. 190 pages.

The Economy of Saudi Arabia by Donald M Moliver and Paul J Abbondante. Praeger Publishers, New York, US. 1980. 167 pages.

Saudi Arabia. Energy, developmental planning, and industrialisation edited by Ragaei and Dorothea el-Mallakh. Lexington Books, Massachusetts, US. 1982. 204 pages.

Saudi Arabian Monetary Agency statistical summary SAMA, Riyadh. Published twice yearly.

Foreign trade statistics Ministry of Finance & National Economy, Riyadh. Published quarterly and annually.

Saudi Arabian Monetary Agency annual report SAMA, Riyadh.

Statistical Yearbook Ministry of Finance & National Economy, Riyadh. Published annually.

Middle East Financial Directory edited by Anna Krajewska. MEED. Published annually.

Development planning

Third development plan 1400-1405 AH (1980-85 AD) Saudi Arabia Ministry of Planning, Riyadh. 1980. 503 pages.

Third national development plan, 1400-1405 AH (1980-1985 AD): highlights Middle East Association, London, UK. 1980. 29 pages.

The Third Saudi Arabian development plan 1980-1985: an assessment of opportunities for British consultants, contractors and suppliers Committee for Middle East Trade, London, UK. 1981.

An overview of the third development plan of Saudi Arabia (1400-1405/1980-

1985) by Ragaei el-Mallakh. International Research Centre for Energy & Economic Development, Colorado, US. 1981.

Saudi Arabia: a case study in development by Fouad al-Farsy. Kegan Paul International, UK. 1982. 224 pages.

Saudi Arabia: the development dilemma by Paul Barker. Economist Intelligence Unit, London, UK. 1982. 92 pages.

Saudi Arabia: rush to development by Ragaei el-Mallakh. Croom Helm, London, UK. 1982. 472 pages.

Saudi Arabia's development potential. Application of an Islamic growth model by Robert E Looney. Lexington Books, Massachusetts, US. 1982. 358 pages.

Energy

Discovery: the search for Arabian oil by Wallace Stegner. Export Book, Beirut, Lebanon. 1971. 190 pages.

The world energy book by David Crabbe and Richard McBride. Kogan Press, London, UK. 1978. 259 pages.

Financial Times oil and gas international year book 1983. Longman Group, London, UK. 1983. 592 pages.

OPEC report Petroleum Economist, London, UK. 1979. 301 pages.

Aramco handbook: oil and the Middle East Aramco, Dhahran, 1980. 279 pages.

Objectives of the oil exporting countries by J E Hartshorn. Middle East Petroleum & Economic Publications, Nicosia, Cyprus. 1980. 248 pages.

Search for security: Saudi Arabian oil and American foreign policy 1939-1949 by Aaron David Miller. University of North Carolina Press. 1980. 320 pages.

Saudi Arabian oil and gas by Petromin, Dhahran. 1980. 28 pages.

Overview of Saudi oil and gas industry Ministry of Petroleum & Mineral Resources. 1980. 32 pages.

The myth of the OPEC cartel: the role of Saudi Arabia by Ali D Johany. University of Petroleum & Minerals, Dhahran, and John Wiley & Sons, UK. 1980. 107 pages.

Commerce

Saudi Arabia Chase World Information Corporation, New York, US. 1975. 375 pages.

Saudi Arabia: Business Opportunities compiled and published by Metra Consulting Group, London, UK. 1978. 223 pages.

Saudi Arabia - business profile series The British Bank of the Middle East, London. 1979. 28 pages.

The commercial guide to Saudi Arabia Saudia, Saudi Arabian Airlines Business Advisory Service, Jeddah.

Leading merchant families of Saudi Arabia by J R L Carter (published in association with the D R Llewellyn Group), London, UK. 1979. 190 pages.

Major companies of the Arab world 1979/80 Graham & Trotman, London, UK. 1980. 672 pages.

Buying habits in Saudi Arabia published by Tihama in association with Frith Overseas Research, Jeddah. 1980.

Doing business in Saudi Arabia by Ernst & Whinney. 1980. 27 pages.

Doing business in Saudi Arabia Second edition by Nicholas A Abraham. Tradeship Publishing Company, Boston, US. 1980. 336 pages.

Doing business in Saudi Arabia — international tax and business service Deloitte Haskins & Sells, New York, US. 1982. 123 pages.

Joint ventures in Saudi Arabia by John Walmsley. Graham & Trotman Publishers, London, UK. 1979. 275 pages.

Prospects and procedures for establishing a joint venture in Saudi Arabia Committee for Middle East Trade, London, UK. 1981. 50 pages.

Investors in Saudi Arabia: a reference to private investment by J R L Carter. Scorpion Publications, London, UK. 1981. 452 pages.

Saudi Arabia: keys to business success edited by Kevin R Corcoran. McGraw Hill, UK. 1981. 225 pages.

Prospects for agricultural and project business in the Kingdom of Saudi Arabia British Agricultural Export Council, London, UK. 1981. 51 pages.

Hints to exporters — Saudi Arabia British Overseas Trade Board, Department of Trade, Export Services & Promotions Division, London, UK. 1981/82.

The great silver bubble by Stephen Fay. Hodder & Stoughton, London, UK. 1982. 275 pages.

Saudi Arabia: a MEED special report July 1982.

Saudi Arabia trade directory Saudi Advertising International, Jeddah. Published annually.

Industry

Middle East industrialisation by Louis Turner and James M Bedore. Published for The Royal Institute of International Affairs by Saxon House, Teakfield, Hampshire, UK. 1979. 219 pages.

Development of the industrial cities of Jubail and Yanbu in the kingdom of Saudi Arabia Committee for Middle East Trade, London, UK. 1979. 100 pages.

A Guide to Saudi Arabian manufactured products Saudi Industrial Development Fund. 3rd edition, 1980.

Guide to industrial development 6th edition. Saudi Consulting House, Riyadh. 1981.

Trends of the construction industry in Saudi Arabia 1976-1979 Local Industrial Development Department, Aramco, Dhahran. 1981. 21 pages.

Laws and regulations

Bylaws of the Saudi Basic Industries Corporation Riyadh. 1976. 40 pages.

Saudi Arabia: company and business law edited by M N Nafa Arab Consultants, London, UK. 1977. 441 pages.

Business laws of Saudi Arabia — Vol 1 and II translated from Arabic into English by N H Karam (official translation expert for the courts of Lebanon). Graham & Trotman, London, UK. 1979 (revised). 360 pages.

Regulations for income tax, road tax and zakat (up to the end of September 1978) Kingdom of Saudi Arabia Ministry of Finance & National Economy, Zakat and Tax Department, 1980.

Trading with Saudi Arabia, a guide to the shipping trade, investment and tax laws by Leslie Alan Glick. Croom Helm, London, UK. 1980. 595 pages.

Detailed guidelines to company law and practice within the kingdom of Saudi Arabia by E M Emmanuel. Hawk Publishing, Ajman, UAE. 1980. 104 pages.

Saudi-isation: the law and the practice by Vernon A A Cassin. AMR-MEED Conference 1981.

Arbitration — procedures and risks in Saudi Arabia by Dr Abdulla al-Munifi. AMR-MEED Conference 1981.

The general principles of Saudi Arabian and Omani company laws (statutes and Sharia) by Nabil A Saleh. Namara Publications, London. 1981. 338 pages.

Tax and the subcontractor — Saudi Arabia by Khalil Kashef. AMR-MEED Conference 1981.

Middle East Executive Reports: a monthly legal and business guide Published by Middle East Executive Reports, Washington DC. US.

Flora and fauna

Wild flowers of Central Arabia by Betty Lipscombe Vincette.

Inland birds of Saudi Arabia by Jill Silby. Immel Publishing, London. 1980. 160 pages. Illustrated.

Red Sea coral reefs by Gunnar Bemert and Rupert Ormand. Kegal Paul International, UK. 1981. 192 pages. Illustrated.

Wildlife of Arabia by Stacey International, London. 1981. 96 pages. Illustrated.

The birds of Saudi Arabia: a checklist by Michael C Jennings. Privately published. 1981. 112 pages.

Language and culture

The Macmillan Arabic Course, Books 1 & 2 by T Francis and M Frost. Macmillan Press, London, UK. 1980. Book 1 — 224 pages; Book 2 — 288 pages.

Spoken Arabic in Saudi Arabia by Omar Saeed Ibrahim, Saudi Publishing House. 1975. 111 pages.

Falconry in Arabia by Mark Allen. Orbis Publishing, London, UK. 1980.

Traditional crafts of Saudi Arabia by John Topham and others. Stacey International, London, UK. 1981. 192 pages. Illustrated.

The art of bedouin jewellery — a Saudi Arabian profile by Heather Colyer Ross. Kegan Paul International, UK. 1982. 132 pages. Illustrated.

The art of Arabian costumes — a Saudi Arabian profile by Heather Colyer Ross, Kegan Paul International, UK. 1982. 188 pages. Illustrated.

Arabic culture through its language and literature by M H Bakalla Kegan Paul International, London, UK. 1982. 365 pages.

Monuments of South Arabia by Dr Brian Doe. Oleander Press, Cambridge, UK. 1983.

Middle East general

A handbook of Arabia (Geographical Handbook Series), Admiralty Great Britain, Naval Intelligence Division, HM Stationery Office, London, UK. 1917. 709 pages. Maps.

The Middle East: a geographical study by Peter Beaumont, G H Blake, J M Wagstaff. Wiley & Sons, Sussex, UK. 1976. 572 pages. Maps.

The Middle East (seventh edition) by W B Fisher. Methuen & Company, London. 1978. 615 pages.

Arabian government and public services directory 1982 Beacon Publications, UK. 1980. Over 320 pages.

The New Arabians by Peter Mansfield. J G Ferguson Publishing Company, Chicago, US. 1981. 274 pages.

History of the Arabs, Philip K Hitti. Macmillan Press, London, 1981. 852 pages.

Arabian essays by Ghazi al-Gosaibi, Industry & Electricity Minister, Kegan Paul International, London, UK. 1982. 120 pages.

Arabia and the Gulf in original photographs by Andrew Wheatcroft 1880-1950. Kegan Paul International, London, UK. 1982. 200 pages.

Triumph of the bedouin by Andrew Vicari. Kegan Paul International, London, UK. 1983.

Middle East Review World of Information, Essex, UK. Published annually. 432 pages.

MEED Annual Review published by MEED, London, UK. Published annually.

Gulf guide and diary Middle East Review Company, Essex, UK. Published annually.

MEED Express Diary Middle East Economic Digest Consultants in association with Express International, Beirut. Published annually.

Saudi Arabia: world bibliographical series vol 5 by Frank A Clements. Clio Press, Oxford, UK. 1979. 195 pages.

Saudi Arabia and the Gulf states: sources of statistics and market information — 7 (revised), published by Statistics and Market Intelligence Library, Department of Trade, Export House, London, UK. 1979. 48 pages.

OUR MOTTO: Efficiency and Personal Service

While in the Eastern Province call on us

THE TRAVELLER'S

TRAVEL AND TOURISM

TEL: 8944100 ALKHOBAR

King A. Aziz Ave. 24th Int. Dawood Bld. — Tel: 8944100 — Alkhobar — P.O. Box: 654, (Dhahran Airport) — Al-Khobar — Saudi Arabia

INDEX

Abalkhail, Mohammad Ali 2
Abdul-Aziz Khogeer Hotel 141
Abdul-Aziz, King (Ibn Saud) 3,5,7-13,87
Abdul-Aziz, Crown Prince Abdullah Ibn 2,3
Abdul-Aziz, Prince Abdulillah Ibn 51
Abdul-Aziz, Prince Abdul-Mujid Ibn 51, 261
Abdul-Aziz, Prince Abdul-Musin Ibn 51
Abdul-Aziz, Prince Ahmad Ibn 2, 3
Abdul-Aziz, Prince Khalid Ibn Faisal Ibn 51
Abdul-Aziz, Prince Majid Ibn 2, 51
Abdul-Aziz, Prince Moutib Ibn 2
Abdul-Aziz, Prince Mugrin Ibn 51
Abdul-Aziz, Prince Nayef Ibn 2
Abdul-Aziz, Prince Salman Ibn 3, 51, 213
Abdul-Aziz, Prince Sultan Ibn 2, 3-4
Abdel-Wahab, Muhammad Ibn 5-6
Abdel-Wasi, Abdel-Wahhab Ahmad 2
Abha 317
Abqaiq 87,88,288,299,306-308,310
Abraham, the Prophet 135,136
Accidents 61,71-72, see also Hospitals for Emergency services
  Traffic, 56,71-72,80,168
Address, forms of 64
Administrative divisions 51
Adultery 79
Agents 121-125, 127-128
Agriculture 28,84,115-117
Agriculture & Water Ministry 2,154,211
Ahmad M Baqadir Park 145
Ain Zubaydah 147
Air freight 132

Air travel 56
  Dhahran/Al-Khobar 279-282
  Hail 260
  Jeddah 159-162
  Khamis Mushait 328
  Al-Madinah 149
  Makkah 139
  Riyadh 213-216
  Tabuk 261-262
  Taif 200
  Yanbu 202
  see also Travel Agents
Airconditioners 238
Ajyad Castle 147
Ajyad Market 143
Alcohol 50,71,79
Altitude 49
Ambulances 61,168
Amphibians 33-35
Amusement parks
  Makkah 145
  Jeddah 153
Al-Angari, Ibrahim Ibn-Abdullah, 2,118
Anayzah 253,256-258
Animal life 29-35
Antiques 177-179,226
Antiquities and archaeology 39-40,192-193,194,223, 251,265-269,270-271, 311-312,331
Antiquities & Museums Directorate-General 39,40
Arab-British Chamber of Commerce 55
Arabic 62-65,70,129,185
  courses 185,301
  bibliography 342
Arafat 21,146
Aramco 87-90,333,335
  staff compounds 306-309
Archaeology & Ethnography Museum 39,40,233
Architecture
  Anayzah 256-258
  Asir region 319-320
  Jeddah 182-183
  Makkah 138
  Najran 271-272
Area 49

Armed forces 111-112
Art galleries 172,179,233
Asir 24-25, 51,317-325,339
Asir National Park 321
Atlantis II Deep 37,38
Al-Ayenah 248
Ayn Dhila 250
Ayn Hit 250
Ayn Semha 250
Aziziyah 144

Baby sitting 206
Badminton 303
Badr, Fayez 2
Al-Baha 51,317
Banking 98-101,
  hours 51
  Aramco 307
  Jeddah 188-190
  Jubail 314
  Khamis Mushait 328
  Makkah 142
  Riyadh 244
  Yanbu 205
Batha Souq 227
Batik making 240
Bauxite 38
Bedu, traditional lifestyle 7-8,27,41
Bereavement 72-73
Bilharzia 76
Bill of lading 126
Billiards 217,303
Birds 29-30,342
Al-Birkah 195
Blasphemy 80
Block visas 52
Blood money 72
Book fair, Riyadh 233
Bookshops
  Al-Khobar/Dhahran/Dammam 297
  Jeddah 176-177
  Jubail 315
  Riyadh 225-226
  Taif 200
Bowling 217,241,307,308
Bribery 79-80
Bridge clubs 188,205,240, 301,302,316
British Council 185

British embassy and consular
   offices
   Jeddah 159
   Al-Khobar 276
   Riyadh 212
Buraydah 253,254-256
Burglary 72
Bus system 56
   Eastern province 56,276
   Jeddah 56,162
   Al-Madinah 56,149
   Riyadh 56,216
   Taif 56
   Yanbu 202
Business 119-133
   bibliography 341,342
   etiquette 41-42
   events 132-133
   groups 245,302
   hours 51
   visas 52
Al-Buwayr 197
Buying seasons 128

Calendar, Islamic 19,62,63
Camel market 309
Camel racing, 242-243
Camel souq 227
Camel trails 247-248
Capital city 50
Cars, hire 55
   Eastern province 282
   Jeddah 162-163
   Jubail 313
   Riyadh 216-217
   Yanbu 202
Car insurance 55-56,71
   repair/service 205,296,
      328
   see also Driving
Casoc 87
Catering 205,294, 295 (see
   also Restaurants
Certificate of origin 126
Chambers of Commerce &
   Industry 55,130,149,202
Chemists
   Jeddah 182
   Jubail 315
   Makkah 143
   Riyadh 231
   Taif 200
   Yanbu 205

Children
   activities 205,206,316
   welfare institutions 44-45
Choral and music societies
   188,205,239,240
Cinema 307-308
Climate 24-26,49-50,274
Clothing, expatriate 71,74-75,
   274
Commerce Ministry 2,154,
   211
Commercial Agencies Decree
   127
Commercial invoice 126
Committee for the Settle-
   ment of Commercial
   Disputes 127
Communications Ministry
   2,154,211
Compounds
   Aramco 306-309
   Dhahran/Al-Khobar/
      Dammam 275-276
   Jeddah 182,185,186
Conference facilities
   Dammam 285
   Dhahran 286
   Jeddah 164,166
   Jubail 313
   Khamis Mushait 326
   Al-Khobar 283-284
   Al-Madinah 149
   Makkah 139
   Riyadh 218,219,220
Construction 84,90-94,104,
   110-112,114
Cooling systems 238-239
Copper 37,38
Coral stone 38
Corniche, Jeddah 152-153
Council of Saudi Chambers
   of Commerce & Industry
   130
Courier services 126
   Dammam 287
   Hofuf 287
   Jeddah 168-169
   Jubail 313
   Khamis Mushait 326
   Al-Khobar 287
   Makkah 142
   Riyadh 221
   Tabuk 262
   Taif 200
   Yanbu 203
Credit, business 127
Credit cards 50
Creek, Jeddah 153
Cricket 186,241-242,303
Cuisine, Saudi 46-48

Currency 50
Customs and manners
   41-42,64,70-71,278
Customs, offences 78-79
   regulations 50

Dammam 86-87,273-305
Dancing group 188
Darb Zubaydah 195
Date preserve 48
Days of week 65
Debt collection 127
Defence 106-107,
   110-112
Defence & Aviation
   Ministry 2, 154, 221,
   328
Dental care
   Aramco 307
   Jeddah 181
   Khamis Mushait 329
   Al-Khobar 299
   Riyadh 230
   Yanbu 205
   see also Hospitals
Dependents' visas 52-54, 70
Desert driving 65-67
Desert, geography and
   vegetation 25-28
Dhahran 56, 87-88, 273-308
Al-Dhana waterfall 323
Dhu-l-Hijjah 21, 51, 62
Dialect 63
Diarrhoea 75
Diplomatic services
   Dhahran/Al-Khobar/
      Dammam 276
   Jeddah 154-159
   Riyadh 212-213
Dir'iya 246-247
Al-Dirs 324
Distances, road 57
Doctors, see Medical care
Domestic help 227, 275
Drama groups 188, 239,
   240, 302, 316
Dress, expatriate 71, 74-75,
   274
Drinking water 67, 75,
   204, 237
Driving 55-56, 71-72
   accidents 56, 71-72, 80,
      168
   Aramco compounds 306
   desert 65-67
   licence 55, 56
   offences 80

345

Drug stores
　Jeddah 182
　Jubail 315
　Makkah 143
　Riyadh 231
　Taif 200
　Yanbu 205
Drug offences 71, 79
Dry cleaning 145, 176, 224, 295

Eastern Province 26, 51, 273-333, 339
Economy 1-2, 13-14, 83-117, 333-336, 340-341
Education 45, 62, 85, 117-118, 134, 183-185, 204, 233-235, 299-301, 329, 330, 337
Education Ministry 2, 154, 211
Electricity supply 50-51, 204, 236, 297, 329
Embassies and consular offices
　Dhahran/Dammam/Al-Khobar 276
　Jeddah 154-159
　Riyadh 212-213
Emergency services 61, 168, 306
　see also Hospitals
Employment
　law 129
　permit 53
　statistics 128
Empty Quarter (Rub al-Khali) 25
Entry requirements 52-55
Estate agents 77-78
　Jeddah 182
　Al-Khobar/Dammam 297
　Riyadh 235
European contractors 92
Exchange rates 50
　regulations 50
Exhibitions 132-133
Exit visa 53
Expatriates, advice to 69-81

Facsimile (fax) machines 61
Fahd, King 1, 2, 3, 17
Fahd peace plan 1, 17, 106
Faifa 324-325
Fairgrounds 145, 153
Faisal, King 3, 13-16
Al-Faisal, Prince Saud 2, 4
Al-Faisal, Prince Turki 4

Family life, Saudi 43-44
Farasan Island 331
Farming 28, 115-117
Fasting 20

Al-Fau 265-269
Fauna 29-35
Al-Fayez, Ali 2
Finance & National Economy Ministry 2, 154, 211
Financial institutions 98-101, 142, 188-190, 205, 244, 307, 314, 328
Fire service 61, 168
Firearms 71, 79
Fishing 206, 277, 316
Five Pillars of Islam 20-21
Flag 6, 49
Flora 26-28
Food, Saudi 46-48, 278
Food shops 171-176, 200, 203, 211, 223-225, 255, 274-275, 292-293, 307, 314, 327-328
Foreign Affairs Ministry 2, 55, 154
Forwarding agents 297
Freight forwarding 131-132

Gardening 205, 239, 277, 302
　supplies 176, 205, 225, 277, 293, 307
Gas, domestic 236-237
General Organisation for Technical Education & Vocational Training (GOTEVT) 117-118
General practitioners, see Medical care
Geneva fountain 152
Geography 24-26
Gold 36-37, 38
　souqs 143, 199, 211, 226, 275
Golf 186, 241, 316
Al-Gosaibi, Ghazi Abdel-Rahman 2, 97
Gourmet Club 218
Government 2, 49
　expenditure 83-85, 94-97, 134
　ministries 2, 154, 211-212
Governors, provincial 51
Granite 38
Great Mosque, Riyadh 211

Guides & Scouts 205-206, 316
Gulf Co-operation Council (GCC) 1, 16, 17
Gymnastics 217, 218, 303

Habalah 320, 322
Hail 51, 259-260, 339
Al-Hair 249
Hajj (pilgrimage) 19, 21, 136-137
Hajji camp 225
Hanakiyah 192-193
Handicrafts 185, 205, 240
Harrat Rahat 191-192
Hasa 26, 273-333, 339
Hauta 262
Health Ministry 2, 154, 211
Health care 55, 73-76
　Aramco 307
　Dammam/Dhahran/Al-Khobar 278, 298-299
　Jeddah 179-182
　Jubail 315
　Khamis Mushait 329
　Al-Madinah 149
　Makkah 145
　Riyadh 227-232
　Taif 200
　Yanbu 204-205
Health regulations 55, 73
Hejaz 24, 191, 339
　railway 196-197
Hepatitis 73
Higher Education Ministry 2, 211
History 5-18
　bibliography 339-340
Hofuf 51, 309-310
Holidays, public 20-21, 51, 62, 129
Holy Mosque 135, 137
Holy Mosque library 147
Horaymilah 252
Horse racing 243
Hospitality 8, 41-42, 278
Hospitals
　Aramco 307
　Dammam/Dhahran/Al-Khobar 278, 298-299
　Jeddah 179-181
　Jubail 315
　Khamis Mushait 329
　Al-Madinah 149
　Riyadh 228-230, 231
　Taif 200
　Yanbu 204-205

Hotels
   Al-Baha 317
   Dammam 284-285
   Dhahran 286
   Jeddah 164-168
   Jizan 331
   Jubail 313
   Khamis Mushait 325-326
   Al-Khobar 283-284
   Al-Madinah 148-149
   Makkah 139-142
   Riyadh 217-220
   Taif 198, 199-200
   Yanbu 202-203
Housing 77-78
   Aramco 308
   Jeddah 185-186
   Khamis Mushait 329
   Al-Khobar/Dammam 297
   Riyadh 235-239
   Yanbu 204
Hubble-Bubble Souq 227
Humidity 49-50

Al-Ibrahim, Shaikh Ibrahim Ibn-Abdul-Aziz 51
Id'abi 325
Identity cards 54
Ijma 22-23
Ikhwan 9-10, 11, 12
Immigration regulations 52-55, 70
Import regulations 50, 78-79
Imprisonment 80-81
Industry 84, 91-97, 342
Industry & Electricity Ministry 2, 154, 212
Information Ministry 2, 154, 212
Inoculation 55, 73
Insect repellent 75
Insurance
   certificate 127
   car 55-56, 71
Interior Ministry 2, 154, 212, 329
Interpreters 63
Investment companies, see: Financial institutions
Investment
   government 83, 85 94-97, 109-110, 134
   incentives 129-130
Iqama 52
Iron 38
Islam 18-23, 49, 51, 273-274
   women in 22, 43-45

see also Makkah, Al-Madinah, History
Islamic calendar 19, 62, 63
Islamic law 19, 22-23, 49, 69, 78-81

Jabal Faifa 324-325
Jabal Guyan 37
Jebel al-Qara 310
Jabal al-Safra 37
Jabal Said 37
Jabal Sawdah 321
Jabal Shammar 259, 260
Jebel Shiba 323
Jails 80
Japanese contractors 92
Jarash 323
Al-Jawf 51
Al-Jazairi, Hussain Abdel-Razzaq 2
Jeddah 56, 159-190, 191-197, 338
Jellyfish poisoning 76
Jiluwi, Prince Abdel-Muhsin Ibn 51
Jiluwi, Prince Abdullah Ibn Abdul-Aziz Ibn Musaid Ibn 51
Jiluwi, Prince Mohammad Ibn Fahd Ibn 51
Jizan 51, 330-331
Juaymah export terminal 88
Jubail 96-97, 312-316
Jurayd Island 316
Justice Ministry 2, 154, 212

Ka'aba 21, 135, 137
Karate 206, 303
Kayyal, Alawi Darwish 2
Keep-fit 185, 186
Keswa factory 147
Khaled, King 16-17
Khamis Mushait 51, 325-330
Al-Kharj 250, 262
Khaybar 195-196
Al-Khobar 87, 273-305
Khurays 309
Al-Khuwaiter, Abdel-Aziz al-Abdullah 2
King Abdul-Aziz airport 56, 159-160
King's Camel Race 242-243
King Saud University 232
Korean contractors 90-91
Kuba 148

Labour law 129, 342
Labour & Social Affairs Ministry 2, 154, 212
Language 62-65, 70, 129
   bibliography 342
Language courses 185, 301, 302
   English 185, 301, 302
   French 185
   German 185
   Spanish 301
Law 19, 22-23, 49, 69, 78-81, 129, 342
Lawyers 190, 244-245, 305
Lead 38
Leaving Saudi Arabia 53, 54
Letters of credit 127
Leyla 263-264
Libraries 204, 233, 307-308
Literature, banned 71, 79
Luna Park 152

Al-Madinah 51, 148-149, 339
Magnesite 38
Mahala 322
Mahd adh Dhanab 36-37
Majlis 41
Majlis al-Shoura 16
Makkah 51, 135-147
   Hajj 19, 21, 136-137
   liberation of 11-12
   occupation of Mosque 1979, 16
Makkah Road Souq 226
Malaaz 224, 235
Malaria prevention 55, 75-76
Mammals 30-33
Manners and customs 41-42, 64, 70-71, 278
Manufacturing 84, 94-97
Marble 38
Marwah 21
Marwah market 143
Al-Masane 37
Mashwi 47
Masjid al-Fatah 148
Masoud, Mohammad 2
Maternity leave 129, 278
Media 188, 206, 305, 308-309, 315
Medical care
   Aramco 307
   Dammam/Dhahran/ Al-Khobar 278, 298-299
   Jeddah 179-182
   Jubail 315
   Khamis Mushait 329

347

Al-Madinah 149
Makkah 145
Riyadh 227-232
Taif 200
Yanbu 204-205
Medical insurance 76
Al-Milhim, Mohammad Abdel-Latif 2
Mina 21
Mineral resources 35-38
Mining 35-38
Ministries 2, 154, 211-212
Missions, diplomatic
Dhahran/Al-Khobar/Dammam 276
Jeddah 154-159
Riyadh 212-213
Mohammad, the Prophet 18-19, 20, 22, 136-137, 146, 147, 148
Monarchy, see Ruling family
Monetary unit 50
Money changers 100
Months, Islamic 64
Mortuary services 72
Motoring, see Driving
Mount Uhud 148
Mountain of Light (Jabal al-Nur) 146
Mountain of Mercy (Jabal al-Rahma) 146
Mudaa market 143
Municipal & Rural Affairs Ministry 2, 154, 212, 329
Museums 39-40, 233, 303
Mushayt, Abdul-Aziz Ibn Said Ibn 51
Music societies 186, 205, 239, 240
Muslim law, see Sharia
Musmak fort 209, 210
Muwahhidun 5-6
Al-Muzdalafah 21

Al-Nadir 324
Nafud 26, 259-260
Najd 24, 246-253
Najran 51, 269-272
Natural History Society 188
Nazer, Hisham 2
Al-Nesab 322
Newspapers 206, 309, 315
Northern borders 51
Numbers, Arabic 65
Nuqrah 37, 38
Nuzhah 144

Oil and gas 13, 16, 86-90, 201, 333-335, 341
Oil revenues 83-85, 334
Olayan 225, 235-236
Ophthalmologists 230, see also Hospitals
Opticians 231, see also Hospitals
Ordnance Corps Programme 112
Oryx 32-33
Otaybiah Hejoun 144
Ottoman, rule of Najd 7
Overtime 129

Painting classes 185, 205
Palestinians, Saudi support for 1, 13, 15, 16, 17
Pan-Arab unity 1, 13-14, 16, 17
Partner, choosing a 121-125
Passports 52-54
Payment, terms of 127
Permits 52-54
Pest control 182, 239, 297
Petrol 205
Petroleum & Minerals Ministry 2, 35, 154, 212
Petromin 88-89
Pets 204, 278
Pharmacies
Jeddah 182
Jubail 315
Makkah 143
Riyadh 231
Taif 200
Yanbu 205
Philatelic Society 188, 316
Photography 70
club 205, 316
Pilgrimage Affairs & Awqaf (Religious Endowments) Ministry 2, 154, 212
Planning Ministry 2, 154, 212
Plant life 26-28
Poisonous creatures 76
Police 61, 168
Population 50, 62
Pork products 71, 79
Pornography 71, 79
Post offices
Dammam 286
Jeddah 168
Jubail 313
Khamis Mushait 326
Al-Khobar 286
Riyadh 220-221
Taif 200

Yanbu 203
Post office boxes 61
Posts, Telegraphs & Telecommunications Ministry 2, 58, 154, 212, 329
Postal codes 61
Prayer 6, 18, 20, 51
Printers 297
Prophet's Mosque 148
Provinces 51
Public transport 56, 149, 162, 202, 216, 243-244, 276
Public Works & Housing Ministry 2, 154, 212

Qara 322
Qaryat al-Fau 265-269
Qassim 51, 253-258
Qatif 311
Qiyas 22-23
Quran 18-23, 44, 79
Qurayyat 51
Quwayah 251

Rabadiya Oasis 258
Rabies 73
Radio 305, 309, 315
Railways
Hejaz 196-197
Riyadh-Dammam 243-244
Rainfall 24-26, 27, 28, 49
Ramadan 20, 51, 55, 62
Ras Tanajib 89
Ras Tanura 87, 88, 95, 306-308
Al-Rashid family 7
Rates of exchange 50
Recreation
Aramco 307-308
Eastern Province 276-278, 301-304
Jeddah 185, 186, 188
Jubail 315-316
Khamis Mushait 330
Makkah 145
Riyadh 239-243
Yanbu 205-206
Regions
administrative 51
geographic 24-26
Removals 295
Reptiles 33-35
Restaurants
Dammam/Dhahran/Al-Khobar 289-292
Jeddah 169-171

STATCO
SAUDI TRAVEL & TOURIST AGENCY

HEAD OFFICE

Kaaki Building, King Khaled Street, Alkhobar, Saudi Arabia.
Tel: 8641930/8641931, 8647256, 8644342. P.O. Box 179, Dhahran Int. Airport. Cables: STATCO-ALKHOBAR. Telex: 670034 ARGTB.
ALKHOBAR — Talal Street. Tel: 8941300, 8645095, 8644390.

BRANCHES:

AL QATIF	—	Alkhalifa Omar Ibn Alkhattab Street. Tel: 8557564 8557808, 8552535. Cable STATCO.
JEDDAH	—	Prince Nawwaf Building, King Abdul Aziz Street Tel: 642-5612, 642-5999. Cable: STATCO. Medina Rd., Al Shuhada Street, (Kilo "3") Algithmi Bldg. Tel: 6517756, 6511962
RIYADH	—	Aziziah Building, King Faisal Street. Tel: 402-2820, 403-1752. Cable: STATCO—GOSAIBI. Salmaniya, 30th Street, Jamjoum Bldg. Tel: 4658222, 4658229.
AL KHARJ	—	Alsaal Building, 16th Street. Tel: 447000, 448550.
SAFWA	—	Main Street. Tel: 6642380, 6642376.

General Sales Agents:

GULF AIR (SAUDI ARABIA)

SYRIAN ARAB AIRLINES (Dhahran)

SAUDIA (Safwa & Al Kharj)

KOREAN AIRLINES (Dhahran)

**TRAVEL & TOURIST AGENTS
TICKETING/ HOTEL RESERVATIONS**

SAWARY

A LEADER IN THE POWER BUSINESS.

POWER PLANTS FROM 1 MW TO 100 MW.

GENERATING SETS FROM 2 KW TO 750 KW.

CABLES OF ALL KINDS.

DESIGN, INSTALLATION, MAINTENANCE & SERVICE.

SOLE DISTRIBUTOR FOR:

FOR INFORMATION CALL:
JEDDAH TEL. 6437558, 6421549/RIYADH 476420.
BURAIDA 4780/DAMMAM 8574255.

Jubail 314-315
Khamis Mushait 327
Makkah 142
Riyadh 221-222
Taif 200
Yanbu 203
see also Hotels
Riding 242, 304
Riyadh 8, 51, 56, 207-245, 246-253, 339
Riyadh Group of British Businessmen 245
Riyal 50
Road distances 57
Rock carvings 192-193, 194, 251
Royal Commission for Jubail & Yanbu 201, 206, 316
Royal palace 147
Rubbish collection 204
Ruling family 3-4, 13-17, 340
Rusaifah 144

Safa 21
Sales representatives 121-125
Salman, Prince Salman Ibn Abdul-Aziz 3, 51, 213
Sandstone 38
Saud, House of, see Historical background
Saud, King 13
Saud, Muhammad Ibn 5, 6
Saud, Prince Saud al-Faisal 2, 4
Saudi Arabian Agricultural Bank 116
Saudi Arabian Monetary Agency 99-101
Saudi Arabian Public Transport Company 56, 162, 202, 216, 276
Saudi Basic Industries Corporation 95-96
Saudi Industrial Development Fund 95-96
Saudia
   Dhahran 279, 282
   Hail 260
   Jeddah 161-162
   Khamis Mushait 328
   Al-Madinah 149
   Makkah 139
   Riyadh 216
   Tabuk 262
   Taif 200
   Yanbu 212
Sawdah Mountains 321

Scorpion stings 76
Scouts and guides 205-206, 316
Sea freight 131-132
Sea life, dangerous 76
Sea sports
   Eastern province 277, 303, 304
   Jeddah 153, 186-187
   Jubail 316
   Khamis Mushait 330
   Riyadh 242
   Tabuk 262
   Yanbu 206
Servants 227, 275
Al-Shaer, Ali Hassan 2
Shaib Awsat 249
Shaib Laha 249
Al al-Shaikh family 6
Al-Shaikh, Abdel-Rahman Ibn-Abdel-Aziz Ibn-Hasan 2
Al-Shaikh, Hasan Ibn Abdullah 2
Al-Shaikh, Ibrahim Ibn-Mohammad Ibn-Ibrahim 2
Sharia 19, 22-23, 49, 69, 78-81
Shia 23
Shipping certificate 127
Shopping
   Aramco 307
   Buraydah 254-255
   Dammam/Dhahran/Al-Khobar 274-275
   Jeddah 171-179
   Jubail 314, 315
   Khamis Mushait 327-328
   Makkah 142-145
   Riyadh 211, 223-227
   Taif 198-199, 200
   Yanbu 203
Shopping hours 51
Sibilla, Battle of 12
Sick leave 129
Silver 37, 38
Sindi, Kamel 2
Snakes 34-35
Snakebite 76
Social customs 41-42, 64, 70-71, 278
Souk 'Aiban 325
Souqs
   Buraydah 254-255
   Dammam/Dhahran/Al-Khobar 275
   Hofuf 309-310
   Jeddah 174-175, 178
   Jubail 314

Khamis Mushait 328
Makkah 143-144
Qatif 311
Riyadh 211, 225, 226-227
Taif 198-199
Yanbu 203
Souq al-Jamal 227
Al-Souq al-Saghir 143
Sponsorship 52, 69-70, 121-125
Sport
   Aramco 307-308
   Eastern Province 276-277, 303-304
   Jeddah 186-187
   Jubail 316
   Khamis Mushait 330
   Riyadh 217-218, 241-242
   Tabuk 262
   Yanbu 206
Standard Oil Company of California (Socal) 86-87
Standards of manufacture 124
Station of Abraham 135, 136
Stomach upsets 75
Stone fish poisoning 76
Al-Sudairi, Amir Abdul-Rahman Ibn Ahmad Ibn Muhammad 51
Al-Sudairi, Amir Fahd Ibn Khalid 51
Al-Sudairi, Hassa Bint-Ahmad 3
Al-Sudairi, Amir Sultan Ibn Abdul-Aziz 51
Sudd Hashquq 196
Sudd al-Khasid 196
Sudd al-Qasaibah 195-196
Al-Solaim, Sulaiman Abdel-Aziz 2
Sulaiyil 264-265
Sulaymaniyah 235
Sultan, Prince Sultan Ibn-Abdel-Aziz 2, 3-4
Sunnah 22-23
Sunnis 23
Supreme Petroleum Council 2
Survival pack 67
Swimming pools 186, 206, 236, 303, 307, 308, 316
   see also Hotels

Tabuk 51, 261-262
Taekwondo 303

349

Taher, Abdel-Hadi 2
Taif 198-200
   rock carvings 194
Tarut island 311-312
Taxis 202, 276
Telegrams
   Aramco 306
   Jeddah 168
   Jubail 313
   Khamis Mushait 326
   Al-Khobar 286-287
   Riyadh 220
Telephone system 58-60, 102-103
   Aramco 306
   Jeddah 168
   Jubail 313
   Khamis Mushait 326
   Taif 200
   Yanbu 203
   directory enquiries 61
   dialling codes 58, 60
Television 206, 305, 309, 315
Telex 61
   Aramco 306
   Jeddah 168
   Jubail 313
   Khamis Mushait 326
   Al-Khobar 286-287
   Riyadh 220
   Taif 200
   Yanbu 203
Temperature 49-50, 274
Theft 79
Tihama coastal plain 322-333
Time differentials 61
Tipping 50
Titles 64
Tours
   Asir region 317-324
   Eastern region 309-312
   Jeddah region 191-197
   Najd region 246-272
   Towqi 252-253
Trade
   with France 112-115
   with UK 103-106
   with US 105-112
Traffic accidents 56, 71-72, 80, 168
Training of Saudi nationals 2, 85, 117-118, 232, 337
Trans-Arabian Pipeline 87-88
Translation services 63, 299
Transport of goods 131-132
Travel 55-57
   groups 239, 277-278, 303, 316
   words and phrases 64
   see also air travel, driving, buses, taxis, railways
Travel agents
   Abqaiq 288
   Dammam 287, 288
   Dhahran 287, 288
   Jeddah 168
   Jubail 287, 313-314
   Al-Khobar 287, 288
   Ras al-Khafji 287
   Ras Tanura 287
   Riyadh 221
   Taif 200
   Yanbu 203
Tumair 252
Turki, Prince Turki al-Faisal 4
Typing 302

Udhailiyah 88, 306-308
Ukhdud 270-271
Umm al-Qura, see Makkah
Umrah 144
   pilgrimage 137
US Army Corps of Engineers 110-112
US contractors 91-92
Universities 62, 117, 134, 232, 301, 337
Uqair 310-311
Usfan 191, 194

Vaccination 55, 73
Valley of the Iris 252
Vegetation 26-28
Vehicles, see Driving
   for desert driving 65-67
Vets 181, 231
Video 79, 241
Visas 52-54, 70
Vocational training 85, 117-118, 337
Voltage 50-51
   Khamis Mushait 329
   Al-Khobar/Dammam 297
   Riyadh 236
   Yanbu 204

Al-Wabah 195
Wadi Ain 220
Wadi Dirs 323-324
Wadi Fatima 191-192
Wadi Hanifa 248-249
Wadi Horaymilah 251-252
Wadi al-Jafi 250-251
Wadi Rima 253-254
Wadi Sawawin 38
Wadi Shaah Turkish fort 324
Wadi Tindaha 322
Wages, minimum 129
Wahhabism 5-6
Water supply 75, 204, 237, 329
   while stranded in desert 67
Water sports
   Eastern province 277, 303, 304
   Jeddah 153, 186-187
   Jubail 316
   Khamis Mushait 330
   Riyadh 242
   Tabuk 262
   Yanbu 206
Weather 24-26, 49-50, 274
Weaver's Guild 316
Weights and measures 50
Welfare institutions 44-45
Wildlife 29-35, 342
Women
   expatriate 278
   Muslim 22, 43-45
Women's groups 188, 205, 240, 301, 302, 315, 316
Workforce 85, 128
Work permit 53
   visa 52
   hours 129

Al-Yamama 220
Yamani, Ahmad Zaki 2
Yanbu 201-206
   industrial plant 96-97, 201
Yanbu al-Bekkah 206
Yanbu al-Nakhl 206
Al-Yanfa 322
Yoga 185, 205, 240

Al-Zabira 38
Al-Zahir Gardens 145
Zakat 20
Zam Zam, Well of 135
Zarghat 38
Zinc 37, 38